*The Gospel of John in Cultural
and Rhetorical Perspective*

The Gospel of John in Cultural and Rhetorical Perspective

Jerome H. Neyrey

WILLIAM B. EERDMANS PUBLISHING COMPANY
GRAND RAPIDS, MICHIGAN / CAMBRIDGE, U.K.

© 2009 Jerome H. Neyrey
All rights reserved

Published 2009 by
Wm. B. Eerdmans Publishing Co.
2140 Oak Industrial Drive N.E., Grand Rapids, Michigan 49505 /
P.O. Box 163, Cambridge CB3 9PU U.K.

Library of Congress Cataloging-in-Publication Data

Neyrey, Jerome H., 1940-
The Gospel of John in cultural and rhetorical perspective / Jerome H.
Neyrey.
p.   cm.
Originally published: New York: Cambridge University Press, 2007.
ISBN 978-0-8028-4866-6 (pbk.: alk. paper)
1. Bible. N.T. John — Socio-rhetorical criticism.   I. Title.

BS2615.52.N495   2009
226.5′077 — dc22

2009022381

www.eerdmans.com

Contents

*Preface: The Gospel of John in Cultural
and Rhetorical Perspective* — viii

Acknowledgments — xiv

Abbreviations — xvi

PART ONE
The Anatomy of the Fourth Gospel: Major Perspectives

1. Encomium vs. Vituperation — 3
   Contrasting Portraits of Jesus in the Fourth Gospel

2. Role and Status in the Fourth Gospel — 29
   Cutting through Confusion

3. Spaces and Places, Whence and Whither, Homes and Rooms — 58
   "Territoriality" in the Fourth Gospel

PART TWO
Narrative Episodes in Focus

4. "Are You Greater than Our Father Jacob?" — 87
   Jesus and Jacob in John 1:51 and 4:4-26

CONTENTS

5. "He Must Increase, I Must Decrease" (John 3:30) — 123
   A Cultural and Social Interpretation

6. What's Wrong with This Picture? — 143
   John 4, Cultural Stereotypes of Women, and Public and Private Space

7. "Equal to God" (John 5:18) — 172
   Jesus and God's Two Powers in the Fourth Gospel

8. The Trials (Forensic) and Tribulations (Honor Challenges) of Jesus — 191
   John 7 in Social Science Perspective

9. Jesus the Judge — 227
   Forensic Process in John 8:21-59

10. Secrecy, Deception, and Revelation — 252
    Information Control in the Fourth Gospel

11. The "Noble" Shepherd in John 10 — 282
    Cultural and Rhetorical Background

12. "I Said: You Are Gods" — 313
    Psalm 82:6 and John 10

13. "In Conclusion ..." — 332
    John 12 as a Rhetorical "Peroratio"

14. The Footwashing in John 13:6-11 — 356
    Transformation Ritual or Ceremony?

15. Worship in the Fourth Gospel — 377
    A Cultural Interpretation of John 14–17

16. "Despising the Shame of the Cross" — 412
    Honor and Shame in the Johannine Passion Narrative

Contents

PART THREE
Jesus vis-à-vis God: Agent or Equal?

17. "My Lord and My God"   441
 The Heavenly Character of Jesus in John's Gospel

18. "I Am the Door" (John 10:7, 9)   454
 Jesus the Broker in the Fourth Gospel

Index of Topics   477

Index of Passages in John's Gospel   483

PREFACE

The Gospel of John
in Cultural and Rhetorical Perspective

The essays here, all previously published, are gathered together in the hope of providing a different and coherent type of reading of the Fourth Gospel. Commentaries on this Gospel are always severely constrained as to space and can only make succinct remarks about the story and its characters. These essays, however, are article-length studies of most of the chapters in the Gospel, interpreting it in terms of classical rhetoric or through the lenses of cultural anthropology. The aim of these studies is not novelty for its own sake, but a fresh interpretation by means of materials that belong in any interpreter's toolbox, both rhetorical and cultural.

The essays are carefully arranged into a meaningful sequence of three parts. The initial three chapters serve as introduction to the distinctive perspective of this volume, namely, the interpretation of the Fourth Gospel in terms of cultural concepts and ancient rhetoric. These provide a view of the Gospel from these perspectives: an encomium for Jesus (chapter 1), the role and status of the significant characters in the narrative (chapter 2), and the sociology of space (chapter 3).

The essays in the core section of this collection (chapters 4-16) examine individual chapters of the Gospel from a variety of perspectives: 1) cultural models, 2) midrashic and background materials, and 3) classical rhetoric. In brief, the reader will find studies of the vision promised in John 1:51, the voluntary decrease in honor by John the Baptist (3:30), the midrash which illustrates how Jesus is "greater than our father Jacob" (4:10-26), Jesus' conversation with the Samaritan woman (4:7-26), the charge that he "makes himself equal to God" and his defense against it (5:18-29), his conflict at Tabernacles in forensic and cultural perspective (7:8-51), his assumption of the role of judge (8:21-59), the cultural contents of what makes for a "noble" shepherd (10:1-19), Jesus' midrashic employment of Psalm 82 (10:31-36), the structure of John 12 as a rhetorical "conclusion," the footwashing (13:6-11) viewed culturally in terms of ritual studies, the model of worship in John 14–17 viewed culturally, and the death of Jesus through the lens of honor and shame (John 18–19). These in-depth interpretative studies of the main narratives are the heart of this book.

The third part of the book contains two essays on Jesus, on what is ordinarily labeled "christology." Chapter 17 gathers together all that is said of Jesus as a heavenly figure, as "equal to God," and even as "god." These materials, moreover, are interpreted in the light of ancient Judean lore and modern scholarship. Readers will see that in the Fourth Gospel reflection on the status of Jesus sees him as a figure who is more than a mere human but less than God, who is Father. How would the recipients of this Gospel have heard this language? What commonplace notions of a true god are operative — Judean and Greco-Roman? Balancing this is the final essay (chapter 18), which examines Jesus' role as a "broker," that is, as the one who bridges the patron and the clients. We normally call this figure "mediator" (1 Tim 2:5; Heb 8:1-2, 6) and even "priest" (Heb 7:23-27).

What lens is used to interpret the Fourth Gospel? Inasmuch as the aim of these studies has always been to interpret the Gospel in its proper cultural context, we have found the following materials of particular utility.

Judean Background

Study of the Judean background of the Fourth Gospel has yielded a wealth of rich materials for understanding this Gospel in its historical and cultural contexts. The author of the Fourth Gospel mandates this mode of reading when his characters explicitly ask "Are you greater than our father Jacob?" (4:12) and "Are you greater than our father Abraham?" (8:53). The author responds by employing what rhetoricians call a "comparison," a comparison/contrast between Jesus and the premier patriarchs of Israel. Answering the questions "greater than Jacob . . . greater than Abraham" requires knowing what the original audience knew of the midrashic embellishments of the Scriptures on these matters. My research into the midrashic background of Abraham and Jacob is crystallized in chapters 4 and 9. Indeed, Jesus is even greater than Moses, who only gave the Law (1:17), who, unlike the Son of man, only ascended and then descended (3:13) and who wrote of Jesus (5:46). This type of thinking seems to be behind the constant replacement by Jesus of Israelite feasts and cultic objects and sacred spaces — he is indeed "greater than" the best of Israel's past.

PREFACE

It would be impossible to understand the meaning and function of Ps 82:6 ("I said: 'You Are Gods'") in John 10 without resort to its interpretation in Judean midrash. In John 10 the psalm functions to deflect the charge of blasphemy arising from the crowd's accusation that Jesus makes himself equal to God (10:33; see 5:18). If the psalm calls figures who are not god "gods," then Jesus might escape the hostility. The midrash on "You are gods" is presented in chapter 12. Similarly, one must ask what the Evangelist meant when he put on the lips of Jesus and other characters names and claims that indicate that Jesus is a heavenly figure. Chapter 17 investigates the Israelite background of numerous ways in which Jesus' heavenly-ness is expressed: 1) God gave Jesus his two basic powers: creative and eschatological; 2) the name "God" corresponds to the creative power, and "Lord" to the eschatological power; 3) Jesus has no beginning and no end, and this eternity is a mark of a true deity; and 4) his official use of God's name "I AM" meshes integrally with the other aspects of his "equality with God."

Greek Rhetorical Background

Much has been made of the Judean background of the Fourth Gospel, but the Gospel is also rich in terms of Greco-Roman rhetoric. Three chapters included here discuss the rhetorical background of certain topics and forms that are easily known from rhetorical education. First, the encomium (and vituperation) is a rhetorical genre studied in the progymnasmata, that is, the school exercises of those receiving education higher than that of slaves and socially unimportant people. Writers are taught stereotypical categories that must be treated in searching to augment the praise of someone (or their shame): 1) origins: geography (place of birth) and generation (parents and ancestors), 2) education and training, 3) virtues, 4) noble death, and 5) posthumous honors. We argue in chapter 1 that the Gospel contains both a positive take on these topics in regard to Jesus, in contrast to the record of shame and blame that outsiders and opponents construct for him.

The shepherd in John 10 is "noble," not "good." "Noble" *(kalos)* belongs to the pallet of praise and honor; "good" to that of virtue and morality. Research shows that the Greeks had a notion of *euthanasia* (dying with honor), as well as "noble death," the prerogative of warriors. Those who eulogized warriors at Athens's annual memorial used stereotypical criteria for acclaiming that a death was "noble," which include these topics: 1) *voluntary* choice of death, 2) death which *benefits* the polis, 3) death which *exemplifies virtue*, both *justice* (duty to the polis) and *courage*, 4) the boast that the fallen are in fact *victorious*,

x

5) *posthumous honors,* and 6) *immortality* through undying fame. The Greek materials are applied to John 10 in chapter 11.

A third turn to Greek materials occurred in the consideration of John 12 as a formal "conclusion" as described in rhetorical handbooks. No one doubts that 1:1-18 is a prologue to the Book of Signs and that a second prologue is found in 13:1-3, which begins the Book of Glory. The conclusion to the first part of the narrative occurs in John 12, which both resumes the basic topics argued in John 1–11 and instructs the reader how to judge the various characters paraded by, loving some and hating others.

Cultural Background

Several of the chapters below are concerned with the cultural context of the Gospel pursued by the use of anthropological and cultural models. Eight different cultural models proved valuable in interpreting the complex themes and issues of the Fourth Gospel. Chapter 18 contextualizes Jesus in the traditional patron-client model as the intermediary, apostle, mediator, and broker who links the Patron, who is God and Father, with the clients, who are Jesus' disciples. In chapter 5, the envy shown to Jesus by the disciples of the Baptizer in John 3 is clarified by recourse to the model of "limited good," according to which all things, honor included, are in limited supply, such that the gain of one means loss by others. Envy is by no means confined to this story, but shows up regularly in the motivation of the elites to kill Jesus. Studies of space, especially public and private space and its relationship to gender, form the background for interpreting John 4. Space, moreover, is by no means confined to public vs. private space, but is an ongoing concern in the Fourth Gospel. Where to worship? What is this about a "house with many rooms"? And what does "dwelling in" mean? These are all addressed in chapter 3.

Throughout the Gospel we are told of confrontations between Jesus and various opponents and of true forensic proceedings against him. All of these are conflicts over honor and are well described according to the choreography of challenge and riposte. The extended narrative around the Feast of Tabernacles is examined in chapter 8, which focuses precisely on the endless thrust and parry of challenge and riposte. And in a dramatic role reversal, Jesus, who is challenged, takes on the role of challenger-judge.

In another reversal, Jesus — the presumed Revealer — plays the role of concealer, as seen in chapter 10. At stake is a full appreciation of the sociology of secrecy: 1) who knows what and when and 2) increasing levels of knowledge as indicators of rising status. Jesus, who knows all things, is highly selective in terms of what he tells any one. The climax of this motif is the proper assessment of what the Beloved Disciple knows and what Jesus tells Mary Magdalene in John 20.

Of all the Gospels, the Fourth Gospel uniquely notes the footwashing in 13:4-11. The problem for us is that the interpretation of footwashing in 13:12-20 is an inadequate explanation of 13:4-11. Peter is prominent in the first, all the disciples in the second; the first washing is absolutely necessary and unrepeatable, whereas the second is a regular feature of the group's gathering. What is needed is a notion of ritual to distinguish changes of status from ceremonial confirmation. Some rituals change role and status, whereas others confirm membership and status. The model of rituals, both change and confirmation, is developed and applied to John 13. Involved is the failed transformation of Peter, which is eventually remedied in John 21.

It is remarkable how much the Fourth Gospel says in passing about worship, on issues concerning sacred space, feast days, objects of petitions, etc. In John 14–17 we find a particularly intense concentration of materials pertaining to worship and prayer. This section of the Gospel, although traditionally identified as a farewell address, is also relentlessly concerned with 1) prayer (petitionary, self-focused, and confessional), 2) homilies, and 3) discussions of Jesus' words and the like. This material is presented in chapter 15 below. A cultural model of prayer and worship is developed there to facilitate our seeing and interpreting the myriad mentions of prayer and worship.

Finally, the trial, crucifixion and death of Jesus were labeled by all as "shame" (Heb 12:1-2). But with a model of honor and shame, we are able to read the narrative ironically and note how the shame inflicted by outsiders is interpreted by insiders as Jesus' honor.

A Johannine Commentary?

The collected materials in this book may be considered in another way, which might make it more attractive as a unified work and not as a mere miscellany. The outline of the chapters at the beginning of the volume immediately indicates that almost all of them form a sequential treatment chapter-by-chapter of the Gospel. The sequence of these chapters begins with John 3 (*"Limited Good"*) and continues with John 4 (*"What's Wrong with This Picture"*), John 7 and 8 (*"Trials and Tribulations"* and *"Jesus the Judge"*), John 10 (*"Noble Shepherd," "You are Gods"*), John 12 (*"Conclusion"*), John 13 (*"Footwashing"*), John 14–17 (*"Worship in the Fourth Gospel"*), John 18–19 (*"Honor and Shame"*), and John 21, the conclusion of the footwashing narrative. Moreover, the article *"My*

Lord and My God" contains significant material on the exposition of the argument "equal to God" in John 5, as well as 8, 10, and 11.

In addition to interpreting individual chapters, the book contains other essays which consider topics and data that run through most of the chapters. For example, the first three chapters examine how Jesus is either praised or blamed according to the conventional topics of an encomium. Then the various characters in the story are considered in terms of their role and status, all the while gaining insight into the value system of the group. Third, Jesus and his world are interpreted in terms of "territoriality," the social model of classifying, communicating, and control of space. The final two chapters consider Jesus' own role and status. On the one hand he enjoys exceedingly high status, even that of "equal to God," and on the other, his sole, unique role is that of "broker" between God and the disciples and between the disciples and God.

Because the contents of the eighteen chapters cover in detail most of the text and its most important values, we invite readers to consider this as a textbook, a study which can go into greater detail than is allowed in a traditional commentary.

Acknowledgments

Augsburg-Fortress Press

"The Foot Washing in John 13:6-11 — Transformation Ritual or Ceremony?" *The Social World of the First Christians. Essays in Honor of Wayne A. Meeks*, ed. L. Michael White and O. Larry Yarbrough (Minneapolis: Fortress, 1995) 198-213 appears with the kind permission of the press.

Biblica

"Jesus the Judge: Forensic Process in John 8:21-59," *Biblica* 68 (1987): 509-42 appears with the kind permission of the journal.

Biblical Theology Bulletin

"What's Wrong with This Picture? John 4, Cultural Stereotypes of Women, and Public and Private Space," *BTB* 24 (1994): 77-91
"The Trials (Forensic) and Tribulations (Honor Challenges) of Jesus: John 7 in Social Science Perspective," *BTB* 26 (1996): 107-24
"Spaces and Places, Whence and Whither, Homes and Rooms: 'Territoriality' in the Fourth Gospel," *BTB* 32 (2002): 60-74
"Worship in the Fourth Gospel: A Cultural Interpretation of John 14-17," *BTB* 36 (2006): 107-17
"Rhetorical *Peroratio* and John 12," *BTB* 37 (2007): 101-13
appear with the kind permission of the journal.

Acknowledgments

Catholic Biblical Quarterly

"Jacob Traditions and the Interpretation of John 4:10-26," *CBQ* 41 (1979): 419-37
"The Jacob Allusions in John 1:51," *CBQ* 44 (1982): 586-605
"'He must increase, I must decrease' (John 3:30): Cultural and Social Interpretation." with Richard L. Rohrbaugh, *CBQ* 63 (2001): 464-83
"'I Am the Door' (John 10: 7, 9): Jesus the Broker in the Fourth Gospel," *CBQ* 69 (2007): 271-91

appear with the kind permission of the journal.

Journal of Biblical Literature

"I Said: 'You Are Gods': Psalm 82 and John 10," *JBL* 108 (1989): 647-63
"The 'Noble' Shepherd in John 10: Cultural and Rhetorical Background," *JBL* 120 (2001): 267-91
"Encomium and Vituperation: Praising and Blaming Jesus in the Fourth Gospel," *JBL* 126 (2007): 529-52

appear with the kind permission of the journal.

Scholars Press

"'My Lord and My God': The Divinity of Jesus in John's Gospel," *SBLSP* 1986: 152-71
"Despising the Shame of the Cross: Honor and Shame in the Johannine Passion Narrative," *Semeia* 69 (1996): 113-37
"The Sociology of Secrecy and the Fourth Gospel," in *What Is John? Volume II. Literary and Social Readings of the Fourth Gospel*, ed. Fernando Segovia (Atlanta: Scholars Press, 1998) 79-109

appear with kind permission of Scholars Press.

Sheffield Academic Press

"Role and Status in the Fourth Gospel: Cutting Through the Confusion," in *The Impartial God: Essays in Biblical Studies in Honor of Jouette M. Bassler*, ed. Calvin J. Roetzel and Robert L. Foster (Sheffield: Sheffield Phoenix Press, 2007) 36-65

Abbreviations

AB	Anchor Bible
ABD	David Noel Freedman, ed., *Anchor Bible Dictionary*
Abr.	Philo, *On the Life of Abraham*
Ag. Ap.	Josephus, *Against Apion*
Agr.	Philo, *On Agriculture*
AJP	*American Journal of Philology*
AJS	*American Journal of Sociology*
Alleg. Interp.	Philo, *Allegorical Interpretation*
ANRW	*Aufstieg und Niedergang der Römischen Welt*
Ant.	Josephus, *Antiquities of the Jews*
ATR	*Anglican Theological Review*
AusBR	*Australian Biblical Review*
AUSS	*Andrews University Seminary Studies*
b.	Babylonian Talmud
BAGD	Walter Bauer, *Greek-English Lexicon of the New Testament*, revised and edited by Frederick W. Danker
BASOR	*Bulletin of the American Schools of Oriental Research*
BETL	Bibliotheca ephemeridum theologicarum lovaniensium
Bib	*Biblica*
BJRL	*Bulletin of the John Rylands Library*
BSac	*Bibliotheca Sacra*
BTB	*Biblical Theology Bulletin*
BVC	*Bible et vie chrétienne*
BZ	*Biblische Zeitschrift*
BZNW	Beihefte zur Zeitschrift für die alttestamentliche Wissenschaft

Abbreviations

CBQ	Catholic Biblical Quarterly
Cher.	Philo, On the Cherubim
CJ	Classical Journal
CQ	Classical Quarterly
CTJ	Calvin Theological Journal
CTM	Concordia Theological Monthy
CurrTM	Currents in Theology and Mission
DR	Downside Review
Dreams	Philo, On Dreams
Drunkenness	Philo, On Drunkenness
EBib	Études bibliques
Embassy	Philo, Embassy to Gaius
EvQ	Evangelical Quarterly
Exp	Expositor
ExpT	Expository Times
Flacc.	Philo, Against Flaccus
Flight	Philo, On Flight and Finding
GCS	Griechische christliche Schriftsteller
Good Person	Philo, That Every Good Person Is Free
GRBS	Greek, Roman and Byzantine Studies
Heir	Philo, Who Is the Heir?
HR	History of Religion
HTR	Harvard Theological Review
HUCA	Hebrew Union College Annual
IDB	G. A. Buttrick, ed., Interpreter's Dictionary of the Bible
IDBSup	Supplementary volume to IDB
IEJ	Israel Exploration Journal
IESS	International Encyclopedia of the Social Sciences
Inst. Orat.	Quintilian, Institutio Oratoria
Int	Interpretation
JAAR	Journal of the American Academy of Religion
JBL	Journal of Biblical Literature
J.E.	Jewish Encyclopedia
JECS	Journal of Early Christian Studies
JETS	Journal of the Evangelical Theological Society
JLT	Journal of Literature and Theology
Jos.	Philo, On the Life of Joseph
JQR	Jewish Quarterly Review
JSI	Journal of Social Issues
JSJ	Journal for the Study of Judaism

ABBREVIATIONS

JSS	*Journal of Semitic Studies*
JSNT	*Journal for the Study of the New Testament*
JSNTSup	Journal for the Study of the New Testament Supplement Series
JSOTSup	Journal for the Study of the Old Testament Supplement Series
JTS	*Journal of Theological Studies*
LAB	Pseudo-Philo, *Liber antiquitatum biblicarum*
LSJ	Henry Liddell, Robert Scott, and Henry Jones, *A Greek-English Lexicon*
LXX	Septuagint
m.	Mishnah
Migr.	Philo, *On the Migration of Abraham*
M-M	James Moulton and George Milligan, *The Vocabulary of the Greek Testament*
Mos.	Philo, *On the Life of Moses*
MT	Masoretic Text
Names	Philo, *On the Change of Names*
NDIEC	*New Documents Illustrating Early Christianity*
NedTTs	*Nederlands theologisch Tijdschrift*
Neof.	Neofiti
Neot	*Neotestamentica*
NIDNTT	Colin Brown, ed., *New International Dictionary of New Testament Theology*
NovT	*Novum Testamentum*
NovTSup	Novum Testamentum Supplement Series
NT Apoc.	Edgar Hennecke and Wilhelm Schneemelcher, eds., *New Testament Apocrypha*
NTS	*New Testament Studies*
Onq.	Targum Onqelos
OTP	James H. Charlesworth, ed., *The Old Testament Pseudepigrapha*
Pesiq. Rab.	Pesiqta Rabbati
PG	*Patrologia Graeca*
Plant.	Philo, *On Planting*
Post.	Philo, *On the Posterity of Cain*
Ps.-J.	Pseudo-Jonathan
QE	Philo, *Questions and Answers on Exodus*
QG	Philo, *Questions and Answers on Genesis*
Rab.	Rabbah
RAC	*Reallexikon für Antike und Christentum*
RB	*Revue Biblique*
REJ	*Revue des études juives*

Abbreviations

ResQ	Restoration Quarterly
RevScRel	Revue des sciences religieuses
Rhet.	Aristotle, Rhetoric
RHR	Revue de l'histoire des religions
RivB	Rivista Biblica
RSRev	Religious Studies Review
RTP	Revue de Théologie et Philosophie
Sacr.	Philo, *On the Sacrifices of Cain and Abel*
SBLDS	Society of Biblical Literature Dissertation Series
SBLSP	Society of Biblical Literature Seminar Papers
SC	Sources chrétiennes
Scr	Scripture
SJLA	Studies in Judaism in Late Antiquity
SNTSMS	Society for New Testament Studies Monograph Series
Sobr.	Philo, *On Sobriety*
Spec.	Philo, *On the Special Laws*
ST	Studia Theologica
Str-B	H. Strack and P. Billerbeck, *Kommentar zum Neuen Testament*
SVF	Stoicorum Veterum Fragmenta
t.	Tosefta
TAPA	Transactions and Proceedings of the American Philological Association
TBT	The Bible Today
TDNT	G. Kittel and G. Friedrich, eds., *Theological Dictionary of the New Testament*
Tg.	Targum
TLZ	Theologische Literaturzeitung
TRu	Theologische Rundschau
TS	Theological Studies
TTZ	Trier Theologische Zeitschrift
TynB	Tyndale Bulletin
TZ	Theologische Zeitschrift
USQR	Union Seminary Quarterly Review
VC	Vigiliae Christianae
VD	Verbum Dei
Virt.	Philo, *On the Virtues*
VT	Vetus Testamentum
Vulg.	Vulgate
War	Josephus, *Jewish War*
Worse	Philo, *That the Worse Attacks the Better*
WTJ	Westminster Theological Journal

ABBREVIATIONS

WUNT	Wissenschaftliche Untersuchungen zum Neuen Testament
Yer I, II	*Targum Yerushalmi I* and *II*
ZKT	*Zeitschrift für Kirche und Theologie*
ZNW	*Zeitschrift für die Neutestamentliche Wissenschaft*
ZRG	*Zeitschrift für Religion und Grenzgebiet*
ZTK	*Zeitschrift für Theologie und Kirche*

PART ONE

The Anatomy of the Fourth Gospel: Major Perspectives

1

Encomium vs. Vituperation

Contrasting Portraits of Jesus in the Fourth Gospel

1.0 Topic and Hypotheses

Past consideration of Johannine characters regarded them as either symbolic or representative figures;[1] now they are studied according to literary theory.[2] This study contributes to those efforts with insights drawn from ancient rhetoric, in particular from the encomium genre of the *progymnasmata*. The encomium, to my knowledge, has been rarely used in interpreting the Gospels, although it ought to be, because it is the most common form in antiquity for praising a person according to fixed, regular categories (origins, parents, nurture, virtues, and death). Anyone who learned to write would most likely have learned it as a key element in being schooled to write materials for public persuasion. Moreover, this conventional and stereotypical[3] view of persons can be

---

1. Raymond Collins, "Representative Figures in the Fourth Gospel," *Downside Review* 94 (1976): 26-46, 118-13; R. Alan Culpepper, *Anatomy of the Fourth Gospel: A Study in Literary Design* (Philadelphia: Fortress, 1983) 99-148; Craig R. Koester, *Symbolism in the Fourth Gospel: Meaning, Mystery, Community* (Minneapolis: Fortress, 1995) 32-73.

2. Dorothy A. Lee ("Partnership in Easter Faith: The Role of Mary Magdalene and Thomas in John 20," *JSNT* 58 [1995]: 37-49) states: "The central role that Mary Magdalene and Thomas play comes . . . from the revelation and confession of faith in which each participates." Both begin with defective faith but end in full-throated confession of faith.

3. "Stereotype" originated as the term which described a type mold from which myriad pages might be printed. It came to mean something mechanically repeated, but wound up in the last century as a sociological term for a pejorative designation of ethnic groups and races. In antiquity, as we shall see, some places and cities enjoyed an honorable or shameful cachet. In terms of their origins, some peoples were noble *(generation)* and some places noble *(geography)*. Moreover, these stereotypes were reinforced in exercises in the *progymnasmata* where students

found in Judean[4] as well as Greco-Roman literature.[5] The encomium, therefore, is the viewpoint of the ancients themselves, the report of a native informant who indicates what conventional topics and contents need be covered to amplify praise for an honorable ancient person. This study, then, is no mere add-on to Johannine scholarship, but a worthy contribution because it examines the most likely honorable terms that author and audience of the Fourth Gospel would recognize.

Under the umbrella of the rhetorical presentation of characters in antiquity, I propose to argue these two hypotheses. First, the author of the Fourth Gospel knows the traditional code for praising persons as is found in the encomium exercise in the *progymnasmata*. Second, the Fourth Gospel uses this rhetorical code in a sly and clever manner because there are *two encomia* in the narrative: one characterizes *outsiders* who see things literally and inadequately (= vituperation) and another represents *insiders* who know what is going on, glory in their secrets and smirk at the outsiders (= encomium).

From Aristotle to Quintilian, epideictic rhetoric focused on "praise" (ἔπαινος) and "blame" (ψόγος), or in Latin *laus* and *vituperatio*.[6] Of them Aris-

---

memorized traditional gnomai and topoi to this effect and learned the conventional forms of encomia in which such stereotypes regularly appear. Thus the conventionality of stereotypical and popular labels used of certain ethnic and sub-ethnic groups becomes common currency in the Mediterranean. See John Harding, "Stereotypes," *IESS* 15.259.

4. Louis Feldman's "portraits" of Israelite heroes described in Josephus's *Antiquities* at the start did not refer to the formal shape of the encomium, although he intuitively identified its conventional topics. See "Josephus as an Apologist to the Greco-Roman World: His Portrait of Solomon," in Elizabeth Schüssler-Fiorenza, ed., *Aspects of Religious Propaganda in Judaism and Early Christianity* (Notre Dame, IN: University of Notre Dame Press, 1976) 69-98; "Josephus' Portrait of Saul," *HUCA* 53 (1982): 45-99; "Hellenizations in Josephus' *Jewish Antiquities*: The Portrait of Abraham," in *Josephus, Judaism and Christianity*, ed. Louis Feldman and Gohei Hata (Detroit: Wayne State University Press, 1987) 133-53; "Josephus' Portrait of Jacob," *JQR* 79 (1988): 101-51; "Josephus' Portrait of David," *HUCA* 60 (1989): 129-74; "Josephus' Portrait of Hezekiah," *JBL* 111 (1992): 597-610. Eventually Feldman discovered the encomium, which provided him with clarity for organizing the data in these "portraits" according to the exact topics described in the encomium. Similarly, Philo's *Mos.* describes Moses according to the same encomiastic topics. See Thomas R. Lee, *Studies in the Form of Sirach 44-50* (Atlanta: Scholars Press, 1986).

5. The topics in the encomium used for amplifying praise are generally found in biographies (βίοι) in antiquity. See Arnaldo Momigliano, *The Development of Greek Biography* (Cambridge, MA: Harvard University Press, 1971) 17; David E. Aune, "Greco-Roman Biography," *Greco-Roman Literature and the New Testament: Selected Forms and Genres* (Atlanta: Scholars Press, 1988) 109-110; Christopher Pelling, *Character and Individuality in Greek Literature* (Oxford: Clarendon, 1990); and Bruce J. Malina and Jerome H. Neyrey, *Portraits of Paul: An Archeology of Ancient Personality* (Louisville: Westminster John Knox, 1996) 10-18, 100-108, 153-201.

6. Paul knows this contrast of "praise" and "blame": In 1 Cor 11:2 he praises the community, but in 11:17 he blames them.

totle says: "The topics for praise and also those for blame . . . the qualities are *much the same as regards both praise and blame*" (*Rhet.* 1.9.1). Later, he remarks: "These are the things from which speeches of praise and blame are almost all derived, as well as what to look for when praising and blaming; for if we have knowledge of these [sources of praise] the opposite is clear, for blame is derived from its opposite" (*Rhet.* 1.9.41). The same categories, then, that argue for the praise of people may equally be used to their shame. Quintilian, following Aristotle's discourse on the rhetoric of praise and blame, provides us with this important idea: "The same method [for praise] will be applied to denunciations as well, but with a view to the opposite effect" (*Inst. Orat.* 3.7.19). The same aim and method became encoded in the encomia of the *progymnasmata*, which taught students to praise and to denounce. In this article we equate encomium with "praise," and vituperation with "blame." The argument, then, has two parts: 1. exposition of the contents of the encomium in the *progymnasmata*; 2. description of the antithetical encomia of Jesus in the Fourth Gospel, a vituperation by outsiders and a genuine encomium by insiders.

2.0 Contents of the Encomium

The *progymnasmata* was the collection of exercises taught those in the second level of education to train youths for public discourse.[7] Recent study of education in antiquity urges us to nuance the conventional, three-stage model found in current scholarship, which Robert Kaster summarized and to which he offered his qualifications. It is generally thought that ancient education consisted of:

> . . . the "primary" school overseen by the "primary" teacher, where one learned "letters" — the elements of reading and writing — and some arithmetic; the "secondary" or "grammar" school, where one received thorough and systematic instruction in language and literature, especially poetry, under the grammarian; and the school of rhetoric.[8]

Kaster offers the following corrections to this. Ancient education was

---

7. Although there has been much attention given to the progymnasmata in recent times, we do not find much scholarly investigation of the encomium and its relationship to Israelite and Christian literature. See Jerome H. Neyrey, "Josephus' *Vita* and the Encomium: A Native Model of Personality," *JSJ* 25 (1994): 177-206; Malina and Neyrey, *Portraits of Paul*, 19-63; and Richard A. Burridge, *What Are the Gospels? A Comparison with Graeco-Roman Biography* (Cambridge: Cambridge University Press, 1992) 109-53.

8. Robert A. Kaster, "Notes on 'Primary' and 'Secondary' Schools in Late Antiquity," *TAPA* 113 (1983): 323-46, here 323.

... a socially segmented system laid out along two essentially separate tracks. The most important formal distinction here is the division between the two tracks or segments: the *ludus literarius*, providing common literacy for students of relatively humble origins on the one hand;[9] and the *scholae liberales*, catering to a more privileged part of the population on the other.[10] The *scholae liberales* began with instruction in writing for a public or municipal audience, especially epideictic rhetoric so necessary for civic life.[11]

As we know, the collection of exercises for public speech and writing, namely, the *progymnasmata*, contained the cultural rules and values for the encomium, that is, the literary expression of the rhetoric of praise and blame.

Extant *progymnasmata* typically contain the following exercises:[12] 1. myths, 2. chreia,[13] 3. refutation and confirmation, 4. commonplaces on virtues and vices, 5. encomium and vituperation, 6. comparison,[14] 7. prosopo-

---

9. For an enlightening look into this level of literacy, see Raffaella Cribiore, *Writing, Teachers, and Students in Graeco-Roman Egypt* (Atlanta: Scholars Press, 1996) 129-37.

10. Kaster, "Notes on 'Primary' and 'Secondary' Schools in Late Antiquity," 337.

11. What level of education would the Gospel writers have reached? Matthew seems to have been formally trained in Israelite and Hellenistic ways; he employs the form of the encomium with considerable finesse; see Jerome H. Neyrey, *Honor and Shame in the Gospel of Matthew* (Louisville: Westminster John Knox, 1998), and "The Social Location of Paul: How Paul Was Educated and What He Could Compose as Indices of His Social Location," in *Fabrics of Discourse: Essays in Honor of Vernon K. Robbins*, ed. David B. Gowler, L. Gregory Bloomquist, and Duane F. Watson (Harrisburg, PA: Trinity Press International, 2003) 126-64. Readers may have a fresh appreciation of the author of the Fourth Gospel after seeing what he could write.

12. The book of George A. Kennedy (*Progymnasmata: Greek Textbooks of Prose Composition and Rhetoric* [Atlanta: Society of Biblical Literature Press, 2003]) contains fresh translations of all of the extant progymnasmata. For individual authors, see James R. Butts, *The "Progymnasmata" of Theon: A New Text with Translation and Commentary* (unpublished dissertation: Claremont, 1986); Hermogenes of Tarsus in Charles S. Baldwin, *Medieval Rhetoric and Poetic* (New York: Macmillan, 1928) 23-38; Menander Rhetor in Donald A. Russell and Nigel G. Wilson, *Menander Rhetor* (Oxford: Clarendon Press, 1981); Aphthonius of Ephesus in Ray Nadeau, "The Progymnasmata of Aphthonius in Translation," *Speech Monographs* 19 (1952) 264-85; and more recently Patricia P. Matsen, Philip Rollinson, and Marion Sousa, eds., *Readings from Classical Rhetoric* (Carbondale: Southern Illinois University Press, 1990) 266-88. We include Quintilian, *Inst. Orat.* 3.7.10-18 in this category.

13. The best introduction to the *chreia* is still that of Ronald F. Hock and Edward N. O'Neill, *The Chreia in Ancient Rhetoric*. Volume I: *The Progymnasmata* (Atlanta: Scholars Press, 1986).

14. See F. Focke, "Synkrisis," *Hermes* 58 (1923): 327-68; Philip A. Stadtler, "Plutarch's Comparison of Pericles and Fabius Maximus," *GRBS* 16 (1975): 77-85; David H. J. Larmour, "Making Parallels: Synkrisis and Plutarch's Themistocles and Camillus," *ANRW* II.33.6 (1996) 4154-4200; Christopher Forbes, "Comparison, Self-Praise and Irony: Paul's Boasting and the Conventions of Hellenistic Rhetoric," *NTS* 32 (1986): 1-30; Peter Marshall, *Enmity at Corinth: Social Conventions in Paul's Relations with the Corinthians* (Tübingen: Mohr, 1987) 53-55, 325-53.

poieia,[15] 8. description, 9. thesis for or against something, and 10. legislation, for or against a law. Although "praise and blame" runs through most of them, it is formally and explicitly taught in the "encomium." The conventional encomium instructs students where to find reasons and data for praise (or blame), which genre is found widespread in the Greco-Roman and Israelite literary worlds. With great consistency, the encomium instructed authors how to praise someone in terms of the following five categories:

I. Origin
   A. Geography and Generation: country, race, ancestors, parents
   B. Birth: phenomena at birth (stars, visions, etc.), oracles
II. Nurture and Training
   A. Education: teachers, arts, skills, laws, mode of life
III. Accomplishments
   A. Deeds of the Body: beauty, strength, agility, might, health
   B. Deeds of the Soul: justice, wisdom, temperance, courage, piety
   C. Deeds of Fortune: power, wealth, friends, fame, fortune
IV. Comparison
V. Noble Death and Posthumous Honors

Let us now examine what the ancients understood by some of the categories.

2.1 Origin

Each category of the encomium was itself a commonplace understood by all the ancients. All knew the basic, invariable content of "origins," i.e., origin in a noble land *(geography)* and from noble stock *(generation)*. A synopsis of four encomiastic instructions on geography and generation yields this uniform content.

Hermogenes	**Aelius Theon**	**Aphthonius**	**Quintilian**
ethnic affiliation	ethnic affiliation	ethnic affiliation	ethnic affiliation
nation/city-state	nation/city-state	home locale	country
	government		
clan/tribe		ancestors	ancestors
		fathers	parents

---

15. See Joseph M. Miller, "Concerning Ethiopia," *Readings in Medieval Rhetoric* (Bloomington: Indiana University Press, 1973) 33-36; Stanley K. Stowers, "Romans 7:7-25 as a Speech-in-Character (προσωποποιία)" in *Paul in His Hellenistic Context*, ed. Troels Engberg-Pederson (Minneapolis: Fortress, 1995) 180-202.

Thus a person's origins are expressed by two topics: geography *(ethnos, polis, patria)* and generation *(genos, pateres, progonoi).*

Geography. The ancients were acutely aware of the meanings carried by geography, which was rooted in their theory of elements. Places were known to be wet, dry, hot and cold,[16] which elements also indicated character. A person with excessive heat would be such-and-such type of person, whereas people with more coldness would be another type (see Hippocrates, "Air, Water and Places," 24.1-40). Aristotle's version of this applies the four-element theory to specific geographical regions and their capacity for ruling, arguing once more that geography equals character.

> Let us speak of what ought to be the citizens' natural character. This one might almost discern by looking at the famous cities of Greece and by observing how the whole inhabited world is divided up among the nations. The nations inhabiting the cold places and those of Europe are full of spirit but somewhat deficient in intelligence and skill, so that they continue comparatively free, but lacking in political organization and capacity to rule their neighbors. The peoples of Asia on the other hand are intelligent and skillful in temperament, but lack spirit, so that they are in continuous subjection and slavery. But the Greek race participates in both characters, just as it occupies the middle position geographically,[17] for it is both spirited and intelligent, hence it continues to be free and to have very good political institutions, and to be capable of ruling all mankind if it attains constitutional unity. (*Politics* 1327b.1-2; see Plato, *Laws* 5.747d)

Thus "Europe," which is north and west of Greece, is "cold," full of spirit, but deficient in intelligence and skill; while "free" themselves, the people there lack the political skills to rule others. Place = element = character! Asia, east of Greece, is unlike Europe in that it has intelligence and skill, but lacks spirit, with the result that the people there are content with subjection and slavery. Greece, which is geographically centered, contains a balance of all four elements and so

---

16. Malina and Neyrey, *Portraits of Paul,* 113-25.

17. Greece's "middle position" is know as geocentrism or as the "omphalos myth." At times Greece enjoyed this preeminence for it considered the "navel" at Delphi to be the center of the world; for example, consider the remark of Strabo: "Now although the greatest share of honor was paid to this temple because of its oracle, since of all oracles in the world it had the repute of being the most truthful, yet the position of the place added something. For it is almost in the center of Greece taken as a whole, between the country inside the Isthmus and that outside it, it was also believed to be in the center of the inhabited world, and people called it *the navel of the earth,* in addition fabricating a myth, which is told by Pindar. . . . There is also a kind of navel to be seen in the temple" (*Geography* 9.3.6).

is intelligent, skilled, with great spirit, good political institutions and capacity to rule all mankind. Place = all four elements = character.

In time a series of stereotypes developed characterizing various places and the people dwelling in them, which served as an index of snobbery: some places were inherently honorable and noble, but others ignoble.[18] For example, "Cretans are always liars, evil beasts, lazy gluttons" (Titus 1:12), whereas Paul boasts that he comes from a no low-status city (Acts 21:39). Menander Rhetor, a progymnastic author, provides a cogent summary of the logic of geography in praise:

> You will come to the topic of his native country *(patris)*. Here you must ask yourself whether it is a distinguished country or not [and whether he comes from a celebrated and splendid place or not]. If his native country is famous, you should place your account of it first, and mention it before his family.... If the city has no distinction, you must inquire whether his nation as a whole is considered brave and valiant, or is devoted to literature or the possession of virtues, like the Greek race, or again is distinguished for law, like the Italian, or is courageous, like the Gauls or Paeonians. You must argue that *it is inevitable that a man from such a [city or] nation should have such characteristics*. (II.369.18-370.5)[19]

Certain places characteristically breed people with specific praiseworthy traits: Greeks in literature and virtue, Italians in law, and Gauls in courage.[20] The pre-

---

18. The classification of someone on the basis of place of origin was a standard element of the way persons were described; see Aristotle, *Rhet.* 1.5.5; Cicero, *De Inventione* 1.24.34-35; Quintilian, *Inst. Orat.* 3.7.10-11; 5.10.24-25.

19. In one of his satires, Lucian caricatures several ethnoi, each known in terms of some characteristic behavior: "Whenever I looked at the country of the Getae I saw them fighting; whenever I transferred my gaze to the Scythians, they could be seen roving about in their wagons; and when I turned my eyes aside slightly, I beheld the Egyptians working the land. The Phoenicians were on trading venture, the Cilicians were engaged in piracy, the Spartans were whipping themselves and the Athenians were attending court" (*Icaromenippus* 17). Various places, then, had certain characteristics: Scythians roam, Egyptians farm, Phoenicians trade, Cilicians rob, and Greeks attend court.

20. Not just virtue, however, but also vice. The following illustrations come from Bruce J. Malina (*The New Testament World: Insights from Cultural Anthropology* [3rd edition; Louisville: Westminster John Knox, 2001] 64-65). "The Egyptian is by nature an evil-eyed person, and the citizens of Alexandria burst with envy and considered that any good fortunes to others was misfortune to them" (Philo, *Flacc.* 29); "Scythians delight in murdering people and are little better than wild beasts" (Josephus, *Ag. Ap.* 2.69). Modern readers are not unfamiliar with this classification, for we speak of Arabian stallions, Russian wolfhounds, Irish sheepdogs, and the like.

supposition behind this lies in the belief that "it is *inevitable* that a man from such a city or nation should have such characteristics." Yes, "inevitable!" Thus knowing the geography of a person's origins tells the ancients about the person's worth and value.[21]

Generation. Much as we value the pedigree of animals produced through select breeding, so too the ancients in regard to people. Quintilian sums it up: "Persons are generally regarded as having some resemblance to their parents and ancestors, a resemblance which leads to their living disgracefully or honorably, as the case may be" (*Inst. Orat.* 5.10.24). Lists of the culturally specific values in parents that were popularly praised may be found in most rhetoricians; Aristotle provided just such criteria which warrant praise:

> Now good birth in a race or a state means that its members are indigenous or ancient; that its earliest leaders were distinguished men, and that from them have sprung many who were distinguished for qualities that we admire. The good birth of an individual implies that both parents are free citizens, and that, as in the case of the state, the founders of the line have been notable for virtue or wealth or something else which is highly prized, and that many distinguished persons belong to the family, men and women, young and old. (*Rhet.* 1.5.5)

Aristotle expresses the common expectation that "children will be chips off the old block" (see Deut 23:2; 2 Kings 9:22; Isa 57:3; Hos 1:2; Ecclus 23:25-26; 30:7), either like father, like son (e.g. Matt 11:27) or like mother, like daughter (e.g. Ezek 16:44). If the parents or ancestors were "landed" or citizens of a free *polis*, then the root stock of the family was noble; virtuous ancients should be expected to breed virtue. Plato says: "They were good because they sprang from good fathers" (*Menexenus* 237). Confirmation of this is found in the endless introduction of biblical characters as "son of so-and-so." To know the father is to know the son. The honor rating of the father indicates the honor rating of the son.

Birth. Important, honorable births were announced by celestial phenomenon (stars, comets) and accompanied by oracles and prophecies. Modern readers already know this from comparisons of biblical and classical materi-

---

21. Describing the "honor rating" of the cities Paul is said to have visited, Jerome H. Neyrey ("Luke's Social Location of Paul: Cultural Anthropology and the Status of Paul in Acts," in *History, Literature, and Society in the Book of Acts*, ed. Ben Witherington [Cambridge: Cambridge University Press, 1996] 268-76) called attention to the vanity and rivalry of cities in the matter of rank and titles, such as "metropolis," "first and greatest," "autonomous," "Warden of the (Imperial) Temple," "friend of Rome," and the like.

als,[22] but we now locate it in its proper rhetorical context, a key element of the encomium. Menander Rhetor gives typical instructions on this topic:

> If any divine sign occurred at the time of his birth, either on land or in the heavens or on the sea, compare the circumstances with those of Romulus, Cyrus, and similar stories, since in these cases also there were miraculous happenings connected with their birth — the dream of Cyrus' mother, the suckling of Romulus by the she-wolf. (2.371.5-14)

Whatever happened in the macrocosm of the sky mirrored and foretold what was soon to occur in the microcosm of the earth. Such phenomena, then, served as status markers.

2.2 Nurture and Training

There were a right way and a wrong way to educate and socialize a son.[23] Moreover, independent of the family, one might inquire what events shaped the person's character. Our native informant, Marcus Tullius Cicero, instructs us:

> Under *manner of life* should be considered with whom he was reared, in what tradition and under whose direction, what teachers he had in the liberal arts, what instructors in the art of living, with whom he associates on terms of friendship, in what occupation, trade or profession he is engaged, how he manages his private fortune, and what is the character of his home life. (*De Inventione* 1.24.35)

Sons can never exceed the nobility of their fathers, but they can hope to match them, if they are reared in the traditions of the clan. In addition to Cicero's commonplace on "nurture and training," Josephus demonstrates in his *Life* the content of this topic, declaring that he made "great progress" in his education and "gained a reputation for an excellent memory and understanding" (8). When fourteen years old, he "won universal applause for his love of letters," such that the "chief priests and leading men of the city used constantly to come to me for precise information on some particular of our ordinances" (8-9). He

---

22. A collection of background parallels may be found in David R. Cartlidge and David L. Dungan, eds., *Documents for the Study of the Gospels*, revised and enlarged edition (Minneapolis: Fortress, 1994) 129-36. It is curious that they never considered the encomium form as the basis for collecting parallels.

23. John J. Pilch, "'Beat His Ribs While He Is Young' (Sir 30:12): A Window on the Mediterranean World," *BTB* 23 (1993): 101-13.

tells us that he investigated the manner of life of the three major sects of Judea, Pharisees, Sadducees and Essenes, submitting himself to hard training and laborious exercises. Finally, he apprenticed himself to Bannus and became schooled in the values and structures of the Israelite purity system (11). It is essential for Josephus that he present himself not only as gifted intellectually and highly cultured, but also as "nurtured and trained" as an observant Israelite.

2.3 Comparison

Comparison may be a distinct exercise of its own in the *progymnasmata* or it may be part of the encomium. Nevertheless, its purpose and mode of argument are identical in both. As one *progymnastic* author states:

> Comparison is a composition made comparative by the process of placing side by side with the subject that which is greater or equal to it . . . to place fine things beside good things or worthless things beside worthless things or small things beside the greater. The comparison is a double encomium or an invective combined with an encomium. There are as many proper subjects for a comparison as there are for both invective and encomium: persons, things, times, places, animals, and also plants.[24]

Comparison generally compares persons and things similar in honor or prowess (= two encomia) or contrasts them (= encomium and vituperation). Those making comparisons, moreover, are instructed to use the same categories of the encomium which we have just surveyed, so that persons are compared in terms of birth, origin, nurture and training, etc.

> When we compare characters, we will first set side by side their noble birth, their education, their children, their public offices, their reputation, their bodily health, as well as whatever else I said earlier, in the chapter "On Encomia," about bodily good qualities and external good qualities.[25]

2.4 Death and Posthumous Honors

A death was "noble" if accompanied by posthumous honors, such as public celebration of the dead in games or by monuments, as Demosthenes describes: "It

---

24. Aphthonius in Matsen and Rollinson, *Readings from Classical Rhetoric,* 279-80.
25. Butts, *The "Progymnasmata" of Theon,* 10.113.

is a proud privilege to behold them possessors of deathless honours and a memorial of their valour erected by the State, and deemed deserving of sacrifices and games for all future time" (*Funeral Oration* 36).[26] The very funeral orations themselves are structured out of the encomium to glorify the dead, first by giving a public evaluation of their worth and later by an annual burnishing of their reputation.[27] Hence, we frequently find the claim that those being celebrated are in one sense like the gods, because their glory too is now deathless and everlasting.

3.0 The Vituperation of the Outsiders

With our knowledge of the encomium, let us turn to the Fourth Gospel. Two things will occur simultaneously in this part of the article. We will bring forward in sequence each of the five major topics of the encomium and show that in the Fourth Gospel the author constructs not one, but two encomia about Jesus, one representative of how outsiders view Jesus (= vituperation, because it seeks to vilify him) and another characteristic of insiders (= encomium, because it claims maximum honor for Jesus on the same encomiastic points).

The author, who is responsible for all that the outsiders say about Jesus, structures their remarks, not haphazardly, but according to the main topics of the encomium, not as praise for Jesus, but as blame. Hence he creates for outsiders not an encomium, but a vituperation whose purpose is to shame and dishonor Jesus. The data used in this vituperation are not entirely erroneous in terms of geography and generation, but represent outsider thinking which is fleshly, from below, judged according to appearances and lacking in knowledge.[28] They know very little, and construe this in a hostile manner. Finally, in

---

26. See John E. Ziolkowski, *Thucydides and the Tradition of Funeral Speeches at Athens* (Salem, NH: Ayer Company, 1985) 126-28.

27. The following inscription was a public decree, read aloud at the tomb of a certain Theophilos and subsequently carved in white marble: " worth . . . of very noble ancestral stock, having contributed all good-will towards his country, having lived his life as master of his family, providing many things for his country through his generalship and tenure as agoranomos and his embassies as far as Rome and Germany and Caesar, being amicable to the citizens and in concord with his wife Apphia, now it is resolved that Theophilos be honoured with a painted portrait and a gold bust and a marble statue," *NDIEC* 2 (1982): 58-60.

28. These are the folks who continually misunderstand, take things literally, and fail to see or hear irony. See D. A. Carson, "Understanding Misunderstanding in the Fourth Gospel," *TynB* 33 (1982): 61-91; Earl Richard, "Expressions of Double Meaning and Their Function in the Gospel of John," *NTS* 31 (1985): 96-112; and Bruce J. Malina, "John: The Maverick Christian Group: The Evidence of Sociolinguistics," *BTB* 24 (1994): 167-82.

their vituperation against Jesus, the author provides grounds for judging them (see 12:31-36, 46-50).

3.1 Geography

The author formally raises the topic of Jesus' "origins" by staging a controversy over "whence" Jesus comes and "whither" he goes. Readers are introduced to this pattern by Nicodemus,[29] who arrived knowing that Jesus "came from God," but left knowing nothing at all. After making a critical distinction between ways of "knowing," namely, "flesh" versus "spirit" (3:6), Jesus plays with the word "spirit" (as earthly wind or heavenly phenomenon), to illustrate those two ways of knowing: "The wind blows . . . and *you do not know* whence it comes and whither it goes" (3:8). Although not about Jesus' "origins," this introduces[30] a formal pattern: 1. "know" (or not know); 2. "whence" and "whither." The quotations below illustrate the most significant uses of the pattern concerning "whence" Jesus comes.

> The Jews murmured at him because he said, "I am the bread which **comes down from heaven.**" They said, "Is not this Jesus, the son of Joseph, whose father and mother *we know?* How can he now say, 'I have **come down from heaven**'?" (6:41-42).

> "*We know* where this man **comes from**, but when the Christ appears, *no one will know* **whence he comes.**" So Jesus proclaimed, as he taught in the temple, "*You know me, and you know* where **I come from**? But I have not come of my own accord; he who sent me is true, and him *you do not know. I know him,* for **I come from him**, and he sent me" (7:27-29).

> "Is the Christ to **come from Galilee**?" . . . "*Search* and you will *see* that no prophet is **to rise from Galilee**" (7:41-42, 52).

> Jesus answered, "Even if I do bear witness to myself, my testimony is true, for *I know* **whence I have come** and whither I am going, but you *do not know whence I come or whither I am going*" (8:14).

---

29. Actually, when Nathanael first appears, he, too, shared the geographical presumption of the baseness of Jesus' "origins": "What good can come from Nazareth?" (1:46), but he was recruited to "come and see." Thus he dropped the outsider view of Jesus' origins and began to see like an insider (1:47-51).

30. Still earlier, the steward at the wedding in Cana tasted the wine, but he "did not know whence it came" (2:9).

[Pharisees:] "*We know* that God has spoken to Moses; but as for this man, *we do not know* **where he comes from**." The man answered, "Why, this is a marvel! *You do not know* **where he comes from**, and yet he opened my eyes. . . . If this man were **not from God** he could do nothing" (9:29-30, 33).

In each of these incidents, the author structures the discourse as a challenge/riposte exchange according to the formal pattern of two elements: 1. knowing/not knowing and 2. whence Jesus comes. Outsiders claim to know, but Jesus accuses them of culpable lack of knowledge. Like Nicodemus, they "know" only in earthly, fleshly ways, but Jesus claims that his "origins" are from the heavenly world. Thus, his "origins" refer both to Jesus' "locale" and authorization (agent/apostle).

At this point we know several things. First, the author knows the category of "origins" and its role in honoring or shaming, depending on the nobility or baseness of geography. Second, "origins" is an obligatory encomiastic topic, for the author makes it the formal point of controversy between outsiders and Jesus. Third, the author structures the contrast between the vituperation of outsiders and the encomium of insiders in terms of "knowing" (or claiming to know) and "not knowing." Outsiders "know" according to the flesh and think earthly thoughts; for them "whence" can only mean a peasant father and mother, Nazareth, Galilee, and the like. Moreover, it is Jesus who tells them that they are completely wrong. Thus the author knows the topic, handles it traditionally, and advances it from its confinement at the beginning of an encomium to a topic of great significance which pervades the narrative (see 19:9).

3.2 Generation

Outsiders know Jesus' father and mother as peasants from no distinguished clan whose offspring, therefore, cannot be persons of honor. The outsiders think it enough to rebut Jesus' remark about "coming down from heaven" by simple reference to his mortal parents: "Is not this Jesus, the son of Joseph, whose father and mother we know? How does he now say, 'I have come down from heaven'?" (6:42). If the parents, moreover, come from Nazareth of Galilee, q.e.d. Even Jesus' family, whatever its low status, dishonors him in several ways. "His own did not receive him" (1:11), and his brothers seek to manipulate him, indicating a breakdown of kinship relations (7:1-7). It is always shameful when kin or family show disrespect to one of their own. In the outsider's vituperation, Jesus must be a charlatan and a deceiver because he has no nobility whatsoever, either from the mean place of his birth or from his undistinguished parents.

3.3 Training/Education

Paul claims respect because he studied under Gamaliel (Acts 22:3); in contrast, Peter and others were shamefully dismissed as "uneducated, common men" (Acts 4:13). So too with Jesus, outsiders mock him for his lack of education and training: "How is it that this man has learning, when he has never studied?" (John 7:15). A man without learning has no voice in the company of those who have it (see Luke 2:46-47).[31] Jesus' challengers consistently argue that he says, teaches, preaches his own message, which is self-serving and deceitful.

3.4 Deeds of the Soul

As regards deeds of the soul, outsiders see no virtue whatsoever in Jesus, only vice. Some label him a "deceiver": "He leads the people astray" (7:12), proof of which appears when those sent to arrest Jesus do not return with this "deceiver" but declare that they were captivated by his words: "No man ever spoke like this man!" (7:46). With good reason the Pharisees grumble that these men too are victims of Jesus "deception" (7:47). Others label Jesus as demon-possessed (8:48, 52), the implication of which is that he cannot be God's agent, but is rather the agent of God's enemy. And they consider him a lawbreaker because he violates the Sabbath law by healing on the Holy Day (chs. 5, 9), which leads some to brand him a "sinner": "This man is not from God, for he does not keep the Sabbath" (9:16, 24). Finally, Jesus in their eyes commits the sin of sins, blasphemy, by making himself equal to God (5:18; 10:30-33).

3.5 Death

To them, his death cannot be "noble," for as a sinner he justly gets what he deserves. Although Jesus evades attempts to stone him for his blasphemy (8:59; 10:31), the Jerusalem elite finally capture him and hand him to the Romans to be crucified. In this scenario, Jesus' body is mutilated and denied posthumous honors, as is fitting. Eternal glory is out of the question and his end is unrelieved shame.

---

31. It should not be presumed that every male had "voice" in village or city. In a study of Luke 4:1-30, Richard L. Rohrbaugh ("Legitimating Sonship — A Test of Honour: A Social-Scientific Study of Luke 4:1-30," in *Modelling Early Christianity: Social-Scientific Studies of the New Testament in Its Context*, ed. Philip F. Esler [London: Routledge, 1995] 187-89) argues about who may say what, where and when. Not all have "voice," which is a matter of honor and status.

Outsiders, therefore, find no reason whatsoever to praise Jesus. On the contrary, on every topic that matters in considering the honor or worth of a person, they see only grounds to dismiss and revile Jesus. No noble origin; no honorable parents; no education/training; only vice and sin, and an appropriately shameful death. For him only vituperation is suitable.

4.0 The Insiders' Encomium

The author, however, creates a true encomium for Jesus; that is, he creates a portrait of praise for Jesus which represents the insiders' viewpoint, which is the complete antithesis of the outsiders' vituperation. Here we find praise, honor and glory for Jesus in terms of the same topics, categories, and contents used to construct the outsiders' vituperation. Moreover, the contents of generation and geography, the key topics for evaluating Jesus, are always revealed by Jesus himself, which means that only insiders have and understand this esoteric knowledge.

4.1 *Geography*

Jesus' *geography* as reported by and for insiders is the complete obverse of what outsiders know. "Whence" means so much more to them:

> The true light that enlightens every person was *coming into the world* (1:9).

> The word became flesh and dwelled among us (1:14).

> No one has ascended into heaven but he who *descended from heaven*, the Son of man (3:13).

> He who *comes from above* is above all . . . he who *comes from heaven* is above all (3:31).

> I have *come down from heaven*, not to do my own will, but the will of him who sent me. . . . This is the bread which *came down from heaven*. . . . I am the living bread which *came down from heaven*. . . . This is the bread which *came down from heaven* (6:38, 50-51, 58).

> What if you were to see the Son of man ascending *where he was before*? (6:62).

> You know me and you know *where I come from*? But I have not come on my own accord, but he who sent me is true, and him you do not know (7:28).

> You are from below, *I am from above;* you are of this world, *I am not of this world* (8:23).
>
> Jesus, knowing that . . . he had *come from God* and was going to God . . . (13:3).
>
> Now, Father, glorify me in your own presence with the glory *which I had with you before the world began* (17:5).

Outsiders' claims to know "whence" Jesus comes are always reduced to the fact that he is a mere mortal. They indeed claim to know whence he comes: "You know me and you know *where I come from?*" (7:28). In contrast, insiders understand Jesus' "whence" as a claim that he is truly "from above" and "not of this world." "Whence" means that he "came down from heaven" into this world. In key rhetorical places, such as the prefaces for the Books of Signs and Glory, the audience is told the secret. The Word, who was eternally and who was face-to-face with God in the beginning, descended into the world and became one of us (1:9, 14). The author again tells us this secret of secrets on the eve of Jesus' departure: "Jesus, knowing that . . . he had come from God and was going to God . . ." (13:3). Insiders, then, know "whence" and even "whither" Jesus goes. Nazareth and Galilee are low-status places, hardly the "bosom of the Father" (1:18) or the house of the Father with many rooms (14:2); this is premier real estate.

Although controversy clouds discussion of Jesus' true "origins," Jesus and the insiders truly know "whence" he comes; they alone revel in the great secret of knowing "whence he comes and whither he goes." It is inevitable that a man from such an honorable place as the bosom of the Father should have the characteristics of that place.

4.2 Generation

As regards *generation,* mention of "Joseph and his mother" (6:42) hardly exhausts this important category.[32] Jesus also has a Father in the heavenly

---

32. Apart from the passing remark in 6:42, we know nothing about Joseph, but we have several views of the mother in 2:1-12 and 19:25-26. A question arises: is the mother a worthy parent such that her son takes honor from her? This is debated among scholars such as Raymond E. Brown, *Mary in the New Testament* (Philadelphia: Fortress, 1978) 182-94, and Raymond Collins, "Mary in the Fourth Gospel: A Decade of Johannine Studies," *Louvain Studies* 3 (1970): 99-142.

world.³³ Because this Father is the noblest person in heaven and on earth, Jesus as "Son of God" or "Son of man" or "Son" is greatly to be praised and honored. According to the adage "like father, like son," one would expect Jesus to share in the nobility of his Father in many ways, such as: 1. "equality with God" (5:17; 10:30), 2. coming and acting in the "name of the Father" (5:43; 10:25), and 3. "receiving . . . manifesting . . . making known" God's name (17:6, 11-12, 26). Moreover, this Father holds Jesus in high regard inasmuch as he is the "only" or "unique" Son of this Father (1:14, 18; 3:16, 18),³⁴ the Son whom the Father loves (3:35; 5:20; 15:9).

4.3 Nurture and Training

Although outsiders dismiss Jesus because he lacks education and training, insiders know otherwise. In fact, his supremely noble Father has groomed this Son with great care. To outsiders, the untrained and uneducated, Jesus is simply a deceiver. But insiders frequently address him as "rabbi" (1:38, 49; 4:31; 6:25; 9:2; 11:8) or as "teacher" (1:38; 11:28; 13:13-14; 20:16). The author gives considerable attention throughout the narrative to Jesus as "word" (1:1-2) and authorized agent, who has been schooled by God in what to say and what to do. Jesus is supremely "in the know," because God gives him secrets and esoteric knowledge, shows him all that he does, and teaches him what to say.

God makes Jesus who he is. The Father *gives* Jesus all things, especially heavenly secrets and exclusive knowledge: "No one has ever seen God; the only Son, who is in the bosom of the Father, he *has made him known*" (1:18). "Not that any one has seen the Father except him who is from God; he has *seen* the Father" (6:46). The Son is unique in that he alone has seen the Father, the source of wisdom and knowledge, and because he alone makes known this God. But he is remarkably "in the know."

God teaches Jesus what to do. The Father *shows* Jesus all that he does, so that he *does* what the Father *does*: "Truly, truly, I say to you, the Son can do nothing of his own accord, but only *what he sees the Father doing;* for *whatever he does, that the Son does likewise.* For the Father loves the Son, and *shows him*

---

33. Marianne Meye Thompson, *The God of the Gospel of John* (Grand Rapids: Eerdmans, 2001) 69-72.

34. The parent is honorable and so according to the principle of generation the son draws honor from this. Moreover, Jesus is the "unique" or "only" son, which is rhetorical shorthand for acclaiming this son as most honorable. See Jerome H. Neyrey, "'First,' 'Only,' 'One of a Few,' and 'No One Else': The Rhetoric of Uniqueness and the Doxologies in 1 Timothy," *Bib* 86 (2005): 59-87.

all that he himself is doing; and *greater works* than these *will he show him,* that you may marvel" (5:19-20). Jesus does not spy on God or steal God's secrets. On the contrary, he has had superior nurture and training. Moreover, if we understand "do" and "does" as mastercraftsman's skills, then Jesus has completed his apprenticeship and is a certified master craftsman on a par with his teacher.

God teaches Jesus what to say. The Father *teaches* Jesus and gives him the words he should say: "He who is of the earth belongs to the earth, and of the earth he speaks; he who comes from heaven is above all. *He bears witness to what he has seen and heard.* . . . For he whom God has sent *utters the words of God*" (3:31-34). Again he refers to his "education" by God: "*My teaching* is not mine, but *his who sent me;* if any man's will is to do his will, he shall know whether *the teaching is from God* or whether I am speaking on my own authority" (7:16-17).[35] How important it is in this Gospel that Jesus does not act as an earthly person speaking on his own: "For I have *not spoken on my own authority;* the Father who sent me has himself given me commandment *what to say and what to speak.* And I know that his commandment is eternal life. What I say, therefore, *I say as the Father has bidden me*" (12:49-50).

Simply put, Jesus has been taught to act as the exclusive agent of God and so to bring God's words and wisdom. Emphatically Jesus states that he is *not* self-educated *nor* promoting his own teaching. Rather, Jesus himself "witnesses" to what he has seen and heard; he speaks as the Father "taught" him; he obeys God's command as to what to say and what to speak. Although "nurture and training" were treated lightly in the outsider's vituperation, this topic becomes a major source of honor for Jesus in the insiders' encomium. Thus we find yet another encomiastic topic which the author knows and formally expands as a key component in his encomium.

4.4 Deeds of the Soul

As regards virtues or deeds of the soul, the author and the insiders attest that Jesus acts virtuously.[36] He honors his Father (8:49, 54) by doing always what is pleasing to him (7:29), obeys his commandment (10:17; 12:27) and keeps his will (4:34; 5:30; 6:38). In a culture where the virtue of sons was linked with the com-

---

35. See also "When you have lifted up the Son of man, then you will know that . . . I speak thus as the Father taught me" (8:28). "I speak of what I have seen with my Father, and you do what you have heard from your father" (8:38).

36. For a comparable treatment of Jesus' "deeds of the soul," see Neyrey, *Honor and Shame in the Gospel of Matthew,* 106-26.

mand "honor your father," Jesus' exemplary respect for and loyalty to his Father stand out as an issue of great importance. It serves as the refutation of the charges made by outsiders that he dishonors God by his sins and deceptions. Although the term "justice" hardly appears in the Fourth Gospel (16:10), this topic was a commonplace taught in rhetorical handbooks of Aristotle and in the *progymnasmata*, which we think has relevance here.

> The parts of justice are piety, fair dealing and reverence: piety toward the gods, fair dealing toward men, reverence toward the departed. Piety to the gods consists of two elements: being god-loved and god-loving. The former means being loved by the gods and receiving many blessings from them, the latter consists of loving the gods and having a relationship of friendship with them. (Menander Rhetor 1.361.17-25)[37]

Piety to the gods, Menander says, consists of two elements: being god-loved and god-loving. Although our author does not use these precise terms, he nevertheless develops these two topics. Repeatedly the author tells us that Jesus is "beloved of God":

The Father *loves* the Son, and has given all things into his hand (3:35).

The Father *loves* the Son, and shows him all that he himself is doing (5:20).

The Father *loves me*, because I lay down my life, that I may take it again (10:17).

As the Father has *loved* me, so have I loved you (15:9).

I desire that they . . . behold my glory which thou hast given me *in thy love for me* before the foundation of the world (17:24).

I made known to them thy name, and I will make it known, *that the love with which thou hast loved me* may be in them, and I in them (17:26).

Despite what outsiders think, the encomium of the insiders emphatically argues that God indeed "loves" Jesus. Exemplifying this, the Father bestows great

---

37. Most rhetoricians from Aristotle to Cicero present a stereotypical definition of "justice." In addition to that of Menander Rhetor in the text, consider this: "First among the claims of righteousness are our duties to the gods, then our duties to the spirits, then those to country and parents, then those to the departed; among these claims is piety, which is either a part of righteousness or a concomitant of it. Righteousness is also accompanied by holiness and truth and loyalty and hatred of wickedness" (Ps.-Aristotle, *Virtues and Vices*, 5.2-3).

benefaction on Jesus who is "god-loved" ("all things," "all that he himself is doing"), who in turn displays loyalty and obedience to him ("command . . . lay down my life," "made known to them thy name"). For his part, Jesus is God-loving: "I do as the Father has commanded me, so that the world may know that *I love the Father*" (14:31). Far from being a person thirsting for glory, Jesus insists that all he does is for the glory of his Father (5:30; 6:38; 7:18). Thus the accusations that he "makes himself anything" (5:18; 8:53; 10:33; 19:7, 12) are utterly false; God authorizes him entirely.

Jesus, moreover, brokers this "loved by God" benefaction: "He who has my commandments and keeps them, he it is who loves me; and he who loves me will be loved by my Father" (14:21). And "If a man loves me, he will keep my word, and my Father will love him, and we will come to him and make our home with him" (14:23). In fact the only way to become "loved by God" is by loving God's agent.

Jesus' justice toward his Father is in fact acknowledged by God in various ways: the Father has affirmed Jesus' worthiness by setting his seal on him (6:27) and by glorifying him (5:41, 44; 8:50, 54). The correct conclusion, then, is that Jesus manifests to a high degree the most noble of the deeds of the soul, "justice." He displays faithfulness and loyalty to God, obeys his commands, and dedicates himself solely to the honor of God. And, not surprisingly, he is both "God-loved" and "loving God."

4.5 Comparison

Many encomia contain rules for a *comparison*. Indeed Plutarch's *Lives* are formally structured on this pattern. Generally *progymnastic* rules for a comparison instruct authors to compare similar persons or objects, which seems to be the manner of the Fourth Gospel. Thus two persons receive praise, not blame, but in varying degrees. First, John the Baptizer and Jesus are compared and distinguished. While John is first in time, i.e., "before" Jesus, in terms of precedence, Jesus "was" before John, because he enjoys uncreated eternity in the past (1:15). Moreover, John is but the witness to the light, not the light itself (1:8), the friend of the bridegroom (3:29); he is not "the Christ, Elijah, or a prophet" (1:20-21), but the voice of one crying in the wilderness (1:23). God directed John to witness to Jesus (1:33-34); thus his entire worth and so his honor rest in honoring Jesus. The comparison of John and Jesus, then, serves to distinguish Jesus as a figure worthy of superior honor. Second, Jesus is asked twice in a pejorative tone "Are you greater than" Jacob or Abraham? Jacob gave the Samaritans the well at Sychar, but Jesus gives them living water. As great as Jacob was, Jesus is greater.³⁸ Third, the discourse in John 8 centers around "father Abraham," contrasting true sons who resemble their father by showing hospitality to visitors from afar (Genesis 18) with slave sons whose *generation* includes Ishmael, Cain, and finally Satan, who is a murderer and liar from the beginning.³⁹ But Abraham also functions in Jesus' argument as a figure who "came into being" (8:58) and "died" (8:52), that is, Abraham is a contingent being; in comparison, Jesus is uncreated in the past and imperishable in the future, namely "I AM" — "before Abraham came into being, I AM" (8:58). Yes, Jesus is greater than Abraham. Finally, the author repeatedly compares Jesus and Moses. If "the law was given through Moses, grace and truth came through Jesus Christ" (1:17), thus affirming that Jesus is a superior broker of better blessings. If Moses can be said to have ascended to heaven, Jesus is superior because he first descended from there and later returned (3:13). And if Moses lifted up a serpent which saved Israel from death by snakebite, Jesus must be lifted up to save humanity from death itself by giving it "eternal life" (3:14-15). Finally the author metamorphoses Moses the advocate into Moses the accuser. Moses, Jesus claims, "wrote of me" (5:46). Jesus, moreover, is the judge of Israel, but Moses is only its accuser. Thus four distinct times the author compares Jesus with Israel's greatest patriarchs or with the Christian hero, John. These figures, as the rules for a comparison instruct, are not shamed or demoted, rather Jesus is shown superior to them.

4.6 Death and Posthumous Honors

The death of an honorable person is noteworthy when it conforms to the tradition of a "noble death" or when it results in posthumous honors. *Noble death* refers to the topos found extensively in Greek funeral orations in which various criteria are cited to argue why a slain warrior is worthy of praise, honor and glory, even if killed in battle.⁴⁰ Not all who died in battle warrant this, but only

---

38. For a detailed argument on how Jesus supplants the biblical supplanter, see Jerome H. Neyrey, "Jacob Traditions and the Interpretation of John 4:10-26," *CBQ* 41 (1979): 419-37.

39. On the comparison of true sons of Abraham vs. false sons, see Jerome H. Neyrey, "Jesus the Judge: Forensic Process in John 8:21-59," *Biblica* 68 (1987): 520-28.

40. The ancients spoke about a "good" or "easy" death, but especially a "noble" death to honor fallen soldiers; see Jerome H. Neyrey, "The 'Noble' Shepherd in John 10: Cultural and Rhetorical Background," *JBL* 120 (2001): 267-91. In addition to the wealth of Greco-Roman illustrations of this, 1, 2, and 4 Maccabees also belong in this discussion. See Jan van Henten, *Martyrdom and Noble Death: Selected Texts from Graeco-Roman, Jewish and Christian Antiquity* (London: Routledge, 2002); David Seeley, *The Noble Death: Graeco-Roman Martyrology and Paul's Concept of Salvation* (Sheffield: JSOT, 1989); Arthur J. Droge, *A Noble Death: Suicide and Martyrdom among Christians and Jews in Antiquity* (San Francisco: Harper, 1992).

those displaying *aretē*, that is, a kind of nobility prized by elites. Seven criteria for a noble death emerge from the speeches: a death is noble which 1. benefits others, 2. displays justice to the fatherland and courage, 3. is voluntarily accepted, 4. presents the fallen as having died unvanquished and undefeated, 5. contains contrasts between people courageous or cowardly and those who fight or flee, 6. produces posthumous honors, and 7. leads to immortal glory. This material greatly aids the interpretation of the "noble shepherd" in John 10:11-18. The following synopsis illustrates that the author of the Fourth Gospel knows the topos of "noble death" and formally applied it to the "noble" shepherd.

Rhetorical Tradition about "Noble Death"	John's Discourse on the Noble Shepherd
Death *benefited* others, especially fellow citizens	Death *benefited* the sheep: he lays down his life for them
Comparison between courage/cowardice, fight/flight, death/life, honor/shame	*Comparison* between shepherd/hireling: courage/cowardice, fight/flight, death/life, honor/shame
Manly *courage* displayed by soldiers who fight and die	Manly *courage* displayed by shepherd who battles the wolf and dies
Voluntary death is praised	*Voluntary* death repeatedly claimed: "I lay it down of my own accord"; "No one takes it from me"; "I lay it down; I take it up again"
Justice in death: soldiers uphold the honor of their families and serve the interests of the fatherland: duties served = justice	*Justice*: the shepherd manifests loyalty to his sheep and his Father/God (10:14-15); he has a command from God: duties served = justice

By means of the rhetoric of "noble death" the author argues that Jesus' death was not as outsiders thought, but richly noble in all the ways that humans can conceive of an honorable death. No shame here, only honor (Heb 12:2).

4.7 Posthumous Honors

Because the Gospel states that he was returning whence he came (the heavenly world of the Father), Jesus is restored to his former glory: "Father, glorify me in your own presence with the glory which I had with you before the world was made" (17:5). According to insider logic, Jesus' death itself was "glory" (12:23; 13:31-32). In Johannine anti-language, Jesus' death (i.e., being lifted up) is also his being lifted from this world to that of the Father (3:14; 8:28; 12:32). Outsiders, as we have come to expect, cannot imagine that glory awaits Jesus. At best, when Jesus says that he goes away and that they cannot find him, outsiders think either that he is exiting Israel for the Diaspora (7:35) or that he will kill himself (8:22). The grave is the only future they see for Jesus, and a shameful one at that. But insiders know that Jesus' death is but the beginning of his return to glory. The following data on "whither" Jesus goes speak to his posthumous glory.

> "Return": "I go to him who sent me" (7:33); "Knowing that he had come from God and was returning to him" (13:3)
> "Lift up": ". . . so must the Son of man be lifted up" (3:14); "When you have lifted up the Son of man . . ." (8:28; see 12:32)
> "I go away": ". . . to prepare a place for you" (14:2-3); ". . . I am going to the Father" (14:12); ". . . I go to the Father" (14:28)
> "Glory . . . glorify": ". . . when Jesus was glorified" (12:16); "Now is the Son of man glorified. . . . God will also glorify him in himself, and will glorify him at once" (13:31-32); "Glorify your Son. . . . Father, glorify me in your own presence with the glory which I had with you before the world was made" (17:1, 5); "Father, I desire that they also . . . behold my glory which you have given me in your love for me before the foundation of the world" (17:24)

Sometimes we are told that Jesus is "going" or "returning" (7:33; 13:3) to where he was before. Sometimes he says that he is "going away," not traveling to another place or killing himself as the outsiders think, but entering the presence of the Father (14:12, 28; 17:11) so as to "prepare a place" for the insiders. If the outsiders consider his death consummate shame, the insiders label it as "glory." Indeed, throughout the Farewell Discourse, the author prefers to interpret Jesus' death as "glory" and "being glorified." Jesus himself announces this interpretation at the departure of Judas: "Now is the Son of man glorified. . . . God will also glorify him in himself, and will glorify him at once" (13:31-32). "Glory" in this context must refer to the alchemy of the crucifixion in that what outsiders consider shame, God sees as glorious and honorable. Moreover, if Jesus in and after his death achieves glory, this glory is simply the glory which he enjoyed with God from the very beginning: "Father, glorify me in your own presence with the glory which I had with you before the world was made" (17:1, 5). And again, Jesus desires that "they also . . . behold my glory which you have given me in your love for me before the foundation of the world" (17:24). Posthumous honors, glory and eternal life, await Jesus.

5.0 Summary and Further Questions

We now know the formal structure of the encomium, its regular topics and the traditional content of each. We know, moreover, that the encomium was a familiar genre in the Greco-Roman and Israelite world. Other genres of literature, such as *bioi*, funeral orations, and similar forms of epideictic rhetoric, frequently organize their materials according to the formal topics of the encomium. The data presented above are persuasive that the author of the Fourth Gospel learned to write an encomium. Second, the encomium was hardly unknown to early Christian writers, for both Matthew and Luke employ the topics and contents of the encomium and Paul in three of his letters uses the topics of generation and nurture (see Gal 1:11-17; Phil 3:2-11; 2 Cor 11:21-12:10).[41] Third, we have seen in the Fourth Gospel that the stereotypical topics which make up the encomium are all fully and formally present: origins, birth, nurture and training, deeds of the soul, comparison, and death-posthumous honors. These are explicit topoi which do not depend on the intuition of a clever reader. The author fully appreciates these topics and uses them to augment praise for Jesus (or blame). Fourth, we have argued that the author created two encomia, actually a vituperation (outsiders) and an encomium (insiders). The very fact that we find controversy on each of the encomiastic topics indicates that they and their contents are well known, that the topics are not miscellaneous items, but coherent parts of a larger pattern. The controversial topics, moreover, make scant sense when seen independent of each other. But when appraised as the topics of an encomium, they are logically welded together and take on a meaning they do not have if considered independently.

Although Matthew and Luke begin their narratives with "origins and birth," our author seems haphazardly to take up this or that topic, even coming back to it later in the story. Does this argue against his knowing the encomium? By no means, for Quintilian himself says that in praising someone there are two modes of organizing arguments: chronological order from birth to death and emphasis on certain points:

> It has sometimes proved the more effective course to trace a man's life and deeds in due chronological order, praising his natural gifts as a child, then his progress at school, and finally the whole course of his life, including words as well as deeds. At times on the other hand it is well to divide our praises, dealing separately with the various virtues, fortitude, justice, self-control and the

---

41. Malina and Neyrey, *Portraits of Paul*, 33-63; see George Lyons, *Pauline Autobiography: Toward a New Understanding* (Atlanta: Scholars, 1985).

rest of them and to assign to each virtue the deeds performed under its influence. We will have to decide which of these two methods will be the more serviceable, according to the nature of the subject. (*Inst. Orat.* 3.7.15)

Sequence from birth to death is by no means a requirement.[42]

What then is the benefit of this study? In addition to appreciation of the form of the encomium and the conventional contents of its topics, we learn a genre which can surface in the Fourth Gospel various data which can then be classified according to the conventions of the ancients. No other type of reading can illuminate the categories of the encomium embedded in the Fourth Gospel; nothing else can gather and interpret them as a native would. In addition, the clusters of data can then be appreciated, not simply as individual items, but as conventional topics related together in the ancient mind. We learn the pieces as well as the whole, or the whole is greater than the sum of its parts. We are then, interpreting the Fourth Gospel accurately as the ancients would have heard it.

Furthermore, when the Fourth Gospel is read in light of the encomium, we discover parallel, but antithetical encomia, a vituperation shaming Jesus and an encomium praising him. Both the vituperation and the encomium develop the same conventional topics; for, as the rhetoricians indicate, the same sources of information can be used to elevate or denigrate a person. Hardly miscellaneous topics, those of the encomium are the very ones that a writer or speaker is expected to develop. The figure which follows summarizes the major argument of the paper, namely, two contrasting accounts of Jesus, one a vituperation and the other an encomium.

Outsiders: Vituperation	Insiders: Encomium
Geography: Nazareth and Galilee	*Geography:* heavenly world; bosom of the Father
Generation: Joseph, his mother, some brothers	*Generation:* unique son of the Father
Nurture and Training: no schooling at all	*Nurture and Training:* elaborate apprenticeship with God who taught him

---

42. In no classical funeral oration will we find a chronological treatment of a hero's life; the authors introduce topics when suitable or for rhetorical advantage. See Ziolkowski, *Thucydides and the Tradition of Funeral Speeches at Athens*, and Nicole Loraux, *The Invention of Athens: The Funeral Oration in the Classical City* (Cambridge, MA: Harvard University Press, 1986).

Deeds of the Soul:
sinner, deceiver, law breaker

Deeds of the Soul:
courage, justice, obedience, loyalty

Comparison:
absent

Comparison:
are you greater than Moses, Jacob, Abraham; noble shepherd vs. hireling

Death and Posthumous Honors:
none: death is fitting punishment for crimes; shame; death permanently ends his career; no glory! no posthumous honors!

Death and Posthumous Honors:
many and great: a "noble" death (à la "noble Shepherd"); power over death: I have power to lay down my life and power to take it back; death is status elevation ritual whereby Jesus returns to prior glory or is glorified by God

The very same encomiastic topics afford outsiders grounds to vilify Jesus and insiders opportunities to honor and glorify him. Inasmuch as Jesus himself speaks to the audience the contents of each topic, the audience learns remarkable secrets, revelation, and knowledge. They think spiritually, are "taught by God" (6:45).

2

Role and Status in the Fourth Gospel

Cutting through Confusion

1.0 Introduction: Problem, Solution and Hypothesis

Scholarship on characters in the Fourth Gospel has exploded in recent times, but like most explosions, the energies released travel helter-skelter with no coordination of method or agreed results. We are told of symbolic,[1] representative,[2] and even "narrative"[3] study of Johannine characters,[4] all of which avoid any analysis of them in terms of their social and cultural role and status. Even when some current studies of Peter treat his "role" or "status," the interpreters do not bother to tell us what is meant by "role" and "status."[5] Comment on Mary Magdalene and the Samaritan woman labors with imprecision because of misguided efforts to ascribe to them some role. Part of the problem lies in the way such scholars value only "role," but not "status." Hence we find Mary Magdalene variously described as an "apostle," a quasi-apostle, an apostle to the apostles, a mediator, and a witness.[6] Moreover, some explicitly refuse to use so-

---

1. Craig R. Koester, *Symbolism in the Fourth Gospel: Meaning, Mystery, Community* (Minneapolis: Fortress Press, 1995) 32-73.

2. Raymond Collins, "Representative Figures in the Fourth Gospel," *Downside Review* 94 (1976): 26-46, 118-32.

3. R. Alan Culpepper, *Anatomy of the Fourth Gospel* (Philadelphia: Fortress, 1983) 10-48.

4. Even anonymous characters are studied, as in David R. Beck, *The Discipleship Paradigm: Readers and Anonymous Characters in the Fourth Gospel* (Leiden: Brill, 1997); W. W. Watty, "The Significance of Anonymity in the Fourth Gospel," *ExpT* 90 (1979): 209-12.

5. For example, in Arthur Droge's article ("The Status of Peter in the Fourth Gospel: A Note on John 18:10-11," *JBL* 109 [1990]: 307-11), he uses the term "status" only in the title and never in the text, so it is difficult to know how he understands it.

6. See Raymond E. Brown, "The Role of Women in the Fourth Gospel," *TS* 36 (1975): 688-

cial and cultural materials, in favor of a reading free from academic controls and constraints:

> This article is an attempt to outline some significant female features in the picture as a whole and as far as possible in an article of limited extent to indicate a coherent view of the roles and functions of women in the Gospel of John. My emphasis is on description rather than on explanation, the description not being dependent on any specific terminology or methodological frame of reference.[7]

Result: impressionistic guesses. Thus previous use of social concepts such as "role" and "status" to interpret Johannine characters is either absent, imprecise, or rejected. What readers need, then, is rigor in their reading of the dramatis personae of the Fourth Gospel, which we propose to do by means of careful use of the social concepts of "role" and "status."

In most of the studies I have examined, even if "role" and "status" are mentioned, these concepts are not well understood and so are used loosely, resulting in imprecision and vulnerability to exaggeration or ideological advancement. Moreover, one finds a bias in scholarship that values only "role," but ignores "status" — a perilous opinion in regard to the Fourth Gospel. But if we employ formal notions of "role" and "status," what problem will this solve? What advantage is gained from it? First, precision, which can rescue the project from the Kingdom of Hunch and Guess. In place of the conflicting and subjective interpretations mentioned above, shared critical understanding of "role" and "status" will provide a solid basis for clarifying the confusion. Second, the ancient world was acutely aware of roles and statuses. In a world whose pivotal value was honor, worth, regard, and esteem, "role" and "status" located people in horizontal relationships as well as vertical evaluation. This "self-knowledge" was vital for all those playing the game.

99, reprinted in *Community of the Beloved Disciple* (New York: Paulist Press, 1979) 183-98. Elizabeth S. Fiorenza (*In Memory of Her* [New York: Crossroads, 1985] 326, 332-33) labels Magdalene an "apostolic witness," whereas in another place she calls her the "apostle to the apostles": "Mary Magdalene: Apostle to the Apostles," *USQR*, April 1975, pp. 22-27; this is similar to the description of her by Colleen M. Conway (*Men and Women in the Fourth Gospel: Gender and Johannine Characterization* [Atlanta: Society of Biblical Literature, 1999] 198), who says of her: "It is clear that the message Jesus gives to Mary to proclaim is the Johannine kerygma.... she assumes the role of mediator." See Sjef van Tilborg, *Imaginative Love in John* (Leiden: Brill, 1993) 200-206.

7. Turid Karlsen Seim, "Roles of Women in the Gospel of John," in Lars Hartman and Birger Olsson, eds., *Aspects of the Johannine Literature* (Uppsala: Almquist & Wiksell, 1986) 56-73, citation from p. 56.

In this study, we will argue the following hypotheses:

1. "Status" is vastly more important in the Fourth Gospel than "role."
2. Characters who in the Synoptics enjoy identifiable roles *lack them* in the Fourth Gospel. *It is almost as if this Gospel were anti-traditional in terms of leadership roles.*
3. In fact, although there are many roles evident in the Fourth Gospel (kinship and political roles), there are *few roles in view* within the Jesus Group.
4. We can identify *eleven criteria for status,* which are not all of equal importance; nor does it matter if characters do not have all such status markers, provided they have the right ones.

Eventually, this study will yield a social map, a *ranking of persons as having elite, moderate, or low status* within the Jesus group.

And so, our argument contains four steps: 1. *clarify* the meaning and use of "role" and "status," for which we turn to social and cultural studies; 2. *apply* the concepts of "role" and "status" to seven figures: the Samaritan woman, the man born blind, the "Beloved" family at Bethany, the disciples, Mary Magdalene, Simon Peter, and the Beloved Disciple; 3. *extract criteria* for evaluating status; 4. *draw a social map* locating by status hierarchies the Johannine characters as enjoying elite, moderate and meager status, based on the eleven criteria identified.

2.0 Role and Status: The Theory

2.1 Role

The concept of "role," borrowed from the stage, involves behavior and the socially recognized position of a person, entailing rights and duties. A role implies a set of expectations for interaction between a person who holds one position in a group and another person who holds a reciprocal position.[8] In other words, there can be no role of "leader" without a "follower" role, no mother without child.[9] As several anthropologists define it, "role" is

---

8. A. Paul Hare, "Groups: Role Structure," *IESS* 6.283. Bruce Malina ("Social Levels, Morals and Daily Life," in *The Early Christian World,* ed. Philip F. Esler [London: Routledge, 2000] 1.371) clarifies this remark, "The roles that an individual plays point to statuses within the overall system. In this sense social roles point to stereotypical, presumed entitlements and responsibilities."

9. Hare, "Groups: Role Structure," 6.283.

... a set of expected behavior patterns, obligations, and norms attached to a particular status. The distinction between status and role is a simple one: you "occupy" a certain status, but you "play" a role ... as a student you occupy a certain status that differs from that of your teacher, administrators, or other staff. As you occupy that status you perform by attending lectures, taking notes, participating in class, and studying for examinations. This concept of role is derived from the theater and refers to the parts played by actors on the stage. If you are a husband, mother, son, daughter, teacher, lawyer, judge, male or female, you are expected to behave in certain ways because of the norms associated with that particular status.[10]

Thus the role of "mother" refers to her status and duties to her children; in politics, kings vis-à-vis subjects; in economics, bankers to borrowers; and in education, teachers to students.[11] As Malina states, "roles are indicative of institutional location, hence of the status of that person within that institution."[12]

Examination of certain roles in the Fourth Gospel can put flesh to this abstraction. Here we are considering various roles identified in the institution of *kinship*. We know of family roles, those of Jesus and then of other characters.[13] Jesus' family consists of Joseph his father (6:42), God his Father, (Mary) his mother (2:1-12; 19:26-27), his aunt (19:25), and his brothers (7:3-5). Other blood relationships include: the brothers Andrew and Peter (1:40), the sisters Martha and Mary and their brother Lazarus (11:1), and the sons of Zebedee (21:2). All persons in familial roles have reciprocal duties and their roles last as long as the relationship does.

Furthermore, in the institution of *Israelite politics,* various roles of Jesus are either acknowledged or denied such as "prophet" (6:14; 7:52; 9:17), "king" (6:15; 12:13; 18:33-37), "Messiah" (1:41; 4:25-26; 7:31, 41-42), and "teacher" (1:38; 3:2; 20:16). On the other hand Jesus has interaction with political figures, both Judean and Roman. We recognize the role played by a Judean leader (3:2) and

---

10. Raymond Scupin and Christopher De Corse, *Anthropology and Global Perspective* (2nd ed.; Englewood Cliffs, NJ: Prentice Hall, 1995) 280. It is commonly said that statuses are polar or reciprocal; any particular status always implies at least one other to which it is related, e.g., mother-child, employer-employee, doctor-patient.

11. Ralph H. Turner ("Role: Sociological Aspects," *IESS* 13.552) says of "role" that "it provides a comprehensive *pattern* for behavior and attitudes; it constitutes a *strategy* for coping with a recurrent type of situation; it is *socially identified,* more or less clearly, as an entity; it is subject to being placed recognizably by *different individuals;* and it supplies a major basis for *identifying* and *placing* persons in society."

12. Malina, "Social Levels, Morals and Daily Life," 1.371.

13. On the family of Jesus, see Tilborg, *Imaginative Love,* and Jan G. Van der Watt, *Family of the King: Dynamics of Metaphor in the Gospel according to John* (Leiden: Brill, 2000) 304-40.

by high priests (11:49-51; 18:13-26); Joseph of Arimathea belongs here as well, because of his wealth (19:40-41). Similarly, we know of roles in the institution of *imperial politics*, Caesar and the Roman prefect of Judea, who owes his role to his being an imperial "friend" (19:12). Of concern to this study are the potential roles played by the seven characters of the Jesus group mentioned above.

2.2 *Status*

Whereas persons *play* certain roles, they *occupy* or *have* status. "Status" differs from "role" in that status is "a recognized position that a person occupies within society . . . [which] determines where he or she fits in relationship to everyone else."[14] In addition, one scholar defines status as "a quality entailing deference and precedence in interaction, a quality of professional or public honor. . . . Status systems are generated by bases or dimensions of honor — power, wealth, knowledge."[15] "Status" suggests verticality, a ranking of people according to cultural criteria of worth or excellence.[16] It indicates the honor, respect, or worth a person enjoys.[17] Thus statuses are thought of as "polar or reciprocal: any particular status always implies at least one other to which it is related."[18] For example, some statuses may be first or last, highest or lowest, most or least, or best or worst.

To visualize "status," imagine an elongated pyramid (e.g, the Transamerica tower in San Francisco). By custom, the higher one's office, the more elevated one's status; low status occupations are normally on the lower levels. The Bank

---

14. Scupin and DeCorse, *Anthropology and Global Perspective*, 280.

15. Andrew Abbott, "Status and Status Strain in the Professions," *AJS* 86 (1981): 820. For an easy introduction to the meaning of status, see John J. Pilch, *Introducing the Cultural Context of the Old Testament* (Mahwah, NJ: Paulist Press, 1991) 117-50.

16. "Status" has been defined as: "A quality entailing deference and precedence in interaction, a quality of professional or public honor. . . . Status systems are generated by bases or dimensions of honor — power, wealth, knowledge. . . . Status has come to be a synonym of any 'position in a social system.' . . . Whereas formerly superiority of status could mean any sort of hierarchical ordering — of power, wealth, or honor — to many it now refers only to esteem, prestige, honor, respect, that is, to various forms of evaluation. . . . What matters is not what you really are but what people believe you to be" (M. Zelditch, "Status, Social," *IESS* 15.250).

17. Paul Humphreys and Joseph Berger, "Theoretical Consequences of the Status Characteristics Formulation," *AJS* 86 (1981): 954-55, and Malina, "Social Levels, Morals and Daily Life," 1.369-80.

18. Robin M. Williams, *American Society: A Sociological Interpretation* (3rd ed.; New York: Alfred A. Knopf, 1970) 42.

of the Universe occupies the top ten floors, and its CEO has his office on the very top floor; twenty floors below is the office of Dewey, Cheetum and Howe, Esq., and near ground level we find the office of the political action committee to reelect Arnold.

It will help if we add another piece of information to this status pyramid, taken from the inscriptions on the temple at Delphi. On the entrance to the temple at Delphi three pithy sayings were engraved: "Know thyself" (γνῶθι σεαυτόν), "Nothing overmuch" (μηδὲν ἄγαν), and "A pledge, and ruin is nigh."[19] The man who "knows himself" knows his status and so his social position on the pyramid. This is social knowledge, not conscience or self-awareness. The wise man who "knows himself" avoids extremes, that is, he does not strive for higher status nor allow himself to be pushed below what society deems appropriate for a person of his social location (Plutarch, *Letter to Apollonius* 116D-E).[20] Thus all persons should know just where they belong and so give deference to those above and expect the same from those below.

To assess status, an examiner must know the particular criteria used for ranking and evaluation, either 1) extrinsic-institutional criteria or 2) intrinsic-personal criteria. *Extrinsic criteria* evaluate someone in terms of basic societal institutions, which in ancient Judea consisted of politics and kinship. Hence, in the system of *politics*, people may be ranked as powerful or weak ("Do you not know that I have power to crucify you?" John 19:10);[21] in *kinship*, one is either a blood relative or an outsider ("It is not right to take the children's bread and give it to dogs," Matt 15:26); in *economics*, few are rich, but many are poor ("a rich man clothed in purple and fine linen who feasted sumptuously every day," Luke 16:19).[22] In the world of antiquity, status was immediately related to these three binary opposites: male-female, Greek-barbarian, and free-

---

19. Diodor of Sicily, 9.10.1-4; Plutarch, *Letter to Apollonius* 116D-E; *Dinner of the Seven Wise Men* 164B-C; *Talkativeness* 511A-B; see Helen North, *Sophrosyne: Self-Knowledge and Self-Restraint in Greek Literature* (Ithaca: Cornell University Press, 1966).

20. He will not allow others to praise him too much (Plutarch, *Dinner of the Seven Wise Men* 164C). For, as was popularly thought, "Fortune has a knack, when men vaunt themselves too highly, of laying them unexpectedly low and so teaching them to hope for 'nothing in excess'" (Diodor of Sicily 15.33.3). The practice of moderation or "nothing to excess" was hallowed in Horace's ode on "golden mediocrity" (*Ode* 2.10.1-12). See R. G. M. Nisbet and Margaret Hubbard, *A Commentary on Horace: Odes: Book II* (Oxford: Clarendon, 1978) 160-61. See also Kurt Scheidle, *Modus Optimum. Die Bedeutung des "Rechten Masses" in der römischen Literatur* (Frankfurt am Main: Peter Lang, 1993).

21. In the political world of Rome, the stratification of males consisted of emperor, senator, equestrian, *decurio*, citizen, subject, slave; in Judea, high priest, high priests, priests, Levites, landowners, peasants, artisans (Malina, "Social Levels, Morals and Daily Life," 1.372).

22. Malina, "Social Levels, Morals and Daily Life," 1.371-72.

slave.²³ Males, simply by birth, were thought to have a position in life superior to that of females, as is evident from study of the pervasive, radical gender division characteristic of antiquity.²⁴ Greeks considered themselves the only civilized people in the world, all others being barbarians; free elites with leisure ranked over the working poor, who ranked over slaves, who Aristotle said were not human at all.

Intrinsic criteria look to personal qualities or achievements. *Personal* qualities evaluate an person in terms of cultural values (beautiful, witty, wise, strong, pious, possessed by spirits).²⁵ For example, A. W. K. Adkins describes how in an early period of life in Greece the "aggressive virtues" were valued, but with stable polis life, the "agreeable virtues" rose in importance. More to our point, persons in the Fourth Gospel are regularly evaluated in terms of values such as courage, whether one associates with Jesus in daylight or nighttime (3:1-2) or whether one publicly confesses him or remains silent in fear (9:4-33 vs. 9:22; 12:42). *Achievements* speak to culturally valued acts, for example, endurance of pain or deprivation (ascetic achievements of monks and hermits), prowess (military, athletic, or aesthetic), skills, intellectual insight or commercial successes.²⁶

---

23. One should reckon also the added status accruing to older members of society simply because they are old and the lack of status of young people. This is commonly expressed in discussions of *pietas* and εὐσέβεια; see also Thomas M. Falkner and Judith de Luce, eds., *Old Age in Greek and Latin Literature* (Albany, NY: SUNY Press, 1989); Tim G. Parkin, *Old Age in the Roman World: A Cultural and Social History* (Baltimore: The Johns Hopkins University Press, 2003); Thomas M. Faulkner, *The Poetics of Old Age in Greek Epic, Lyric, and Tragedy* (Norman: University of Oklahoma Press, 1995); and Bessie Ellen Richardson, *Old Age among the Ancient Greeks* (New York: Greenwood Press, 1969).

24. For a record of the ancients on gender division, see Jerome H. Neyrey, "Jesus, Gender and the Gospel of Matthew," in *New Testament Masculinities*, ed. Stephen D. Moore and Janice C. Anderson, *Semeia* 45 (2003): 43-53.

25. Instructors in the rhetoric of honor describe the culturally specific values which are deemed praiseworthy: "Then, you will bring out the most important topic of the encomium, the achievements, which you will divide into the spirit, the body, and fortune — the spirit like courage or prudence, the body like beauty, swiftness, or strength, and fortune, like power, wealth and friends." Aphthonius (trans. Ray Nadeau, "The Progymnasmata of Aphthonius in Translation," *Speech Monographs* 19 [1952]: 264-85). Aristotle: "The parts of virtue are justice, manly courage, self-control, magnificence, magnanimity, liberality, gentleness, prudence, and wisdom" (*Rhet.* 1.9.5, trans. George Kennedy, *Aristotle On Rhetoric* [Oxford: Oxford University Press, 1991], 80).

26. One's reputation or worth may be either ascribed (bestowed or inherited) or achieved. This basic idea of honor informs the way status is evaluated: "Ascribed status is that which is inherited, such as sex, race, or ethnicity, or over time, age, and is crucial for defining the basic patterns of people's lives [birth, physical features, genealogy]. Achieved status, on the other hand, is acquired through personal effort or chance, possibly from occupational or educational attainment [marriage, occupation, perceived acquisitions]" (Charlotte Wolf, "Status," *IESS* 13.826).

Persons may be further evaluated in terms of their position in each kinship and political institution. Thus they may be ranked as highest or lowest, first or last, and rich or poor. Moreover, even when power is stratified, various roles can be ranked. The Fourth Gospel knows of 1) Caesar, the Emperor, 2) Pilate, procurator and "friend" of Caesar, 3) Roman soldiers and slaves.[27] Kinship roles are always highly stratified: at the head, the father or patriarch of the family, his wife and the mother of his children; among these children sons rank higher than daughters and among the sons one stands out as major.

2.3 Classical Examples of Reckoning Status

To give flesh to the abstract definition of status, let us examine several Greco-Roman texts which can illustrate the matter. In one place Josephus describes the composition of a deputation:

> The scheme agreed upon was to send a deputation comprising persons of different classes of society but of equal standing in education. Two of them, Jonathan and Ananias, were from the lower ranks and adherents of the Pharisees; the third, Jozar, also a Pharisee, came of a priestly family; the youngest, Simon, was descended from high priests. (Josephus, *Life* 196)

So, we identify three levels of status or three floors in our pyramid: lower, priestly, and high priestly strata. Josephus presumes that all will know how to rank these levels of status in their proper hierarchy, from lowest to highest.

Similarly Cicero distinguishes various levels of his society in terms of their honor rating. First he states that it is our duty to honor men "conspicuous for conduct in keeping with their high moral standards, and who, as true patriots, have rendered or are now rendering efficient service to their country." Continuing with persons worthy of honor, "it is our duty also to show proper respect to old age, to yield precedence to magistrates, to make a distinction between a fellow citizen and a foreigner, and, in the case of the foreigner himself, to discriminate according to whether he has come in an official or a private capacity" (*De Officiis* 1.149). Next "in regard to trades and other means of livelihood," Cicero distinguishes which are to be considered "becoming to a gentleman and which are vulgar." He then catalogues the "vulgar" trades at great length:

---

27. For the structure of the social system of the early empire, see Géza Alföldy, *The Social History of Rome* (Baltimore: The Johns Hopkins University Press, 1988) 94-186. See also Ramsey MacMullen, *Roman Social Relations* (New Haven, CT: Yale University Press, 1974) 88-120.

> First, those whose means of livelihood are rejected as undesirable... as those of tax-gatherers and usurers. Unbecoming to a gentleman, too, and vulgar are the means of livelihood of all hired workmen whom we pay for mere manual labor, not for artistic skill.... Vulgar we must consider those also who buy from wholesale merchants to retail immediately; for they would get no profits without a great deal of downright lying; and there is no action meaner than misrepresentation. And all mechanics are engaged in vulgar trades; for no workshop can have anything liberal about it. Least respectable of all are those trades which cater for sensual pleasures: "Fishmongers, butchers, cooks, and poulterers, and fishermen," as Terence says. (*De Officiis* 1.150)

In view here is the old prejudice that those who work with their hands have insufficient leisure to be literate and so civilized. Yet in contrast to "vulgar" laborers, Cicero describes "professions" *(artibus)* which are honorable:

> The professions in which either a higher degree of intelligence is required or from which no small benefit to society is derived — medicine and architecture, for example, and teaching — these are proper for those whose social position they become. Trade, if it is on a small scale, is to be considered vulgar; but if wholesale and on a large scale, importing large quantities from all parts of the world and distributing to many without representation, it is not to be greatly disparaged.... But of all the occupations by which gain is secured, none is better than agriculture, none more profitable, none more delightful, none more becoming to a free man. (*De Officiis* 1.151)

Thus Cicero identifies and ranks those whom we have a duty to honor: elites conspicuous for high moral standards or service of the state; elites, of course, do not labor for wages, which characterizes a low social group performing "vulgar" labors, who are then contrasted with a middle group whose "professions" require artistry and skill. These three groups, we suggest, occupy different statuses (not roles) in Cicero's elite perspective.

2.4 Status in the Fourth Gospel

If roles in the Fourth Gospel were easy to spot, not so status. Our task now is to discover the criteria whereby the author of the Fourth Gospel evaluates the people in his narrative. In the Gospel, we find two antithetical sets of evaluative criteria: those representative of insiders in the Jesus group and those of the dominant society outside the group (i.e., Temple and synagogue).²⁸ Depending on one's point of view, each group divides the world into insiders and outsiders. Insiders and outsiders are recognizable according to the criteria of honor and shame: for one group, such-and-such is praiseworthy, even if reviled by its opponents; and one group may hold in contempt what the second one honors. In the eyes of his followers, Jesus the Insider deserves great honor, worth, and respect. In addition to statements that God has glorified Jesus and will glorify him again (8:54; 12:23; 13:31-32; 17:1, 4), God himself mandates that "All . . . honor the Son just as they honor the Father. Anyone who does not honor the Son does not honor the Father" (5:23). But in the eyes of outsiders Jesus is a disgrace, and they refuse his credentials. Like most prophets, Jesus receives no respect in his homeland (4:44). Some even accuse him of demon possession (8:48). The Evangelist provides a culturally based reason for denial of honor: many value more what the synagogue or their neighbors think of them than what God thinks. Hence they prefer the "glory that comes from one another" (5:44) to the praise of God. Our task, then, is to determine who is an insider or outsider in terms of antithetical criteria for honor and shame. The Fourth Gospel provides an insider point of view, from which we distinguish insiders and outsiders and the criteria by which insiders are worthy of honor and respect and outsiders little or no honor.²⁹

This article cannot hope to examine all of the *dramatis personae* in the narrative, and so we focus on certain insiders to see more accurately why they are honored: the Samaritan woman, the disciples, the man born blind, Martha, Mary and Lazarus, the Beloved Disciple, Mary Magdalene, and Peter. We begin by according these persons insider status, which means that they are all honorable persons in the Johannine Jesus Group in differing ways, some more than others. By what criteria can we know status in the Fourth Gospel? In our reading of the seven characters mentioned above, we will look for what makes them special or distinctive. And, as each character is examined, we would expect to

---

28. Malina ("Social Levels, Morals and Daily Life," 1.370) identifies four ranking orders relative to our task: 1) the ranking structure of the non-elite quarters of a specific local community (e.g., Corinth or Alexandria); 2) separate ranking structures in small communities in specific localities inhabited by similar people (e.g., Judean communities in Hellenistic cities); 3) ranking structures covering the total regional society, of cities and of concern to persons and groups in regional central places (e.g., the tetrarchy of Herod and Agrippa); 4) an empire-wide ranking system (e.g., Roman elites), of little interest to most of the people in the empire.

29. Robert Kysar (*John, the Maverick Gospel* [Louisville: Westminster John Knox, 1993]) rightly named this document "maverick" not only for its antithetical stance to the synagogue, but also its apparent conflict with other Jesus groups. Thus it may not be just different from others, but emphatically so.

find similar identifying markers. What to look for in the first place? Readers of the Fourth Gospel are schooled already concerning what virtues and vices count here; and because we are so often urged to compare and contrast characters, we gain assurance of what is important or detrimental. This study ends with an extended synopsis of the characters being studied, in which the major section deals with role and status, especially an inventory of criteria. If readers desire, they are welcome to peek.

3.0 Reckoning the Role or Status of Important Characters

3.1 The Samaritan Woman

Role. At least one role of the Samaritan woman is clear, wife/spouse, which she has played at least five times, but no longer (4:18). Her household duties included clothing production, child rearing, and food preparation, the last of which explains her presence at the well.[30] But some scholars have touted her as "witness" and "apostle." *Apostle?* Although Jesus said "Go, call your husband" (4:16), he did not commission her to recruit the inhabitants of Sychar; nor do we know if she in fact "called her husband." If a speaking role was authorized, why does the author not deal with the novelty of a woman addressing non-related males in public? If Jesus did not authorize her, she acts on her own and without authorization. Schneiders delights in this, namely, that she "assumes on her own the mission of witness."[31] But "making yourself something" is a vainglorious claim in ancient cultures and was universally considered folly, and is especially so in the Fourth Gospel.[32] Look at the threats to kill Jesus for "mak-

---

30. The duties of a wife/mother are consistent among Greco-Romans and Judeans: "These are works which the wife must perform for her husband: grinding flour and baking bread and washing clothes and cooking food and giving suck to her child and making ready his bed and working in wool" (*Mishnah Ketubot* 5.5). "Before anything else I should speak about the occupations by which a household is maintained . . . to the wife those which have to do with spinning and the preparation of food, in short, those of a domestic nature" (Hierocles, *On Duties* 4.28.21ff.).

31. Sandra Schneiders, "Women in the Fourth Gospel and the Roles of Women in the Contemporary Church," *BTB* 12 (1982): 39.

32. One thinks of Theophrastus's characters and the stock characters of Greek and Roman comedy (i.e., ἀλαζονεία and κενοδοξία); the premise of Plutarch's "On Inoffensive Self-Praise" is that self-promotion is a serious social affront. In the first line of the writing it says: "It is agreed that to speak to others of one's own importance or power is offensive" (538A); "praise of ourselves is for others most distressing" (539D). It provokes envy and so discord. The Samaritan Woman is not "praising herself," but claiming an honor utterly and hopelessly beyond her status.

ing himself" equal to God (5:18; 10:33), Son of God (19:7), and king (19:12; see 8:53). When authorization is important, the author hammers us with the information that God established Jesus in his ascribed role and status,[33] but nothing is said about the woman's authorization. To claim that she "makes herself a witness" and the like is simply a bad idea. The following chart compares and contrasts the Samaritan woman with others who are formally "sent."

Figure	Authorization	Role and Purpose
John the Baptist	"... a man *sent from God*" (1:6); "... he who sent me to baptize with water" (1:33).	1. *role:* witness par excellence 2. specific *content* of witnessing (1:15, 29, 30, 33-34) 3. purpose: "that all might believe" (1:7) 4. duration: until he died 5. audience: specific people suitable for baptism
Samaritan woman	"Go, call your husband" (4:16) — not formal authorization as witness	1. *role???:* recruiter? bringer of news? 2. *content:* "he told me everything I ever did," "can this be the Christ?" 3. *no purpose* of "calling" stated by Jesus in 4:16 4. *duration:* after two days, her witness is outgrown and ceases 5. *audience:* "call your husband"; but also the people of Sychar?
Disciples	"*I sent* you to reap that for which you did not labor" (4:38); "As *you sent* me into the world, so *I have sent* them into the world" (17:18); "As the *Father has sent* me, even so *I send you*" (20:21-23)	1. *role:* agents 2. *content* of role: purification but presumably other tasks if they are "sent" as Jesus was sent 3. *purpose:* to harvest believers and to effect purification 4. *duration:* presumably until they die 5. *audience:* those already evangelized; insiders

---

33. Peder Borgen, "God's Agent in the Fourth Gospel," in *Religions in Antiquity*, ed. Jacob Neusner (Leiden: Brill, 1968) 137-48; A. E. Harvey, "Jesus as Agent," in L. D. Hurst and N. T. Wright, eds., *The Glory of Christ in the New Testament* (Oxford: Clarendon Press, 1987) 239-50. See Karl H. Rengstorf, *Apostleship* (London: Adam and Charles Black, 1952) 11-24; George W. Buchanan, "Apostolic Christology," *SBLSP* (1986): 172-82.

Role and Status in the Fourth Gospel

Figure	Authorization	Role and Purpose
Mary Magdalene	"*Go* to my brethren and *say* to them, I am ascending to my Father and your Father, to my God and your God" (20:17)	1. *role:* witness 2. specific *content* of message (20:17) 3. *purpose:* sharing unique revelation with fictive kin 4. *duration?* 5. *audience:* "my brethren" and so insiders

John, the disciples, and Mary Magdalene are authorized for a specific purpose, sometimes the dissemination of some revelation or message,[34] but the Samaritan woman has neither message nor revelation to declare (she speaks in "questions"). Finally, the villagers themselves terminate whatever "witness" she bore (4:39), for they surpass her when they have immediate access to Jesus. They declare, moreover, Jesus to be superior to whatever she said about him (4:42). If she has a "role," it is extremely short-lived.

If not an "apostle," then a "witness"? "Witnesses" are always insiders who may speak to insiders or outsiders. Most witnesses speak as forensic defenders of Jesus in public (1:19-28; 5:31-40; 7:7; 16:8-11) and occasionally spread propaganda about Jesus (1:32-34). The narrative, moreover, pays considerable attention to what makes a good forensic witness: multiple witnesses (8:13-18) and the noble standing of witnesses (5:31-37) and deeds (10:25), none of which apply here, because she is not a forensic witness. The propaganda quality of "witnessing," moreover, should contain specific content (some acknowledgment of the role and status of Jesus: 1:34; 9:17). Informants "witness" about Jesus (11:46). And indeed the villagers state that they came to believe because of her "witness" (4:39), i.e., the λόγος she spoke to them. But in the parameters of the narrative, this strange λόγος is her thricefold argument that Jesus might be the Christ because "He told me everything I ever did" (4:29, 39), namely, her sexual history. One might glory in a benefaction, but touting one's sexual history? Something indeed has happened in Sychar, but it does not result from her authorization as apostle or witness.

Might she have an informal role, such as recruiter or one who carries news or one who brings gossip? In regard to *recruitment,* in 1:35-51 we find a pattern whereby a believer speaks a word about Jesus and invites the hearer to "come and see" (John to Andrew, Andrew to Peter, Philip to Nathanael). They are cer-

---

34. Nowhere in the Fourth Gospel do we find the kind of formal commissioning of the disciples that we find in Matt 10:5-15; Mark 6:7-13; and Luke 9:1-6. There the disciples repeat Jesus' specific message, "The Kingdom of God is at hand," and imitate Jesus by being mighty in word and deed. None of this is found in the Fourth Gospel.

tainly not "apostles" here, even if they recruit others. In regard to those who *carry news,* we find a pattern whereby X tells Y some news: Martha tells Mary that Jesus is there (11:28; see 11:3); Philip tells Andrew about the Greeks and both tell Jesus (12:21-22); the disciples tell Thomas about the risen Jesus (20:25). In a world without media, news is spread informally by means of a *"gossip network."*[35] "Gossip" as news network is the right term here. If the Samaritan woman has a recognized place in her social network, it is most likely that of one who brings news or one who plugs into a gossip network.

Status. One of the premiere status markers in the Fourth Gospel is knowledge: what has been told or revealed to one; what secrets one knows; and what selected disclosures one enjoys. Although Jesus says many things to her, what she does *not know* remains a significant problem at the end of conversation. For half of the dialogue she misunderstands Jesus (4:7-14); even at 4:15, she reckons Jesus' "water" to be only a permanent thirst-quencher. In 4:16-26 she does not strictly misunderstand Jesus so much as spar with him. Jesus is not fooled by her attempted deception of her shamelessness, "I have no husband." He is the character with all knowledge. She mocks his revelation of her sexual history by calling him "Mr. Know-it-all," a prophet, and challenges him to solve the divisive issue of where to worship. After he informs her, she again challenges him with a Samaritan claim to ultimate knowledge: "We know that the Messiah will tell us everything" (so much for your knowledge!). But "I am the Messiah." What does she know? As the saying goes, "Not much." Prophet and Messiah are not revelations to her or acknowledgments by her, but agonistic and sarcastic remarks in her interminable sparring match. How much did Jesus' revelation penetrate? Inasmuch as she subsequently refers to Jesus only in interrogative terms ("Can this man be the Messiah?" 4:29), what does she know? How surprising, then, is Schneiders' claim that she is "remarkable for the clarity and completeness of the presentation of the revelation process in the Fourth Gospel."[36] Her status, then, rests on what she knows and how much she understands of what was said to her. Finally, her status takes a hit when her villagers dismiss her "witnessing." Hence, we acknowledge for her a role such as informal recruiter and bringer of news, but her status never rises to the level of the later great figures.

---

35. See Richard L. Rohrbaugh, "Gossip in the New Testament," in John J. Pilch, ed., *Social Scientific Models for Interpreting the Bible* (Leiden: E. J. Brill, 2001) 239-59; Deborah Jones, "Gossip: Notes on Women's Oral Culture," *Women's Studies International Quarterly* 3 (1980): 193-98; Don Handelman, "Gossip in Encounters: The Transmission of Information in a Bounded Social Setting," *Man* 8 (1973): 210-27; Sian Lewis, *News and Society in the Greek Polis* (Chapel Hill, NC: University of North Carolina Press, 1996).

36. Schneiders, "Women in the Fourth Gospel," 39.

What of the other status markers? As a representative or symbolic character, her narrative characteristics would normally be considered markers of very low status: a female, a Samaritan, an unclean person, a sinner, and even an adulteress. Ironically these are ignored or even utilized positively in the narrative.[37] She might well typify that the last is first, the outsider is an insider, unclean is clean, etc. Even if she does not enjoy high status, she is certainly superior to Nicodemus, whom the author holds in contempt.[38] Her juxtaposition with Nicodemus increases her status: he came to Jesus in darkness (cowardice?), but she appears in sunlight; he never ceased misunderstanding Jesus, but with her there is some progress; the best he said about Jesus was "teacher," whereas, even if in interrogative mode, she declares Jesus "Messiah"; both mock Jesus, but she is never mocked by him. Once more, role is less significant than status.

3.2 The Disciples

Included in this group are true and consistent insiders such as the first persons to follow Jesus who then recruit others (1:35-51); those labeled "followers/disciples" (2:2, 11; 4:27; 13:5; 20:20-26; 21:1-2), "the Twelve" (6:67-71), and people like the man born blind, who is shamed for being "his disciple" (9:28). Others were once disciples or claimed to be so: people who claim to believe but are liars ("If you continue in my word you are my disciples," 8:32) and people who were once disciples but have dropped out of the group (6:60-65). Some are named (Andrew, Simon, Philip and Nathanael, Thomas, Judas not Iscariot, and Judas the traitor), while others are anonymous. The Fourth Gospel, which mentions the traditional disciple Andrew three times (1:35-40; 6:8-9; 12:22), gives special attention to disciples less well known in other Gospels: Philip (1:43; 6:5-7; 12:21; 14:8-10), Nathanael (1:45-50; 21:2), and Thomas (11:16; 14:4-6; 20:24-29; 21:2). The premiere "disciples" have been with Jesus from the beginning, seen his signs and are visited by the Risen Jesus. We focus only on the named, abiding followers, who are genuine insiders.

As regards their *role*, Jesus "sends" them, either to harvest where they have not sown (4:38) or to purify in virtue of the Spirit Jesus gives them (20:21-23). Both tasks are directed to insiders: "reaping" refers to what others sowed, so the

---

37. See Jerome H. Neyrey, "What's Wrong with This Picture? John 4, Cultural Stereotypes of Women, and Public and Private Space," pp. 143-71 in the present volume.

38. All agree that she should be understood as the antithesis of Nicodemus; see Mary Magdalene Pazdan, "Nicodemus and the Samaritan Woman: Contrasting Models of Discipleship," *BTB* 17 (1987): 145-58.

harvest is that of insiders; and forgiving and retaining sins refers to the purity of the group, that is, to insiders. There can be no forgiveness of "the world" and its ruler. In addition to these formal authorizations, they are told to assist at the feeding and to gather up the fragments. But these commands (6:10, 12), symbolically significant as they may be, are not authorized as duties or repeatable tasks as are the "reaping" and "forgiving" of sins. According to the purpose for which they are "sent" and the commands given them, they are portrayed as laboring only within the group.³⁹ Although they function in the process of recruitment (1:36-51) and as brokers for people seeking Jesus (12:20-23), they seem not to have a role to outsiders, neither traveling to them nor heralding a word to win adherents.⁴⁰ In John, unlike the Synoptic Gospels, they are not sent out on an apprentice mission (Matt 10:1-15//Mark 3:13-19), nor are they formally commissioned by the risen Jesus, "Go, make disciples of all nations" (Matt 28:19; see Luke 24:44-49). We are, then, reluctant to call them "apostles," the role in favor among Paul and others.

As regards *status*, because Jesus makes a parallel between the Father "sending" him and his "sending" them ("As you sent me into the world, so I have sent them into the world" [17:18; see 20:21]), we consider them sub-brokers of Jesus, the premiere broker of God.⁴¹ This suggests considerable status. Peder Borgen argued that we consider Jesus as "agent" of God. The basic principle of the Israelite institution of agency is "an agent is like the one who sent him."⁴² Hence the disciples are "like" the one who sends them, i.e., Jesus. Second, the disciples receive selected disclosure of special Johannine gnosis. They are promised a unique vision of the Son of Man enthroned in heaven (1:51), a high status marker. They are present at three of Jesus' signs: the multiplication of water-wine in 2:1-12 and loaves in 6:5-13 and the raising of Lazarus, the last and great-

---

39. The Fourth Gospel differs from the Synoptics on several points: whereas in them Jesus often "sends" (ἀποστέλλω, Matt 10:5, 16) them and even calls them "apostles" (ἀπόστολος, Mark 3:14; 6:30; Luke 6:13; 9:10; 17:5; 22:14; 24:10), in the Fourth Gospel ἀποστέλλω is used primarily of Jesus. It is used only in an extended sense once in regard to the disciples: "A servant is not greater than his master, nor is he who is sent greater than the one who sent him" (13:16). "Apostle," then, is a restricted term, whose primary referent is Jesus.

40. Only in one place are the disciples referred to as "witnesses"; the Spirit will "bear witness" to Jesus and "you are also witnesses, for you have been with me from the beginning" (15:27).

41. This Gospel restricts imitation of Jesus to the disciples in terms of washing the feet of one another ("I have given you an example, that you should do as I have done to you," 13:15) and laying down one's life ("love one another as I have loved you," 15:12). The focus is inward, toward insiders.

42. Borgen, "God's Agent in the Fourth Gospel," 122, and Buchanan, "Apostolic Christology," 172-82.

est sign. They hear the controversial discourse about the Bread of Life (6:29-59). In the Farewell Discourse, they are instructed about Jesus' "whence" and "whither," prayer, judgment, and future crises. Disclosure of special information, moreover, is a high status marker. Third, they are exhorted to practice the two premier Johannine virtues, "remain" and "love," loyalty being another status marker. Fourth, they are promised another Advocate, who will broker knowledge of Jesus to them, either past things that Jesus said or future things (14:25-26 and 15:26). They receive manifestations of the risen and ascended Jesus (20:19-23, 24-29 and 21:1-23). Clearly they are insiders of considerable status. But the status markers just noted are just that, status markers, not authorizations to engage outsiders.

In summary, they are positioned at both the entrance and exit of the group: recruiting others and determining if sins are forgiven or retained. There seems to be no command to *speak* to outsiders. Their status, moreover, seems more important than any role they play in the community.

3.3 The Man Born Blind

Does the remark of Jesus to the man born blind ("Go, wash in the pool of Siloam," 9:7) serve as a commission to play a role? Superficially it resembles Jesus' remark to the Samaritan woman, "Go, call your husband" (4:16), in that both are *commands* to do a specific thing; but no role is in view. After fulfilling the command, the man is transformed from blind to sighted, but still no role is in view. But when re-aggregated with his family and neighbors, he begins to play the role of "witness," although the technical term "witness" is not applied to him, nor was he authorized to do so. He publicly answers a series of questions: "Is this not the man?" "I am"; "Where is he?" "I do not know"; "The Pharisees asked how he received his sight," "He put clay on my eyes." Finally, when asked about Jesus, he says "He is a prophet." His speech, while not formally authorized, is clearly a full, bold, public acknowledgment of Jesus, especially when juxtaposed to his parents' fear of public "confession" (9:22). At this moment the audience knows that a forensic proceeding is occurring, and the "witnessing" will become sharp and pointed. His interrogators "know" that Jesus is a sinner (9:24), a judgment from which he dissociates himself ("Whether this man is a sinner, I do *not* know"). Instead he "knows" a legal fact, "though I was blind, now I see" (9:25), and that it was commanded by Jesus, even though it was the Sabbath. After the court reviles him, he utters some of the best lines in the drama: "You do not know where he comes from, and yet he opened my eyes. . . . If this man were not from God, he could do nothing" (9:30-33). As a witness, he defends Jesus to hostile outsiders and constructs the perfect argument about the source and meaning of Jesus' signs. For him Jesus is a prophet and the one authorized by God. As regards his role, he speaks as a forensic witness on Jesus' behalf at a trial before outsiders — and without authorization. He is one of the heroes of the Fourth Gospel.

He enjoys, moreover, very high status for several reasons. First, he is the beneficiary of a unique miracle ("Never since the world began has it been heard that anyone opened the eyes of a man born blind," 9:32). Second, in contrast to those afraid to confess Jesus publicly (9:22; 12:42; Nicodemus and Joseph of Arimathea), by his feisty dialogue he manifests great courage. Third, he suffers for his witness by being subject to the very sentence which his parents sought to avoid, being ostracized from the synagogue, which Jesus predicts will also be the fate of authentic disciples (16:1-2; see 12:24-25). Finally, he receives a special revelation from Jesus (9:35-38). Jesus "found" him and asked him: "Do you believe in the Son of man?" To his honest reply, "Who is he ...?" Jesus then makes a selected disclosure of unique information: "You have seen him ... it is he who speaks to you" (9:37), to which he appropriately responds, "Lord, I believe" (9:38). Thus the status of the man born blind hinges on four elements: 1. he is favored with a remarkable sign (9:32); 2. he makes a bold, public acknowledgment of Jesus; 3. he suffers for the sake of Jesus, and 4. he is a recipient of special revelation. His role is that of witness; he enjoys very high status.

3.4 The Beloved Ones

The author tells us of a crisis in Bethany in a family consisting of one brother and two sisters. Lazarus, Martha, and Mary already enjoy high status inasmuch as they are all called "beloved" of Jesus. Do any of them play a *role?* Lazarus plays no role. Yet his status seems to be quite high. First, he is "beloved" by Jesus and the beneficiary of Jesus' last and greatest sign. Because sitting at table with Jesus is so rare in this Gospel, his sitting beside Jesus in 12:1-2 signals significant status. Finally, we are told that the chief priests plan to put Lazarus to death because he is a living and public witness to Jesus' power (12:9-11). He is targeted, then, to suffer and die for Christ. So, in one sense he will die because of Jesus and even die with Jesus, very high status indeed (see 12:24-25). Thus, Lazarus, while playing no role, nevertheless enjoys very high status.

That the sisters send news of Lazarus's illness to Jesus does not of itself indicate that they have a role (11:3). Many bring news to others but have no formal role, such as the unnamed person who tells Martha that Jesus has come to town

(11:20).⁴³ We focus, then, on the conversation between Jesus and Martha in 11:20-27. Formally, this looks like another statement-misunderstanding-clarification exchange, suggesting that Jesus teaches and Martha learns. She begins the dialogue with a reproach ("If you had been here, my brother would not have died") and a petition ("I know that whatever you ask from God, God will give you"). Her "I know" is no empty claim and acknowledges Jesus' close relationship to God. Jesus' statement to her seems obvious: "Your brother will rise again." Martha, however, misunderstands Jesus' words in terms of traditional knowledge about "resurrection" and "the last day." She knows old knowledge, but not the new knowledge of Jesus. He then makes a clarification, which is a select disclosure of remarkable knowledge: "I am the resurrection and the life . . ." (11:24-25). But the narrative suggests that Martha does not entirely understand what Jesus said to her. At first her response is of a lower order than Jesus' self-revelation: "I believe that you are the Christ, the Son of God, he who is coming into the world" (11:27). The problem is that in this Gospel the claim to be or have "resurrection and life" is part of an elitist understanding based on Jesus' claim that he enjoys full eschatological power and so equality with God. Martha's response includes nothing of this sort. Yet, asked if she believes this, she states that she does, a significant confession, though not what she was invited to know. Thus as a student she cannot be said to have learned her lessons well.⁴⁴

According to the criteria for *status*, she is neither lowest nor highest. First, she enjoys special status as "beloved" because of a relationship with Jesus. Second, she is the recipient of revelation which, alas, she does not grasp. Third, her brother will be favored with the greatest of signs, although she will need coaching at tomb-side (11:39). "Beloved" is balanced by mediocre understanding of revelation and need for coaching.

3.5 Mary Magdalene

Most recent discussion of Mary Magdalene centers around whether she has a role and if so, which one. We know that Jesus sent her to an elite group in a

---

43. Martha will shortly play the respectable role of "diakonos" at the meal when the three Beloved Disciples host Jesus (12:2). This sounds quite similar to Luke's portrayal of Martha in Luke 10:41-42. In John, however, Martha is both meal server and conversation partner with Jesus, whereas Mary is Jesus' interlocutor in Luke.

44. The exchange between Jesus and Martha in 11:38-40 confirms this imperfect knowledge; Jesus said that "I am the resurrection," which Martha has quickly forgotten when the tomb is to be opened.

speaking capacity with a specific message: "Go to my brethren and say to them, I am ascending to my Father. . . ." She is authorized to speak, and in this regard she is similar to the disciples whom Jesus sends to retain or release sins (20:23) and to Peter whom Jesus established as the shepherd to "feed my lambs . . . sheep" (21:15-18). All of these, moreover, are directed *ad intra,* that is, to insiders of the group. Except in 15:27 and 17:18, the Fourth Gospel mentions no authorization to speak to outsiders, unlike Matt 28:18-20.

What *role?* Either "witness" or "apostle" or "prophet." Inasmuch as no other person in the Fourth Gospel other than Jesus is ever considered an "apostle,"[45] *prima facie* we find it extremely difficult to ascribe this role to Mary. We are also hesitant to ascribe the role of "witness" to her. Witnesses may speak to outsiders as well as insiders, but they speak of what they already know and do so at special times and circumstances. Mary goes to tell "my brethren" unique knowledge, which no one else knows. She is, then, a conduit of specific information of the highest significance. This distinguishes her speaking role from all others in the Fourth Gospel. Her "message" is not just news, but the handing on of a unique disclosure. She has, then, a speaking role which I consider a *prophetic* role. Although the Spirit will come and remind the disciples of words Jesus spoke long ago, her role comes immediately from the Risen Jesus; and she conveys new information, not old. Her role, moreover, needs to be measured against Jesus' remarks to the disciples who are authorized twice according to the formula "As the Father has sent me, so I send you" (17:18; 20:21). Mary does not belong in this chain of authorized command: God → Jesus → disciples; she is the mouthpiece for Jesus and speaks as his agent, his prophet.

If Mary were thought to have a public speaking role, some gender considerations are in order. First, *speech.* In general, females spoke only with the males of their households or kinship groups (1 Tim 2:12; 1 Cor 14:33-36), but not with males apart from these groups. She, however, speaks to "my brethren," a fictive kin group whom she presumably knows and who know her. Second, *travel.* Whereas the commissioning of male disciples in the Synoptics implies that they will travel from city to city and town to town speaking to strangers of the House of Israel in "public" space, Mary is not thus commissioned. She will not speak to strangers, especially strange males, but to "my brethren," whom she knows and who know her. Despite modern attempts to transport Mary Magdalene to the Western Mediterranean in the mid-first century, there is no reliable record that she left Judea. Third, *word/gospel.* Witnesses and apostles will deliver the official message about Jesus again and again as they go from group to group (Matt 28:19). But Mary speaks only one word, albeit an extraordinary revela-

---

45. Buchanan, "Apostolic Christology," 179-81.

tion. But having spoken it, she will have fulfilled her duty to Jesus. Fourth, *duration*. Whereas the roles of witness and apostle endure as long as their holders live, can the same thing be said of Mary? The Gospel only says that she spoke to "my brethren"; did she repeat her word daily to them or does her role cease after delivering her message? Her role, therefore, is dissimilar to that of other "witnesses" in the Fourth Gospel; in fact, it is difficult to be precise about what role she plays.

Yet Mary is unique in the narrative. I think we go in the wrong direction if we insist on establishing a *role* for her; she is like no one else, which might be the point. Instead of role, the issue seems to be one of *status*. Her status rests on several criteria: 1) courage: presence at the cross; 2) attention to the body of Jesus, even attempts to touch/hold it; 3) being called by name; and 4) receiving the most significant information about Jesus.

Why is *status* more important than role for Mary? On the one hand, if we insist on ascribing to her a role, it would seem to end as soon as it started. Having fulfilled Jesus' command to "go and tell my brethren," now what? What duties has she? What audience will she subsequently address? Roles have time limits of a sort, but status does not. Once a "beloved" of Jesus, always a "beloved" of Jesus. Once fortunate to receive a selected disclosure of the highest order, always a favored one. We mentioned above four criteria for high status, and there is no doubt that she enjoys exceptionally high *status*.[46]

We have argued that what one knows serves as an excellent index of one's *status*. Mary Magdalene has unique knowledge of extraordinary importance. From the earliest parts of the narrative, the most important piece of information concerns knowledge of *whence* Jesus comes and *whither* he goes. Most characters struggle with this problem. In two key places, the prologues in 1:1-18 and 13:1-3, we are told that Jesus comes from God (whence) and returns to God's bosom (whither, 1:14, 18; 13:1-3). Only insiders can accept this; to outsiders it is a blasphemous claim. *Whence?* Jesus himself tells characters that he comes from above, that is, descends from heaven: "No one has ever ascended but the one who first descended from heaven" (3:13); "I am the bread which came down from heaven" (6:38, 41); "[king] . . . for this I have come into the world" (18:37). Others have clues and arguments about his "whence," some insightful ("if this man were not from God . . . ," 9:33) or misleading ("son of Jo-

---

46. Martin Hengel ("Maria Magdalena und die Frauen als Zeugen," in *Abraham unser Vater. Juden und Christen im Gespräch bei die Bibel*, ed. Martin Hengel and Peter Schmidt [Leiden: E. J. Brill, 1963], 150-52) argues that Mary enjoys very high status among the female disciples; that is, she has the same priority among the female disciples that Peter does among the males: she is mentioned in all the lists of female witnesses, and first in the Synoptics. This is status, but not role.

seph," 6:42) or biased ("what good can come from Nazareth?" 1:46; "no prophet will come from Galilee?" 7:26-27, 41-42, 52), or shallow ("a teacher come from God," 3:2). *Whither?* Jesus promises a vision of himself when he has returned whither he came: "You will see the heavens opened and the angels of God ascending and descending on the Son of man" (1:51). Again it is Jesus who remarks, "What if you were to see the Son of man ascending where he was before?" (6:62), and he prays to be "glorified in your presence with the glory which I had with you before the world was made" (17:5). How hard it is for outsiders to get this straight, for when Jesus says "I go to him who sent me . . . where I am you cannot come" (7:33-34), some interpret this as departure for the Dispersion (7:35) or even suicide (8:22). Hence, only Jesus knows "whence I have come and whither I am going" (8:14). But by telling Mary that "I am returning to my Father and your Father," he provides her with knowledge about *"whence"* and *"whither"*: he is *returning* whence he came. There is, moreover, no indication that she does not understand what he said, unlike Nicodemus, the Samaritan woman, and Martha. This indicates *very high status*, which is more significant than any role she might play.

3.6 Simon Peter

In the Synoptics Peter plays the role of "fisher of men," i.e., an agent of recruitment of outsiders, and the "rock" upon which Jesus builds his assembly (Matt 16:18). When Peter was gathered with the Twelve, Jesus authorized him to say and do what Jesus said and did: preach the kingdom, heal, and cast out demons (Mark 3:13-15). But in the Fourth Gospel, all consideration of Peter's role is muted or absent until 13:4-38 and 21:1-19. The purpose of Jesus' washing of Peter's feet is to transform him from ordinary to extraordinary disciple. No mere cleansing rite, this should transform him to a new *status*, that is, the status of an elite disciple who is willing to lay down his life for Jesus.[47] But shortly thereafter Peter fails and must wait for another time to attempt to gain this status. Yet we learn that he has ambitions for a particular *role*, namely that of shepherd, i.e., successor of the Noble Shepherd. This becomes evident in the similarities of the dialogue at the beginning and ending of the scene in John 13. Recall that the qualification for a "noble" shepherd is that he lay down his life for his sheep (10:11, 15).

---

47. Jerome H. Neyrey, "The Footwashing in John 13:6-11: Transformation Ritual or Ceremony?" in *The Social World of the First Christians: Essays in Honor of Wayne A. Meeks*, ed. L. Michael White and O. Larry Yarbrough (Minneapolis: Fortress, 1995) 206-9.

13:6-8	13:36-38
"Lord, do you wash my feet?" (13:6)	"Lord, where are you going?" (13:36)
Jesus answered, "What I am doing you do not know now, but afterward you will understand" (13:7).	Jesus answered him: "Where I am going you cannot follow now, but afterward you will follow" (13:36b).
Peter said to him: "You shall never wash my feet" (13:8)	Peter said to him: "Lord, why cannot I follow you now? I will lay down my life for you" (13:37).
Jesus answered him: "Unless I wash you, you have no part in me"(13:8).	Jesus answered: "Will you lay down your life for me? The cock will not crow, until you have denied me three times" (13:38).

As we fast-forward to John 20–21, we see that the traditional role of "fisher of men" seems to be in view. Simon gathers others to go fishing with him — his initiative, his role. Blessed with an extraordinarily huge catch, Simon leads the way by "hauling the net ashore full of large fish" (21:11). Seemingly he is confirmed in his role of chief fisherman, a role directed to those outside the group. Next Jesus serves them fish and bread. While the text does not explicitly say that Peter participated in serving this meal, the fact is that he will immediately be told to "Feed my lambs. . . . Feed my sheep." Thus even in the beach breakfast scene, Peter is an apprentice host, learning from Jesus how to "Feed my lambs." Finally, Jesus purifies him of his failure by a triple question about loyalty, balancing Simon's triple denial. When purified, Simon is finally qualified to play the *role* of shepherd, another inward-looking role.[48] Thus, Simon's roles are successively identified: fisherman, food provider, and shepherd. If explicit authorization is important, Jesus commands and so commissions Peter three times to take the *role of shepherd*. And by the end of the narrative, Peter plays even the role of "noble" shepherd of the group.[49]

But *status*? Does Peter enjoy respect and status? Until John 20, very little is said of Peter that indicates high status; on the contrary, a veritable avalanche of negative status markers buries him. If comparisons are made, he is inferior to Andrew who called him. The Beloved Disciple surpasses him in loyalty, knowledge, closeness to Jesus, etc. But as the story ends, although Peter is commis-

---

48. See A. H. Maynard, "The Role of Peter in the Fourth Gospel," *NTS* 30 (1984): 531-47, and Conway, *Men and Women in the Fourth Gospel*, 163-77.

49. Jerome H. Neyrey, "The 'Noble' Shepherd in John 10: Cultural and Rhetorical Background," *JBL* 120 (2001): 267-80.

sioned to an important role, it remains unclear what kind of status this traditional figure enjoyed in the non-traditional Johannine group.⁵⁰

3.7 Beloved Disciple

Whoever this person was, does he have a *role* in the narrative? Reclining so close to Jesus at the supper and having access to the identity of the traitor are important *status* markers, but not indicative of a role. At the cross, however, Jesus authorizes him for a most significant role, namely "son" to his mother. The Beloved Disciple assumes the role of the male formally responsible to protect the honor, reputation, and well-being of this important female. This role, moreover, is strictly an internal role within the circle of disciples.

The Beloved Disciple, moreover, has another *role,* namely sub-broker of Jesus to the disciples. Brokers mediate between patrons and clients goods such as power, loyalty, material gains, and information. One would expect in this Gospel to find an emphasis on the group's most important commodities, that is, commitment ("beloved," "son") and information (revelations, manifestations, etc.). The Beloved Disciple is uniquely positioned on Jesus' bosom to ask him for significant information, the identity of the traitor (13:25); his role is that of go-between as he seeks the answer to Peter's question from the one who knows all. He brokers entrance for Peter into the palace of the high priest (18:15-18), and he brokers for Peter and others the recognition of Jesus on the shore (21:7). He is not formally authorized as the purveyor of information, but that again may be irrelevant. As a charismatic figure, he has knowledge, insight, and wisdom.

As regards *status,* the Beloved Disciple is identified by many significant markers. First, at his initial appearance, he was "lying close to the breast of Jesus" (13:23), and since physical proximity to Jesus is a significant status marker, he begins exceptionally well placed. Moreover, he is privy to restricted information, the identity of the traitor. Third, he manifests courage and loyalty superior to all of the other disciples, first by entering the high priest's palace and by standing publicly in support of Jesus at his cross. The only disciple there, he puts his life on the line for Jesus. Fourth, he displays alacrity, running fast to the tomb; after seeing all that Simon saw, he has great insight ("he saw and he believed," 20:8). He believes despite seeing nothing that Peter had not seen; hence Jesus' makarism declaring those "blessed" who believe without seeing (20:29) would extend to him. He is, then, a "blessed" as well as a "beloved" one. Fifth, a rumor in the group suggested that the Beloved Disciple would not die

---

50. On this problem, see Brown, *The Community of the Beloved Disciple,* 81-84.

(21:22). The very hint that so eminent a person would escape death and "remain" until Jesus comes would distinguish him as a unique, remarkably favored disciple. All of this indicates that whatever role he has, he has *exceptionally high status*.

4.0 Summary and Conclusions

The following chart gathers the bits of information about the characters surveyed and assesses it comparatively. From this, we seek to confirm roles and statuses argued earlier. After this summary, we will try to rank in importance the characters in the Gospel in terms of their statuses.

Person	Authorization	Status	Roles and Duties	Duration
Samaritan woman	*Authorization:* none; "Go, call your husband and come here" (4:16) is *not* authorization for a role.	*Elite, but medium status:* Markers = 1. what she comes to know, 2. her recruitment of others, 3. her remarks about Jesus, 4. symbolism as a character who upsets expected norms.	Role: 1. "wife"; 2. recruiter and news bringer *Duties:* food preparation	*Duration:* quickly terminated (4:42)
Disciples	*Authorization:* "I send you to reap that for which you did not labor; others have labored" (4:38; 17:18)	*High status:* but someone has already sown the word; they are in second place	Roles: 1. agents to the insiders; 2. sub-brokers of Jesus *Duties:* "to reap," to allow others to enter	*Duration:* Continues over time
	"For I have set you an example, that *you also should do* as I have done to you" (13:15)	*High status:* imitation of Jesus; only leaders perform this action	Roles: 1. servants of hospitality: a role restricted to leaders of group *Duties:* to extend hospitality; to perform servant tasks	Continues over time
	"As the Father has sent me, so I send you." When he had said this, he breathed on them and said to them, "Receive the Holy Spirit. If you forgive the sins of any . . ." (20:21-23)	*High status:* Extension of Jesus' role	*Roles:* agents who control entrance and exit of group *Duties:* to serve as gatekeepers vis-à-vis insiders; guardians of group's boundaries	Continues over time

Person	Authorization	Status	Roles and Duties	Duration
Man Born Blind	*Authorization:* none	*Very high status:* markers = 1. unique healing; 2. bold acknowledgment of Jesus (vs. parents); 3. suffers for Jesus; 4. prime articulator of the logic of the signs; 5. recipient of unique revelation by the "Son of man"	*Role:* 1. forensic witness defending Jesus *Duties:* steadfast loyalty to Jesus for his healing	*Duration:* no way to know duration after becoming an insider
Martha	*Authorization:* none	*Medium status:* markers = 1. labeled "beloved"; 2. receives disclosure of unique knowledge; 3. acknowledges Jesus with good, but unimpressive title	*Role:* none	n/a
Lazarus	*Authorization:* none	*High status:* markers = 1. labeled "beloved"; 2. recipient of greatest sign; 3. seated next to Jesus at table; 4. destined to die for Jesus	*Role:* none	n/a
Mary Magdalene	*Authorization:* "Go to my brothers and *say* to them . . ." (20:17)	*Very high status:* markers = 1. loyalty: standing at the cross; and visiting the tomb; 2. seeking to recover and honor Jesus' body; 3. called by name; 4. receives an appearance of the Risen Jesus; 5. attempts to touch him; 6. receives a disclosure of great significance; 7. bringer of important message to the "brethren"	*Role:* prophet with important information *Duties:* to bring Jesus' revelation to the "brothers"	*Duration:* difficult to know since task is completed in 20:18
Simon Peter	*Authorization:* "Feed my lambs. . . . *Tend* my sheep. . . . *Feed* my sheep" (21:15-17)	*Ambiguous status:* positive markers = 1. long encounter with Risen Jesus; 2. seeks physical presence of Jesus; 3. finally becomes "shepherd" and even "noble" shepherd; negative markers = 1. called second; 2. lukewarm acknowledgment of Jesus; 3. failure in washing transformation ritual; 4. withdraws all loyalty to Jesus in courtyard	*Role:* not just fisherman and table server, but shepherd *Duties:* to be Noble Shepherd (pasture; defense);[51] to lay down his life for the sheep (21:18-19)	*Duration:* Continues over time

51. Although the tradition knows of an anonymous disciple drawing a sword in the garden,

Role and Status in the Fourth Gospel

Person	Authorization	Status	Roles and Duties	Duration
Beloved Disciple	*Authorization:* "Woman, behold your son.... Behold your mother" (19:26-27)	*Very high status:* 1. physical contact with Jesus; 2. secret knowledge of the traitor; 3. courage and loyalty at Jesus' death; 4. "blessed" because he believed and did not see; 5. alone recognizes the Risen Jesus; 6. rumor that he will not die	*Role:* as fictive kin, "son" of Jesus' mother *Duties:* honor, protect, and defend the mother of Jesus	*Duration:* as long as Jesus' mother lives

From these data we distill the following information about roles. On the basis of the persons examined in this study, we judge that formal roles within the Jesus group were few and of modest significance: witness, agent, prophet, fisherman, and shepherd, along with informal roles such as recruiter and news-bringer. Only the witnessing of the man born blind is directed to outsiders; all other roles look to insiders already within the group. We conclude, then, that *roles were not important in the group. Far more significant for the Johannine group is status.*

As regards status, we have come to identify the following markers of status in the Fourth Gospel.

1. reception of revelations and christophanies (1:51; 9:34-36; 20:16-18),
2. disclosure of esoteric information (10:25; 14:1-17:26; 20:17),
3. being labeled "beloved" by Jesus (Martha, Mary and Lazarus and BD),
4. praise from Jesus and being labeled as "blessed" (13:17; 20:29),
5. bold public confession (man born blind vs. his parents, 9:22),
6. loyalty and faithfulness (Mary Magdalene, the Beloved Disciple at the cross),
7. recipient of unique healing (man born blind, Lazarus),
8. imitation of Jesus; suffering for him (12:9-11, 24-25),
9. fictive kin: son and mother (19:26-27)
10. actual/attempted physical contact with Jesus (Mary, 12:1-8; the Beloved Disciple, 13:25; Mary Magdalene, 20:17),
11. never dying (21:19-23)

But let us ask another question: Who's Who in the Johannine Group? Can we discern an order of precedence? It seems easy to distinguish three levels of

---

the Fourth Gospel identifies this figure as Simon Peter; hence he is showcased as trying to defend Jesus, one of the marks of a shepherd; yet he is rebuked for this and Jesus remains the shepherd who is to negotiate the escape of his disciple/sheep (18:8-9).

status of Johannine characters: elites, traditional figures, and marginal or fringe dwellers. At the top of the pyramid we find the following elites, who are positioned, not because of any role played, but according to status markers. I feel confident about ranking the Beloved Disciple, Mary Magdalene, and the man born blind as enjoying very high status; but it becomes difficult to rank the other elites.

1. Beloved Disciple: physical closeness to Jesus; special knowledge; courage — cross; "son" of Jesus' mother; perhaps deathless
2. Mary Magdalene: courage; physical closeness to Jesus; called by her own name; special manifestation; revelation of the most elite knowledge
3. Man born blind: unique healing; forensic witness for Jesus; bold, public speech on Jesus' behalf; suffers for Jesus; receives a christophany
4. Lazarus: beloved; recipient of greatest sign; targeted for death because of Jesus
5. Martha: beloved; special knowledge but modest acknowledgment of Jesus
6. Mary: beloved; physical closeness (anoints feet)

Other characters display admirable characteristics, but weaknesses as well. It is unclear how to rank these in terms of status.

7. Thomas: knowledge (non-receptive interlocutor with Jesus: 11:16; 14:5); physical closeness (demands to touch Jesus' hands and side); confession, "My Lord and my God"
8. Nathanael: overcomes difficulties to come to Jesus, praised by Jesus, revelation from Jesus, acknowledgment of Jesus, promised a christophany
9. Peter: never credited with being "in the know"; disloyalty eventually canceled by confession of loyalty; eventually becomes "shepherd"; dies to glorify God
10. Andrew: first disciple; recruits others; not noticeably "in the know"; no bold speaking about Jesus
11. Philip: recruits another; brokers "the Greeks" to Jesus; receives special information
12. Samaritan woman: never quite knowing what Jesus is saying; always challenging Jesus; delivering an ambivalent confession of Jesus

Finally, the narrative tells of still other characters who lack courage, learn nothing from encountering Jesus or fail in converting "sign" into faith. These would have no little or no status in the eyes of the members of the group.

13. Nicodemus: earthly knowledge; total failure to understand Jesus, lacks courage (at night)
14. Joseph of Arimathea: no courage ("secret disciple," 19:38)
15. Crippled man in 5:1-15: no loyalty to Jesus as a result of his healing; ultimately a "witness" against Jesus to Jesus' enemies.

Gathering the threads of this investigation, certain conclusions suggest themselves. First, in general, *roles* seem considerably less important than *status*. Moreover, with the exception of forensic witnessing, the roles are directed to insiders, as opposed to Synoptic and Pauline apostolic roles to spread the gospel to outsiders. They are, moreover, roles involving speech of some sort. This relates to the scholarly discussion that the Fourth Gospel is a maverick gospel, in which high-status elites stand in opposition to or superior to those with traditional roles, such as the apostles and especially Peter. One wonders, moreover, if there is a tension between what the earthly Jesus did and what the Risen Lord said, for the disclosure of remarkable secrets and the demonstration of public courage are most evident in Jesus' death and resurrection. There can be no denying that knowledge, selected disclosure, revelations, and christophanies are the coin of the realm: persons can be ranked in terms of what they know, when they know it, and how they know it. And "knowing" in this Gospel is a status marker, not a role.

3

Spaces and Places, Whence and Whither, Homes and Rooms

"Territoriality" in the Fourth Gospel

1.0 Introduction: Topic, Focus, and Hypothesis

The Fourth Gospel names many spaces and places, some geographical and some not. After scholars noted the geographical contrast between "Galilee" and "Judea/Jerusalem," they then inquired what meaning the Evangelist invested in both locations: how are "Galilee" and "Judea" classified in the symbolic world of the author? If not as real places, then what do they mean? Similarly, when the Samaritan woman declares that her people consider "this mountain" the correct place of worship, whereas Judeans worship in "Jerusalem" (4:20), her remarks reflect an investment of meaning given each respective mountain by Samaritans and Israelites. Jesus' response, however, dis-invests both places of significance for worship (4:21-24). Furthermore, in the Fourth Gospel various narrative characters enjoy physical closeness to Jesus. Some anoint his feet, attempt to cling to him, or rest on his chest. This suggests that a person's place relative to Jesus' physical body might serve as an index of status within Jesus' group. Finally, controversy surrounds "whence" Jesus comes and "whither" he goes. Characters considered "outsiders" by the Evangelist invariably interpret "whence" as the village where Jesus was born or the region where he lived. These folk also misunderstand "whither" he goes, guessing that he is departing the land of Israel for the "Dispersion among the Greeks" (7:35). Answers such as these expose their proponents as outsiders who think literally and physically about places such as Nazareth, Galilee, or the Diaspora. But in the eyes of the Evangelist, the answers to "whence" Jesus comes and "whither" he goes are not geographical places.

These and other significant data about place in the Fourth Gospel deserve to be treated as redundant examples of the phenomena called "territoriality." I propose to use the model of "territoriality" found in current anthropology because it is suited both to gathering data and to assessing their social significance. This enterprise will make a contribution to Johannine studies, inasmuch as many spatial data relate to the Gospel's high christology and membership in the group, not to geography in the Fourth Gospel. This mapping process of the Johannine author reinforces the view of Jesus as an alien and his disciples as living in "no where."

2.0 The Anthropological Model "Territoriality"

What is "territoriality"? Robert Sack, a representative of modern research into this area, defines it as:

> the attempt by an individual or group to affect, influence, or control people, phenomena, and relationships, by delimiting and asserting control over a geographic area.... Territories require constant effort to establish and maintain.[1]

His emphasis rests on the attempt to *control* some place or persons. Control presumes that the controlling group has in some way *labeled* or *classified* some place in relationship to itself. Sack notes that the controlling group tries to "affect, influence or control" places and that the object of control might be "people, phenomena, relationships." "Territory," then, may be geographical or transgeographical.

If we know some of the history of the development of the model of "territoriality," we may better understand it and its utility. Modern research into "territoriality" began with studies of animal behavior, especially that of birds.[2] From early on, certain concepts emerged which remain integral parts of all models of territoriality. Birds could be observed performing some conspicuous behavior which was interpreted as communication of an exclusive claim to a certain area, which was intended to exert control of that territory. For example,

---

1. Robert D. Sack, *Human Territoriality: Its Theory and History* (Cambridge: Cambridge University Press, 1986) 19; Ralph B. Taylor, *Human Territorial Functioning: An Empirical Evolutionary Perspective on Individual and Small Group Territorial Cognitions, Behaviors and Consequences* (Cambridge: Cambridge University Press, 1988) 6. See also, Michael J. Casimir, *Mobility and Territoriality: Social and Spatial Boundaries among Foragers, Fishers, Pastoralists, and Peripatetics* (Oxford: Oxford University Press, 1992).

2. Edward T. Hall, *The Hidden Dimension* (New York: Doubleday, 1966) 7-22, and John Calhoun, "The Role of Space in Animal Sociology," *JSI* 22 (1966): 46-58.

a male bird becomes intolerant of other males as he confines himself to a certain area for the purposes of ensuring an adequate food supply and safe nesting space for his mate.[3] Even as anthropologists later focused on human patterns of "territoriality," the three foci of the model remain: 1) *classification* of places, 2) *communication* of this classification, and 3) *control* of the places so classified.

2.1 Classification Systems

The classification system, the key to the model, refers to the ways in which humans invest space with meaning or label it for some purpose. For example, people declare this space "ours" but that space "yours," thus making "our" space sacred and set apart from other, profane spaces. Parents often classify their bedroom as "off-limits" for their children, thus distinguishing adult from family space. Muslims and Israelis both claim that the Temple Mount in Jerusalem is their own sacred space and thus see the presence of the other there as profaning it.

Anthropologists provide many general patterns for classifying territory, all of which contain binary opposites which set certain spaces apart as restricted and unrestricted, ours and yours, holy and profane, and the like. These labels are intended to have dramatic impact on how we and others think of and behave in regard to a certain space. A sample inventory of classification systems would include: 1) public-private, 2) sacred-profane, 3) honorable-shameful, 4) clean-unclean, 5) fixed-fluid sacred space, 6) center-periphery, and 7) civilization-nature. Inasmuch as only the first five have direct bearing on this study, they alone will be examined here.

1. *Public and Private.* The Greco-Roman world used labels such as "public-private," "open-covered," "outdoors-indoors" to indicate gender-divided space, with males in public, in open space, and out of doors and females in covered space and indoors. But they also distinguished occasions when males attended to civic affairs in the *boulē* or *agora* as "public" from occasions when males attended symposia, etc. as "private." Philo's stereotypical description of gender-divided "public and private" space embodies this classification found commonly in the Greco-Roman world:[4]

---

3. C. R. Carpenter, "Territoriality: A Review of Concepts and Problems," in *Behavior and Evolution*, ed. Anne Rose and George Simpson (New Haven: Yale University Press, 1958) 224-50.

4. Jerome H. Neyrey, "Jesus, Gender and the Gospel of Matthew," in *New Testament Masculinities*, ed. Stephen D. Moore and Janice Capel Anderson, *Semeia* 45 (2003): 43-66, and "'Teaching You in Public and from House to House' (Acts 20:20): Unpacking a Cultural Stereotype," *JSNT* 26 (2003): 69-102.

Marketplaces and council-halls and law-courts and gatherings and meetings where a large number of people are assembled, and open-air life with full scope for discussion and action — all these are suitable to men both in war and peace. The women are best suited to the indoor life which never strays from the house (*Spec.* 3.169; see Xenophon, *Oeconomicus* 7.19-22; Hierocles, *On Duties* 4.28.21; *On Marriage* 4.22.21-24).

The same "public-private" might apply to the situation whereby honorable men speak boldly in public, while others spread rumor and sedition in private. Jesus boasts to Annas that he has spoken publicly *(παρρησίᾳ)* in synagogue and temple and has *not* spoken in private *(ἐν κρύπτῳ)* (18:20). Thus he has acted honorably according to expected male behavior in culturally appropriate space for males. While some uses of "public-private" in antiquity pertain to male vs. female space, this classification in the Fourth Gospel seems to concern males only, whether speaking publicly or privately within friendship or kinship groups.

2. *Sacred and Profane.* These categories tend to have religious connotations. Mircea Eliade, for example, declared that a theophany or revelation transformed a profane space into a sacred one, and thus it became locally fixed.[5] Jonathan Z. Smith countered that sacred space is founded through ritual and thus is a human choice based on cultural distinctions.[6] He goes on to say: "Within the temple, the ordinary (which to any outside eye or ear remains wholly ordinary) becomes significant, becomes sacred, simply by being there . . . there is nothing that is inherently sacred or profane."[7] Bruce J. Malina provides a more functional definition; he attempts to give modern college students a broad, cross-cultural sense of "sacred" in their lives. Sacred = something set apart, such as a temple or a house, vestments, or even my jeans and my toothbrush.[8] The Samaritan woman's remark about "this mountain" and the one in Jerusalem as places of worship depends on some notion of the sacredness of each place. Ethnic myths about each mountain contain the reasons that each is classified as holy/not common and as sacred/not profane space. Samaritans and Judeans, then, created a "there" there.

---

5. Mircea Eliade, *The Sacred and the Profane: The Nature of Religions: The Significance of Religious Myth, Symbolism, and Ritual within Life and Culture* (New York: Harcourt, Brace and World, 1959) 23.

6. Jonathan Z. Smith, *To Take Place: Toward Theory in Ritual* (Chicago: University of Chicago Press, 1987) 96-116.

7. Smith, *To Take Place,* 104.

8. Bruce J. Malina, *The New Testament World: Insights from Cultural Anthropology* (3rd ed.; Louisville: Westminster/John Knox, 2001) 161-64; see Colin House, "Defilement by Association: Some Insights from the Usage of κοῖνος/κοινόω in Acts 10 and 11," *AUSS* 21 (1983): 143-53.

3. *Honor and Shame.* All of us are familiar with Nathanael's slur about Jesus' home: "Can any good come from Nazareth?" (1:46), an excellent example of a classification which denies honor to someone based on an honorless home-of-origin. Correspondingly, Paul boasts of being "a Judean from Tarsus in Cilicia, a citizen of no low-status city" (Acts 21:39). These are representative examples of a pattern taught in rhetoric on how to write an encomium. Villages, moreover, are mean places in which to live, utterly lacking the facilities found in Greco-Roman cities for elite citizens. Richard Rohrbaugh cites Pausanias about what it takes to make an honorable city, emphasizing how honor is tied to the city's public architecture:

> . . . if indeed one can give the name of city to those who possess no public buildings, no gymnasium, no theater, no market-place, no water descending to a fountain, but live in bare shelters just like mountain huts on the edges of ravines. (*Descriptions of Greece*, 10.4.1)[9]

4. *Pure and Polluted.* Students of Second Temple Judea know that Jerusalem's holy Temple was polluted when a non-Israelite conqueror sacrificed an unclean animal on the altar there (see 1 Macc 1:54; 2 Macc 6:1-2). The undoing of this pollution was commemorated at the Feast of the Rededication, which John 10:22 cites as the occasion of one of Jesus' arguments with the Jerusalemites. A holy place may be made polluted and then re-sanctified.

Similarly, when they hand over Jesus to Pilate, the behavior of the high priest and cohorts illustrates this classification. "They themselves did not enter the praetorium so that they might not be defiled, but might eat the Passover" (18:28). This passage contains both a *classification* of Pilate's official space by elite Judeans according to their elaborate purity system and an ironic twist given to this idea by the author. The *praetorium* is unclean, and the mere entering of it contaminates. By remaining outside, the elite Judeans communicate this and claim respect for observing the purity code.[10] The author, however, sees irony in the fact that while they observe one aspect of the purity code, they nevertheless instigate the murder of Jesus, which is vastly more defiling than entering Pilate's chambers. Thus both the author and his characters label space clean-unclean, but from different classification systems.

5. *Fixed-Fluid Sacred Space.* Anthropologists and students of religions have

---

9. Richard L. Rohrbaugh, "The Pre-Industrial City in Luke-Acts," in *The Social World of Luke-Acts: Models for Interpretation*, ed. Jerome H. Neyrey (Peabody, MA: Hendrickson, 1991) 127.

10. Malina, *The New Testament World*, 164-80; Jerome H. Neyrey, "The Idea of Purity in Mark's Gospel," *Semeia* 35 (1986): 91-128.

developed various versions of this classification.[11] Jonathan Smith, for example, contrasts two types of space, *locative* and *utopian*.[12] *Locative* space focuses on a "center"; it is closed and centrifugal in direction.[13] *Utopian* space refers to an "open" society, periphery (not center) in focus and centripetal in thrust. At heart Smith's energies and insights are with *utopian* space, characterized by rebellion, freedom, and breaking of limits and boundaries by humankind. Yet his insights do not offer the usefulness of an explanatory model such as one finds in the works of Bruce J. Malina. Malina operates out of Mary Douglas's model of "group/grid," which provides him with many descriptive characteristics of *fixed-fluid* sacred space. Since this material is pivotal for classification of space in the Fourth Gospel, let us take time to digest these insights. Of *fixed* sacred space, Malina writes:

> Just as persons have their statuses by ascription and perdure in that status indefinitely, the same holds true for places. The topography of the main places where people in this script live out their lives is rather permanent. A palace location, a temple location, and a homestead stay in the same place and with the same lineage through generations.[14]

Thus *fixed* sacred space correlates with *fixed* roles and statuses. All of this is characterized by redundant aspects of stability, permanence, and continuity. The temple-city of Jerusalem exemplifies this well. Of *fluid* sacred space, Malina writes:

> This situation of porous boundaries and competing groups stands in great contrast to the solid, hierarchical, pyramidal shape of strong group/high grid [fixed space] . . . as groups form and re-form anew, permanence is no longer to be found outside the group; and where the group is, there is stability. Sacred space is located in the group, not in some impersonal space like a temple. The group is the central location of importance, whether the Body of Christ, the church, for Christians, or the synagogue gathering for Jews, or the philosophical "schools". . . . Discourse within these groups, whether the words of a portable Torah, the story of Jesus, or the exhortations of the

---

11. Stanford M. Lyman and Marvin R. Scott, "Territoriality: A Neglected Sociological Dimension," *Social Problems* 15 (1968): 240-41; Jonathan Z. Smith, *Map Is Not Territory: Studies in the History of Religions* (Leiden: E. J. Brill, 1978) xi-xv and 67-207.

12. Jonathan Z. Smith, *Divine Drudgery: On the Comparison of Early Christianities and the Religions of Late Antiquity* (Chicago: University of Chicago Press, 1990) 121-42.

13. Smith, *Map Is Not Territory*, 101, 186-87.

14. Bruce J. Malina, *Christian Origins and Cultural Anthropology: Practical Models for Biblical Interpretation* (Atlanta: John Knox Press, 1986) 31.

philosopher-teacher, becomes the mobile, portable, exportable focus of sacred place, in fact more important than the fixed and eternal sacred places.[15]

For our purposes, we note four things. 1) "Group" becomes the equivalent of fluid space, and so the social dynamics of a "group," such as loyalty *(pistis, alētheia)*, love *(agapē)*, service, etc., rise in importance. 2) Since stability and permanence are not found outside the group, we are clued to consider the "spatial" quality of "remain" in the Fourth Gospel. 3) The group might be a scholastic enterprise, either a philosophical school or a midrashic one. If worship entails the reading and hearing of sacred writings, it can occur anywhere; thus sacred space is mobile and portable. 4) The group, then, is the central location of importance; and so it is not accidental that the New Testament often calls the Christian group "temple" and "household of God."

2.2 Communication and Control

Communication of these classifications could be relatively simple. All a prosperous city need do to communicate that it is honorable or civilized space is to build a wall around itself with a well-guarded gate (e.g., Josh 2:1-21). The same would apply to sections within cities where various trades or occupations or ethnic groups were separated from each other and from the elites by interior walls and gates (e.g., Acts 19:23-25). Non-elites are thus kept away from the urban elites as well as from other non-elites with whom there might be rivalry or conflict. Similarly, what a wall and gate are to a city, a barred door manned by a guard would be for a house or residence (see John 18:15-17; 20:19, 26; Acts 28:16). Perhaps the most dramatic example we have of this principle of communication and control is the balustrade in the Jerusalem Temple which prohibited Gentile access to the court of the Israelites. Recent Temple archaeology has recovered samples of the inscription carved on the balustrade, which reads: "No foreigner is to enter within the forecourt and the balustrade around the sanctuary. Whoever is caught will have himself to blame for his subsequent death."[16]

Both Philo and Josephus comment on this, indicating that it was a well-known device for controlling access within the Temple (Philo, *Embassy to Gaius* 212; Josephus, *Ant.* 12.146; 15.417; *War* 5.193-94). Thus by the very building of a door to close a building, a fence and gate to protect animals or property, and a

---

15. Malina, *Christian Origins and Cultural Anthropology*, 38.
16. Peretz Segal, "The Penalty of the Warning Inscription from the Temple of Jerusalem," *IEJ* 39 (1989): 79-84. See also Philo, *Embassy* 212; Josephus, *Ant.* 12.146; 15.417; *War* 5.193-94.

wall and gate around a city, people communicate that the space within is "ours," "sacred," "pure," etc. The major reasons for control of space seem to be protection and taxation.[17]

3.0 Johannine "Territoriality"

We turn now to the Fourth Gospel, and from the many instances of place we have found in the Gospel we choose the following six as the most significant. 1) "Galilee" and "Judea" seem at first to refer to actual geographical places, but study of this Gospel's symbolic world turns us in another direction. 2) "Public and private" depend on cultural notions of appropriate male behavior. 3) "Not on this mountain, not in Jerusalem" urges us to think of fluid sacred space. 4) "Whence" Jesus comes is understood by some characters in terms of actual places; but the true "whence" and "whither" of Jesus take us out of this world. The same applies to the antitheses Jesus makes between "above" vs. "below" and "*not* of this world" vs. "of this world." 5) Where do disciples "worship in spirit and truth"? In the Father's house with its "many rooms"? 6) Finally we must consider the repeated assertions that some persons are "dwelling in" or "being in" another — the cryptic basis of the Evangelist's definition of sacred space for the group.

3.1 Galilee and Judea

Our questions about these two places are not at all topological or traditional.[18] We ask instead with what meanings the author has invested each place, their "symbolic" meaning if you will.[19] Yet this study is not simply redaction criti-

---

17. Most of our illustrations will come from Greco-Roman materials, but it is noteworthy that the same "public" vs. "private" classification of space is also found in the Mishnah and Talmud. For example, "Our Rabbis taught: There are four domains in respect to the Sabbath: private ground, public ground, *karmelith* and a place of non-liability" (*b. Šabbaṭ* 6a). The passage then goes on to define each space in exacting detail. See also *b. Baba Baṭra* 11a-b; *b. ʿErubin* 22b-23a, 101a-b.

18. Karl Kundsin, *Topologische Überlieferungstoffe im Johannes-Evangelium* (Göttingen: Vandenhoeck & Ruprecht, 1925); C. H. Dodd, *Historical Tradition in the Fourth Gospel* (Cambridge: Cambridge University Press, 1963) 233-47; Wayne A. Meeks, "Galilee and Judea in the Fourth Gospel," *JBL* 85 (1963): 159-63.

19. Robert T. Fortna, "Theological Use of Locale in the Fourth Gospel," *ATR* Supp 3 (1974): 58-95; H. H. Charles, "Johannine Geography," *Studies in Religion* 11 (1982): 77-84; Donatien Mollat, "Remarques sur le vocabulaire spatial du quatrième évangile," in *Studia Evangelica* 1 = *Texte und Untersuchungen* 73, ed. K. Aland (Berlin: Akademie, 1959) 321-28.

cism of John, although such studies will be valuable in the course of this inquiry. It has been observed that while Jesus is described as "remaining" in various towns in Galilee and even in Samaria, he never "remains" in Jerusalem. Using "remain" (μένειν) as a clue, we notice that the disciples "remain" with Jesus (1:38-39) and that Jesus "remains" at Cana (2:12) and Samaria (4:40) and in Galilee (7:9).[20] Moreover, he urges his disciples to "remain" in the vine (15:4), in Jesus himself (15:5-7), and in his love (15:9-10). Thus, if "remaining" indicates loyalty and adherence to Jesus, then the Gospel tells us that this happens in "Galilee," wherever that might be. But it does not happen in "Judea." Thus we best assess these two places, not as geographical locations, but as "symbolic" places: in "Galilee" Jesus is accepted, gains disciples, and remains; in "Judea" he is harassed, put on trial, and killed.[21] He does not remain in "Judea."

But what contribution does "territoriality" bring to this conversation? It facilitates learning the *classification* or meaning invested by the author in these two places. The author labels each place in terms of some dualism or binary opposite: "love-hate" or "friendly-hostile" or "remain-not remain." The *communication* of this is made in the course of the narrative: it is a matter of discovering what place is welcoming or hostile; by noting whether Jesus "remains" or not, one learns the code. But even in "Galilee," there are friendly, safe places such as Cana and hostile ones such as the synagogue in Capernaum (6:59). In general Jesus finds hostility in "Judea," although not in Bethany (11:1ff.; 12:1-8). As regards *control* of these spaces, the author does not prohibit disciples from residing in any place, nor does he encourage them to migrate to other places. Unlike Mark 13:14, Jesus does not urge the disciples to leave Jerusalem; nor is it clear that he wishes them to flee to Galilee and safety. He prays not that God take them out of the world (17:15), but that God protect them from the evil one. Thus "Galilee" and "Judea" indicate that the disciples have friends and foes everywhere, and the *control* that issues from the classification governs the disciples' association with this or that *group*, not this or that *place*.

Yet if a disciple goes to certain places, such as the local synagogue, this may result in being expelled from it for one's confession of Jesus (9:22; 12:42; 16:1-2), presumably according to the synagogue's *classification* based on notions of purity-pollution. Thus the synagogue would be classifying its gathering as a place where Jesus should *not* be acclaimed; and it exercises its *control* by expelling anyone who does so.

---

20. Raymond E. Brown, *The Gospel According to John* (Garden City, NY: Doubleday, 1966) 1.510-12.

21. Jouette Bassler, "The Galileans: A Neglected Factor in Johannine Research," *CBQ* 43 (1981): 243-57.

Spaces and Places, Whence and Whither, Homes and Rooms

What is communicated by "Galilee" and "Judea," therefore, is *classification* not of real or topological space, but rather of social space, the Jesus gathering and the Judean synagogue. Moreover, groups need not have a fixed place, as they can meet in various places at diverse times. Yet "Galilee" and "Judea" are genuine *classifications*, informed by the dualistic system which contrasts friend and enemy, ours and theirs, or love vs. hate. Some *control* is exercised because this classification creates a sharp boundary between disciples and foes which functions as a dividing wall or a fence/gate which constitutes a sheepfold (10:1-11).

3.2 Public and Private: παρρησίᾳ-κρύπτῳ

Investigation of Johannine territoriality leads us to a native *classification* of space which is *communicated* by Jesus himself. When questioned about his teaching, Jesus answered: "I have spoken openly (παρρησίᾳ) to the world; I have always taught in synagogues and in the temple. . . . I have said nothing in secret (ἐν κρύπτῳ)" (18:20; see 10:23-24). This juxtaposition of "public" vs. "private" may be taken in two ways: 1) acceptable speech = "public," but subversive speech = "private," and 2) authorized speaking role = "public," but unauthorized speech = "private." In general, the classification "public" pertains to males gathered in public places such as courts and assemblies who have "public voice" to speak on certain matters.[22] The issue of who has "public voice" is no minor matter in the Fourth Gospel, as the questioning of John in 1:19-23 indicates. Furthermore, if it could be maintained that Jesus lacks appropriate schooling (7:15), then he should not be acclaimed as "teacher" (3:2; 13:13-14) or "Rabbi" (1:38, 49; 4:31; 6:25; 9:2; 20:16). Only Jesus' disciples call him "rabbi," never his enemies; Nicodemus, a would-be disciple, addresses him as "teacher." Moreover, if Jesus breaks the Law by violating the Sabbath, he should be disqualified from public speech as a deceiver. From ch. 5 on, most of Jesus' "public speech" is a forensic duel with his accusers, Jesus both defending himself and judging his judges.[23]

Jesus often claims "public voice" on the basis of his authorization.[24] "He

---

22. Richard L. Rohrbaugh, "Legitimating Sonship — A Test of Honour: A Social-Scientific Study of Luke 4:1-30," in *Modelling Early Christianity: Social-Scientific Studies of the New Testament in Its Context*, ed. Philip F. Esler (London: Routledge, 1995) 183-97.

23. Jerome H. Neyrey, "Jesus the Judge: Forensic Process in John 8:21-59," *Biblica* 68 (1987): 509-42, and "The Trials (Forensic) and Tribulations (Honor Challenges) of Jesus: John 7 in Social Science Perspective," *BTB* 26 (1996): 107-24.

24. Peder Borgen, "God's Agent in the Fourth Gospel," in *Religions in Antiquity*, ed. Jacob

whom God has sent utters the words of God" (3:34; see 5:30, 38; 7:18; 8:42). God precisely authorized him "what to say and what to speak" (12:48-49; 7:16-17). Finally, in his Farewell Address, Jesus honorably claims "I have given them your word" (17:14). What precisely is Jesus authorized to say? He claims authorization: 1) to proclaim God's word, 2) to conduct a *cognitio* of those who claim to be his disciples (3:3-20; 8:31-58), and 3) to mount a public defense of his claims and actions (5:19-46; 10:25-39; see 9:8-34). Jesus, one might say, speaks as long as he pleases and where he pleases. That he continues speaking in public despite the extreme displeasure this causes for the Temple elite is narrated to the audience. In 7:15, the elites challenge his right to speak; in 7:32 they send soldiers to seize him and thus silence him; in 7:43-48, the painful persuasiveness of his "public" speech draws a sharp rebuke from the Pharisees. Later at the Feast of the Rededication, the same elites demand that Jesus speak boldly about whether he is the Christ (10:24), only to have him foil their traps. Alternately, those who accept Jesus as "prophet" accord him "public voice" (7:40); they argue that he must be from God (3:2; 9:17; 10:21). His "speech," moreover, results in his hearers having eternal life (5:24) and in being made clean (15:3). The Evangelist, then, *classifies* Jesus as authorized for public speech, which is *communicated* by Jesus' bold public behavior (παρρησία). This classification builds on the gender-division of space whereby males are in public but females in private; but it also discriminates over which males have public voice. The *control* of space from the point of view of the narrator seems to be the celebration of Jesus' bold public speech, with a corresponding censure of those hiding in private who will not publicly show allegiance to him. Public speakers receive honor, but cowardly non-speakers, shame. The issue of public space, then, is situational: in certain circumstances (and places) public speech is both legitimate and expected.

Many, however, deny Jesus "public voice," for they consider him a deceiver and a false prophet who leads the people astray.[25] At Tabernacles the crowds divide in their judgments of Jesus: the positive evaluation of him ("he is a good man") is countered by those who claim that "he leads the people astray" (7:12; 7:43; 10:19-21; see 9:16). If the latter claim were sustained, then Jesus would surely be removed from the Temple. More proof that "he leads the people astray" comes with the failure of the troops sent to capture Jesus; they blame it on his speech: "No man ever spoke like this man!" (7:46), which the Pharisees

---

Neusner (Leiden: E. J. Brill, 1968) 137-48; George W. Buchanan, "Apostolic Christology," *SBLSP* (1986): 172-82.

25. Bruce J. Malina and Jerome H. Neyrey, *Calling Jesus Names: The Social Value of Labels in Matthew* (Sonoma, CA: Polebridge Press, 1988) 34-67.

interpret as further evidence that Jesus deceives the people (7:47). It goes without saying that in the Fourth Gospel the Pharisees and the Jerusalem elite *classify* public space in the Temple as sacred or restricted, such that Jesus should have no "public voice" there. They *communicate* this in a variety of ways: 1) by questioning Jesus' credentials, 2) by sending soldiers to arrest him, 3) by charging him with breaking the Sabbath, (4) by scrupulous examination of his speech to find errors so as to discredit him, and (5) by direct questioning of him (10:22-25). On the side of the Temple elite one finds a series of cultural norms which allow "public voice" only to adult males (not women and children), and only to males of a certain status (to elites, but not to non-elites, and to rabbis/Pharisees/teachers but not to the ʽam ha-ʼareṣ; see Acts 4:13). Thus they seek to *control* Jesus' speaking in the Temple and elsewhere in Jerusalem, labeling him as a nonobservant, self-important sinner and deceiver.

So much for "in public." But what if Jesus only had nighttime conversations with people "in private"? What if, for fear of the repercussions that speech "in public" would bring, either Jesus or his disciples "hid themselves" (8:59; 12:36) or met secretly? This Gospel repeatedly *classifies* such "private/secret" space as cowardice for fear of discovery, and so the sanctions imposed on disciples of Jesus (see 9:22; 12:42). Thus when the reader hears of Nicodemus coming to Jesus "at night," that is, "in private," and addressing him as "a teacher come from God," the author is classifying Nicodemus as a cowardly person. Later when Nicodemus appears in public, carrying spices to bury Jesus, even then he retains the stigma of the one "who had at first come to him by night" (19:39). "In private," then, is *classified* for the Johannine group as unholy, unvirtuous space. Both Jesus' public behavior and the scorn directed against those afraid to speak (9:22; 12:42) *communicate* this evaluation. *Control* in this instance means urging or requiring bold public speech by authentic members and scornful sanctions against those afraid to speak. It is doubtful how welcome such persons would be in the circle of disciples.

In summary, the *classification* "in public" is clear and meaningful to all the characters in the narrative. On the side of Jesus, it was *communicated* by Jesus himself, who claimed ascribed authority from God about "what to say and what to speak." Since "in public" refers to many specific places such as synagogue, Temple, and the like, *control* over them means for Jesus that he and others demand access to places where they are not wanted. In short, they insist that boundaries be porous, not firm. In contrast, the Pharisees and the Jerusalem elite dog Jesus whenever he appears "in public." Because they *classify* the public areas of the Temple as holy and sacred, they judge the presence of a deceiver such as Jesus as a pollution. The *communication* of their classification may be observed in 7:13, where people are afraid to speak of Jesus "for fear of the Jews" (once more: 9:22; 12:42). *Control* means the attempt to remove Jesus from public space, as in 7:32, 45-49, and finally to kill him (11:45-50).

3.3 "Not on This Mountain Nor in Jerusalem..."

Struck by Jesus' knowledge of her sexual history, the Samaritan woman says with sarcasm: "Sir, I perceive that you are a prophet" (4:19). In light of this she challenges his prophetic opinion concerning the *classification* of "this mountain" or Jerusalem as "the place where one should worship." Both mountains long competed for the label "holy," "sacred," and "set apart." Jesus, however, completely *declassifies* both mountains as "holy" or "sacred" space (4:21), even as he *classifies* a replacement for temple-situated sacred space when he declares that "true worshipers will worship in spirit and truth" (4:23).[26] *Communication* of this facilitates the process whereby the Samaritans later acclaim Jesus as "the Savior of the world" (4:42). By Jesus' dealings with the Samaritans, which we are told are contrary to custom (4:9), and by the declassification of both Judean and Samaritan temples, we learn that there is *no* "holy land," *no* sacred turf, and thus *no* chosen place. Classification of space, then, replicates classification of people. We note, moreover, that a "temple" on sacred ground consists of more than a building and implies a system of worship: 1) a building complex, 2) a high priest, 24 courses of priests, Levites, an army of people to maintain the compound, as well as temple police, 3) objects to offer, 4) taxes, tithes, and offerings to support the whole system (see 8:20), 5) an articulated calendar of feasts, 6) a myth about the temple's origins, which justifies it, and 7) a succession of barriers and walls to keep priests separate from worshipers, males from females, and Israelites from Gentiles. In *declassifying* all and every space, Jesus also *declassifies* the entire system represented by a temple and so logically abolishes *control* of "this mountain" and "Jerusalem."

"True worshipers will worship the Father in spirit and in truth" (4:23), but is there a specific fixed place for this? The disciples do not appear to have a fixed sacred place for worship, but what have they? At Jesus' first Passover, he creates an incident which leads to a double-meaning remark: "[You] destroy this temple and in three days I will raise it up" (2:19).[27] His opponents misunderstand him to mean the physical Temple, thus proving themselves to be outsiders who

---

26. Hendrikus Boers, *Neither on This Mountain Nor in Jerusalem* (Atlanta, GA: Scholars Press, 1988) 198-200.

27. Richard Bauckham, "Jesus' Demonstration in the Temple," in *Law and Religion: Essays on the Place of the Law in Israel and Early Christianity*, ed. Barnabas Lindars (Cambridge: James Clarke and Co, 1988) 72-89.

take his words literally (2:20). In the most famous aside in this Gospel, the author communicates the spiritual, hidden meaning of Jesus' word: "He spoke of the *temple of his body*" (2:21). Thus from the beginning, the author *classifies* a place (Jesus' body) as "holy," even as the new "temple." The author *communicates* that this equation of new temple and body of Jesus will be made clear after Jesus' resurrection. Thus the body of the Risen Jesus is in view. In what sense is this "new temple" a place? Inasmuch as Jesus shows himself bodily after his resurrection in a great variety of places, there is no fixed sacred space like Mount Zion. It is a fluid sacred space, which materializes (so to speak) at no fixed time or place. But is there *control* of the Risen Jesus? Since only insiders believe that he was raised, they alone have access to Jesus. In this first remark about temple, the audience learns that the "body" of the Risen Jesus is its new temple, which is not located in Jerusalem or any other fixed geographical place.

We turn to John 20–21 only because the author links the "new temple" with the body of the Risen Jesus (2:21-22). At first, the Risen Jesus seems to discourage access to his body by telling Mary Magdalene: "Do not hold me, for I have not yet ascended . . ." (20:17). But the obvious fact is that she sees his body and would touch it: the temple, once destroyed, is now raised up. And since she is the first person to be so close to Jesus/temple, her significance is celebrated by this proximity. Inasmuch as temples were often sites where oracles and revelations were delivered, Mary receives a remarkable revelation from Jesus and about him, that he is "ascending" to the holiest of all holy places, the presence of Father/God (20:17b). Later Jesus shows his disciples "his hands and his side" (20:20), proof that the temple destroyed is reconstituted. And holy things again happen in this temple: a commission is given along with a unique gift of spirit for purification purposes (20:21-23), one of the Temple's primary functions. Thomas flippantly demands to probe the wounds in Jesus' hands and side, an offer on which Jesus takes him up (20:25, 27). This, too, is proof of a new temple; and in Thomas' case, we hear a most profound confession or holy prayer addressed to Jesus, "My Lord and my God" (20:28). Each of these appearances might well be classified as a "christophany," a manifestation by a heavenly being who on occasion delivers an oracle or commission. Moreover, the "bodily" appearances of the heavenly Jesus occur 1) in a variety of otherwise non-sacred places (garden, graveyard, room, the Sea of Galilee and its shore), 2) at irregular times (20:19, 26; 21:1), but 3) with important representative characters in the narrative (Mary Magdalene, Thomas, Simon Peter, the Beloved Disciple, Nathanael, and James and John). 4) Certain disciples are favored with commissioning by Jesus (20:21-22; 21:15-19), that is a status transformation to a new role and status within the group. On most occasions in John 20–21, the body of the Risen Jesus, whether touched or just viewed, is linked with 1) great revelations

(Mary), 2) exalted confessions (Thomas), and 3) authorization to forgive sins (disciples). These types of activities, we suggest, take place in the new temple, which is the risen Jesus; these are the stuff of worship.

Jesus' risen body is a "temple" or holy space, wherever Jesus chooses to appear. Hence it is not a fixed place that can be suitably labeled and thus controlled. This space, while eminently holy, cannot be *classified* or *controlled*, as are temples built on fixed sites. Such is the nature of fluid sacred space. Wherever the Risen Jesus is, there is the new temple. But the Gospel has more to say about this temple space, as we will see in the sections "My Father's House" and "'In-Dwelling' and 'Being-In' Another."

3.4 Whence and Whither

Johannine territoriality addresses not only space and place, but also the directional markers which indicate the place whence Jesus came and whither he goes. This pair of markers, moreover, functions like other double-meaning words, admitting a literal and so erroneous meaning, as well as a symbolic, correct meaning. "Whence" and "whither" have everything to do with Jesus' fundamental "territoriality," the bosom of the Father (1:18; 17:5).

When outsiders hear about or ask whence Jesus came, their literal meaning serves as a *classification* which would *control* Jesus by disqualifying him as prophet or Christ. For example, Philip told Nathanael that "we have found him of whom Moses in the Law and also the prophets wrote, Jesus of Nazareth, the son of Joseph" (1:45). The fact that Jesus comes from Nazareth trumps the claim that he could be the unique person Philip proclaimed: "Can anything good come out of Nazareth?" (1:46). The classification of someone on the basis of place of origin was a standard element the way persons were described.[28] Nathanael's *classification* of whence Jesus comes argues against Jesus having any significant role or status. It is to Nathanael's credit that when he discarded this erroneous classification, he could come to Jesus and earn his praise as one "without guile." Later, when some bystanders wonder if the authorities believe that Jesus is the Christ, they resolve the issue by claiming to know whence Jesus comes. But "when the Christ appears, no one will know whence he comes"(7:26-27). An arbitrary *classification* it would seem, but one which would *control* Jesus' activity by rejecting his role as "Christ." In the same episode, some acclaim Jesus as the

---

28. Bruce J. Malina and Jerome H. Neyrey, *Portraits of Paul: An Archeology of Ancient Personality* (Louisville: Westminster/John Knox, 1996) 25, 113-25; see also Aristotle, *Rhet.* 1.5.5; Cicero, *De Inventione* 1.24.34-35; Quintilian, *Inst. Orat.* 3.7.10-11; 5.10.24-25.

Spaces and Places, Whence and Whither, Homes and Rooms

Christ, but others counter that with, "Is the Christ to come from Galilee?" (7:41-42), a mantra repeated by the Pharisees: "Search and you will see that no prophet is to rise from Galilee" (7:52). The very act of speaking like this to would-be believers in Jesus *communicates* a *classification*. And on the basis of this, Jesus' role and status are degraded and he is *controlled*. Similarly, when Jesus claims to be the "bread come down from heaven" (6:38, 41-42), the audience refuses one meaning of the remark ("come down *from heaven*") by countering it with a literal explanation of Jesus' "whence," namely, his parents: "Is not this Jesus, the son of Joseph, whose father and mother we know?" Thus their *classification* of his origin *controls* their crediting him with a public role and voice.

But the Fourth Gospel offers another *classification* of Jesus' place of origin, this time from the side of the author. At a low level of argument, Jesus' signs are read as his authorization by God in, for example, Nicodemus's statement "We know that you are a teacher come 'from God' for no one can do these signs that you do unless God is with him" (3:2). Although all parts of this confession seem correct, it is inadequate, because Nicodemus clearly does not believe that Jesus descended from heaven into this world (3:13). Similarly the crowd at one point declares: "When the Christ appears, will he do more signs than this man has done?" (7:31). Favorable, but not enlightened. On the right track is "If this man were not *from God*, he could do nothing" (9:33). In contrast, the Gospel tells us that he came into the world *from heaven* (1:9); he is both the bread which came *down from heaven* (6:38) and the Son of Man who first descended from heaven into this world (3:13). Thus, Jesus' true "whence" is heaven, the realm of God. Both Jesus and his Evangelist *communicate* the full, spiritual sense of "whence" Jesus came, which serves as the legitimation of Jesus' works and words, thus *controlling* access to Jesus. Only insiders, drawn by the Father, will know this knowledge, by which they are admitted to, but others excluded from, enlightened group membership. Thus false understandings of "whence" Jesus comes discredit outsiders, whereas correct understandings both exalt Jesus and authenticate the disciples who accept this. Thus group access is *controlled* on the true *classification* of "whence" and "whither."

"Whither" does Jesus go? Like "whence," "whither" serves as a double-meaning word which admits some and excludes others from the group. The classic instance of this arises in the chaotic narrative of Tabernacles. After hearing of the misunderstanding of "whence" Jesus comes (7:26-27), we observe a comparable difficulty with "whither" he goes: "I will go to him who sent me; you will seek me and you will not find me; where I am you cannot come" (7:33-34). The outsiders guess that Jesus "intends to go to the Dispersion among the Greeks" (7:35), but in fact they do not know what he means when he says "Whither I am going you cannot come" (7:36). Later the crowd offers another literal, but dumb interpretation, suggesting that Jesus' "going away" means that he will kill himself (8:22). These and other *classifications* are *communicated* to the Gospel's characters and audience. Were they successful, they would *control* Jesus by wishing him off the scene (to the Diaspora, dead), gone from their midst, and thoroughly discredited.

As with the positive meanings of "whence," so also we have positive *classifications* of "whither." Although the parabola of descent-ascent occurs often in the Gospel (1:1-18; 8:14; 13:1), the Farewell Discourse provides the richest source of ore on "whither" Jesus goes. Jesus "goes away," the disciples are told, "to prepare a place for them" (14:2-4). True, the disciples do not understand completely, but then they do not interpret him basely and literally like the outsiders. In fact, Jesus explains his "whither," *classifying* and *communicating* it to his disciples and the audience. He is going to God "to prepare a place for you" (14:2); "I am going to him who sent me" (16:5). Finally, Jesus delivers the most complete and candid explanation of "whither" he goes: "Father, glorify me in your presence with the glory which I had with you before the world was made" (17:5). This insider, positive *classification* of Jesus' "whither" means the bosom of God (1:18); it is of course *communicated* only to insiders. And it thus *controls* their loyalty during his passion by affirming that they have "rooms" in God's house and thus God's benefaction and protection.

One might assess this in a more abstract vein and conclude that true knowledge of Jesus' "whence" and "whither" distinguishes two groups in the Gospel: insiders and outsiders. It functions as barrier or wall which cannot be spanned or crossed. Thus knowing "whence" and "whither" serves to *control* authentic or elite membership in the Johannine circle by defining that as group sacred space.

Do "whence" and "whither" designate a real place? Insofar as journeys are made from heaven and back to heaven, it is a true, genuine place. It is conceptualized the same as any territory on earth: according to Revelation, it has a wall with twelve gates, a temple in its midst and a throne room for its Sovereign. Presumably, this is the place a vision of which is promised in 1:51. It is to this place that those whom Jesus raises from the dead will go (5:28-29) as well as those who have eaten the bread of life which comes down from heaven. It is a place known only by the Johannine elite, to which only they will go.

3.5 In My Father's House There Are Many Μοναί

Since God wants "true worshipers" to "worship in spirit and truth" (4:23), does the Gospel provide any clues about a sacred "place" for this worship? One attempt to answer this takes us to parts of the Gospel where God is said to have a dwelling. The earliest mention of this is found in Jesus' demand that "unless one is born again . . . of water and of spirit," one cannot either see or enter "the kingdom of God" (3:3, 5). This "kingdom," which is *classified* as sacred and holy because it is God's, is also *controlled* by admission restricted only to those born "from above." But this is hardly a place such as the land of Israel. Sverre Aalen argued that we best take "kingdom" as referring to God's "house" or household, which may be entered here on earth. It is "there" that "the goods of salvation are available and received."[29] Thus, birth by water and spirit serves as the entrance rite into the household of God. And where God is, there too are the "goods of salvation." Thus God's "kingdom" is where initiated disciples gather, the household of God.[30]

Later Jesus states that "in my Father's house (ἐν οἰκίᾳ) there are many 'rooms' (μοναί)" (14:2). Moreover, he goes "to prepare a place (τόπον) for you," after which he declares "I will take you to myself, that where (ὅπου) I am you may be also" (14:2-3). Does "my Father's 'house'" tell us anything different from "kingdom of God"? Aalen says no: "The 'house of the Father' in John xiv.2, as well as in viii.35, is simply another expression for the kingdom of God."[31] Again, the reference would be to a "household," that is, a community of disciples. But James McCaffrey argues that "house" and "rooms" here are readily explained by reference to the complex of courts, porches, and chambers in the Jerusalem Temple.[32] He calls attention to the parallel expression in 2:16 and 14:2, namely "my Father's house," concluding that since "house" meant "temple" in 2:16, it likely means the same thing in 14:2. I am hesitant at this point to accept "temple," if this means the heavenly temple such as one finds in Colossians, Hebrews, and Revelation. A heavenly temple out of reach and sight of the disciples is misleading, but if it were thought of as a fluid sacred place where disciples worship in and through Jesus, I would accept οἰκία as "temple." Then Jesus' remark that he would come and "take you *to myself*" is adequately explained in terms of the risen Shepherd gathering his sheep around him — something that takes place here, not in heaven.

What, then, are the μοναί in the Father's house? Gundry argues that John 14:2 does not speak of a heavenly hotel for transients, especially since the language of chs. 14–15 emphasizes "dwelling" as a present spiritual experience:

29. Sverre Aalen, "'Reign' and 'House' in the Kingdom of God in the Gospels," *NTS* 8 (1962): 223.
30. See Sjef van Tilborg, *Imaginative Love in John* (Leiden: E. J. Brill, 1993).
31. Aalen, "'Reign' and 'House' in the Kingdom of God in the Gospels," 238.
32. James McCaffrey, *The House with Many Rooms: The Temple Theme of Jn. 14,2-3* (Rome: Pontifical Biblical Institute, 1988) 67-70.

("the Father . . . dwells in me," 14:10; "the Paraclete dwells in you, and will be in you," 14:17; also 15:4-7, 9-10).[33] If we accept οἰκία as household/temple, then μοναί indicate ample space for the disciples in God's residence. Jesus, of course, is going to prepare a τόπος for the disciples, which suggests that he secures insider status for them. I find the meaning of "house," "rooms," and "place" adequately explained by reference to household, ample residence, and insider status. Despite McCaffrey's argument, "temple" would only be adequate if it referred to the controlled and secure gathering of the disciples around Jesus, who is their liaison with God. Jesus does not promise to *take* the disciples to the μοναί in the Father's house; for he only says "I will take you *to myself,* that where I am you may be also" (14:3). Just as 2:18-20 spoke of Jesus' body as the new temple, so too being attached to him means belonging to "the Father's house(hold)." Thus, we should not think of the "Father's house" as heaven, but as God's family or household here on earth, a common enough metaphor found throughout the New Testament. It is a social, but not necessarily a spatial metaphor.[34]

Clearly Jesus *classifies* a certain place as sacred, the very dwelling place of God. His discourse in 14:2 and 23 *identifies* the place and *communicates* its sacred quality. Inasmuch as only disciples are told of this, *control* operates here in the sense of exclusivity: insiders vs. outsiders, which we take as a replication of the classification systems sacred-profane and holy-polluted. But there is no "there" there because God's "house" with many "rooms" is not a building erected on a sacred mountain, nor is it a heavenly temple. Rather it is fluid sacred space which is only occasionally realized in time and place when the disciples gather in the name of the risen Jesus. Nevertheless we learn of a place where worship will take place. A remark like 14:2-3, moreover, may take on added significance in the light of the disciples being ex-synagoged (9:22; 12:42; 16:1-2) and excluded from the Jerusalem Temple.

3.6 "In-Dwelling" and "Being In" Another

Certain words in the Fourth Gospel carry an enriched meaning, such as "light," "hour," "true," and "dwelling" (μένειν), the verb from which μονή comes. Raymond Brown's classification of "dwelling" yields two basic meanings: 1) perma-

---

33. Robert H. Gundry, "In My Father's House Are Many Μοναί," *ZNW* 58 (1967): 70.

34. On the equation of "church" and "temple," see Bertil Gärtner, *The Temple and Community in Qumran and the New Testament* (Cambridge: Cambridge University Press, 1965) 47-98; David C. Verner, *The Household of God: The Social World of the Pastoral Epistles* (Chico, CA: Scholars Press, 1983) 128-79.

nence and 2) immanence/relationship.[35] For example, the Spirit of God "dwelled/remained" on Jesus (1:33), indicating a permanent relationship with him (see 8:35; 12:34; 15:16); Jesus, on the other hand, promises to "dwell" with his disciples (14:25) and demands that they "dwell" in the vine (15:4, 5, 7) — all of which expresses both permanence and closeness. The majority of the references to "dwell" occur in the Farewell Address and function to balance Jesus' unsettling remarks about "going away" and "coming back" with a strategy of loyalty and faithfulness. Several important usages then emerge: "dwell" refers to "the Father dwelling in me" (14:10), implying that Jesus is like a shrine or temple where the presence of God dwells. But turning to the disciples, Jesus commands them to "dwell" in him in an immanent relationship as branches remain in the vine. Aspects of this relationship include 1) having "the Spirit dwelling in you" (14:17) or the "words of Jesus dwelling" in you (15:7) and 2) "dwelling in Jesus' love" (15:9, 10), which is achieved by keeping his commandments. Thus "dwell" connotes strong relational ties, but not spatial location. Yet, we were told, "dwelling" in Jesus means corresponding proximity to the Father who "dwells" in Jesus. This dwelling-as-relation is not located in any fixed place, yet it is treated as such. Truly it points to Jesus as *pontifex*, mediator, broker, and priest uniting God and the disciples.

The relationship is *classified* (God in Jesus and both of them in the disciple = maximally holy) and *communicated* by Jesus' very discourse and with *control* envisioned (members only). The unfruitful branches, on the other hand, are "taken away and cast forth" (15:2) and "gathered, thrown into the fire and burned" (15:6). Fruitful branches remain, even if they are purified (15:2).

In addition to "dwell in," the author speaks about persons "being in" another, which resembles the immanence/relationship idea of "dwell in." For example, one stream of this speaks of "being in" God and Jesus: "Believe me that I am in the Father and the Father is in me" (14:10, 11). This expresses a profound relationship: "I am in the Father" states that Jesus is with, alongside, in the bosom of, or in union with the Father — the holiest possible position in all the world (see 1:18). If that expression looks to the world above from which Jesus descended, then the second part, "the Father is in me," seems to reverse that direction and envision God enfolding Jesus and empowering him with powers to do God's works (10:38; 14:10) while on earth. Again, Jesus is positioned as the bridge between the heavenly and earthly worlds.

Several highly significant references remain. Jesus states that on a future day the disciple will "know" the ultimate knowledge: "I am *in my Father* and you are *in me* and I *in you*" (14:20; see 14:10-11; 17:21, 23). The triple "being in"

---

35. Brown, *The Gospel According to John*, 1:510-12.

expression, of course, refers to relationships. "I am in my Father" and "I am in you" describe Jesus' bridge position as the link binding him to the Father and then to the disciples. Thus the Father is intimately joined to the disciples *through Jesus*. Other New Testament writings call Jesus "mediator" (1 Tim 2:5) and "priest" (Heb 7:26-28), two different ways of explaining his *pontifex/bridge* role. But where is this? Although the Fourth Gospel does not talk of a heavenly temple, a sacred space is localized when disciples gather to worship as God's household and when the risen Shepherd gathers them around himself.

3.7 Two Different Worlds, We Live in Two Different Worlds

In his conversation with Nicodemus, Jesus divided the world into two halves: "that which is born of flesh is flesh and that born of spirit is spirit" (3:6). Since the issue is being "born," we learn that some are born to flesh and others to spirit, who alone may "enter the kingdom of God." We have here an instance of boundary language which separates insiders from outsiders, namely, those born of spirit with relationship to God's household are juxtaposed to those born of flesh, who know only this world. Note how this boundary language replicates the *whence* and *whither* categories. "The wind blows where it wills and you hear the sound of it, but you do not know 'whence' it comes and 'whither' it goes" (3:8). Those born of flesh know something, but not "*whence* the wind comes and *whither* it goes." Others born of water and spirit know quite accurately whence and whither Jesus comes and goes. We have authentic Johannine dualisms here that separate two different worlds, two kinds of people, and insiders from outsiders.

But is "territoriality" involved here? This antithesis of two different worlds truly serves as a *classification* of groups, i.e., insiders and outsiders. Its very *communication* to Nicodemus serves to *control* his access to Jesus. Because Nicodemus knows in a limited, fleshly manner, he is shown *not* to be a denizen of the real world of spirit, but of the world of flesh. The Johannine elites, who look down upon the Nicodemuses of this world, have access to the world of spirit and true gnosis, that is, the "kingdom of God." Two different worlds, and the insiders live in the better one.

This mechanism of boundary-making and separation matures later in the narrative when Jesus is confronted by enemies who seek to arrest him, lie to him, or kill him. He says: "You are from below, I am from above; you are of this world; I am not of this world" (8:23). The issue has escalated from incomprehension of Jesus' words to open hostility to him. Jesus' remark serves to *classify* each world, one as worthy and holy and the other as worthless and profane. The

Spaces and Places, Whence and Whither, Homes and Rooms

manner in which Jesus *communicates* this classification creates a legal norm, whose sanction is to "die in your sins" (8:24). Thus Jesus *controls* entrance into the kingdom of God, which is "above" and "not of this world." Being "from below" and "of this world" now are sins or crimes, which preclude one's access to God and God's world.

What makes Jesus' remark so frightening and definitive is a quick glance at how the "world" is treated in this Gospel. We all know the beginning of the story, how "God so loved the world that he sent his only Son . . ." (3:16). Classified as the object of God's compassion, this world does not experience *control*, that is, no attempt is made to keep heaven and earth separate or saints and sinners apart. For the Son came to save all in the world (3:17; 4:42; 12:47), to give life to the world (6:33, 51), to be the Lamb which takes away its sin (1:29), and to be its light (8:12; 9:5). In this view, while heaven is still separated from earth, the boundary between them is porous and allows the benevolence of God to enter the world.

This changed, of course, as the world proved to be a hostile place. As Brown remarked, "The reaction of those who turned from Jesus was one not simply of rejection but also of opposition."[36] Correspondingly the world came to be seen as controlled by Satan, who enters into a disciple of Jesus (6:70; 13:2, 27) and whose offspring both lie and murder like their father (8:44). Balancing statements that Jesus did not come into the world to judge (3:17) are statements insisting that he does judge (9:39; 12:31). Thus, the *classification* of this world changes. It becomes a place of unmitigated hostility and obtuseness; in terms of the Judean purity system as classification, this world is profane, corrupt, polluted, and ruled by the evil one. The *communication* of this occurs when Jesus unmasks its crimes and stands in judgment of it. In this context, 8:23, with its declaration of two different worlds, both *communicates* the new labeling of "the world" and establishes *control* over it in the sense that a radical boundary is drawn between "above" and "below"/"*not* of this world" and "this world." Later Jesus prays for his own, but *not* for the world (17:9). Because he gave the disciples God's word, the world hates them because they are not part of it (17:14). He does not pray that God take them out of the world, but only that God keep them from the evil one (17:15). Thus Jesus' *classification* creates a boundary radically separating him and his disciples from their enemies. Because it would definitively *control* access to God's world, it must be taken with utmost seriousness. But it also means that Jesus and his disciples are out of place here. They are aliens in an alien land.

On this topic, Meeks described how Jesus was an alien in the world and

---

36. Brown, *The Gospel According to John*, 1.509.

then how his followers find themselves comparably situated: "The depiction of Jesus as the man 'who comes down from heaven' marks him as the alien from all men of the world. Though the Jews are 'his own,' when he comes to them they reject him, thus revealing themselves as not his own after all but his enemies; not from God, but from the devil, from 'below,' from 'this world.'"[37] Of the disciples he says: "The book defines and vindicates the existence of the community that evidently sees itself as unique, alien from the world, under attack, misunderstood."[38] The experience of the alien leader-hero Jesus is replicated in the comparable alienation of his followers.

But where is this other world? The world "below" may be some specific place such as Jerusalem, the Capernaum synagogue, and the like. But in fact, "this world" and "below" really refer to wherever Jesus is rejected, such as we saw earlier in the classification of "Judea" and "Jerusalem." Two different worlds, then, are not so much about space as about welcome to and acceptance of Jesus and disciples.

4.0 Summary, Conclusions, and Further Questions

4.1 Summary

The model of "territoriality" allows us to see things in the narrative of John which would otherwise go unnoticed and undigested. Moreover, it enables us to relate and coordinate data that are generally treated discretely. The model, we saw, consisted of three items: 1) *classification* of space, 2) *communication* of the classification, and 3) *control* of it. In regard to *classifications*, the Fourth Gospel uses the following: public-private, sacred-profane, honor-shame, pure-polluted, and fixed-fluid. Many of these relate directly to Jesus: 1) Jesus' speech is always in "public" and not in "private," thus *classifying* him as a male with public voice. 2) His homeland (Nazareth and Galilee) is *classified* by others as "shameful," a classification that would *control* his ability to function as sage, prophet, or Christ. His true "whence," however, is in the presence of God, hence "honorable," sacred, and pure. 3) "Sacred-profane" refers to what many narrative characters considered the most dedicated and most "pure" place on earth, the Temple. But Jesus *declassifies* (i.e., profanes) all temples and mountains as sacred, even as he presents his own body as the new temple, the new sacred space. Hence his body becomes the dwelling of God which is most "sacred" and

---

37. Wayne A. Meeks, "The Man from Heaven in Johannine Sectarianism," *JBL* 91 (1972): 69.
38. Meeks, "The Man from Heaven in Johannine Sectarianism," 70.

"pure." But other classifications, such as "public-private," relate both to Jesus and the disciples, namely public speech on Jesus' behalf. But the most useful classification of space in the Fourth Gospel is fixed-fluid sacred space. This shifts our focus to the group which is truly no-where: neither in the Temple nor the synagogue. When it meets, it does so around Jesus-the-temple, and here worship of God takes place through prayer, by listening to Scripture, the words of Jesus, and utterances of prophets. It is likely that this group has entrance rituals as well as sacred meals. Yet this remains fluid space, as the components of sacred space disperse immediately after worship; and the gathering site could be anywhere.

Each of these *classifications* would exercise *control* over the place so classified. "In public" is a value statement that urges disciples to imitate Jesus in bold, public speech, even if it results in expulsion from synagogue space. Similarly, knowing "whence" Jesus came and "whither" he goes belongs to elite insiders in the group, a mark of distinction. Inasmuch as this is insider knowledge, *control* in this case means that it is off-limits to all non-members and non-elites. They cannot enter the kingdom of God, nor do they have dwellings in the Father's house. *Classified* as creatures "of this world" and "of the world below," they are *controlled* in the sense that they cannot know Jesus' "whence" and "whither" nor find this "way." Knowledge, then, becomes a door, a wall, a gate, a boundary.

Jesus' very group is space that is variously *classified* as pure ("kingdom of God"), honorable (true children of Abraham) and sacred (vine). Aalen's article argued that these classifications overlap in meaning: kingdom = household, son of Abraham = legitimate member of the household, and vine = the people. Access to Jesus and to the household of God is *controlled* by many "unless . . ." demands: "unless one is born of water and the spirit . . ."; "unless one eats my flesh and drinks my blood . . ."; "unless you confess that 'I AM'. . ."; "unless I wash you. . . ." These function as doors, barriers, and checkpoints which prohibit admission unless the criteria are met. And *control* also functions in Jesus' boundary-making remark: "No one can come to me except the Father draw him" (6:44, 65) — the most radical of all boundaries.

4.2 Conclusions

What do we know if we know this? First, there is relatively little geographical or topological space of concern in the Fourth Gospel. "Galilee" and "Judea" are not real places but code names for welcome or rejection. "Not of this world . . . not from below" likewise indicate non-geographical but social space. The very classification of these spaces in this manner reinforces the group's sense of dislocation in synagogue and Temple, and its positioning of itself totally with Jesus.

Second, we call attention to the classification which distinguishes between *fluid* and *fixed* sacred space. Although current anthropology of space does not pay much attention to this, it is a classification of considerable use to New Testament scholars who note that the Jesus group is regularly called "house," "household," and "temple," but not in the sense of fixed sacred space. It provides a scenario for imagining how, when the disciples gathered, they formed a sacred space, albeit a fluid one, which reverted to profane use after their gathering was completed. Thus the Jesus group becomes the prime example of fluid sacred space.

Third, with his *declassification* of the temples on Mount Gerizim and Mount Zion, Jesus erased the category of *fixed* sacred space for the Fourth Gospel's audience. We saw, however, that he replaced what the old Temple represented with his body, which, because of the nature of bodies, is *fluid*. This new temple is not a place to which disciples make pilgrimage but what comes into being when the circle of disciples is gathered. In Johannine terms, this group can be called "household," "kingdom," or the place where one "worships in spirit and truth." This is *fluid* sacred space, for the group can gather anywhere. The alternative space is the synagogue, to which Johannine disciples may not go any more.

Fourth, many of the spatial categories we examined point to a new temple in which worshipers will worship in spirit and truth. "Dwelling in" and "being in" either God or Jesus refers to their presence with the disciples. Jesus' body, which is now a temple, is "where" God comes and is found. Finding the risen Jesus, one finds the presence of God. Jesus is understood in the role of mediator (or priest), thus forming a link between God/Patron and disciples/clients. Jesus serves as consummate broker between heavenly patron and earthly group.

Fifth, ultimately "there is no 'there' there." There is no mountain or building where the Johannine group worships. Even Jesus' remarks about above-below and "*not* of this world"–"of this world" do not point to specific geography, but classify and communicate a cosmic dualism. Jesus may return whence he came, but again there is no "there" in the sense of fixed sacred space. When he "goes away" and "comes back," it is to meet disciples in a variety of places, none of which appear to be canonized as pure, sacred space. Hence consideration of where Jesus is by John 20–21 indicates that his presence and so the presence of God is attached to the group of his disciples. Again, there is no "there" there; the classification labels are transferred to the social body of disciples.

Are the disciples any different, then, from the synagogue? In one sense, no. The synagogue which gathers in a regular place, would be accustomed to classify this space as "ours," which is made "sacred" when Torah is read and prayers are made. Yet the synagogue members could likewise make the pilgrimage feasts to Jerusalem and its Temple. In contrast, the Johannine disciples likewise have gathering space, but increasingly less and less in the local synagogue; and one wonders if they continued to attend the pilgrimage feasts in Jerusalem. What is different between disciples and synagogue is the rejection, hatred, and excommunication the disciples experience. This increases their self-understanding as "aliens in an alien world."

4.3 Further Questions

This chapter considered only the main spatial references in the Fourth Gospel. A complete study would consider motifs such as *congregational places* that become off-limits to Jesus and his disciples (Temple, synagogue) and *houses* (where the wedding was held in Cana, where Jesus was staying in 3:2, the house of Mary, Martha, and Lazarus, and the houses of Annas and Caiaphas). Since the disciples are likened to a flock of sheep, it would matter if they were gathered safely together (10:15-16; 12:32) or scattered (10:12; 16:32). One suspects that Johannine interest in houses and households (4:53; 8:35; 14:2) provides further definition to what we are calling *fluid* sacred space.

Consideration of the type of social group represented in the Fourth Gospel offers a further sharpening of our analysis of *fluid* space. Scholars now generally agree that the Johannine group can profitably be called a sect.[39] "Faith in Jesus, in the Fourth Gospel, means a removal from 'the world,' because it means transfer to a community which has totalistic and exclusive claims."[40] But although they are not of this world, they must remain in it as greater hostility rises against it. Such experiences affect how a group understands itself and locates itself. Moreover, if the cultic hero is an alien here below, this is replicated in the way the disciples likewise experience hostility. They too are aliens, but unlike Jesus they may not leave the world.

Worship, although not strictly a spatial concern, would mimic a temple system. With the rejection of fixed sacred space, other aspects of the system likewise fall away: there is no need for an order of priests, animal or grain sacrifices, calendar, sacred garments and vessels, and tithes or taxes for support. Important in this context is the role of Jesus as the ideal broker between God-Patron and the disciples-clients.

---

39. Raymond E. Brown, *Community of the Beloved Disciple* (New York: Paulist Press, 1979) 14-16, 61-62, 89-91; but see Meeks, "The Man from Heaven in Johannine Sectarianism," 69-70.
40. Meeks, "The Man from Heaven in Johannine Sectarianism," 70-71.

Jesus' remark to Annas about speaking only in public might well be extended to the circle of disciples to see if any of them speaks boldly and in public about Jesus. We know that Pharisees tried to *control* confessional behavior in some synagogues by declaring that anyone who acknowledged Jesus as the Christ would be expelled (9:22; 12:42). And this enjoyed considerable success, if we examine who kept their mouths shut "for fear of the Jews": both the parents of the man born blind, but also "many even of the authorities believed in him but for fear of the Pharisees did not confess it" (12:42). The otherwise noble Joseph of Arimathea, who buried Jesus, was "a disciple of Jesus, but secretly, for fear of the Jews" (19:38). These characters did not imitate Jesus' bold, public speech and did not have courage to violate the control extended by the Pharisees. Yet, of course, there are other characters, such as the man born blind, who speak boldly about Jesus and for this are thrown out. *Classification* and *control* are most evident here.

Finally, I would suggest a closer look at physical proximity to the body of Jesus. Not just anyone may touch Jesus; this is reserved for special characters such as Mary (12:1-8), the Beloved Disciple (13:23), the Magdalene (20:17), and Thomas (20:27-29). Among these characters some are identified as those whom Jesus loved: Mary and Martha and Lazarus (11:5) and the Beloved Disciple (13:23; 19:26; 20:2; 21:7, 20). They are also most intimate with his person: Mary anoints his feet, the Beloved Disciple leans on his chest. We are invited, then, to arrange the status of the disciples in terms of physical proximity to Jesus, thus envisioning a fully articulated map of persons.

PART TWO

Narrative Episodes in Focus

4

"Are You Greater than Our Father Jacob?"

Jesus and Jacob in John 1:51 and 4:4-26

Introduction and Hypothesis

In the Fourth Gospel we find one explicit and one implied reference to Jacob. In 4:12 the Samaritan woman asks Jesus in a sarcastic tone if he is "greater than our father Jacob." And in 1:51 Jesus promises his disciples a heavenly vision which has considerable similarities with Jacob's vision of a ladder linking the heavenly and earthly worlds (Gen 28:12-13). Both references to Jacob function only insofar as the Gospel's audience knows enough about the Jacob story to make the connections and comparisons. Since the Evangelist is a considerate author, he works with materials which he can reasonably presuppose that he shares with his audience. What materials? The core narrative for Jacob that we will examine is found in Genesis 28 and 32, but elaborations of it are common in targum and midrash. What does the audience of these stories need to know to appreciate them as the Evangelist's original audience did? What background is presumed in the vision promised in 1:51 and in the question in 4:12?

1.0 Seeing What Jacob Saw (John 1:51)

Many have noted that the promise of a vision of the heavenly Son of man in 1:51 is an odd conclusion to the dynamics of 1:36-50,[1] an observation that deserves fresh attention. My hypothesis about John 1:51 is as follows: 1) 1:51, indeed, be-

---

1. Rudolf Bultmann, *The Gospel of John* (Philadelphia: Westminster, 1971) 105-6; see Raymond E. Brown, *The Gospel according to John* (Garden City, NY: Doubleday, 1966), 1.89.

longs to a stratum of the Gospel distinguished by its high christology; 2) the Jacob allusion designates the disciples as Jacob-like visionaries who will see a theophany, as Jacob did; and 3) the title "Son of man" refers to the descending and ascending Jesus (see 3:13-14), hence a heavenly figure.

What, however, is the evidence for the secondary character of 1:51?[2] First, there is a shift in 1:50-51 from singular "you" (Nathanael) to plural "you" (the disciples); Jesus now addresses all the disciples. Furthermore, if we ask when these promises of Jesus were fulfilled, we find diverse possible answers. The signs-source material and the Cana miracle in particular might be said to fulfill the promise to Nathanael that he would see "greater things than these" (1:50). The promised vision of 1:51, however, is never literally fulfilled in the Gospel,[3] yet the disciples later are given special *information about Jesus' origin and destiny*, which may be construed as "seeing" his heavenly character; hence they have "insight" rather than mere "sight" (see 1:1-2; 20:28).[4] The climactic title "Son of man," which is introduced here by Jesus himself, is juxtaposed to the list of titles previously confessed by others ("Lamb of God," 1:36; "Messiah," 1:41; "Son of God, King of Israel," 1:49). The manner of presentation of the titles changes between 1:36-50 and 51: formerly they named Jesus to others; but now he identifies himself. The basic content of the titles differs. Disciples who in 1:35-49 evangelize other disciples announce to each other the various titles, which J. Louis Martyn has shown are distinguished as titles of a "low christology," i.e., an early confession which basically states that Jesus is but a man, albeit Messiah, Prophet, and King.[5] But in 1:51 Jesus himself reveals the new title, "Son of man," which as we shall see, reflects the Gospel's high christology, the confession of Jesus as a descending heavenly figure.

A pattern, moreover, is established in 1:35-50 which is broken by v. 51. First, in 1:35-50 a succession of spokesmen announce Jesus as they speak to their relatives and friends. Second, they name Jesus by an honorific title. Third, they in-

---

2. Bultmann, *The Gospel of John*, 105-7; Brown, *The Gospel according to John*, 1.88-89; idem, "'Other Sheep Not of This Fold,'" *JBL* 97 (1978): 5-22; see J. L. Martyn, "Glimpses into the History of the Johannine Community," *L'Évangile de Jean. Sources, rédaction, théologie*, ed. M. de Jonge (BETL 44; Gembloux: Duculot, 1977) 149-75.

3. E. Schwarz, "Aporien im vierten Evangelium," *Nachrichten der göttingischen gelehrten Gesellschaft der Wissenschaften* (1908): 517; H. Windisch, "Angelophanien um den Menschensohn auf Erden," *ZNW* 30 (1931): 226-27.

4. This suggestion, of course, is not new; see Bultmann, *The Gospel of John*, 106; R. Schnackenburg, *The Gospel according to St. John* (New York: Herder and Herder, 1968), 1.321; F. Lentzen-Deis, "Das Motif der 'Himmelöffnung' in verschiedenen Gattungen der Umweltliteratur des Neuen Testaments," *Bib* 50 (1969): 315. See also Jerome H. Neyrey, *The Gospel of John* (Cambridge: Cambridge University Press, 2006) 60-61.

5. Martyn, "Glimpses," 157-60.

vite the hearers to "come and see" for themselves. Finally, when the hearers do come and see, Jesus confirms their interest either by inviting them to stay with him (1:39), by giving them a new name (1:42), or by praising them (1:47).[6] In contrast, 1:51 is a plural address directed not to any individual but to all the followers who already form Jesus' group. It is neither an invitation to come and see nor an evangelization of them; rather, it is a proclamation of a future vision to be seen by them. It is formally prefaced by the "amen" formula.[7] The earlier "come and see" pattern is transcended, for they have indeed come and seen Jesus, but there is still more to see. Jesus himself takes the initiative in revealing a new title for himself — a title that surpasses all previous attempts to identify him.

It is especially in the Jacob allusion that 1:51 can be seen to be different from 1:35-50. Nathanael was praised as a "true Israelite . . . without guile" (1:47). As Bultmann has shown, this need not be anything more than a popular designation of praise.[8] On the level of the story, Nathanael is an "Israelite," a term which contrasts him with Jesus' enemies, "the Judeans."[9] His guilelessness, moreover, is to be explained from the pattern of his faith, which is contrasted with the rejection of Jesus by unbelievers. Nathanael knows the preaching about Jesus, especially the claim that Jesus fulfills the Scriptures (1:45); but he poses objections to applying the Scriptures to a peasant from Nazareth (1:46). Yet these objections do not prevent him from further inquiry, for he "comes and sees" for himself — difficulties notwithstanding (1:46b). In this he is sharply contrasted with "Judeans," who likewise hear the proclamation but object to Jesus' messiahship using the very Scriptures as arguments (see 7:27, 41-

---

6. Brown, *The Gospel according to John*, 1.78-80.

7. On the significance of the Amen sayings in John, see K. Berger, *Die Amen Worte Jesu* (BZNW 39; Berlin: de Gruyter, 1970) 28; B. Lindars, *Behind the Fourth Gospel* (London: SPCK, 1971) 44, 52. B. F. Westcott (*The Gospel according to St. John* [London: John Murray, 1908] 48) remarked on the double "Amen": "The words by their emphasis generally presuppose some difficulty or misunderstanding to be overcome; and at that time mark the introduction of a new thought carrying the divine teaching further."

8. Bultmann, *The Gospel of John*, 104 n. 6; see W. Michaelis, "Joh. 1, 51, Gen. 28, 12 und das Menschensohn-Problem," *TLZ* 85 (1960): 567.

9. The "Judeans" are under considerable censure from the point of view of John's Gospel, and yet "Israel" is a favorable term (see 1:31; 3:10; 12:13). John seems to reflect the same favorable use of "Israel" as found in Rom 9:4; 11:1; 2 Cor 11:22; Gal 6:16 (see 1QS 9:6); see S. Pancaro, "The Relationship of the Church to Israel in the Gospel of St John," *NTS* 21 (1974-75): 396-405, esp. pp. 398-401; R. T. Fortna, "The Theological Use of Locale in the Fourth Gospel," *Gospel Studies in Honor of Sherman Elbridge Johnson* (ed. Massey H. Shepherd, Jr., and Edward C. Hobbs; *ATR* Supplementary Series 3; 1974) 89-95. A comparable debate occurs in John 8 over who are the authentic offspring of Abraham — Christians or (unbelieving) Judeans; see T. B. Dozemann, "*Sperma Abraham* in John 8 and Related Literature," *CBQ* 42 (1980): 342-58.

42, 52) and so fail to come to Jesus.[10] Nathanael, then, typifies both a wisdom process of "searching the Scriptures" for Jesus (see 5:39, 46-47) and the overcoming of objections that the Scriptures could not possibly refer to the peasant from Nowheresville. Nathanael is like Jacob, moreover, not the devious character who grabbed his brother's heel at birth and stole his brother's birthright and blessing, but the perfect Jacob, the man of wisdom. Like Jacob, Nathanael comes "second," after the founding apostles; he must labor for his reward; and he is clever and enterprising (see Genesis 29–30). There is simply no evidence to suggest at this level of the story that Nathanael is like Jacob as "one who sees God."

In 1:51, explicit allusion is made to Jacob's theophany in Gen 28:12. Not just Nathanael, but all the disciples are promised a vision such as Jacob had. Indeed, they are like Jacob, not in guilelessness or cunning, but in virtue of a gratuitous promise made by Jesus that they would see a comparable heavenly vision, a christophany. They are the true "Israel" — they will "see God." Thus, in virtue of the juxtaposition of "you" (singular) and "you" (plural), the difference in the titles in 1:35-50 and 51, the broken pattern, and especially the Jacob allusions in 1:47 and 51, the last verse of the first chapter should be judged as a secondary addition to the passage.

1.1 Christophanies of the Heavenly Logos, Jesus

It is commonly agreed that John 1:51 in some way alludes to Jacob's vision in Gen 28:12.[11] The points of comparison and contrast deserve close consideration. In Gen 28:12 three statements are made: 1) a *ladder* on earth reaches to heaven; 2) *angels* ascend and descend on it; and 3) the *Lord* stands on it (atop it) and reveals himself. In John 1:51, however, 1) the heavens are opened, but there is *no mention of a ladder* or anything or anybody linking heaven and earth; 2) *angels* ascend and descend, not on the absent ladder, but stream from all parts of heaven toward the Son of man; and 3) Jesus corresponds to "the Lord" of Jacob's theophany. This comparison allows us to sift out worthy suggestions from the welter of interpretations offered by commentators on the use of Gen 28:12 by John.

The author is not comparing Jesus with Jacob in John 1:51. Jacob saw a

---

10. See R. F. Collins, "Representative Figures in the Fourth Gospel," *Downside Review* 94 (1976): 34-36.

11. See C. F. Burney, *The Aramaic Origin of the Fourth Gospel* (Oxford: Clarendon, 1922) 115-16; H. Odeberg, *The Fourth Gospel* (Uppsala: Almqvist and Wiksells, 1929) 33-36; C. K. Barrett, *The Gospel according to St. John* (2d ed.; Philadelphia: Westminster, 1978) 186-87; and Michaelis, "Joh. 1. 51, Gen. 28, 12 and das Menschensohn-Problem," 561-78.

heavenly vision; Jesus offers one. The disciples, however, are cast in the role of Jacob, for they will see a heavenly vision just as Jacob did. Commentators often suggest that the function of the vision in John is to be understood in terms of some sort of mediation or communion between heaven and earth.[12] But the ladder, which figures so prominently in Jacob's dream, is not mentioned, nor is it needed in John 1:51. The disciples will look directly into heaven and have an immediate recognition of a heavenly figure. Still other commentators suggest that, from traditions about Gen 28:12 found in targum and midrash, Jesus is depicted in 1:51 as the Shekinah made present,[13] as Bethel,[14] or as the glory of God.[15] These are important suggestions for they call attention to the object of the vision, and suggest that the heavenly Jesus corresponds to the appearing Lord in Gen 28:12. Thus far the allusions to Gen 28:12 in John 1:51 suggest that the focus is on a vision of a heavenly figure; that the angels ascend and descend toward this heavenly figure, not on a ladder; and that Jesus corresponds to the appearing Lord in Jacob's theophany.

The last suggestion must be seen in the light of several other arguments in John. First, it is emphatically maintained that "no one has ever seen God" (1:18).[16] This absolute exclusion would seem to apply to Moses; for, as Wayne Meeks has argued, John 5:37 would seem to be undercutting even Moses' Sinai visions.[17] Nor has anyone ever ascended to heaven to see God or receive heavenly revelations (3:13).[18] But this negative insistence poses a question. If Moses, the patriarchs, and the prophets did not see God, how are we to read the Scriptures that tell of theophanies to them? John's answer to this is direct: they saw the heavenly Logos, Jesus; they received christophanies. Abraham, for example,

---

12. See Bultmann, *The Gospel of John*, 105 n. 3; see also Schnackenburg, *The Gospel According to St. John*, 1.320-21; Michaelis, "Joh. 1.51, Gen. 28.12 und das Menschensohn-Problem," 575. According to proponents of these ideas, Jesus is the gate of heaven, the ladder, the mediator. The issue of mediation will be taken up formally in the concluding chapters of this book.

13. Both in the prologue (1:14) and later on (12:41), Jesus is described as the Shekinah made present; see Brown, *The Gospel according to John*, 1.486-87.

14. See I. Fritsch, "'Videbitis . . . angelos Dei ascendentes et descendentes super Filium hominis' (Io. I, 51)," *VD* 37 (1959): 3-11; R. H. Lightfoot, *St. John's Gospel* (Oxford: Clarendon, 1956) 99; Schnackenburg, *The Gospel according to St. John*, 1.320; O. Cullmann, "Die Berufung des Nathanael," *Angelos* 3 (1928): 2-5.

15. See Bultmann, *The Gospel of John*, 106.

16. See R. Bultmann, "Untersuchungen zum Johannesevangelium," *ZNW* 29 (1930): 169-92.

17. Wayne A. Meeks, *The Prophet-King* (NovTSup 14; Leiden: Brill, 1967) 299-300; see also Brown, *The Gospel according to John*, 1.25-26, 30-36; N. A. Dahl, "The Johannine Church and History," *Jesus in the Memory of the Early Church* (Minneapolis: Augsburg, 1976) 108-9; see M. R. D'Angelo, *Moses in the Letter to the Hebrews* (SBLDS 42; Missoula: Scholars, 1979) 95-123, 182-85.

18. See W. A. Meeks, "The Man from Heaven in Johannine Sectarianism," *JBL* 91 (1972): 52-54.

"saw the day" of Jesus (8:56). As Nils A. Dahl has shown, this refers to an experience of Abraham during his life on earth, such as the covenant of the pieces (Genesis 15).[19] Although Abraham is credited with prophetic visions of the future (see Matt 13:17; Heb 11:10), John's text is *not* referring to a vision of Jesus who-is-to-come-as-Messiah. For the text continues with the astounding statement that Jesus was not a mere future figure revealed to Abraham but rather a contemporary of Abraham, nay, a preexistent figure: "Before Abraham came into being I AM" (8:58). The arguments in favor of reading "I AM" in 8:58 as the divine name[20] are cogent. But in designating himself as "I AM" Jesus is not making himself identical with Yahweh but identifying himself as the appearing figure of Old Testament theophanies. According to John's own argument, Abraham did not see God; nevertheless he saw "I AM," i.e., Jesus.

Likewise, in John 12:41 it is stated that Isaiah "saw his glory." Although Isaiah prophesied about future events (see Sir 48:24-25),[21] it is commonly argued that John's text refers to a time in Isaiah's life when "he saw his glory," namely, the vision in the Temple (Isaiah 6).[22] Since Isaiah, like Abraham and Moses, did *not* see God, what he saw must have been the appearing Jesus. Thus an argument is established in John: 1) no one has ever seen God;[23] 2) but the patriarchs and prophets saw someone, namely, the heavenly Jesus, in their theophanies.

Returning to John 1:51, we are led to conclude that the text apparently presents the disciples of Jesus as playing the part that Jacob previously played: they are promised a vision just as Jacob had. The Gospel does not state explicitly that Jacob saw the heavenly Jesus, but that is a safe inference both from the examples of Abraham and Isaiah and from the argument in the text that *no one* (Jacob included) has ever seen God.

The possibility of interpreting scriptural theophanies as appearances of Jesus is not unique to John, and it will be helpful to examine some parallel materials which establish the currency of interpreting Old Testament theophanies as appearances of a figure other than God/Yahweh.

---

19. See Dahl, "The Johannine Church and History," 110.

20. See Odeberg, *The Fourth Gospel*, 309-10; C. H. Dodd, *The Interpretation of the Fourth Gospel* (Cambridge: University Press, 1968) 94; and Brown, *The Gospel according to John*, 1.536-538. See also Neyrey, *The Gospel of John*, 166-67.

21. Bultmann (*The Gospel of John*, 451) claims that Isaiah saw only the future glory of Jesus; on the visionary character of Isaiah in late Judaism, see F. W. Young, "A Study of the Relation of Isaiah to the Fourth Gospel," ZNW 46 (1955): 215-21.

22. See Dahl, "The Johannine Church and History," 106-8; A. Loisy, *Le quatrième évangile* (Paris: Émile Nourry, 1921) 378-79.

23. One might trace in Israelite sources the qualification of Old Testament texts which indicate that Moses saw God face to face; see M. R. D'Angelo, *Moses in the Letter to the Hebrews*, 97-123.

The testimony of Justin in the early second century stands as a powerful witness to such a reading of Scripture which I am claiming for John's Gospel. One of the main points of his *Dialogue with Trypho* is the argument that Jesus appeared to the patriarchs:

> Reverting to the Scriptures, I shall endeavor to persuade you, that he who is said to have appeared to Abraham, and to Jacob, and to Moses, and who is called God, is distinct from him who made all things. (*Dial.* 56)[24]

Justin then systematically argues that 1) Abraham's theophanies were appearances of Jesus (*Dial.* 56, 59), 2) that Moses' visions as well were (*Dial.* 56, 59, 60, 126; *1 Apol.* 63), and 3) likewise Jacob's visions (*Dial.* 58, 60, 86, 126). Therefore, at the end of his work, Justin is confident that he has proved:

> ... neither Abraham, nor Isaac, nor Jacob, nor any other man, saw the Father and ineffable Lord of all and of Christ, but (saw) him who was according to his will his Son, being God, and the Angel because he ministered to his will. (*Dial.* 127)

Thus Justin's argument includes three items: 1) no one has seen God, 2) but the patriarchs did see someone, namely Jesus, 3) who is rightly called "God."

For completely different reasons, Philo also explains that the theophanies in the Scriptures were not visions of God. He accepts the statement in Exod 33:20-23 that no one can see God (*Spec.* 1.8; *Post.* 48). Therefore the theophanies were revelations of God's word or of a potency of God. In the case of Abraham, Gen 17:1 states that "the Lord was seen of Abraham," and Philo shows that the designation "Lord" in the text refers, not to God himself, but to one of the two powers in God (*Names* 3). In regard to Moses' famous request, "Show me *thyself*" (Exod 33:13, LXX),[25] Philo repeatedly insists that Moses did not see God, but rather the "back of God" (see Exod 33:23; *Post.* 48; *Names* 21, *Flight* 29). When finally he explains what Moses saw when granted a vision of the "back of God," Philo states that Moses saw the glory of God, the "powers that keep guard around you" (*Spec.* 1.8), the same powers that Abraham saw.[26]

---

24. The translation is by A. Roberts and J. Donaldson in *The Ante-Nicene Fathers* (reprint, Grand Rapids: Eerdmans, 1950), 1.223; cf. *PG* 6.600.

25. The MT of Exod 33:13 reports that Moses asked, "Show me thy ways," which was changed in the LXX to "show me yourself" (Vulg.: *ostende mihi faciem tuam*). Philo interpreted 33:13 LXX as a request to see God's essence; for discussion of this text, see M. R. D'Angelo, *Moses in the Letter to the Hebrews*, 179-80.

26. For a fuller treatment of Philo's doctrine on the "powers of God," see A. F. Segal, *Two Powers in Heaven* (SJLA 25; Leiden: Brill, 1977) 159-81; and A. F. Segal and N. A. Dahl, "Philo and the Rabbis on the Names of God," *JSJ* 9 (1978): 1-28.

Finally, in regard to Jacob Philo gives us a fuller description of what the patriarch saw in his theophany. Although Philo admits that according to Exod 33:20-23 no one can see God,[27] he likewise accepts the scriptural etymology of Jacob's special name "Israel" as "the one who sees God" (Gen 32:28-30).[28] According to Philo's religious epistemology, Jacob/Israel is the one who sees not God's real nature but only *that* God is (*Rewards* 7). And in explaining the theophanies to Jacob, Philo maintains that, while Jacob is truly called "Israel," he did *not* see God. Hence, in regard to Jacob's first famous vision (Gen 28:12), Jacob "saw 'the place'" (Gen 28:11). Although "the place" properly refers to God, Jacob saw the divine word, the second meaning of "place." When Jacob saw the ladder and "the Lord standing firmly upon it" (Gen 28:12), the "Lord" whom Jacob saw was not God, but one of the powers of God (*Dreams* 1.11-12).

In regard to another dream of Jacob (Genesis 31), in which he is told to return to the land of his birth, Philo reproduces the LXX of Gen 31:13 and proceeds to give an unusual and careful exegesis of this passage. The MT reports God as saying only "I am the God (of) Bethel," but the LXX changed this to "I am the God who appeared to you in the place of God." Evidently "in place of God" is translating Beth-el, "house (place) of God"; but there is no clear reason why the LXX introduced the phrase "who appeared to you." Surely the LXX intended to say no more than the MT, that the deity who confronted Jacob in chap. 31 was the same one who appeared to him at Bethel in ch. 28. But Philo reads the text quite differently, for he interprets "in place of God" to mean that it was not God who appeared to Jacob (in either ch. 28 or ch. 31) but a heavenly being who appeared *in place of God*. This substitutionary interpretation of 31:13 then explains what Jacob saw in 28:12.

Philo's substitutionary reading of "in place of God" creates a problem for him: "Are there two Gods, for we read 'I am the God that appeared to you,' not 'in my place' but 'in the place of God'?" (*Dreams* 1.39). The solution for Philo lies in the subtlety of the text, which distinguishes "God" with the article (ὁ Θεός) from the anarthous form (θεός).

> Accordingly the holy word in the present instance has indicated him who is truly God by means of the article saying "I am the God" (Gen 31:13), while it omits the article when mentioning him who is improperly so called, saying

---

27. *Drunkenness* 11; *Migr.* 36; *Names* 5, 12.

28. See *Allegorical Interp.* 2.9; 3.66; 3.75; *Sacrifices* 39; *Posterity* 18, 261; *Confusion* 13, 16, 28; *Migration* 20, 22, 36; *Heir* 15; *Prelim. Studies* 10; *Flight* 38; *Dreams* 1.21, 27; 2.6, 26; *Abraham* 12; 57; *QG* 3.49; 4.233. See further J. Z. Smith, "The Prayer of Joseph," in *Religions in Antiquity*, ed. J. Neusner (Leiden: Brill, 1968) 265-66.

"Who appeared to you in one place" not "of the God," but simply "of God." (*Dreams* 1.39)[29]

This means that Scripture "gives the title of 'God' to his chief Word" (ibid.). Thus the divine Word, "God" in an improper sense, appeared to Jacob in chs. 28 and 31. And so Jacob/Israel saw only "the image," not God's Self (*Dreams* 1.41).

Philo and Justin are clear examples of the kind of exegesis of the Old Testament theophanies that we seem to find also in John. The form of the argument in Philo and Justin is likewise important for, like that in the Fourth Gospel, it maintains that 1) no one has seen or can see God, 2) therefore the Old Testament patriarchs saw a divine Logos (Philo) or Jesus (Justin) and 3) the appearing figure is "god" — according to Philo, the Logos who is given the title "god," and, according to Justin, Jesus, who is called God. This type of exegesis will become normative in later Christian writers, but Philo indicates that it already existed early in the first century.

This part of the investigation of John 1:51 may be summarized: 1) the disciples are like Jacob and are promised a vision like Jacob's; 2) according to Gen 28:12, Jacob received a theophany, a vision of a revealing God, and since Jacob's vision in Genesis 28 is alluded to in John 1:51, John would seem to be promising a comparable theophany: the heavens opened and the Son of man revealed himself; but 3) as Jacob and the other patriarchs did not see God-Yahweh but the Logos-god, so the disciples are promised a vision of the divine Jesus.

1.2 *The Son of Man*

Since the disciples in 1:51 are promised a vision of the Son of man, several questions arise apropos of the title in the context of this paper: 1) What is the meaning of the title? 2) From what level of the Johannine community's history does it come? 3) What relationship, if any, exists between the Son of man, Jacob, and Gen 28:12?

Most studies of the Son of man title concentrate on its occurrences in the Synoptic Gospels, and so discussion of the Johannine Son of man sayings is usually measured according to those documents. Classification of Synoptic usage tends to be threefold: 1) the earthly Son of man with authority, 2) the rejected and crucified Son of man, and 3) the vindicated and returning Son of

---

29. Philo repeats the same substitutionary interpretation of Gen 31:13 in *Dreams* 1.40, apropos of justifying anthropomorphic language about God; see A. F. Segal, *Two Powers in Heaven*, 159-60.

man.[30] But John's understanding is totally different, for he understands the title as referring to a figure who first descends into the world and then ascends out of it.[31] And so the Son of man, who in the Synoptics is "vindicated" by God's raising him from the dead, is according to John returning to that glory which he enjoyed before the creation of the world. He begins and ends in the bosom of God, something impossible in the view of the other Gospels.

The content for the title Son of man depends on John 3:13-14, where Jesus tells us two quite different facts about this figure. The Son of man is unique: *no one* has ever ascended to heaven except the one who descended from there.[32] Charles Talbert cited this rabbinic text which argues for the exclusivity of the descent and ascent of the Son of man: "R. Jose says, Behold it says, 'The heavens are the heavens of the Lord, but the earth he has given to the children of men' (Ps 115:16). Neither Moses nor Elijah ever went up to heaven, nor did the Glory come down to earth."[33] R. Jose claims that there has been no commerce whatsoever between heaven and earth. This disallows the claims of Moses and Elijah, as is implied in John 3:13. But someone does descend and will ascend, namely the Son of man, who was in origin a heavenly figure, who alone sees God, who appears in place of God, and who ultimately returns to his former glory. This profile is equivalent to the statements about the divine Logos in John's prologue,[34] and it evidently reflects the high christology of the later Johannine community, which confessed that Jesus is God (20:28).

Juxtaposed to John 3:13, however, is another Son of man saying which gives us a different piece of information: "the Son of man must be lifted up" (3:14). This reflects the same kind of tradition found in Mark 8:31, which speaks about

---

30. See R. Bultmann, *The Theology of the New Testament* (New York: Scribner's, 1951), 1.30.

31. See E. M. Sidebottom, "The Ascent and Descent of the Son of Man in the Gospel of John," *ATR* 39 (1957): 115-22. For a summary of the current discussion of the Johannine Son of man, see F. J. Moloney, *The Johannine Son of Man* (Rome: LAS, 1976) 1-22. The remarks of Meeks ("The Man from Heaven in Johannine Sectarianism," 65-72) about the "Son of man" as an alien figure who originally descends before he re-ascends are essential for interpretation of this figure; see also Peder Borgen, "The Son of Man Saying in John 3:13-14," *Philo, John and Paul* (Atlanta: Scholars Press, 1987) 110-12.

32. See Meeks, "The Man from Heaven in Johannine Sectarianism," 52, esp. n. 32; see Moloney, *The Johannine Son of Man*, 51-59.

33. *Mekilta de Rabbi Ishmael*, trans. Jonathan Z. Lauterbach (Philadelphia: Jewish Publication Society of America, 1976) 2.224, as cited by Charles Talbert, *Reading John: A Literary and Theological Commentary on the Fourth Gospel and the Johannine Epistles* (New York: Crossroad, 1992) 101.

34. For an extended comparison of the divine Logos in the prologue with the Son of Man in John 3, see my article "John III: A Debate over Johannine Epistemology and Christology," *NovT* 23 (1981): 115-28; and O. Cullmann, *The Christology of the New Testament* (London: SCM, 1963) 184-87.

the rejected and suffering Son of man, who is eventually vindicated. Rejection and vindication describe the son of man in Daniel 7, a pattern found elsewhere. But the author of the Fourth Gospel has here in John 3:14 metamorphosed Mark's presentation to suggest that the lifting up of the Son of man is really exaltation, indeed return to the glory Jesus had before the world's creation (see John 12:32-33; 17:5).

John 3:13-14, then, contain two quite different understandings of the title in John. And they reflect a shift in Johannine christology from consideration of Jesus as a rejected, suffering and vindicated man to the proclamation of him as a heavenly figure, who descends from heaven and ascends back.

The author states in John 5:27 that God gave Jesus authority to judge because he is the Son of man. This usage of the title reflects the kind of tradition found in the Synoptics about the future judgment by the Son of man (see Mark 8:38 and 13:26), a tradition apparently reinterpreted by John.[35] First, 5:27 occurs in an apologetic passage where Jesus' heavenly powers are being defended. The charge is made in 5:18 that Jesus "made himself equal to God," and while the defense concedes that Jesus is, in fact, "equal to God," it insists that Jesus does not "make himself" thus. "Equal" is God's doing: 1) God shows him all that he does (5:20); 2) as the Father raises the dead and gives life, so does the Son (5:21); 3) the Father gave all judgment to the Son so that, as all honor the Father, they should likewise honor the Son (5:23); 4) as the Father has life in himself, so he gave the Son to have life in himself (5:26); and 5) God gave him his own authority for judgment (5:27). This Son of man saying, therefore, functions apologetically in 5:19-29 in defense of Jesus' equality with God,[36] not at all what the Synoptics argue.

Second, this authority to judge is not a future endowment of Jesus, as it is in the Synoptics, for the bestowal has already happened ("has given," 5:22, 27). This authority is not to be confused with the authority of the earthly Son of man to forgive sins (see Mark 2:10) because in 5:19-29 the Johannine Son of

---

35. See B. Lindars, "The Son of Man in the Johannine Christology," in *Christ and Spirit in the New Testament*, ed. S. S. Smalley and B. Lindars (Cambridge: University Press, 1973) 51-52; S. Schulz, *Untersuchungen zur Menschensohn-Christologie im Johannesevangelium* (Göttingen: Vandenhoeck & Ruprecht, 1958) 111-13; J. Louis Martyn, *History and Theology in the Fourth Gospel* (Nashville: Abingdon, 1979), 129-31. For a general discussion of the eschatology of this passage, see R. Bultmann, "The Eschatology of the Gospel of John," *Faith and Understanding* (New York: Harper & Row, 1969), 1.164-83, and R. Kysar, *The Fourth Evangelist and His Gospel* (Minneapolis: Augsburg, 1975) 207-14.

36. For a full discussion of this "eschatological power" given to Jesus, see Jerome H. Neyrey, *An Ideology of Revolt: John's Christology in Social-Science Perspective* (Philadelphia: Fortress, 1988) 18-35.

man, who is primarily a heavenly figure, has the power to judge along with other eschatological powers normally associated with Final Judgment. The giving of authority — like other marks of Jesus' equality with God — was done while Jesus was in heaven, *before* his descent. It would appear, then, that a traditional statement about the Son of man's judgment has been reinterpreted by John; the differences in the meaning of the title (the man Jesus vs. the heavenly Jesus) reflect the shift in John's community from low to high christology.

Likewise, after the Bread of Life discourse, when Jesus is rejected both by the synagogue (6:60) and by some of his disciples (6:61), he confronts his scandalized followers and says: "[what] if you were to see the Son of man ascending to where he was before?" (6:62). On one level, the saying reflects the tradition found in certain Synoptic sayings such as Mark 14:62, where the rejected one is vindicated at God's right hand. But here it is colored with typical Johannine elements, such as: 1) the Son of man first descends from heaven (see 3:13; 6:33, 41-42, 51, 58), inasmuch as 2) the Son of man was originally 3) a heavenly figure. In 6:62, then, we find a tradition about the Son of man (rejected on earth, vindicated in heaven) which is recast in Johannine terminology to indicate that the rejected one is first and foremost a heavenly figure who descends into the world.[37]

In the confrontation with the Jews in John 8, Jesus states "when you have lifted up the Son of man, then you will know that I AM" (8:28). This basically reflects the suffering Son of man statements of the Synoptics (see 3:14 above),[38] but again, couched in Johannine terms. First, the Judeans reject Jesus and try to kill him because he makes himself equal to God (8:37, 40, 59; see 10:33). Second, the lifting up of the Son of man here functions as a Johannine double-meaning expression which to outsiders means "lifting up on a cross," that is, death, but to insiders refers to his glorification, that is, his return to his former glory (see 12:23, 34; 13:31).[39] Third, the link of Son of man and "I AM," when seen in the light of 8:58, indicates that as a heavenly being who "has life in himself," Jesus transcends time and mortality. In 8:58, the author juxtaposes Jesus' eternity, "I AM," with Abraham's contingent being, who came into being and subsequently died.

This examination of four major Son of man passages in John suggests several conclusions. First, there is embodied in John a stream of tradition about a human figure who is rejected and killed, which is judged to be a confession co-

---

37. See Smalley, "The Johannine Son of Man Sayings," 294-95; in general, commentators on 6:62 tend to stress the aspects of Jesus' ascension or preexistence in this verse; yet see Moloney, *The Johannine Son of Man*, 121-23.

38. Moloney, *The Johannine Son of Man*, 135-37.

39. See Dodd, *The Interpretation of the Fourth Gospel*, 246-47; Brown, *The Gospel according to John*, 1.145-46; Meeks, "The Man from Heaven in Johannine Sectarianism," 62-64.

"Are You Greater than Our Father Jacob?"

herent with the low christology of the early Johannine community. Second, this usage is juxtaposed to or overlaid with references to a heavenly figure who is timeless, a person who descends from glory into the world and ascends back to glory. With this in mind, let us turn back to 1:51.

1.3 Seeing into Heaven

According to 1:51 the disciples will see directly into heaven ("see the heavens opened"). When biblical passages say "the heavens opened," then either 1) someone or something descends to earth (Matt 3:16; Isa 64:1; 3 Macc 6:18; Acts 10:11), or 2) a visionary on earth sees a heavenly figure in heaven (Acts 7:56; Rev 11:19; 15:5; 19:11; Ezek 1:1).[40] Here the disciples are to see "the angels of God," who in this case are not messengers descending to earth for various tasks (see Acts 5:19; 8:26; 10:3; 12:7-11), but are angels ministering around a heavenly figure, presumably an enthroned one.[41] The angels, moreover, ascend and descend; since they are already in heaven, they ascend more intimately into heaven's center or descend toward it,[42] all focusing on the heavenly throne. Their ascent and descent in heaven designates them as belonging to the circle of heavenly figures around the throne of God (see Rev 4:4, 6-8; 5:11). The pattern of ascent and descent, of course, resembles the precise direction of the angels' movement in Gen 28:12, and it seems that John intends the reader to take the detail quite seriously. The angels of God in John 1:51 first ascend[43] and then descend; inasmuch as they are already in heaven (see "heavens opened"), they ascend toward the throne on which the Son of man is seated.

What are the angels doing? A midrash on Gen 28:12 gave specific tasks to these angels. For example, *Tg. Yer. I* and *II* indicate that angels who accompa-

---

40. See F. Lenten-Deis, "Das Motif der 'Himmelsöffnung' in verschiedenen Gattungen der Umweltliteratur des Neuen Testament," 301-27, and W. C. van Unnik, "Die 'geöffneten Himmel' in der Offenbarungsvision des Apokryphon des Johannes," in *Apophoreta*, ed. W. Eltester (BZNW 30; Berlin: Töpelmann, 1964) 269-80.

41. See B. Lindars, *The Gospel of John* (Greenwood, SC: Attic, 1972) 121-22.

42. M. Black (*An Aramaic Approach to the Gospels and Acts* [2d ed.; Oxford: Clarendon, 1954] 85) argued that ἐπί in John 1:51 should be translated as "toward"; hence he writes, "The picture we have then is of the heavens opened and angels from above and beneath converging on the Son of Man, the central figure." For another discussion of the throne-centrality of the passage, see G. Quispel, "Nathanael und der Menschensohn (Jn 1:51)," *ZNW* 47 (1956): 282-83.

43. Certain midrashic texts (*Gen. Rab.* 68:12, 14) insist on the prior ascent of the angels. Inasmuch as there is no ladder mentioned in John 1:51, the angels are not starting from earth; nor are we ever told in John that angels ascend from earth. Unlike Gen 28:12, the starting-point of the vision in John 1:51 is not earth but heaven itself.

nied Jacob on his journeys first ascended to tell angels still in heaven that the image of the one they guarded on earth is the same as the image which the heavenly angels see on the heavenly throne:

> And behold, angels that had accompanied him from the house of his father ascended to bear good tidings to the angels on high, saying, "Come and see a just man whose image is engraved on the throne of glory, whom you desired to see." And behold angels from before the Lord were ascending and descending and observed him. (*Tg. Neof.* Gen 28:12)

Midrashic texts speak of angels taking Jacob up (ascending) and bringing him down (descending),[44] exalting him and debasing him.[45] The angels in John 1:51 are not messengers, nor do they compare the throne image with the human likeness, nor do they lift up and lower the Son of man. Their ascent and descent, I suggest, functions in two ways: 1) it points to the locus of the Son of man figure, viz., seated in the center of heaven,[46] and 2) it suggests the exalted status of the Son of man, viz., a heavenly figure whose home is the bosom of the Father.

The focus of John 1:51, therefore, is not on the angels but on the figure of the Son of man. As regards the tradition history of this statement, it is probably based on an earlier Synoptic tradition about the enthroned Son of man,[47] but a tradition that has been completely reinterpreted by John. For example, in Mark 14:62 the enemies of Jesus who reject him as Christ are promised a vision: "You will see the Son of man seated at the right hand of the throne and coming on the clouds of heaven." This vision will cause terror and fear in Jesus' enemies, for it functions as proof by means of allusion to the persecuted and vindicated son of man in Daniel 7, just how shameful were their dealings with God's agent.[48] John's version differs from Mark 14:62 on many points: 1) the vision is not promised to enemies but to intimate friends; 2) it is not a threat but a blessing for their "coming and seeing"; 3) it is not intended to strike fear for rejecting

---

44. *Gen. Rab.* 68:18; 70:12.
45. *Gen. Rab.* 68:12, 13.
46. See Quispel, "Nathanael und der Menschensohn (Joh 1:51)," 282.
47. Brown, *The Gospel according to John*, 1.89; H. Windisch, "Angelophanien um den Menschensohn auf Erden," 218; idem, "Joh. 1, 51 and die Auferstehung Jesu," *ZNW* 31 (1932): 199-204; Schulz, *Untersuchungen zur Menschensohn-Christologie*, 122-23; Barrett, *The Gospel according to St. John*, 155; and S. S. Smalley, "Johannes 1, 51 and die Einleitung zum vierten Evangelium," in *Jesus and der Menschensohn*, ed. R. Pesch and R. Schnackenburg (Freiburg: Herder, 1975) 300-314.
48. See C. F. D. Moule, "From Defendant to Judge — and Deliverer: An Enquiry into the Use and Limitations of the Theme of Vindication in the New Testament," *Bulletin of the Studiorum Novi Testamenti Societas* 3 (1952): 44-47.

"Are You Greater than Our Father Jacob?"

Jesus but is offered as a reward for and the climax of faith in him; and 4) it does not tell of vindication after the example of Daniel 7 but is shaped as a theophany after Gen 28:12.

This comparison of John 1:51 with the Synoptic tradition of the enthroned Son of man yields the following conclusions. Whether John 1:51 is related in any way to the tradition found in Mark 14:62, it now makes a distinctive claim. Second, since John's version relies more on Gen 28:12 than on Daniel 7, the purpose of the appearing Jesus utterly differs from that found in the Synoptics. The Son of man in John before his descent was "face-to-face with God" (1:2) and in his ascent he returned to "the lap of God" (1:18). Finally, the disciples are certainly not seeing the earthly Jesus, for they are looking into the "opened heavens" and so at a heavenly figure; nor are they seeing the Jesus of the parousia who comes to judge the living and the dead, a tradition which is totally absent from John's Gospel.[49]

What is the function of this figure? In the Synoptic traditions the enthroned Son of man functioned in many ways. To his persecutors Jesus promised a scene of heavenly vindication (Luke 22:69; Mark 14:62); to suffering Christians Jesus appeared in exaltation (Acts 7:56), presumably to comfort his followers in their trials.[50] John's text reflects these traditions when the expelled blind man receives a mysterious appearance of the Son of man and is strengthened in his expulsion from the synagogue (9:35-38); likewise in 8:28 Jesus' enemies are promised a vision of vindication when the crucified one will be revealed as the heavenly Son of man (see Rev 1:7). But the promised vision in 1:51 functions not as a vindication in the face of enemies, nor is it evidently an exhortation to persecuted disciples. The fact that this Son of man saying draws more from Gen 28:12 than from Daniel 7 suggests that John 1:51 describes a theophany, a revelation of the heavenly locus and status of the Son of man. It climaxes the coming to faith of the chief members of the Johannine church in 1:35-50 and points to the ultimate confession of Jesus in that Gospel as a heavenly figure.

1.4 The Son of Man, Jacob, and Gen 28:12

In *Midrash Rab.* we find several instances of a reading of Gen 28:12 that interpret the vision in an unusual way. The MT says that when the ladder was set up, the

---

49. See Schulz, *Untersuchungen zur Menschensohn-Christologie*, 99-103.
50. See Barrett, "Stephen and the Son of Man," *Apophoreta*, 32-38; R. Pesch, *Die Vision des Stephens* (Stuttgart: Katholisches Bibelwerk, 1966) 38-58.

NARRATIVE EPISODES IN FOCUS

angels ascended and descended "on it" (28:12), which is interpreted in the midrash to say that the angels ascended and descended "on him," i.e., Jacob.[51] This midrash has often been cited apropos of John 1:51, for the Gospel says that the angels ascend and descend "on the Son of man" rather than on a ladder.[52] Following this hint, one would be led to say that Jesus is like Jacob: the angels will ascend and descend *on him*, just as they did *on Jacob*. This raises an important issue: Is there any relationship between the title Son of man, Jacob, and Gen 28:12? Is Jacob ever called "Son of man"? Is he ever considered a heavenly figure?

Returning to the midrash, we read that the angels discover a marvelous correspondence when they descend "on Jacob": his image on earth is the same as an image engraved on the Merkabah:

> Is it thou, (said the angels) whose features are engraved on high; they ascended on high and saw his features, and they descended below and found him sleeping. (*Gen. Rab.* 68:12)

There is some midrashic evidence that Jacob's image was thought to be engraved on the Merkabah.[53] What image, however? Ezekiel's vision of the heavenly throne described four faces engraved thereon: "a man," a lion, an ox, and an eagle (Ezek 1:10).[54] Somehow the midrash came to equate the image of the "man" in the throne vision with Jacob. Although the explanation for this is unclear, there are other bits of evidence that may shed some light on this. First, apropos of Gen 28:12, *Gen. Rab.* 68:13 interprets "the ladder" which was set up as "an image," inasmuch as "ladder" *(sulâm)* is similar in Hebrew to "image" *(semel)*.[55] The midrash then goes on to identify two such images: 1) the "image" which Nebuchadnezzar set up as a rival to God (see Dan 3:1) and 2) the "image" of Jacob on the throne.[56] Second, Jacob is occasionally called "man"; e.g., in in-

---

51. See *Gen. Rab.* 68:12 (and see *Exod. Rab.* 42:2). In commenting on Gen 28:13 ("the Lord stood on him"), *Gen. Rab.* 69:3 debates the proper meaning of *ʿālāyw* and offers an interpretation which says that God stood "on him," i.e., Jacob.

52. See Odeberg, *The Fourth Gospel*, 33-36; Burney, *The Aramaic Origin of the Fourth Gospel*, 115-17; Bultmann, *The Gospel of John*, 105-6; Schnackenburg, *The Gospel according to St. John*, 1.320.

53. On the relationship of John 1:51 and Merkabah mysticism, see Quispel, "Nathanael und der Menschensohn (Joh. 1.51)," 282.

54. See J. Jervell, *Imago Dei* (Göttingen: Vandenhoeck & Ruprecht, 1960) 117 for an explanation of the heavenly image of Israel-Jacob based on Ezek 1:26.

55. See Odeberg, *The Fourth Gospel*, 35-36; Dodd, *The Interpretation of the Fourth Gospel*, 245-46; and Barrett, *The Gospel according to St. John*, 187.

56. See *Gen. Rab.* 68:12; 82:2; *Tg. Yer. I* and *II* on Gen 28:12; *b. Hullin* 91b; *Pesiq. Rab.* 27; 28:2; *Pirqe Rabbi Eliezer* 35.

"Are You Greater than Our Father Jacob?"

terpreting Gen 28:13, the rabbis cited Prov 27:17 ("a man sharpens a man") and so called Jacob "man":

> "A MAN" alludes to Jacob: as soon as our father Jacob arose, "A man was together with the face of his friend," for the Shekinah attached itself particularly to him, as it says, AND, BEHOLD, THE LORD STOOD BY HIM (Gen 28:13). (*Gen. Rab.* 69:2)

Third, a particular midrash actually calls the patriarchs the "chariot of God." Interpreting ʿālāyw ("upon him/it") in Gen 28:13, R. Simeon b. Lakish said:

> The patriarchs are the chariot (of God), as it says, "And God went up *from upon* Abraham" (Gen 17:22); and "God went up *from upon* him" (Gen 35:13); AND, BEHOLD, THE LORD STOOD UPON HIM (Gen 28:13). (*Gen. Rab.* 69:3)

Thus there is evidence that in some discussions of Gen 28:12-13 Jacob was called "man" in the sense that the image of Jacob was on God's throne; thus "Jacob/man" would be considered a heavenly figure. But what kind of heavenly figure?

Jacob might be considered a heavenly figure because he was a preexistent being.[57] There is a curious stream of material which boldly calls Jacob "god" (*El*). Much of this material is attached to Gen 33:20, which states, "There he erected an altar and called it El-Elohe-Israel." In *b. Meg.* 18a the argument is set forth:

> How do we know that the Holy One, blessed be He, called Jacob *El*? Because it says *And the God of Israel called him* (Jacob) *El* (Gen 33:20). For should you suppose that (what the text means is that) Jacob called the altar *El*, then it should be written, "And *Jacob* called it." But (as it is not written so), we must translate "He called Jacob El." And who called him? The God of Israel.

Needless to say, this interpretation was very disturbing, with the result that in the midrash we find attempts to moderate the scandal of calling Jacob *El*. For example, commenting on Gen 33:20, R. Simeon b. Lakish remarked: "He (Jacob) declared to him: 'Thou art God in the celestial spheres, and I am god in the terrestrial spheres'" (*Gen. Rab.* 79:8 and 80:4). This explanation is identical with Philo's treatment of the troublesome text in Exod 7:1 where Moses is called "god" ("See I make you god to pharaoh"). Because of Moses' excellence, he is

---

57. See *Gen. Rab.* 72:7; Smith, "The Prayer of Joseph," 268-69; according to *Gen. Rab.* 72:7, the patriarchs are part of the Merkabah, hence preexistent; Str-B 2.257-58.

made "god," but *only on earth:* "He appointed him as god, placing all the bodily region and the mind . . . in subjection and slavery to him" (*Sacr.* 9).[58]

In connection with another text Jacob is acclaimed god. In one midrash, Gen 49:1 is cited ("Jacob called his sons"); to this is attached a second text from Ps 57:2 ("cry to God ['El] Most High"), and then the parallel between the two texts is drawn: Jacob can be called "god":

> Another interpretation: "I will cry out to God Most High" refers to Jacob. When his sons entered from their blessings, he began to confer distinctions upon them. (*Gen. Rab.* 96, new version)

Still another bit of evidence occurs in a passage where Jacob commanded his body to be taken up from Egypt back to Israel lest the Egyptians worship it:

> BURY ME NOT, I PRAY, IN EGYPT (Gen 47:29) . . . another reason why Jacob did not wish to be buried in Egypt was they should not make him an object of idolatrous worship. (*Gen. Rab.* 96:5)

From this investigation, then, we cull two main interpretations of John 1:51 available to us. I argued earlier that the disciples are like Jacob, for they see what Jacob saw, the heavenly Jesus. Alternately, the midrash on Jacob suggests the possibility that Jesus is Jacob (the angels descend on him as they do on Jacob), and that the disciples see the image of Jesus, Son of man, just as the image of Jacob-man was found on the Merkabah. But it is time to submit this last suggestion to a critique.

The dating of the midrash presents a first set of problems. The composition of these works is quite late, although many traditions contained in them may be dated much earlier, even to the first century.[59] But in the case of the Jacob midrashic materials cited above, there is no evidence that any of those traditions existed in the first century. Hence we cannot use them reliably as interpretive background for John 1:51.

---

58. E. R. Goodenough, "The Political Philosophy of Hellenistic Kingship," *Yale Classical Studies* 1 (1928): 68, 76-77, 83-84, explains the use of a topos in Philo's description of Moses as ideal king, especially in reference to Moses as a "god" on earth; for a further discussion of Philo's portrait of Moses as "god," see C. R. Holladay, *Theios Aner in Hellenistic Judaism* (SBLDS 40; Missoula, MT: Scholars, 1977) 109-29; for an Israelite interpretation of Exod 7:1, see Str-B 2.462-64.

59. Discussion of the date of composition of the midrashic works cited in this study may conveniently be found in the appropriate articles in the *Encyclopedia Judaica* (New York: Macmillan, 1971). But for a critical guide to the proper use of these works, especially in establishing the antiquity of traditions within the midrash, see R. Block. "Note méthodologique pour l'étude de la littérature rabbinique," *RSR* 43 (1955): 194-227.

Moreover, the Jacob materials we have examined represent two distinct streams: 1) via Gen 28:12, Jacob's image is in heaven, and 2) via Gen 33:20, Jacob is called *El*. It would be a mistake to merge these two traditions without further ado. It would be rash to say that Jacob's image in heaven was thought of as a divine figure. Even when Jacob is called *El*, he is never cited as acting like God, let alone revealing himself in theophanies. But John's understanding of the title Son of man is that of a heavenly figure who has appeared to the patriarchs, Jacob included.

Turning back to John's text, we should note the numerous elements there which also invite a negative judgment on the Jacob-Jesus identification from the side of the Gospel's imagery. John never mentions *the ladder spanning earth and heaven* (Gen 28:12) or the dual image, and the vision in 1:51 focuses exclusively on a *heavenly figure in heaven*. Hence there is nothing in John to indicate that the angels descend to earth and see an image that is also on the Merkabah. In John, the *disciples* will see the vision in the center of heaven, whereas in the midrash the *angels* see the image. Jesus is never *equated* with Jacob in the Gospel; rather the question is asked, "Are you *greater* than our father Jacob?" (4:12), but the answer boldly comes back that Jesus *supplants* Jacob and so is *superior* to him. Jesus, in fact, is never compared *with* any patriarch (see 8:53) but is proclaimed as the one who appeared *to* them. And as attractive as it might be to link Jacob with the image of *"man"* on the Merkabah, there is no evidence that Jacob is called *"Son of man"*[60] or that this possible association would be intelligible to Johannine circles.

1.5 Summary

According to the literary evidence, John 1:51 is a later addition to 1:35-50. In alluding to Gen 28:12, John 1:51 draws a parallel between the disciples and Jacob, indicating that they, like Jacob, will see a heavenly vision. As Jacob saw Jesus in his visions, so the disciples will also receive a theophany of the heavenly Jesus, the Son of man. This should be understood in light of the pattern in John whereby it is maintained that Jesus, not God, appeared to the patriarchs and prophets of the Old Testament. The angels in 1:51 are heavenly courtiers who stream toward the throne of God. They are not traveling to and from earth, for

---

60. Yet Odeberg (*The Fourth Gospel*, 36) would link Gen 28:12 with Isa 49:3 in terms of the glorified Son of man; Dodd (*The Interpretation of the Fourth Gospel*, 246) followed up this idea. *Midrash Ps.* 8:4 calls Isaac "Son of man"; only in *Midrash Ps.* 80:8 (on Ps 80:17, "for the son of man whom thou hast chosen for thyself") is there any possible connection between Jacob and "son of man."

no ladder is mentioned. The figure of the Son of man in John undergoes a metamorphosis. Whereas in the Synoptics he is an earthly figure who is rejected and then vindicated in heaven, in the Fourth Gospel he is a figure who abides in heaven and then descends to earth and ascends back to where he was before. It would seem that the phrase "a true Israelite" should likewise be interpreted to designate the disciples not as guileless but as "those who see God." The promise of 1:51, although not literally fulfilled, is realized in the vision of faith of the Johannine community which confessed Jesus as the divine Son of man, equal to God (5:18), and as Lord and God (1:1-2; 20:28).

2.0 "Are You Greater than Our Father Jacob?" (4:12)

2.1 Introduction and State of the Question

The Fourth Gospel twice records people asking Jesus if he is "greater than" one of Israel's founding patriarchs: "Are you greater than our father Jacob?" (4:12) and "Are you greater than our father Abraham?" (8:53). Both questions, like most questions, are intended to challenge Jesus so as to reduce his honor,[61] for such is the basic function of questions in antiquity. They also establish a *synkrisis* or comparison, a very common way of extolling or debasing the virtues or accomplishments of someone, as we see in Plutarch's *Parallel Lives* or even Paul's comparison of the Corinthian virtues (1 Cor 12:30-13:13).[62] For such a laudatory comparison to work, the audience must know enough about both figures or items to follow the logic. This is especially true with "Are you greater than our father Jacob?" What could the audience be expected to know about Jacob such that in comparison Jesus is "greater"?

Although the affairs of Jacob are narrated throughout the second half of Genesis, the events of importance for comparison are found earlier, in Genesis 27–32, which provide basic information about Jacob. Yet what specific events would the first-century audience of the Evangelist know? How did they interpret the biblical story? What legendary accretions to the Jacob story did they know?

---

61. Jerome H. Neyrey, "Questions, Chreiai, and Challenges to Honor: The Interface of Rhetoric and Culture in Mark's Gospel," *CBQ* 60 (1998): 657-81.

62. See F. Focke, "Synkrisis," *Hermes* 58 (1923): 327-68; Christopher Forbes, "Comparison, Self-Praise and Irony: Paul's Boasting and the Conventions of Hellenistic Rhetoric," *NTS* 32 (1986): 1-8; David H. J. Lamour, "Making Parallels: *Synkrisis* and Plutarch's 'Themistocles and Camillus,'" *ANRW* II.33.6 4154-4204; D. A. Russell, "On Reading Plutarch's Lives," *Greece and Rome* 13 (1966): 150-51; P. A. Stadter, "Plutarch's Comparison of Pericles and Fabius Maximus," *GRBS* 16 (1975): 77-85.

The question in John 4:12 seems rarely to have been studied in terms of what specific Jacob materials are operative in the comparing of Jesus and Jacob.[63]

2.2 Jacob in Scripture and Legend

As we noted above, the question asked in John 4:12, "Are you greater than our father Jacob?" formally resembles the one put to Jesus in 8:53, "Are you greater than our father Abraham?"[64] Together the two questions belong to a theme in the Gospel which asserts Jesus' superiority to the founding fathers of traditional Israelite faith (see 1:17-18; 5:38; 6:32).[65] The thrust of the questions suggests not only that Jesus replaces Jacob,[66] Abraham, and Moses vis-à-vis God's revelation, but that an absolute claim is made on his behalf: he is greater than all of these in that he supplants them with new revelation.

The question in 4:12, moreover, should be seen in relation to other statements in the Gospel which proclaim the distinctiveness of Jesus vis-à-vis Israel's past experiences and personages. Jesus is the *true* vine and the *true* light (1:9; 6:32; 15:1). Even in the "I am + predicate" formulae ("*I am* the living bread," "*I am* the door," "*I am* the noble shepherd"), Jesus is linked in an exclusive manner with certain events or elements.[67] Often in the Gospel the demonstrative "this" or "that" is used apropos of Jesus to underscore his uniqueness or superiority, as in "*This* is he" (1:30, 33, 34), "*This* is the Savior of the world" (4:42), "*This* is the prophet who is to come into the world" (6:14).[68] The question in 4:12, then, belongs to a mode of discourse in the Gospel which both as-

---

63. Recent commentaries have all but ignored the Palestinian background about Jacob implied in the question; see R. Schnackenburg, *The Gospel According to St. John* (New York: Herder & Herder, 1968) 429; B. Lindars, *The Gospel of John* (London: Oliphants, 1972) 182; but see J. Ramón Díaz, "Palestinian Targum and the New Testament," *NovT* 6 (1963): 76-77.

64. Birger Olsson, *Structure and Meaning in the Fourth Gospel* (Lund: Gleerup, 1974) 162-73.

65. Other comparisons are possible. Two recent studies from Yale University have examined respectively the Jesus-Moses and Jesus-Abraham material in John; see W. Meeks, *The Prophet-King*, and B. Schein, *Our Father Abraham* (unpublished Yale dissertation, 1973).

66. In Luke 11:31 and Matt 12:41-42 Jesus is clearly proclaimed as "greater than Solomon." The allusions to Jacob in John 1:47-51 belong to a different theme in John than the one under consideration here. Just as Abraham's and Moses' visions were in fact visions of Jesus, so Jesus promises Nathaniel, the true Israelite (i.e., the new Jacob) that he will see a vision similar to that of Jacob at Bethel, viz., Jesus himself enthroned in heaven; see Nils Dahl, "The Johannine Church and History," in *Current Issues in New Testament Interpretation*, ed. W. Klassen and G. F. Snyder (New York: Harper, 1962) 134-36.

67. Brown, *The Gospel According to John*, 1.534; see John 6:35, 51; 8:12; 10:7, 9, 11, 14; 11:25; 14:6; 15:1.

68. John 1:30, 33, 34; 3:19; 4:42; 6:14, 50, 58; see 1 John 1:5; 2:25; 3:11, 23; 5:3, 4, 9, 11, 14; 2 John 6.

serts the superiority of Jesus over Israel's patriarchs and makes an absolute claim on his behalf.[69]

2.3 Jacob's Well and Jacob the Supplanter (4:10-15)

Because it is the clearest point of comparison, let us begin with the question in 4:12, "Are you greater than our father Jacob, *who gave us this well?*" The Genesis accounts do not record that Jacob ever dug a well, much less that he gave a well to any of his sons; the text, however, does mention that Jacob bought Shechem and then gave it to Joseph (Gen 33:19; 48:22), and Shechem is the location of Jacob's well (see John 4:2).[70]

The trend of some traditions was to associate Jacob not with any particular well but with the traveling well tradition (see 1 Cor 10:4): "Jacob was seventy-seven years old when he went forth from his father's house, and *the well went with him.*"[71] And this same source also tells us that at one point Jacob left this traveling well at Bethel: "There he *left the well.*"[72] The legend of the traveling well should, of course, be linked primarily with Miriam's well in Numbers 21.[73] But as the targums on Numbers 21 indicate, Miriam's well was itself simply the old patriarchal well which had been lost and was only then rediscovered:

> And from thence was given them the living well, the well concerning which the Lord said to Moses, assemble the people and give them water. Then, behold, Israel sang the thanksgiving of this song, at the time that the well which had been hidden was restored to them through the spirit of Miriam: *Spring up, o well, spring up, o well! sang they* to it, and it sprang up: the well which the fathers of the world, Abraham, Isaac, and Jacob, digged; the princes who were of old digged it, the chiefs of the people, Moses and Aaron, the scribes

---

69. Yet in the Gospel, it is still maintained that the Father is "greater than" Jesus (see John 10:29; 14:26); see W. Thüsing, "Die johanneische Theologie als Verkündigung der Grösse Gottes," *TTZ* 74 (1965): 321-31.

70. In Gen 29:1-12, however, Jacob is associated with a specific well, not his own but Laban's. Here he meets Rachel, waters her flock, and woos her. *Tg. Yer. I* Gen 29:1 indicated that Jacob worked a miracle here by having the water automatically flow from the well.

71. *Pirqe Rabbi Eliezer* 35 (trans. G. Friedlander [London: Kegan Paul, Trench, Trubner, 1916] 263).

72. *Pirqe Rabbi Eliezer* 35 (Friedlander, 267).

73. See 1 Cor 10:4; *LAB* 10.7; 11.15; 20.8; E. Earle Ellis, "A Note on First Corinthians 10:4," *JBL* 76 (1957): 53-56; R. Le Déaut, "Miryam, soeur de Moïse, et Marie, mère du Messie," *Bib* 45 (1964): 209-13.

of Israel, found it with their rods; and from the desert it was given to them for a gift.[74]

It is presumably this very well which was said to have been one of the ten things created before the world's founding.[75] Hence, while there is nothing in the legends to suggest why Jacob specifically should be associated with a given well at Bethel or Shechem, he is linked to the general well tradition. The well in John 4:12 might be called Jacob's well simply because it lies in Jacob country, at Shechem.

A second item in the discourse seems to presuppose more specific knowledge of Jacob legends. Jesus remarked that the woman should ask him for water (4:10), to which she replied, "You don't have a bucket and the well is deep; how do you get this living water?" (v. 11). The legends about Jacob mention a miracle whereby water would automatically surge to the top of Jacob's well and overflow, a phenomenon well-attested in the targums of Genesis 28 and in other midrashic accounts: "Five miracles were wrought for our father Jacob at the time that he went forth from Beersheba.... The fourth sign: the well overflowed, and the water rose to the edge of it, and continued to overflow all the time he was in Haran."[76] The woman's remarks to Jesus that he has no bucket for a deep well sets the stage to ask how Jesus expects to draw water from the well. Without a bucket, the only alternative would be to perform a miracle like Jacob's. Jacob's miraculous drawing of water, therefore, seems to be presupposed in the dialogue in 4:11.

A third item in the discourse might allude to Jacob material, namely, the remark by Jesus in 4:10. If only the woman knew "the gift of God and who it is that speaks to you," then she would ask and he would "give you living water." The allusion may lie in the interpretation of the well itself as "gift." The text of Num 21:16 indicates that when the Israelites arrived at Beer, God promised Moses, "I will give them water." After finding a well in this place, the Israelites traveled on to Mattanah, Nahaliel, Bamoth, and Moab (21:18-20). The point is that the place name, Mattanah, is interpreted in targumic expansions according to its perceived root *(ntn)* as "gift." The interpretation, of course, would logically be understood in the light of Num 21:16c ("I will give them water"). Whereas the MT on Num 21:18c reads "And from the wilderness they went on to

---

74. *Tg. Yer. I* Num 21:17-18.
75. *Tg. Yer. I* Num 23:31; see *Pirqe Abot* 5:9; *Num. Rab.* 19.25.
76. *Tg. Yer. I* and *II* and *Tg. Neof.* Gen 28:10. The targums to Gen 29:10, 12 actually describe the miracle happening at Laban's well when Jacob meets Rachel there and waters her flocks; on this miracle, see *Pirqe Rabbi Eliezer* 36 (Friedlander, 268); *Midrash Ps.* 91.7. This Jacob legend was noted by J. R. Díaz, "Palestinian Targum and the New Testament," 76-77.

Mattanah," it was changed in the LXX to "and from the well to Manthanain," and finally in the targums to Num 21:18, "*Mattanah*" is read, not as a place name, but as "*gift*."[77]

> Tg. Neof.:   and from the wilderness it was given to them *as a gift*
> Tg. Yer. I: and from the desert it was *given* to them
> Tg. Yer. II: and from the desert it was *given* to them *as a gift*

This reading is also found in another midrash on this passage:

> *And from the Wilderness at Mattanah.* This implies that it was *given (nittĕnâ)* to them in the wilderness to serve their needs.[78]

The midrashic interpretation of the place name as "gift" is still more evident in the targumic reworkings of Num 21:19. Whereas the MT reads only place names ("from Mattanah to Nahaliel and from Nahaliel to Bamoth . . ."), all the targums expand on the gift quality of the well.

> Tg. Neof.:   and after the well had been *given to them as a gift* . . .
> Tg. Onq.:   and from thence *it was given to them* . . .
> Tg. Yer. I: and from thence *it was given to them* at Mattanah

Thus the miraculous well was interpreted as "gift of God."

Now when Jesus told the woman, "if only you knew the *gift* of God," on one level the "gift" might be the general recognition of the true well of Israel's history which God gave the people (see Num 21:16). But Jesus qualifies the statement so that the allusion is not simply to the well but to himself: "If only you knew the gift of God and *who it is* who says to you 'Give me a drink.'" Thus the person of Jesus is an integral part of the woman's knowing and is put in parallel to "the gift of God." The giving of special waters by Jesus is developed later in the Gospel (see 7:37-39; 19:34).

Thus far the comparison of Jesus and Jacob seems to presuppose knowledge of two items: a miraculous welling up of water and designation of the well as a gift. The point of the comparison, of course, has been to show that Jesus is certainly "greater than our father Jacob"; and Jesus' superiority is explained in response in 4:13-14, where an absolute claim is made on his behalf.

---

77. A. Diaz Macho, *Neophyti I* (Madrid: Consejo Superior de Investigaciones Cientificas, 1974) *IV, Numeros*, 581, n. 13; see R. Le Déaut, "Miryam, soeur de Moïse, et Marie, mère du Messie," 211.

78. *Num. Rab.* 19.26.

"Are You Greater than Our Father Jacob?"

> Everyone who drinks of this water will thirst again,
> but whoever drinks of the water that I will give him will never thirst.

The form of the response is significant because it represents a pattern of antithetical statements that characterizes Jesus' mode of discourse in the Gospel and that claims superiority for him or asserts his absolute importance.[79] The assertion made here resembles the statement about the superiority of Jesus' bread from heaven to Israel's manna (see 6:49-51), especially in its claim to produce an eternal result *(eis ton aiōna)*.

According to 4:13-14 Jesus claims that he is not just a latter-day Jacob or even that Jacob was a type of Christ. A more radical claim is made: Jesus supplants/replaces Jacob. The woman's question in 4:12 seems to contain a pun, implying that Jesus is supplanting Jacob the Supplanter, thus doing to Jacob what he did to Esau. According to Gen 25:26, Jacob's name means "to grab by the heel" or "to supplant"; Jacob is so proficient at being "jacob," that he supplants Esau in birth (25:26), birthright (25:34), and blessing (27:36). In one sense, he is just one more example of the traditional experience in Israel of the younger son supplanting the elder, a pattern found in the case of Isaac and Ishmael, Jacob and Esau, Joseph and his brothers, Ephraim and Manasseh, David and his brothers, and Solomon and his siblings, and later applied by Paul to Gentile Christians vis-à-vis the Jews (Rom 11:7-12).[80] But in a writer like Philo, Jacob's sobriquet is, as his name suggests, "the Supplanter."[81] Hence in the first century, Jacob was still known as "jacob," the supplanter.[82] Hence, Jesus is supplanting Jacob, i.e., "greater than our father Jacob."

---

79. See John 3:6, 12, 20-21, 36; 6:49-51; 11:9-10; also 1 John 2:23; 3:8-9, 14-15; 4:2-3, 7-8.

80. See R. N. Whybray, *The Succession Narrative* (London: SPCK, 1968) 10-55.

81. Philo, *Cher.* 67; *Alleg. Interp.* 1.61; 2.89; 3.15, 93, 180; *Names* 81; *QG* 4.163; *Dreams* 1.171.

82. Despite the deviousness ascribed to Jacob in Genesis, in the first century the figure of Jacob was considerably restored and polished; his lies and deceptions are explained away (Philo, *QG* 4.172, 201, 206). Wisdom, not craftiness, comes to him (Wis 10:10; Sir 24:8; 1 Bar 3:36-37). According to Philo, Jacob is the archetypal "practicer" of virtue (*Sacr.* 17; *Alleg. Interp.* 3.18, 22, 93) who supplants passion (*Alleg. Interp.* 3.93, 190; *Sacr.* 42; *Names* 81; *Heir* 252-53); he is the true lover of virtue (*Dreams* 1.45, 69, 127, 159), first in virtue (*Alleg. Interp.* 3.192), and living full of wisdom in a house of virtue (*Alleg. Interp.* 3.2). In *Pesiq. Rab.* 26.1 Jacob is a "perfect man," one of the four "supremely perfect creatures whom God Himself had formed." The vehicle for this rehabilitation seems to be tied to a fresh reading of Gen 25:27 in which *tam* is translated no longer as "quiet" but as "perfect."

2.4 Jacob's Courtship at the Well (4:16-18)

Is there an allusion to Jacob in 4:16-18? The Old Testament background suggests a parallel between the courtship meetings at wells of Abraham's servant and Rebekah (Gen 24:1ff.), Jacob and Rachel (Gen 29:1-14), Moses and Zipporah (Exod 2:15-22),[83] and Jesus and the Samaritan woman. In Josephus's account of these encounters at a well, only the Jacob-Rachel story contains a story of a tender and elaborate courtship (*Ant.* 1.286-92). Justin was quick to see Jacob's marriages as types of what Christ was to accomplish: Leah was the synagogue who was replaced by Rachel, the church (*Dialogue with Trypho* 134). Any matrimonial allusions in John 4:16-18, therefore, would seem to cast Jesus in the role of groom and the woman (Samaritan church?) as the bride.

Using allegorical methods of interpretation, critics have attempted to identify the five husbands (4:18) with the five books of the Samaritan Pentateuch[84] or with the five gods (*ba'al* as husband/god) which the Samaritans were said to worship,[85] but such interpretations have fallen into disfavor.[86] The thrust of such investigations has been primarily in terms of Samaritan traditions, whereas our focus is the Jacob traditions.

If there is a Jacob allusion operating here, it would be primarily in terms of courtship at a well. Courtship would imply that Jesus replaces the former "husbands" of the woman with the true *ba'al*, viz., himself. Since the woman is portrayed as accepting Jesus as Messiah (4:39), he effectively becomes her *ba'al*; and he replaces Samaritan expectations when they confess him as "Savior of the world" (4:42). The Jacob matrimonial allusions, however, are tenuous and are not truly rooted in any Jacob tradition.

2.5 The Right Place to Worship and Visions of the Future (4:19-20)

The woman's response in 4:19-20 reflects a shift in the dialogue: "Sir, I perceive that you are a prophet. Our fathers worshiped on this mountain; and you say

---

83. The link between the well and matrimony is well attested not only in biblical texts but in later midrash as well; see *Song of Songs Rab.* 4.12.3: "Thy God will one day make thee like a park of pomegranates (Song 4:13) in the Messianic era. What is that? The well [of Miriam]. Whence did the Israelites procure wine for drink offerings all the forty years that they spent in the wilderness? R. Johanan said: From the well."

84. Origen, *In Johannem* 13.8 (GCS 10, 232).

85. See 2 Kgs 17:29-34; *b. Yebamot* 64b; Josephus, *Ant.* 9.288; Philo, *Migr.* 188-206; see Brown, *The Gospel According to John*, 1.171, n. 18.

86. Schnackenburg, *The Gospel According to St. John*, 433; Lindars, *The Gospel of John*, 185-87; Brown, *The Gospel According to John*, 1.171.

that in Jerusalem is the place where people ought to worship." The operative images turn from well and water to worship, especially knowledge pertinent to worship. Jesus' remark about the woman's many husbands prompts a sarcastic response: if you know so much, Mr. Know-it-all, then solve this unsolvable problem. Sarcastic and challenging, indeed, but a lead-in to a very serious matter, the right place of worship.[87] The knowledge of Jesus, therefore, seems to function as the mediating link between the two halves of the discourse. It distinguishes him from the woman *who does not know* (4:10) and it looks forward to his identification as Messiah *who knows all* (4:25, 39). But does the second half of the dialogue (vv. 19-26) allude to or presuppose allusions to Jacob? If not to specific Jacob legends, then might Jesus continue to "supplant" older traditions? That is, does he still function as "jacob"?

In her riposte to Jesus that he is a know-it-all, "a prophet," the woman challenges him to settle a political issue of significance, namely, the right place of worship, which maintained a hostility between Samaritans and Jews. Northern and Samaritan traditions did not accept Jerusalem as "the place where I will put my name."[88] The most obvious evidence of this disagreement with Jerusalem was the erection of the golden calf at Bethel in the days of Jeroboam (1 Kgs 12:28-29). The deuteronomic redactor was likewise reluctant to localize God in any one place, especially Jerusalem (see Deut 12:5, 11, 14, 18, 21, 26), a polemic which is found also in the redaction of 1 Kgs 8:28ff.

Besides this general orientation of non-Judah tribes,[89] there are passages in the Jacob stories which could be read in support of an alternate site to Jerusalem as the legitimate place of worship. Jacob experienced a vision of a ladder stretching from heaven to earth; when he awoke he designated the spot of the vision as "the place": "Surely the Lord is in this place; and I did not know it ... how awesome is this place! This is none other than the house of God and the gate of heaven" (Gen 28:16-17). Samaritan traditions which supported worship on Mount Gerizim interpreted Jacob's vision as occurring on that mountain.[90]

---

87. See 1 Macc 4:46; 14:41.

88. It is customary to associate Stephen's speech in Acts 7 with Jesus' remarks in John 4, the link being a Samaritan anti-temple bias; see W. F. Albright and C. S. Mann, "Stephen's Samaritan Background," *The Acts of the Apostles*, ed. J. Munck (AB 31; Garden City: Doubleday, 1967) 285-300; O. Cullmann, "L'Opposition contre le temple de Jérusalem, motif commun de la théologie johannique et du monde ambiant," *NTS* 5 (1958-59): 157-73, and more recently in *The Johannine Circle* (Philadelphia: Westminster, 1976) 16, 39-53.

89. R. E. Clements, "Deuteronomy and the Jerusalem Cult Tradition," *VT* 15 (1965): 303-8; see 2 Macc 5:19.

90. See John Macdonald, *The Theology of the Samaritans* (Philadelphia: Westminster, 1964) 327-33; Josephus, *Antiquities* 18.85-87; Hans Kippenberg, *Garizim und Synagoge* (Berlin: W. de Gruyter, 1971) 258-59, 263.

Also supporting the Samaritan claim is Gen 33:19-20, Jacob's building of an altar at Shechem. Thus Jacob is certainly a factor in a northern and Samaritan tradition which asserted that Gerizim is the legitimate place of worship.

Recent archaeological research on Mount Gerizim has uncovered a massive building under a Roman temple, a building which has subsequently been identified as the Samaritan temple.[91] Moreover, in an important article on Samaritan traditions of the temple's "hidden vessels," M. Collins has shown that in the first century there was strong expectation that an eschatological prophet would recover the hidden vessels on Gerizim and thus restore true worship there as the rightful place.[92] Collins's article has shown that Josephus's account of Samaritan attempts to meet on Mount Gerizim in the first century (see *Ant.* 18.85-87) reflect a live religious issue, which focuses our attention on the woman's question in John 4:19-20, especially her remarks about a prophet.[93]

Beyond the use of Jacob's vision as foundational for a Samaritan tradition of Mount Gerizim as the place of worship, the same vision of Jacob (Gen 28:16-18) was used in Israelite sources as validation of Jerusalem's claims for Mount Zion. *Gen. Rab.* 69.7 notes that the spot of Jacob's ladder was the very site of the temple; *Tg. Yer. I* Gen 28:17 explicitly connects Jacob's site with Jerusalem: "This place is not profane but the holy house of the name of the Lord, the proper spot for prayer, set forth before the gate of heaven, founded beneath the throne of Glory."[94] The essentials of this reading are found also in two variant readings of *Tg. Neof.* Gen 28:17.[95] Although such targumic expansion may be of later date, inasmuch as it reflects a period after the fall of the Temple in 70 A.D. when sacrifice would be replaced by prayer, nevertheless the use of Jacob's vision to validate a particular spot is clearly very old. Proof of this claim comes from a passage in *Jubilees* which, dealing with Jacob's vision of the ladder, emphatically restrains him from consecrating Bethel as the legitimate place of worship. It is emphatically insisted that the dream site is "*not* the place."

---

91. The literary evidence for the Samaritan temple may be found in Josephus, *Antiquities* 11.322; 13.254; see H. H. Rowley, "Sanballat and the Samaritan Temple," *Men of God* (London: Nelson, 1963) 246-76; Kippenberg, *Garizim und Synagoge*, 48-59, 188-200. Archeological evidence may be found in R. J. Bull, "The Excavation of Tell er Ras (Mt. Gerizim)," *BASOR* 190 (1968): 11-18; idem, "An Archeological Footnote . . . ," *NTS* 23 (1977): 460-62.

92. M. F. Collins, "The Hidden Vessels in Samaritan Traditions," *JSS* 3 (1972): 97-116.

93. Collins, "The Hidden Vessels in Samaritan Traditions," 110-12, 115-16.

94. *Tg. Yer. I* Gen 28:11 commented that Jacob "prayed in the place of the house of the sanctuary." *Pirqe Rabbi Eliezer* 35 (Friedlander, 266) linked Gen 28:12 explicitly to Jerusalem: "Hence thou canst learn that every one who prays at Jerusalem is (reckoned) as though he had prayed before the Throne of Glory, for the gate of heaven is there and it is open to hear the prayers of Israel, as it is said 'And this is the gate of heaven' (Gen 28:17)."

95. A. Diez Macho, *Neophyti 1, I. Genesis*, 181.

> Do *not* build this place.
> Do *not* make it an eternal sanctuary;
> Do *not* dwell here;
> this is *not* the place. (*Jub* 32:22)

Thus Jacob traditions were generally operative in the politics of locating the correct place of worship. But as "greater than Jacob," Jesus is challenged about his knowledge, one aspect of which was knowledge for settling the disputed location of Jacob's vision vis-à-vis the legitimate place of worship.

Just as Jacob was linked to a specific place of worship in virtue of Gen 28:16-18, he is likewise treated as a visionary according to midrashic developments of several other Jacob texts in Genesis. The passage from *Jubilees* that we just examined expands the vision of Jacob's ladder in the direction of his receiving heavenly secrets about the future of Israel. Gen 28:12-15 tells only of a vision of a ladder and of the Lord promising to establish a covenant concerning the land with Jacob and sons. But the retelling of this vision in *Jub* 32:21-24 supplements the divine oracle with an angelic messenger bringing seven tablets of heavenly secrets for Jacob to read: "And he read them and knew that all that was written therein which would befall him and his sons throughout the ages" (v. 21). And the text continues with the angel commanding Jacob to record his special revelations: "Write down everything as you have seen and read" (v. 24). Thus in virtue of Gen 28:12-15, Jacob was considered privy to heavenly revelations as well as purveyor of them (see *Jub* 32:26).[96]

Another Jacob text (Genesis 49) also became the occasion for claiming that Jacob possessed special heavenly knowledge. The MT of Gen 49:1 describes the dying Jacob gathering his sons together "that I may tell you what shall befall you in the days to come." The LXX puts a different nuance to the text by translating "following days" as "to the end of the days." This verse became the locus of considerable expansion in targum and midrash[97] as Jacob was credited with visions of the eschatological future. Typical of this expansion is *Tg. Neof.* Gen 49:1: "I

---

96. The targums to Gen 28:12 tell of a different sort of expansion of the Jacob story. He is revealed to the angels in heaven as the one "whose likeness is engraved on the throne of Glory, and whom you (angels) have so greatly desired to see" (*Yer. I* and *II, Neof.* Gen 28:12). In these passages, however, Jacob seems to be linked with strains of merkabah mysticism.

97. The targums to Gen 49:1-2 contain a confusion over whether Jacob actually revealed mysteries and secrets. *Yer. I* and *Neof.* Gen 49:1-2 both record that important mysteries were withheld from Jacob; for example, *Neof.*: "when the mystery was revealed to him, it was closed to him." *Yer. I* Gen 49:1-2, however, while attributing some revelations to Jacob, insists that others were "hidden from him"; see *b. Pesaḥim* 56a; *Gen. Rab.* 93.3. The fact that later traditions seem to emphatically circumscribe Jacob's knowledge suggests that they are reacting to other traditions that do credit Jacob with heavenly revelations.

will tell you the concealed secrets, the hidden ends, the giving of rewards of the just and the punishment of the wicked and what the happiness of Eden is."[98]

J. M. Allegro published a text from Qumran (4QpGn49) that contains Jacob's visionary blessing of Judah (Gen 49:10) interpreted as a messianic prophecy.[99] Jacob foresees the coming Messiah ("a ruler from the tribe of Judah") who, it appears, will be associated with the "Interpreter of the Law" for the sectarian community. Allegro argued from 4QFlor that this "Interpreter of the Law" in 4QpGn49 is himself a messianic figure, citing 4QFlor as evidence: "He is the Shoot of David, who will arise with the Interpreter of the Law."[100] Granting the Qumran doctrine of a royal as well as a priestly Messiah,[101] we have clear pre-Christian evidence of Jacob's vision (Genesis 49) functioning as the locus of speculation concerning a royal Messiah as well as an official interpreter of Israelite law and worship.

Other Jacob texts link him with special revelations, especially knowledge concerning the future place of worship. Attached to Isaac's blessing of Jacob (Gen 27:27) we find the following midrash:

> This verse teaches that the Holy One, blessed be He, showed him (Jacob) the Temple built, destroyed, and rebuilt. Thus: *See the smell of my son* is an allusion to the Temple built, as in the verse, "a sweet smell unto Me shall ye observe" (Num 28:2). *As the smell of the field* suggests it when destroyed, as in the verse, "Zion shall be ploughed as a field" (Mic 3:12); *which the Lord hath blessed* — this hints at it being rebuilt and perfected in the Messianic future, as it is said, "For there the Lord commanded the blessing, even life for ever." (Ps 133:3)[102]

---

98. The proper background of Jacob's deathbed revelations is the somewhat loose genre of testimonies and farewell addresses; see E. Stauffer, "Abschiedsreden," *RAC* 1.29-35; Johannes Munck, "Discours d'adieu dans le Nouveau Testament et dans le littérature biblique," *Aux Sources de la Tradition Chrétienne* (Neuchâtel: Delachaux et Niestlé, 1950) 150-70; Aelred Lacomara, "Deuteronomy and the Farewell Discourse (John 13:31-16:33)," *CBQ* 36 (1974): 65-84.

99. J. M. Allegro, "Further Messianic References in Qumran Literature," *JBL* 75 (1956): 174-75; for further literature on this text, see J. Fitzmyer, "A Bibliographical Aid to the Study of the Qumran Cave IV Texts 158-186," *CBQ* 31 (1969): 71.

100. J. M. Allegro, "Further Messianic References," 176.

101. See J. Starcky, "Les quatres étapes du messianisme à Qumran," *RB* 70 (1963): 481-505; J. Fitzmyer, "The Aramaic 'Elect of God' Text from Qumran Cave 4," *CBQ* 27 (1965): 348-72, and R. E. Brown, "J. Starcky's Theory of Qumran Messianic Development," *CBQ* 28 (1966): 51-57.

102. *Gen. Rab.* 65.23. Several of the targums to Gen 27:27 record another form of this association of Jacob with worship, but omit the mention of the temple destroyed. With slight differences, *Neof.* and *Yer. I* both describe the smell of Jacob "as the smell of incense of good perfumes which will be offered upon the altar of the mountain of the sanctuary." Other midrashim which associate Jacob with visions of the temple include *Pesiq. Rab.* 30.3; 17.2; *Midrash Pss.* 78.6; *Sipre*

"Are You Greater than Our Father Jacob?"

Although such traditions speak of a period after the fall of the Temple in A.D. 70, nevertheless the ease with which they are attached to Jacob suggests a prior readiness to link such materials to the patriarch.

Other sources say that Jacob revealed the history of Judah until, but not including, the coming of the Messiah, who would then know and tell everything:

> The tribe of Judah — the wise and great among them — possessed a tradition from our father Jacob as to all that would befall the whole tribe until the days of the Messiah. Everyone of the tribes similarly possessed such traditions from their father Jacob as to what would happen to them until the days of the Messiah.[103]

Thus Jacob, while credited with special revelations as well as visions, was expected to be supplanted in turn by the Messiah when he came, which tradition seems pertinent to understanding the woman's remark in 4:25: "I know that the Messiah, when he comes, will show us all things." Thus, there seems to be a foundation for proclaiming that Jesus, as prophet and Messiah, would have greater knowledge than Jacob.

But the dialogue in John 4:21-24 does not consider Jesus as a latter-day Jacob whose visions decide long-standing disputes as to the right place of worship. Jesus supplants that entire discussion by invalidating Jacob's visions of the ladder as the place ("*neither* on this mountain *nor* in Jerusalem").[104] And Jesus supplants Jacob's revelations of the future of Israel and its worship by declaring a new time ("the hour is coming . . . and is now here") and a new cult ("true worshipers will worship in spirit and truth").

2.6 Worship in Spirit and Truth (4:21-24)

Jesus' first response in the second half of the discourse (4:21) categorically rejects both Mount Gerizim *and* Mount Zion as "the place where one must worship." His subsequent remarks may allude to other Jacob traditions. In Gen 28:16-18, when Jacob awoke from his dream-vision he exclaimed: "The Lord is

---

Num. 119. The same vision is not always credited to Jacob; see *Gen. Rab.* 2.5; *Pirqe Rabbi Eliezer* 51; it is even ascribed to Abraham in *Gen. Rab.* 56.10.

103. *Num. Rab.* 13.14.

104. Besides *Jubilees* 32:22, further evidence of a polemic against Samaritan worship can be found in *LAB* 25.10, where it is noted that seven idols were found at Shechem, suggesting that the area was always considered as a place of false worship (see 1 Kgs 12:25-29). See R. E. Brown, "Johannine Ecclesiology — the Community's Origins," *Int* 31 (1977): 389.

in this spot and *I did not know it.*" In 4:22 Jesus tells the woman, "You worship *what you do not know,* we worship what we know." The question is: did Jacob know or did he not?

According to some Samaritan traditions, Mount Gerizim was "the place"; and in certain strands of that tradition it is positively asserted that "Jacob *knew* it," probably a corrective apology to rival Israelite readings of Gen 28:16, "I did *not know* it." But in this context, in which John's community asserts both the superiority of Israelite to Samaritan traditions and Christian superiority to both, the remark "you do not know" undercuts all previous claims, Samaritan and Israelite, by reasserting Jacob's statement about "*not knowing.*" And it affirms the replacement of Jacob's concern with the "place of God" with Christian claims concerning true worship, viz., "what we know." The thrust of the replacement, moreover, is again in the direction of an absolute claim on behalf of Jesus.[105]

Another item in Jesus' response presses forward the absolute claim made by Jesus: "true worshipers worship the Father in spirit and truth" (v. 23a). The dialectical language continues the contrasts of vv. 21-22; when the woman asked about the correct "place," Jesus denied in principle that there is such a place; previous claims to know were invalidated by the charge that "you do not know," whereas "we know." Now former eras are negated in favor of a new time, "the hour is coming and is now here." False or incomplete cultic actions now give way to "true worshipers" who supplant the old mode of worship by "worshiping in spirit and truth." Indeed the old tradition is totally supplanted.[106]

But is there a specific Jacob allusion in 4:23? Is the operative factor still the supplanting of Jacob by Jesus? Or is there a possible link between the two halves of the discourse, such that well/water (4:10-14) tends to be linked with spirit and revelation (4:21-24) in Israelite literature? In general it can be said that spirit was metaphorically linked with water in the Old Testament, especially in phrases such as "pour out my spirit" (Isa 32:15; Joel 2:28). In Ezek 36:25-27, the water which purifies is associated with a new spirit of God:

---

105. The thrust of the argument in John 4:21-23 is not simply the denial that God can be localized or contained in space but the supplanting of older traditions of cult and worship; on God as "place," see J. A. Montgomery, "The 'Place' as an Appellation of Deity," *JBL* 24 (1905): 17-26.

106. It is worth noting that at this point in the Gospel Jesus has already offered a replacement for Israelite purification rites (2:6-11; 3:25-30); in fact his water-made-wine is clearly said to be superior to what was previously used (2:10). The Temple is likewise replaced (2:13-22) by Jesus' own body. Later in the Gospel Jesus' death as the Passover Lamb will replace the old ritual; see A. Guilding, *The Fourth Gospel and Jewish Worship* (Oxford: Clarendon, 1960) 58-68, 154-66; Brown, *The Gospel According to John* 2.953-56; C. H. Dodd, *The Interpretation of the Fourth Gospel* (Cambridge: Cambridge University Press, 1968) 233, 424; and Meeks, *The Prophet-King,* 76-78, 91-95.

I will sprinkle clean water upon you, and you shall be clean from all your uncleannesses, and from your idols I will cleanse you. A new heart I will give you, and a new spirit I will put within you; and I will take out of your flesh the heart of stone and give you a heart of flesh. And I will put my spirit within you and cause you to walk in my statutes and be careful to observe all my ordinances.[107]

Spirit, water, and purification are linked in 1QS 4:21. Thus there was a solid basis in Israelite symbols for associating well/water with spirit and purification, which is just the link that John seems to have made.

Despite its problematic dating, the following midrash on Gen 29:1 reflects the tradition we have seen which associates well/water with spirit and worship, in this case cultic festivals. Concerning the well of Jacob we read:

> Another interpretation: *And behold a well in the field* symbolizes Zion; *And lo three flocks of sheep* — the three Festivals (Passover, Pentecost, Tabernacles); *For out of that well they watered the flocks* — from there they imbibed the divine spirit; *And the stone . . . was great* — this alludes to the rejoicing of the place of the water drawing. R. Hoshaya said: Why was it called the rejoicing of the place of drawing water? Because from there they imbibed the divine spirit. *And thither were all the flocks gathered* — they all came, "from the entrance of Hamath unto the Brook of Egypt" (1 Kgs 8:65). *And they rolled the stone from the well's mouth in its place: it was lying for the next Festival.*[108]

As well and water are associated with spirit and worship, the same complex imagery is also linked with special knowledge and revelation. There are passages from 1 Enoch that speak of "fountains of wisdom" (1 En 48:1) or of "wisdom poured out like water" (1 En 49:1).[109]

The Damascus Document is another important text, for it links well and instruction. The exclusive interpretation of Israelite practice by the community to which the Damascus Document belonged is seen as supplanting the corrupt practices of Jerusalem. Holiness and purity are found only in the sect; of old, God "revealed hidden things" to the holy remnant about "holy Sabbaths, glori-

---

107. Olsson, *Structure and Meaning in the Fourth Gospel*, 215, and Odeberg, *The Fourth Gospel*, 153.

108. *Gen. Rab.* 79.8.

109. Odeberg, *The Fourth Gospel*, 152-56, 158-60; Olsson, *Structure and Meaning in the Fourth Gospel*, 214. *Tg. Isaiah* records two differences from the MT that are relevant here: 1) at 12:3 "draw water from the well" (MT) becomes "receive a new teaching from the chosen," and 2) at 55:1 "let everyone who thirsts come to the waters" is changed to "everyone who would learn let him come. . . ."

ous feasts, testimony of righteousness and ways of truth" (CD 3:14-15). This revelation, moreover, is expressed in the metaphor of a well: "He opened (this) before them and they dug a well of abundant waters and whoever despises these waters shall not live" (3:16-17). The sect recognized that one aspect of their exclusive claim to holiness was accurate knowledge of who the true priests were (4:1-6) and of who had defiled the sanctuary (4:18; 5:6-7). The authentic tradition of Torah was attributed to the teachers of the sect, who dug a well from which they drew their teaching of truth:

> And God remembered the covenant of the Patriarchs
> and raised out of Aaron men of understanding
> and out of Israel sages,
> and He caused them to hear (His voice) and they dug the well:
> *The well which the princes dug,*
> *Which the nobles of the people delved with a rod.*
> The well is the Law,
> and those who dug it are the converts of Israel
> who went out from the land of Judah
> and were exiled in the land of Damascus. (CD 6:2-5)

The general symbolic linkage between well/water and special knowledge is found in Philo, who explicitly ties these associations to Jacob's well (Gen 29:1). The spring is divine wisdom (*Flight* 195-96; *Posterity* 138) or God himself, as in Jer 2:13 (*Flight* 197), from whence come ever-flowing waters (*Flight* 197; *Posterity* 136; *Dreams* 1.11) so that whoever drinks the waters of the divine spring gains ultimate knowledge and understanding (*Flight* 195-96; *Posterity* 136, 138). God's waters, moreover, are waters of life, even of immortality (*Flight* 198-99). The "wise ones," Abraham, Isaac, and Jacob, dug the wells of divine wisdom (*Flight* 200). Moses likewise witnesses to the "wisdom of the well" in Numbers 21 (*Drunkenness* 112), although it is Rebecca, the figure of Sophia, who gives the waters of the wisdom of God to those who would learn from her (*Post.* 136; *QG* 4.98-108). For Philo, a well is often a "symbol of education and knowledge" (*QG* 4.191; *Dreams* 1.6; 2.271).

Before explaining Jacob's dream of the ladder in Gen 28:12-15, Philo insisted on investigating three items: 1) the well of the oath, 2) Haran, and 3) "the place" (*Dreams* 1.5). The well symbolized knowledge (*Dreams* 1.6, 11); Haran, according to the epistemological allegory, represents the "mother city of the senses," which even the wise man depends upon. The reprehensible thing is to live always on the sense level, like Laban. Jacob, like Abraham, only spends a brief time on the sense level before fleeing it for realms of true knowledge

(*Dreams* 1.41-47). The "place" mentioned in Gen 28:11 cannot mean the "place of God," for God, who contains all things, cannot be contained in "a place"; according to Philo, "place," when it appears in statements like Gen 22:3 and 28:11, must refer to the *logos* (*Dreams* 1.61-64). When Jacob encountered "the place," he was in contact with "the Word of God, showing, as it does, the way to the things that are best, teaching, as it does, such lessons as the varying occasions require" (*Dreams* 1.68). In Philo, then, we find the same general identification of Jacob with well, water, and divine teaching as was observed in the Old Testament and targumic material.

3.0 Summary and Conclusion

This examination of Jacob traditions throws light on several statements in John 4:10-26. The text was shown to presuppose allusions to Jacob's miracle of well water automatically rising and to the identification of the well as God's "gift." The primary Jacob allusion, however, seems to be the etymological appreciation of Jacob as "supplanter." Hence, the fundamental point of 4:12 is to assert that Jesus supplants Jacob and all the traditions associated with Jacob, in particular Jacob's legitimation of a correct place of worship and knowledge of the days to come. Being "greater" means in fact that Jesus supplants Jacob in an absolute way. He gives water such that the one who drinks it will *never thirst* (4:14), for the new water will well up to "eternal life."

The background of 4:19-20 would seem to include allusions to Jacob both in terms of his vision (Genesis 28) and possibly in terms of his knowledge (Genesis 49). Jacob's vision, which was part of the legitimating process for both Mount Gerizim and Mount Zion, is supplanted by the revelations from the new prophet-Messiah, Jesus.

In 4:21-24 there seems to be an allusion to Jacob's remark in Gen 28:16 ("I did not know"), whereby Jesus supplants Jacob's vision and knowledge by "what we do know." The discussion of 4:23-24 showed that well and water are frequent ciphers for Torah, spirit, and knowledge of worship and that these symbols are indeed tied to Jacob's well, as the midrash on Gen 29:1 indicated. Thus the two halves of the discourse are consistent in their presentation of Jesus' new water, which is deciphered as the new teaching on "worshiping in spirit and truth." Even in the second half of the discourse at the well (4:19-26), the fundamental allusion to Jacob is still that of supplanter. The sectarian Johannine community is not simply claiming that Jesus is supplanting Jacob's well; rather Jesus as the supplanter is invalidating all previous cultic places and rites and is replacing them with a worship centered in Jesus' own person (4:42).

Thus it is not a question of comparison between Jesus' and Jacob's waters that is at issue (4:12-15). Absolute claims are made by the Johannine community on behalf of Jesus, claims which deal with no less than "true worship" of God.

Why Jacob? Of all the Hebrew patriarchs, Jacob is most closely associated with cult, either the place of worship or knowledge about worship (Gen 28:11-17). This association is utilized by John as he systematically asserts the superiority of Jesus to Moses, Abraham, and all other founding fathers of Israel's religion.

5

"He Must Increase, I Must Decrease" (John 3:30)

A Cultural and Social Interpretation

1.0 State of Inquiry and Thesis for Investigation

The episode in John 3:22-30 regularly gets short shrift from commentators.[1] That is especially true of the Baptizer's striking remark in v. 30, which at best is praised but never interpreted.[2] Nor has anyone taken notice of how foreign to Mediterranean culture that remark really is. Hence to our knowledge no one has ever felt the need for or found suitable ancient, non-biblical parallels that might be brought to bear on its interpretation. In the discussion that follows, however, we shall examine relevant parallel material that is indeed illuminating. Yet we do not do so as just another history-of-religions investigation. Instead, we bring to the task models from comparative anthropology that enable us to assess John 3:30 in its proper cultural and social context.

It is also true that this passage is rarely compared with other materials in the Fourth Gospel that might offer clarification. Monographs and commentar-

---

1. Typical of commentaries is that of Martin Stowasser, *Johannes der Täufer im Vierten Evangelium* (Klosterneuburg: Österreichisches Katholisches Bibelwerk, 1992). He pays close attention to the logical and rhetorical shape of the material, text-critical problems, and the history of the tradition of the material. Yet his focus, like that of most commentators, rests on the bridegroom metaphor in 3:29 (pp. 184-90).

2. From the time of the Church Fathers, the typical commentary on 3:30 pointed to the astral parallel of *auxanein* — *elattousthai* with the careers of Jesus and John. See Rudolf Bultmann, *The Gospel of John* (Philadelphia: Westminster, 1971); Raymond E. Brown, *The Gospel According to John* (AB 29; Garden City: Doubleday, 1966) 1.153; Rudolf Schnackenburg, *The Gospel According to St. John* (New York: Herder and Herder, 1968) 1.417.

This study was coauthored with Richard L. Rohrbaugh, who deserves equal praise for it.

ies typically investigate the links between John and Jesus in John 1 and indicate the continuance of those links in John 3:22-30. Yet we will argue that at least in 11:45-52 we find an important but unnoticed parallel to 3:22-30. Whereas John the Baptist did not suffer envy at Jesus' success, the Jerusalem elite did so. The interpretive key to that contrast, we argue, lies in the sociology of perception ("limited good") and the anthropology of envy.

Our thesis is that in this story John's disciples are on the verge of envying Jesus and his disciples. Like most people in antiquity, they appear to share the view that all goods are limited in quantity and already distributed. There is only so much land, gold, fame, or praise existing in the world. Thus if someone seems to be gaining any of these, inevitably others must be losing — possibly me or one of my friends. In other words, the world is a zero-sum game: for some to increase, others must decrease. The Baptizer himself steps apart from the game, but not so his disciples. For them, Jesus' success appears to be a gain that implies their loss. It is this cultural concept of "limited good" and relevant ancient instances of it that we bring to our interpretation of John 3:30.

2.0 Preliminary Reading of John 3:22-30

The scene begins with notice that both Jesus and John are baptizing in Judean territory,[3] which sets the stage for the controversy that follows. The disciples of John engage in a "controversy" with someone[4] over purification. The key term here, *zētēsis*, can have such neutral meanings as philosophical inquiry or investigation, but also a more highly charged meaning such as controversy or legal investigation.[5] The sense in 3:25 is that of controversy and even of envy. These disciples then go to John to voice their interpretation of the *zētēsis*: "Rabbi, he who

---

3. Some scholars have suggested a relationship between Acts 18:25; 19:1-7 and John 3:22-30. For example, Raymond E. Brown suggests that John had many disciples who continued his teaching and baptismal practice after his and Jesus' death. Indeed they were in conflict with the Johannine community; see Brown's *Community of the Beloved Disciple* (New York: Paulist Press, 1979) 29-30 and 69-71. We do not consider this for two reasons. First, it is a historical question but we are asking social questions. Second, even if Brown is correct, there is no impact on our treatment of 3:22-30. Our focus is on "he must increase, but I must decrease," which in John's narrative serves to undercut an expected pattern of limited good and agonistic behavior.

4. There is uncertainty about the identity of the *Ioudaiou* in v. 25. Brown (*Gospel According to John*, 1.150) translates it as "a certain Jew." The reading of P66* (*et al.*) is *Ioudaiōn*. Rudolf Bultmann (*The Gospel of John*, 171) claimed that the controversy is between John's disciples and Jesus; for a more recent argument that the conflict is between the Baptizer's disciples and Jesus, see John W. Pryor, "John the Baptist and Jesus: Tradition and Text in John 3:25," *JSNT* 66 (1997): 15-26.

5. See H. Greeven, "*zētēsis*," *TDNT* 2.756-57; BAGD 339.

"He Must Increase, I Must Decrease" (John 3:30)

was with you beyond the Jordan, to whom you bore witness, here he is, baptizing and *all are going to him*" (v. 26).[6] Their complaint clarifies the subject of the *zētēsis* as a rivalry between Jesus (and his disciples) and John (and his disciples).

The nub of the *zētēsis* resides in the perception that Jesus' growth in fame and reputation comes at the expense of John and his disciples. In many ways John's disciples voice the same kind of remark as do Jesus' enemies in 11:47-48 at the growth of Jesus' fame because of his raising of Lazarus: "This man performs many signs. If we let him go on like this, *everyone will believe in him*...." In both stories some people perceive that their own worth diminishes precisely as Jesus gains greater respect and honor. In fact, Jesus' increase *causes* their decrease.

The audience of the Fourth Gospel has been carefully prepared how to assess remarks such as those of John's disciples. No fewer than three times John announced Jesus' superiority to himself, indicating that he and Jesus are not in competition but that John's career is precisely to herald Jesus.

1:15	"He who comes *after me ranks before me*, for he was before me."
1:26-27	"... among you stands one whom you do not know, even *he who comes after me, the thong of whose sandal I am not worthy to untie*."
1:30	"This is he of whom I said, 'After me comes a man who ranks before me, for he was before me.'"

John, then, has already declared his position on the success of Jesus; he himself does not see the situation in terms of limited good, nor will he engage in envy.

John, however, steps apart from this typical game of envy by making several critical remarks. First, he declares that Jesus has not achieved anything on his own. No one, including Jesus, has anything but "what is given him from above" (3:27). Thus in the jargon of honor and shame, the honor Jesus enjoys is ascribed by God, with whom mortals may not disagree (Acts 5:39). In this way John states that he himself does not share his disciples' perception of a controversy since it is God who gives Jesus his status and fame. Second, he reminds his disciples of his own earlier testimony to Jesus (3:28; see 1:19-23), indicating that his major role has been to herald and acknowledge Jesus' honorable precedence before all. John has always promoted Jesus; it is his mission to see that Jesus increase. Third, he describes his relationship to Jesus as the "friend" *(philos)* who stands close by and

---

6. Only one study of this passage has noticed the social implications of the disciples' reaction: Robert L. Webb, *John the Baptizer and Prophet: A Socio-Historical Study* (JSOTSup 62; Sheffield: Sheffield Academic Press, 1991) 74, remarked, "In hyperbole derived from envy, they state 'all are coming to him' (3:26)."

"rejoices greatly at the groom's voice" (v. 29).[7] Surely groom and "friend" are not rivals; nor does the "friend" lose anything if the groom is happy. In fact, as John says, "this joy of mine is now full"; it has in no way diminished because of Jesus' success. Thus John disputes his own disciples' interpretation of the situation. Whereas they see only loss in Jesus' growing success, John sees "fullness of joy" at Jesus' fame, just as the *philos* revels in the voice of the groom.

Finally, John makes one of the most counter-cultural statements in the New Testament: "He [Jesus] must increase, but I must decrease" (v. 30). Why "counter-cultural"? What is taking place between the characters of the story and the reader and his audience? How would readers know that John has made a remark so unusual as to turn their world upside-down? To answer this we must borrow from cultural anthropology a model for assessing social perceptions of gain and loss in honor-shame (agonistic) societies.

3.0 The Cultural Model of "Limited Good"

Decades ago the anthropologist George Foster[8] described how peasants perceive that all good things in the world exist in limited supply:

> By "Image of Limited Good" I mean that broad areas of peasant behavior are patterned in such a fashion as to suggest that peasants view their social, economic, and natural universes — their total environment — as one in which all of the desired things in life such as land, wealth, health, friendship and love, manliness and honor, respect and status, power and influence, security and safety, exist in finite quantity and are always in short supply, as far as the peasant is concerned. Not only do these and all other "good things" exist in finite and limited quantities, but in addition there is no way directly within peasant power to increase the available quantities.[9]

For peasants, ancient as well as modern, the world exists as a zero-sum game in which land provides the basic analogy for understanding the world. There is

---

7. In Greek the phrase literally means "friend of the bridegroom." In Israelite society the term (*šušbinim*) referred to close friends of similar age who formed associations for mutual aid in putting on a wedding. The obligations incurred were always reciprocal.

8. George M. Foster, "Peasant Society and the Image of Limited Good," *American Anthropologist* 67 (1965): 293-315; see his "Interpersonal Relations in Peasant Society," *Human Organization* 19 (1960): 177, and "Cultural Responses to Expressions of Envy in Tzintzuntzan," *Southwestern Journal of Anthropology* 21 (1965): 24-35.

9. Foster, "Peasant Society," 296. The world of biblical scholarship is indebted to Bruce J. Malina for bringing Foster's work to our attention; see his *The New Testament World: Insights from Cultural Anthropology* (revised ed.; Louisville: Westminster/John Knox, 2001) 81-107.

only so much arable land in the world, and it is already completely distributed. If one person gets more, someone else has to get less. Moreover, the same is true of all other good things in the world including water, food, wealth, and respect and fame. Thus Foster argues that "any advantage achieved by one individual or family is seen as a loss to others, and the person who makes what the Western world lauds as 'progress' is viewed as a threat to the stability of the entire community."[10]

The key here is the perception that everything good is already all distributed and cannot be increased. Foster suggests that when people view the world in this way, two things will happen: 1) they "are reluctant to advance beyond their peers because of the sanctions they know will be leveled against them," and 2) anyone "who is seen or known to acquire more becomes much more vulnerable to the envy of his neighbors."[11] Social relations become heavily dependent not just on maintaining what one has in life but also on avoiding the perception of gaining more. To gain is to steal from others. Thus peasants will not tolerate neighbors who acquire beyond what they themselves have. Because goods are limited, envy follows acquisition as surely as night follows day. Two things, then, are at stake in our discussion of John 3:25-30: 1) the *perception* of limited good, such that one's gain comes at another's expense, and 2) the reaction of envy to prevent this gain/loss.[12]

3.1 Cultural Illustrations of "Limited Good" in Greco-Roman Antiquity

While the notion of limited good was formulated by a modern scholar studying modern peasant societies, it has direct relevance for interpreting a host of ancient texts, both Greco-Roman and biblical.[13] These examples, once appreci-

---

10. George M. Foster, "The Anatomy of Envy: A Study in Symbolic Behavior," *Current Anthropology* 13 (1972): 169.

11. Foster, "Anatomy of Envy," 169.

12. This material has been successfully applied to aspects of ancient Greek culture; see Peter Walcot, *Envy and the Greeks: A Study in Human Behavior* (Warminster: Aris & Phillips, 1978) 22; David Cohen, *Law, Sexuality, and Society: The Enforcement of Morals in Classical Athens* (Cambridge: Cambridge University Press, 1991) 183-98; idem, *Law, Violence and Community in Classical Athens* (Cambridge: Cambridge University Press, 1995) 26, 63-70; J. Elster, "Norms of Revenge," *Ethics* 100 (1990): 862-85; John J. Winkler, "Laying Down the Law: The Oversight of Men's Sexual Behavior in Classical Athens," in *Before Sexuality: The Construction of Erotic Experience in the Ancient Greek World*, ed. David M. Halperin, John J. Winkler and Froma I. Zeitlin (Princeton: Princeton University Press, 1990) 174.

13. For a biblical example, see Richard L. Rohrbaugh, "A Peasant Reading of the Parable of the Talents: A Text of Terror?" *BTB* 22 (1993): 32-39.

ated, illustrate the presence of the concept in antiquity and thereby confirm the appropriateness of using an anthropological model for interpretation of biblical documents. Thus our argument is that ancient expressions of limited good can serve as interpretative parallels for understanding John 3:25-30.

We begin with an ancient saying of Iamblicus which fully expresses what we saw in regard to the attitude of John's disciples: "People do not find it pleasant to give honor *(timē)* to someone else, for they suppose that they themselves are being deprived of something."[14] Evidently, those described here ("people") perceive the world in the same way as do Foster's peasants: everything is limited, especially "honor," such that another's gain comes at one's own loss. Of course this naked quotation tells us nothing of the reaction of those who are "deprived of something"; but since this gain is perceived as an injury or insult of some sort, the common social reaction would likely be anger and/or envy to stop the loss and restore the former balance.

Plutarch (*On Listening to Lectures* 44B) describes a situation of "limited good" when he remarks that some persons hear a speaker and react in envy at his success: "As though commendation were money, he feels that he is robbing himself of every bit that he bestows on another."[15] Here again the issue is one of reputation or respect, and the perspective is that of "limited good." Another's gain means "robbery" of oneself. While Plutarch does not say that this situation results in agonistic behavior, it remains a distinct possibility. In another place (*Old Men in Public Affairs* 787D) Plutarch states: "And whereas men attack other kinds of eminence and themselves lay claim to good character, good birth, and honour, as though they were depriving themselves of so much of these as they grant to others." Obviously honor is to be both sought and defended. But a pattern is also emerging here: a grant of honor to another means depriving oneself of honor in equal measure. The perspective is one of "limited good," and agonistic reactions would likely follow.

In a number of places Josephus also describes situations that presume some sort of perception of "limited good." First, when he describes the envy of John, son of Levi, at his own rise in fortune, he comments:

> ... believing that my success involved his own ruin, he gave way to immoderate envy. Hoping to check my good fortune by inspiring hatred of me in those under my command, he tried to induce the inhabitants of Tiberias, Sepphoris, and Gabara — the three chief cities of Galilee — to abandon their

---

14. *Anonymus Iamblici* in H. Diels, *Die Fragmente der Vorsokratiker,* ed. W. Kranz (5th edition; Berlin: Weidmannsche Buchhandlung, 1935) 2.400.

15. All translations are from the Loeb Classical Library (Cambridge: Harvard University Press).

"He Must Increase, I Must Decrease" (John 3:30)

allegiance to me and go over to him, asserting that they would find him a better general than I was. (*Life* 25)

The issue is once again honor or reputation, and the perception is again that of "limited good." Josephus's "success" meant John's "ruin." The result was "envy" and an attempt by John to win back what he saw Josephus as taking from him.

In another place Josephus reports how Herod demanded that his sons be treated each according to his particular honor, because to give honor unfairly to one son was to take it unjustly from a deserving son: ". . . let the honours you award them be neither undeserved nor unequal *(anōmalos)*, but proportioned to the rank of each; for in paying deference to any beyond the deserts of his age, you gratify him less than you grieve the one whom you slight" (*War* 1.23.5). Once more, the focus is honor and the perception that of "limited good": the deference given one son is seen as another's loss. Feuding among the royal sons is sure to follow in an attempt to redress the perceived wrong.

Josephus's account of Moses' peril clearly reflects his own appreciation of "limited good" (*Ant.* 2.11.1). Even as certain Egyptian nobles urged Pharaoh to put Moses to death, "He [Pharaoh] on his own part was harbouring thoughts of so doing, alike from Moses' generalship and from fear of seeing himself abased, and so, when instigated by the hierarchy, was prepared to lend a hand in the murder of Moses." As we have come to expect, honor is the "limited good": Pharaoh perceived that Moses' reputation came at his own expense ("fear of seeing himself abased"), and the appropriate envious reaction was to kill Moses and thus restore himself to prominence.

Finally, in Josephus's account of Korah's revolt (*Ant.* 4.2.4), he comments: "It were monstrous that Korah, in coveting this honour, should deprive God of the power of deciding to whom He would accord it." Not accidentally the issue is over "honor," and the perception, at least of Josephus, is that of "limited good": Korah's acquisition of status and honor in this regard comes at God's expense. The deity must and will respond to this threat.

In one place, Philo contrasts people of insight with those with mere earthly vision (*Drunkenness* 28). The wise and all-seeing soul, he says, stretches toward God and interprets created things as benefactions of God; moreover, he honors God as the only Cause of these material benefactions. In contrast, the man of undiscerning vision, whose eye is blinded, does not perceive the Cause at all, but considers material benefits as causes of what he hopes to receive. Hence, he worships many gods, building idols of stone and wood. Philo then makes a claim that relates this material to his perception of "limited good": "Polytheism creates atheism in the souls of the foolish, and God's honour is set at naught by those who deify the mortal . . . they even allowed irrational plants and animals to share in the honour which belongs to things imperishable" (*Drunkenness* 28). As we have come to see, "honor" — in this case, God's honor — is proportionately diminished as more creatures are honored as gods; the honor of the imperishable God wanes insofar as honor is given to perishable beings. It is clear, therefore, that there is only so much honor in the cosmos, and when honor is unworthily given to some, it diminishes the legitimate honor of others. For this reason Philo labels the just honoring of God as *hosiotēs*, but the improper honoring of creatures *asebeia*.

Fronto's letter to Marcus Aurelius provides another striking illustration of the phenomenon we are investigating. Fronto begins by comparing Orpheus's ability to charm "sheep and doves with wolves and eagles" with that of a political leader who gathers together different nations endowed with diverse characteristics. Orpheus's following, nevertheless, lived sociably together in unity and concord, "the gentle with the fierce, the quiet with the violent, the meek with the proud, the sensitive with the cruel." While Fronto exhorts the emperor to the same achievement, he concedes that at court the emperor faces "a far harder task than to charm with the lyre the fierceness of lions and wild beasts." His endeavors, then, should be focused on this: "Set yourself to uproot and utterly stamp out one vice of mutual envy and jealousy among your friends, that they may not, when you have shown attention or done a favor to another, *think that this is so much taken from or lost to themselves*. Envy among men is a deadly evil and more fatal than any, a curse to enviers and envied alike."[16] The stage is the imperial court, where clients seek the emperor's patronage, thus competing and climbing the fragile ladder of honor and shame. Despite the fact that Fronto talks about imperial elites and not peasants, the social perception is the same as it was in Philo and Josephus: all things are limited, and the success of one is perceived as another's loss. However a new element emerges here: the explicit remark that envy follows the perception of another's success. That is so because all are grasping for the same prize. All seek a high reputation in the eyes of their peers.

3.2 Israelite and Christian Illustrations of Limited Good

At this point we turn from the Greco-Roman world to examine some of the evidence in the Hebrew and Christian scriptures. The story of Esau's lost blessing in Gen. 27:30-40 provides a good starting place. Esau returns from hunting and

---

16. Fronto, *Correspondence of Marcus Cornelius Fronto* 4.1, as cited in Stanley K. Stowers, *Letter Writing in Greco-Roman Antiquity* (Philadelphia: Westminster, 1986) 81-82.

"He Must Increase, I Must Decrease" (John 3:30)

asks his father's blessing. But as a result of Jacob's deceit, Isaac has already blessed his younger son. Thus, when Esau returns and Isaac truly recognizes him, he is distraught. Esau pleads, "Bless me, me also, father!" But Isaac cannot. There is only one blessing and it is already distributed. So too are the servants, grain, and wine that go with it and sustain it. Esau's second plea (27:38) to his agitated father is even more telling. It makes clear the limited nature of the good: "Have you only one blessing, father?" Indeed he does. Esau receives a curse instead.

When Gideon and his army were prepared to go into battle, the Lord said to him: "The people with you are too many for me to give the Midianites into their hand, lest Israel vaunt themselves against me, saying, 'My own hand has delivered me'" (Judges 7:2). The point of view is that of the person who stands to lose honor by the actions of another. The deity perceives that if Gideon wins the victory with a large army, the likely result is the rise of Gideon's reputation as a great warrior and Israel's reliance on him. This, it is implied, comes at God's expense. Hence the command is given to reduce Gideon's troops by two-thirds so that the victory will remain with God.

Similarly, David was returning to Saul from "slaying the Philistine" and was acclaimed in city after city by women who came out "singing and dancing, with timbrels, with songs of joy, and with instruments of music." And they sang: "Saul has slain his thousands, and David his ten thousands" (1 Sam 18:6-7). The narrative states that when Saul heard this, he was "very angry, and this saying displeased him, 'They have ascribed to David ten thousands, and to me they have ascribed thousands; and what more can he have but the kingdom?'" (18:8). This represents a classic situation of the birth of envy. Saul, like so many other figures we have seen, perceives that David's success comes at his own expense. Moreover, the issue continues to be one of honor, in this case a reputation for military valor and success. Obviously Saul calculates that David will not be satisfied with this honor but will in time aim to have Saul's very throne: "What more can he have but the kingdom?" Thus from that time on, we are told, "Saul eyed David,"[17] indicating that he continued to interpret David's every plan or success as wounding his own honor.

Next we turn to Mark's account of Jesus' teaching in the synagogue of his home village (6:1-6//Matt 13:53-58; Luke 4:16-30).[18] His public act of speaking in so formal a setting as "the synagogue" at the most significant of times ("on the

---

17. This is almost certainly a reference to the evil eye, the essence of which is envy.
18. For a discussion of the Lukan version of the story in terms of honor and shame, see Richard L. Rohrbaugh, "Legitimating Sonship: A Test of Honor: A Social Science Study of Luke 4:1-30," in *Modelling Early Christianity*, ed. Philip F. Esler (London: Routledge, 1995) 183-97.

Sabbath") embodies a claim of qualification to do something that he apparently did not have prior to his departure. Now disciples follow him! Evidently Jesus has changed radically since he left Nazareth and has become a person of considerable stature and honor. But his public speech immediately provokes a negative reaction: "they were astonished."[19] In a string of questions the villagers voice their objections to Jesus' public behavior.[20] First, they call attention to what they find most offensive in Jesus, namely his newly found capabilities and the corresponding honor they bring him:

> Where did this man get all this?
> What is the wisdom given him?
> What mighty works are wrought by his hands? (6:2)

Evidently such actions would hardly be expected of a peasant artisan. They are perceived as increases in Jesus' status vis-à-vis his former neighbors. Such a quantum leap in honor is apparently processed via the perception of "limited good," which adequately explains the hostile reaction to Jesus. His gain is interpreted as their loss.

In antiquity, the chief cultural grounds for an individual's status are pegged to his kin, since a man's origin and birth ordinarily provide a reliable index of his worth for the rest of his life.[21] Hence, the question "where did he get all this?" implies that Jesus could not have gotten "wisdom" and "powers" from his family, who are ordinary peasants: "Is not this the carpenter, the son of Mary and brother of James and Joses and Simon and Judas, and are not his sisters with us?" (6:3). This means that their social location in the village environment is that of typically poor peasants and artisans.[22] Born of humble stock,[23] Jesus has no reason in their eyes to deserve any new honor. As an arti-

---

19. LSJ (517) translates the verb here *(exeplēssonto)* as connoting a sense of distance created by someone or something ("drive away from") or hostile reaction to something ("shocked" or "amazed"); BAGD (244) give as meanings for this verb "astound, overwhelm," sometimes with the sense of joy and at other times suggesting fear or fright.

20. For a study of questions as aggressive and challenging weapons, see Jerome H. Neyrey, "Questions, *Chreiai,* and Challenges to Honor: The Interface of Rhetoric and Culture in Mark's Gospel," *CBQ* 60 (1998): 657-81.

21. Ancient rhetoric of praise and blame and the progymnastic exercise called the encomium both indicate how offspring were ascribed the same social status as their parents and ancestors; for examples of this, see Bruce J. Malina and Jerome H. Neyrey, *Portraits of Paul: An Archaeology of Ancient Personality* (Louisville: Westminster John Knox Press, 1996) 23-27, 92-93, 158-60; Jerome H. Neyrey, *Honor and Shame in the Gospel of Matthew* (Louisville: Westminster John Knox Press, 1998) 37-40, 78-80, 91-101.

22. See George W. Buchanan, "Jesus and the Upper Class," *NovT* 7 (1964): 195-209.

23. We must not forget the humble status of "Nazareth," as voiced by Nathaniel in John

san he received no schooling (John 7:15),[24] and so the qualifications for his public voice in the village synagogue remain uncertain. And yet here he is enjoying a most favorable and increasing reputation. Jesus' increase in respect throughout Galilee lifts him high above his village peers, a situation which his neighbors perceive as an intolerable and unbalancing force that means their corresponding loss of honor in proportion to Jesus' gain.[25] Although the term "envy" does not appear here, the complete recipe for it is present, as we shall shortly see.

What do people do who perceive a serious imbalance in the zero-sum game of honor and status? Luke concludes his version of the Nazareth episode with an attempt on Jesus' life (Luke 4:29). Resort to violence is an open admission of loss.[26] Matthew and Mark both record a hostile reaction, although not life-threatening: "they took offense at him." In short, they deny his claim to public voice; they attempt to cut him down to size. Jesus has the final word, quoting a common proverb that "A prophet is not without honor except in his own country and in his own house." Granted that Jesus' remark is a generic sort of maxim that is sufficiently broad to apply to many situations, nevertheless it does have to do with role and status ("prophet"), honor, and peer envy, items regularly found in a "limited good" perspective. We do not think it far from the mark to translate Jesus' remark as "a person of distinction [prophet] lacks no acknowledgment of his role/status [honor] except in situations of 'limited good,' where his closest associates and relatives [in his own country and in his own house] perceive themselves as losing honor precisely as his increases."[27]

1:46; on the degree to which the city of one's birth can contribute to an individual's status and reputation, see Malina and Neyrey, *Portraits of Paul*, 113-24, 131-32; Neyrey, *Honor and Shame in the Gospel of Matthew*, 91-97; Jerome H. Neyrey, "Luke's Social Location of Paul: Cultural Anthropology and the Status of Paul in Acts," in *History, Literature, and Society in the Book of Acts*, ed. Ben Witherington (Cambridge: Cambridge University Press, 1996) 251-79.

24. In the encomium and other rhetorical sources, a person's education was routinely noted; no student could hope to match, much less surpass, his teacher; but at least the reputation and honor of the teacher would become the source of the disciple's ascribed honor. See Neyrey, *Honor and Shame in the Gospel of Matthew*, 8-9, 80, 102-4.

25. All of the Gospel writers repeatedly anticipate and counteract negative responses to Jesus because of his low status at birth. For a discussion of the strategies each Gospel writer uses in addressing this problem, see Richard L. Rohrbaugh, "Locating Jesus: Strategies for Persuasion" in *The Early Christian World*, ed. Philip F. Esler (London: Routledge, 2000) 85-101.

26. Rohrbaugh, "Legitimating Sonship," pp. 185-86.

27. Evidently Jesus' remark in Matt. 13:57 is a rhetorical *sententia* or maxim; its success in this *chreia* rests on its being a common explanation of the phenomenon we are observing, namely peer envy based on a perception of limited good. For Hellenistic parallels see M. Eugene

In Mark's Gospel we find several other stories that reflect the perception of limited good. In the story about the Canaanite woman (Mark 7:24-30), Jesus first refuses her request, saying: "Let the children first be fed, for it is not right to take the children's bread and throw it to the dogs." The plain meaning of his words states that there is only so much bread, and it belongs to the "children." To give any to the dogs means that the children's share will necessarily shrink. But the woman argues in response that "even the dogs under the table eat the children's crumbs." She effectively neutralizes the limited good perspective by stating that she is not encroaching on the children's portion (bread), but wishes to share in that part of the portion that has always been fed to dogs (the bread crumbs). The story depends on the audience understanding "limited good" to grasp both Jesus' words and the woman's argument.

In Mark's Gospel we also hear John the son of Zebedee reporting to Jesus about a situation that resembles the dialogue between John the Baptizer and his disciples. John and others saw a man who was not a disciple use Jesus' name in successfully casting out a demon (9:38), and they forbade him. Jesus' disciples evaluate what they observe in terms of some notion of "limited good," and so the focus is on the "name" of Jesus and the honor that this non-disciple gains. His success means that Jesus (and his disciples, of course) suffers some corresponding loss; and to stanch this flow, the disciples "forbade him." Jesus, however, does not perceive the incident in terms of "limited good" and in turn criticizes the disciples' actions: "Do not forbid him." Far from being a proclamation of tolerance,[28] Jesus' words admit of a different interpretation, namely, that Jesus continues to gain an honorable reputation when another uses his name. When and until this other person speaks ill of Jesus, the Teacher experiences a net gain in honor. What is clear is that the disciples evaluate the episode in terms of "limited good," seeing the exorcist's success coming at their and Jesus' expense. Jesus does not contradict the evaluation of "limited good" so much as indicate that currently he and his disciples continue to experience a net gain in honor. Hence, "do not forbid him" indicates that Jesus does not feel envy and thus hostility.

One further example from Mark 10:35-45 concludes our survey of parallel materials. Two disciples who are already prominent among the Twelve (Mark 5:37; 9:2) approach Jesus and request further special favors. They wish "to sit at his right hand and his left hand in his glory" (10:37). Today we consider some-

---

Boring, Klaus Berger, and Carsten Colpe, *Hellenistic Commentary to the New Testament* (Nashville: Abingdon Press, 1995) 96, and for Israelite parallels see Joseph A. Fitzmyer, *The Gospel According to Luke* (Garden City: Doubleday, 1981) 527-28.

28. See D. A. Nineham, *Saint Mark* (Baltimore: Penguin Books, 1963) 253; and C. F. D. Cranfield, *The Gospel According to Mark* (Cambridge: Cambridge University Press, 1959).

one at the right hand of the boss to have extraordinary status; so also was that true in antiquity. Psalm 110:1 states it quite clearly: "The Lord said to my Lord: 'Sit at my right hand.'" Thus James and John have asked for a truly unique honor. However Jesus persuades them to accept his new calculus of honor, which is "the cup" of sufferings that he will drink and the "baptism" of his passion and death. Instead of receiving what they asked for, James and John are given the honor of sharing Jesus' fate.

But the damage has been done. The other ten disciples hear of the request and react in anger. Their reaction makes perfect cultural sense in terms of "limited good" because, if James and John were to receive the honor status they requested, there would be little or no special honor left for them. The success of two would come at the expense of ten. Thus the ten understand that the request of James and John will hurt themselves. Moreover, the indignation and anger with which they react was understood as the appropriate emotional response to a sense of injury. The episode, we are told, does not escalate into a situation of envy and agonistic behavior because Jesus intervenes (10:42-45). But all the elements of a battle born of "limited good" perceptions are present.

Yet as Jesus did with James and John (10:38-40) he now does with all of the Twelve (10:43-45). He redefines honor such that "limited good" makes no sense. He criticizes positions of power and status by reminding the Twelve that people in such situations despoil those below themselves. In his circle of disciples, Jesus states, the "great" one is the servant of the rest and the "first" person is the slave of all. Ambition for these particular status positions is acceptable, for no one loses anything; all gain. Jesus then concludes by presenting himself as an honorable example of what he is saying: "the Son of man came not to be served, but to serve, and to give his life as ransom for many."

In sum, the ancient illustrations of "limited good" we have examined exhibit the following traits. First, they all clearly indicate the perception of a zero-sum game in which one's success means another's failure. A causal connection is invariably perceived between the gains of one person and the losses of another. In addition, almost all of the illustrations indicate that the commodity being contested is "honor," that is, commendation by another, reputation, precedence, role and status, attention or favor from a high-ranking person. The result is that in most instances those who perceive themselves as losing because of another's success take hostile action to redress the imbalance. Sometimes active harm is done, including gossip and vilification, or murder or dismissal and disdain. Finally, many of the illustrations describe a situation of envy, a most important element in the social dynamics of ancient Greeks, Romans and Israelites. The data thus appear as follows:

Ancient Illustrations of Limited Good

Author and Work	Expression of "Limited Good"	Commodity in Dispute	Reaction, Especially Envy	Agonistic Redress
Iamblicus	clearly stated	honor	not mentioned	not mentioned
Plutarch: *Listening* 44B	clearly stated	honor	implied	not mentioned
Plutarch: *Old Men* 787D	clearly stated	honor	implied	attack
Josephus, *Life* 122-23	clearly stated	success, good fortune	immoderate envy	inspiring hatred and defection
Josephus, *Ant.* 4.32, 51	clearly stated	honor	not mentioned	divine judgment
Philo, *Drunkenness* 110	clearly stated	honor	not mentioned	not mentioned
Fronto, *Letters* 4.1	clearly stated	attention, favor	explicitly mentioned	"deadly and fatal"
Judg 7:2	clearly stated	honor	not mentioned	not mentioned
1 Sam 18:8-9	clearly stated	reputation, honor	implied	"eyed" David
Mark 6:1-5	implied	reputation, honor	implied	"took offense at him"
Mark 7:24-30	implied	patronage, honor	not mentioned	bestowed favor
Mark 9:38-41	implied	reputation, honor	implied	"they commanded him to stop"
Mark 10:35-45	implied	status, honor	implied	"they became angry at James and John"

4.0 "Limited Good" and Envy

Although only two of the passages discussed above explicitly state that "envy" follows the perception of "limited good," we assert that it is implied in all the others. We base this on our analysis of envy in the ancient world as well as our investigation of "limited good." Let us briefly examine envy in terms of five issues: 1) what is envy, 2) what is envied, 3) who envies whom, 4) how one envies, and 5) how one avoids envy.

1. In his analysis of the emotions speakers typically arouse, Aristotle (*Rhet.* 2.10.1) *defines envy* as "a kind of pain at the sight of [another's] good fortune," a distress which comes not from any effort to match the success of the person envied, but simply "because others possess it." Cicero (*Tusculan Disputations* 4.8.17) repeats this centuries later: "Envy is distress incurred by reason of a

neighbour's prosperity." In Plutarch's words (*On Being a Busybody* 518C), "Envy is pain at another's good." Envy, then, means pain or distress at another's success, a sense of being injured, which seeks redress.

2. The *object of envy* seems always to be "honor" in one of its manifestations. Rhetoricians declare that "success" *(eupragia)* is envied, a judgment verified by authors who describe the arousal of envy.[29] We suggest that whatever patronage someone received, wealth one acquired, status one enjoyed, reputation one earned, prowess one displayed, in short, the Greco-Roman contents of the cultural value of honor, caused the distress and pain which describe envy.

3. *Who envies?* Basically peers, as Aristotle (*Rhet.* 2.10.1) said: "Envy is defined as a kind of distress at the apparent success of one's peers." Cicero (*De Oratore* 2.52.209) echoes this: "People are especially envious of their equals, or of those once beneath them, when they feel themselves left behind and fret at the other's upward flight." Envy, we are told, also arises within families: "Kinship, too, knows how to envy" (Aristotle, *Rhet.* 2.10.5). Foster's excellent study of envy indicates that "every society designates those of its members who are deemed eligible to compete with each other for desired goals," that is, "conceptual equals."[30]

4. Although Cicero (*Tusculan Disputations* 4.8.17) states that envy does not always *translate into harmful behavior* toward the envied person, we find in numerous instances that it does.[31] When we ask how enviers typically envy, our research indicates six ways: 1) ostracism, 2) gossip and slander, 3) feuding, 4) litigation, 5) the evil eye, and 6) homicide.[32] Saul's "eyeing" David after he heard of "Saul's thousands and David's ten thousands" likely illustrates ocular malevolence,[33] which festered until Saul attempted to kill David. Jesus' endless contro-

---

29. Aristotle states that the "good fortune" *(eupragia)* of another occasions envy (*Rhet.* 2.10.1); Josephus describes in his *Life* how his personal success *(eupragia)* causes "immoderate envy" in others (122).

30. Foster, "Anatomy of Envy," p. 170.

31. The observation of Alvin W. Goulder (*Enter Plato* [New York: Basic Books, 1965] 57) is striking: "In one manner or another, Greece usually finds occasion to punish its greatest men — Aristides, Alcibiades, Anaxagoras, Cimon, Demosthenes, Phidias, Pericles, Themistocles, Xenophon — while Aeschylus and Euripides die in self-imposed exile. However novel Socrates' life in other respects, his fate at the hands of the Athenians is scarcely unique. G. C. Field remarks that by the fourth century B.C., 'one thing that strikes anyone . . . is the extraordinary sense of insecurity which all public men, orators and generals alike, must have felt. Hardly anyone of prominence escaped trial at some period of his career, and few avoided condemnation either to payment of a heavy fine, or even to death.'"

32. Anselm C. Hagedorn and Jerome H. Neyrey, "'It Was Out of Envy That They Handed Jesus Over' (Mark 15:10): The Anatomy of Envy and the Gospel of Mark," *JSNT* 69 (1998): 32-34.

33. In a series of studies on the "evil eye," John H. Elliott has made clear the presence and

versies with Pharisees and others represent feuding at its most savage level, for Jesus cannot say or do anything without incessant criticism and carping from his rivals. Likewise the various reactions to Jesus at Nazareth are examples of either ostracism (Mark and Matthew) or attempted homicide (Luke). Jesus' enemies spread slanderous gossip about his empty tomb (Matt 28:11-15).[34] And Jesus is the formal object of judicial proceedings before the Sanhedrin and the Roman procurator.[35]

5. *How does one avoid envy?* Foster's study indicates four ways to avoid envy: 1) concealment, 2) denial, 3) the "sop," and 4) true sharing.[36] If one does noble deeds in secret and hides one's prowess, then no one will know of any reason for feeling envy. But Jesus' mission is to proclaim the kingdom of God (Mark 1:14-15) in all the towns of Galilee (Mark 1:35-39), for which he must be as public as possible. Moreover, Jesus instructed his disciples in a parable about putting a lamp on a lampstand and not under a bushel (Mark 4:21-23), virtually prohibiting them from concealment, a strategy he himself followed.[37] Second, Jesus appears to use the strategy of "denial" when he refuses the compliment of the rich man, "Good Teacher, what must I do?" (Mark 10:17). He instructs this man "Why do you call me good? No one is good except the one God" (Mark 10:18). Third, a "sop" refers to some form of forced sharing of goods to placate a group likely to envy the success that earned the goods, such as the "liturgies" in an-

---

importance of this social phenomenon, which is generally related to envy. See "The Fear of the Leer: The Evil Eye from the Bible to Li'l Abner," *Forum* 4.4 (1988): 42-71; "Paul, Galatians and the Evil Eye," *CTM* 17 (1990): 262-73; "The Evil Eye in the First Testament: The Ecology and Culture of a Pervasive Belief," in *The Bible and the Politics of Exegesis*, ed. D. Jobling, G. Sheppard, and P. Day (Cleveland: Pilgrim Press, 1991) 147-59; "Matthew 20:1-15: A Parable of Invidious Comparison and Evil Eye Accusation," *BTB* 22 (1992): 52-65; "The Evil Eye and the Sermon on the Mount," *Biblical Interpretation* 2 (1994): 51-84.

34. For a study of gossip in the New Testament see Richard L. Rohrbaugh, "Gossip in the New Testament," *Social Scientific Models for Interpreting the Bible: Essays by The Context Group in Honor of Bruce J. Malina*, ed. John J. Pilch (Leiden: Brill, 2001) 239-59.

35. For a fuller account of the ways in which Jesus was envied in Mark, see Hagedorn and Neyrey, "It Was Out of Envy," 38-54.

36. Foster, "The Anatomy of Envy," 175-82; see also Hagedorn and Neyrey, "It Was Out of Envy," 36-38.

37. Yet it must be admitted that Mark contains some instances where Jesus seems to keep secret his presence (7:24) or his actions (1:44; 7:36). But these are significantly outweighed by commands to broadcast news about healings he has done (5:19-20) and by reports about him that circulate widely (1:28, 45; 2:1-2; 3:7-8; 4:1, etc.). Thus we do not wish to perpetuate the mistaken construct of a "messianic secret." See John Pilch, "Secrecy in the Mediterranean World: An Anthropological Perspective," *BTB* 24 (1994): 151-57; John Pilch, "Lying and Deceit in the Letters to the Seven Churches: Perspectives from Cultural Anthropology," *BTB* 22 (1992): 126-34. On prohibition of secrecy, see Matt 5:14-16.

cient Greece.[38] One can only speculate about the remarks in Mark 6:5-6 that Jesus "could not work any power there because of their unbelief." No possibility of sharing his benefaction of wisdom and power is available to Jesus, and it is odious to imagine that Jesus allowed himself to be a victim or to be pressured into buying off his critics. Jesus, then, offered no "sop" to avoid envy. Finally, the rich deposit of Markan references to Jesus' healing power and his lavish feeding of the multitudes argue that Jesus almost continually engaged in true sharing of God's benefaction. Thus, except for Jesus' refusal of the compliment in 10:17, he appears to have engaged in several of the classical strategies of avoiding envy.

We remarked earlier about the widespread prevalence of the perception of "limited good" in the ancient world. Now we argue that in the context of "limited good" envy is the logical and socially expected next step in the sequence of events that occur when the ancients perceive that another's gain means their own loss. This is expressed and clearly implied in the catalogue of materials that illustrate both the existence of a "limited good" perception in antiquity and lay bare its anatomy. This implies a continuous, conflictual social dynamics, which modern scholars label as an agonistic society.[39] For example, biblical scholars readily point out how the principal literary form of the Gospels, the *chreia*, embodies agonistic behavior.[40] The "responsive" type of *chreiai* typically begins with criticism of a sage's behavior and teaching or with a hostile question put to him. Thus provoked, the sage must respond with sharp wit. This native rhetorical form corresponds to what cultural anthropologists describe as situations of challenge and riposte, where the claims of some to honor (prowess, precedence,

---

38. See Friedrich Oertel, *Die Liturgie. Studien zur ptolemäischen und kaiserlichen Verwaltung ägyptens* (Leipzig: Teubner, 1917); N. Lewis, *The Compulsory Public Services of Roman Egypt* (Florence: Edizioni Gonnelli, 1983); S. R. Llewelyn, "The Development of the System of Liturgies," *NDIEC* 7 (1994): 93-111.

39. Jean-Pierre Vernant, *Myth and Society in Ancient Greece* (New York: Zone Books, 1988) 29-56; Peter Walcot, *Envy and the Greeks*, 52-76; and Gouldner, *Enter Plato*, 41-77; and now Cohen, *Law, Violence and Community*, 70-75, 90-101, 128.

40. Any student of *chreiai* in the Gospels is well aware of the agonistic setting of them. Some hostile remark, such as a criticism, or some aggressive question is put to a sage to challenge and possibly defeat him. See Ronald F. Hock and Edward N. O'Neil, *The* Chreiai *in Ancient Rhetoric*. Volume I: *The Progymnasmata* (Atlanta: Scholars Press, 1986); on Markan *chreiai* see Burton L. Mack and Vernon K. Robbins, *Patterns of Persuasion in the Gospels* (Sonoma, CA: Polebridge Press, 1989). Both Mack and Robbins have contributed individual essays on the *chreiai*: Burton Mack, *Anecdotes and Arguments: The Chreiai in Antiquity and Early Christianity* (Occasional Papers 10; Claremont, CA: Institute for Antiquity and Christianity, 1987); Vernon Robbins, "The Chreiai," in *Greco-Roman Literature and the New Testament*, ed. David E. Aune (SBLSBS 21; Atlanta: Scholars Press, 1988) 1-23; idem, "Pronouncement Stories and Jesus' Blessing of the Children," *Semeia* 29 (1983): 43-74.

power) are challenged, generally by a peer who finds the other's honor painful or distressing to himself.[41]

When one reads the narrative of Mark and identifies the responsive *chreiai* and their cultural shape as challenge-riposte episodes, it becomes clear that the narrative episodes in the story of Jesus contain a pervasive sense of antagonism, whether the reader analyzes them in terms of rhetoric as responsive *chreiai* or in terms of cultural anthropology as challenge-riposte exchanges. Thus, we conclude, there was a widespread perception of "limited good" by the ancients generally and by the characters of the Gospels specifically. This perception generally aroused envy in the perceiver, which frequently issued in hostile behavior to cut down to size the person perceived as gaining honor. This gives rise to the constant tension between claimants of honor and those who envy them that is typical of an agonistic society. These perceptions, the envy they arouse, and the agonistic behavior they give rise to are expressed in the ubiquitous rhetorical form of the responsive *chreiai*, an exercise taught even to young students. Thus both the model of social dynamics drawn from cultural anthropology and the forms of ancient rhetoric tell a similar story.

5.0 John 3:22-30 in Cultural Context

The materials we have just surveyed and the model of agonistic social dynamics that we have described can be brought to bear on John 3:22-30 with considerable profit. First, the *zētēsis* in which John's disciples are involved should be described as an envious reaction. They perceive the situation in terms of "limited good" in that they interpret Jesus' rise in reputation and fame as causing decrease in that of John the Baptist and thus their own. Their complaint that "all are going to him" means that fewer are flocking to John and so John is losing popularity. This perception, then, causes in them what is expected in that society: pain at another's good fortune and distress at his success. Since injury must be answered, they are poised to act out their envy in some hostile way.

That of course is exactly what happens in 11:45-52. There we get the culturally expected response when the perception of loss (limited good) leads to envy and eventually to hostile action. In 3:27-30, however, John stops the spiral of envy. He corrects one part of his disciples' perception when he declares that God is the source of Jesus' honor and success (3:27); human beings should in no way challenge God's sovereignty as benefactor. When God is gracious and causes an

---

41. See Hagedorn and Neyrey, "It Was Out of Envy," 43-46; see also Neyrey, "Questions, *Chreiai* and Challenges," 664-70.

"He Must Increase, I Must Decrease" (John 3:30)

increase, no fault accrues to the recipient of his favor. Thus John reminds his envious disciples that he himself has never felt injured or distressed by Jesus; in fact, his greatest honor has been to witness to Jesus (1:19-23).[42] In other words, he does not perceive the present situation in terms of "limited good," as do his disciples. Jesus' success means his own success as herald of or witness to the Lamb of God (1:29-34). Indeed, John himself pointed Jesus out to two of his disciples, who then heard and followed Jesus (1:35-39).[43] Evidently John was pleased that Jesus succeeded, even if it meant "loss" of two of his own disciples.

By way of the metaphor of a wedding party John totally denies any rivalry between himself and Jesus. John, the *philos* of Jesus the bridegroom, listens to the bridegroom's voice and "rejoices with joy" at it (3:29a). No pain at Jesus' good fortune here! No distress at his success! "My joy is now filled" (3:29b). If there is no perception of "limited good," then there is likewise no sense of pain or distress, nor is any envy aroused that leads to agonistic behavior. John, then, completely contradicts his disciples' perception of the situation.

John concludes his response to his disciples with an utterly counter-cultural remark: "He must increase, I must decrease" (v. 30). Most commentators read the "must" here as a statement of divine necessity, signaling God's will that Jesus increase.[44] This final remark repeats what John said earlier about the contentment that the *philos* should have at the bridegroom's taking of a wife. But it also addresses the heart of the cultural model we have been studying. Jesus' success in fact means that John's reputation and significance wanes. The fundamental perception of "limited good" is again validated, but in this case it does not lead to envy and hostility. In this way it is counter cultural. For John insists that he is not pained or distressed at Jesus' "increase." And so he readily surrenders his reputation and honor, which belong to Jesus by right. Rarely does one find in Greek or Israelite literature a public figure who willingly and peacefully allows his honor and prestige to diminish without envy and hostile reaction.[45] Therefore, it is only when readers appreciate the cultural perception

---

42. Morna Hooker ("John the Baptist and the Johannine Prologue," *NTS* 16 [1970]: 354-58) makes the case that John's primary role in John 1:6-8, 19-34 is to witness (*martyrein*) to Jesus, a role secondary to that of a reforming prophet with a special washing rite.

43. On John's active recruitment for Jesus, see Walter Wink, *John the Baptist in the Gospel Tradition* (Cambridge: Cambridge University Press, 1968) 91.

44. For example, Brown (*The Gospel According to John*, 1.146 and 153) likens the "must" in 3:14 to comparable expressions in the Synoptic passion narrative; the "must" in 3:30 has the same sense of divine necessity.

45. Speaking of marks of honor, Aristotle states: "And to take vengeance upon enemies and not to be reconciled; for to retaliate is just" (*Rhet.* 1.9.24). On the common expectation that hurts and injuries would be repaid, see Neyrey, *Honor and Shame in the Gospel of Matthew*, 203-5.

of "limited good," which leads to a sense of pain and distress and issues in envy, that they hear what the characters are saying and understand the strikingly unusual response of John to his disciples.

6

What's Wrong with This Picture?

John 4, Cultural Stereotypes of Women, and Public and Private Space

1.0 Introduction and State of the Question

For some, much is "wrong with this picture" of the Samaritan woman. Certain critics focus on marriage or sexual aspects of the story.[1] For example, they identify many double entendres regarding wells, living waters, and springs as metaphors for sexual intercourse.[2] These double entendres suggest that something is "wrong with this picture" in that the woman and Jesus appear to be engaged in a sexual game in violation of the cultural conventions for shame-guarding females in antiquity.

Others attend to "what is right with this picture."[3] Sometimes they focus on the role the woman plays in bringing the word about Jesus to her village, thus suggesting that she assumes the role of a "missionary" or "apostolic witness."[4] Conversely, they often argue that nothing is "wrong with this picture": the Samaritan woman should not be construed as a whore, nor should females be reduced to their sexuality; her "five husbands" need not be men in the village but false gods worshiped by the Samaritans.

---

1. Calum M. Carmichael, "Marriage and the Samaritan Woman," *NTS* 26 (1980): 332-46.

2. Lyle Eslinger, "The Wooing of the Woman at the Well: Jesus, the Reader and Reader-Response Criticism," *JLT* 1 (1987): 167-83.

3. Elizabeth Schüssler-Fiorenza, *In Memory of Her* (New York: Crossroad, 1984) 327-28; Turid Karlsen Seim, "Roles of Women in the Gospel of John," in *Aspects on the Johannine Literature*, ed. Lars Hartman and Birger Olsson (Coniectanea Biblica New Testament Series 18; Uppsala: Almqvist & Wiksell, 1987) 56-73; and Sandra M. Schneiders, *The Revelatory Text: Interpreting the New Testament as Sacred Scripture* (San Francisco: Harper, 1991) 186-94.

4. Raymond E. Brown, "Roles of Women in the Fourth Gospel," *TS* 36 (1976): 688-99.

Are the different readings of John 4 merely reflections of the gender of the commentators? It is easily verified that male critics tend to accentuate the sexual and marriage allusions in the story while feminist readers focus on aspects of the story with potential for elevating the status of Christian women. Nevertheless, if the aim of biblical criticism is the recovery of the communication of the sacred author, the conversation about John 4 must continue. As we become aware of the gender perspectives of authors ancient and modern, we should likewise take into account the cultural background of the ancient writer. Admittedly this ancient Mediterranean, pre-industrial cultural background might well clash with our modern Western, post-industrial world. And this will raise difficulties for contemporary males and females in their interpretation of biblical materials. But a full and honest reading of John 4 must take into account the ancient cultural expectations concerning males and females. Such cultural matters may even be part of the "good news" of the story.

When we recover the general cultural expectations concerning gender in antiquity, we must ask "what, if anything, is wrong or right about this picture in John 4?" In light of prevailing gender customs, does the author perceive a transgression of them in the story? What is the author's rhetorical stance toward this? A reimposition of gender rules? A transformation of them? Merely to point out how John 4 accords with or violates gender expectations is only part of this investigation. We must investigate what rhetorical stance the author takes in regard to this issue. What is needed, then, for a full conversation on John 4 is a more accurate description of the general cultural expectations for males and females in antiquity as the appropriate background of the narrative.

2.0 Hypothesis of This Study

We argue here that the basic rhetorical strategy in John 4 requires of us an appreciation of the cultural stereotypes of gender in the ancient world. Knowing this, as did the males and females in that world, we can observe with them how the author plays with "what's wrong with this picture?" Initially, from a cultural perspective, everything appears "wrong with the picture" in John 4: unrelated males and females are meeting in the "public" world at an unusual time of day. As we shall see, the ancients construed the world as radically gender divided: males in the "public" and females in the "private" world. Males in that culture, moreover, were expected to be sexually aggressive, whereas females were deemed virtuous in terms of their defense of their sexual exclusivity.[5] In John 4,

---

5. Bruce J. Malina and Jerome H. Neyrey, "Honor and Shame in Luke-Acts: Pivotal Values

all social taboos customarily separating males and females into separate worlds are systematically recognized, but broken and transformed. This upsetting of cultural taboos, moreover, is conscious and intentional; it constitutes an essential part of the communication of the author. We must, then, initially assess "what is wrong with this picture."

But finally, all may not be "wrong with this picture," if modern readers attend to several more pieces of the cultural background of John 4. First, the author intends the scenario described there to be perceived as the "private" world of kinship groups. It may be narrated as occurring "out of doors," but the encounters of Jesus and the woman (4:7-26) and the woman and the villagers (4:39-42) should ultimately be seen as the formation of fictive-kinship groups, and so they are governed by the customs of the "private," not the "public" world. Something, then, may take place "out of doors" and yet be "private," not "public." And thus nothing may be "wrong with this picture," if the space is understood by the characters as "private."

We recall the fact that the early church never attempted to form a "public" *ekklesia*, but gathered in households and modeled itself after the "private" institution of the family, household, and kinship group.[6] If the "private" world of the kinship group is what the author has in view, then nothing is "wrong with this picture." But this judgment will depend on whether we perceive the events as part of either the "public" or the "private" world.

Second, how are we to assess the male/"public" and the female/"private" worlds? Most of our ancient documents were written by males and often portray the "public" world positively; conversely, they view the "private" world as a less important arena. With our dearth of evaluations of the "private" world by females in antiquity, we are generally left with only one voice in the matter: the "public" is better than the "private" world. This viewpoint is reinforced in some modern discussions of the place of males and females in our world. In the eyes of many, the "private" world of today's household can mean second-class status for females, lack of respect for their talents, and numbing drudgery. Thus, if we argue that Jesus invited people into the "private" world of a kinship group, this might appear to some to be a reactionary statement, that Jesus would resist welcoming females into the "public" world. Such a view would misconstrue the narrative in John 4. There was no "public" Christian world for males or females.

---

of the Mediterranean World," in *The Social World of Luke-Acts: Models for Interpretation*, ed. Jerome H. Neyrey (Peabody, MA: Hendrickson, 1991) 40-44.

6. John H. Elliott, *A Home for the Homeless: A Social-Scientific Criticism of I Peter, Its Situation and Strategy* (Minneapolis: Fortress Press, 1990) 165-207; David C. Verner, *The Household of God: The Social World of the Pastoral Epistles* (SBLDS 71. Chico, CA: Scholars Press, 1983) 27-81.

All Christians met in "private" space and adopted the customs appropriate for households and kinship groups.[7]

What seems to be needed is a more culturally sensitive evaluation of the "public" and "private" worlds in antiquity. Some ancient writers reflect that the "public" world was characterized as an agonistic place where males engaged in constant honor challenges.[8] Hierocles, admittedly a male voice who may idealize the "private" world, questions the prevailing myth of the "public world":

> [T]hose gloomy circumstances of life which involve the forum or the gymnasium or the country or, in general, all our anxieties while we are occupied with our friends and spend time with our associates are at the time not obvious to us, since they are obscured by inevitable distractions.... But when a wife is present she becomes a great comfort in these circumstances by asking her husband about non-domestic matters or bringing up and considering together with him matters concerning the home, thus causing him to relax, and she cheers him up by her unaffected enthusiasm. (*On Duties, On Marriage* 5.22.21-24)

If nurturing, security, and mutuality for females and males can be found anywhere in antiquity, they are more likely to occur, not in the "public" world, but in the "private" world of kinship relationships. Thus, further appreciation of the "private" world of the fictive-kinship group may be necessary to appreciate what the author of John 4 is doing by welcoming the Samaritan woman into a new network of social relations.

We should, then, attend to the cultural clues in the narrative. To do this, we must re-create the cultural world of the author and begin to see things as he and other males and females saw them. In true reader-response criticism, how would ancient readers hear this story? What aspects of their culture are inextricably embedded in the narrative, which we of another culture cannot readily see? What do modern readers need to know of that culture to be informed and respectful tourists in another country?

That the ancients viewed the world and everything in it as radically gender divided implies consequent cultural expectations about honorable males and shame-respecting females. To grasp this, we need knowledge of the typical and

---

7. For a further development of the ancient cultural meanings of "public" and "private," see Jerome H. Neyrey, "Jesus, Gender and the Gospel of Matthew," in *New Testament Masculinities*, ed. Stephen D. Moore and Janice C. Anderson, *Semeia* 45 (2003): 43-66; idem, "Teaching You in Public and from House to House' (Acts 20:20): Unpacking a Cultural Stereotype," *JSNT* 26 (2003): 69-102.

8. Malina and Neyrey, "Honor and Shame in Luke-Acts," 35-38, 49-52.

ordinary cultural expectations about the behavior of males and females in antiquity. In short, we need to develop a stereotype of that gender-divided world. Implied in all of this is a clearer assessment of what constitutes a "private" world and what social dynamics are appropriate there.

3.0 Ancient Cultural Expectations: Gender Division of Society[9]

Cultural anthropologists argue that the ancient peoples of the eastern Mediterranean viewed all reality in terms of gender division, that is, in terms of honor and shame, especially as these applied to males and females. We examine, then, the ancient distinction between "public" and "private," with the attendant focus on the kinship network as the prime example of the "private" world.[10] We begin this by gathering and examining instances of the ancient *topoi* on the topic in which the cultural stereotypes of male and female are described.

3.1 Gender Commonplaces in Antiquity

Philo offers a clear summary of what we call a gender division of society. He distinguishes both male and female space as well as corresponding male and female tasks:

> Market-places and council halls and law-courts and gatherings and meetings where a large number of people are assembled, and open-air life with full scope for discussion and action — all these are suitable to men both in war and peace. The women are best suited to the indoor life which never strays from the house, within which the middle door is taken by the maidens as their boundary, and the outer door by those who have reached full womanhood. (*Spec.* 3.169)

The proper place for males is in public, doing public things, whereas females belong in private space. Although Philo does not spell out what women do "in private," in another place he comments on the popular perception of male and female physiology: "how unlike the bodily shapes of man and woman are, and

---

9. John Davis, "The Sexual Division of Labour in the Mediterranean," in *Religion, Power and Protest in Local Communities: The Northern Shore of the Mediterranean*, ed. Eric Wolf (New York: Moulton Publishers, 1984) 17-50.

10. An exposition of the numerous semantic terms used to label "public" vs. "private" may be found in Neyrey, "Teaching You in Public and from House to House," 75-83.

each of the two has a different life assigned to it, to the one a domestic, to the other a civic life" (Philo, *Virt.* 19). Thus we learn that females do tasks associated with private space or the domestic life ("the house"), namely, food preparation, clothing production, and child rearing.

Philo's description of the gender-divided world of antiquity is itself a first-century *topos* easily traced back to classical Greek writers, who themselves only reflect common opinion on the topic. Xenophon's summary is worth noting:

> [H]uman beings live not in the open air, like beasts, but obviously need shelter. Nevertheless, those who mean to win store to fill the covered place, have need of someone to work at the open-air occupations; since plowing, sowing, planting and grazing are all such open-air employments; and these supply the needful food. Then again, as soon as this is stored in the covered place, then there is need for someone to keep it and to work at the things that must be done under cover. Cover is needed for the nursing of the infants; cover is needed for the making of corn into bread, and likewise for the manufacture of clothing from the wool. And since both the indoor and the outdoor tasks demand labour and attention, God from the first adapted the woman's nature, I think, to the indoor and man's to the outdoor tasks and cares. (*Oeconomicus* 7.19-22)

Space is divided according to gender: males in "open air" space and females in "covered" space, males "without" and females "within." Their respective tasks are gender-divided as well: males work at "open-air occupations" such as plowing, sowing, grazing, etc. and females at "indoor occupations," such as child rearing, food preparation, and clothing production.

A third example of this commonplace illustrates how the ancients generally perceived the world divided according to cultural notions of gender:

> Before anything else I should speak about the occupations by which a household is maintained. They should be divided in the usual manner, namely, to the husband should be assigned those which have to do with agriculture, commerce, and the affairs of the city; to the wife those which have to do with spinning and the preparation of food, in short, those of a domestic nature. (Hierocles, *On Duties* 5.28.21ff.)

The world of the ancients, then, was divided according to cultural perceptions of gender into "male" and "female" space. In male space (marketplaces, public squares, open fields), males did male occupations, whereas in female space (houses, wells, ovens), females did female occupations. Objects, moreover, were likewise classified as male or female, depending on whether they were for "public" or "private" use: agricultural implements and weapons of war were male, whereas domestic implements, cooking utensils, and looms were female.[11] We must next ask about the implications of ascribing to females "private space" and how this contributes to a stereotype of ideal female behavior.

3.2 Private Space = Female Space

This commonplace in the gender division of the world invites a closer examination of female space. As noted above, females are perceived as part of the "private" world, that is, the house and spaces related to household duties, such as ovens and wells. From our research we have discovered a number of specific terms for male and female space; inasmuch as our interest here is with female space, we focus on the most common of these terms, *gynaikōnitis* or "women's quarters." What we learn from a series of examples aids our reconstruction of a stereotype of ideal female space and behavior in antiquity.

What, then, are the cultural expectations about a typical female space? The three *topoi* quoted above indicate that females are expected to dwell in "private" space, primarily their homes and secondarily places where female tasks are performed. But even in regard to homes or "private" space, Xenophon describes the typical household in which women's quarters are separated from men's and bolted to maintain that important cultural division: "I showed her the women's quarters too, separated by a bolted door from the men's quarters, so that nothing which ought not to be moved may be taken out, and that the servant may not breed without our leave" (Xenophon, *Oeconomicus* 9.5). He observes that male and female clothing is itself carefully separated and stored in its proper gender-specified place: "After that we put together the women's holiday finery, and the men's holiday and war garb, blankets in the women's quarters, blankets in the men's quarters, women's shoes, men's shoes" (*Oeconomicus* 9.6). Women's quarters might be on the second story of a house (Lysias, *On the Murder of Eratosthenes* 9) or in a part of the house guarded by a strong wall (Plutarch, *Sayings of the Spartans* 230C). Peasant houses were unlikely to have so defined a "women's quarter."

Infants and children were kept in these quarters. Plutarch describes how Charon's son resided in the women's quarters: "He brought his son from the women's apartments, a mere boy as yet, but in beauty and bodily strength surpassing those of his years" (*Pelopidas* 9.5). Lucian likewise describes the

---

11. Harry A. Hoffner, "Symbols for Masculinity and Femininity: Their Use in Ancient Near Eastern Sympathetic Magic Rituals," *JBL* 85 (1966): 326-34.

women's quarters as the place where children are raised: "You come in too, Micyllus, and dine with us. I'll make my son eat with his mother in the women's quarters so that you may have his room" (*The Cock* 11).

Our survey of this term for women's quarters indicates that it: 1) describes living arrangements of Greeks, Persians, Egyptians, Romans, and Israelites, albeit elites (see *War* 5.198-200, especially 199), and 2) covers at least the period from 400 B.C.E. through the first century C.E.

Cornelius Nepos indicates that gender expectations about females in the Greek East were modified somewhat in the Latin West, at least by some elite females:

> Many actions are seemly according to our code which the Greeks look upon as shameful. For instance, what Roman would blush to take his wife to a dinner-party? What matron does not frequent the front rooms of her dwelling and show herself in public? But it is very different in Greece; for there a woman is not admitted to a dinner-party, unless relatives only are present, and she keeps to the more retired part of the house called "the women's apartment" (*gynaeconitis*), to which no man has access who is not near of kin. (Cornelius Nepos, *praef.* 4-7)

In her recent book, Kathleen Corley discusses the prevailing cultural expectations concerning "private" women at "public" meals, the relaxation of those rules for elite Roman women, and the subsequent social reaction to those changes.[12] Although she focuses on the presence of women at meals, her data confirm the general stereotype of a gender-divided world described here. Appreciation of the cultural expectations for females in a gender-divided world should help us to grasp the intended shock in John 4 of a noonday meeting between Jesus and the woman in public space.

3.3 House and Household Tasks

Ancient discussions of female tasks tend to contrast what is proper to them with what is expected of males. Xenophon provides a useful example. Males, whose proper gender space is the "open air," do tasks appropriate to that space: "plowing, sowing, planting and grazing are all such open-air employments." But females, whose proper gender place is "covered," do the basic tasks which support the household: "Cover is needed for the nursing of the infants; cover is

---

12. Kathleen E. Corley, *Private Women, Public Meals: Social Conflict in the Synoptic Tradition* (Peabody, MA: Hendrickson, 1993) 24-66.

needed for the making of corn into bread, and likewise for the manufacture of clothing from the wool" (*Oeconomicus* 7.21).[13] The remark of Hierocles quoted above repeats the commonplace that males engage in public affairs whereas females "have to do with spinning and the preparation of food, in short, those of a domestic nature." The Mishnah likewise lists tasks appropriate to females (*Ketubot* 5.5; see also *Shabbat* 7.2).

3.4 Female Chastity, Shame-guarding, and Dealings with Males

One corollary of the gender division of space and labor is the inevitable separation of males and females who are not kin. Below is a sampler of the cultural expectations of females vis-à-vis males outside the household or kinship group. Although further historical studies are needed on the antiquity and pervasiveness of the veiling of females in public, Dio Chrysostom speaks about it as an ancient custom still valid in his time:

> Many of the customs still in force reveal in one way or another the sobriety and severity of deportment of those earlier days. Among these is the convention regarding feminine attire, a convention which prescribes that women should be so arrayed and should so deport themselves when in the street that nobody could see any part of them, neither of the face nor of the rest of the body, and that they themselves might not see anything off the road. (*Oration* 33.48-51)

The veil replicates the wall or barrier which spatially enclosed the "women's quarters" discussed above.

If the purpose of the veil was to keep men from gawking at women,[14] then one might expect that other strategies for separating the genders were intended to keep women not only out of the gaze of men, but out of their speech as well. Although Plutarch disagrees with Thucydides, he witnesses to the conventional view of that older historian:

> I do not hold the same opinion as Thucydides ["Great is your glory if you fall not below the standard which nature has set for your sex, and great also is hers of whom there is least talk among men whether in praise or blame" 2.45.2] that the best woman is she about whom there is least talk among per-

---

13. See Aristotle, *Oeconomica* 1.3.4, 1343b 30–1344a 9; Eva C. Keuls, *The Reign of the Phallus: Sexual Politics in Ancient Athens* (San Francisco: Harper and Row, 1985) 228–65.

14. Blake Leyerle, "John Chrysostom on the Gaze," *JECS* 1 (1993): 159–65.

sons outside. Regarding either censure or commendation, feeling that the name of the good woman, like her person, ought to be shut up indoors and never go out. (*In Praise of Women* 242E)

Yet even Plutarch notes other cultural norms concerning male talk about females:

But to my mind Gorgias appears to display better taste in devising that not the form but the fame of a woman should be known to many. Best of all seems the Roman custom, which publicly renders to women, as to men, a fitting commemoration *after the end of their life*. (*In Praise of Women* 242F, emphasis added)

We note the expectation that males will talk about the "form" of a female, with all its sexual overtones. Plutarch, however, would restrict any talk of a woman *until after her death*, when her sexual exclusivity cannot be threatened (see also Plutarch, *Camillus* 8.3.133A; Livy, *Ab Urbe Condita* 5.50.7; Cicero, *De Oratore* 2.11.44). But the general rule was: "There ought to be no random talk about fair and noble women, and their characters ought to be totally unknown save only to their consorts" (Plutarch, *Sayings of the Spartans* 217F). And again, "In regard to a woman's endowments, there should be absolutely no talk among those outside the family" (220D). Since female sexual exclusivity was a primary value in the ancient gender-divided world, whatever kept women from seduction or the mere threat of it was valued and became constitutive of the stereotype of the ideal female and her proper place and behavior. How anomalous, then, would seem the triple mention of the Samaritan woman's sexual "past" in the presence of males not her kin (John 4:16-18, 29, 39).

3.5 Female Public Silence

If it is deemed shameless for a male to talk about a female not of his kinship circle, it goes without saying that females should not speak to unrelated males, especially in public space.[15] This aspect of the gender expectations of females seems to be true of Rome as well as Greece and for all periods of history. "What have women to do with a public assembly? If old-established custom is preserved, nothing" (Valerius Maximus, *Factorum et Dictorum Memorabilium* 3.8.6; see Philo, *Spec.* 3.174).

---

15. M. I. Finley, "The Silent Women of Rome," in his *Aspects of Antiquity: Discoveries and Controversies* (New York: The Viking Press, 1968) 129-42. See also Ramsey MacMullen, "Women in Public in the Roman Empire," *Historia* 29 (1980): 208-18.

What's Wrong with This Picture?

For females to speak with unrelated males in public spaces would be interpreted as "putting on men's airs," as Plutarch notes:

> [T]heir women, it is said, were too bold, putting on men's airs with their husbands even, to begin with, since they ruled their houses absolutely, and besides, on public occasions, taking part in debate and the freest speech on the most important subjects. But Numa, while carefully preserving to the matrons that dignified and honourable relation to their husbands which was bestowed on them by Romulus . . . enjoined great modesty upon them, forbade them all busy intermeddling, taught them sobriety, and accustomed them to be silent; wine they were to refrain from entirely, and were not to speak, even on the most necessary of topics, unless their husbands were with them. (Plutarch, *Lycurgus and Numa* 3.5)

The flip side of this cultural prescription of female silence in public is found in the stereotype of ancient females as gossips and busybodies. Juvenal provides a convenient example of this derogatory stereotype:

> Better that your wife should be musical than that she would be rushing boldly about the entire city, attending men's meetings, talking with unflinching face and hard breasts to Generals in their military cloaks, with her husband looking on! This same woman knows what is going on all over the world: what the Chinese and Thracians are after, what has passed between the stepmother and the stepson; she knows who loves whom, what gallant is the rage; she will tell you who got the widow with child, and in what month; how every woman behaves to her lovers, and what she says to them . . . she picks up the latest rumors at the city gates, and invents some herself. (*Satires* 6.398-409)

The cultural expectation of female silence in public should provide modern readers with an adequate scenario for assessing the potential impropriety of the conversation between the Samaritan woman and Jesus, as well as her subsequent colloquy with the men of the village.

3.6 The Stereotype: Context, Constancy, and Validity

It goes against the grain for historically trained commentators to deal with stereotypes,[16] for the prevailing scholarly paradigm instructs us to look at what is

---

16. Peter Burke, *Sociology and History* (London: George Allen and Unwin, 1980) 13-14.

unique and different. Yet study of cultural stereotypes should have an important place in the study of a culture which itself relies on commonplaces, *topoi, gnōmai, sententiae,* doxographies, and other types of summary statements. Edward Hall, moreover, has called our attention to cultures where stereotypes play an important role. He distinguishes between "low context" and "high context" societies.[17] "Low context" societies, such as the industrial West, produce detailed texts which spell out matters in considerable detail and leave little to the imagination. One thinks of legal contracts with all their fine print. "High context" societies, however, produce sketchy texts, leaving much to the reader's imagination. For example, 2 Sam 11:1 mentions kings going out to war in the spring and thus presumes knowledge of a culture which divides the year into rainy and dry seasons. Kings go out to war after the late rains. So, too, with gender expectations. They are presumed as part of the cultural context. It is, then, an appropriate piece of historical and critical inquiry to ask about general cultural expectations, especially in regard to one of the prime values (honor and shame) and its structural implications (gender division of society).[18]

In brief, all reality was divided according to gender. Males belonged in public places, performing male tasks, using male instruments and animals. Females belonged in private places, attending to female tasks, and using female implements. Cultural notions of honor and shame dictated that males be sexually aggressive, but that females be shame-conscious and defensive of their sexual exclusivity.[19] Hence, all intercourse between non-related males and females should be viewed with suspicion and rigorously controlled.

Although historians note some relaxation of these rules in Rome during the late republic, it is safe to say that the cultural expectations regarding females remained constant throughout antiquity, in particular in villages and towns,

---

17. Edward T. Hall, *Beyond Culture* (Garden City, NY: Doubleday, 1976) 91-101; idem, *The Dance of Life: The Other Dimensions of Time* (Garden City, NY: Doubleday, 1983) 59-77.

18. Maureen J. Giovannini, "Female Chastity Codes in the Circum-Mediterranean: Comparative Perspectives," in *Honor and Shame and the Unity of the Mediterranean,* ed. David D. Gilmore (American Anthropological Association special publication 22; Washington: American Anthropological Association, 1987) 61-74.

19. The same public-private distinction was applied to the respective male-female genitals. Herophilus and Galen testify to the ancient belief that male and female genitals were classified as "public" and "private." Although it was argued that male and female sexual organs are similar, the difference was significance: male genitals are outside the body, whereas female genitals are within the body. Thus Galen writes: "All the parts, then, that men have, women have too, the difference between them lying in only one thing... namely, that in women the parts are within the body, whereas in men they are outside, in the region called the perineum" (*Usefulness of the Parts of the Body* 14.6). External vs. internal classification of the genitals, then, replicates the larger stereotype of a gender-divided world.

where gender expectations hardly changed. Furthermore, what was expected of elite, urban females was likewise expected of non-elite, rural females insofar as space and wealth allowed. The very documents of the New Testament, which are *klein Literatur* or non-elite documents, witness to the pervasiveness of gender expectations among urban artisans and village peasants (e.g., 1 Cor 14:33-35; 1 Tim 2:11-15; 5:10-14). The stereotype, then, can be said to have validity for Greeks and Romans and Israelites as well as elites and non-elites.

4.0 What's Wrong with This Picture?

From the perspective of stereotypical female behavior for this cultural world we initially ask "What's wrong with this picture?"

4.1 Time and Place (4:6-7)

Jesus encountered the woman "at the sixth hour," which was roughly midday.[20] This seemingly innocuous detail, however, indicates that the woman came to the well at an unusual hour — for females, that is. Women at wells were a common phenomenon, since water was needed for cooking, but they came only at certain hours, namely, morning or evening (Gen 24:11; see Gen 29:7). Midday is a culturally "wrong" time for females to be at a well for domestic purposes. The woman, moreover, appears not to be in the company of other women, as would have been the custom (see 1 Sam 9:11).

What's wrong with this picture? 1) She comes alone at an unusual hour 2) to a place, which, when many women are gathered, is gender appropriate, but at midday and alone would suggest deviance on her part. The anomalous time, her isolation, and the public nature of the well at midday suggest that she has been shunned by the women of the village for some behavior (4:16-18), and so she acts alone when other women are dutifully at work elsewhere.

4.2 Speech with a Strange Man in Public (4:7-26)

The characters themselves tell us how strange this encounter appears. The woman remarks to Jesus: "How is it that you, a Judean, ask a drink of me, a Samaritan woman?" (4:9). The narrator dilates on this issue with the aside, "For

---

20. Norman Walker, "The Reckoning of Hours in the Fourth Gospel," *NovT* 4 (1960): 69-73.

Judeans have no dealings with Samaritans" (4:9). But more is at stake than ethnic differences. When the disciples return from the village and see Jesus conversing with this female, they react with astonishment: "They marveled that he was talking to a woman" (4:27a). Their shock lies in the fact that a male and a female were conversing alone in public.[21] The narrator then voices the questions that should have been asked, but were not, by the characters: "but none said, 'What do you (Jesus) wish with her? or 'Why are you talking with her?'" (4:27b). The questions are there nonetheless, because the encounter of Jesus and the woman at face value suggests improper behavior.

What were Jesus and the woman talking about? Although it is not the whole of their dialogue, they spoke considerably about the woman's lack of sexual exclusivity, i.e., her shamelessness. When Jesus told her to go and call her husband, she responded that she had no husband (4:17a), when in fact she had had five husbands already. So we learn that she is no maiden, but a sexually seasoned woman. Her current male companion is *not* her husband and so has no responsibility to guard her shame or to defend her sexual exclusiveness, which is the only basis for her honor in the village. Although she might have been widowed five times (see Mark 12:20-23), her current non-marital relationship with a sixth male suggests either adultery or concubinage. In any case, she clearly lacks the exclusivity upon which her reputation and honor depend in a gender-divided world. Moreover, when the woman recounts her conversation with Jesus back in the village, she focuses on one point only, his remark about her sexual history: "Come and see a man who told me everything I have ever done" (4:29). The villagers were impressed with her testimony that "He told me everything I have ever done" (4:39), which can only refer to Jesus' remarks in 4:17-18 about the six men in her life. The author insists on keeping the lack of sexual exclusivity before his audience. What, then, is wrong with this picture? It is bad enough that a female is conversing with an unrelated male in a public place at an unusual hour. Worse, the reader is told repeatedly the most significant item in her conversation with Jesus is his remark on her shameless sexual behavior.[22]

4.3 Speech with Other Men in Public Space (4:28-30)

Although Jesus commands her to go and call her husband (4:16), she goes into the village marketplace where all the men are gathered. She does not go to her

---

21. Seim, "The Roles of Women in the Gospel of John," 59.
22. Mary Margaret Pazdan, "Nicodemus and the Samaritan Woman: Contrasting Models of Discipleship," *BTB* 17 (1987): 145-48.

own house, nor does she bring her water jar home (4:28). House-to-house canvassing seems highly unlikely, since she seems to the women in the village to be a sexual pariah. The narrative does not say "marketplace," but from our knowledge of that culture, it would be culturally accurate in imagining males gathered together in an open-air space, such as a marketplace (see Philo and Hierocles, cited above). She does not return to private space at all, but goes into public space, to the one place where males could be expected to congregate. From our knowledge of the gender division of space, females should not be present in this public space when males are there. Rather they should be with the other females of the household attending to household matters in appropriate private space.

Moreover, this woman speaks to these males and tells them of her conversation with another man, a Judean stranger. And as we noted above, she tells the village males that this new male knew about her sexual shamelessness, "all that I ever did" (4:29, 39). What, then, is wrong with this picture? Absolutely everything. The details of this narrative are at odds with the commonly expected behavior of shame-guarding females in the ancient world of honor and shame. And as vv. 9 and 27 indicate, even the characters in the narrative are aware of these breaches of gender rules. So the readers and hearers are carefully reminded of the impropriety of the conversation. The story loses its power and punch if these critical details are ignored and dismissed.

4.4 Other Women at Wells: A Comparison (Conventions Confirmed)

A comparison of John 4 with other narrative scenes at wells confirms that we should attend to cultural customs regarding females in this context. Hall's remarks on "low context" are appropriate here, for much is presumed concerning women at wells. The Old Testament narrates three scenes of males and females meeting at wells (Gen 24:10-49; 29:4-14; Exod 2:15-22), and the *Protoevangelium of James* (11:1) records another. In all of these, the narrators present prospective brides either to their husbands or their agents. And since the key element of a worthy wife is virginity or sexual exclusivity, the narratives all make a point that the social intercourse at the well is strictly in accord with cultural customs.[23] The females are shy, obedient, and defensive of their virtue; they speak respectfully to the males and obey when commanded; they seek the shelter of the "private" world as soon as possible. In short, the narratives record that everything is "right with this picture." Yet from other sources we know that females risked

---

23. Robert Alter, *The Art of Biblical Narrative* (New York: Basic Books, 1981) 51-58.

being molested at wells.[24] These data confirm that scenes of females at wells normally contained a sexual component which required viewers to attend to what was "wrong" or "right" about the picture.

5.0 The Rhetorical Shape of the Narrative

Feminist scholars pay close attention to rhetorical criticism, by which they mean the ideological context of authors and their intent.[25] What, then, is the rhetorical stance of the author of John 4 in regard to "what's wrong with this picture"? The narrator recounts the dialogue part of the story (4:7-26) in terms of a recurring pattern characteristic of this Gospel, namely, "statement . . . misunderstanding . . . clarification."[26] Jesus makes a statement, which is misunderstood, but that leads him to speak again in clarification. This dialogue may function either as an invitation, so that addressees are led to insight and so to a change of status as "insiders" (4:6-15; 11:20-27), or as a distancing mechanism, so that addressees are proven to be ignorant and blind and so are confirmed as "outsiders" (3:1-21) who experience no status transformation. Some significant examples are:

Statement	Misunderstanding	Clarification
3:3	3:4	3:5
6:41	6:42	6:43-48
8:21	8:22	8:23-30
11:11	11:12	11:13-15
12:27-28	12:29	12:30
14:4	14:5	14:6

5.1 John 4:7-15

The pattern functions here as an invitational dialogue describing how the Samaritan woman is progressively enlightened and experiences a change of status from radical "outsider" to "insider." The pattern here has a cyclical movement, in that Jesus' "clarification" of the woman's "misunderstanding" serves

---

24. See *Mishnah Ketubot* 1.10; Aristophanes, *Lysistrata* 327-31; see Keuls, *The Reign of the Phallus*, 235-40.
25. Schneiders, *The Relevatory Text*, 185.
26. Jerome H. Neyrey, *An Ideology of Revolt: John's Christology in Social-Science Perspective* (Philadelphia: Fortress Press, 1988) 42-44 and 234.

as his new "statement" for her further "misunderstanding" and so for his added "clarification":

Statement	Misunderstanding	Clarification
4:7	4:9	4:10
4:10	4:11-12	4:13-14
4:13	4:14	4:13
4:32	4:33	4:34

Jesus states: "Give me to drink" (4:7). She responds with surprise that a Judean male would ask a Samaritan female for a drink. On one level she is correct, for this is highly unusual; on another level she misunderstands Jesus. He confirms that she misunderstands, remarking *"If only you knew..."* (4:10). If she were "in the know," the issue of who gives whom a drink would be irrelevant, and she would ask him and he would give her water: "If you knew the gift of God, and who it is that is saying to you 'Give me a drink,' you would have asked him and he would have given you living water" (4:10). A male giving a drink to a female?! Thus the dialogue already encodes gender expectations, but treats them in terms of "misunderstandings" which need "clarification."

Jesus' clarification in 4:10 of her misunderstanding becomes a new statement which provokes another cycle of this pattern. She misunderstands him when she comments about buckets and deep wells. Jesus clarifies that "those who drink of the water that I will give them will never be thirsty" (4:14). This clarification serves as a new statement, which is again misunderstood. The woman asks Jesus for his water, rejoicing that she will "never have to keep coming here to draw water" (4:15) from this well. Just how much have her misunderstandings been clarified? Yet, her "misunderstandings" are portrayed as progress of some sort, not as confirmation of obtuseness, as was the case with Nicodemus. In terms of rhetorical patterns, she moves from the position of *asking questions* (4:9, 11, 12), to that of *speaking imperatives* ("give me," 4:15). Indeed she even mouths the original words of Jesus:

Jesus: "Give me to drink"
Woman: "Give me this water"

Jesus remarked earlier, "if you only knew, *you would ask...*"; finally she *asks* him for his water. But how impressive is this? Like Nicodemus, she is understanding Jesus at an earthly, material level because she wants well water "so that I may not thirst, nor have to come here for water" (4:15). There is nothing of the spiritual about her self-serving request. Her words may repeat Jesus' words, but she is still very far from his communication. She is, however, a work in progress; Jesus speaks to her selected disclosure of important materials; her character is in the process of change. Unlike Nicodemus, she keeps in conversation with Jesus, even if she does not go very much below the surface of Jesus' words. Finally, by asking Jesus for his water, she is on track to become an "insider," that is, one who shares Jesus' food and drink.

Is this a "public" or a "private" scene? Ostensibly it begins in public and is played according to public rules. The woman's "saucy" speech has all the trappings of a challenge-riposte exchange; she and Jesus meet at a public place in male time. But the rhetorical pattern suggests that a transformation of some sort is taking place, not just of the status of the woman, who is in process of becoming an insider, but also of the nature of the space that they occupy. Inasmuch as Jesus is speaking significant words to her, he is welcoming her into his "private" world, the sphere of fictive-kinship. There males share food and beverage with females ("give me to drink") and exchange information ("are you greater than . . . ?"); there honor challenges as well as "saucy" speech are absent. The change in the rhetorical patterns of the woman's speech and her asking Jesus for a drink are indications that the space in which she and Jesus have intercourse is ceasing to be "public" and becoming "private." She is being transformed into an "insider," one whom Jesus receives into his fictive-kinship "private" world.

5.2 John 4:16-26

Jesus again makes a statement, in this case, a command that the woman "Go, call your husband and come here" (4:16). Something new happens, for she neither questions Jesus nor misunderstands him. The modification of the form indicates that the period of obtuse misunderstanding is over (4:7-15). When she states openly "I have no husband," Jesus praises her twice for speaking the truth: "You are right in saying 'I have no husband' . . ." (4:17) and "What you have said is true" (4:18). From now on, the woman speaks with some claim to insight: "I see . . ." (4:19) and "I know . . ." (4:25). Truthfulness and praise characterize this "private" world. The pattern, however, does not indicate a kinship relationship because her speech takes on the character of challenging, even sarcastic, speech. As in all challenge-riposte exchanges, Jesus responds, trumping her claim.

Tone of voice seems impossible to determine in an ancient text. Her next remark, however, is by no means an acknowledgment of Jesus as prophet but a challenge to "Mr. Know-It-All." With Jesus' exposure of her sexual history, she challenges Jesus with a vexing question for which there is no answer. "Our ancestors worshiped on this mountain, but you say that the place where people must worship is in Jerusalem" (4:20). Despite her sarcastic use of the role of "prophet," prophets in fact are in the know, both about the hidden evils of the human heart and about proper worship of God. Jesus takes up the challenge and gives her special knowledge that worship in the future will not be "public" worship at civic shrines, as in Judea and Samaria, but "private" worship, namely, worship in households which are traditional "at-home" space for females. It is not accidental that the only mentions of "houses" and "households" in the Fourth Gospel include prominent women such as Martha and Mary (11:20, 31; 12:2-3). But she is by no means finished with her challenges to Jesus: "Messiah will announce all things to us" (4:25). This is surely a claim that Samaritans are to be honored by Messiah and especially by his knowledge. Jesus challenges her claim with a most unusual revelation of his identity: "I who speak to you am he" (4:26). Although the woman is no longer portrayed as misunderstanding Jesus (4:9-15), she still does not possess knowledge that would make her an insider or a disciple. Indeed, in 4:17-25 she "sees" and "knows," but this functions as a challenge to Jesus, not as an acknowledgment of his role and status. Nevertheless she is told remarkable information, which the narrative indicates that she understood, unlike the water in 4:15.

But is she an insider? Does she ever acclaim or acknowledge Jesus? Indeed she asks the people of the town "can this be the Christ?" (4:29) not on the basis of the information in 4:9-24, but on the basis of Jesus' knowledge of her sexual history (4:16-17). She voices a question, not a declarative statement as did John, Andrew, and Philip (1:36-50). Finally, her question about Jesus proves too weak for the Samaritans, who "have heard for ourselves and know indeed that this is the Savior of the world" (4:42). Nothing about the woman's speech in John 4 should be credited as authentic, sure knowledge; if she is not utterly misunderstanding Jesus (4:9-15) she is sarcastically challenging Jesus (4:16-26).

There are gender considerations here. First, the topic is about males, her current male companion (*not* her husband) and her five previous husbands. She talks of prophets, traditional male prophets because the topic discussed is the correct place of worship (4:19-20). The only extant records of discussion of that topic come from male prophets. She comments about "Messiah," who is male. It might also be the case that political topics such as the correct place of worship and the coming Messiah are male subjects of conversation (see Plutarch, *Lycurgus and Numa* 3.5, cited above), since they pertain to the "public" world of males. Yet this woman engages in them unreservedly. Thus her conversation is *always about men:* this Judean man (Jesus), our father Jacob, husbands, prophets, and Messiah. If this were a "public" forum, these remarks would be improper because they violate the cultural expectations of females in the male sphere. But since this is becoming the "private" world of Jesus' discipleship circle, astute cultural readers will not perceive them as inappropriate.

Although the woman is no longer portrayed as misunderstanding Jesus (4:9-15), she still does not possess knowledge that would indicate that she is an insider or a disciple. In 4:17-25 she claims knowledge, i.e., she "sees" and "knows"; but this knowledge functions as an aggressive challenge to Jesus. Her challenges, moreover, are trumped, for Jesus does know the mysterious place of worship and declares that he is the knowledgeable Messiah she boasted about.

The rhetorical exchange in 4:16-26 is proper to the "private" world. Information is freely exchanged. The dialogue here is not yet one of mutuality and self-revelation, which are proper to kinship networks, for the woman retains an aggressive stance. But she will immediately begin telling the local people about this person Jesus. Perhaps unwittingly, she becomes a spokesman for Jesus and emphasizes the "private" world she enjoyed with him; she has nearly finished her entrance into the circle of Jesus. In the process, she has found a new home and new honor; people take her seriously. She enjoys a measure of respect.

5.3 Clues in the Rhetoric

Our investigation of the rhetoric of the dialogue between Jesus and the woman yields many thematic points. 1) The narrative begins by calling attention to a sharing of vessels that contravenes cultural expectations about ritual purity,[27] thus indicating the breaking of a boundary. 2) The narrative explicitly attends to cultural expectations about ethnic boundaries (4:9), which are likewise broken. 3) This Samaritan female, moreover, is perceived by other characters in the narrative as violating the gender expectations of that culture (4:27), thus breaking a gender boundary. 4) At one point the narrative indicates a certain role reversal; the male figure who asks this female for a drink (4:7) becomes the serving figure who offers water to the woman (4:15). More breaking of gender boundaries. 5) Although Jesus commanded her "Go, call your husband" (4:16), she did not obey him. Cultural expectation of ideal females would celebrate their obedience to males, not such a strange performance as hers. Indeed the woman went and spoke, but her action is hardly what Jesus commanded.

---

27. David Daube, "Jesus and the Samaritan Woman: The Meaning of *sygchraomai*," *JBL* 69 (1950): 137-47.

Jesus' Command (4:16)	The Woman's Actions (4:28-30)
Go,	So the woman left her water jar,
	and went away into the city,
call your husband	and said to the men:
	"Come, see a man who told me all that I ever did. Can this be the Christ?"
	And they went out of the city
and come here.	and were coming to him.

Since she "left her water jar" at the well (4:28), she did not go home, but went to a place where many people were gathered, namely, the public square or agora, where the village males would be gathered. Instead of entering her house (i.e., private space where females may speak freely with the males of their kinship group), she enters "the city" (i.e., public space), and speaks with the males there. Instead of "calling her husband," she speaks enthusiastically about another man, namely Jesus. She insists, moreover, that "he told me all that I ever did," which contextually refers to her five previous husbands and her current male companion, and so keeps referring to her sexual history, and that to other men (see also 4:39). Yet the narrative does not censure her for this, but endorses her behavior (4:37-38). Again cultural expectations of female behavior are being ignored or transcended.

6) The form in which the dialogue is cast indicates that the woman is undergoing a change of status. Not only is she transformed from "*not* in the know" to "in the know," she moves from being a true "outsider" (Samaritans have no dealings with Judeans) to an "insider." The rhetoric, then, supports the conclusion that the woman has moved from "public" space to the "private" world of Jesus' kinship circle. Behavior that might properly be considered "wrong in this picture" in the "public" world becomes appropriate within the "private" world of discipleship. Thus the transformation narrated is also that of the space where the characters meet, no longer viewed as public, but as private.

The rhetoric, therefore, aids the reader in appreciating "what's wrong with this picture?" From the perspective of cultural expectations of gender space and behavior, the woman is portrayed as violating and at variance with all gender expectations regarding time, place, tasks, and persons *insofar as this is public space*. But, as the rhetoric indicates, the dialogue reflects the transformation of the scene at the well into "private space"; and so from the viewpoint of Jesus' kinship network, nothing is "wrong with this picture."

Since the narrator consciously calls attention to the gender issues and their impropriety, we argue that his treatment of them is part of the communication. Such cultural conventions do not restrict Jesus' mission (4:7-26) or that of the

Samaritans (4:28-29, 39-42); their transformation is itself part of the message. No person is excluded from kinship with Jesus because of gender, ethnicity, or social status. Discipleship is a matter of the "private" world, not the "public" world, where different social dynamics are appropriate.

6.0 The Author's Agenda: How to Think about This Woman

What, then, is the author communicating there? How are we to think about this woman? It has been maintained that the Johannine *dramatis personae* can be seen as "representative figures,"[28] which asks us to think about their stereotypical nature. Of what might they be types? How should we think about the Samaritan woman?

Gentile. Ethnic boundaries are broken (4:9); non-Judeans become insiders. This aspect is evidently highlighted when the narrative climaxes in 4:42 with the proclamation of Jesus as "the Savior *of the world.*" Then follows an episode in which Jesus bestows a benefaction on an "official's son" (4:47-54), a figure often considered to be a Gentile. This Gospel, moreover, formally proclaims Jesus as available to Israelites, Greeks, and Romans (12:20, 32; 19:20). This editorial thrust, moreover, resembles the traditions in the Synoptic Gospels about the impartiality of God's blessings to all peoples and their inclusion in the covenant community, e.g., the Syrophoenician woman (Matt 15:21-28) and the commission to make disciples of all nations (Matt 28:19).

Unclean, polluted. Jesus expresses willingness to drink from the same jug as the woman, risking ritual uncleanness. When he discourses on the proper way to worship, he sets aside issues of the right place (Jerusalem or this mountain). Thus Jesus regularly supplants the purity rules of his world by working on the Sabbath (5:16; 7:23; 9:16) or by using the jars normally containing purification water for wine (2:6). Thus Jesus is portrayed as disregarding the purity system of his Judean culture.[29] This material resembles materials in the Synoptics about Jesus' touching a leper, spitting on the eyes of a blind man, being touched by a menstruating woman, and taking a corpse by the hand. Furthermore, the Synoptic Gospels indicate that he "ate and drank with tax collectors and sinners" (Mark 2:15-17; Matt 11:19; Luke 19:7). Commensality with the unclean was a flagrant violation of the purity code. Yet Jesus offers the woman a drink of his water and is willing to drink from her jug.

---

28. Raymond Collins, "The Representative Figures in the Fourth Gospel," *DR* 94 (1976): 26-46, 118-32.

29. Jerome H. Neyrey, "The Symbolic World of Luke-Acts: 'They Turn the World Upside Down,'" in Neyrey, *The Social World of Luke-Acts,* 274-89.

Sinner, even adulteress. Piggybacking on Jesus' breaking of purity regulations is his studied unconcern for the "sinful" status of the woman, who appears to be either a concubine or an adulteress (the sixth man with whom she is living is *not* her husband). Corley has shown that, according to the tradition, Jesus was also the friend of "courtesans."[30] Hence, up to this point, the Samaritan woman could be the Johannine "representative" of Jesus' inclusion of *Gentile* disciples, even those culturally labeled *unclean,* including "*sinners*" and even "*courtesans.*" She would, then, typify the most radical instance of inclusivity in the circle of Jesus' disciples.

Female. If the cultural background of John 4 has any bearing on our understanding of the social dynamics of the story, we might ask a further question concerning the representative nature of the Samaritan woman. She speaks about Jesus to others, presumably males, and leads them to him. In this does she embody a typical role recognized by the Johannine group? If so, is this a role uncharacteristically given to a female in this culture? We can compare her with two other Johannine characters, Mary Magdalene and the first disciples of Jesus, to see if she is "representative" of anything further.

In making comparisons, we are guided by sociological theory of "role" as "a set of expectations for interaction" between a person who holds one position in a group and another person who holds a reciprocal position.[31] A "role" is commonly defined as "the socially recognized position of a person which entails rights and duties." Roles might be formal (i.e., king, priest, teacher, mother) or informal. Paul, for example, claimed the formal role of "apostle" (1 Cor 9:1; 15:8-11), which entailed certain "rights" (1 Cor 9:4-12) and "duties" (9:16-17). Can the Samaritan woman be said to have a socially accepted "set of expectations"? Does she have "rights"? "Duties"? Is she recognized by the other characters as having these? If she has a "role," is it one in the "public" or "private" world?

Formal spreading of the word. Form-critical studies show that appearances of the Risen Jesus function as explicit commissionings of certain male disciples as leaders within the group as well as spokesmen to the "public" world.[32] This is also the case with John 20:25 and 21:15-18.[33] Compared with these narratives, John 4 should not be read as a formal commissioning. Although the author knows the rhetorical form of a commissioning, he has not cast the narrative of the Samaritan woman in it.

30. Corley, *Private Women, Public Meals,* 152-58.
31. A. Paul Hare, "Groups: Role Structure," *IESS* 6.283.
32. Benjamin J. Hubbard, *The Matthean Redaction of a Primitive Apostolic Commissioning: An Exegesis of Matthew 28:16-20* (SBLDS 19; Missoula, MT: Scholars Press, 1974) 102-12.
33. Jerome H. Neyrey, *The Resurrection Stories* (Wilmington, DE: Michael Glazier, 1988) 67-91.

Yet this Gospel contains another appearance of the Risen Jesus, this time to Mary Magdalene. In her case (20:11-17) we seem to be dealing with a formal role, but not necessarily one in the "public" sphere. When we compare Mary with the Samaritan woman, we learn the following:

1. In both cases Jesus has intercourse with solitary females outside a city in public space, apart from their private space, namely, their houses (see also 11:20, 28-30).
2. In both the women struggle with incomprehension or misunderstanding: Mary thinks Jesus is a gardener; the Samaritan woman just cannot grasp Jesus' initial remarks to her (see 11:23-26).
3. To both Jesus reveals his identity (see 11:25).
4. To both he issues a command to go and speak (see 11:28):
   – 4:16 Go *(hypage)* call your husband
   – 20:17 Go *(poreuou)* say to my brothers
   He gives Mary specific, significant lines to speak, "Say, 'I am ascending to my Father and your Father, to my God and your God'" (20:17). In terms of the high christology of this Gospel, she conveys a remarkable piece of information to the group. But Jesus does not tell the Samaritan woman what to say when he says "Call your husband." Nothing profound here at all, no specific message. Nor can it be said that she is an insider in 4:16-17. Moreover, when she speaks, she emphasizes words of Jesus that he did *not* authorize her to speak: "He told me all that I ever did" (4:29, 39), which we know to be her sexual shamelessness.
5. Mary made clear pronouncements ("He told me 'thus-and-such'"), which differs formally from the Samaritan woman's tentative question ("Can this be the Christ?").
6. Mary obeyed Jesus' command; she "went and said to the disciples . . . 'He said thus-and-such to me'" (20:18). The case is less clear with the Samaritan woman, who went and spoke, not to her husband, but to the men of the village, and wondered "Can this be the Christ?" (4:29). Jesus had commanded her, "Go, call your husband, and come here"; but she went to the village square and spoke to others. The rhetorical form of the commissioning of Mary urges readers to recognize her as having a formal role within the fictive-kinship group. Mary's "commission-fulfillment" contrasts with the Samaritan woman's "command–quasi-obedience." Not every command entails a formal commissioning to a role.
7. Both are sent to the "private" world to speak, Mary to Jesus' "brethren" and the Samaritan woman to "your husband." Neither is formally commissioned to speak to the "public" world. In terms of gender-specific behavior,

Mary's actions comply with what we have come to know as the cultural expectations of shame-guarding females in the "private" sphere. It is permissible for a female to speak with the males of her household or kinship group (1 Tim 2:12; 1 Cor 14:33-36).[34] Mary does not speak in public to strange men but in private to members of Jesus' fictive-kinship group ("my brothers"). She is not sent to "public" space, i.e., to other countries or villages to speak to unknown men. In comparison, the Samaritan woman likewise operates in the "private" world. As I have argued, she does not go as commanded to her house or kin, but to the village square; she speaks to whoever is there, which in that culture would mean the males of the village. Her relationship to at least six men of the village might position her as a person with contacts to many households and thus aid in networking. As a person who has lost her sexual exclusivity, she is not an anomaly in this "public" world. Although she appears in the marketplace or "public" space, we are not to imagine that she remains there. After all, Jesus has told her that true worship would occur, *not* in "public" space ("this mountain or Jerusalem"), but in "private" space, namely, households where kinship groups gather. The direction, then, of the woman's speech is not to create a "public" forum where she would have a "public" role. Rather, she moves from "private" space (her household) to "public" space (the marketplace), but then back to "private" space (the circle of Jesus' disciples).

8. The story about Mary is cast in terms of a formal commissioning narrative, and so she might be considered a "representative character." But the same cannot be said of the Samaritan woman, who is not formally commissioned by Jesus to say specific words to a specific group of people. Nor is she recognized by the townsfolk as having a role with duties and rights. If she has a "duty," it is to obey Jesus' command to "call your husband." She has no duty to say specific words to other people. Thus it cannot be maintained that she was *sent*, much less into the "public" world.

Informal spreading of the word. Yet does she have an "informal" role? In the rhetoric of the narrative, her conversation with the villagers is told with approval (4:31-38).[35] Is this indicative of an "informal" role? If so, is it a role which belonged only to males? Is it a role in the "public" or "private" sphere? Is her "rushing to bring the news home" a convention of typical well scenes, as Alter describes them?[36]

---

34. Stephen Barton, "Paul's Sense of Place: An Anthropological Approach to Community Formation in Corinth," *NTS* 32 (1968): 225-46.
35. Seim, "Roles of Women in the Gospel of John," 70.
36. Alter, *The Art of Biblical Narrative*, 52 and 58.

In two rhetorically significant places in this Gospel, readers are told of disciples spreading the news about Jesus in an informal manner. Both at the story's beginning and ending, those who have come to know Jesus tell others about him and even lead them to him for purposes of joining his circle. At the beginning John the Baptizer tells two of his disciples about Jesus (1:35-36), who then "follow" him to learn "private" information: "Where do you stay?" He tells them "Come and see" (1:39), and so they enter his "private" world. Subsequently they find others, tell them about Jesus, and invite them to "come and see." John tells Andrew, who tells Simon; Philip tells Nathanael. Thus, a clear pattern emerges, which is repeated again and again in the Fourth Gospel:[37] 1) Martha tells Mary that Jesus is present (11:28); 2) Philip tells Andrew about the Greeks seeking Jesus, and both tell Jesus (12:21-22); 3) the ten disciples, to whom the Risen Jesus manifests himself, tell the absent Thomas: "We have seen the Lord" (20:25). Jesus never authorizes any of these people to spread news about himself, nor is any formal role indicated by this pattern.

In a world without media, news is spread informally in a "gossip network," a technical term used by anthropologists to describe the spread of information in a media-less world.[38] Spreading news does not seem to entail any *formal* role; there emerges no recognized system of rights and duties, which are characteristic of "roles." But let us note how in the passages we are investigating certain gender expectations continue to prevail: men speak to men (1:35-46; 12:20-22; 20:25) and women to women (11:28). The speakers are either kin (Andrew and Simon are brothers, Martha and Mary are sisters) or members of the same village ("Philip was from Bethsaida, the city of Andrew and Peter," 1:44) or fictive kin (the ten and Thomas, whom Jesus calls "my brothers" in 20:17).[39] This suggests that the informal network we are observing reflects village social dynamics, as well as customary gender expectations, and occurs fully within the conventions for kinship-related persons. Again, the dominant institution is the "private" world of the household, where valuable information is shared, not the

---

37. Schüssler-Fiorenza, *In Memory of Her*, 327-28.

38. Don Handelman, "Gossip in Encounters: The Transmission of Information in a Bounded Social Setting," *Man* 8 (1973): 210-27; Deborah Jones, "Gossip: Notes on Women's Oral Culture," *Women's Studies International Quarterly* 3 (1980): 193-98; Richard L. Rohrbaugh, "Gossip in the New Testament," in *Social-Scientific Models for Interpreting the New Testament: Essays by the Context Group in Honor of Bruce Malina*, ed. John J. Pilch (Leiden: Brill, 2001) 239-59; Sian Lewis, *News and Society in the Greek Polis* (Chapel Hill: University of North Carolina Press, 1996); Robert F. Goodman and Aaron Ben-Ze'ev, eds., *Good Gossip* (Lawrence, KS: University of Kansas Press, 1994).

39. Nathanael was from Cana in Galilee (21:2); the only other mention of Cana in the Fourth Gospel is the location of the wedding in 2:1-12.

"public" world, where unrelated males contest with each other for prestige and honor.

These observations pertain to John 4 as well, but with some variation. The woman spreads the "gossip" about Jesus. She went to but one place, her village. Once she has spread the news, her place in the network vanishes. At first the Samaritans believe "because of the word of the woman" (4:39), but as the circle of disciples grows they believe "because of his word" (4:41). After Jesus stays with them, moreover, they remark to her: "It is no longer because of your words that we believe, for we have heard for ourselves and we know that this is indeed the Savior of the world" (4:42). Like the male figures illustrative of this pattern, she too ceases to play a part once the "gossip" about the Messiah is delivered.

We should look more closely at 4:39-42. I have maintained that Jesus and his disciples gathered others into fictive-kinship relationships. We should, then, consider 4:39-42 in terms of a new circle of Jesus' disciples, even a fictive-kinship group. "Many Samaritans," we are told, "believed in him" (4:39), and so joined the woman in the immediate circle around Jesus. When the text says "they asked him to stay with them" (4:40), we should understand "stay" as a characteristic Johannine term indicating close affiliation with and loyalty to Jesus, namely, membership in his circle (1:28-29; 5:28; 8:31; 12:46; 15:4-7). Then "many more believed" and joined the group (4:41). This gathering, then, is not a "public" group in a "public" forum; it is a fictive-kinship group and so must be considered "private."

Thus the woman is really engaged in "private" speech to newly related males in the emerging kinship group (4:39). If the appropriate scenario is one of kinship, then the woman brings her non-related male associates into a new social relationship which is not "public" at all but the "private" world of the fictive-kinship group. In that context, nothing is "wrong with this picture."

Conclusions

Of what might the Samaritan woman be a "representative"? Looking at 4:6-26, we argue that the narrator has concentrated in this one figure many of the characteristics of the marginal persons with whom Jesus regularly deals in the Synoptic Gospels. She is an amalgam of cultural deviance. In terms of stereotypes, she is a *non-Judean*, who is ritually *unclean;* she is a *"sinner,"* a publicly recognized *"shameless"* person, even someone with whom Jesus has *commensality*. As a *shameless* woman, she embodies most of the social liabilities which would marginalize her in her society. At a minimum, she represents the gospel axiom that "least is greatest" or "last is first." Ultimately, she represents the inclusivity of the Christian group in a most radical way. The stereotype of gender expectations serves to portray her precisely as the quintessential deviant, the last and least person who would be expected to find favor with God. Her status transformation in 4:6-26 is basically that of a person moving from "*not* in the know" and from challenging attacks on Jesus' knowledge to bringing the news about Jesus to her village. She began as an outsider, but in the story becomes an insider.

Does it matter if we note "what's wrong with this picture"? Throughout the story, she violates the cultural expectations of her society. But this intentionally and continually casts her in a deviant role as the most unlikely person on the cultural horizon to be welcomed into Jesus' kinship network. The initial violations of gender expectations (4:6-17) as well as the later ones (4:27-30) consistently stereotype the Samaritan woman as deviant, but this deviance does not matter to the narrator, which is the rhetorical point of the story. The Gospel goes to unlikely people; it might even be spread in the gossip network by unlikely persons (see Acts 4:13; John 4:36-38). As we note "what's wrong with this picture?" the Samaritan woman becomes that much stranger and that much more unlikely a candidate for inclusion. Then how much more extraordinary she is as an example of God's inclusivity and Jesus' reform of social conventions!

"What's wrong with this picture?" Gender stereotypes, then, initially work in the narrative to label the Samaritan woman as the ultimate outsider: non-Judean, unclean, sinner, shameless. The author, then, has created a stereotype of the ultimate *outsider* and the quintessential *deviant*, only to have the stereotype broken, but basically in the direction of the inclusivity of *outsiders* and *deviants*.

Looking at 4:27-30 and 39-42, however, we are told more about this woman. Here she functions as a mediating figure in spreading the news about Jesus to the Samaritans. Although Mary Magdalene may accurately be said to have a formal role as the bearer of a sacred formula to specifically designated persons, we have seen that her role still conforms to the gender expectations of that culture and occurs within the "private" world of the kinship group. The Samaritan woman may occupy a structural place in a "gossip network," but this entails no formal role. Even if on one occasion she speaks to non-kinship-related males, we should not conclude that this is a new pattern, for it is not confirmed by the gender dynamics between characters in the "gossip network," i.e., Martha and Mary (11:28) or the Ten and Thomas (20:24-25).

Do gender considerations play a part in how we understand the Samaritan woman vis-à-vis her townsfolk? As we have seen, gender considerations must be nuanced in terms of "public" and "private" worlds. What is appropriate in one sphere is not in the other. At the beginning of the story, the woman is clearly in the "public" sphere and relates to Jesus in a fashion that tells us much is "wrong with this picture." But as Jesus leads her into his "private" world, her behavior becomes less challenging and more typical of the "private" world. Thus less and less is perceived as "wrong with this picture." Not only is the individual transformation of the woman narrated, but the nature of the social relationships between her and Jesus is also changed. As the woman is welcomed into Jesus' "private" world, she sheds her "public" sauciness and brings good news about Jesus to her village. She then begins to model behavior appropriate to the "private" world of Jesus' fictive-kinship circle, and so she represents much that is "right with this picture." But "wrong" and "right" are contingent on whether the space is "public" or "private." Thus gender considerations remain important throughout.

7

"Equal to God" (John 5:18)

Jesus and God's Two Powers in the Fourth Gospel

Introduction

The materials in John 5 are like most narratives of healings in the Gospels. The initial incident is a miracle Jesus worked on the Sabbath (5:1-15) which metamorphosed into a charge that he had "violated the Sabbath" (5:16) and then an accusation, which necessitated an apologetic defense of his action and his person (5:30-47). This, of course, closely resembles Sabbath healings which become controversies in the Synoptics (Mark 3:1-6; Matt 12:9-14; Luke 6:6-11; 13:10-17; 14:1-6). Such healings would seem to be part of strata of the tradition when miracles and signs functioned as propaganda for Jesus. Between the healing and the defense (5:1-16 and 30-47) we find a strange passage in which another accusation is made, far more serious than mere breaking of the Sabbath, in which Jesus' opponents construe his remark in 5:17 as outrageous because they interpret it as a claim that "He makes himself equal to God." This too requires a response which explains the accusation, approving part of it ("equal to God") but rejecting another part of it ("he makes himself"). A defense, nevertheless, is made to explain in what precise ways Jesus truly is "equal to God" (5:19-29).

Thus in John 5 we read of two trials of Jesus, one accusing him of being a sinner for violating the Sabbath and another accusing him of blasphemy and unparalleled arrogance. The two charges are answered by two apologetic responses, one that depends on witnesses called to testify to Jesus' holiness (5:30-47) and another that explains in great detail just how Jesus is "equal to God" (5:19-29). Two very different christologies are in view, the prophetic identity of the healer Jesus and the heavenly character of the Son who is "equal to God."

"Equal to God" (John 5:18)

Our focus will rest on the middle part (5:18-29), namely, the charge and defense that Jesus is "equal to God." But some preliminary remarks about the trial which issues from the Sabbath healing deserve attention first.

1.0 A Miracle Becomes a Controversy

1.1 The Typical Form of Miracle Stories

The healing at the pool called Bethzatha, as well as three other healings in the Fourth Gospel, follows a traditional pattern for telling such stories. The basic purpose for telling a miracle story is the celebration of the healer and the bestowing of honor and respect on him. After all, honor is more precious than gold in that world. To enhance the honor of the healer, mention is typically made of the severity of the challenge facing him, in this case, a paralysis lasting thirty-eight years — truly a hopeless case. Whereas many folk healers employ salves, roots, and other *materia medica*, Jesus' preferred mode of healing is a simple command. Whereas typically folk healings end with amazement and praise of the healer, not so in the Gospels, where they often result in censure, challenge, and controversy.

We are fortunate to have many examples of this form from the time of the early church. And it seems appropriate to examine one. The Judean apologist Josephus honors Solomon as the source of Israelite healing and wisdom, telling a story which contains the typical elements of a miracle story: 1) setting, 2) severity of the disease, 3) cure, 4) proof, and 5) result: praise of the healer and Solomon.

> And God granted him (Solomon) knowledge of the art used against demons for the benefit and healing of men. He also composed incantations by which illnesses are relieved, and left behind forms of exorcisms with which those possessed by demons drive them out, never to return. And this kind of cure is of very great power among us to this day, for I have seen a certain Eleazar, a countryman of mine, in the presence of Vespasian, his sons, tribunes and a number of other soldiers [*setting*], free men possessed by demons [*severity*], and this was the manner of the cure: he put to the nose of the possessed man a ring which had under its seal one of the roots prescribed by Solomon [*cure: materia medica*], and then, as the man smelled it, drew out the demons through his nostrils, and when the man at once fell down, he adjured the demon never to come back into him, speaking Solomon's name and reciting the incantations which he had composed. Then, wishing to convince the by-

standers and prove to them that he had this power [*proof*], Eleazar placed a cup or foot-basin full of water a little way off and commanded the demon, as it went out of the man, to overturn it and make known to the spectators that he had left the man. And when this was done, the understanding and wisdom of Solomon were clearly revealed,[1] on account of which we have been induced to speak of these things, in order that all men may know the greatness of his nature and how God favoured him, and that no one under the sun may be ignorant of the king's surpassing virtue of every kind [*honor and praise*]. (Josephus, *Ant* 8.45-48; see Lucian, *Lover of Lies* 16)

The following chart puts four miracles stories in the Fourth Gospel in synoptic form, which allows us to grasp quickly how the Johannine author is indeed following the conventional manner of telling healing stories. Yet it should be noted that very little praise comes to Jesus in the Fourth Gospel for his healings and miracles. Even the acclamation of "Prophet" leads to attempts to manipulate Jesus.

Typical Form	**John 5:1-15**	**John 6:1-15**	**John 9:1-34**	**John 11:1-44**
Setting	Sheep Gate	Galilee, Passover, mountainside	Jerusalem and the Pool of Siloam	Bethany
Severity	ill for thirty-eight years	5000 hungry people	a man born blind	dead for four days
Cure (with or without materials)	word of command: rise, take up your mat and walk	words of blessing: he took the loaves, gave thanks, and distributed	materials: "he spat on the ground and made a clay with the spittle and anointed the man's eyes . . . go wash"	word of command: "Lazarus, come forth"
Proof	he took up his mat and walked	twelve baskets of fragments left	he went, washed, and came back seeing	the dead man came out of the tomb
Public Reaction	censure of Jesus: "this is why the Judeans persecuted Jesus, because he did this on the Sabbath"	manipulation of Jesus: "This is indeed the Prophet who is come into the world"	divided reaction: Jesus is a sinner vs. he is a prophet from God	trial to kill Jesus: "It is expedient for you that one man should die for the people"

---

1. Dennis Duling argues that when Jesus is called "Son of David" the reference is to Solomon, the miracle worker, who is son of David: "Solomon, Exorcism, and the Son of David," *HTR* 68 (1975): 235-52; idem, "The Eleazar Miracle and Solomon's Magical Wisdom in Flavius Josephus' *Antiquitates Judaicae* 8.42-48," *HTR* 78 (1985): 1-25.

"Equal to God" (John 5:18)

1.2 No Good Deed Goes Unpunished

Never is a word of praise said about Jesus for the healing at the pool. Rather, the story progresses to the point where he is formally charged with malice. Whereas the healed man should logically sing Jesus' praises, he is immediately caught up in controversy: "It is the Sabbath; it is not lawful for you to carry your mat" (5:10). The man makes a typical denial of malice, claiming that some unknown man told him to do it (i.e., "blame him, not me"). Even when the man finds out Jesus' identity, it is not to celebrate it but simply to relay it to the prosecutors: "He told the Judeans that it was Jesus who had healed him" (5:15). Far from resulting in any praise of Jesus, hostility follows: "This is why the Judeans persecuted Jesus, because he did this on the Sabbath" (5:16).

Jesus stands accused of sinfulness, which would utterly subvert his claims to be God's son and agent, if the charge is true. We find ourselves in the midst of a trial — a forensic proceeding against Jesus — to which he must and will respond. It will help us to appreciate the shape of trials/forensic proceedings in the ancient world. One thinks of Susanna: 1) accusation, 2) by respectable elders, 3) proof = testimony by honorable people, 4) verdict, and 5) sentence.[2] While not all the pieces of this process are present in John 5, an accusation is made (violation of the Sabbath) by respectable people (Judean elders), the proof of which is the very man carrying his mat around. No formal verdict or sentence is mentioned because this event is only the beginning of the forensic proceedings against Jesus which will climax much later with his trial before Pilate.

False Charge, False Judgment. Charged with sinfulness, Jesus pleads "not guilty" because he acted not on his own authority but in obedience to the authority of the holy God (see Acts 5:29). In fact, his Sabbath action is a virtuous, holy action: "My judgment is just, because I seek to do not my own will but the will of him who sent me" (5:30). Hence, he is no maverick, but an observant and obedient person. But do not take his word for it: listen to what witnesses say on his behalf.

The essence of ancient trials resided in the testimony of witnesses for or against the accused. What counted was the word of honorable, noble people known to the court.[3] But the testimony of a person speaking on his own behalf

---

2. A. E. Harvey, *Jesus on Trial* (Atlanta: John Knox, 1976) 46-66; and Jerome H. Neyrey, "Jesus the Judge: Forensic Process in John 8,21-59," *Bib* 68 (1987): 509-18.

3. A. E. Harvey (*Jesus on Trial*, 20) describes the weight of witnesses as evidence: "Whose word can we trust? If a citizen who enjoyed the respect of society solemnly affirmed that something was the case, this is all one could ask for. If two or three such citizens gave identical evidence (and stood up to cross-examination), this was sufficient even to condemn a man to death. . . . The all-important question was the character of the witnesses."

has little standing in the court (8:13). Furthermore, whereas two or more witnesses are needed (see 8:17-18; Deut 19:15; *Mishnah Ketubot* 2.9), Jesus now calls *five* witnesses to testify on his behalf, all of very high status.

John, the Perpetual Witness (5:33-36). John enjoys excellent standing in this court, because it once sent to John for testimony (1:19-28; see 1:6-8, 15) and accepted his word: "He was a burning and shining lamp, and you were willing to rejoice for a while in his light" (5:35). John, then, is a witness acceptable to both the accused and the court. He testified to Jesus' holiness and authorization by God (1:32-34). But Jesus has "a testimony greater than John's" (5:36).

Actions Speak Louder than Words (5:36). Jesus' second witness is the "works" God gave him to do: "The very works that I am doing, testify on my behalf that the Father has sent me." The man born blind in John 9 will develop this argument when he explains the sign which Jesus performed on the Sabbath: "We know that God does not listen to sinners, but he does listen to one who worships him and obeys his will. If this man were not from God, he could do nothing" (9:31-33). Jesus' works, then, attest that he is God's agent.[4]

The Best Possible Witness (5:37-38). "The Father who sent me has himself testified on my behalf." Obviously, this "Father" is God, whose knowledge of the human heart is perfect and whose judgment is true. Hence, the perfect witness testifies on Jesus' behalf that he is not a disobedient or nonobservant sinner as charged, but holy in the paramount way holiness was assessed, total faithfulness and obedience to God.[5] But where do we find God's testimony? In his works, as noted above, but also in the Scriptures. Yet many people are unable to read them correctly. For understanding God's testimony in the Scriptures depends on how one knows.

At this point, the dynamic changes: the trial of Jesus now becomes the trial of his judges. When Jesus says that "You do not *have his word abiding* in you, because you *do not believe him* whom he has sent" (5:38), he accuses his accusers of a terrible sin: this court neither has God's word nor does it believe in God. They, the arbiters of Israel's relations with God, are sinners and evildoers. And it gets worse: "You have *never* heard his voice or seen his form" (5:37). While this may be read as a denial that Moses and Israel saw God at Sinai ("no one has ever seen God," 1:18; 6:46), it likewise charges Jesus' accusers with being utterly deaf to God's word, in whatever form it comes. They, then, are the disobedient sinners, not Jesus.

---

4. Even Nicodemus made some connection between God's favor and Jesus' actions: "No one can do these signs that you do, unless God is with him" (3:2).

5. See James M. Reese, "Obedience (submission)," in *Handbook of Biblical Social Values*, ed. John J. Pilch and Bruce J. Malina (Peabody, MA: Hendrickson, 1998) 142-43.

Israel's Sacred Writings (5:39). Israel lived and died according to its understanding of the Scriptures. Jesus notes this practice: "You search the Scriptures because you think that in them you have eternal life." But they read with a fatal bias. Earlier Nathanael mocked the testimony that a peasant from Nazareth could be the one of whom Moses and the prophets wrote (1:45-46). Later, we hear of a divided judgment about Jesus on the basis of the Scriptures (7:40-43), a debate which ends with a hardened judgment: "Search and you will see that no prophet is to arise from Galilee" (7:52). Except for Nathanael, very few others who search the Scriptures find the truth about Jesus. Hence, this must be construed as a judgment on Jesus' judges: they cannot understand their own Scriptures.

And Then There Was Moses (5:46-47). The last witness for the defense is Israel's most reliable defender, Moses. Of him Jesus claims: "If you believed Moses, you would believe me, for he wrote about me" (5:46). But why do Jesus' accusers not find him attested to in the Scriptures? The reason is the same as expressed in 5:37-38, namely hardness of heart and blindness: "But if you do not believe what he wrote, how will you believe what I say?" (5:47). The tables are turned and the accusers are now accused.

To What Do These Witnesses Testify? They do not support the defense of Jesus in 5:19-29 that he is "equal to God." No witnesses were called in that defense, because no witnesses can testify there, only God. But in 5:30-47 Jesus' witnesses function in his defense against the charge of being a sinner and lawbreaker (5:16). Five acceptable, high-status witnesses attest to Jesus' agency from God and his holiness: he is a saint, not a sinner.

The Tables Are Turned.[6] Trials can be turned upside-down; the accused becomes the accuser and the judges are judged — which is what happens in 5:31-47. Jesus is *not* a sinful person, but his accusers are sinners. When Jesus said, "I know that *you do not have the love of God* in you" (5:42), he accuses them of grave sinfulness, especially since they are the leaders and guardians of Israel's faith. He offers *proof* of their sinfulness: "I have come in my Father's name, and you do not accept me" (5:43). Not to receive a king's agent is to insult the king, because according to the ancient principle of agency: "an agent is like the one who sent him" and "the agent of the ruler is like the ruler himself."[7] Indeed, "how can you believe" when you seek not God's glory but your own (5:44)?

---

6. Urban C. Von Wahlde, "The Witnesses to Jesus in John 5:31-40 and Belief in the Fourth Gospel," *CBQ* 43 (1981): 385-404.

7. Peder Borgen, "God's Agent in the Fourth Gospel," in *Religions in Antiquity*, ed. Jacob Neusner (Leiden: Brill, 1968) 137-48; A. E. Harvey, "Jesus as Agent" in *The Glory of Christ in the New Testament*, ed. L. D. Hurst and N. T. Wright (Oxford: Clarendon Press, 1987) 239-50; see Karl H. Rengstorf, *Apostleship* (London: Adam and Charles Black, 1952) 11-24.

The Defender Becomes the Accuser: Although Moses acted as advocate for Israel before God,[8] Jesus claims that this advocate will become their accuser. "Do not think that I will accuse you before the Father; your accuser is Moses, on whom you have set your hope" (5:45). *Charge:* Jesus declares: "You do not have the love of God within you" (5:42) and "You do not have his word abiding in you" (5:38). *Verdict:* guilty. *Sentence:* Instead of finding in the Scriptures "eternal life" (5:39), these sinners will find eternal death.

2.0 Ascribed, Not Achieved Honor

As the following synopsis shows, the new charge in 5:18 is not simply a doublet of the old charge in 5:16. The prosecution by the Judeans is significantly heightened ("they sought to kill him") and a fresh, cogent reason is offered for this ("he makes himself equal to God").

Old Charge (5:16)	*New Charge (5:18)*
sinful action:	blasphemy:
violation of Sabbath	he makes himself equal to God

Old Apology (5:30-47)	*New Apology (5:19-29)*
five prominent witnesses testifying to Jesus' obedience and sinlessness	careful validation of the claim that Jesus truly is "equal to God"

The key to understanding the new apology (5:19-29) is to deal critically with the new charge. Part of it is erroneous and must be rejected ("He makes himself"), but part of it is true ("equal to God"), which requires defense and careful explanation.

"He Makes Himself Equal to God."[9] The charge that "He makes himself (something)" is frequently leveled at Jesus in this Gospel, as the following examples illustrate:

10:33 You, though only a human being, are *making yourself* God.

---

8. Moses functioned as Israel's defender before God (Exod 32:11-14; Num 14:13-19), a tradition found in Philo, Josephus, and the Midrashim; see Wayne A. Meeks, *The Prophet King* (Leiden: Brill, 1967) 159-61, 200-204, 254-56.

9. Wayne Meeks ("Equal to God" in *The Conversation Continues: Studies in Paul and John in Honor of J. Louis Martyn*, ed. Robert Fortna and Beverly Gaventa [Nashville, TN: Abingdon, 1990] 309-21) asks three questions of John 5:18. First, what did Jesus' accusers understand by "equal to God"? Second, what did the Johannine disciples understand by the phrase? And third, how could Jesus' disciples make themselves so odious by proclaiming this declaration?

19:7	He ought to die because he *made himself* to be the Son of God.
19:12	Everyone who *makes himself* a king sets himself against Caesar.[10]

This charge implies not only that Jesus acts ambitiously for honor and glory, but, worse, that he is stealing this glory from the glorious persons of the world, Caesar and God. Because honor and glory are limited goods, were Jesus to acquire them, others must lose them.[11] Caesar executes such upstarts; God destroys such vainglorious fools. So, the Evangelist labors to show that this part of the charge is utterly false: Jesus does *not* make himself anything, for God makes him what he is.

In answer to the charge in 5:18, Jesus disowns acting independently of God, much less contrary to God's law, for "of himself the Son can do nothing." Rather, he does "what he sees the Father doing," which does not mean that he spies on God and steals heavenly secrets (like Prometheus). On the contrary, "the Father *loves* the Son and *shows* him all that he does" (5:20). Thus the charge is untrue that Jesus arrogantly assumes power or status ("... making himself"); for as the defense argues, God *loves* the Son and God *shows* the Son what he does. That is, God *makes him equal*.

The defense in 5:19-27 provides ample argument for this "equality."

5:19	Whatever the Father *does*, the Son *does* likewise.
5:20	The Father *shows him all* that he himself is doing.
5:21	*As the Father* raises the dead and gives them life, *so the Son* gives life.
5:22	The Father judges no one but *has given all* judgment to the Son.
5:23	All must *honor the Son* just as *they honor the Father*.
5:26	As the Father *has life in himself*, so he has *granted* the Son *to have life in himself*.
5:27	He has *given him* authority to execute judgment.

Thus, as regards the second part of the charge, the author maintains the claim that Jesus is, indeed, "equal to God": "What the Father does, the Son does likewise" (5:19b) and the Father shows him "All that he himself does" (5:20a). It is not true that Jesus "makes himself" anything.

Therefore, since Jesus enjoys the same honor as God, the same authority, and the same extraordinary powers, he is undeniably "equal to God." And this equality with God is not Jesus' vainglorious self-extension; rather it is God's

---

10. See Jerome H. Neyrey, *The Gospel of John* (Cambridge: Cambridge University Press, 2007) 106-9.

11. Readers are referred back to the discussion of limited good and honor in 3:21-30.

will that he be so recognized and respected. In summary, the claim that Jesus "makes himself" anything is false and must be rejected. *And God wills that he be honored equally with himself — that is, acknowledged as "equal to God."* Contrary to the charge in 5:18, the proper statement should be "God makes Jesus equal to himself."

3.0 God's Two Powers: Creation and End Time

The complete apology in 5:19-29 attributes to Jesus two different powers.[12] God's creative power is given to Jesus as he labors on the Sabbath just as God does (5:18). Raising the dead, however, judging, and having life in oneself refer to a different power which is associated with the end time, namely God's eschatological power.

3.1 Creative Power

In 5:17 Jesus claimed that "My Father is working still and I am working." This statement functions as an apology for *not* resting on the Sabbath; and it implies that God also did *not* stop creating on the seventh day but continued working.[13] Apropos of the healing in 5:1-9, Jesus defends himself by claiming two things: 1) God continues to work on the Sabbath, hence Jesus is imitating God's continued creative work by his healing on the Sabbath, and 2) God shows him all that he does, empowering him for works of creation and providence. And *all* of God's deeds of creation/providence Jesus does likewise. The Gospel has already attributed all creation to the Logos (1:1-3) and we should see 5:1-9, 17-20 as the continuation of that theme. Jesus, who is truly "equal to God," has God's full creative power.

---

12. C. H. Dodd (*The Interpretation of the Fourth Gospel* [Cambridge: University Press, 1968] 322-23) argued that two powers are alluded to, but he described them inaccurately as *zōopoiein* and *krinein;* comparably, R. Schnackenburg, *The Gospel According to St. John* (New York: Crossroad, 1982) 2.106. These studies need to be corrected in the light of the present discussion of God's two powers, creative and end-time.

13. See Philo, *Cher.* 88-89; *Alleg. Interp.* 1.5; *Gen. Rabbah* 11.10; *Exod. Rabbah* 30.6. The Judean material on this topic can be found in C. K. Barrett, *The Gospel According to St. John* (2nd ed.; Philadelphia: Westminster, 1978) 256, and C. H. Dodd, *Interpretation of the Fourth Gospel*, 320-21.

3.2 End-Time Power

The long list of powers dealing with the end time overpowers the sole mention of creative power, which immediately suggests that it is the more important of the two for the author's argument. The list below itemizes the powers God gave Jesus to be in charge of the end time, all of which, we shall shortly see, constitute one power only, i.e., eschatological power.

> *Make alive:* As the Father raises the dead and gives them life, so the Son *makes alive* whom he wills (5:21).
> *Judgment:* The Father has given all *judgment* to the Son (5:22).
> *Honor:* . . . that all may *honor* the Son just as they *honor* the Father (5:23).
> *The dead hear and live:* The *dead* will *hear* the voice of the Son of God and those who *hear* will *live* (5:25).
> *Life in himself:* As the Father has *life in himself,* so he has granted the Son also to have life in himself (5:26).
> *Judgment:* . . . and has given him authority to execute *judgment,* because he is the Son of Man (5:27).
> *The dead raised and judged:* All in the tombs will hear his voice and come forth, those who have done good, to the *resurrection* of *life,* and those who have done evil to the *resurrection* of *judgment* (5:28-29).

It is clear that *giving life, judging, speaking to the dead (who hear), bringing them to life,* and *raising the dead for a resurrection of life or judgment* all pertain to the end time. But how do equal *honor* with God and *having life in himself* belong to this scenario? "Honor" has to do with Jesus being "equal to God." Hence *honoring* Jesus means honoring God and vice versa. And *honoring* Jesus means crediting him with God's two powers. "Having life in himself" pertains to the end time in that Jesus has total and complete power over death, starting with himself. We are told in 10:17-18 that Jesus has power to lay down his life and power to take it up; this, moreover, is a command of God. The first and best proof of his end-time power is his raising of himself from death, which greatly surpasses the power involved in calling Lazarus from the tomb.

3.3 Why Two Powers? Which Powers?

What is the significance of insisting that Jesus has God's two powers? Discussions of God in Israel frequently focused on God's two powers.[14] Since all theol-

---

14. See *Alleg. Interp.* 2.68; *Cher.* 27-28; *Sacr.* 59; *Plant.* 86-87; *Heir* 166; *Flight* 95, 100; *Abr.* 124-

ogy dealt with God's operations in the world, it was axiomatic that these two powers encompassed all of God's actions in the world. The same is true of Hellenistic theology, where the deity is fundamentally described in terms of his providence (kindness and justice), which is manifested by creation and maintenance of the world and by justice.[15] Philo expresses this most clearly in his exposition of God's two powers: *dynamis poiētikē* and *dynamis basilikē*.[16] Through the *dynamis poiētikē* God "creates and operates the world" (*Quaestiones in Gen.* 4.2); and by the *dynamis basilikē* God is described as having sovereignty to rule over all that God has created. The same dual aspect of God's total powers may also be found in Rom 4:17, where Abraham's great faith consists of belief in God who 1) called being out of non-being (creative power) and 2) made the dead alive (end-time power).[17] Creation and eschatology, then, encompass all of God's actions.[18] John's Gospel, moreover, reflects just this tradition of God's two basic powers in 5:19-29 when it attributes creative (5:19-20) and end-time (5:21-29) power to Jesus.[19]

In Philo and the Rabbis, moreover, the two powers of God are associated respectively with God's two names.[20] For Philo, the beneficent, creative power (*dynamis poiētikē*) is called "*Theos*" (the equivalent of Elohim in the LXX) and the royal, ruling power *(dynamis basilikē)* is called "*Kyrios*" (the equivalent of the tetragrammaton in the LXX). For example, in explaining the cherubim atop the ark (Exod 25:18), Philo identifies the two powers of the deity and names them accordingly:

25; *Mos.* 2.99; *QE* 2 64-66. See also Harry Wolfson, *Philo* (Cambridge: Harvard University Press, 1948) 1.218-22.

15. This resembles the doctrine of God's providence as this is discussed in Greco-Roman philosophy; see Jerome H. Neyrey, "The Form and Background of the Polemic in 2 Peter," *JBL* 99 (1980): 407-31.

16. See *Alleg. Interp.* 2.68; *Cher.* 27-28; *Sacr.* 59; *Plant.* 86-87; *Heir* 166; *Flight* 95, 100; *Dreams* 1.159-163; *Abr.* 124-25; *Mos.* 2.99; *Embassy* 4, 6; *QE* 2.62, 64-66, 68. See also Wolfson, *Philo*, 1.218-25; Erwin R. Goodenough, *By Light, Light* (New Haven: Yale University Press, 1935) 24-29.

17. See Halvor Moxnes, *Theology in Conflict: Studies in Paul's Understanding of God in Romans* (NovTSup 53; Leiden: Brill, 1980) 231-82.

18. Other examples of God's two powers may be found in 2 Macc 7:23, 28-29; 3 Macc 2:3; Hebrews 1; Acts 17:24-31; and Theophilus, *ad Autolycum* 1.4.

19. It should be noted that whereas Philo and the rabbis speak of God's "executive" power (*dynamis basilikē*), John has already broadened this category to include end-time issues such as resurrection, judgment, and "having life in himself," and so the second power of God is expanded to include end-time issues.

20. The study by Alan Segal and Nils Dahl ("Philo and the Rabbis on the Names of God," *JSJ* 9 [1978]: 1-28) presents a contemporary discussion of this material; see also A. Marmorstein, "Philo and the Names of God," *JQR* 22 (1931-32): 295-306.

"Equal to God" (John 5:18)

> I should myself say that they (the Cherubim) are allegorically representations of the two most august and highest potencies (*dynameis*) of Him that is, the creative and the kingly. His creative potency is called God (*Theos*), because through it He placed and made and ordered this universe, and the kingly is called Lord (*Kyrios*), being that with which He governs what has come into being and rules it steadfastly with justice. (*Mos.* 2.99).[21]

The Rabbis likewise associated the two powers with God's two names, although for them the creative power was linked with the tetragrammaton and judgment with Elohim.[22] But the tradition is clear that God's two powers tend to be linked respectively with God's two names. Is this true in John?

In the Gospel's prologue, where Jesus is credited with creative power, he is called *"theos"* (1:1-3). Ch. 5 also deals with Jesus' creative "working," in which context he is alleged to be "equal to God" (*Theos*, 5:18). "*Theos*," then, is the appropriate name for Jesus when he exercises creative power. "*Kyrios*," however, is much more difficult to deal with; for while Jesus is often acclaimed "*Kyrios*" in John, this title is constantly open to the minimalist interpretation of "sir" or "master." There is, however, one climactic place in the Gospel when he is acclaimed "My Lord *(Kyrios)* and my God *(Theos)*" (20:28). Surely at this point "*Kyrios*" should be treated as a cultic title, its full force acclaiming Jesus as having divine power because he has power to raise the dead.[23] But what is intended by acclaiming Jesus as "*Kyrios*" after his resurrection? Is his exercise of a certain power implied and acknowledged? Creative power is not only claimed but demonstrated (1:1-18; 5:1-9, 19-20), and so Jesus is rightly called "*Theos*." Eschatological power is initially claimed only in 5:18, 21-29, and its demonstration remains the task of the rest of the Gospel, especially the next several chapters.

Therefore, from this investigation of ch. 5, we draw the following conclusions:

1. Jesus is properly called "equal to God,"
2. because he has God's two basic powers (creative and end-time);
3. he is properly called *"Theos"* in virtue of having God's creative power and *"Kyrios"* in virtue of God's executive or end-time power.
4. Jesus does not falsely "make himself" anything,
5. for God gave him these powers and so wants Jesus to be honored even as God is honored.

---

21. For other places in Philo where the two powers of God are called by God's two names respectively see *Plant.* 86-87; *Abr.* 124-25, *Dreams* 1.160, 163, and *QE* 2.62.

22. For a summary of the differences between Philo and the Rabbis, see Segal and Dahl, "Philo and the Rabbis on the Names of God," 1-3.

23. See Rudolf Bultmann, *The Gospel of John* (Philadelphia: Westminster, 1971) 695.

4.0 Eschatological Power in Subsequent Chapters

As is characteristic of the Fourth Gospel, a sentence or statement frequently serves as the text, topic, or agenda of subsequent discussion. 5:18, 21-29 is just such a topic statement.[24] As the following chart shows, the seven items contained in 5:18-29 are formally explained and treated in chs. 6, 8, 10, and 11.[25]

Eschatological Power	John 6	John 8	John 10	John 11
Equal to God: ". . . making himself equal to God" (5:18)			10:30, 33	
Son gives life: "Just as the Father raises the dead and gives them life, so also the Son gives life to whomever he wishes" (5:21)	6:27, 33, 47-50, 54, 57, 58	8:51	10:28	11:25a
Judgment: "The Father . . . has given all judgment to the Son" (5:22); "he has given him authority to execute judgment, because he is the Son of Man" (5:27)		8:21-30	10:29	
Equal honor: "all honor the Son just as they honor the Father. Who does not honor the Son does not honor the Father" (5:23)		the name "I AM"	(10:31; 10:39)	11:4
The dead hear and live: "the dead will hear the voice of the Son of God, and those who hear will live" (5:25)			(10:3-5)	11:43-44
Life in himself: "just as the Father has life in himself, so he has granted the Son also to have life in himself" (5:26)	6:51	8:24, 28, 58	10:17-18, 34-36	11:25a
Resurrection and life: "all who are in their graves will hear his voice and come out — those who have done good, to the resurrection of life, and those who have done evil, to the resurrection of condemnation" (5:28-29)[26]	6:40, 44, 54			11:25-26

---

24. See Jerome H. Neyrey, "John III — A Debate over Johannine Epistemology and Christology," *NovT* 23 (1981): 115-17.

25. It would be interesting to include the remarks in the Bread of Life Discourse in this discussion. Three strange statements there seem to be saying something more than that Jesus' bread gives life: in 6:39, 44, 54 Jesus claims that he will "raise up on the last day" those who eat his bread of life, which might be further evidence of a new and special claim to have end-time power such as was made in 5:28-29.

26. See Nils A. Dahl, "'Do Not Wonder!' John 5:28-29 and Johannine Eschatology Once More," in *The Conversation Continues: Studies in Paul and John in Honor of J. Louis Martyn*, ed. Robert Fortna and Beverly Gaventa (Nashville, TN: Abingdon, 1990) 322-36.

"Equal to God" (John 5:18)

4.1 Eternal Life, Life-in-Oneself, and Raising from the Dead (John 6:26-59)

We focus here exclusively on the statements made by Jesus which pertain to his claim to have God's full end-time power. A generic statement about "life" fixes the topic: "The bread of God is that which comes down from heaven and gives life to the world" (6:33). Whether one "eats" the bread of life or believes that Jesus is that "bread come down from heaven," the results are the same: "that I should lose nothing of all that he has given me, but raise it up on the last day . . . that all who see the Son and believe in him may have eternal life, and I will raise them up on the last day" (6:39-40). We take "not lose" to mean that Jesus will protect those God has given him from judgment at the resurrection (see 5:28-29) and from being snatched by the Angel of Death and so avoid perishing (10:28-29). But the naked claim that "I will raise them up on the last day" (6:39-40) unabashedly refers to the most royal of the end-time powers enumerated in 5:21-29. Again, Jesus states that those whom the Father draws to Jesus, "I will raise that person up on the last day" (6:44).

Indeed Jesus is "the bread of life" in a way that elevates him above all breads eaten in the past. Some bread is *not* "self-rising": "Your ancestors ate the manna in the wilderness, and they died" (6:49). Not so Jesus' bread, which is "self-rising": "I am the living bread that came down from heaven. . . . one may eat of it and not die. Whoever eats of this bread will live forever" (6:50-51). Manna did not have "life in itself," but Jesus, the bread of life, does (see 5:26). Hence, "whoever eats this bread will live forever" (6:51), that is, have "life in oneself" because of Jesus, who is truly "self-rising." "Not die" cannot mean a literal avoidance of death (see 21:20-23 and 8:52-58), but avoidance of "death" after death, as the multiple references to "I will raise them up on the last day" imply.

Two aspects of Jesus' eschatological power are subsequently joined. It is only those who "eat my flesh and drink my blood" who have eternal life, and "I will raise them up on the last day" (6:53-54). Thus those who eat Jesus' bread, which has life in it, will themselves have "eternal life" within themselves. And once more, Jesus has the power to call them from the tombs and raise them to a resurrection of life. In summary, a significant thread may be followed through the Bread of Life discourse which shapes a discourse parallel to but independent of manna-bread-Eucharist. We notice that three different aspects of eschatological power are highlighted here:

The Son Gives Life: "The bread of God . . . *gives life* to the world" (6:33); "Those who believe *have eternal life*" (6:47); "I am the bread *of life* . . . the *living bread* . . . if anyone eats of this bread he will *live forever*" (6:48-51); "who eats and drinks *has eternal life*" (6:54); "who eats me will *live because of me*" (6:57); "who eats this bread will *live forever*" (6:58). When summarized, these verses state that Jesus *gives life*, that people *live because of him*, and that the life he gives is *eternal life*.

Life in Himself: Jesus speaks of earthly bread without "life in itself": "Your ancestors ate the manna in the wilderness, and they died" (6:48, 58). Alternately he heralds bread with "life in itself": "This is the bread that comes down from heaven, so that one may eat of it and not die. Whoever eats of this bread will live forever; and the bread that I will give for the life of the world is my flesh" (6:50-51). Since it is claimed that God gave only to Jesus to "have life in himself," the only bread capable of giving life must be that identified with Jesus.

Resurrection and Life: Four times Jesus claims power to raise the dead at the end time: "I will raise him up at the last day" (6:39, 40, 44, 54). Therefore, given the fact that the previous discourse boldly claimed for Jesus extensive eschatological powers (5:21-29), we take the passages mentioned in John 6 as further specification of three distinct powers: 1) to give life, 2) to have life in oneself, and 3) to raise up on the last day.

4.2 More End-Time Powers in John 8

Much indeed happens in John 8, but as was the case with John 6, we focus here only on what we consider to be aspects of eschatological power.

Power to Judge. Twice in the pivotal discussion of God's end-time powers Jesus claimed that God gave him power to judge: "He has given all judgment to the Son. . . . He has given authority to execute judgment" (5:22, 27). Despite the fact that Jesus boasts that "I judge no one" (8:15), he shortly claims that "I have much to say about you and much to judge" (8:26), a remark which shapes the rest of John 8 as a trial of those who are both liars and murderers. Jesus performs the role of judge in two parts of John 8. First he proposes a new law with a severe punishment for failure to comply (8:21-29), and second he examines the testimony of those who claim compliance, namely, that they "believed in him." As judge, he will examine their responses to his remarks only to uncover that they and their father were murderers and liars from the beginning (8:30-47). The discourse in 8:30-47 is a classic example of a judge's *cognitio*, his scrutiny of the remarks of persons on trial.

"I AM" as Eternally Existing. Three times in 8:21-58 Jesus refers to himself using the expression "I AM." As will be shown, "I AM" is the name of the appearing deity in the Scriptures, as well as a claim to be uncreated in the past and imperishable in the future — that is, a claim to be eternally existing. The first two usages, in 8:21-24 and 28, occur in a context of open hostility to Jesus (see 7:19, 25, 32, 44). The second use of "I AM" is relevant to our inquiry be-

cause it refers on the one hand to Jesus' death ("when you have lifted up the Son of Man") but also to his imperishability ("you will know that I AM"). We take this as a claim that Jesus has life in himself, and even if his enemies kill him, he will be eternally living. This reading of "I AM" is supported by the comparison of Jesus and Abraham at the end of the scene. Of Abraham we know that he came into being by birth and passed out of existence by death, both aspects functioning as important elements in the subsequent argument. In contrast to Abraham's contingent being, "I AM" already existed: "*before* Abraham came into being, "I *AM*." Jesus, then, is an utterly different kind of being from Abraham and all the prophets. Taking them together, we see that the reference to "I AM" in 8:28 situates it in the context of imperishability (looking forward), whereas in 8:58 "I AM" is shown to be eternal in the past, uncreated (looking backward), and so to claim to "have life in himself." One more thing should be noted in regard to "I AM." In 5:23 it was stated that Jesus is to be honored just as God is honored. The confusion at first and then the formal rejection of the application of "I AM" to Jesus should be interpreted as a total failure on the part of the audience in 8:21-58 to honor Jesus as God wants him to be honored.

4.3 Power to Lay Down His Life and to Take It Back: John 10

Because these materials will be discussed thoroughly in chapter 11 below, we will bypass them here except to note where the relevant passages are found:

Equal to God: "You, though only a human being, are making yourself God" (10:33).

Judgment (judge's *cognitio* and verdict): "You do not believe because you do not belong to my sheep" (10:26).

Equal Honor: "The Father and I are one" (10:30) — rejected: "Can you say that the one whom the Father has sanctified and sent into the world is blaspheming because I said, 'I am God's Son'?" (10:36).

Give eternal life, never perish, no snatching of them: "I give them eternal life, and they will never perish. No one will snatch them out of my hand" (10:28).

Life in Himself: "For this reason the Father loves me, because I lay down my life in order to take it up again. No one takes it from me, but I lay it down of my own accord. I have power to lay it down, and I have power to take it up again. I have received this command from my Father" (10:17-18).

4.4 Calling the Dead from their Tombs: John 11

The story begins with the report of a "beloved" disciple falling ill. The supposition is that Jesus will act promptly to prevent Lazarus's death, thus manifesting his power to "give life."

Equal Honor and Glory. Jesus normally accrues glory because of his signs and wonders. At Bethany, however, his actions are "for the glory of God, so that the Son of God may be glorified by means of it" (11:4). Equal glory? Equal honor?

Contrasting End-Time Scenarios. Readers are primed to expect something dramatic, something far beyond the raising of Jairus's daughter (Mark 5:41-42) or of the widow of Nain's son (Luke 7:14-17). We learn that Lazarus has indeed died, but is now four days in the tomb (11:17); thus bodily corruption must be advanced by now ("he stinks," 11:39), which makes the situation that much more complicated. Yes, even a beloved disciple will taste death.

We find a rather fulsome discussion of end-time scenarios in the conversation between Jesus and Martha. She functions in three ways: 1) she reproaches Jesus for inaction, 2) she petitions Jesus to do something, and 3) she serves as spokesperson for traditional ideas about the end time. Her petition is curious: "I know that God will give you whatever you ask of him" (11:22). Implied is the understanding that Jesus himself does not have the powers to remedy the situation and must petition God. This is not what Jesus said in 5:21-29; he already has the necessary powers. His next remark is another clever double-meaning phrase such as is found throughout the narrative: "Your brother will rise again" (11:23) may be taken with 1) Jesus' meaning: calling Lazarus from the tomb, and 2) Martha's traditional understanding: "rise in the resurrection on the last day" (11:24). Her remark, although traditional, is not adequate here.

Have Life in Himself and Give Life. Jesus tells Martha of his endowment of end-time power: "I am the resurrection and the life. Those who believe in me, even though they die, will live, and everyone who lives and believes in me will never die" (11:25-26). Minimally, the claim to have "life in himself" is contained in "I am the resurrection." The claim to "give life" explains "even though they die, they will live . . . will never die." They will live, die, but then live eternally because Jesus gives life, just as God gives life (5:21). The statement that disciples will "die" and "live" suggests a power over the disciples to take them from death, that is, to raise them from the dead (see 12:25-26).

Calling the Dead from Their Tombs. The events at Lazarus's tomb give the strongest proof of Jesus' end-time power. First the author indicates the severity of the problem facing Jesus: "Lord, by this time there will be an odor, for he has been dead for four days" (11:39). Nevertheless, Jesus demonstrates that "the dead will hear the voice of the Son of God, and those who hear will live" (5:25). The dead (e.g., Lazarus) hear the voice of the Son of God: "Lazarus, come forth," and live. Lazarus exits the tomb and sheds his grave clothes.

In summary, we find in the Bethany story many aspects of Jesus' end-time power on display. First, Jesus has life in himself ("I am the resurrection"); second, by virtue of this miracle, Jesus will share in the glory of God; third, traditional understandings of resurrection unto judgment as voiced by Martha are surpassed by Jesus' demonstration of power to call the dead from their tombs; fourth, Jesus gives life, just as God does. Finally, whereas other aspects of Jesus' end-time power are merely claimed or discussed, two of them are subject to verification. Jesus' having life in himself can be demonstrated when he lays down his life and takes it back (10:17-18). Jesus' power to call the dead from their tombs is certified when he says "Lazarus, come forth."

Conclusions

As an exposition of John 5, this study indicates that there was an original "sign" performed by Jesus, which was metamorphosed into a controversy story — not an unusual circumstance in this Gospel. But only in John 5 are elements of a forensic process clearly in evidence: charge, defensive witnesses, and failure to reach a verdict, much less a sentence. But another part of John 5 deals with a different charge, one that warrants death ("tried to kill him"). No witnesses can be called to attest to the truth of Jesus' "equality with God," and so Jesus' defense divides the charge and rejects "he makes himself" but explains the disturbing "equal to God."

Jesus claims to have God's two basic powers, creative and end-time power. Proof of his possession of creative power is the Gospel's prologue (1:1-3) and his working as God is working (5:17). The focus, we have seen, rests on the many aspects of end-time power given to Jesus: to give life, to judge, to deserve equal honor with God, to have life in himself, to call the dead from their tombs, and to raise them to a resurrection. Hence, the claim that Jesus is "equal to God" is shown to be an extraordinary and valid description of Jesus.

We consider it highly significant that the claim to end-time power is not dropped or forgotten. In fact, it became part of the skeleton of the following chapters. Not only do we learn more about the meaning of the end-time power, but we are presented with demonstrable proof that Jesus indeed has these powers.

Does it matter if the discussion of God's two powers only begins in ch. 5 and terminates with the raising of Lazarus? As regards creative power, Jesus demonstrates that he has this in the initial verses of the Gospel. And if miracles and healings illustrate this power, then the transformation of water into an extraordinary amount of wine should be seen in this light. Another Sabbath miracle, the healing of the man born blind, likewise belongs here, especially Jesus' paste of clay and water applied to the man's eyes. At the other end of the Gospel, it has been argued that Jesus' death scene illustrates his control of the when and how of his death. "It is accomplished/perfected" (19:30) is spoken to God and should be taken as a self-focused prayer that Jesus is indeed "laying down my life."

Finally, the most important element of this chapter is to make readers aware of the Israelite discussion of God's two powers and how the Johannine author formally ascribes these powers to Jesus.

8

The Trials (Forensic) and Tribulations (Honor Challenges) of Jesus

John 7 in Social Science Perspective

Topic, Focus, and Hypothesis

Even the most casual reading of the Fourth Gospel indicates that Jesus is constantly engaged in tribulations, which the narrator most frequently portrays as a formal trial or forensic proceeding against Jesus.[1] We first saw this in 5:17-45, where Jesus is charged with crimes, for which he delivers a defense and calls witnesses on his behalf. The Gospel, moreover, narrates how in 10:22-39 he is again put on trial, charged with blasphemy, and obliged to defend himself. The Pharisees, the chief priests, and the Council later try him in absentia (11:45-53). Of course, one should include the final trial of Jesus before Pilate in the Passion Narrative. In addition to this, an inquiry is held with the man born blind, which in effect is a surrogate trial of Jesus; for in ch. 9 Jesus is charged with breaking the Sabbath; witnesses are called concerning his action; a judgment is rendered about Jesus and his witness, the man born blind. The sentence in this case is expulsion from the synagogue. Yet the proceedings, while they focus on the man born blind, are all about Jesus.

The events narrated in John 7–8 fit into this pattern in the Gospel of the trials (forensic) and tribulations (honor challenges) of Jesus: he is charged and put on trial and judgments are rendered concerning him. Needless to say, this

---

1. By "trial" we mean the occasions when accusations are made against Jesus (Sabbath violation or "making himself equal to God") by authorities and when either Jesus or someone else responds with a defense of his actions; trials of Jesus, if successful, might end with attempts to kill or stone him. See A. E. Harvey, *Jesus on Trial* (Atlanta: John Knox, 1975); J. D. M. Derrett, "Law in the New Testament: The Parable of the Unjust Judge," *NTS* 18 (1971): 178-91; A. T. Lincoln, *Truth on Trial: The Lawsuit Motif in the Fourth Gospel* (Peabody, MA: Hendrickson, 2000).

Gospel can be said to favor telling the story of the tribulations of Jesus in terms of forensic proceedings. It is in light of this large pattern that we wish to read in detail the narrative of Jesus' tribulations and trials in John 7.

Many commentators have experienced great difficulties in "seeing a coherent and logical progression" through John 7.[2] We suggest that a careful reading of the narrative in terms of the setting at the Feast of Tabernacles and in light of typical forensic proceedings can go a long way into solving many of the alleged problems of coherence and logic. But it is especially in terms of the way that the tribulations of Jesus are portrayed in the Fourth Gospel that we can learn not only about John 7 but also about the parallel prosecutions in the rest of the Gospel.

It is now apparent that in the Synoptic Gospels the endless conflict between Jesus and his adversaries is portrayed in terms of the *chreia*, in particular the "responsive *chreia*."[3] This type of narrative showcases the wit and cleverness of a sage; hence "honor" and "praise" are its formal aims. Moreover, the *chreia* works by having some hostile question asked of the sage or some criticism made of him and his practice, to which he necessarily responds with cleverness so as to vanquish his questioners and critics. In the Fourth Gospel, the ubiquitous *chreia* is metamorphosed into a formal forensic proceeding against Jesus, which transforms the hostile questions and criticism into legal charges, which if sustained, would end in Jesus' ruin. From the view of conflict in the narrative, both *chreiai* and forensic proceedings demonstrate agonistic attacks on Jesus. In contrast to the Synoptics, John favors the forensic form over the *chreia* to narrate the trials and tribulations of Jesus.

To appreciate the trials and tribulations of Jesus described in John 7, we need an appropriate set of analytical tools and adequate cultural scenarios. When we examine ch. 7 in terms of its narrative craft, we will benefit by considering it according to the conventions of forensic proceedings in ancient Judea, that is, as the trial (forensic) of Jesus. It is a fact that the Johannine narrative repeatedly presents Jesus on trial before Judeans, and thus the forensic proceeding in John 7 should be examined in terms of this formal, redactional literary presentation. Then, if we would fully appreciate the cultural meaning of the tribulations of Jesus, we should interpret the same disputing process in terms of the pivotal cultural value of the ancient world, namely, the struggle to gain honor and to avoid shame. This level of analysis invites us to examine the nar-

---

2. Harold W. Attridge, "Thematic Development and Source Elaboration in John 7:1-36," *CBQ* 42 (1980): 160-70.

3. Burton L. Mack and Vernon K. Robbins, *Patterns of Persuasion in the Gospels* (Sonoma, CA: Polebridge Press, 1989). See also Jerome H. Neyrey, "Questions, *Chreiai*, and Challenges to Honor: The Interface of Rhetoric and Culture in Mark's Gospel," *CBQ* 60 (1998): 657-81.

rator and his characters in terms of a world of cultural meanings given to their behavior, not just by anthropologists, but by the ancient culture itself. "For Jesus testified that a prophet has no honor in his own country" (4:44). Thus characters in the Gospel both grant "honor" to Jesus and withhold it from him.

It is our hypothesis that the narrator chose to present Jesus continually in situations of conflict to highlight how alien both Jesus and his disciples were to their respective worlds. The narrative choice of forensic proceedings, moreover, follows a regular pattern in which Jesus-the-accused honorably turns the tables on his accusers and conducts his own trial of them — he is no mere victim. Thus in response to intense conflict, both Jesus and his disciples acquit themselves honorably, at least on the narrative level. Finally, in view of the shame of the cross (Heb 12:2), the narrator fully appreciates the need to present Jesus in cultural terms as a victorious person, a winner, and so an honorable man. Thus the levels of analysis (forensic trials and tribulations of honor) are two compatible and necessary ways of reading John 7 to appreciate how honorable Jesus is, so that people may join themselves to him and become his loyal disciples.

1.0 The Unity of John 7: Form and Context

1.1 Tribulation Everywhere: Formal Unity

The narrative in John 7 begins with an abrupt statement: "After this, Jesus went about in Galilee; he would not go about in Judea, because the Jews sought to kill him" (7:1). Readers know that this refers back to the conflict narrated in John 5. The remark in 7:1, then, simply describes the latest stage of a conflict already existing in the narrative. The narrator assumes that readers will recall the cause of this hostility from the earlier trial of Jesus, which occurred at another feast in Jerusalem: "This is why the Jews sought all the more to kill him, because he not only broke the Sabbath, but also called God his own Father, making himself equal to God" (5:18). Although his adversaries put Jesus on trial then, they did not resolve that conflict, which resurfaces now on the occasion of another pilgrimage feast in Jerusalem, namely Tabernacles.[4]

---

4. On the link between John 5 and 7, see Raymond E. Brown, *The Gospel According to John* (AB 29; Garden City: Doubleday, 1966) 1.307; J. Louis Martyn, *History and Tradition in the Fourth Gospel* (2d ed.; Nashville: Abingdon, 1979) 68-74; Urban C. Von Wahlde, "The Witnesses to Jesus in Jn 5:31-40 and Belief in the Fourth Gospel," *CBQ* 43 (1981): 385-404; idem, "Literary Structure and Theological Argument in Three Discourses with the Jews in the Fourth Gospel," *JBL* 103 (1984): 575-84.

Following the narrative announcement that "the Jews' Feast of Tabernacles was at hand" (7:2), conflictual relationships between Jesus and two groups of people immediately appear. First, the brothers of Jesus urge him to attend the feast "that your disciples may see the works that you do" (7:3). If these "brothers" were true disciples, we might take their advice seriously; but inasmuch as the Evangelist remarks that "even his brothers did not believe in him" (7:5), the narrative audience perceives serious conflict between Jesus and them, which Jesus expresses in terms of "hate." These brothers are evidently *not* in conflict with "the world" as Jesus is: "The world cannot hate you, but it hates me" (7:7). Hence, the brothers belong to "the world" which "hates" Jesus. The conflict between Jesus and the "brothers" is resolved by the command that they go to the feast, but he will remain in Galilee.

Second, Jesus indeed goes to Judea, where "the Jews sought to kill him." Despite what he said to his "brothers," he ostensibly aims "to be known openly." The result is that, while Jesus cannot be said to initiate the tribulations in John 7, he courts conflict by positioning himself face-to-face with his adversaries on a special occasion and in a highly public place: "About the middle of the feast Jesus went up into the temple and taught" (7:14). The smoldering conflict now explodes into a full-blown dispute because Jesus publicly confronts the temple elite. Formal forensic proceedings against Jesus begin again, but now attempts are made to arrest and silence him.

Thus John 7 presents first a conflict between Jesus and his brothers, and then with the Jews in Jerusalem. Tribulation and conflict aptly describe a redundant set of conflictual relationships that Jesus has in John 7: his "brothers," "the world," and "the Jews" of Jerusalem.

1.2 Narrative Unity: The Feast of Tabernacles

Yet in addition to the record of tribulations, 7:2-3 indicates that "the Feast of Tabernacles" was at hand, for which many pious Israelites would make a pilgrimage to Jerusalem. His brothers command "Leave here and go to Judea," obviously for the feast. To them, at least, Jesus refuses to participate in the feast (7:3-9), and so he misses the beginning of the festivities. Eventually he makes the pilgrimage up to Jerusalem, albeit in secret (7:10), and makes a grand entrance into the Temple "about the middle of the feast" (7:14), at which time the hostilities described in 7:11-36 begin. Finally, "on the last day of the feast, the great day" (7:37), Jesus makes a bold public claim.

Because Tabernacles was basically a harvest feast, the rituals pertinent to that feast correspond to the basic necessities of an agricultural community: a prayer for the winter rains (water) and for the renewal of sunlight (light).[5] Apropos of these two foci, *Mishnah Sukkah* tells us about "the water libation," in which a large golden flagon was filled at the Siloam spring and brought to the Temple for libations (4.9). The same tractate tells of giant golden candlesticks that burned during the festival (5.1), the wicks of which were made of discarded priestly garments (5.3). These two foci of water and light seem to be alluded to in the narrative when Jesus declares on the last day of the feast a promise of *new water* ("If any one thirsts, let him come to me and drink," 7:37) and when he claims to be the *prayed-for light* ("I am the light of the world; whoever follows me . . . will have the light of life," 8:12).[6]

The narrative, then, positions Jesus in the midst of a major feast claiming to replace the benefactions prayed for at that time.[7] In one sense the Gospel has presented Jesus repeatedly replacing the Temple, its feasts, and its cultic objects, which, to say the least, causes significant grievance among the Temple elite. Yet this replacement motif does not seem to function as a formal irritant in John 7; the conflict is about old matters, namely, healing on the Sabbath (5:10, 18; 7:21-23). Nevertheless, the Evangelist indicates that Jesus is not above giving further provocation to his adversaries, and in the most public fashion. To speak boldly and publicly as he does is the mark of an honorable male (see 18:20). He does nothing to mitigate the conflict, first by showing up in the Temple and teaching and then by claiming to be the very things prayed for at the feast, namely, water and light. We would have to say that Jesus acts very provocatively here, which is part of the narrative strategy.

One immediate result of examining the Johannine narrative in terms of the Feast of Tabernacles is the connection between the forensic proceedings against Jesus in 8:12-20 and comparable actions in ch. 7. Just as the conflict in John 7 reaches a climax with Jesus' claim to be the prayed-for *water*, so the trial in John 8 occurs in the context of Jesus' claim to be the prayed-for *light* (8:12). The formal structure of chs. 7 and 8 witnesses to repetitive elements of a typical forensic process: some Jerusalemites 1) formally *charge* Jesus (7:19-23), 2) *examine* his testimony (7:16-18; 8:13-18), 3) *judge* him (7:24; 8:15), and 4) try to *arrest* him (7:32, 44, 45-47; 8:20). This is prima facie evidence of a scene of a continuous conflict and forensic proceedings clustering around the two thematic elements of the Feast of Tabernacles, *water* and *light*.

---

5. Eduard König, "Tabernacles, Feast of," *The Jewish Encyclopedia* 11.656-62; Louis Jacobs, "Sukkot," *Encyclopedia Judaica* 15.496-502.

6. Hakan Ulfgard, *Feast and Future: Revelation 7:9-17 and the Feast of Tabernacles* (Coniectanea Biblica NT series 22; Stockholm: Almqvist & Wiksell, 1989) 19.

7. See A. T. Lincoln, "Trials, Plots and the Narrative of the Fourth Gospel," *JSNT* 56 (1994): 3-30; Jerome H. Neyrey, "Jesus the Judge: Forensic Process in John 8,21-59," *Bib* 68 (1987): 512-15.

2.0 A First Reading: Forensic Proceedings

2.1 John 7 and Johannine Forensic Imagery

A series of narrative clues in John 7 asks considerate readers to connect this chapter with the forensic proceedings described in ch. 5. The accusation of Sabbath violation (5:10, 16) continues to be the primary forensic *charge* against Jesus (7:21-23). The *"court"* which tried and sentenced him ("sought to kill Jesus," 5:18) still seeks to kill him (7:1, 19) and so engineers his *arrest* (7:32, 45). *Witnesses* bear testimony both for and against him (7:12, 25-27, 40-43), which is climaxed by a rump *trial* of Jesus who is absent (7:50-52). In addition, Jesus gives formal instructions to the judges, urging them to judge correctly: "Do not judge by appearances, but judge with right judgment" (7:24; see 8:15). Now in six brief scenes in ch. 7 the adversaries of Jesus constantly render both informal and formal judgments about Jesus as his trial continues. Thus, a cursory reading of John 7 indicates a considerable unity to the chapter in terms of two narrative features: first, the chronological framework created by the Feast of Tabernacles, but especially the extensive forensic proceedings against Jesus.

Let us be clear about what constitutes a typical "trial" or forensic proceeding in the narrative world of the Fourth Gospel. From the trial of Jesus before Pilate, we learn a great deal about Roman judicial process.[8] The following diagram indicates the formal elements in Jesus' trials, as seen in the accounts of both Luke and John[9]:

Forensic Elements	Luke 23:14-15	John 18:1–19:4	John 19:5-16
arrest	23:14a	18:1-11	
charges	23:14b	18:29-30	19:7
judge's *cognitio*	23:14c	18:33-38	19:8-11
verdict	23:14d	18:38	19:12
sentence	23:15b	19:4	19:13-16
judicial warning	23:15c	19:1-4	

This procedure is also evident in the trials of Paul before the Roman governors Felix and Festus.[10] There the identity and authority of the judge, who is the

---

8. A. N. Sherwin-White, *Roman Society and Roman Law in the New Testament* (Oxford: Oxford University Press, 1963); Henry J. Cadbury, "Roman Law and the Trial of Paul," in *The Beginnings of Christianity*, ed. F. Jackson and K. Lake (reprint, Grand Rapids, MI: Baker Book House, 1979) 5.295-337.

9. Sherwin-White, *Roman Society and Roman Law*, 24-27; Jerome H. Neyrey, *The Passion According to St. Luke* (New York: Paulist Press, 1985) 80-82.

10. Jerome H. Neyrey, "The Forensic Defense Speech and Paul's Trial Speeches in Acts 22-

chief civil and/or military magistrate, are evident from the beginning. The core of the process consists in the judge's *cognitio*, that is, the face-to-face interrogation of the accused by the judge, in which the judge evaluates the testimony of the defendant in response to the charges alleged against him. In Acts, moreover, we have formal forensic speeches, both those of Paul's accuser Tertullus (24:2-8) and those of Paul the defendant (22:1-21; 24:10-21; 26:1-23), which are readily intelligible in terms of classical forensic rhetoric.

But Jesus and many of his early followers were engaged in forensic proceedings with Judeans as well as Romans. Judean forensic process differed from Roman in three principal areas:[11] *Legal authority*: the "judges" may not necessarily be civic magistrates with clearly defined roles but simply the leading men or elders of city or village.[12] For example, although Jesus is tried before the Sanhedrin, which consisted of the chief priests, scribes and elders, Susanna was tried simply before the elders of the city.

Matter for Judgment: as Harvey points out, some trials might focus on establishment of facts, as in the case of murder or theft, for which purpose eyewitnesses are indispensable. But many forensic situations deal only with allegations or claims by witnesses (see 1 Kgs 21:12-14), in which the brunt of the process consists of the testimony of honorable witnesses and the scrutiny of these, as in the case of Susanna and the elders. No new evidence is presented before the judging elders, only the discrediting of the accusing witnesses, whose testimony is shown to be contradictory and therefore false, and the acceptance of testimony from honorable witnesses.[13] Considerable attention will be placed, then, on the social status of the witnesses as proof of their reliability.

Witness and Character: testimony from an honorable, educated, and prominent person simply commands more credibility in forensic situations than that of a slave, a woman, or an uneducated person (see Acts 4:13).[14] Judean forensic process, then, was much less formally structured than Roman procedure. The judges might well be the elders of the city or village, assembled in the city gate,

---

26: Form and Function," in *Luke-Acts: New Perspectives from the Society of Biblical Literature Seminar*, ed. C. H. Talbert (New York: Crossroad, 1984) 210-24.

11. Z. W. Falk, *Introduction to Jewish Law of the Second Commonwealth* (Leiden: Brill, 1972) 98-110; Derrett, "Law in the New Testament," 178-91.

12. D. A. McKenzie, "Judicial Procedure at the Town Gate" *VT* 14 (1964): 100-105.

13. Harvey, *Jesus on Trial*, 20-21; Paul R. Swarney, "Social Status and Social Behaviour as Criteria in Judicial Proceedings in the Late Republic," in *Law, Politics and Society in the Ancient Mediterranean World*, ed. Baruch Halpern and Deborah Hobson (Sheffield: Sheffield Academic Press, 1993) 137-55.

14. See A. A. Trites, "The Concept of Witness in the Fourth Gospel," in his *The New Testament Concept of Witness* (Cambridge: Cambridge University Press, 1977) 78-127.

who attend primarily to the testimony of witnesses and their character. Obviously both Roman and Judean forensic procedures are similar in that "judges" assemble to hear "charges" and investigate the truth of the "witnesses" in the case. Finally, even the narrative of John 7 indicates that other customs pertaining to trials seem to be in view, such as requiring that the accused face his accusers (see John 7:51; Acts 25:16; see Josephus, *War* 1.209; *Antiquities* 14.167).

All of this has a bearing on how we view the proceedings in John 7. First, the narrator intends us to view a formal forensic process under way, which includes *arrest* (7:32, 44, 45), *charges* (7:21-23 and vv. 12, 47), *testimony*, either for the defense (7:15-24, 51) or for the prosecution (vv. 25-27), all of which should issue in a *verdict* and a *sentence* (see 8:59; 11:49-53). Although many will give testimony in the scenes of this extended trial, we must ask whether any of it is subject to a *cognitio*, or scrutiny by the judges. Furthermore, we must be careful to ascertain who the judges are in any given sequence and who is on trial.

We must immediately recognize that this forensic material in the Fourth Gospel comes to us through several filters, that is, two distinct readings of judgment materials. On the one hand, God gave Jesus all authority to judge (5:22, 27), and, in fact, Jesus does act as judge in certain scenes (i.e., 8:21-58).[15] But, on the other hand, in a second stream the opponents of Jesus take the role of judges. Their evaluation or judgment of Jesus ironically becomes the basis of a judgment about them: as they judge, so they are judged (Matt 7:2).[16] These judges, moreover, are warned at the start: "Do not judge by appearances, but judge with right judgment" (7:24; 8:15). This second stream of judgment material seems to be especially operative in John 7. Who, then, is really on trial, Jesus or his judges? Hence, the narrative audience, who sees and hears the "trial of Jesus" by his opponents, also judges those judges.

Who's on Trial? Who's Judging Whom? Let us examine the six scenes which comprise the narrative of Jesus' visit at the Feast of Tabernacles. Since we are viewing an extended trial of Jesus by various "courts," we should consider each scene formally in terms of the traditional elements of a forensic proceeding, which was noted above.[17]

---

15. Neyrey, "Jesus the Judge," 515-19. But in some places we find disclaimers by Jesus that he does *not* judge (3:17; 8:15; 12:47).

16. On the widespread usage of "measure for measure" in both Jewish and Christian literature, see Hans Peter Rüger, "Mit welchem Maß ihr meßt, wird euch gemessen werden," *ZNW* 60 (1969): 174-82.

17. At this point readers know only that Jesus' rivals attempt to shame him; what is not yet clear is the risk taken by them because such a fragile situation not uncommonly leads to the accused accusing his accusers. Thus those who sought to shame Jesus are themselves shamed at

2.2 The First Scene (7:10-13)

The narrator intends us to associate the group that controls the action at the announcement of the Feast of Tabernacles ("the Judeans *sought* [*ezētoun*] to kill Jesus," 7:1) with the group who appears at the outset of the first trial scene: "The Jews *sought* him at the feast, saying 'Where is he?'" (7:11). Note the double meaning of "seek," which could mean friendly association with Jesus (1:38-39), but in this context more likely means hostile assault on him.[18] The announcement that "the Jews" are "seeking" Jesus (7:11) presents an ominous hint that the subsequent events in Jerusalem could result in his arrest and execution, as indeed they do (8:59; 10:39; 11:45-53). The narrative informs us that a formal judgment has already been rendered by "the Judeans" who seek to kill him, which is sufficiently public that the crowd knows of it: "For fear of 'the Judeans' no one spoke openly of him" (7:13). Readers, then, initially identify these "Judeans" as people evaluating Jesus with hostility and acting as his "judges."

There are other people on stage, namely, "the crowds," who are "murmuring" about Jesus. The last "murmurers" in the narrative were the "dropouts" who criticized every one of Jesus' claims in the Bread of Life discourse (6:25-65; see "murmuring" in 6:41, 43, 61). "Murmuring" in the Scriptures, moreover, is a very judgmental action. Not everyone in this "crowd," however, appears hostile to Jesus. For, in fact, the crowd's reaction is "divided": some say "He is a good man," while others insist that "He leads the people astray" (7:12).[19] The crowd, then, seems to function as witnesses in the trial, testifying either on Jesus' behalf ("he is a good man") or on behalf of the prosecution ("he leads the people astray"). The presence of this divided testimony indicates that, despite the previous judgment against Jesus, his trial is still very much in progress and a final judgment has not yet been reached.

2.3 Second Scene (7:14-24)

As long as Jesus remains in private (7:10), no one can arrest and prosecute him. But he boldly appears in public in the Temple (7:14), with the result that his trial immediately resumes (see 10:22). That he teaches openly in the Temple serves as

---

the end. See J. M. Kelly, "'Loss of Face' as an Inhibiting Factor," in his *Studies in the Civil Judicature of the Roman Republic* (Oxford: Clarendon, 1976) 93-111.

18. D. A. Carson, "Understanding Misunderstandings in the Fourth Gospel," *TynB* 33 (1982): 59-91; Earl Richard, "Expressions of Double Meaning and Their Function in the Gospel of John," *NTS* 31 (1985): 96-112.

19. Martyn, *History and Tradition in the Fourth Gospel*, 73-81.

the grounds to reopen the case against him as a false prophet (7:12): "How is it that this man has learning, when he has never studied?" (7:15). From a forensic point of view, this question serves as a *charge* against Jesus because it calls into question his status as a valid teacher. Jesus has already been *charged* with "leading the people astray" (7:12), which in the biblical idiom is equivalent to an accusation that he is a false prophet, the sentence for which is death. This *charge* argues that Jesus cannot know the Law and teach correctly, for he has no formal education. The rhetorical importance of famous and noble teachers is well established in ancient rhetoric.[20] In effect, to his accusers he is a self-made imposter, who vainly claims special status.

A first reading of 7:14-24 indicates that it is a trial of Jesus by others. In this vein, the "Judeans" are judging Jesus, charging him with the crime of being a false prophet who leads the people astray. Hence we recognize Jesus' remarks in 7:16-24 as a defense against their charges, with appropriate testimony on behalf of the honorable person who sent Jesus to teach. In defense, Jesus testifies that he indeed has "schooling," when he claims to have teaching from a learned and powerful authority: "My teaching is not mine, but his who sent me" (7:16). As proof of this, he continues: "If any man's will is to do his will, he will know whether my teaching is from God or whether I am speaking on my own authority" (v. 17). Thus he denies that he is a self-made imposter, for his argument rests on the legal principle accepted even by this court: "Whoever speaks on his own authority seeks his own glory; but he who seeks the glory of him who sent him is true, and in him there is no falsehood" (7:18; see also 8:12-13). According to the normal roles assumed at a trial, Jesus acts as both accused and witness on behalf of the one who sent him, in contrast to the "Judeans," who play the role of judges.

What makes a trustworthy *witness* (see 8:13-14)? Why should anyone believe Jesus in this trial? First of all, he does not seek glory for himself, nor does he "make himself" equal to God or "make himself" king. He is but the agent of a most prominent person, even the God of Israel. His teaching is not his own, that is, idiosyncratic, false prophecy, but the authentic word of God. In this witness "there is no falsehood." Thus the first part of the charge that "he leads people astray" is rebutted and proven false. Those who held and continue to hold this judgment have judged wrongly. Such judges will be judged for this false judgment.

A second reading of the scene is warranted by a number of narrative clues.

---

20. Bruce J. Malina and Jerome H. Neyrey, *Portraits of Paul: An Archeology of Ancient Personality* (Louisville: Westminster/John Knox Press, 1996) 27-28, 41-43; see also Jerome H. Neyrey, *Honor and Shame in the Gospel of Matthew* (Louisville, KY: Westminster John Knox, 1986) 80.

For example, Jesus makes his own bold accusation against his critics/judges. He accuses them of failing to keep the Law of Moses: "Did not Moses give you the law? And not one of you keeps it" (v. 19). Presumably he is speaking of circumcision on the Sabbath (see 7:22-23), but this may cryptically refer to other aspects of Moses' Law, such as just judgment (see 7:24; 8:15; Deut 19:15-21) or the prohibition against murder and lying. Why murder and lying? In the continuation of this trial in John 8, Jesus will formally accuse these accusers of both *murder* and *lying*. Those whom Jesus addresses are shown to be not children of Abraham, who received heavenly messengers, but rather offspring of the devil:

> You are of your father the devil, and your will is to do your father's desires. He was a *murderer* from the beginning, and has *nothing to do with the truth*. . . . When he *lies*, he speaks according to his nature, for he is a liar and the father of lies. (8:44)

This has a direct bearing on how we should read the exchange in 7:19-20 between Jesus and his judges. He raises both of these issues, *murder* and *lying*.[21] First, he asks "Why do you seek to *kill* me?" (v. 19), which accuses them of *murder*. Their defense is to *lie*: "Who is seeking to kill you?" (v. 20). Readers know that this is a *lie* because the Evangelist's inaugural remark stated that people were in fact trying to *murder* Jesus: "He would not go about in Judea because the Jews *sought to kill* him" (7:1). The crowds in Jerusalem, moreover, all know that murder is afoot: "Is not this the man whom they *seek to kill?*" (7:25). *Murder* and *lying*, therefore, characterize these judges of Jesus, despite what they say. Thus, we suggest that when Jesus begins his countercharge in 7:19, the true accusation which he makes is the double charge of both murder and lying. Soon, in 8:44, Jesus will demonstrate that his audience are offspring of the devil, who is both *murderer* and *liar from the beginning*. Admittedly, this is not apparent at a first reading of 7:19, but will become so only in time and through the intense scrutiny of the remarks of others, which in forensic jargon is called the judge's *cognitio*. Thus, in terms of roles, Jesus no longer acts as the accused, but begins to judge his judges; they in turn change from judges to accused.

Most of us think that the meaning of the remarks in 7:19 has to do with healing on the Sabbath, which was the formal charge against Jesus at the previous trial on the occasion of the previous feast in Jerusalem (5:10-17). And indeed such is the clear meaning of the continuation of the exchange in 7:21-23. "I

---

21. Readers familiar with the culture of the Levant know how pervasive lying was; see John J. Pilch, "Lying and Deceit in the Letters to the Seven Churches: Perspectives from Cultural Anthropology," *BTB* 22 (1992): 126-34; idem, "Secrecy in the Mediterranean World: An Anthropological Perspective," *BTB* 24 (1994): 151-57.

did one deed, and you all marvel at it" (7:21) — this must refer back to the healing on the Sabbath in 5:1-10. At the time, no formal defense was made to the charge of Sabbath violation, but rather to the more important accusation that Jesus "made himself equal to God" (5:18, see the discussion in chapter 7 above). Now Jesus offers a defense as he compares what he did on the Sabbath with Moses' command to circumcise on the eighth day, even if it falls on a Sabbath (7:22-23). He offers a defense using a standard argument of *qal waḥomer* or *a fortiori* reasoning. If Jesus is guilty for healing on the Sabbath, then they too are guilty for circumcising on the Sabbath. According to Jesus, his judges judge hypocritically since they act on the Sabbath to circumcise Judean males and are not held guilty for it. If they harm a very small bodily organ so as to make the body "whole" for membership in the covenant group, how can they object to Jesus' making a man "whole" as well?

But let us not be distracted by 7:22-23; it may seem like an appropriate defense for violation of the Sabbath, but it actually provides the warrant for the true accusation against these judges, namely, that they judge unjustly. Their very accusation against Jesus as a sinner and Sabbath violator is a false judgment, which Jesus has now exposed. The truly important remark here is Jesus' statement on the absolute need to judge justly: "Do not judge by appearances, but judge with right judgment" (7:24). According to this principle, then, Jesus has taken over the role of the judge who judges the local judges. He has accused them of a very serious crime, judging unjustly, the sentence for which was death.

My reading of this second scene, then, would require in fact two readings. On the surface, the Jerusalemites are judging Jesus, accusing him of crimes worthy of death, for which he defends himself. But typical of this Evangelist, there is a cryptic second meaning to Jesus' remarks and behavior, for he becomes the accuser and judge while the judges are themselves judged. The charges against Jesus (false prophecy, Sabbath violation) pale in comparison to his charges against them, which I take to be *murder, lying,* and unjust judgment. The reader who is attentive to the narrative clues recognizes both the attempts at murder and the lie, but especially the erroneous and false judgment of Jesus by his judges.

2.4 Third Scene (7:25-30)

The dramatis personae shift from the Temple elite to "the people of Jerusalem." At first, it seems that they are simply one more voice in the divided crowd in 7:12-13; but upon closer inspection, we discover that they are allies of Jesus' judges. In 7:13 we were told that "for fear of the Judeans no one spoke openly of him," that is, favorably about him. And they are openly speaking about him; for, in 7:25-26 they comment, "Is not this the man whom they seek to kill? And here he is, speaking openly, and they say nothing to him!" But are they speaking favorably or unfavorably? We will see that their conversation about Jesus is not favorable. While they may not be formally part of the party of Jesus' judges, their negative evaluation of Jesus identifies them as being in sympathy with those who judge Jesus. But what forensic role do they play in the narrative? Are they "judges" as well? Or perhaps "witnesses" for the prosecution? In any event, the narrator would have us put them in the same camp as Jesus' judges.

Although they *testify* about Jesus, their *testimony* supports the prosecution, not the defense. They are aware of the previous forensic proceeding against Jesus: they know the *judges* ("the authorities"), the *charges* ("the [false] Christ"), and the proposed *verdict and sentence* ("seek to kill him"). Their remarks, moreover, are neither a confession of Jesus' identity nor *testimony* on his behalf. Rather they voice a question, "Can this be the Christ?" which they immediately answer in such as way as to bring *testimony* against Jesus: "We know where this man comes from. When the Christ appears, no one will know where he comes from" (v. 27). In effect, they mount an argument that Jesus must be a false Christ. He cannot be the real one because their lore indicates that no one will know where the true Christ comes from.[22] Yet their testimony is subject to scrutiny, as Jesus himself mounts his own *cognitio* of their testimony. The person who conducts a *cognitio* generally plays the role of judge, which signals the reader that this scene entails a reversal of roles: although they seem to judge Jesus, he in fact is judging them and will judge them on the basis of the demand voiced in 7:24, namely, that judges judge rightly and not according to appearances.

The narrative plays with the phrase about "knowing" Jesus. Having claimed to "know Jesus," they are shown *not* to know him authentically or truly. Jesus remarks with heavy irony, "So you know me and you know where I come from?" indicating that they "judge by appearances" when they claim to know whence Jesus comes, either from Galilee (7:41, 52) or from peasant parents in Nazareth (6:42; Nathanael made the same error in judgment in 1:45-46). In any other context this would be important and valuable knowledge about the character of a person.[23] But here Jesus shows that it is both inadequate and even er-

---

22. Marinus de Jonge, "Jewish Expectations about the 'Messiah' according to the Fourth Gospel," in his *Jesus: Stranger from Heaven and Son of God* (Missoula, MT: Scholars Press, 1977) 77-116.

23. Malina and Neyrey, *Portraits of Paul*, 23-26, 113-25.

roneous knowledge. They are "judging according to appearances," bearing false testimony about Jesus — false, that is, from the perspective of the narrator.

Genuine knowledge of Jesus, we are told, consists in acknowledging the one who has authorized him and sent him: "I have not come on my own accord; he who sent me is true, and him *you do not know*" (v. 29). As Jesus did with the accusation in 7:19, so he issues a *countercharge* to those who testify against him here. They "do not know" God, and so they "do not know" the one whom God sent. This is no mere gap of information or fallible ignorance which remedial education will repair. Not in the Fourth Gospel! *Not to know* comprises a serious *charge* by Jesus and this Gospel's community (see 8:47, 55). In this Gospel, failure to know certain things merits a terrible sentence (see 8:24).

This segment of the forensic proceeding ends with an attempt to "arrest him" (v. 30). Actually the technical term here is *"seek,"* the same verb used in 7:1, 19, 25, 34, 36, usually in the sense of *"seek to kill."* Linguistically, then, this "court" is linked with others in the narrative who have judged that Jesus is a false prophet or false Christ. And the very fact that this group seeks to "arrest" Jesus reveals them as allies of Jesus' judges and thus Jesus' enemies. Their judgment agrees with other false judgments of Jesus. In terms of forensic roles, then, the narrator has turned the tables: the judges of Jesus are themselves judged, and Jesus, the judged one, becomes the judge. The crime now is their failure to act according to the law enunciated by Jesus in 7:24, namely, "to judge rightly and not by appearances." Claiming to know Jesus, they judge only according to appearances, and so judge unjustly. Thus these witnesses for the prosecution bring judgment upon themselves for that false judgment.

2.5 Fourth Scene (7:32-36)

The process against Jesus quickens as the Jerusalem elites respond to the crowd. Although "some of the people in Jerusalem" bear testimony against Jesus (7:25-27), yet others "believed in him" and said "When the Christ appears, will he do more signs than this man has done?" (7:31). In reaction to this testimony on Jesus' behalf they "sent officers to arrest him" (7:32). Thus in terms of forensic roles, "the chief priests and the Pharisees" serve as judges with power to arrest and prosecute, and Jesus remains the accused defendant who continues to speak and bear testimony.

Yet when Jesus speaks in 7:33-34, he is not defending himself against a specific charge as he did in 7:14-23; nor is he conducting a *cognitio* of the false testimony of hostile witnesses as he did in 7:25-29. His remarks now serve as testimony on his behalf and as proof of the evil of his accusers. Hence, his role is more than accused defendant as it metamorphoses into that of accusing judge. Let us examine more closely the three parts of his public declaration in 7:33-34: 1) "I shall be with you a little longer, and then I go to him who sent me"; 2) "you will seek me and you will not find me"; and 3) "where I am you cannot come." We notice first of all the signature literary pattern occurring in which Jesus makes a *statement*, which is *misunderstood*, and this leads him to offer a *clarification*.[24] Jesus speaks in 7:33-34, but is completely misunderstood by his hearers in 7:35-36. In this instance, he offers no clarification, which is a highly significant change in the pattern. This pattern of *statement-misunderstanding-(clarification)* functions in two ways in the Fourth Gospel: in most instances, it describes how outsiders become insiders as they move from "*not* being in the know" about Jesus to insight, knowledge, and finally loyalty. Yet on occasion it serves to clarify for the audience that the person to whom Jesus speaks is and remains an outsider, that is, someone who is impervious to Jesus' revelation and who cannot hear his voice, because he or she is not one of the sheep (3:1-12; 10:24-27; 18:37-38). Let us call this a judicial function: remaining in ignorance and being impervious to Jesus' word proves that the person addressed by Jesus is not one of his sheep, does not hear his voice, and does not believe in him — all serious charges in this non-ecumenical Gospel, charges that warrant a terrible sentence. And the fact that Jesus does not offer a *clarification* here is further evidence that he judges those who *misunderstand* him to be hopelessly obtuse and irrevocably fixed in evil.

In addition to the form of the exchange, we attend to the content of Jesus' remarks. What is ignored by the hearers and what is misunderstood? Why does the audience say what it says? Inasmuch as Jesus earlier accused them of both murder and lying, we should not presume good faith and candor now.

Jesus' Statement (7:33-34)	*Their Misunderstanding (7:35-36)*
I shall be with you a little longer, and then I go to him who sent me.	Where does this man intend to go that we shall not find him? Does he intend to go to the Dispersion among the Greeks and teach the Greeks?
You will seek me and you will not find me.	What does he mean by "You will seek me and you will not find me"?
Where I am you cannot come.	"Where I am you cannot come"?

We consider it highly significant that this "court" ignores Jesus' remarks about "going to him who sent me" (7:33), just as others in this extended forensic pro-

---

24. Herbert Leroy, *Rätsel und Missverständnis* (Bonn: Peter Hanstein, 1968) 45-47, 53-67.

cess likewise ignore all of Jesus' testimony about God who sent him (7:16-18, 28). Since Jesus acts as God's agent, speaks what God has authorized him to speak, and performs the signs God deputized him to do, it is utterly shameful for his judges and critics to ignore this part of his testimony (see 9:31-33). Moreover, by ignoring Jesus' testimony about God who authorizes him, the hearers prove a very important thing, namely that they do *not know* God, which is a terrible evil. Jesus earlier laid down the principle of judgment operative behind all these remarks: "If any man's will is to do his will, he *shall know* whether the teaching is from God or whether I am speaking on my own authority" (7:17). Hence, only those who know and are faithful to God will judge Jesus correctly; how terrible then not to know God or the one whom God has sent. Part of Jesus' constant accusation against these very judges has been that "you do *not know* him":

> He who sent me is true and *him you do not know* (7:28).
> You *know neither me nor my Father;* if you knew me, you would know my Father also (8:19).
> The reason why you do not hear them [my words] is that you are *not of God* (8:47).
> You have *not known him;* I know him. If I said, I *do not know him,* I should be a liar like you (8:55).

We find here relentless accusations by Jesus that his judges "do not know God," who sent Jesus. And by ignoring Jesus' remark "I go to him who sent me" (7:33), the interlocutors provide dramatic proof of their studied refusal to attend to this significant legal datum. The audience that ignores Jesus' testimony refuses to know God. Out of their own mouths they are convicted.

Furthermore, Jesus' statement contains cryptic references to an important theme in this Gospel, namely, *whence* Jesus comes and *whither* he goes. We saw in regard to 7:27 that outsiders regularly "judge by appearances" and so constantly misunderstand *whence* Jesus comes (see also 7:41-42, 52). Similarly, they fail to understand *whither* he goes. The narrator and his informed audience know that Jesus comes from heaven and from God, his true *whence,* and that he goes back to God and to heaven (1:1-18; 13:1-3; 17:5). Dolts like Nicodemus cannot understand whence wind comes and whither it goes (3:8); if he cannot understand earthly things, he will never grasp heavenly things (3:12). Similarly Jesus' critics and judges simply do not know "whence are you?" (19:9), or think they do know (6:41-42; 7:27, 41-42, 52). In 7:33-36, the audience does not even attend to *whence* Jesus comes and utterly fails to understand *whither* he goes. Here they think that he will leave Judea and go among the Dispersion (7:35), but in 8:22 they think that he will commit suicide.

But let us examine more closely their misunderstanding of *whither* he goes. They claim not to know what Jesus means by "you will seek me." But is that true? Granted we are dealing with fictional characters, but has the narrator given us sufficient clues to know whether they are honestly asking "What does he mean by saying, 'You will seek me'?" out of ignorance? Consider the following series of statements about people "seeking" Jesus:

The Jews *sought to kill* him (7:1).
The Jews *sought* him at the feast (7:11).
Why do you *seek to kill* me? (7:19).
Who *seeks to kill you?* (7:20).
Is this the man whom they *seek to kill?* (7:25).
They *sought* to arrest him (7:30).
You *will seek* me and you will not find me (7:34).
What does he mean by *"You will seek me"?* (7:36).

"Seeking" Jesus, then, means either seeking to kill him or seeking to arrest him as the prelude to killing him. "Seeking" in John 7 is tantamount to murder. From the narrative point of view, then, this audience is either unbelievably obtuse as to the public controversy over Jesus or is lying when it says that it does not know what Jesus means about "seeking" him. I favor the latter interpretation for two reasons. In 7:20 the judges and critics of Jesus already lied by asking "Who seeks to kill you?" when the narrator has clearly informed his readers that they are in fact "seeking to kill him" (7:1); Jesus knows this and so asks, "Why do you seek to kill me?" (7:19). Moreover, Jesus will shortly expose many of his audience as sons of the devil, who is both liar and murderer *from the beginning* (8:44). Hence, we read the crowd's question in 7:35-36 as a lie about murder; they are "seeking" Jesus to arrest and kill him, but now they are lying about it.

But what did Jesus mean about "seeking and not finding"? In the other Gospels, those who seek find (Matt 7:7//Luke 11:9); seeking and finding have to do with the kingdom of God. Like so many other double-meaning terms in John, this admits of a wide range of meanings. On occasion it describes how others find positive benefit by finding Jesus themselves or by finding others whom they bring to Jesus (1:41, 43, 45) or finding pasture (10:9) or fish (21:6). Jesus "found" the man healed of his disease, who reports him to the Jews (5:14), and "found" the man born blind, who was excommunicated for his testimony on Jesus' behalf (9:35); only in the latter case is this a positive thing. In forensic circumstances, moreover, Pilate twice does *not* "find" any cause to execute Jesus (18:38; 19:4). Still none of these meanings fits John 7. Rather, what Jesus says is "you will *not find* me," which we take to refer to their impotence in arresting and killing him. The officers sent to arrest him in 7:32 return empty-handed in 7:45; and because his hour has not come, those who try to arrest him in 8:20 cannot; and when the crowd takes up stones to throw at him, Jesus hides (8:59); nor when they try to arrest him in 10:39 can they succeed.

In summary, at first it seemed that Jesus was still acting in the role of the accused who testifies once more in his defense. But the more we let ourselves be educated by the Evangelist, the clearer we learn to "judge justly" as Jesus commanded. By this we perceive that roles are being reversed here: Jesus begins to act as judge by accusing this audience of evil and proving it to be sinful because 1) it does not know God, who sent Jesus, and 2) it lies publicly to cover up murderous intent. The ostensible judges do *not* judge justly, but "judge by appearances" when they assess *whence* Jesus comes and *whither* he goes. And so the judges are judged.

2.6 Fifth Scene (7:37-44)

Jesus bears new *testimony* in 7:37-39 that he is the desired "water" for which pilgrims pray at the feast of Tabernacles. Again people must judge his testimony, whether it is true or false, and again the Gospel records a divided judgment, "Some people said. . . . Others said. . . ." In the court of public opinion, some accept his testimony and render a positive verdict about Jesus, "This is really the prophet. . . . This is the Christ" (7:40-41a), but others simply dismiss him (7:41b-42). In substance this testimony repeats the earlier negative judgment of Jesus in 7:26-27.

John 7:26-27	John 7:41b-42
this is the Christ?	This is the Christ
yet we know where this man comes from;	come from Galilee?
When the Christ appears, no one will know where he comes from.	Has not the Scripture said that the Christ is descended from David and comes from Bethlehem, the village where David was?

In each sequence, a claim is made to know whence Jesus comes. By now the audience knows how to evaluate these judgments. In both cases, these people judge Jesus "according to the flesh," for they clearly do not know "whence Jesus comes" (see 7:28). Thus we judge those who falsely judge Jesus and condemn them. By wanting to "arrest him," moreover, they are allied with Jesus' judges and enemies (7:30, 32, 45) and become equally guilty of attempted murder.

2.7 Sixth Scene (7:45-52)

The forensic character of the whole narrative becomes most apparent in 7:45-52. The *arrest*, which was engineered earlier (7:32), fails when the guards sent to arrest Jesus bear favorable *testimony* on his behalf: "No man ever spoke like this man!" (7:46). The judges, however, reject their *testimony*, "Are you led astray, you also?" (7:47). In fact, this only confirms the original *charge* against Jesus, namely, "He is leading the people astray" (7:12). Here is further proof for the judges that Jesus is a false prophet, a danger to Israel.

The judges also dismiss the positive *testimony* from the crowd on behalf of Jesus (7:12b, 40-41a): they are "accursed" (v. 49). In the judges' *cognitio*, therefore, the crowd's *testimony*, like that of the guards sent to arrest Jesus, is not acceptable in this court. But another person stands and speaks, someone with standing in the court. Nicodemus, "a ruler of the Judeans" (3:1), raises a point of law: "Does our law judge a man without first giving him a hearing and learning what he does?" (7:51). How should the reader take this? As further *testimony* on behalf of Jesus?

Commentators point out the ambiguity of Nicodemus in this context.[25]

> he is "one of them," that is, a member of the group judging Jesus;
> he says nothing favorable about Jesus; he does not acclaim him "a good man," a "prophet" or the "Christ"; he only asks a point of law;
> he is already characterized for the reader as the person "who had gone to him before" (7:50), but "at night" (3:2; 19:39).

Since he cannot be said to be testifying on Jesus' behalf, he neither refutes the charge that Jesus is a false prophet nor judges Jesus justly (i.e., as a true prophet). Thus he is not giving *testimony* on Jesus' behalf; he only raises a point of law.

Yet he serves an important function in the forensic proceedings, for he calls

---

25. Jouette M. Bassler, "Mixed Signals: Nicodemus in the Fourth Gospel," *JBL* 108 (1989): 635-46; Marinus de Jonge, "Nicodemus and Jesus: Some Observations on Misunderstanding and Understanding in the Fourth Gospel," in his *Jesus: Stranger from Heaven and Son of God*, 29-47.

attention to the judges' false judgment. Nicodemus is correct that a true and just trial demands the face-to-face accusation of an alleged malefactor and a formal investigation of the charges, something which is denied Jesus both here and in 11:45-53.[26] By speaking up, Nicodemus shows that this important element of a just judgment is *not* being followed here. As such, he functions as a witness against the judges. Moreover, he occasions the further false judgment of the judges, who continue to judge "according to the flesh": "Search and you will see that no prophet is to rise from Galilee" (7:52). The *judges*, then, have passed *judgment*. But the narrative tells us clearly that they have judged unjustly. And so these judges bring judgment upon themselves.

2.8 Summary and Conclusions

The narrator instructs us to read the entire story of Jesus at the Feast of Tabernacles in terms of an extended forensic process (8:12-59 included). Sometimes the proceedings are informal, as when "the people" or "the crowds" evaluate Jesus and testify for or against him (7:12, 40-43); at other times, a more formal process is envisioned (7:14-24, 45-52). In terms of the formal elements of a forensic process, we can identify the following:

1. *arrest*, only attempted (7:30, 32, 44, 45-46);
2. *charges* against Jesus: a false prophet who "leads the people astray" (7:12, 41, 47), a sinner who violates the Sabbath (7:21-24);
3. *judges*, the Pharisees and chief priests (7:32, 45-52) or "the Judeans" (7:13, 15);
4. *testimony*, either on Jesus' behalf (7:12b, 16-18, 21-24, 40-41, 46) or against him (7:12c, 27, 41-42);
5. *cognitio*: either the judges' examination of Jesus' testimony (7:14-15, 37-43) or Jesus' scrutiny of the testimony of others (7:28-29);
6. *verdict*: a guilty verdict implied in vv. 30 and 44 when the court officials "seek to arrest" Jesus;
7. *sentence*: the references to "seeking" Jesus refer to a death sentence, i.e., they "seek to kill" him (7:1, 19, 34).

The judges, moreover, are formally instructed on the principles of right judgment (7:24), and one participant instructs them about valid legal procedure (7:51). On the narrative level, there is no doubt that there are *judges* and a *defen-*

---

26. See Severino Pancaro, "The Metamorphosis of a Legal Principle in the Fourth Gospel: A Closer Look at Jn 7,51," *Bib* 53 (1972): 340-61.

dant. In keeping with the informality of forensic proceedings in Jesus' time, the "court" might be constituted by the public crowds and located in the city (7:11-12, 25-31, 40-43) or by the Pharisees and chief priests and situated in the Temple (7:14-24, 32, 45-52). People indeed render *testimony* about Jesus and pass *judgment* on him. The whole narrative, then, should be read as an extended forensic process.

On the level of the Gospel's narrative rhetoric, however, all these judges are themselves on trial. As they judge, so they will be judged. And so another trial occurs, not just the trial of Jesus, but that of his judges. It is no accident that the narrative keeps a strict record of the right and wrong judgments made about Jesus:

Contrasting Judgments about Jesus

a saint:	*not a saint:*
"a good man" (v. 12)	"you have a demon" (v. 20)
	lawbreaker (v. 21)
the Christ:	*not the Christ:*
"when the Christ comes, will he do more signs than this man?" (v. 31)	"we know where he comes from" (v. 27)
"this is the Christ" (v. 41)	"the Christ . . . comes from Bethlehem" (v. 42)
a prophet:	*not a prophet:*
"this is really the prophet" (v. 40)	"he leads the people astray" (v. 12)
	"are you led astray?" (v. 47)
	"no prophet is to rise from Galilee" (v. 52)

Thus readers can judge the judges and test whether they are judging according to appearances or justly. As one judges, so is one judged.

3.0 A Second Reading: Challenge and Riposte in an Honor-Shame Culture

As illuminating as a formal study of John 7 in terms of forensic proceedings might be, such a reading is not enough. It tells us some things, perhaps many things, but it remains at the level of interesting, but surface description. Such a literary and formal reading of the trials (forensic) of Jesus does not and cannot tell us about the pervasive social and cultural tribulations of Jesus narrated in the Gospel. If we choose to ask different questions, we must do a second reading of the material. What questions? Social and cultural ones such as: Why do these people fight constantly? What is their conflict about? How do they generally fight, because only rarely are people put on trial? When we ask these questions we are inquiring about the cultural world of the Fourth Gospel, of which conflict is a familiar aspect. The best way to examine the cultural nature of the tribulations of Jesus described in the Fourth Gospel is to employ concepts and models from the cultural anthropology of honor and shame. The pervasive tribulations of Jesus in the Fourth Gospel, we maintain, are about the honor of Jesus, that is, his worth, respect, standing, and status and role. As Aristotle and other ancient informants tell us, any successful person in that cultural world will be subject to envy and attacked in any number of ways (*Rhet.* 2.10.1).[27] Trials (forensic) are but one form of this envious conflict.[28] Let us then begin to read John 7 in terms of honor and shame and the conflict over reputation, worth, and fame which is dramatized there.

3.1 The Meaning of Honor and Shame

Over the years, many articles have been published using the model of honor and shame to interpret biblical documents.[29] It is not necessary to repeat the entire model, but only to make salient remarks to guide our second reading. In essence, honor is the abstract, general term for the positive worth, value, reputation, and fame of a person. It refers to the public evaluation of an individual in terms of the ancient code of excellence *(aretē)* or cultural norms for success. Classicists and anthropologists of the Mediterranean world both ancient and

---

27. John H. Elliott, "Matthew 20:1-15: A Parable of Invidious Comparison and Evil Eye Accusation," *BTB* 22 (1992): 58-60.

28. David Cohen, *Law, Violence and Community in Classical Athens* (Cambridge: Cambridge University Press, 1995) 61-118.

29. Halvor Moxnes is an important interpreter of the New Testament using the cultural model of honor and shame: "Honor and Shame," *BTB* 23 (1993): 168-77; "Honour and Righteousness in Romans," *JSNT* 32 (1988): 61-77; "Honor, Shame and the Outside World in Paul's Letter to the Romans," in *The Social World of Formative Christianity and Judaism*, ed. Jacob Neusner (Philadelphia: Fortress Press, 1988) 207-18; and "The Quest for Honor and the Unity of the Community in Romans 12 and in the Orations of Dio Chrysostom," in *Paul in His Hellenistic Context*, ed. T. Engberg-Pederson (Minneapolis: Fortress Press, 1995) 203-30; Matthew S. Collins, "The Question of *Doxa*: A Socioliterary Reading of the Wedding at Cana," *BTB* 25 (1995): 100-109; and John H. Elliott, "Disgraced Yet Graced: The Gospel according to 1 Peter in the Key of Honor and Shame," *BTB* 25 (1995): 166-78.

modern consider honor a pivotal value in this cultural world.³⁰ Greeks and Romans alike were driven by a love of honor, which inspired them to boldness and success. This positive public evaluation might be expressed in a variety of ways, as Aristotle notes:

> Honor is a sign of reputation for doing good. . . . The components of honor are sacrifices [made to the benefactor after death], memorial inscriptions in verse or prose, receipt of special awards, grants of land, front seats at festivals, burial at the public expense, statues, free food in the state dining room, among barbarians such things as *proskynesis* and rights of precedence, and gifts that are held in honor in each society; for a gift is a grant of a possession and sign of honor, and thus those ambitious for money or honor desire them. Both get what they want: those ambitious for money get a possession, those for honor an honor. (Aristotle, *Rhet.* 1.5)³¹

Yet, what is honor? A leading authority on the topic describes it as both a claim to worth and the public acknowledgment of that claim:

> Honour is the value of a person in his own eyes, but also in the eyes of his society. It is his estimation of his own worth, his *claim* to pride, but it is also the acknowledgment of that claim, his excellence recognized by society, his *right* to pride.³²

By this he means that people present themselves to their peers and neighbors as worthy. This might be an individual claiming for himself respect because of some prowess or benefaction or a family claiming for its offspring the same regard in which the family itself is held. Yet claims mean nothing unless acknowledged by some public; for honor is reduced precisely to this public grant of worth and respect. If claims are publicly acknowledged, then a grant of honor is bestowed. Should claims be rejected or challenged, shame becomes a possibility. For shame refers to denial of respect and worth or to loss of them.

---

30. J. G. Peristiany, ed., *Honor and Shame: The Values of Mediterranean Society* (Chicago: University of Chicago Press, 1966); Julian Pitt-Rivers, "Honor," *IESS* 6.503-11; Bruce J. Malina, *The New Testament World: Insights from Cultural Anthropology* (3rd ed.; Louisville, KY: Westminster John Knox, 2001) 27-57; Pierre Bourdieu, "The Sentiment of Honour in Kabyle Society," in Peristiany, ed., *Honor and Shame*, 191-241; and David Gilmore, ed., *Honor and Shame and the Unity of the Mediterranean* (American Anthropological Association Special Publication 22; Washington, D.C.: American Anthropological Association, 1987).

31. The translation is that of George A. Kennedy, *On Rhetoric: A Theory of Civil Discourse* (Oxford: Oxford University Press, 1991) 59-60.

32. Julian Pitt-Rivers, *The Fate of Shechem or the Politics of Sex: Essays in the Anthropology of the Mediterranean* (Cambridge: Cambridge University Press, 1977) 1.

3.2 Sources of Honor

How does one get public respect and worth? Reputation and evaluation occur in two ways, either ascribed worth or achievement based on merit. *Ascribed honor* is like an inheritance: simply by birth (or adoption) into an honorable family, appointment to office by an elite, or consecration for sacred tasks, worth, status, and regard are given to someone independent of actions or merit. Ascribed honor becomes a lifelong trait, such that the person is always and in every situation viewed by some appropriate title or status (e.g., "father," "king," "master"). Conversely, individuals could *achieve* a reputation and fame through merit, excellence *(aretē)*, and prowess. Prowess in military, athletic, and literary competitions earned ancient Greeks battle trophies and laurel wreaths, as well as celebration in literature (besides Homer, see 1 Sam 18:7-8; 21:11; 29:5). Aristotle, writing about urban elites, describes how honor is earned through civic benefaction.

All of these examples depict how an elite person might perform socially recognized deeds of excellence in public and receive official recognition of success and worth. What of achievement by non-elites in very modest circumstances? Honor, worth, respect, and reputation were generally achieved even by non-elites in the ubiquitous and constant game of push-and-shove which characterized the agonistic nature of ancient societies. Not simply on the battlefield or at the Olympic games or at the royal court did individuals merit the praise of others; they might just as well seek and earn it in the ordinary intercourse of daily life through the game of challenge and riposte. But why does honor involve challenge? How does it necessarily imply conflict?

3.3 An Agonistic World: Conflict over Limited Goods

Honor leads invariably to conflict because of the way those who pursue it understand their world. Classicists often describe the ancient world as a highly agonistic society.[33] They observe how the ancients competed vigorously and continuously for success and thus for the reputation and honor which it brings. It takes little imagination to recall how Jesus is constantly engaged in conflict, whether we describe this in terms of responsive *chreia* in the Synoptics or forensic proceedings in the Fourth Gospel. In all the Gospels, we maintain, this conflict was a competition for respect and honor. Yet this combat and conflict

---

33. Jean-Pierre Vernant, *Myth and Society in Ancient Greece* (New York: Zone Books, 1988) 29-56; Peter Walcot, *Envy and the Greeks: A Study in Human Behaviour* (Warminster: Aris and Phillips, 1978) 52-76; and Alvin W. Goulder, *Enter Plato: Classical Greece and the Origins of Social Theory* (New York: Basic Books, 1965) 41-77.

needs to be understood in terms of a cultural perception of "limited good" if we are to understand why it was so pervasive and intense and why the stakes so high. George Foster, the premier expositor of the cultural perception of limited good defines it like this:

> By "Image of Limited Good" I mean that broad areas of peasant behavior are patterned in such a fashion as to suggest that peasants view their social, economic, and natural universes — their total environment — as one in which all of the desired things in life such as land, wealth, health, friendship and love, manliness and honor, respect and status, power and influence, security and safety, *exist in finite quantity* and *are always in short supply,* as far as the peasant is concerned. Not only do these and all other "good things" exist in finite and limited quantities, but in addition *there is no way directly within peasant power to increase the available quantities.*[34]

What are the likely outcomes if one perceives the world in this fashion? Foster suggests an intense conflict motivated by envy: "[A]ny advantage achieved by one individual or family is seen as a loss to others, and the person who makes what the Western world lauds as 'progress' is viewed as a threat to the stability of the entire community."[35] Why? If the supply of good things is radically limited, the gain by one person must come through loss by another. And if the "good" for which people are competing is "honor," which exists in a very limited supply, then any claim to worth by another will inevitably be seen as threat to the worth and standing of others. Jesus' success, then, was perceived by many of the people around him as their personal loss. And no honorable person can afford to lose the most precious thing he has, namely, his honor or public reputation, without a fight. Failure to stem the loss of public reputation would itself be shame, which is the equivalent of social death.

Although Foster describes modern peasant villages in Latin America, the same perception seems equally true of the Greco-Roman and Semitic worlds of antiquity. For example, an anonymous fragment of Iamblicus states: "People do not find it pleasant to give honor to someone else, for they suppose that they themselves are being deprived of something."[36] Plutarch describes the discomfort which people experience listening to a successful lecturer which he credits

---

34. George M. Foster, "Peasant Society and the Image of Limited Good," *American Anthropologist* 67 (1965): 296.

35. George Foster, "The Anatomy of Envy: A Study in Symbolic Behavior," *Current Anthropology* 13 (1972): 165-86.

36. Cited in H. Diels, *Die Fragmente der Vorsokratiker* (5th ed.; Berlin: Weidmannsche Buchhandlung, 1935) 2.400.

to their own perceived loss of worth at the lecturer's rise in reputation: "As though commendation were money, he feels that he is robbing himself of every bit that he bestows on another" (*On Listening to Lectures* 44B). Finally, Josephus not only tells of the envious discomfort of his rival as his own success increased, but of the behavioral consequences of thinking this way, namely, aggressive envy and rivalry:

> But when John, son of Levi . . . heard that everything was proceeding to my satisfaction, that I was popular with those under my authority and a terror to the enemy, he was in no good humour; and, believing that my success involved his own ruin, gave way to immoderate envy. Hoping to check my good fortune by inspiring hatred of me in those under my command, he tried to induce the inhabitants of Tiberias, Sepphoris, and Gabara — the three chief cities of Galilee — to abandon their allegiance to me and go over to him, asserting that they would find him a better general than I was. (Josephus, *Life* 122-23)

The perception of limited good can be observed in two incidents in the Fourth Gospel, both of which are invitations to conflict. First, the disciples of the Baptizer are outraged by the rising success of Jesus, for they rightly perceive that his gain is their loss (3:25-26). Their very complaint to their leader and mentor indicates that they are poised to combat Jesus' success in some fashion. But the Baptizer untypically accepts his loss at Jesus' gain and refuses to act agonistically and in envy of Jesus: "He must increase, but I must decrease" (3:30). In this rare instance, combat is avoided because the person losing honor interprets the loss as divinely authorized; after all, John "was not the light, but came to bear witness to the light" (1:8). It was John's role to "bear witness to him, and cry, 'This is he of whom I said, "He who comes after me ranks before me, for he was before me"'" (1:15). He dutifully fulfilled that role by pointing out Jesus to his own disciples: "Behold, the Lamb of God" (1:29, 36), with the inevitable consequences that Jesus would increase at his expense. Not so the Pharisees and the Jewish council! They too perceive Jesus' success and interpret his gain as their loss in public worth (11:47-48). But unlike the Baptizer, they act agonistically and in envy to destroy Jesus (11:49-53). Both Mark and Matthew indicate that "it was out of envy that they handed Jesus over" (Mark 15:10//Matt 27:18). They acted true to their culture in envying Jesus' success and seeking to reduce his stature and even crush him. Jesus' gain meant their loss, and they were not mandated by God to allow this.

Why, then, do the ancients, both Greek and Semite, fight? They perceive all the world's goods to exist in a very limited supply — including and especially honor — such that the rise in another's fame and reputation necessarily means loss to others and to themselves. The conflict, moreover, is over the most valuable of all "goods," namely, honor and public worth. Such a perception necessarily leads to envy and the desire to level the successful person. As David Cohen has noted, in classical Athens the envious and competitive ancients use the law courts as the forum and vehicle of expressing this conflict and envy, a point which has relevance for the forensic proceedings against Jesus.[37] Thus even the Fourth Gospel is no stranger to this cultural pattern of perception and action, and so it should come as no surprise to find Jesus engaged in endless tribulations (honor challenges) from those who perceive themselves to be losing in the competition for this very limited good.

3.4 Challenge and Riposte

Given the cultural facts of an agonistic world, the cultural perception of limited good and the inevitable envy which arises, we are in a position now to describe in a general way the shape and aim of the dynamics of conflict in antiquity, that is, challenge and riposte. In describing the kinds of challenges that occur in an honor-shame world, Bruce Malina distinguishes between positive and negative challenges.[38] For our purposes, we focus on the negative. Negative challenges describe the actions of an enemy or adversary who explicitly seeks to humiliate or slight or offend another. They can occur when someone physically or verbally attacks another person, engages in sexual aggression against another man's wife, or drags him to court. These actions all have but one purpose: to harm the reputation of the successful person and so to level them or at least to reduce their prestige to an acceptable level.

A typical challenge situation tends to have the following four steps: 1) a claim to honor, often implicit, 2) a challenge to that claim, 3) a riposte to the challenge, and 4) a public verdict of honor or shame bestowed by the audience which must be present during the contest.[39] Inasmuch as "honor" comprises the ability to defend what is one's own (property, wife, reputation, etc.), a riposte must be given to an honor challenge, lest the person so challenged be dismissed as a wimp or a patsy or an easy mark. With this cultural model of

---

37. Cohen, *Law, Violence, and Community in Classical Athens*, 61-142.
38. Malina, *New Testament World*, 33-36; Bruce J. Malina and Jerome H. Neyrey, "Honor and Shame in Luke-Acts: Pivotal Values of the Mediterranean World," in *The Social World of Luke-Acts: Models for Interpretation*, ed. Jerome H. Neyrey (Peabody, MA: Hendrickson, 1991) 25-67.
39. Bourdieu, "The Sentiment of Honour in Kabyle Society," 215.

conflict in mind, let us reread the trials (forensic) of Jesus in terms of honor challenges.

4.0 Conflict in John 7: Challenge and Riposte in an Honor-Shame World

4.1 Technical and Equivalent Terminology for "Honor" in John 7

Earlier in the narrative, Jesus declared that it was the will of God that he be honored with an exceedingly great honor. God had put all judgment in Jesus' hands "that all may honor the Son, even as they honor the Father. He who does not honor the Son does not honor the Father who sent him" (5:23). This claim was made to Jesus' very critics, who, far from acknowledging it, prosecute him as a sinner and seek his shame, even his death (5:18). Given the narrative link between chs. 5 and 7, the same claim to honor remains before both the narrative characters and the readers. Although the technical term "honor" does not occur in John 7 (see 4:44), equivalent expressions focus the challenge-riposte dynamics in terms of assessing Jesus' worth, status, and reputation. Jesus himself articulates a key principle in the game of honor: "He who speaks on his own authority seeks his own glory; but he who seeks the glory of him who sent him is true" (7:18). "Glory" *(doxa)* is often and correctly translated as "reputation" or "fame"; it means "public opinion" quite simply, that is, "honor" (for *doxa*/glory as a synonym of honor, see Rom 16:25-27; Eph 3:20-21; Jude 24-25; 2 Pet 3:18). As Jesus states the case, ambitious *achievers* seek honor for themselves, while those with *ascribed honor* seek honor for the ascriber. Aristotle and other rhetoricians do not praise but rather blame people who act for idiosyncratic and selfish motives (*Rhet* 1.9.17-18). Therefore, the narrative maintains that Jesus does not seek his own honor and "glory," but according to the virtue of righteousness seeks what rightfully belongs to his Patron-Father who sent him. He is not, then, acting out of "love of honor" or ambition.

In regard to "shame," although the technical term does not appear in John 7, the actions of Jesus' adversaries all converge on destroying his reputation and discrediting him from social life. Negative labels such as "deceiver" (7:12b, 47) and "demon possessed" (7:20), if sustained, would utterly dis-value Jesus; negative evaluations of Jesus' place of origin likewise discredit him: "a nobody" come from "nowheresville."

Putting Jesus "on trial" may be the appropriate narratological and form-critical classification of the story in John 7. But being "on trial" is precisely a test of Jesus' reputation, worth, and status, in short, a test of his honor. The very demand of Jesus that the audience "not judge by appearances, but judge with right judgment" (7:24) is an unequivocal demand that his honor claims be properly assessed and publicly acknowledged. Hence, the narrator frames the rhetorical issue in John 7 as an issue of the honor and shame of Jesus or the acknowledgment or rejection of his claims. Readers as well as the characters in the narrative must make evaluative judgments about Jesus, judgments of his worthiness or baseness, which are the grounds for praise or blame.

4.2 Ascribed or Achieved Honor in John 7?

Three native criteria for *ascribed honor* are clearly in the foreground of John 7: origins, teachers, and authorization. Does Jesus come from an honorable city or region? — a typical topic whereby the ancients evaluated people in terms of their origins.[40] In terms of the honor one derived from being born and raised in a certain city, we cite the rules from the *progymnasmata* of Menander Rhetor for composing an encomium on a city. These rules were educational commonplaces in antiquity; all who learned to write Greek were schooled in them. They represent, moreover, the general cultural code of honor of the Hellenistic world. The very first thing an author should note when composing an encomium on someone is the honor which accrues simply from being born in an honorable city (or country). Because of its relevance for this study, we cite Menander in full:

> If the *city* has no distinction, you must inquire whether his *nation* as a whole is considered brave and valiant, or is devoted to literature or the possession of virtues, like the Greek race, or again is distinguished for law, like the Italian, or is courageous, like the Gauls or Paeonians. You must take a few features from the nation . . . arguing that it is inevitable that a man from such a [city or] nation should have such characteristics, and that he stands out among all his praiseworthy compatriots. (Menander Rhetor, *Treatise 2* 369.17-370.10)[41]

Thus it was "inevitable" that a person from such an honorable city would have its honorable characteristics. In the Fourth Gospel and in Acts, Jesus and Paul

---

40. Jerome H. Neyrey, "Josephus' *Vita* and the Encomium: A Native Model of Personality," *JSJ* 25 (1994): 177-206; idem, *Honor and Shame in the Gospel of Matthew* (Louisville, KY: Westminster John Knox, 1998) 91-97.

41. The translation is that of D. A. Russell and Nigel Wilson, *Menander Rhetor* (Oxford: Oxford University Press, 1981) 79.

are evaluated in terms of their origins: Jesus was dismissed by Nathanael simply because he came from the village of Nazareth (John 1:46), whereas Paul claimed honorable status because he was from Tarsus, a "no low-status city" (Acts 21:39) and had visited Philippi, "the leading city of the district of Macedonia" (16:12).[42]

In regard to the second criterion for ascribed honor, has Jesus been taught by a wise and respected teacher? Again, in the rules for composing an encomium in the *progymnasmata*, writers and speakers are instructed to pay attention to a person's "nurture and training," which consisted of an evaluation of the person's education *(paideia)*, his teachers, arts, and skills *(technē)*, and grasp of laws *(nomoi)*. We cite again Menander Rhetor:

> Next comes "nurture." Was he reared in the palace? Were his swaddling-clothes robes of purple? Was he from his first growth brought up in the lap of royalty? Or, instead, was he raised up to be emperor as a young man by some felicitous chance? If he does not have any distinguished nurture (as Achilles had with Chiron), discuss his education, observing here: "In addition to what has been said, I wish to describe the quality of his mind." Then you must speak of his love of learning, his quickness, his enthusiasm for study, his easy grasp of what is taught him. If he excels in literature, philosophy, and knowledge of letters, you must praise this. If it was in the practice of war and arms, you must admire him for having been born luckily, with Fortune to woo the future for him. Again: "In his education, he stood out among his contemporaries, like Achilles, like Heracles, like the Dioscuri."[43]

In terms of ascribed honor, we highlight several things here. Individuals were thought to be shaped, molded, and formed by their mentors and teachers, whose stamp they henceforth bore. Given the reverence for the past and the importance of tradition and the cultural expectation of living up to the customs of the ancestors in ancient culture, young men were only as good as their teachers and those who formed them in the social values enshrined in their past culture. This correlates with the preceding notion of family stock. If the parents were noble, so must the children be; if the teachers were excellent, so must the pupil be.

Hence, when the question is raised, "How is it that this man has learning, when he has never studied?" (7:15), several things are in view. First, it seems to

---

42. On the honorable status of cities and regions, see Jerome H. Neyrey, "Luke's Social Location of Paul: Cultural Anthropology and the Status of Paul in Acts," in *History, Literature, and Society in the Book of Acts*, ed. Ben Witherington (Cambridge: Cambridge University Press, 1996) 251-79.

43. Menander Rhetor, *Treatise* 2.371.17-372.2.

be a public fact, at least in the Johannine narrative world, that Jesus did not have a formal *paideia* and did not sit at the feet of any teacher, as Paul did (Acts 22:3). This fact, moreover, implies that Jesus' worth can only be as good as the quality of his teachers; hence, if he had no teachers at all, much less distinguished ones, then how can he have any learning? His claims to learning, then, seem presumptuous and vain. The dispute over whether he speaks "on his own authority" or on the "authority of another" expresses the controversy over his education quite plainly; this may be simply a case of vainglory if Jesus falsely and foolishly claims to know something (see 1 Cor 3:18; 8:2); but because he has not engaged in the process which leads to wisdom and knowledge, he speaks on his own authority, which is empty and pretentious. Finally, formal lack of education was a cause for public shame even in the New Testament, to judge by the treatment of Peter and John in Acts 4:13.

The third indicator of ascribed honor is raised by Jesus himself, who claims neither to be acting on his own authority nor to be seeking his own glory, but to be "sent" and to speak on the authority of another and to seek the glory of his sender (7:16-18).[44]

We might summarize the argument in John 7 by noting that Jesus' adversaries credit him with ambitiously trying to *achieve honor* and respect, albeit vainly and erroneously. They refuse to acknowledge any claims to achieved honor and see no grounds for conceding ascribed honor, especially honor deriving from culturally correct education. The narrator, on the other hand, presents Jesus' status and worth in terms of *ascribed honor*, which is likewise continually rejected by Jesus' adversaries. The precise debate over "judging by appearances" (7:24) might be accurately paraphrased as a controversy over the correct assessment of the source of Jesus' honor and worth: is it *achieved* or at least claimed on the basis of achievement, as some interpret the scene? or is it *ascribed* to Jesus by the most honorable person in the cosmos, as the narrator claims? John 7 presents a public debate with a "divided" crowd and hence a divided verdict: "While some say, 'He is a good man,' others said, 'No, he leads the people astray'" (7:12), and "So there was division among the people over him" (7:43).

4.3 Challenges to Jesus

We will understand the challenges to Jesus in proportion to our appreciation of the claims made by him or for him. The narrator addressing the fictional audi-

---

44. Peder Borgen, "God's Agent in the Fourth Gospel," in *Religions in Antiquity*, ed. Jacob Neusner (Leiden: E. J. Brill, 1968) 137-48; and Jerome H. Neyrey, "'I Am the Door' (John 10:7, 9): Jesus the Broker in the Fourth Gospel," *CBQ* 69 (2007): 271-91.

ence has already made substantial claims on Jesus' behalf. He is "the Word" who is face-to-face with God and actually in the lap of God (1:1, 18). John the Baptizer, "a burning and shining lamp" (5:35), bore testimony on Jesus' behalf as a superior person who "ranks before me, for he was before me" (1:15, 27, 30). Most of the narrator's claims on Jesus' behalf can be discerned when we see whether characters in the story acknowledge or reject Jesus in any way. Again the Baptizer is the greatest acknowledger of Jesus' honor: "I have seen and have borne witness that this is the Son of God" (1:34) and "Behold, the Lamb of God!" (1:29, 36; see also 5:32-35). Nathanael, an Israelite in whom there is no guile, acknowledges Jesus: "Rabbi, you are the Son of God! You are the King of Israel!" (1:49). Others acknowledge Jesus' role and status as King or Prophet or Son of man or Christ. Truly exalted claims are made by Jesus in 7:37-39: he is the replacement for the prayed-for water and rains during the feast of Tabernacles; but the author does not record any reaction whatsoever to these claims. Yet claims to worth and status are constantly being made throughout the Fourth Gospel and even in John 7.

Of course, this record of acknowledgment and testimony on Jesus' behalf is hardly the entire story of the Fourth Gospel, as most scenes and episodes deal with refusals to acknowledge his claims to honor. According to the choreography of honor and shame interchanges, these refusals are formal challenges to him. We focus here only on the challenges to Jesus in John 7, which are both numerous and deadly serious. The entire narrative consists of an escalating series of challenges to Jesus. First, his brothers urge him to go publicly to the feast, which we consider as a challenge for several reasons. As the narrator indicates, "even his brothers did not believe in him" (7:5). They belong to the world which hates Jesus (7:7); hence they belong to the camp of Jesus' adversaries and so their remarks should be seen as hostile. Their implied motivation, while it is not to see Jesus arrested and killed, appears to be self-serving, namely, that he continues to gain a great reputation, which will enhance their own standing as "brothers." Their "challenge," then, is to seek to take a large share of Jesus' reputation and fame, which, as we saw in the discussion of limited good, means that Jesus must lose as they gain.

Second, challenges to Jesus in John 7 are typically cast in terms of the forensic process waged against Jesus. Most obvious are the charges leveled against him by the various "courts" who evaluate and judge him. For example, as we have seen, Jesus is engaged in a forensic process in 7:15-24, where the residual charge against him appears to be his previous healing on the Sabbath (5:10, 16): "I did one deed, and you all marvel at it" (v. 21). Other forensic judgments are made about him which attack his popularity and public reputation, such as, "He is leading the people astray" (7:12) and "How is it that this man has learning, when he has never studied?" (7:15).

Third, in keeping with the forensic process, others challenge Jesus when they testify against him and present arguments which attack his claims. For instance, some argue that Jesus cannot be the Messiah because they know whence he comes, but when the Messiah comes no one will know where he comes from (7:27). Others point to the fact that Jesus is from Galilee, but as all know, the Christ is to come not from there, but, being "descended from David," from Bethlehem, "the village where David was" (7:41-42). Finally, the Pharisees and chief priests contest Jesus' role and status as a prophet by declaring that "No prophet is to rise from Galilee" (7:52). Thus any claims made that Jesus is the Messiah (7:31, 41) or a prophet (7:40, 52) are challenged outright.

Thus his "brothers" and his formal adversaries and the crowds each challenge Jesus, but in different ways. Yet in their challenges, each completely misses and thus fails to acknowledge the core of Jesus' claims, namely, his ascribed role and status: that he has an "hour" assigned him for his works (7:6), that he is authorized to do what he does (7:16-18) and that he "comes from" an exalted person who ascribes him great honor (7:25-29).

4.4 Always Answer a Challenge

Challenges must be answered; failure to deliver a riposte normally results in loss of honor. As we shall see, the ripostes come first and foremost from Jesus himself, with occasional assistance from others. The narrative presents Jesus adroitly giving a riposte to each of the three challenges just noted above. First, he flatly rejects the suggestion from his "brothers" that he perform more signs or honor claims at this time; it may be "their time," but his hour has not yet come (7:6). They, in effect, belong to "the world" which hates Jesus, which only serves to distance him and his true disciples from his adversaries (see 15:18-25). Jesus effectively dismisses them with a command, "Go to the feast yourselves" (7:8); he refuses their challenge to manipulate him for their own honor. He defends his honor by not being put upon or manipulated.

As we noted above, 7:15-24 contains a number of key strategic moves characteristic of a defense in forensic proceedings. Presuming that the charges against Jesus and the current public hearing are themselves challenges to him, Jesus mounts a careful riposte to the charges. His teaching and thus his authority to heal on the Sabbath come from God; and this God is "true, and in him there is no falsehood" (7:18). Jesus has adequate "learning" to speak, hence he is no false prophet who leads the people astray. Moreover, he only seeks God's honor, not his own advancement; hence he acts honorably, not dishonorably (7:18) in speaking as he has been commanded. Moreover, in defense of his healing on the Sabbath, Jesus offers a legitimate defensive argument: if Moses authorizes circumcision on the Sabbath, surely making a broken man whole on the Sabbath is permitted (7:23). Each and every accusation or insinuation is answered directly, often by simply being denied.

Again, as noted above in the section on forensic proceedings, it is characteristic for the narrator of the Fourth Gospel to present a "turning of the tables" during forensic proceedings against Jesus. Jesus himself articulates the shape of his riposte when he commands his judges, "Do not judge by appearances, but judge with right judgment" (7:24; 8:15). The judges themselves are put on trial and judged according to the judgment they make, that is, by whether they truly know whence Jesus comes. In the choreography of honor and shame dynamics, this means that forensic proceedings *against someone* are effectively challenges to them, and that the turning of the tables means that the defendant's riposte consists of conducting the same proceedings *against his accusers*. Thus the narrative of the forensic trial equals a challenge to Jesus; but by the "turning of the tables" on the judges, he issues the groundwork for a fitting riposte.

In this vein, we interpret Jesus' bold accusations against his accusers as appropriate ripostes to challenges to him. If they accuse him of leading the people astray and violating the Sabbath, he returns the compliment by accusing them of murder (7:19) and lying (7:20). These countercharges are more than the turning of the tables. Judging according to appearances is an evil, but it is not in the same category as murder and lying.

In the third instance (7:26-29), Jesus rebuts certain false claims to know whence he comes with a question, which we noted above often serves as a rhetorical index of a challenge. "You know me, and you know where I come from?" (7:28). The impact of Jesus' response depends on the audience appreciating the irony of the moment: very few people truly know "whence Jesus comes," although many claim to know. According to the narrative, their claim is false and Jesus mocks it (7:28), thus beginning his riposte. The rebuttal continues when he says "I have not come of my own accord; he who sent me is true, and *him you do not know*. I know him for I come from him" (7:28-29). Aside from the fact that we have claims and counterclaims to correct knowledge, it is simply insulting on Jesus' part to call his audience both stupid and lying. Yet, such "insults" according to the choreography of honor represent a legitimate riposte to a prior challenge. The narrator emphasizes the power of the insult-riposte when he tells that as a result of Jesus' testy remark "they sought to arrest him" (7:30).

Apart from Jesus' personal ripostes to challenges, two other narrative characters come to his defense and participate in the process of delivering a riposte to challenges to Jesus. The officers sent by the chief priests and Pharisees to arrest Jesus return empty-handed (7:32, 45). Why? "No man ever spoke like this man!" (7:46). On the narrative level, it is always a coup of honor for an accused or executed person to elicit a final grant of honor and respect from his executioner (see Matt 27:54 and Luke 23:47). It does not matter if these officers are dismissed as people "led astray" and "accursed" (7:47, 49); they have borne their testimony which challenges Jesus' challengers. Second, whether a true disciple or only one in secret, Nicodemus proposes a legal question which works on Jesus' behalf, "Does our law judge a man without first giving him a hearing and learning what he does?" (7:51). However we evaluate this as a formal defense of Jesus, it serves to call in question the legitimacy of the challenges to Jesus, thus embarrassing them for their envious challenge in the first place. In the narrative, it was perceived as a gross insult to which a curt and stinging riposte is returned: "Are you from Galilee too? Search and you will see that no prophet is to rise from Galilee" (7:52).

Moreover, despite the official censure of public discussion of Jesus, the officials do not have their way in silencing all defense and praise of Jesus, which challenges the negative evaluations and judgments. In contrast to the accusation that Jesus leads the people astray, some declare that "He is a good man" (7:12-13); and juxtaposed to those who argue that Jesus cannot be the Christ, others state "When the Christ appears, will he do more signs than this man has done?" (7:31); and, canceling the judgment that Jesus cannot be the Christ because he is not from Bethlehem, some acclaim him favorably: "This is really the prophet!" and "This is the Christ" (7:40-41). Thus the "schism" or divided judgment about Jesus contains both challenges and ripostes on his behalf. The challenges just will not stick, and so Jesus' honorable role and status remain acknowledged, at least by some.

5.0 Conflict in Two Keys: Summary and Conclusions

This chapter has focused on conflict in John 7, both the trials (forensic) and tribulations (honor challenges) of Jesus. We hope to have shown that the narrative in John 7 (along with 8:12-59) enjoys a distinctive unity in terms not only of the temporal context, which is the Feast of Tabernacles, but especially in terms of the extended forensic proceedings occurring. From a literary and formal consideration, John 7 consists of an extended trial of Jesus. Knowing the conventions of a forensic proceeding, we are able to identify the various characters in the narrative according to their proper role in a trial, thus learning how to read the story more accurately in light of the author's formal shaping of the narrative and his ideological perspective.

But it would have been shameful to rest contented with this literary, form-critical reading. For if we would truly understand the record of conflict described in the story, we need more social tools to sort out the cultural elements which go into an adequate reading of the conflict. To this end, we turned to the anthropology of honor and shame. This culturally appropriate model instructed us on things which could never be gleaned from even the most exacting literary and formal-critical analysis. We learned what the conflict was all about, namely the worth, reputation, and status of Jesus — his honor rating. Moreover, we learned more about the code of honor, that is, the typical things which the ancients considered in evaluating someone's worth, in this case the cultural importance of "origins/birth" ("whence") and "nurture and training" (*paideia* or education). The forensic model of analysis simply cannot tell us the importance of such things. Furthermore, we learned about the social and cultural patterns of Jesus' world, how they assessed honor in terms of *ascription* or *achievement*, how they perceived the limited character of all goods, including and especially honor, how success inevitably breeds envy, and finally how they typically fight by means of the choreography of challenge and riposte. John 7 is that much richer for reading it in two keys, literary-formal and cultural. With this perspective we begin to see that conflict, pure and simple, is the dominant game in town, whether it is expressed literarily in terms of *chreiai* or in terms of forensic proceedings.

Finally, what do we know if we follow these interpretative leads? First and foremost, the rhetorical strategy of the Gospel writer has been and remains the honoring of Jesus as a person of incalculable worth, status, and prestige. For it is the will of God that "all shall honor the Son, even as they honor the Father. Who does not honor the Son does not honor the Father who sent him" (5:23). Hence, not only are the signs of Jesus told to elicit honor, but also the stories of conflict in which Jesus acquits himself nobly. The signs were performed and narrated "so that you may believe that Jesus is the Christ, the Son of God" (20:31); they manifest his "glory" or honor (2:11). They are, then, his claims to worth and status. But his forensic trials serve to highlight that his claims are truly defensible and that Jesus, the honorable man, knows how to defend his honor and thus earn our continual esteem and praise. The author, then, presents Jesus according to the value system and cultural code of his world, namely, honor and shame. And he portrays Jesus as a fully honorable person, both in terms of ascribed honor (origins/birth, education, authorization) and in terms of his ability to claim and defend his honor. If honor is the pivotal or premier value of the author's cultural world, then Jesus should be reckoned as a most exalted and worthy and celebrated person. This kind of value statement simply cannot be gleaned from a mere study of the forensic process.

9

Jesus the Judge

Forensic Process in John 8:21-59

This study of John 8 takes its cue from what appears to be a contradiction in the text. In 8:15 Jesus states that "I judge no one," a fair statement in light of the fact that he is himself being judged by others (see 7:32, 45-52). But in 8:26, the situation is reversed, as Jesus states "I have much to say about you and much to judge." It is my hypothesis that John 8:21-59 contains a considerable amount of forensic imagery and that its narrative is formally structured as a forensic process, a trial in which Jesus is no longer the accused but the judge. While a forensic approach to the Fourth Gospel is scarcely new,[1] John 8:21-59 has not been examined in this regard, an important thematic perspective which thoroughly pervades the Fourth Gospel.

1.0 Typical Forensic Process

If, according to the hypothesis of this study, John 8:21-59 is structured as a typical forensic process, we must know what that process looked like. For only when we know that can we identify and interpret the forensic elements of John 8 and see how they conform to the cultural expectations of a trial. From the Roman trial of Jesus by Pilate, however, we learn a great deal about Roman judicial

---

1. Interest in the forensic aspects of the Fourth Gospel has grown steadily: Rudolf Bultmann, *The Gospel of John* (Philadelphia: Fortress, 1971) 84-97 and 237-84; J. Louis Martyn, *History and Theology in the Fourth Gospel* (2d ed.; Nashville: Abingdon, 1979) chapters 3 and 4; A. E. Harvey, *Jesus on Trial: A Study of the Fourth Gospel* (Atlanta: John Knox, 1977); and A. T. Lincoln, *Truth on Trial: The Lawsuit Motif in the Fourth Gospel* (Peabody, MA: Hendrickson, 2000).

process.² The following diagram indicates six formal elements in Jesus' Roman trial, as seen in the accounts of both Luke and John:

Forensic Elements	Dramatis Personae	Luke	John	John
1. Arrest	police/soldiers	23:14a	18:1-11	
2. Charges	accusers and accused	23:14b	18:29-30	19:7
3. Witnesses	false witnesses (Matt 26:59-61), true witnesses (Matt 27:19)		18:20-21	
4. *Cognitio:* judge's examination of accused	judge: magistrate, elders, or other	23:14c	18:33-38	19:8-11
4. Verdict	judge's task	23:14d	18:39	19:6
5. Sentence	judge's task; others execute sentence	23:15b		19:12-16
6. Judicial Warning	judge's task; others perform task	23:15c	19:1-4	

In the previous chapter, "Trials (Forensic) and Tribulations (Honor Challenges) of Jesus," we presented a detailed description of the typical sequence of events and the roles of the dramatis personae in a trial. There is no need to repeat those materials here.

2.0 Jesus Does Not *Judge* (8:12-20)

Before we can examine the forensic procedure in 8:21-58, we must attend to 8:12-20, which is itself a forensic process, but of a different kind. In 8:12-20, Jesus insists that he does not judge (8:15), whereas he shortly proclaims that he has "much to judge" (8:26). This important *aporia* might be taken as a clue to different layers of tradition in the Fourth Gospel. At present, let us examine 8:12-20 in terms of the forensic process presented there.

Regarding 8:12-20, scholars agree that it is of a piece with John 7.³ The occasion is still the Feast of Tabernacles (7:2), and Jesus claims to offer Christian replacements for the water (7:37-39) and light (8:12) which are prayed for at this feast. More importantly, the forensic process begun in ch. 7 continues in 8:12-20, as the following synopsis indicates:

---

2. The standard work on Roman legal process in the provinces of the empire is A. N. Sherwin-White, *Roman Society and Roman Law in the New Testament* (Oxford: Oxford University Press, 1963); this replaced the study by H. J. Cadbury, "Roman Law and the Trial of Paul" in F. Jackson and K. Lake, eds., *The Beginnings of Christianity* (London: Macmillan, 1933) 5:295-337.

3. For example, Raymond E. Brown, *The Gospel According to John* (AB 29; Garden City, NY: Doubleday, 1966) 1.342-45; Rudolf Schnackenburg, *The Gospel According to St. John* (New York: Herder, 1982) 2.187-96.

Jesus the Judge

1. Legal Claim
   claim: Jesus = light: "I am the light of the world. Whoever follows me will not walk in darkness but have the light of life" (8:12).
   claim: Jesus = water: "If any thirst, let them come to me and drink" (7:37). "Whoever believes in me, as the Scriptures say, 'Out of his heart shall flow rivers of living water'" (7:38).
2. Basis for Testimony: Firsthand Knowledge
   "Even if I bear witness to myself my testimony is true; for I know whence I have come and whither I am going" (8:14).
3. Demand for Impartial Judgment
   "You judge according to the flesh; I judge no one" (8:15).
   "Do not judge according to appearances but judge with right judgment" (7:24).[4]
4. Acceptable Testimony: Two Witnesses
   "Yet even if I do judge, my judgment is true, for it is not I alone that judge, but I and he who sent me. In your law it is written that the testimony of two witnesses is true. I bear witness to myself and the Father who sent me bears witness to me" (8:16-18).
   "My teaching is not mine but his who sent me; if anyone's will is to do his will, he will know whether I am speaking on my own authority" (7:16-17).
5. Authorized Testimony: Agent Sent from God
   "'Where is your Father?' Jesus answered: 'You know neither me nor my Father; if you knew me, you would know my Father also'" (8:19).
   "Who speaks on his own authority seeks his own glory; who seeks the glory of him who sent him is true and in him there is no falsehood" (7:18).
6. Setting of the Scene: the Temple
   "These words he spoke in the treasury, as he taught in the Temple, and no one arrested him" (8:20b).
   "Jesus went up to the Temple and taught" (7:14); "they sought to arrest him, but no one laid hands on him" (7:30).

8:12-20 is not only linked with ch. 7 in terms of Jesus' claims to be the replacement of the Feast of Tabernacles, but is formally shaped like ch. 7 according to elaborate forensic procedure. Put simply, Jesus is the accused and the assembled Jews are his judges. In both texts, 1) Jesus makes a claim before the assembly of Israel in its most sacred location, the Temple: he is Israel's water (7:37-39) and its light (8:12). 2) The Temple personnel examine the basis for his claim primar-

---

4. Proof of judging according to appearances is found in the debate over whether the Christ or a prophet can come from Galilee (7:27, 40-44, 52).

ily in terms of the legitimacy of the claimant: a witness should have firsthand information (8:14) or be informed on the topic to which he witnesses (7:15). What makes Jesus an apt witness in this instance is that he is truly "in the know": he knows whence he comes and whither he goes (8:14), while they do not know (7:27). They might be "in the know," if they were devoted to God (7:17). Because of his superior knowledge, Jesus' claim and testimony ought to be acceptable at court. 3) Instructions are given to the judging public to judge justly and fairly; they should not judge with partiality[5] according to the flesh or appearances (8:15; 7:24). 4) The testimony of a single witness is not acceptable in Israel's court (Deut 19:15); yet two witnesses testify to Jesus' claims, Jesus and the one who sent him (8:16-18; 7:26-28). 5) Jesus claims to be a valid witness, deputized by the most honorable person as his personal agent,[6] and so he must be received as an acceptable witness (8:19; 7:18, 28). In form, then, 8:12-20 resembles the kind of forensic procedure typically found elsewhere in the Fourth Gospel, in particular 5:30-46 and 7:13-52.[7]

3.0 A New Trial: Accusing the Accusers

If in 8:12-20 Jesus the accused was questioned by his judges about his claims to be the world's light, this is hardly the case in 8:21ff., where the roles are reversed and Jesus becomes the judge and his audience the accused.

3.1 *The New Trial (8:21-30)*

The discourse in 8:21-30 sets the stage for the new forensic process which will be played out in 8:31-58. Typical of the Fourth Gospel, 8:21 functions on a literary level as the topic statement for the subsequent narrative[8] and consists of three

---

5. See Jouette Bassler, *Divine Impartiality: Paul and a Theological Axiom* (SBLDS 59; Chico, CA: Scholars Press, 1981) 7-27.
6. Peder Borgen, "God's Agent in the Fourth Gospel," in *Religions in Antiquity*, ed. Jacob Neusner (Leiden: Brill, 1968) 137-48.
7. See Urban C. Von Walde, "Literary Structure and Theological Argument in Three Discourses with the Jews in the Fourth Gospel," *JBL* 103 (1984): 575-84; idem, "The Witnesses to Jesus in Jn 5:31-40 and Belief in the Fourth Gospel," *CBQ* 43 (1981): 385-404.
8. Special attention to this rhetorical strategy was given by Jerome H. Neyrey, *The Gospel of John* (Cambridge: Cambridge University Press, 2006) 41-47, 76-78, 89-90, 93-94, 110-11, 124-28, 268-69, 271-72. Peder Borgen (*Bread from Heaven* [Leiden: Brill, 1965]) argued that the text in 6:31 (Exod 16:15) functions as the topic statement which is developed in the rest of the Bread of Life discourse.

items: 1) "I go away and you will seek me," 2) "you will die in your sins," and 3) "where I am going you cannot come." The development of these topic items proceeds in chiastic order, starting with the third item: 3) "Then the Jews said: 'Will he kill himself, since he says *"Where I am going you cannot come"?"'* (8:22). 2) *"You will die in your sins,* for *you will die in your sins* unless you believe that I AM" (8:24). 3) "When you have *lifted up* the Son of Man then you will know that I AM" (8:28).

"Where I am going you cannot come" resembles Jesus' remark in 7:34, but the narrator interprets it quite differently here. Of course, correct knowledge of whence Jesus comes and whither he goes is a major Johannine theme. This knowledge divides insiders from outsiders. The audience "judges according to the flesh," when they misunderstand Jesus' remark as a prediction of his suicide: "Will he kill himself, since he says, 'Where I am going, you cannot come?'" (8:22). Something is askew, as the audience suspects Jesus of suicide, an unholy act which would imply that he is evil and not from God.[10] The truth of the matter is just the reverse; inasmuch as Jesus is "going" back to God, he is going to a world "above," which is "*not* this world" (8:23). "*You cannot come,*" then, is a statement of fact that Jesus and his hearers belong to two different worlds: "You are from below, I am from above; you are of this world, I am not of this world." This is a damning statement in the Johannine idiom, a formal forensic charge. Jesus and his listeners belong to irreconcilable, hostile worlds; he belongs to God's world, which they cannot enter, for they are truly outsiders to God and God's covenant.

"*You will die in your sins.*" As we will see, this functions as the sentence for the crime of failing to acknowledge Jesus as "I AM."[11] Such people never come into God's presence, that is, the world "above." The Law, the breaking of which warrants this censure, is articulated immediately in 8:24: "*Unless they believe that I AM.*" Inasmuch as most "unless" statements function as demands for membership (3:3, 5; 6:53; 12:24; 13:8; 15:4), so too 8:24 is a radical demand for belief of a very high order.[12] In the course of the narrative of the Gospel, this is the

---

9. Many attempts have been made to discern the structure of John 8; see W. Kern, "Der symmetrische Gesamtaubau von Jo 8, 12-58," *ZKT* 78 (1956): 451-54.

10. Josephus, for example, condemns suicide in *War* 3.363-78, calling it "repugnant to that nature which all creatures share, and an act of impiety toward God who created us" (3.369); "This crime, so hateful to God, is also punished by the sagest of legislation" (3.376).

11. For excellent recent discussion of "I Am," see Catrin H. Williams, "'I Am' or 'I Am He'? Self-Declaratory Pronouncements in the Fourth Gospel and in Rabbinic Tradition," in *Jesus in the Johannine Tradition,* ed. Robert T. Fortna and Tom Thatcher (Louisville, KY: Westminster John Knox, 2001) 343-52; also David M. Ball, *'I Am' in John's Gospel: Literary Function, Background and Theological Implications* (Sheffield: Sheffield Academic Press, 1996).

12. Jerome H. Neyrey, *The Gospel of John* (Cambridge: Cambridge University Press, 2006) 79-80, 214-15.

latest and most exalted of the demands issued in the Fourth Gospel and the formula by which Jesus must be acknowledged.

> 3:3 *Unless* one is born anew, one cannot see the kingdom of God.
> 3:5 *Unless* one is born of water and the spirit, one cannot enter the kingdom of God.
> 6:53 *Unless* you eat the flesh of the Son of man and drink his blood, you have no life in you.[13]

Whereas these functioned at one time as formal criteria according to which one is reckoned an insider, 8:24 becomes the newest and most transcendent forensic norm of judgment according to which Jesus' listeners will be judged. The ultimate and fatal sin becomes noncompliance with the demand to acknowledge Jesus according to the special formula "I AM." The original remark of Jesus, *I go away and you seek me*, again sounds similar to a remark in 7:33-34:

8:21	7:33-34
	I shall be with you a little longer
I go away	and then *I go* to him who sent me.
and *you will seek me* and die in your sins,	*You will seek me* and not find me;
for *where I am going*	*where I am*
you cannot come.	*you cannot come.*

But in Johannine logic, 8:21a contains a statement of double meaning,[14] the cryptic significance of which is lost on Jesus' listeners, who are from below and of this world. The narrator finally explains it in 8:28 in terms of Jesus' death. His "going away" and their "seeking" him refer to their attempts to kill Jesus: "When *you have lifted up* the Son of man . . ." 8:21, then, serves as a topic sentence of three items containing Johannine double-meaning words which are subsequently explained in 8:22-30.

In terms of forensic procedure, 8:21-30 represents a forensic scenario different from that found in 8:12-20, as the diagram at the top of p. 233 indicates. Let us not underestimate the aggressive tone of Jesus' remarks here. He has absolutely demanded of his audience that they confess him as "I AM," a life-and-death issue, failure to do so resulting in "dying in sin." Jesus has, moreover, accused his hearers of *not* being of his world: "You are from *this* world, you are

---

13. For more on this type of statement in the Fourth Gospel, see Neyrey, *The Gospel of John*, 79-80 and 214-15.

14. D. A. Carson, "Understanding Misunderstandings in the Fourth Gospel," *TynB* 33 (1982): 59-91; Earl Richard, "Expressions of Double Meaning and Their Function in the Gospel of John," *NTS* 31 (1985): 96-112.

Jesus the Judge

Forensic Aspect	8:12-20	8:21-30
Judge	assembled Jews	Jesus
Accused	Jesus	assembled Judeans
Charge/crime	false claims: water and light	refusal to believe that Jesus is "I AM"
Sentence		die in their sins

from below," harsh statements of fact[15] that Jesus, who knows what is in the human heart (2:25), utters in solemn seriousness.

The audience of Jesus pleads "not guilty" to the charges, for as 8:30 indicates, "As he spoke, many believed in him." But this is just the issue that must be investigated,[16] inasmuch as it belongs to accused to plead innocent. The charge still stands; the testimony of the accused must be tested. The trial, then, has just begun: are these accused telling the truth that they are Jesus' disciples?

The rhetorical function of 8:21 is twofold: it not only functions as the topic statement for the subsequent dialogue, but it also heralds the mode of inquiry and the proof that make up the investigation by Jesus, the judge. The form of 8:21-30 differs from the forensic procedure described in 8:12-20, for it exemplifies the typical Johannine pattern of *statement–misunderstanding–explanation*. Jesus makes an initial *statement* in 8:21 containing a double-meaning remark, which the hearers *misunderstand* because they are outsiders and do not grasp the inner, spiritual meaning of his words (8:22). Jesus then issues an *explanation*, a further word (8:23-30), which exposes the extra meaning coded in his original statement, a pattern found throughout the Fourth Gospel.

Statement	3:3	4:10	4:32	6:41	11:11
Misunderstanding	3:4	4:11-12	4:33	6:42	11:12
Explanation	3:5	4:13-14	4:34-38	6:43ff	11:13-15[17]

---

15. Compare this with the way Jesus treats Nicodemus (3:6, 11-12) and those who followed him because they ate their fill (6:26).

16. Part of the scholarly concern has focused on the relationship of 8:30 with 8:31: Is the audience the same? If people "believe" in Jesus, how is it that Jesus treats them so harshly in 8:31ff.? Alternately, if the discourse in 8:32-58 proves that they are not believers, then are they lying in 8:30 when they claim to believe? The author, I argue, intends 8:30 to be ambiguous so that their claims may be subject to Jesus' *cognitio*. See C. H. Dodd, "Behind a Johannine Dialogue," in his *More New Testament Studies* (Manchester: Manchester University Press, 1968) 42-43.

17. This pattern has been discussed as an example of the way Jesus keeps secrets: he explains misunderstandings to some but to others makes his meaning difficult to grasp; see Jerome H. Neyrey, "The Sociology of Secrecy and the Fourth Gospel," in *What Is John?* Volume

This literary pattern will function in 8:31-58 as the official forensic criterion for testing the truth of the accused's claims of innocence to the charge made in 8:23-24. Jesus makes this plain in 8:31 when he abruptly establishes a test to see whether the claim in 8:30 that "they believed in him" is true. He states, "You are my disciples, if you remain in my word," that is, if they *understand* Jesus' words correctly and *agree* with them.[18] Their reaction to Jesus' words, then, will determine whether the protestations of innocence in 8:30 are true. The testimony of the accused must be tested, a process which is conducted by means of the form *statement–misunderstanding–explanation* which, as the following diagram indicates, regularly structures the flow of the discourse in 8:31-58.

Tests	*first*	*second*	*third*	*fourth*	*fifth*
Statement	8:32	8:38	8:41a	8:51	8:56
Misunderstanding	8:33	8:39a	8:41b	8:52-53	8:57
Explanation	8:34-37	8:39b-40	8:42-47	8:54-55	8:58

The preliminaries of the forensic process are over, and it is time to get on with the substance of the trial.

3.2 The First Test (8:21-30)

This first test of whether the alleged believers "are . . . truly my disciples" is crafted in traditional chiastic form:

    A. If you *remain in my word* (v. 31b)
    B. you will know the truth . . . set you *free* (v. 32b).
    C. We are the *Seed of Abraham* (v. 33a).
    D. We have never been *slaves* (v. 33b).
    D'. Everyone who does sin is a *slave* to sin; the slave does *not remain* in the house forever, but the son *remains* forever (vv. 34-35).
    C'. I know that you are *Seed of Abraham*, but you seek to kill me (v. 37a, b).
    B'. If the Son makes you *free*, you will be truly *free* (v. 36).
    A'. My *word finds no place* in you (v. 37c).

II: *Literary and Social Readings of the Fourth Gospel*, ed. Fernando Segovia (Atlanta: Scholars Press, 1998) 79-109.

18. After charging the audience with being in the wrong place ("from below . . . of this world"), how can the same people pass muster?

Jesus the Judge

The chiastic structure highlights the central issue of the first test: authentic disciples *remain in Jesus' words*. This theme is presented in an *inclusio*: beginning in 8:31b, Jesus makes a conditional statement about authentic discipleship (if you *"remain in my word"*), and in 8:37c, he concludes by stating that at this point *"my word finds no place in you."* By 8:37, the judge has performed his *cognitio* and judges that the audience has failed the first test. This motif of "truly abiding," moreover, is highlighted in the middle of the passage when Jesus states that slaves do not *remain* but sons *remain*, indicating the overriding concern with establishing where the hearers truly stand or remain, i.e. discipleship with Jesus.[19]

The rest of this exchange centers around the second issue, the meaning of the terms *free* and *slave*. Jesus' words alone make for authentic freedom; but the hearers claim that freedom comes by descent from Abraham, indicating by this that belonging to Abraham is more important to them than belonging to Jesus, which implies at the very least that they are loosely attached to him as disciples.

In terms of uncovering the truth of their claims to be Jesus' disciples, the probative force of this exchange comes precisely from the form in which the dialogue is cast, viz., *statement–misunderstanding–explanation*. Jesus issues a *statement*: "If you remain in my word, you will know the truth." They, of course, *misunderstand* his word, insisting that they have "never been slaves" (8:33), implying that they do not need or want Jesus' truth or words which alone make for authentic freedom. Jesus then gives an *explanation* which indicates how wrong they are, that they are truly slaves, not free: "You seek to kill me" (8:37), which must be understood in the Fourth Gospel as the ultimate sin. And, as Jesus indicates, "Everyone who does sin is a slave of sin and the slave does not remain in the house" (8:34-35). *Slaves*, therefore, because *sinners!* The dynamic of 8:31-37, then, is a forensic demonstration that these people who claimed to believe in Jesus (8:30) are *not truly Jesus' disciples* for the following reasons:

1. They do not remain in his word, rather they misunderstand it and reject it.
2. They are not free, but slaves, that is, slaves of sin because they seek to kill Jesus.
3. They prefer affinity with Abraham rather than discipleship to Jesus.
4. They are lying when they say that they believe in Jesus.

---

19. "Remain" *(menein)* indicates relationships of loyalty and affiliation; see J. Heise, *Bleiben. Menein in den Johanneischen Schriften* (Tübingen: J. C. B. Mohr [Paul Siebeck], 1967); Brown, *The Gospel According to John*, 1.510-12.

The correct understanding of the allusions to Abraham in 8:31-37 greatly aids in appreciating the forensic thrust of this passage. A distinction is made between "free" and "slave" and between the son who "remains" and the one who does "not remain." It would appear that we have allusions here to Abraham's two sons, Isaac and Ishmael. According to Gen 16:15, the slave woman Hagar bore Abraham a slave son (Ishmael), whereas in Gen 21:1-8 Sarah bore Abraham a free son (Isaac). According to Gen 21:10, however, the slave son did not remain in Abraham's house, because Sarah demanded, "Cast out this slave woman with her son; for the son of this slave woman shall not be heir with my son Isaac." Evidently, the free son remained in the house.[20]

This material has a direct bearing on the argument in 8:31-37, where the primary issue is: who is truly a disciple of Jesus? who is free? and who remains? As the argument goes, the issue is one of being an authentic member of God's kingdom (see 3:3, 5). Descent from Abraham, of course, was regularly claimed in post-biblical Judaism as grounds for membership in God's covenant.[21] The Q-source passage Matt 3:9//Luke 3:8 and the discussion in Gal 4:21-31 are evidence of the importance in the New Testament both of being of Abraham and of descending from Abraham's true son.[22] While the audience claims to be such when they claim to be "seed of Abraham," such a claim is ambiguous, for Abraham had two sons, and so testing is needed to discover just how the audience is descended from Abraham and according to which son. Apropos of the argument in 8:31-58, Jesus would not seem to object if his audience really were of Abraham, for then they would do what Abraham did (8:39). What Jesus uncovers, however, is that they are not of Abraham's free son, Isaac, who remained in the house, but of Ishmael, the slave son, who did not remain.

True Disciples	*False Disciples*
from Isaac	from Ishmael
free, legitimate	slave, illegitimate
remained in the house	did *not* remain in the house

Claiming to be "Seed of Abraham," the audience passes itself off as authentic members of God's covenant, but their claim contains deception. They descend

---

20. Not all agree that the focus in John 8:31-37 is on the two sons of Abraham; many see it as exemplifying the contrast between Sarah and Hagar (Gal 4:21-31), for example, Brown, *The Gospel According to John*, 1.362-64.
21. See Thomas Dozeman, "*Sperma Abraam* in John 8 and Related Literature," *CBQ* 42 (1980): 344-45.
22. See, for example, C. K. Barrett, "The Allegory of Abraham, Sarah and Hagar in the Argument of Galatians," in his *Studies on Paul* (Philadelphia: Westminster, 1982) 154-79.

from Abraham, but through the slave Ishmael, not through the legitimate and free son Isaac.

But what is wrong with being a descendant of Abraham through Ishmael? While Gen 21:9 in the MT says only that Sarah saw Ishmael "playing" with her son Isaac, this point is elaborately developed in the midrashim. In some streams, Ishmael's "playing" was interpreted as idolatrous worship, whereby he was seducing the young Isaac into sin;[23] in other places, "Sarah has seen how Ishmael took arrows and shot, with the intention of killing Isaac,"[24] a tradition reflected also in Gal 4:29. I suggest that this latter understanding of Ishmael-as-murderer might also be operative in the Johannine argument, for Jesus accuses his hearers of "seeking to kill him" (8:37; see 8:40, 44, 59). In fact, this "seeking" of Jesus functions precisely as the proof that the audience is descended from Abraham not through Isaac, but through Ishmael, for they do what Ishmael did, i.e., attempt to kill. This means that they are sinners, slaves of sin (8:34b), and so will not remain in the house. Besides attempted murder, the audience is guilty of lying, for, while they are "seed of Abraham," they are descended from Ishmael, but would pass themselves off as free sons (8:33). Knowing the Abraham allusions, then, furthers our appreciation of the forensic argument operative in the passage, how their claim to be "seed of Abraham" needs to be tested to determine from which son, Isaac or Ishmael, they are descended.

3.3 A Second Test (8:38-40)

As in 8:31-37, these verses are also crafted in a chiastic arrangement which focuses their meaning.

> A. "I speak of what I have seen with my Father,
>   and you *do* what you have heard from *your father*" (v. 38).
> B. "They answered him: '*Abraham* is our *father*'" (v. 39a).
> B'. "Jesus said to them: 'If you were *Abraham's children*, you would do what *Abraham* did, but now you seek to kill me, a man who has told you the truth which I heard from God'" (vv. 39b-40).
> A'. "This is not what *Abraham did*" (v. 40c).

The key issue in this passage concerns *doing*, either *doing* what "your father told you" (8:38) or *doing* what Abraham did" (8:40c), the argument resting on the

---

23. See *Tg. Ps.-J., Tg. Yer. I*, and *Tg. Neof.* Gen 21:9; see also *Gen. Rab.* 53.11.

24. *t. Soṭa* 6.6 as cited by H. D. Betz, *Galatians* (Philadelphia: Fortress, 1979) 250; see also Roger Le Déaut, "Traditions targumiques dans le Corpus Paulinien?" *Bib* 42 (1961): 37-43.

presumption that one's pedigree and ancestry are established by one's *doing* what one's ancestor did (a chip off the old block). On this point, the passage is picking up a point raised in 8:32-37, that Jesus' audience claims to be "seed of Abraham," a claim partially disputed by showing that the claimants are descended from the slave son Ishmael. But when the audience again claims that "Abraham is our father," are they truly Abraham's offspring in any sense? Whose offspring are they?

The forensic importance of 8:38-40 lies in the way the passage is once more presented in terms of the familiar pattern. Jesus *states*, "I speak of what I have seen with my Father, and you do what you have heard from your father." Indeed this is a cryptic remark, open to many interpretations, the correct one of which only a true disciple will know. The audience *understands* that Jesus is challenging their legitimacy as descendants of Abraham: "Abraham is our father." But they *do not understand* what it means to be offspring of Abraham, because they do not know what the patriarch did. If they understand Jesus' clarification about his father, they surely do not accept it. Shortly, Jesus will clarify his remarks about "their father," who is the devil.

We must ask, however, what did Abraham *do*? Traditionally, this has been interpreted in terms of Abraham's faith, a point clearly made in Romans 4 and Galatians 3. But post-biblical Jewish authors praised Abraham equally for his hospitality,[25] when he received the three heavenly messengers at the oaks of Mamre (Genesis 18). If Abraham were the father of Jesus' present audience, they would do what Abraham did, viz., show hospitality to the present heavenly visitor who has come into their midst, namely Jesus. But as the text indicates, hospitality is far from their minds, which are set on murder, "but now you seek to kill me" (8:40a).

A second time, then, the judge has probed their testimony and found them not to be telling the truth. Again they do not understand Jesus' word, so how can they remain in it? Again, their claim to be legitimate in virtue of descent from Abraham is challenged and refuted. What remains is the second, insistent charge from Jesus that they "seek to kill me" (8:37, 40). If that is the case, then they cannot truly be his disciples.

---

25. Philo, for example, praises Abraham over and over for his hospitality (*Abr.* 107, 114-16, 132, 167), a point mentioned explicitly in Josephus, *Ant.* 1.196; see also *1 Clement* 10.6-8 and *Testament of Abraham* 17.

3.4. A Third Test (8:41-47)

Once again, the author shapes the passage by means of a chiasm which helps to convey its argument:

- A. You *do* what your *father did* (v. 41a).
  - B. They said to him: "We were not born of fornication; we have *one Father, even God*" (v. 41b).
  - B'. Jesus said to them: "If *God* were your *Father*, you would love me, for I proceeded and came forth from *God*; I came not of my own accord, but he sent me . . ." (vv. 42-43).
- A'. "You are of *your father* the devil and your will is to *do your father's* desires. He was a murderer from the beginning, because there is no truth in him. When he *lies*, he speaks according to his own nature" (v. 44).

The key issue is again *doing* what one's *father did*. Linked with 8:39 and the argument that children prove their ancestry by *doing* what their fathers *did*, 8:41-44 begins and ends with Jesus' judicial charge that his audience *does* what its true father *did*, which in this case means murder and lying. Do they *understand* what he is saying? Jesus has twice already in this discourse accused the audience of trying to kill him: "Yet you seek to kill me" (8:37) and "But now you seek to kill me" (8:40). This is true, for they are seeking to kill him — so much for the charge of murder in 8:44. It is equally true that the audience is lying to Jesus constantly, namely, that they are his disciples (8:30), that they are not slaves (8:32-33) and that they are not illegitimate children (8:41). The audience, of course, is lying when it claims to be holy and to be children of God; thus Jesus exposes the lie with his argument that "if God were your father, you would love me," the one whom God sent but whom they seek to kill (8:40a) — hardly a "loving" act. Indeed, they understand all too well what Jesus is saying about their lying and attempting to kill Jesus.

We recognize that there are further allusions to Abraham and his sons in 8:41-44, which have a bearing on the forensic argument here. If we are correct in describing how Jesus has rebutted the claims of authentic membership in God's covenant family because the audience, despite their claims to be "Seed of Abraham," are not descended of Isaac but Ishmael, then we can more easily see how the audience reacts to this slur on their legitimacy, a charge which they truly understand. Defensively they counter in 8:41 that they are "not born of fornication," that is, illegitimate "Seed of Abraham" and so bastards[26] as regards mem-

---

26. What does illegitimacy mean in the cultural world of antiquity? Bastards are symbols

bership in the House of Israel. Are they lying? To be sure! Philo, for one, clearly indicates that Ishmael was a bastard, not a legitimate son and heir.[27] The claim in 8:41, then, is a disclaimer by the audience, but is it true? The testing of this lies in finding out the audience's pedigree by examining what they *do*, for the principle has been established in 8:31ff that sons *do* what their fathers *did*. Now what did Ishmael do?

As noted above, many midrashic texts state that Ishmael tried to kill Isaac. Gen 21:20 indicates that Ishmael was an accomplished archer, a point which is read back into Gen 21:9, viz., that Ishmael "played with" Isaac. He "played with" Isaac by shooting arrows at him, trying to kill him.[28] Gen 16:12, moreover, calls Ishmael a "wild ass of a man," which is interpreted to mean that Ishmael lived in constant conflict with family and neighbors: "His hand against every man and every man's hand against him." Some midrashim even interpret this as Ishmael's "plundering of lives." Such an understanding of Ishmael will become important when we try to understand the remarks in 8:44 that the audience is a murderer, thus taking after their father, *doing* what he *did*. But more on this later. Sufficient now to know that Ishmael was considered a bastard son of Abraham, a son who tried to kill the legitimate son, Isaac. By their deeds you shall know them!

Again the familiar formal pattern we have observed continues to prove that these people who claim to be Jesus' disciples do not remain in his word. Jesus *states* something which all people would understand: "You do what your father did." In one sense they *understand* part of this statement, for they take offense at the slur implied, that they are bastard children of Abraham: "We were not born of fornication!" But they are liars, and so we expect them to tell a lie which would blunt Jesus' charge: "We have one Father, even God." No *misunderstanding* here. Jesus' subsequent remarks indicate that he sees their remarks as a lie and so he proves in 8:42-43 that the audience is not obeying their Father/God as they claim, and so are sinners, a point he made earlier in 8:34. Of course the Fourth Gospel has already declared how one becomes a true

---

of people who reject God's discipline (Heb 12:8), are often the sworn enemies of God's elect (Josephus, *Ant.* 5.233-34), and are not permitted to enter the assembly of the Lord (Deut 23:2). In short they are honorless, base-born outsiders. The remarks of Bruce J. Malina (*The New Testament World: Insights from Cultural Anthropology* [3rd edition, Louisville, KY: Westminster John Knox, 2001] 154) are worth noting: "Given the emphasis on defensive strategy and holy seed, imputations of doubtful lineage are among the gravest insults in the culture, sure to get prompt attention. For example, Jesus calls his contemporaries an 'adulterous generation' (Mark 8:38; Matt 12:39; 16:4), literally 'a generation of bastards,' the offspring of adulterous unions."

27. Philo, *Sobr.* 8; *Names* 148.
28. See Sifre Deut 31; *t. Soṭa* 6.6; Josephus, *Ant.* 1.215.

child of God. In 1:12-13, it is not those born according to material, physical and earthly criteria (i.e., right clan, circumcision or adoption) who are God's children, but those born according to spiritual criteria, such as belief in Jesus. In 3:3-5, moreover, those who qualify to enter God's kingdom are those born *anōthen*, not simply "again" (birth in a literal and material sense), but "from above" (birth by spirit). Having God as Father, then, is a spiritual claim which, according to 1:12-13 and 3:3-6, means acceptance of Jesus. Not believing in Jesus, how can the audience in 8:41 truly claim that God is their Father? They are perpetrating lies and deception.

Jesus' next remarks are certainly not a clarifying explanation, but an undisguised charge that the audience is totally evil. Jesus' remarks in 8:44-47 contain the following four charges:

1. you are of your father the devil;
2. he was a murderer and a liar, and so are they;
3. "you do *not* believe me" (v. 45) and "if I tell you the truth, why do you *not* believe me?" (v. 46);
4. "you are not of God" (v. 47).

Jesus' remarks in 8:45-47 make abundantly clear that this audience is not "remaining in my word." Jesus continues to give them "the word," but it is evident that they are neither accepting that word nor remaining in it. They cannot, then, truly be his disciples! All along they have been lying and trying to kill Jesus. As judge, then, Jesus has performed a classic *cognitio* of their remarks and shown them to be utterly false.

The judge's *cognitio*, moreover, leads to specific formal charges against those being examined. As the trial continues, Jesus formally accuses them of being enemies of God, offspring of Cain and spawn of the devil (8:44).[29] "You do what your father did" (8:41a), a general accusation which includes the specific charges of *murder* and *lying*. Concerning murder, Jesus states, "You are of your father the devil, and your will is to do his desires. He was a murderer from the beginning" (8:44). It is one thing to indicate that their father is the devil and that he was "a murderer *from* the beginning"; but that remark also accuses the devil's offspring of the same crime: "Your will is *to do* your father's desires." The charges of Jesus are, at this point, just that, charges. Proof is needed! If proof is forthcoming, then the main point of this forensic process, the truth or falsehood of the claim in 8:30 to be followers of Jesus, would be settled. If this audi-

---

29. On the devil as the father of Cain, see Nils A. Dahl, "Der Erstgeborene Satans und der Vater des Teufels," in *Apophoreta*, ed. W. Eltester (Berlin: Töpelman, 1964) 70-84.

ence is truly "of the devil" and *does* what the devil *did* (lying, murder), then they cannot be telling the truth in 8:30 and cannot be Jesus' disciples, and so would come under the sentence enunciated in 8:24.

The progress of the forensic proceeding thus far gives strong support to Jesus' charge that his audience is plotting murder. This charge explains the cryptic double meaning in the remark that they were "seeking" Jesus, for while on the surface it might mean that they were seeking the truth, Jesus proves that their "seeking" (8:21, 28, 40) was rather a "seeking to kill" him (8:37). At first Jesus ambiguously remarks, "You will seek me" (8:21), whose sinister meaning is hinted at in the remark, "When you have lifted up the Son of man" (8:28), but which is finally exposed for what it really means, "You seek to kill me" (8:37, 40). When they actually take up stones to throw at him (8:59), they prove the truth of Jesus' charge of murder. Like their father, moreover, they were murderers from the beginning. So much for the charge of murder. They have been lying all along, but it will become thematic in the next part of this trial in 8:48-55.

3.5. A Fourth Test (8:48-55)

The trial which continues in 8:51 is punctuated here with a brief, bitter exchange. Jesus the judge has accused his hearers of lying and of being offspring of the devil. Typical of this type of name calling, they reciprocally accused Jesus of the same thing, under the rubric "It takes one to know one." If *they* are liars, he is an apostate from Israel, "a Samaritan"; if *they* are offspring of the devil, then he too "has a demon" (8:48). At the very least, this outburst clearly demonstrates what the audience really thinks of Jesus, and so they could never have been his disciples. Whereas the audience never attempts to refute Jesus' charge of demonic descent, Jesus himself offers as apology to their slurs the fact that he honors his Father, who is God, something completely incompatible with allegiance with the devil. They come from two different worlds (8:23).

The testing of the audience continues in the form we have come to expect. Jesus makes another *statement*: "If anyone keeps my word, he will *never see death*" (8:51), which is *misunderstood*: "Now we know that you have a demon. Abraham died, as did the prophets; and you say, 'If anyone keeps my word, he will *never taste death*'" (8:52). The *misunderstanding* lies in the way they repeat Jesus' word, indicating that they took it in a literal, material fashion:

> Jesus' word: If anyone keeps my word, he will *never see death*.
> Their version: If anyone keeps my word, he will *never taste death*.

Jesus never stated that his disciples would *never* die, although there is a great deal of confusion on that point in 21:20-23 and 11:21, 37. The probative force of this exchange rests on the original accusation of Jesus that these people are "of this world and from below," that is, not of Jesus' world. Like Nicodemus (3:6, 12), they are flesh, not spirit, and so cannot understand heavenly or spiritual things. By taking Jesus' words literally, they demonstrate that they are not spiritual and that they do not understand spiritual things, thereby proving what Jesus had charged them with, being "of this world" and "from below."

Their misunderstanding is compounded by their reduction to the state of questioning in 8:53. Those who ask questions demonstrate that they do not have answers. By asking "Whom do you make yourself? Are you greater than our father Abraham?" the audience indicates that they do *not* know who Jesus is, even though he told them in 8:24 that he is "I AM." Not knowing even then who he was (e.g. "They said to him, 'Who are you?'" 8:25), they nevertheless claimed to believe in him. Now when they ask "Whom do you make yourself?" they prove that they have never known who he is, neither "greater than Abraham" nor "I AM." Their questioning proves that they were lying from the beginning when they claimed to know Jesus and asserted that they were his followers.

Jesus' *explanation* is not really an explanation but an argument proving the audience's guilt. He indicates how different he is from them, confirming the charge in 8:23 that he is "*not* of this world" nor "from below," although they are. In substance, Jesus proves now what he had charged earlier, viz., that they are liars.

As regards lying, Jesus conducts a complicated demonstration. Of their lying father it was said: "He has nothing to do with the truth, because there is no truth in him. When he lies, he speaks according to his nature, for he was a liar and the father of lies" (8:44). Lying, then, has two aspects: 1) having *nothing to do with the truth* yet 2) *dissembling* that one knows and says the truth. Of the listeners it is argued in fact that they have nothing to do with the truth; for if they were truly Jesus' disciples, "they would know the truth and the truth would make them free" (8:31). They dissemble, moreover, when they claim to be (legitimate) "descendants of Abraham" (8:33) but are not, and boast that they are "sons of God" (8:41) but are not.

Finally in 8:55, Jesus finishes his argument proving them liars. Speaking of God, Jesus claims to be the complete opposite of his audience: "You do not know him; I know him." This judgment of fact serves as the basis for Jesus' next remark: "If I said 'I do not know him' I should be a liar like you; but I do know him." Implied in this comparison/contrast is an accusation that they are liars. Were Jesus to dissemble, he would reverse his statement and say "I do not know him." But Jesus speaks the truth when he claims "but I do know him." The liars, on the contrary, dissemble when they say "I know him (God)," for their judge has persuasively shown that they *do not know God*[30] or understand God's words, despite their dissembling to the contrary.

In proving them liars, Jesus demonstrates the forensic purpose of the entire dialogue in 8:31-58. Recall that Jesus already judged his listeners to be "from below" and "of this world" (8:23). To paraphrase, "they speak according to their nature" (8:44), that is, they naturally dissemble and lie when they say that they believe Jesus (8:30). It belongs to Jesus the judge to ferret out the truth, which in this case is to demonstrate that like their father they are "liars *from the beginning.*" They always were and will be outsiders to God's word and God's covenant.

The reference to Abraham in 8:52-53 functions in the forensic argument. Jesus, of course, has made a claim in his *statement* that "if one keeps my word, he will never see death" (8:51). This claim is easily refuted by the literal, physical argument that all people celebrated in Israel for "hearing" God's word have died. Abraham, canonized because he "believed God and it was credited to him as righteousness" (Gen 15:6), died; the prophets, all of whom received a word of God, died. Despite Jesus' claim, the literal facts seem to speak otherwise, as his audience is quick to point out. But the very fact that they misquote Jesus' words ("not taste death") here also functions as one more proof that Jesus' words do not find a home in them.

At stake here is an important forensic element. We noted at the beginning of this study that the social standing or character of a witness is a pivotal factor in forensic proceedings for evaluating the truth of a testimony given.[31] Jesus makes extraordinary claims, but what of his character? Who is Jesus that anyone should take him seriously? Jesus earlier dismissed the audience because of its base character: they are *not* descended from Abraham through Isaac, but take their lineage through the illegitimate Ishmael and finally from Cain and the devil. Therefore the appropriate question now becomes Jesus' own character or standing: "Are you greater than our father Abraham? Whom do you make yourself?" (8:53). Abraham is an uncontested saint and a thoroughly honorable character, whose holiness and honor exist apart from Jesus' claims. What, then, is Jesus' character that anyone should listen to him, especially when measured by the standard of Abraham?

---

30. John 8 contains an elaborate forensic proof that the hearers "do not know God":
   1. They said to him, "Where is your Father?" Jesus answered: "You *know* neither me *nor my Father;* if you knew me, you would *know my Father*" (8:19).
   2. "They did *not understand* that he spoke to them of his Father" (8:27).
   3. "I proceeded and came forth from God; I came not of my own accord, but he sent me. Why do you not understand what I say?" (8:42-43).
31. Harvey, *Jesus on Trial,* 20-21; Neyrey, "Forensic Defense Speech," 211-13.

Jesus immediately claims to be a holy and honorable person. He disclaims that he is vainglorious,[32] "If I glorify myself, my glory is nothing" (8:54a), and then goes on to assert his character: "It is my Father who glorifies me, of whom you say that he is your God" (8:54b). This affirms his character: he is *honorable*, for God, who is a prominent person, attests to his honor. He is a *holy* person, for the attesting person is the Holy One, Blessed be He. While Jesus' honorable character supports his claims in 8:51, the relationship of Abraham and Jesus remains unexplained, as there is still more to say about them in the rest of the forensic proceeding.

3.6 The Final Test (8:56-59)

Jesus concludes the trial, bringing it back to where it began. In 8:24, he charged that they would die in their sins if they did not confess him as "I AM." In 8:58-59 a final test demonstrates conclusively that they will not accept him as "I AM," for they take up stones to throw at him when he affirms once more that "I AM." 8:56-59, then, clinches the argument and proves beyond any shadow of doubt what the audience really thinks of Jesus.

Jesus makes a final *statement*, "Abraham rejoiced that he was to see my day; he saw it and was glad" (8:56). Not surprisingly, the audience *misunderstands* Jesus' words:

> Jesus' words: "Abraham rejoiced that he was to see my day; he saw it and was glad" (8:56).
> Their understanding: "You are not yet fifty years old, and you have seen Abraham?" (8:57).

In Jesus' version, he is the prominent figure, the one whom Abraham was privileged to see, and so he is in fact "greater than father Abraham." In their version the roles are reversed and Jesus is privileged to see Abraham. Once more, his word does not remain in them; in their eyes, Jesus is some minor figure out of the mainstream of things.

Jesus finishes these proceedings with further comment on his relationship with Abraham, "Before Abraham was coming to be, 'I AM'" (8:58). Thus his superiority to Abraham is reaffirmed, for his being is "to be" *(eimi)* and Abra-

---

32. As we saw in the chapter on John 5, Jesus never "makes himself" anything (5:18; 8:53; 10:33); rather God makes him what he is (5:19-29; 10:17-18). Materials on Jesus as the agent, mediator, and broker of God will be discussed in chapter 18.

ham's is "to become" *(ginesthai)*. Jesus, moreover, claims that his "being" is prior in time to Abraham's "coming to be," a statement of radical precedence (see 1:15, 30). Their question in 8:57 about how a young Jesus could have seen an old Abraham is simply reversed by Jesus' remark that he is the old, ancient, eternal figure who "is" before the recent Abraham "came to be." The audience does not misunderstand Jesus' statement; because they fully recognize what is implied in his statement, they take up stones to kill him. Again, it is now proved beyond a shadow of a doubt that they are not his disciples and lied in 8:30 when they claimed to believe.

The trial has now run its course. Earlier Jesus established a law that all who did not believe that he is "I AM" would die in their sins (8:24). How does the audience plead, guilty or not guilty? Not guilty, of course. Thus Jesus conducted a *cognitio* of his interlocutors, testing whether they truly are disciples, whether his word remains in them, whether they are authentic sons of Abraham. Along the way he makes salient that the audience are inveterate liars and murderers. Finally, he uncovers the root cause of their wickedness, namely, that they are offspring of the devil who was a liar and a murderer from the beginning. In the discourse they repeatedly misunderstand Jesus' words and object to them, proof that his word does not remain in them. Finally, they prove themselves guilty by trying to kill Jesus. The narrative does not explicitly state a guilty verdict, although no other verdict is possible; nor does it record a sentence, although the penalty of "die in your sins" (8:24) was stated earlier.

One more reference to Abraham occurs in this forensic context. The honorable Jesus asserted in 8:56 that "Your father Abraham rejoiced that he was to see my day; he saw it and was glad." There is considerable debate over which theophany in Genesis might be alluded to here, the Covenant of the Pieces (Genesis 15),[33] or the Visit at the Oak at Mamre (Genesis 18).[34] Because of the possible correspondences between Abraham's hospitality in Genesis 18 and John 8:39 and between laughter in Gen 18:12-15 and John 8:56, it seems that the Fourth Gospel alludes to Genesis 18. More importantly, it implies that Abraham received a christophany in the visit at the Oak of Mamre.

In short, Jesus claims to be a character of extraordinary eminence and holiness (recall 8:23, "I am from above . . . I am not of this world"). He claims to be nothing less than the appearing deity who gave christophanies to Abraham, Isa-

---

33. See Nils A. Dahl, "The Johannine Church and History," in his *Jesus in the Memory of the Church* (Minneapolis: Augsburg, 1976) 107-10.
34. L. Urban and P. Henry, "'Before Abraham Was I Am': Does Philo Explain John 8:56-59?" *Studia Philonica* 6 (1979): 157-93.

iah, Moses etc., a topic which will be discussed later in chapter 17. He is superior to Abraham; and so it is important to get straight whether Jesus saw Abraham (lower status for Jesus) or whether Abraham saw Jesus (higher status for Jesus). Jesus is superior in that he is "I AM" *(eimi)*, eternal in the past and imperishable in the future, whereas Abraham has both a beginning, "coming to be" *(ginesthai)* and an ending, "Abraham died" *(apethanen)*, indicating radically contingent being. Jesus' superior character, moreover, is communicated especially in the name "I AM," which must be taken as a reference to the name of the appearing deity of the Hebrew Scriptures. Whereas it might have been conceivable for the audience to fail to understand the content of Jesus' claim in 8:24, that content is now revealed. Thus Jesus as "I AM" is an extraordinary figure both in honor and holiness as the one who bears God's name (see 17:6, 11-12, 26) and who has acted throughout Israel's history as the figure who appeared to the patriarchs. His character as a trustworthy and acceptable witness is unimpeachable; his claims, therefore, must be accepted.

4.0 Resume, Conclusions, Further Questions

4.1 Resume

The Fourth Gospel apparently redacted John 8:21-59 to present the entire episode as an extended forensic process in which are present all of the formal elements of a typical forensic process: a judge, the accused, a norm of judgment or law, testimony from witnesses, the judge's *cognitio*, and forensic proof.

1. Judge and Accused: Although 8:12-20 records the testimony of Jesus as a knowledgeable, deputized witness to his Jewish judges, 8:21-30 portrays a shift in forensic roles whereby Jesus becomes the judge and his listeners the accused.
2. Norm of Judgment: As judge, Jesus establishes a most solemn law ("Unless you believe that I AM") complete with punishment for non-compliance ("you will die in your sins," 8:24).
3. Charge: Along with this, Jesus the judge accuses his hearers of a serious sin, viz., *not* belonging to Jesus' world, which is the world of God: "You are from below, I am from above; you are of this world, I am not of this world" (8:23). This is no exhortation to do better, but an accusation of evil. His audience pleads "not guilty," alleging belief in him (8:30), which would mean that they escape the judgment pronounced in 8:23-24. But is their protestation of belief true?

4. **Judge's *Cognitio*:** In 8:31-59, Jesus as judge conducts an investigation of the speech of the accused to see whether they are in fact telling the truth that they are authentic believers (8:31).
5. **Testimony of Witnesses:** As the judge speaks to them, they bear testimony against themselves, proving that they are liars and so pseudo-believers. In forensic proceedings this is considered to be the best testimony at a trial, when unwilling witnesses testify against themselves.[35] As a result of his *cognitio*, Jesus has discovered that they are really slaves of sin, bastards of Abraham, murderers, liars and sons of the devil.
6. **Forensic Proof:** The proof that they are not genuine believers and true disciples comes in the course of Jesus' *cognitio*: 1) they misunderstand him constantly, 2) they dispute his assertions, and 3) they make false claims. The clinching demonstration comes when they take up stones to throw at him for the revelation that he is "I AM."

By 8:58-59, the audience has been convicted of the law stated in 8:24. Guilty as charged. This is but the latest scene where Jesus acts as judge (3:1-21; 5:16-46; 6:24-66; 7:32-52; 8:21-59; 9:3-41; 10:19-39; and 12:36-50).

4.2 Conclusion: The Social Significance of Jesus' Judgment

If 8:21-59 is presented in the Fourth Gospel in formal forensic terms, how does this function? What does this suggest about the life and setting of the Johannine community? One way of answering this entails reflection on the meaning of "judgment" in the Fourth Gospel and other New Testament writings. What, in fact, goes into "judgment"? On one level, a judge hears charges and claims, which he tests for validity. Yet in the gospel tradition, judgment also has to do with separating the good and the bad. For example, Matthew records at least five parables in which judgment is described as an act of separation:

13:36-43 separation of wheat from tares
13:47-50 separation of good from bad fish
22:11-14 separation of those with from those without wedding garments
25:1-13   separation of wise from foolish maidens
25:31-46 separation of sheep from goats

---

35. See Quintilian, *Inst. Orat.* 5.7.15-18. The clearest example of this can be found in Luke 19:22, where the king condemns the useless servant: "I will condemn you out of your own mouth."

Jesus the Judge

The wicked have no place with the just and must be winnowed out, as chaff is separated from wheat (see Matt 3:12). Jesus' dialogue with the pseudo-believers in 8:31-58 generates an elaborate series of dualistic contrasts which force a separation of 1) true, free sons of Abraham from false, slave sons, 2) sons of God from sons of the devil, and 3) true disciples from false ones.

A. True Covenant Members	A. Pseudo-Covenant Members
1. free	1. slaves
2. legitimate sons who remain in the house	2. slave sons who do not remain in the house
3. descendants of Abraham through Isaac	3. descendants of Abraham, but through Ishmael
4. they do what their father did: hospitality	4. they do what their father did: lying and murder
B. Who is the Father?	B. Who is the Father?
1. my Father, who is God	1. your father is the devil
2. I told you the truth from my Father	2. there is no truth in your father
C. True Disciples	C. Pseudo-Disciples
1. remain in my word	1. my words find no place in you
2. who is of God hears the words of God	2. the reason you do not hear them is that you are not of God
3. I honor my Father	3. and you dishonor me
4. I know him	4. you have never known him

It follows, then, that Jesus' forensic inquiry in 8:31-58 serves to draw firm boundary lines between true and false disciples, between authentic offspring of Abraham and bastard descendants, and between members of God's covenant community and members of Satan's household. In doing this, Jesus the judge has conclusively proved his original charge in 8:23, viz., that his audience belonged to a world totally and completely opposed to his world: he is "from above," while they are "from below"; he is "*not* of this world," while they most assuredly are "of this world." Failing to belong to Jesus' world, the audience is shown to be of a cosmos ruled by the devil. The forensic process, then, serves precisely to separate the evil from the good, a process necessary in a world of ambiguity, masquerade and deception. It belongs to the judge to sift testimony, to read hearts, and to unmask deception, which power is abundantly credited to Jesus in the Fourth Gospel (see 2:23-25).

Jesus' judgment in 8:21-59, moreover, deserves to be seen in connection with the larger pattern of judgment of "the World" which develops in the

Fourth Gospel. Although it is not always perceived so negatively,[36] "the world" came to be viewed as a hostile place which rejects Jesus (1:9-10) and hates him (7:7), precisely because he is not of the world (15:18-19). And so he shifts from being its savior to *its* judge (9:36). Probably as a result of the failure of *its mission*, the Johannine community came to see "the world" as a totally evil place of deceit and sin, over which the "ruler of this world" presided. This point of view reflects the dualistic perspective of a cosmos divided into two worlds, that of God and of Satan, Since one can only serve one master, one is either a member of God's world or of Satan's. Jesus' assumption of the role of judge in 8:21-59 inaugurates in the Fourth Gospel an aggressive stance toward "the world," proclaiming in 8:23 a radical division of the cosmos so that one is either with Jesus in being "from above" and "*not* of this world," for which the reward is holiness and eternal life, or is "from below" and part of "this world," for which the recompense is to "die in sin" (8:24). Jesus' judgment in 8:21-59, then, inaugurates a trial with "the world" which has not accepted him as God's agent, a trial which the Spirit will continue.[37] This is hardly an ecumenical perspective, but reflects the hostile situation of the Johannine community.[38]

4.3 Further Questions

This inquiry raises fresh questions. What is being signaled, for example, when Jesus is formally credited with judgmental powers and portrayed exercising them, when so much of the text insists that he does not judge? Jesus claimed in 5:21-29 that God endowed him with executive or eschatological authority. A plausible suggestion is that the Fourth Gospel credits Jesus with God's two basic powers, one of which is power to judge (5:22, 27), in virtue of which Jesus is acclaimed "equal to God." This material was discussed earlier in the interpretation of John 5. Other aspects of Jesus' eschatological power are also discussed and demonstrated in John 8, namely, his "honor equal to God's" (5:23 = 8:49-50), his "having life in himself" (5:26 = 8:24, 28, 58), and his ability to "give life" (5:21 = 8:51-53). A full study of John 8, then, would try to see Jesus' judgment related to his exercise of God's eschatological power, as described earlier.

36. "The world" was viewed quite benevolently as a place worthy of God's concern and Jesus' mission (3:16-17; 4:42; 6:33; 8:12; 9:5; 11:27; 12:46), but also as inimical to Jesus and his disciples (7:7; 8:23; 15:18-19; 16:8-11).

37. See 16:8-11; D. A. Carson, "The Function of the Paraclete in John 16:8-11," *JBL* 98 (1979): 558-66.

38. See Wayne A. Meeks, "The Man from Heaven in Johannine Sectarianism," *JBL* 91 (1972): 67-71.

Jesus the Judge

This inquiry calls attention to the mutual accusations of demon possession in John 8. Jesus accuses his opponents of being offspring of the devil and doing the deeds of their father (8:44), while they in turn accuse him of demon possession (8:48, 52). The analysis of John 8 in terms of forensic process cannot deal with such questions, but invites a consideration of this phenomenon from the viewpoint of cultural anthropology, which would evaluate such mutual accusations of demon possession as formal "witchcraft accusations."[39]

Not only does Jesus conceal and reveal, i.e., keep secrets, but the analysis of 8:30-59 indicates that defensive lies are being told constantly by those who claim to be believers. Indeed, they are congenital liars who belong to a line of liars going back to their father, the premier Liar. Thus more attention should be given to John 8:30-59 in terms of the phenomena of secrecy and lying. In part the secrecy materials will be taken up in a subsequent chapter in this volume.

Forensic trials, moreover, can be fruitfully analyzed in light of sociology. Accordingly trials function as status degradation rituals whereby an interest group attempts to label someone a "deviant" and to impose censure and penalties by virtue of a process which publicly defames the alleged "deviant."[40] This model invites us to examine 8:21-59 as an attempt by some in the Johannine community to label others (e.g., the alleged "believers") as deviants.

---

39. For a general discussion of witchcraft accusations against Jesus, see Bruce J. Malina and Jerome H. Neyrey, *Calling Jesus Names: The Social Value of Labels in Matthew* (Sonoma, CA: Polebridge Press, 1988) 1-32. But because of the maverick quality of the Fourth Gospel, see R. A. Piper, "Satan, Demons and the Absence of Exorcisms in the Fourth Gospel," in *Christology, Controversy and Community*, ed. David G. Horrell and Christopher Tucker (Leiden: Brill, 2000) 253-78.

40. Malina and Neyrey, *Calling Jesus Names*, 69-92; see also Jerome H. Neyrey, "Witchcraft Accusations in 2 Cor 10-13: Paul in Social Science Perspective," *Listening* 21 (1986): 160-70.

10

Secrecy, Deception, and Revelation

Information Control in the Fourth Gospel

1.0 Focus, Data, and Hypothesis

In spite of the fact that Jesus is identified in the Fourth Gospel as the consummate Revealer of God,[1] there are other data which point to him as the agent of information control and secrecy.[2] Despite Jesus' claim that "I have always taught in the synagogues where all Judeans come together. . . . I have said nothing secretly" (18:20), he holds long, extended conversations in private with select persons in which things are said which are not communicated to the crowds (e.g., 11:20-32). Moreover, on occasion he hides himself (12:36), which hiding is not in self-defense (8:59). People regularly lie to him (8:44, 55), but he also appears to lie to others (7:1-10).[3] He regularly speaks double-

---

1. R. Bultmann, *The Theology of the New Testament* (New York: Charles Scribner's Sons, 1955) 2.66.

2. On the "messianic secret" see W. Wrede, *The Messianic Secret* (Cambridge: J. Clarke, 1971); H. Räisänen, *The "Messianic Secret" in Mark* (Edinburgh: T & T Clark, 1990); and most recently John J. Pilch, "Secrecy in the Mediterranean World: An Anthropological Perspective," *BTB* 24 (1994): 151-56; and W. H. Kelber, "Narrative and Disclosure: Mechanisms of Concealing, Revealing, and Reveiling," in *Genre, Narrative and Theology,* ed. M. Gerhardt and J. G. Williams. *Semeia* 43 (1988) 1-20.

3. Ancient commentators were quite perplexed by Jesus' remarks; some solved the problem by claiming that Jesus was speaking "spiritually and in a mystery" (Epiphanius, *Haer.* 51.25, GCS 31:295; see Jerome, *Against the Pelagians* 2.17). Modern commentators are equally unsure of how to interpret this. R. E. Brown, for example, resorts to "two levels of meaning" to avoid having Jesus tell an outright untruth (*The Gospel According to John* [AB; Garden City, NY: Doubleday, 1966-70] 1.308. R. Bultmann (*The Gospel of John* [Philadelphia: Westminster Press, 1971] 294) sees a contradiction here which he says is impossible to reconcile, yet he attempts to do so by

meaning words, makes frequent statements which are misunderstood and discourses in parables, which are not comprehended. Questions asked of Jesus go unanswered. There are, then, data in the Fourth Gospel which pertain to information control and secrecy. A catalogue of this material proves helpful in appreciating the extent of information control in the Gospel.[4] Most of the keeping of secrets, deceiving and revealing occur in chs. 6–9, which is why this broad-reaching study is positioned here. For we have just seen that certain people lie to Jesus when they claim to be his disciples (8:30), which lies and deceptions Jesus systematically exposes; he reaches the ultimate revelation that they are just like their father, the Prince of Lies, who was a liar and a murderer from the beginning.

The Fourth Gospel will be examined here in terms of a social-scientific model of secrecy or information control. As leading hypotheses, I will investigate the following. First, it is a fact that in this Gospel one finds extensive information control. Not everybody knows all things. Rather, select persons know special things; if they share this information, they inform only a select few others. Second, information control and secrecy serve to establish group boundaries between outsiders and insiders (those "*not* in the know" vs those "in the know") as well as distinctions within the status hierarchy of the Johannine group. Disciples, in fact, may be ranked in terms of *who* knows *what* special or esoteric information. Third, the "sociology of secrecy" model can help retrieve ignored data, coordinate disparate data into an intelligible pattern, and offer insights into the social dynamics of a group.

2.0 The Sociology of Secrecy

Secrecy, spying, espionage, and intelligence services are as ancient as recorded history. Dvornik examined the phenomenon of secrecy from the ancient Near East,

---

noting that Jesus, while he does not go up publicly, goes in secret to the feast and so remains the (hidden) Revealer.

4. Study of the phenomenon of secrecy, lying, and information control in the Hebrew Bible can be found in the works of J. J. Roberts, "Does God Lie? Divine Deceit as a Theological Problem in Israelite Literature," *Congress Volume (Jerusalem)*, ed. J. A. Emerton (Vetus Testamentum Supplements 40; Leiden: Brill, 1988) 211-20; R. A. Freund, "Lying and Deception in the Biblical and Post-Biblical Judaic Tradition," *Scandinavia Journal of the Old Testament* 5 (1991): 45-61; W. Janzen, "Withholding the Word," *Traditions in Transformation*, ed. B. Halpern and J. D. Levinson (Winona Lake, IN: Eisenbrauns, 1981) 97-114; and T. Craven, "Women Who Lied for the Truth," *Justice and the Holy: Essays in Honor of Walter Harrelson*, ed. D. Knight and P. Paris (Atlanta: Scholars Press, 1989) 35-49.

covering Egypt, Assyria-Babylon-Persia, Greece, Rome, and Byzantium.[5] In modern times, scholarly interest in "secrecy" has tended to focus on governmental secrecy, intelligence services (CIA, KGB), and U2 aircraft and spy satellites, with a corresponding development of the genre of spy and espionage fiction. The leaking of governmental secrets has in recent times become an art, especially with the publication of the Pentagon Papers during the Vietnam War; Valerie Plame exemplifies the devastating power of selected disclosure of classified information. Alongside this is found a burgeoning library on "privacy," a topic of particular interest in the United States.[6] Recently, the anthropologist Clifford Geertz studied the social function of secrecy in the operations of the common bazaar.[7] The phenomenon, then, existed in antiquity and continues to demand our attention.

Sociologists trace the systematic analysis of "secrecy" to George Simmel's publication of "The Secret and the Secret Society."[8] Recent scholars have given fresh attention to Simmel's work by examining the phenomenon in cross-cultural perspective.[9] Biblical scholars, too, have begun to employ this material for biblical interpretation, notably John J. Pilch.[10] In surveying the literature on "secrecy," I am attempting to construct a model of the "secrecy process" which will be cross-cultural and so applicable to the Fourth Gospel.

---

5. F. Dvornik, *The Origins of Intelligence Services* (New Brunswick, NJ: Rutgers University Press, 1974).

6. See B. Laslett, "The Family as a Public and Private Institution: An Historical Perspective," *Journal of Marriage and the Family* 35 (1973): 480-92; J. S. Victor, "Privacy, Intimacy and Shame in a French Community," *Secrecy: A Cross-Cultural Perspective*, ed. S. K. Tefft (New York: Human Sciences Press, 1980) 100-103; C. and B. Warren, "Privacy and Secrecy: A Conceptual Comparison," *Secrecy: A Cross-Cultural Perspective*, 25-34.

7. C. Geertz, "The Bazaar Economy: Information and Search in Peasant Marketing," *American Economics Review* 68 (1978): 28-32.

8. G. Simmel, "The Sociology of Secrecy and of Secret Societies," *American Journal of Sociology* 11 (1906): 441-68, reprinted in K. H. Wolff, ed., *The Sociology of George Simmel* (Glencoe, IL: The Free Press, 1950) 305-76.

9. L. E. Hazelrigg, "Reexamination of Simmel's *The Secret and the Secret Society*: Nine Propositions," *Social Forces* 47 (1969): 323-30. Beyond Simmel, other anthropologists have studied the phenomenon; see M. Gilsenen, "Lying, Honor and Contradiction," *Transaction and Meaning: Directions in the Anthropology of Exchange and Symbolic Behavior*, ed. B. Kapherer (Philadelphia: Institute for the Study of Human Issues, 1976) 191-219; J. Du Boulay, "Lies, Mockery and Family Integrity," *Mediterranean Family Structures*, ed. J. G. Peristiany (Cambridge: Cambridge University Press, 1976) 200-221.

10. John J. Pilch, "Lying and Deceit in the Letters to the Seven Churches: Perspectives from Cultural Anthropology," *BTB* 22 (1992): 126-35; see also J. H. Neyrey, "Deception, Lying, Secrecy, Hypocrisy, Ambiguity and Revelation: The Cultural Character of Divine Judgment in Matthew," *When Judaism and Christianity Began*, ed. A. Avery-Peck, D. Harrington, and J. Neusner (Leiden: Brill, 2004) 199-230.

2.1 The Secrecy Process

Stanton Tefft defines secrecy as "the mandatory or voluntary, but calculated, concealment of information, activities, or relationships."[11] Secrets, moreover, are "a social resource (or adaptive strategy) used by individuals, groups, and organizations to attain certain ends."[12] As a strategy, secrecy may be employed *aggressively* against rivals or *defensively* against attackers.[13] Secrecy enables certain types of associations to avoid political persecution or destruction; it allows other groups to maintain an exclusive monopoly on esoteric knowledge. As an adaptive device, then, secrecy allows individuals and groups to attain certain ends, such as control of one's environment and the prediction of others' actions.[14] Tefft, who takes a broad view of the phenomenon of secrecy, describes it as an adaptive device containing five interrelated processes: 1) security (control of information), 2) entrusted disclosure, 3) espionage, 4) evaluation of spying, and 5) post-hoc security measures.

Kees Bolle makes the observation that "Not only is there no religion without secrecy, but there is no human existence without it."[15] Families do not want their plans, embarrassments, intimacies, private interactions, or finances discussed outside their houses — likewise with groups, organizations, and governments. All practice some form of information control, whether they base it on the right to privacy, the nature of interpersonal relations, or the politics of business and administration. All engage in some form of "security," that is, information control, and hence secrecy.

Within families, groups, organizations, or governments, certain people are privy to what is withheld from others. In fact, *who* knows *what* may serve as an index of status or ranking within a group. But not all people know all things. Thus, secrets are entrusted to some, not others. The others may or may not know that there are secrets withheld from them. Hence, one finds within governments the use of degrees of classified information, labels such as "for your eyes only," and the like. Nevertheless, there tends to be an inner circle which is "in the know."

This immediately raises the issue of some sort of "security system" in which it is determined who can or should be entrusted with what secret. It is a

---

11. S. K. Tefft, "Secrecy as a Social and Political Process," *Secrecy: A Cross-Cultural Perspective*, 320.

12. S. K. Tefft, "Secrecy, Disclosure and Social Theory," *Secrecy: A Cross-Cultural Perspective*, 35.

13. Tefft, "Secrecy, Disclosure and Social Theory," 36.

14. Tefft, "Secrecy as a Social and Political Process," 321.

15. K. W. Bolle, *Secrecy in Religions* (Leiden: Brill, 1987) 1.

known fact that group members who develop bonds of mutual loyalty pose less security risk than those of low morale. Nevertheless, groups tend to develop security systems to secure their secrets, simply because not all group members can be counted on to have highly developed bonds of mutual loyalty. Such systems can include a number of steps in securing its secrets, such as: 1) loyalty tests for old and new members, 2) total obedience to the group at the expense of other ties, 3) gradual revelation of secrets to members, and 4) imposition of strict norms of silence.

Secrets invite snooping, espionage, and disclosure. This may in part be due to fear that secrets may be used to harm others (i.e., a planned coup) or to shut others out from certain (unknown) benefits (i.e., technological formulae; discoveries). Thus, it is deemed a vital self-interest to know what others are up to. There may also be a reaction of shame to learn that one is excluded from the honor of being part of the inner circle. Whatever the varied reasons, outsiders tend invariably to engage in some form of espionage to learn the secrets of others.

By "espionage" we simply mean the "acquisition of information held secret by another group or individual."[16] Spying, whether done by persons or technology, will entail a body of people who watch, scrutinize, lie in wait, trap, trick (and so on) others so as to learn their secrets. They may investigate records, interrogate associates, plant informers and spies, or simply set up some form of intelligence service.

If espionage succeeds in gaining access to controlled information, an evaluation process must take place. Is the new information of any value? Is it a cover? A false lead? "Leaks" of information may be intentional to distract those who engage in espionage from more vital secrets or to lull them into thinking that they have cracked the secret.

If individuals, groups, organizations, or governments learn that their secrecy has been breached, they are likely to engage in a post-hoc program to identify the spy, plug the leak, bury the secret deeper, and so forth. New loyalty tests (even polygraph tests) may be demanded. But the "secrecy process" is hardly over, for with the renewed interest in keeping secrets, those who control information invite a new round of espionage and evaluation, which may result, if successful, in new post hoc programs to shore up security. And so the cycle repeats itself again and again and again.

---

16. Tefft, "Secrecy as a Social and Political Process," 333.

Secrecy, Deception, and Revelation

2.2 *The Functions of Secrecy*

If secrecy is an adaptive strategy, a means to protect or to attain certain information in the course of social interaction,[17] then one might inquire about the various functions it can play. First, one should distinguish *manifest* and *latent* secrecy.[18] *Manifest* secrecy describes the formal and overt policy of certain societies or groups to hide ceremonies, rites, information, and the like from the curious and perhaps dangerous eyes of others. In contrast, *latent* secrecy may be practiced by groups as the additional and unintended consequences of certain structural arrangements, such as covering up unintended actions.

Our attention focuses primarily on the specific functions of manifest secrecy. And here one may distinguish the functions of *extra-group* secrecy from *intra-group* secrecy.[19] *Extra-group* secrecy may be practiced for aggressive or defensive purposes.[20] *Aggressive* secrecy, which Tefft judges is best understood under the rubric of "conflict theory,"[21] describes actions and strategy used by alienated secret groups to organize political rebellion or provide secret leadership for revolutionary organizations. Groups subject to coercion by more powerful groups deal with their antagonists by trying to equalize power by hiding information or resources. Alternately, groups often employ *defensive* secrecy strategy to protect themselves. Secret societies such as the Ku Klux Klan, which are in close accord with the values of the dominant society, employ secrecy to disguise illegal activities. Alienated groups, however, which are embattled minorities within a larger hostile society, use secrecy to escape persecution or destruction.[22] One sociologist suggests that "the more intense the conflict the greater efforts to conceal information from antagonists."[23] Thus *extra-group* secrecy is employed in an atmosphere of fear or distrust.[24]

Intra-group secrecy is employed for a variety of purposes.[25] It may prove significant for group formation, insofar as some groups form for the overt purpose of engaging in covert actions, such as secret societies. Likewise, secrecy

---

17. Tefft, "Secrecy, Disclosure and Social Theory," 35.
18. Tefft, "Secrecy, Disclosure and Social Theory," 46.
19. E. Brandt, "On Secrecy and the Control of Knowledge: Taos Pueblo," *Secrecy: A Cross-Cultural Perspective*, 125-27.
20. Tefft, "Secrecy, Disclosure and Social Theory," 36.
21. Tefft, "Secrecy, Disclosure and Social Theory," 49-63.
22. Tefft, "Secrecy as a Social and Political Process," 324; Brandt, "Secrecy and the Control of Knowledge," 131.
23. Tefft, "Secrecy, Disclosure and Social Theory," 51.
24. See P. Erickson and J. Flynn, "Secrecy as an Organizational Control Strategy: Police Planning for a National Political Convention," *Secrecy: A Cross-Cultural Perspective*, 252-54.
25. Tefft, "Secrecy, Disclosure and Social Theory," 51-53.

both sets up group boundaries and, when defended, maintains them. Those "in the know" distinguish themselves from those "*not* in the know," and the very process of guarding this distinction contributes to group cohesiveness. This is often called the "superiority syndrome." Internal secrecy within groups, whereby only select members know certain information, serves to control access to rank, status, and political power. "Elders" or "experts" regularly maintain their special position within groups by monopolizing esoteric information even from other insiders, thus buttressing their own power and status within the group.[26] Groups may employ internal secrecy or information control among members simply as an efficient defensive mechanism to protect the group, for the fewer people who share vital information, the safer the secret. Finally, bureaucracies are notorious for employing internal espionage against insiders to garner information about shifting loyalties.[27]

2.3 Who Knows What? When?

Elizabeth Brandt's study of secrecy in the Taos Pueblo offers suggestive clues to the function of secrecy within a hierarchical group.[28] As most people have observed, information is restricted even within close-knit groups; not all people know everything. If one attempts to plot out status and role within a group, *who* knows something can often serve as an index of public standing. Those "*not* in the know," even within the group, may be spouses brought in by exogamous marriages, and so untrustworthy, or families and tribes who only recently associated with the group. They represent persons of low status, who are not integrated into the social networks within a village. We can contrast them with the few elites in the group, who are privy to the group's secrets and who stand atop the status hierarchy in the group and control it in virtue of their monopoly of esoteric information. It often happens that only those with complete information enjoy full political power within the group. Between these two extremes we can observe a diversity of individuals in terms of the kinds of knowledge they possess.[29]

What Is Known? If persons can be ranked in terms of *what they know*, then one should inquire more closely about what is known and what can be known. Brandt's study of the kinds of knowledge available in the Taos Pueblo surfaces

26. Brandt, "Secrecy and the Control of Knowledge," 130-34.
27. See J. Z. Smith, "No News Is Good News in Late Antiquity," *Secrecy in Religions*, 66-80.
28. Brandt, "Secrecy and the Control of Knowledge," 125-34.
29. Brandt, "Secrecy and the Control of Knowledge," 133; Hazelrigg, "Reexamination," 324.

five that may be group specific to the Pueblo: "1) mystical; 2) theological; 3) liturgical; 4) dogma or catechism; and 5) participatory."[30] "Mystical" knowledge refers to the private, ineffable, and non-verbal communication (i.e., the vision quest); it always remains secret. "Theological" knowledge is a kind of "deep knowledge that penetrates below the surface," thus providing mythical frameworks of interpretation or rationales for perception and action; novelist Tony Hillerman has gained special access to this through informers. "Liturgical" knowledge refers to the correct manner of conducting ceremonies and rituals, i.e., dances and chants, or simply to "behavior" within the group. "Dogma" refers to a superficial form of knowledge about the group; it involves a rote form of learning and represents the official "received" views of the group.[31] "Participatory" knowledge represents for Brandt a miscellaneous category for the various pieces of information that low level performers and spectators have (e.g., liturgical participation in a language foreign to those attending).

Some people know more than others because information is controlled so that certain people know more than others. Those most "in the know" with knowledge of the core myths and rituals rank highest. Those with specialized knowledge of this or that item belong in the middle, while others who know little or understand superficially are ranked lowest. This may be easily verified by inquiring into the degrees of membership in various secret societies, such as the Masons or the Ku Klux Klan.[32]

When Is It Known? In focus here are issues of recruitment, initiation, and advancement within groups. It is a well-known fact that special knowledge is reserved for novices during initiation rituals.[33] Even among novices, there are grades of initiation and corresponding new knowledge, as in the case of the cult of Mithra. Moreover, ancients clearly understood that the life cycle of humans consisted of stages (see Philo, *Cher.* 114) with various knowledge and behaviors appropriate to each stage (Philo, *Alleg. Interp.* 3.159). Furthermore, ancient education itself consisted of graded mastery of knowledge. Thus, people are ranked and classified in terms of their stage of life and its appropriate knowledge (see 1 Cor 3:1-2).

Thus, when we investigate a group or sift through information about them in documents, we may gain vital clues as to the roles and statuses of its

---

30. Brandt, "Secrecy and the Control of Knowledge," 127.
31. Brandt, "Secrecy and the Control of Knowledge," 128.
32. See N. P. Gist, "Dogma and Doctrine in Secret Societies," *Society and Social Research* 23 (1938): 121-30; idem, *Secret Societies: A Cultural Study of Fraternalism in the United States* (Springfield, MO: University of Missouri Press, 1940).
33. See Brandt, "Secrecy and the Control of Knowledge," 137-38; Brandt, "Bizango: A Voodoo Society in Haiti," *Secrecy: A Cross-Cultural Perspective,* 151-52.

members by attempting to answer the questions: who knows what and when does s/he know it?

3.0 The Secrecy Process and the Fourth Gospel

We recall that secrecy is defined as "the calculated concealment of information."[34] What follows is an extensive catalogue of the ways Jesus and others practice a concealment and revealing of select information. Following the formal perspective of the sociology of secrecy/information control laid out above, we will focus on 1) secrecy/information control, 2) espionage, and 3) select disclosure.

3.1 Information Control

Granted that not everyone knows everything all the time, we examine how Jesus, the Gospel's author and certain narrative characters regularly hide and conceal information. The following remark clearly indicates that Jesus himself practices concealment as well as disclosure: "Judas (not Iscariot) said to him, 'Lord, how is it that you will reveal yourself to us, and not to the world?'" (14:22). The ways to conceal knowledge and keep secrets are numerous, as the following catalogue indicates.

Lying. Jesus exposes their lies: "When he [your father, the devil] lies, he speaks according to his own nature, for he is a liar and the father of lies" (8:44, 55); Jesus lies to others: "Go to the festival yourselves. I am not going to this festival, for my time has not yet fully come" (7:8; see 1 John 2:21, 27; 4:1). Thus lies are told on both sides.

Deception: what you see is not what you get. Jesus made himself non-recognizable to go to Tabernacles: "He also went, not publicly but as it were in secret" (7:10). Many accuse Jesus of deception: "No, he deceives the crowds" (7:12); "Surely you have not been deceived too, have you?" (7:47). Accusations of demon possession belong here, because they charge that an evil inner self masquerades behind an upright, deceptive exterior. "The crowd answered, 'You have a demon!'" (7:20); "The Jews answered him, 'Are we not right in saying that you ... have a demon?'" (8:48, 52); "Many of them were saying, 'He has a demon and is out of his mind'" (10:20; see also 7:41; 9:16, 24; 18:30).

Ambiguity. As Gilbert and Sullivan wrote, "Things are seldom what they seem. . . ." For example, two of Jesus' healings apparently violate the Sabbath in

---

34. Tefft, "Secrecy as a Social and Political Process," 320.

the eyes of many. In a supremely ironical moment, the man born blind formulates the right way to remove this ambiguity: "We know that God does not listen to sinners, but he does listen to one who worships him and obeys his will. Never since the world began has it been heard that anyone opened the eyes of a person born blind. If this man were not from God, he could do nothing" (9:31-33). How obvious that Jesus is favored by God! Again one notices how Jesus constantly instructs his judges *not* to judge according to appearance: "Do not judge by appearances, but judge with right judgment" (7:24); "You judge by human standards; I judge no one" (8:15).

Evasion. For defensive purposes, the parents of the man born blind evasively reply: "'We know that this is our son, and that he was born blind; but we do not know how it is that now he sees, nor do we know who opened his eyes. Ask him; he is of age. He will speak for himself.' His parents said this because they were afraid of the Jews; for the Jews had already agreed that anyone who confessed Jesus to be the Messiah would be put out of the synagogue" (9:21-22).

Riddles[35] *and parables*[36] keep important information secret (10:6; 16:25, 29-30).

Double-meaning words.[37] The vocabulary of this Gospel is notorious for the intentional slipperiness of its discourse. Although we are treating this phenomenon in terms of secrecy, others have studied it as an example of "anti-language" which intentionally uses common vocabulary but investing it with a disguising exterior to befuddle enemies.[38] Jesus addresses Nicodemus using a double-meaning word (*anōthen,* which can mean "from above" or "again"): "'No one can see the kingdom of God without being born from above.' Nicodemus said to him, 'How can anyone be born after having grown old? Can one enter a second time into the mother's womb and be born?' Jesus answered, 'I tell you, no one can enter the kingdom of God without being born of water

---

35. H. Leroy, *Rätsel und Missverständnis. Ein Beitrag zur Formgeschichte de Johannesevangelium* (Bonn: Hanstein, 1968); and more recently Tom Thatcher, *The Riddles of Jesus in John* (Atlanta: Society of Biblical Literature, 2000); idem, *Jesus the Riddler: The Power of Ambiguity in the Gospel* (Louisville, KY: Westminster John Knox, 2006).

36. See K. E. Dewey, "*Paroimiai* in the Gospel of John," *Gnomic Wisdom,* ed. J. D. Crossan, *Semeia* 17 (1980): 81-99.

37. See D. A. Carson, "Understanding Misunderstanding in the Fourth Gospel," *TynB* 33 (1982): 61-91; E. Richard, "Expressions of Double Meaning and Their Function in the Gospel of John," *NTS* 31 (1985): 96-112.

38. The pioneer in applying the model of anti-language to the Fourth Gospel is Bruce J. Malina in *The Gospel of John in Sociolinguistic Perspective: 48th Colloquy of the Center for Hermeneutical Studies,* ed. Malina and Herman Waetjen (Berkeley, CA: Center for Hermeneutical Studies, 1985); see also Bruce J. Malina and Richard L. Rohrbaugh, *Social-Science Commentary on the Gospel of John* (Minneapolis, MN: Fortress Press, 1998).

and Spirit'" (3:3-5). Jesus offers the woman at the well a drink of water, which she misunderstands. Balancing that is a confusion over "bread": "The disciples were urging him, 'Rabbi, eat something. But he said to them, 'I have food to eat that you do not know about.' So the disciples said to one another, 'Surely no one has brought him something to eat?'" (4:31-33).

Statement-misunderstanding-(maybe) clarification. Two dozen times we find this pattern. Jesus speaks but his message is not transparent; his receivers hear his words, but always misunderstand them. Jesus then speaks again, which may be a clarification and so a disclosure or a proof that the listener is both impervious and unworthy of his words.

Statement	*Misunderstanding*	*Clarification*
3:3	3:4	3:5
6:41	6:42	6:43-48
8:21	8:22	8:23-30
11:11	11:12	11:13-15
12:28	12:29	12:30
14:4	14:5	14:6

Hiding. "They picked up stones to throw at him, but Jesus hid himself and went out of the temple" (8:59); "After Jesus had said this, he departed and hid from them" (12:36).

Irony (= Disparity of Knowledge). The author and the Johannine audience often know something about the drama before them which the narrative characters do not.[39] Hence some knowledge is kept from some but disclosed to others. 1) Sometimes characters claim knowledge which would dishonor Jesus: "They were saying, 'Is not this Jesus, the son of Joseph, whose father and mother we know? How can he now say, "I have come down from heaven"?'" (6:42); "We know that God has spoken to Moses, but as for this man, we do not know where he comes from" (9:29; see also 7:27, 41-42). 2) Other times people assume something which ironically is false: "The Jews were astonished at it, saying, 'How does this man have such learning, when he has never been taught?'" (7:15). "Has not the scripture said that the Messiah is descended from David

---

39. Part of the irony of this Gospel is that some characters speak true things but do not know the half of what they say. For example, "Everyone serves the good wine first, and then the inferior wine after the guests have become drunk. But you have kept the good wine until now" (2:10). "No one who wants to be widely known acts in secret. If you do these things, show yourself to the world" (7:4-5). "'You do not understand that it is better for you to have one man die for the people than to have the whole nation destroyed.' He did not say this on his own, but being high priest that year he prophesied that Jesus was about to die for the nation" (11:50-51).

and comes from Bethlehem, the village where David lived?" (7:42). "Search and you will see that no prophet is to arise from Galilee" (7:52). "Then the Jews said to him, 'You are not yet fifty years old, and have you seen Abraham?'" (8:57). The outsiders think that they know information prejudicial to Jesus, but in fact the points made are ironically vital to the audience for his knowledge is, in fact, correct.

Knowing in a glass darkly. Outsiders often "think" that they know something. "Rabbi, we know that you are a teacher who has come from God" (3:2). "Yet we know where this man is from; but when the Messiah comes, no one will know where he is from" (7:27). "Indeed, an hour is coming when those who kill you will think that by doing so they are offering worship to God" (16:2).

3.2 *Espionage: Discovering Secrets*

When secrecy exists, it invariably provokes espionage to unveil what is covered over. This endeavor to discover Jesus' secrets is espionage by the Jerusalem elders, and it takes many forms.

Espionage, Always and Everywhere. In his *Gallic Wars*, Julius Caesar identifies a host of figures who function in his extensive intelligence network. In the field, he employs "scouts" *(exploratores)* for reconnaissance of the enemy army, whereas in the city he depends on regular reports by unnamed sources, presumably spies, informants, or sympathizers. In regard to espionage in the Fourth Gospel, however, one does not find specific terms for "scouts," "informers," "spying," or "entrapment," as one does in Luke 20:20 and Gal 2:4 (see Mark 3:2 and Luke 6:7). Nevertheless, one learns of the intense scrutiny of Jesus, the object of which is to discover his secrets (whereabouts, doctrine, disciples, etc.). People regularly "hear about" Jesus, either because of the friendly spread of his reputation (4:47; 12:9, 12) or through hostile reports about him carried by informers and agents of his enemies (4:1; 11:46-47). His movements and speech, then, are carefully monitored.

Certain Judeans alert a network of informers to track Jesus' movements: "Now the chief priests and the Pharisees had given orders that anyone who knew where Jesus was should let them know, so that they might arrest him" (11:57). But the most intense espionage occurs in the tireless questioning of John and Jesus on trial. Two groups of investigators question John the Baptizer; the first group seeks to uncover his identity, "Who are you?" He is not the Christ, Elijah or a prophet. But despite their persistent questions, the only identity he gives them is: "I am the voice of one crying out in the wilderness, 'Make straight the way of the Lord,' as the prophet Isaiah said" (1:23).

Questions and Espionage. In their search for information about Jesus, various people ask questions either directly of him or about him. Questions in an honor-shame society are often challenging actions; while they seek answers and information, questions are far from being neutral in intent (see Mark 11:28-30; 12:13-15).[40] It is an interesting fact that in the Fourth Gospel the term for asking questions *(erōtaō)* occurs three times more frequently than the combined instances of it in the Synoptics, an indication that "asking questions" in this Gospel is a significant feature. In addition to the obvious verb *"to ask,"* the Fourth Gospel contains an elaborate series of questions asked in some form of the interrogatives *"who?"* and *"why?"* and *"how?"*

Who are you? On three occasions designated officials hold a public inquiry concerning John and then Jesus. John the Baptizer is thoroughly investigated by deputized agents of the Jerusalem elite, who ask *"Who are you?"* (1:19-22). Later, the man cured of his paralysis is queried about Jesus, "They asked him, *who is the man* who said to you, 'Take it up and walk'?" (5:12; see 9:21). The officials, then, are constantly engaged in an espionage process concerning Jesus. In addition, Jesus is directly asked about his own identity: *"Who are you?"* (8:25) and *"Who do you make yourself to be?"* (8:53). Twice people ask him, *"Who is this Son of man?"* — once positively (9:36) and once negatively (12:34). Finally in the Gospel's last narrative, no one asks him *"Who are you?"* (21:12), for they are all now "in the know."

What is this? What are you doing? In the espionage process, elites ask certain people questions, such as "What do you have to say about so-and-so," either the Baptizer about himself (1:22) or the man born blind about Jesus (9:17). Facts about Jesus are demanded, either how he healed (9:26) or what crime he allegedly committed (18:29, 35). Other "what" questions seem to frustrate the espionage process of learning Jesus' secrets; for example, when Jesus tells Peter, "What business is this of yours?" (21:22-23; see 2:4), this question continues to keep secret Jesus' purposes. Other "what" questions demand that Jesus reveal the secret of his legitimation, "What sign do you give?" (2:18; 6:30). When others ask "What are we to do?" (11:47), they admit that their espionage against Jesus is failing (see 6:28). Finally, we learn of inquiry into his words, "What does he mean?" — by foe (7:36) and friend (16:17-18). Jesus, then, keeps many secrets, which only provokes others to labor to discover them.

Why are you doing this? Espionage against Jesus often includes inquiry into the reasons why something is done. For example, if John the Baptizer is not the Christ or a prophet, then it is urgent to know "Why do you baptize?" (1:25).

---

40. For a study of "questions-as-weapons," see Jerome H. Neyrey, "Questions, *Chreiai,* and Challenges to Honor: The Interface of Rhetoric and Culture in Mark's Gospel," *CBQ* 60 (1998): 657-81.

When the officials sent to arrest Jesus return empty-handed, they too are asked, "Why did you not bring him?" (7:45). And the man born blind sarcastically asks the Pharisees who keep inquiring about Jesus, "Why do you want to hear it again? Do you too want to become his disciples?" (9:27). Furthermore, people directly ask Jesus "why?" questions: "Why cannot I follow you now?" (13:37) and "Why is it that you will manifest yourself to us and not to the world?" (14:22). Moreover, when Jesus acts as judge of his own judges, he too conducts his own espionage to reveal their secret enmity: "Why do you seek to kill me?" (7:19); "Why don't you understand?" (8:43); "Why don't you believe?" (8:46); "Why do you strike me?" (18:23).

How can this be? How can you say . . . ? Nicodemus asks questions introduced by the adverb "how" in an effort to discover the secret of Jesus' words: "How can this be?" (3:9). Still others ask hostile questions about Jesus' words, which virtually indicate that his secrets are impervious to their espionage.

6:42 "How does he say, 'I have come down from heaven'?"
6:52 "How can this man give us his flesh to eat?"
8:33 "How is it that you say, 'You shall be made free'?"
12:34 "How can you say that the Son of man must be lifted up?"

On one occasion, we are told of intense scrutiny by the Pharisees concerning the manner in which Jesus healed the blind man (9:10, 15, 19, 21, 26). The crowds likewise question how Jesus came by his learning, since he is unlettered (7:15). Clearly, people who ask questions of this sort are not privy to the secret meanings of Jesus' words. Yet, they engage in espionage to find out his secrets or to discredit him. When Jesus acts as judge of his judges, he too conducts his own espionage of them. His "how" questions reveal a serious lack of understanding in his hearers:

3:12 "How can you believe if I tell you heavenly things?"
5:44 "How can you believe, who receive glory from one another and do not seek the glory that comes from the only God?"
5:47 "If you do not believe his [Moses'] writings, how will you believe my words?"

The confines of this investigation prevent me from pursuing a promising lead in the sociology of secrecy. The most common formal element of the Johannine discourses seems to be that of a forensic trial of Jesus. A conservative reading of the document indicates that Jesus is first put on trial in 5:16-18, 31-47, which trial is continued in 7:14-52, 8:12-59, 9:13-34, 10:21-39, and 11:45-53. Forensic trials constitute a hybrid form of the espionage process. The judges solicit testimony, sift evidence, and make inquiry — all to discover the secret of whether the accused is guilty or innocent. Indeed, one of the formal aspects of Roman trials in antiquity was the judge's *cognitio*, in which he personally scrutinized the testimony about and from the accused.[41] These extended forensic proceedings against Jesus, while formal in terms of their literary character, deserve to be treated under the rubric of espionage. They aim at discovering Jesus' secrets. One can conclude, then, that the Fourth Gospel consistently presents Jesus as the object of espionage. His opponents systematically inquire about him, either by interrogating witnesses, his associates, or Jesus himself.

3.3 Select Disclosure

In contrast to espionage which ferrets out secrets, we observe here some of the ways in which knowledge is disclosed.

Gossip network. Some "news" is disclosed by means of the "gossip network." Worlds without media rely on a "gossip network" to spread information.[42] Gossip is regularly spread about Jesus, for the most part friendly communication about his identity and whereabouts. Gossip in this sense, moreover, travels in a network of kin (brothers and sisters) or persons of the same trade and from the same town. Brother speaks to brother (Andrew to Peter, 1:40-42) and sister to sister (Martha to Mary, 11:28). Philip is from Bethsaida, the same village as Andrew and Peter (1:44). The disciples, who are called "brothers" (20:17), speak to fictive kin, namely Thomas (20:24-25; see also 4:28-30; 11:3; 12:21-22).[43] This, however, is communication without any attempt at concealment. The following instances of *selective disclosure* are calculated to give information to others, which may or may not be of significance.

Footnotes and asides are provided for select knowers, namely, insiders.[44]

---

41. See J. H. Neyrey, "Jesus the Judge: Forensic Process in John 8:21-59," *Bib* 68 (1987): 535-36.

42. Don Handelman, "Gossip in Encounters: The Transmission of Information in a Bounded Social Setting," *Man* 8 (1973): 210-27; Deborah Jones, "Gossip: Notes on Women's Oral Culture," *Women's Studies International Quarterly* 3 (1980): 193-98; Richard L. Rohrbaugh, "Gossip in the New Testament," in *Social-Scientific Models for Interpreting the New Testament: Essays by the Context Group in Honor of Bruce Malina*, ed. John J. Pilch (Leiden: Brill, 2001) 239-59; Sian Lewis, *News and Society in the Greek Polis* (Chapel Hill: University of North Carolina Press, 1996); Robert F. Goodman and Aaron Ben-Ze'ev, eds., *Good Gossip* (Lawrence, KS: University of Kansas Press, 1994).

43. Nathanael was from Cana in Galilee (21:2); the only other mention of Cana in the Fourth Gospel is the location of the wedding in 2:1-12.

44. See M. C. Tenney, "The Footnotes of John's Gospel," *BSac* 117 (1960): 350-64; J. J. O'Rourke, "Asides in the Gospel of John," *NovT* 21 (1979): 210-19.

Translation of Semitic terms into Greek: "They said to him, 'Rabbi (which translated means "Teacher"), where are you staying?'" (1:38); "We have found the Messiah (which means Christ)" (1:41); "Now in Jerusalem by the Sheep Gate there is a pool, called in Hebrew Beth-zatha, which has five porticoes" (5:2); "'Go, wash in the pool of Siloam' (which means Sent)" (9:7). "When Pilate heard these words, he brought Jesus outside and sat on the judge's bench at a place called The Stone Pavement, or in Hebrew Gabbatha" (19:13); see also 4:25; 19:17; 20:16.

Special times and customs. Time: "Now the Passover, the feast of the Judeans, was at hand" (6:4); "Now the Judeans' feast of Tabernacles was at hand" (7:2); "At that time the festival of the Dedication took place in Jerusalem. It was winter" (10:22). Customs: "The Samaritan woman said to him, 'How is it that you, a Jew, ask a drink of me, a woman of Samaria?' (Jews do not share things in common with Samaritans)" (4:9). "They took the body of Jesus and wrapped it with the spices in linen cloths, according to the burial custom of the Jews" (19:40).

Eventual disclosure. Many times, although the words of Jesus were spoken in the presence of disciples, their meaning is disclosed later. "His disciples did not understand these things at first; but when Jesus was glorified, then they remembered that these things had been written of him and had been done to him" (12:16). "After he was raised from the dead, his disciples remembered that he had said this; and they believed the scripture and the word that Jesus had spoken" (2:22). The Spirit as special broker of this disclosure: "But the Advocate, the Holy Spirit, whom the Father will send in my name, will teach you everything, and remind you of all that I have said to you" (14:26); "When the Advocate comes . . . he will testify on my behalf" (15:26; see 16:13-14).

Questions asked and maybe answered. Answered: "His disciples asked him, 'Rabbi, who sinned, this man or his parents, that he was born blind?' Jesus answered, 'Neither this man nor his parents sinned; he was born blind so that God's works might be revealed in him'" (9:2-3). Mysterious answer: "Simon Peter said to him, 'Lord, where are you going?' Jesus answered, 'Where I am going, you cannot follow me now; but you will follow afterward'" (13:36).

Disclosure of information for proper interpretation of characters. The first time a character appears in the story is an ideal time to inform the audience about him: "He was speaking of Judas son of Simon Iscariot, for he, though one of the twelve, was going to betray him" (6:71). Also, "Mary was the one who anointed the Lord with perfume and wiped his feet with her hair; her brother Lazarus was ill" (11:2; see 18:10, 14). And the second time a character comes in view important information is repeated, for readers to have the right attitude toward him: "Nicodemus, who had at first come to Jesus by night, also came, bringing a mixture of myrrh and aloes, weighing about a hundred pounds" (19:39). Finally, the Gospel writer testifies to his veracity: "(He who saw this has testified so that you also may believe. His testimony is true, and he knows that he tells the truth)" (19:35; see 21:24).

Secret vs. public disclosure of information. "Jesus answered, 'I have spoken openly to the world; I have always taught in synagogues and in the temple, where all the Jews come together. I have said nothing in secret" (18:20). "How long will you keep us in suspense? If you are the Messiah, tell us plainly" (10:24). "Then Jesus told them plainly, 'Lazarus is dead'" (11:14). "I have said these things to you in figures of speech. The hour is coming when I will no longer speak to you in figures, but will tell you plainly of the Father" (16:25). . . . "His disciples said, 'Yes, now you are speaking plainly, not in any figure of speech!'" (16:29).[45]

Entrusted disclosure. In the light of remarks such as 14:21-22 and 17:6, 11, 12, 26, I accept it as a fact that information is regularly controlled in the Fourth Gospel. Jesus gives select persons secrets and some are even subsequently entrusted with the disclosure of the controlled information to select others. For example, the author introduces us to this pattern in the presentation of the premier witness to Jesus, John the Baptizer, who twice admits that "I did not know him" (1:31, 33); yet, John was ultimately entrusted by God with special information about Jesus: "He who sent me . . . said to me, 'He on whom you see the Spirit descend and remain, this is he who baptizes with the Holy Spirit'" (1:33). Eventually he shares his secret, but with only two of his disciples (1:35-36).

Other examples of this pattern of "entrusted disclosure" include the following. Although the servants at the wedding at Cana know the secret of whence the water-turned-into-wine comes (2:9), Jesus' disciples receive "the manifestation of his glory" (2:11). More significantly, the Samaritan woman is gradually entrusted with secrets about Jesus. She begins the story as a character who was told "If only you knew . . . who it is who said to you 'Give me to drink,' you would have asked him . . ." (4:10). As she is entrusted with more secrets, she does eventually ask "Give me this water" (4:15), and she receives remarkable information (4:20-24), even a christophany of Jesus as the Messiah (4:26). The man born blind likewise receives a special epiphany by Jesus as well as an answer to his question about the Son of man, "Who is he?" (9:36). Martha, who along with Mary and Lazarus is a "beloved disciple," receives very special information about Jesus as "the Resurrection and the Life" (11:25). I mention in passing the disclosure of select information to the inner circle of disciples during Jesus' Farewell Address.

---

45. N. Petersen, *The Gospel of John and the Sociology of Light: Language and Characterization in the Fourth Gospel* (Valley Forge, PA: Trinity Press International, 1993).

In an earlier study of the Samaritan woman,[46] I noted that on occasion those who receive unique shares of this controlled information in turn disclose it to select others. Using concepts from sociology about "gossip networks," I suggested that in media-less cultures information is always spread by word of mouth, although selectively to kin or fictive kin. I offer a clarification of that by indicating here how the information which Jesus discloses to select individuals is in turn controlled in its disclosure to other select people.

Why don't people know?[47] Some are capable only of earthly knowing: "If I have told you about earthly things and you do not believe, how can you believe if I tell you about heavenly things?" (3:12). And, "He said to them, 'You are from below, I am from above; you are of this world, I am not of this world'" (8:23). "Whoever is from God hears the words of God. The reason you do not hear them is that you are not from God" (8:47). Some are blind and prefer darkness to light: "Jesus said, 'I came into this world for judgment so that those who do not see may see, and those who do see may become blind'" (9:39). "Although he had performed so many signs in their presence, they did not believe in him. This was to fulfill the word spoken by the prophet Isaiah: 'Lord, who has believed our message, and to whom has the arm of the Lord been revealed?' And so they could not believe, because Isaiah also said, 'He has blinded their eyes and hardened their heart, so that they might not look with their eyes, and understand with their heart and turn, and I would heal them'" (12:37-40).

4.0 Jesus: Exclusive Revealer

No one knows but Jesus. Jesus enjoys exclusive access to and disclosure of God: "No one has ever seen God. It is God the only Son, who is close to the Father's heart, who has made him known" (1:18). Jesus alone has the words of God: "He whom God has sent speaks the words of God" (3:34). "The words that I say to you I do not speak on my own; but the Father who dwells in me does his works" (14:10). Jesus occasionally discloses his identity: "Jesus said, 'Do you believe in the Son of Man?' He answered, 'And who is he, sir? Tell me, so that I may believe in him?' 'You have seen him, and it is he who speaks to you'" (9:35-37). "Jesus said to her, 'Mary!' She turned and said to him in Hebrew, 'Rabbouni!' (which means Teacher)" (20:16; see 4:25-26; 11:19-26; 20:19-21, 26-29). Jesus makes select disclosures to his disciples: "Jesus said to Martha, 'Your brother will rise again.' Martha said to him, 'I know that he will rise again in the resurrection on the last

---

46. See Neyrey, "What's Wrong with This Picture?" 167-69 in the present volume.
47. Petersen, *Gospel of John and the Sociology of Light*, 72-75.

day.' Jesus said to her, 'I am the resurrection and the life'" (11:23-25); "Go to my brothers and say to them, 'I am ascending to my Father and your Father, to my God and your God'" (20:17).

Jesus knows human hearts. He penetrates disguises. "But Jesus on his part would not entrust himself to them, because he knew all people and needed no one to testify about anyone; for he himself knew what was in everyone" (2:24-25). "Then they said to him, 'Where is your Father?' Jesus answered, 'You know neither me nor my Father. If you knew me, you would know my Father also'" (8:19; see 1:47; 6:26). "But I know that you do not have the love of God in you" (5:42). "Jesus said this to test him, for he himself knew what he was going to do" (6:6). "Now we know that you know all things, and do not need to have anyone question you" (16:30).

Revelations of forthcoming events: "I tell you this now, before it occurs, so that when it does occur, you may believe that I am he" (13:19). "And now I have told you this before it occurs, so that when it does occur, you may believe" (14:29; see 15:11; 16:1-4).

Revelation of God's name: "I have made your name known to those whom you gave me from the world" (17:6). "I made your name known to them, and I will make it known" (17:26).

Revelation of whence he comes and whither he goes: "No one has ascended into heaven except the one who descended from heaven, the Son of Man" (3:13). "Go to my brothers and say to them, 'I am ascending to my Father and your Father, to my God and your God'" (20:17).

Revelation of everything Jesus heard from his Father: "I do not call you servants any longer, because the servant does not know what the master is doing; but I have called you friends, because I have made known to you everything that I have heard from my Father" (15:15). "Now they know that everything you have given me is from you; for the words that you gave to me I have given to them" (17:7-8).

Revelation of the traitor. Although Jesus reveals the fact of a traitor in their midst (13:18, 21), he keeps Judas' identity secret. This in turn prompts the inner circle of his disciples to conduct their own espionage to learn Jesus' secret. Peter asks the Beloved Disciple to get this secret information from Jesus, "Who is it?" (13:24-25), the possession of which knowledge becomes a mark of distinction later (21:20).

In summary, by these patterns the author of the Fourth Gospel labors to indicate just who are the espionage agents spying on Jesus. Those who receive no answer to their questions or who receive in turn double-meaning responses or who judge by appearances or who seek in a hostile manner are all clearly outsiders. Because of their wicked or inferior nature, they cannot understand heavenly and spiritual things. In contrast, true insiders receive answers to their questions or begin to see and know beyond appearances or seek *and find*. They share the controlled information. Nevertheless, information remains tightly controlled, especially against outsiders. The espionage process, however, utterly fails. Jesus' secrets are never discovered. Even if investigative agents hear Jesus speak, they invariably misunderstand him. The information which is being controlled, then, is never at risk, except for the traitor, but then Jesus knew he was a traitor from the beginning (6:64, 70-71; 13:18, 21, 27). Because there is no discovery of secrets by outsiders, there is no post hoc adjustments of the control of information.

5.0 Secrecy and Differentiation of Characters

In the discussion on the model of secrecy, I noted that information is controlled for both outsiders and insiders. Turning to the Fourth Gospel, one quickly observes a recurring pattern which distinguishes two groups, namely, insiders who are "in the know" from outsiders "not in the know." Yet, there are degrees of knowledge among the insiders who are "in the know." The author and his readers, then, can immediately and easily classify narrative characters in terms of *who* knows *what*.

5.1 Outsiders: "Not in the Know"

The narrator employs a number of patterns to help us recognize outsiders as people who are "*not* in the know." Often Jesus bluntly tells his audience that they are "*not* in the know," even though he is then and there speaking to them:

1. "You do not know" (3:10; 7:28; 8:14, 19, 43, 55).
2. "You do not hear/listen to my voice" (8:37, 47; 10:26-27; 18:37).
3. "You do not believe" (8:45; 10:25).
4. "You do not belong" (10:26).

On occasion, the author supplies the information directly to us (8:27; 10:6; 12:37) which has been denied outsiders.

In a variety of ways, the narrative regularly classifies people "*not* in the know." Even when people claim to know something, that claim is often challenged by Jesus: "So you 'know' me, and you 'know' where I come from? But I have not come of my own accord; he who sent me is true, and him you do '*not* know'" (7:28; see 8:52). Furthermore, some of those who ask questions of Jesus never receive an answer, and so they remain in the category of "not in the know." Nicodemus, for example, asks a question of Jesus (3:4), which Jesus answers in a way which reduces Nicodemus to ignorance: "How can this be?" (3:9).[48] Jesus sarcastically answers his second question with a question, indicating that Nicodemus is "*not* in the know": "You, a teacher of Israel, and you do not understand this? . . . If I told you earthly things and you do not believe, how can you believe if I tell you heavenly things?" (3:10, 12; for other unanswered questions, see 7:35-36; 8:19, 22, 25, 53; 10:24). In the case of the man born blind, his interrogators ask questions and repeatedly receive the same answer yet refuse to accept it. Thus, they position themselves as the figures whom Jesus labels as truly blind (9:39-41). Finally, according to the Johannine pattern of "statement/misunderstanding/clarification," some people receive a final word from Jesus. However, it does not serve to "clarify" anything or enlighten them, but rather confirms them in their "misunderstanding" (3; 6:42/43-51, 52/53-58; 9). The author, then, clearly labels a host of characters as outsiders who are "not in the know."

More to our point, both Jesus and the narrator indicate why these outsiders are "*not* in the know" — an epistemology of ignorance, so to speak. Some of Jesus' hearers are earthly people who can barely know "earthly things" *(epigeia)*, but never "heavenly things" *(epourania,* 3:12). When others question Jesus about the meaning of his words, he declares that they cannot know his meanings because they are "from below" and "of this world," whereas he is "from above" and "not of this world" (8:23). Some only "judge by appearances" (*kat' opsin,* 7:24) or "judge according to the flesh" (*kata tēn sarka,* 8:15); they cannot know the truth. Since only Jesus' "sheep hear his voice," those who do not hear his voice are not his sheep (10:4-5, 26-27; 18:37). If "All shall be taught by God" (6:45a) and "Every one who has heard and learned from the Father comes to me" (6:45b), then those who do not understand Jesus are presumably "*not* taught by God" and have "*not* heard and learned from God." Some people, then, do not know because they cannot know by their natures (3:6, 12; 8:24); others do not know because they love darkness rather than light (3:19; see 3:2; 9:39-41; 12:42); still others do not know because they are kept in the dark (12:40).

5.2 Marginal Insiders: "Not in the Know"

On occasion, the narrator tells us about characters who are "*not* in the know," yet who are also in some sense insiders. The mother of Jesus at the Cana wed-

---

48. See J. H. Neyrey, "John III — A Debate over Johannine Epistemology and Christology," *NovT* 23 (1981): 118-22.

ding does not know about Jesus' "hour" (2:4).⁴⁹ She may be functioning as a Johannine stereotype of blood relatives who appear to be insiders, but are not — at least, not yet. Some commentators consider Nicodemus to be an insider of some sort. After all, he comes to Jesus; he claims to know something: "We know you are a teacher come from God"; he speaks on behalf of a fair trial for Jesus (7:51); and he buries Jesus lavishly with spices (19:39). Yet, for all this, he does not know much (3:4, 9, 12); he comes at night; and he thinks that Jesus is utterly and permanently dead. He too may be a typical Johannine stereotype of a quasi-insider, one only very partially "in the know."

5.3 Insiders: Degrees of Being "In the Know"

In the course of the narrative, the author classifies various insiders in terms of different pieces of knowledge. I argue that this is a conscious rhetorical strategy, which allows author and readers to rank the narrative characters according to a hierarchy of knowledge. One's rank in the group or one's place on the ladder of precedence is reflected by what one knows. Not all insiders know the same thing; even among in-group members, information is controlled.

 1. Certain persons are immediately identified as insiders by the very fact that they "come and see." Whether the persons are Andrew and associate (1:39), Nathanael (1:46), the men of Samaria (4:29), or the Greeks (12:20-22), they all come to Jesus and know certain things (1:41, 49; 4:42; 12:23-26). Yet, one should examine what each insider knows, for the author invites us to rank and classify them in terms of what each knows. For example, in the inaugural appearance of Jesus in 1:35-51, the narrator describes a series of people who come "into the know." However, each knows something different about Jesus, and their knowledge is not equal:

Andrew:	We have found the Messiah (1:41)
Philip:	We found him of whom Moses in the Law and also the prophets wrote (1:45)
Nathanael:	Rabbi, you are the Son of God. You are the King of Israel (1:49).

Curiously, Peter never says anything about Jesus, so one does not know what he knows at this point. It is commonly argued that the knowledge encoded in the

---

49. R. E. Brown, et al., eds., *Mary in the New Testament* (New York: Paulist Press, 1978) 191-92.

christological titles grows to the climactic response by Nathanael.[50] The narrator portrays him as a heroic figure who had to combat his previous knowledge of the Scriptures to "come and see" for himself (1:45-46; see also 5:39, 46-47; 7:52). Jesus, moreover, canonizes Nathanael as an "Israelite in whom there is no deceit" (1:47) and promises him even greater secrets, "You shall see greater things than these" (1:50). Nathanael, then, speaks the best lines, plays the juiciest role, and takes the climactic place in the drama. On the narrative level, then, Nathanael is more "in the know" than the others, and so we classify him as enjoying a higher status among the group than the others. This inaugural narrative, moreover, programs the reader to expect certain things: 1) there is differentiation in knowledge about Jesus, which can be mapped according to the sophistication of the titles ascribed to him; 2) some disciples simply know more; 3) disciples "in the know" are wont to impart this knowledge to select others; and 4) disciples "in the know" enjoy more status and prestige in the group than those with lesser knowledge.

2. This classification of knowledgeable insiders is surpassed by the "statement-misunderstanding-clarification" pattern with which the Samaritan woman and Martha are presented. When the Samaritan woman begins her conversation with Jesus, she is told "If only you knew . . ." (4:10). Jesus, who knows everything in the human heart (2:24-25), indicates that at this point she is "not in the know." She progresses, however, from asking questions (4:9, 12), to perceiving accurately (4:19), to learning important information (4:20-24), and finally to receiving a formal revelation (4:25-26). In addition to her coming "into the know" when Jesus "told her everything she ever did" (4:29, 39), she becomes a conduit of information for others (4:16, 28-30, 39). The entire village eventually shares her knowledge. Clearly, she is one of the Johannine heroines, even a foil for the obtuse Nicodemus.

Martha experiences a comparable enlightenment. Unlike the Samaritan woman, who starts her conversation with Jesus "*not* in the know," Martha begins by knowing two things: "I know that whatever you ask from God, God will give you" (11:22) and "I know that he [Lazarus] will rise again at the resurrection of the dead" (11:24). Yet, just as Jesus led the Samaritan woman through "statement," "misunderstanding," and "clarification," so he leads Martha to new and marvelous knowledge:

Statement: "Your brother will rise again" (11:23)
Misunderstanding: "I know he will rise again in the resurrection at the last day" (11:24)

---

50. Brown, *Gospel According to John*, 1.86-88.

Secrecy, Deception, and Revelation

Clarification: "I am the resurrection and the life; he who believes in me, even though he die, yet shall he live" (11:25)

Once "in the know," she too leads others to Jesus, namely her sister Mary (11:28-29). Thus, Martha begins knowing something but ends knowing very important information about Jesus; she also serves as a conduit of special information. Because she begins the story as a "beloved disciple" (11:5) and receives a unique revelation (11:25-27), she stands a notch higher than the Samaritan woman. Even insiders, then, can be differentiated in terms of what they know.

3. The man born blind presents another Johannine hero. Blind from birth (9:1) and at first "*not* in the know" (9:12, 25), he is transformed into a sighted person (9:7) who gains great insight (9:35-38). He comes to know that Jesus is a prophet (9:17), and to the pseudo-wise he proclaims what he knows, "We know that God does not listen to sinners" (9:31). Finally, he knows what others should know: "If this man were not from God, he could do nothing" (9:33). His transformation, moreover, continues when Jesus finds him and reveals himself to him (9:35-38). From knowing nothing, he has progressed to knowing about Jesus and then to acknowledging him. He would serve as a conduit of information to others (9:17, 24, 31-33), but his audience is hopelessly deaf (or blind, 9:39-41). The blind man, precisely because he serves as the narrative foil to the obtuse and unknowing Pharisees (9:39-41), represents an ideal Johannine character,[51] a hero who risks excommunication because of his bold public confession as well as a person supremely "in the know."

For the following reasons I classify him as enjoying a higher status within the group than the Samaritan woman: He speaks on behalf of Jesus before hostile crowds. Not only is he in conflict with Jesus' Pharisaic investigators, he is juxtaposed as well with his parents, who do not know much and are afraid to speak what they do know (9:20-22). The author labels his parents cowards with the comment, "His parents said this because they feared the Jews" (9:22), who threatened excommunication to anyone confessing Jesus to be the Christ. Their son, however, speaks boldly what he knows about Jesus, even when it causes his expulsion from the synagogue (9:34). Finally, he receives a christophany, the central focus of which is a revelation of the "Son of man" (9:35), knowledge which Jesus alone imparts (3:13; 8:28; 12:34) and which represents a more esoteric understanding of Jesus than "Messiah" or "prophet." On the basis of what he knows, the man born blind represents a very high level of sophistication in the Johannine circle. In terms of social ranking within the Johannine group, he should definitely be placed higher than Martha because of the quality of his "knowledge" about Jesus.

---

51. See R. Collins, "Representative Figures in the Fourth Gospel," *DR* 94 (1976): 41-43.

4. Simply in terms of the volume of very secret information shared in a most private setting, the disciples who hear Jesus' Farewell Address (John 13–17) must be classified as consummate insiders with exceptionally high status. Jesus calls them "friends" (or "beloved ones") precisely because "all that I have heard from my Father I have made known to you" (15:15). The formal conventions of Farewell Addresses[52] indicate that the following sorts of information are imparted:

1. Predictions of the Leader's Death (13:31-33; 14:28-31; 16:4-7; 16:16-19)
2. Predictions of the Future
   - a traitor (13:10-11, 18-19 and 21-30)
   - a denier (13:36-38)
   - hard times to come (14:1-4, 6-7, 9; 15:18-25; 16:1-4, 20, 32-33)
   - good times to come (14:1-4, 18-22; 16:21-24)
3. Articulation of Group-Specific Virtues
   - footwashing as hospitality (13:12-17)
   - loving one another (13:34-35; 14:15, 23-24; 15:12-17)
   - abiding (15:3-10)
   - keeping my commandments (14:15, 21; 15:10-13)
4. Announcement of a Successor[53]
   - another paraclete (14:16-17)
   - the Spirit (14:25; 15:26-27; 16:7-15)
5. Prophylactic Quality of This Secret Information (13:19; 15:18; 16:4, 33)

The formal and controlled revelation of this in-group knowledge to select persons should alone justify classifying them as the elite inner circle of the group. In addition to the information communicated through the form of a Farewell Address, we can itemize other materials uniquely revealed to this group:

a. Revelation of a status-specific ritual (13:12-17) as well as a new and higher status (15:14-17).
b. Elaborate knowledge of the traitor in the group (13:18, 21-30).
c. Statement–misunderstanding–clarification for Thomas (14:3-6), Philip (14:7-11), and Judas (14:21-24).

52. See F. F. Segovia, *The Farewell of the Word: The Johannine Call to Abide* (Minneapolis: Fortress Press, 1991) 4-20; See also W. S. Kurz, *The Farewell Address in the New Testament* (Collegeville, MN: Liturgical Press, 1990); J. H. Neyrey, *The Passion According to Saint Luke* (New York: Paulist Press, 1985) 5-48.

53. See J. L. Martyn, *History and Theology in the Fourth Gospel* (New York: Harper and Row, 1968) 135-42.

d. Formal notice that information is highly controlled (14:21-22).
e. The final "I am + predicate" revelations (14:6; 15:1-10).
f. Remembrances of special materials (14:26; 15:20; 16:4, 21).
g. Intense scrutiny of Jesus' words (16:16-24).
h. Speaking "plainly" and no longer "in figures" (16:25-30).
i. Revelation of God's name (17:6, 11, 12, 26).
j. Special knowledge for the disciples (17:7-8, 14, 17, 25).

Thus the audience in John 13–17 receives face-to-face, private, and unique communication from the departing revealer. Jesus, moreover, twice highlights their special status as elite insiders because of their sharing in highly controlled knowledge: "You know what I have done to you . . ." (13:12, 17) and "I call you friends, for all that I have heard from my Father I have made known to you" (15:14-15).

The author, however, further classifies even these members of the inner circle precisely in terms of what they know. One can examine, for example, the narrative figure of Peter. In the Synoptic Gospels, certain details serve to indicate his "knowledge" and his high status: 1) Peter is called first along with his brother Andrew (Mark 1:16-18); 2) he is privy to special revelations by Jesus: a raising from the dead (Mark 5:37-42), his transfiguration and theophany (Mark 9:2-9), special information about tax paying (Matt 17:24-27), secrets about the temple's future and the coming of the Son of man (Mark 13:3-37); 3) he is honored as the recipient of direct heavenly revelation about Jesus' identity (Matt 16:16-17); and 4) he speaks on behalf of the group.

The Fourth Gospel portrays Peter quite differently. He is called second, and not by Jesus himself; his brother Andrew is "first in time" and "first in knowledge" (1:40-41). When we compare Peter's knowledge about Jesus in John 6:67-69 with the Synoptics' record of his confession at Caesarea Philippi, Peter knows something, but this is hardly the climactic or revealed insight described by the Synoptics.

Mark 8:28-29	John 6:67-69
"Who do you say that I am?" "You are the Christ."	"Do you also wish to go away?" "To whom shall we go? You have the words of eternal life; and we have believed and come to know that you are the Holy One of God."

Peter's remark in John contains modest information about Jesus ("Holy One of God"); it lacks the quality of a bold public confession ("To whom should we go?"). He is an insider, but not a particularly enlightened or courageous one. Although he speaks for all the disciples, the reader does not automatically credit Peter with special status because of his lackluster and low-density understanding of Jesus. Nathanael or Martha he is not!

The Johannine portrait of Peter becomes clearer in the Farewell Address. Four times the reader is told that Peter is "*not* in the know":

> 13:7 (concerning the footwashing): "What I am doing you do not know now, but afterwards you will know."
> 13:24 (concerning the traitor): Simon Peter beckoned to him and said: "Tell us who it is of whom you speak."
> 13:36 (concerning Jesus' departure): "Lord, where are you going?"
> 13:37 (concerning Peter's following): "Lord, why cannot I follow you now?"

Yes, he will know later (13:7) and follow later (13:36), but at this point he is simply "*not* in the know." What makes this so damaging a portrayal is the narrator's contrast of Peter with a figure who is incredibly "in the know" (13:21-26) and who will boldly stand by Jesus in his hour, namely, the Beloved Disciple (18:15-17; 19:26-27).

The comparison and contrast of Peter and the Beloved Disciple continue after the Farewell Address.[54] On the morning of the resurrection, the two are again paired and compared. The Beloved Disciple not only runs faster, arrives at the tomb first (20:4-5), and sees all that Peter sees, but he also "saw and believed" (20:8), remarks which position him above Peter. Finally, when the disciples are last described together, no one recognizes Jesus on the shore, except the Beloved Disciple, who shares what he knows with Peter: "That disciple whom Jesus loved said to Peter, 'It is the Lord'" (21:7).

Only at the very ending of the narrative do we find Peter ever coming "into the know," and even there the narrator does not explicitly say that Peter understood Jesus. Jesus reveals to Peter the secret of his future: ". . . when you are old, you will stretch out your hands, and another will gird you and carry you where you do not wish to go" (21:18). The narrator does not say whether Peter understood Jesus' remark, just as he did not indicate whether Peter received the secret about the traitor (13:24). The remark is cryptic. On the narrative level, only the readers are "in the know," because the narrator shares with us the secret: "This he said to show by what death he would glorify God" (21:19). Thus, there re-

---

54. See J. H. Neyrey, "The Footwashing in John 13:6-11: Transformation Ritual or Ceremony?" in *The Social World of the First Christians: Essays in Honor of Wayne A. Meeks,* ed. L. Michael White and O. Larry Yarbrough (Minneapolis: Fortress, 1995) 205-13.

Secrecy, Deception, and Revelation

mains considerable ambiguity about Peter, even at the point where the narrative seems to clarify his precise status in the group. Can we ever confidently say that Peter is "in the know"? Is he ever "in the know" about important christological matters? So we classify Peter lower on the status ladder than the Beloved Disciple for his remarkable lack of knowledge as well as failure of courage. Granted that he is an insider, but he is not worthy of high status or prestige or knowledge.

5. One other disciple deserves consideration in this mapping of the status of knowledgeable insiders. In 20:1-18 Mary Magdalene is portrayed as a figure who is transformed from being a person painfully "not in the know" to being someone who is both well informed about great secrets and informs others. She begins the narrative "not in the know":

20:2	". . . we do not know where they have laid him."
20:13	"I do not know where they have laid him."
20:14	She did not know that it was Jesus.
20:15	"Supposing him to be the gardener . . . 'Tell me where you have laid him.'"

Although clearly "*not* in the know" even when she meets Jesus ("supposing him to be the gardener"), Mary is transformed immediately into a disciple supremely "in the know." Jesus calls her name ("Mary"), a revelation which pulls back the veil of unknowing ("Rabbi," 20:16). This knowledge inaugurates the great revelation of one of the most important secrets in the Gospel: "Go to my brethren and say to them, 'I am ascending to my Father and your Father, to my God and your God'" (20:17). Like other disciples "in the know," she serves as a conduit of esoteric christological information to others, who are also insiders (20:18).

In my scheme of things, Mary enjoys very high status within the Johannine group.[55] Not only is she the first to see the Risen Lord, she is also given access to the most important secrets about Jesus ("whither he goes") and serves in turn as conduit of this controlled information to others. Neither Andrew, Peter, Nathanael, nor the man born blind is so portrayed. Her knowledge, then, indicates a special status within the group.

---

55. The status of Mary and the reasons for it are provided at great length in chapter 2 of this volume.

6.0 Summary and Conclusions

6.1 The Secrecy Process

The sociology of secrecy has proved to be a productive, comprehensive, and enlightening window into the Fourth Gospel. It gathers neglected aspects of the document and differently highlights data which have been regularly examined by commentators. It invites a unified view of the dynamics of revelation and secrecy, which has not been discussed before in any depth or with any accuracy. The model itself derives from cross-cultural examples and has been shown to be quite applicable to ancient societies, especially in view of the elaborate intelligence services employed by Egypt, Assyria, Babylon, Rome, and Byzantium. The model, therefore, is hardly a modern scholarly construct imposed on the ancient documents, but one which is formed and adjusted in dialogue with specific historical cultures. Moreover, many elements of the secrecy process remain constant throughout history.

The sociology of secrecy, with its emphasis on information control, lying, deception, and espionage may strike some as inappropriate to a Gospel popularly thought to be a missionary revelation of truth by the Word of God. Modern religious readers may bristle at the suggestion that secrecy was in any way a conscious strategy of the early Christians. Yet, the ancient world most definitely held different views of deception and lying than we do,[56] and it would be ethnocentric and anachronistic to expect them to conform to our changing and perhaps relative standards of morality in this area. Theirs was not an open, democratic society in which all voters needed maximum information to make informed choices. Their dominant institution was kinship and family, which rigorously kept its secrets to itself; no one else needed to know them nor did there exist a moral duty or explicit laws which required their disclosure.

6.2 The Model and the Fourth Gospel

I would summarize as follows the way the sociology of secrecy can serve as a template for surfacing and integrating various data in the Fourth Gospel:

---

56. The New Testament expects people to encounter liars (Tit 1:12). A liar, moreover, might even be a very popular hero from the Greek epics; see P. Walcott, "Odysseus and the Art of Lying," *Ancient Society* 8 (1977): 1-19; A. J. Haft, "Odysseus, Idomeneus and Meriones: The Cretan Lies of Odyssey 13-19, *CJ* 79 (1983): 289-306; S. Murgnahan, *Disguise and Recognition in the Odyssey* (Princeton: Princeton University Press, 1987); D. Lateiner, "Deceptions and Delusions in Herodotus," *Classical Antiquity* 9 (1990): 230-46.

1. The document employs manifest secrecy, that is, formal, overt information control. God, Jesus, and the Spirit teach, clarify, and remind only certain characters in the document of select pieces of information. This *manifest secrecy* is Janus-faced: it looks both to outsiders as well as insiders.
2. In terms of *extra-group* secrecy, the Johannine group acts in distrust of outsiders and in superiority to them:
   a. Distrust: the world hates Jesus and company; it puts him on trial and seeks to kill him. Questions are unanswered; misunderstandings are not clarified. Crowds are addressed in "parables" and with double-meaning words. This represents a *defensive* strategy in the face of hostility to protect the Johannine circle.
   b. Superiority: as the alien Jesus is "not of this world," even so his disciples. They are superior to what is fleshly and from below; thus they are elite knowers of non-earthly or heavenly things.
3. In regard to *intra-group secrecy*, the Johannine circle engages in quite different social dynamics. Since not all characters know everything, I argue that the narrative presents a hierarchy of dramatis personae precisely in terms of *who* knows *what*. First, the control of information — namely, "secrecy" — builds self-identification boundaries around the Johannine circle, which are strengthened as the group protects its secrets. This sort of internal information control functions both as security for the group's secrets and as a process for classifying roles and statuses within the group (see Matt 11:25-27). Second, within the Johannine circle, select members rank higher than others in terms of their superior information.

I focus specifically on the phenomenon in the Gospel whereby the elite knowers are not the traditional apostolic figures (in particular, Peter), but elite, "beloved" or charismatic figures unknown in the Synoptic tradition. Again, control of information establishes boundaries, namely, *who* knows *what*; this reinforces the distinction between disciples "*not* in the know" and those "in the know." These few elite disciples, moreover, are the conduits for the dissemination of secrets and controlled information to others, thus confirming their status within the group. In short, the sociology of secrecy invites a fresh consideration of the internal tensions and conflict in the sectarian group known as the Johannine circle.

11

The "Noble" Shepherd in John 10

Cultural and Rhetorical Background

Introduction, State of the Question, and Thesis

Interpretation of the death of Jesus in the Fourth Gospel has proved fragmentary and elusive. Some interpreters contrast it with that of Paul,[1] while others focus on different motifs, such as glorification,[2] sacrificial references,[3] ascent and lifting up,[4] or cosmic war.[5] This article adds still another study based on a rhetorical topos from the ancient cultural world of a "'noble' death," which in John applies to the death of the "noble" shepherd in 10:11-18.

Some translate the adjective which describes the shepherd in 10:11 and 14 as "noble,"[6] "ideal,"[7] "model,"[8] "true"[9] or "good."[10] The Greek adjective is καλός,

---

1. Rudolf Bultmann, *Theology of the New Testament* (New York: Scribner, 1955) 2.52-53.
2. Rudolf Bultmann, *The Gospel of John: A Commentary* (Philadelphia: Westminster Press, 1971) 632-33.
3. See B. Grigsby, "The Cross as an Expiatory Sacrifice in the Fourth Gospel," *JSNT* 13 (1982): 51-80; G. Carey, "The Lamb of God and Atonement Theories," *TynB* 32 (1981): 97-122.
4. See Godfrey C. Nicholson, *Death as Departure: The Johannine Descent-Ascent Schema* (SBLDS 63; Chico, CA: Scholars Press, 1983).
5. See Judith Kovacs, "'Now Shall the Ruler of This World Be Driven Out': Jesus' Death as Cosmic Battle in John 12:20-36," *JBL* 114 (1995): 227-47.
6. D. A. Carson, *The Gospel According to John* (Grand Rapids, MI: Eerdmans, 1991) 386.
7. Raymond E. Brown, *The Gospel According to John* (Garden City: Doubleday, 1966) 1.386, 395-96; Barnabas Lindars, *The Gospel of John* (London: Oliphants, 1972) 361.
8. Brown, *The Gospel According to John*, 1.395-96.
9. See Bultmann, *The Gospel of John*, 364; George R. Beasley-Murray, *John* (Waco, TX: Word Books, 1987) 170; and John Painter, *The Quest for the Messiah* (2nd ed.; Nashville: Abingdon, 1993) 349, 353.
10. As another instance of his body-desires vs. mind-philosophy contrast, Philo distin-

not ἀγαθός; and these two words refer to quite different semantic domains,[11] although they were linked together in certain circumstances.[12] The opposite of καλός is shame (αἰσχρός), while the opposite of ἀγαθός is evil (πονηρός). We best understand καλός in terms of the cultural value of honor and shame, which is not the same as the moral sphere of good and evil. The Evangelist, moreover, labels the shepherd "noble" for two reasons, because 1) he lays down his life for the sheep[13] and 2) he knows his sheep (10:14). Commentators add one more reason from 10:17-18 which refers to the "voluntary" character of the death of the shepherd,[14] a traditional criterion of a "noble" death.

These preliminary insights, however, remain scattered and incomplete, and so invite a fuller consideration of the rhetoric and culture behind this text. We suggest that καλός rightly belongs to the cultural world of honor and shame; it qualifies behavior generally recognized as noble or excellent, and so worthy of public praise. We propose to examine Greek rhetorical literature on "noble death" to discover the rich complex of terminology, reasons and motifs whereby the ancients labeled a death as "noble." Our hypothesis is that the labeling of the shepherd as "noble" reflects the rhetorical topos of "noble death" in the Hellenistic world. As a result, we shall come to see that 10:11-18 is not a sequence of miscellaneous remarks, but a formally structured argument based on a commonplace on noble death found in Greek rhetoric.

1.0 An Honorable and Noble Death

The argument that the shepherd dies a "noble death" begins with an analysis of Greek rhetoric on the topic. This consists of 1) anecdotal mention of "noble death" in antiquity to establish that the concept truly existed in the culture of

---

guishes cattle-grazers and shepherds. The shepherd (ἀγαθὸς ποιμὴν) makes an excellent leader. But this line of inquiry is not useful here because Philo has nothing to say about the shepherd's death (Philo, *Agr.* 28-41).

11. See Aristotle, *Rhetoric* 1.3.6. But the ancient rhetorical distinction between καλός and ἀγαθός is blurred by commentators. Some argue that καλός expresses "the highest moral beauty" (Frédéric Godet, *Commentaire sur L'Évangile de Saint Jean* [Neuchatel: L.-A. Momnier, 1970] 3.89) or the perfection of living out the role of shepherd (J. H. Bernard, *A Critical and Exegetical Commentary on the Gospel According to St. John* [New York: Scribners, 1929] 2.357).

12. See Georg Bertram, "Καλός," *TDNT* 3.538-40, 544. See also Walter Dolan, "The Origin of Καλὸς κ'ἀγαθός," *AJP* 94 (1973): 365-74.

13. Brown, *The Gospel According to John*, 1.395; Lindars, *The Gospel of John*, 361; Carson, *The Gospel According to John*, 386.

14. See Leon Morris, *The Gospel of John* (Grand Rapids, MI: Eerdmans, 1971) 510; John Painter, *The Quest for the Messiah*, 356; Raymond Brown, *The Gospel According to John*, 1.399-400.

ancient Greece, 2) Athenian funeral orations celebrating the "noble death" of the city's fallen soldiers, 3) the criteria for praise in epideictic rhetoric, and 4) the rules for an encomium in the progymnasmata which instruct how to draw praise from death.[15]

1.1 Anecdotal Mention

Although the ancients praised success and victory above all, the hard experience of a military culture required that suitable honor be paid to those who died in battle fighting for their city. Extant Athenian funeral orations provide ample data about the expression "noble death."[16] Death is sometimes called "easy," "good," "noble" or "famous"; a life might "end well." 1) *An Easy or Good Death* (εὐθανασία). Anecdotes about the deaths of public figures mention that so-and-so died a "good death."[17] 2) *Noble or Famous Death* (καλῶς ἀποθανεῖν, εὐγενῶς ἀποθανεῖν, εὐκλεῶς ἀποθανεῖν). More commonly ancient authors qualified the verb "to die" with an adverb such as "nobly" or "honorably," often indicating *why* they judged a particular death "noble." For example, Isocrates urges soldiers faced with battle to act nobly, even if this means death: "Strive by all means to live in security, but if ever it falls to your lot to face the dangers of battle, seek to preserve your life, but with honour and not with disgrace; for death is the sentence of all mankind, but to die nobly (καλῶς ἀποθανεῖν) is the special honour which nature has reserved for the good" (*ad*

---

15. Other sources of information about "noble death" include: 1) the epitaph; see Richard Lattimore, *Themes in Greek and Latin Epitaphs* (Urbana, IL: University of Illinois Press, 1942) esp. 237-40; 2) the death of the philosopher-hero resisting the tyrant; see Herbert A. Musurillo, *The Acts of the Pagan Martyrs* (New York: Arno Press, 1979) 236-46; 3) the aretalogies studied by Moses Hadas and Morton Smith in their *Heroes and Gods: Spiritual Biographies in Antiquity* (New York: Harper and Row, 1965); 4) Hellenistic τελευταί and Roman *exitus illustrium variorum* (see A. Ronconi, "Exitus Illustrium Variorum," *RAC* 6 [1996]: 1258-68, which is the primary source for Adela Y. Collins, "The Genre of the Passion Narrative," *ST* 47 [1993]: 3-38); and 5) miscellaneous references such as can be found in the *Rhetoric to Herennius* 3.7.14 and Horace, *The Art of Poetry* 469.

16. Two books have recently been published whose titles include the phrase "noble death": David Seeley, *The Noble Death: Graeco-Roman Martyrology and Paul's Concept of Salvation* (Sheffield: JSOT Press, 1990); Arthur J. Droge and James D. Tabor, *A Noble Death: Suicide and Martyrdom among Christians and Jews in Antiquity* (San Francisco: Harper, 1992). Both books employ the phrase but do not tell their readers whence it comes. Droge and Tabor concern themselves with suicide, while Seeley focuses on vicarious expiation as the background for Paul's doctrine of salvation. In contrast, this study begins with the actual phrase "noble death" as it appears in Greek rhetoric, especially in the Athenian funeral orations.

17. See also Polybius 32.4.3; Philo, *Sacr.* 100; Clement of Alexandria, *Stromateis* 5.11.68.

Dem. 43). His perspective is that of a military society[18] in which courage to fight and die brings honor; in contrast, other actions are shameful, such as cowardly flight. The battle, moreover, was fought in defense of Athens, and so benefited the city's inhabitants. At stake, then, are the issues of honor and shame, which are being publicly reinforced by this funeral oration.[19] Isocrates once more provides an example of the third term being examined. "For we shall find that men of ambition (φιλοτίμους) and greatness of soul (μεγαλοψύχους) not only are desirous of praise for such things, but prefer a glorious death (εὐκλεῶς ἀποθνῄσκειν) to life, zealously seeking glory rather than existence" (*Evag.* 3). This sparkles with terms celebrated in the rhetoric of praise and blame: those who "die nobly" are "lovers of honor" (φιλότιμοι) and "great souled" (μεγαλοψύχοι); they seek "glory," which can be found even in death. In general, then, Greek orators describe as "noble" the death of soldiers in which courage is contrasted with cowardice and where death is declared honorable but flight shameful.[20] *3) Ending Well.* Orators also labeled a death noble by declaring that it "ended well" (καλῶς τελευτεῖν). Herodotus, for example, frequently speaks of warriors ending their lives well in combat or choosing battle rather than flight. He records how Croesus asked Solon if he knew of someone truly blest. Solon told him of a certain Tellus of Athens, whose crowning blessing was to "end well."

> [H]e crowned his life with a most glorious death (τελευτὴ τοῦ βίου λαμπροτάτη): for in a battle between the Athenians and their neighbours at Eleusis, he attacked and routed the enemy and most nobly died (ἀπέθανε κάλλιστα); and the Athenians gave him public burial where he fell and paid him great honour. (*Hist.* 1.30)

18. Although Seeley (*The Noble Death*, 15, 95-96, 107-9, 125-26) identifies "military setting" as one of the tags used by philosophers to give nobility to the struggle between mind and passions, he never investigates occasions when actual soldiers were celebrated for dying a "noble death."

19. Diodor of Sicily provides another example: describing a besieged city, he commented on the reactions of the men there: "Others, as they heard the laments of their wives and helpless children, sought to die like men (εὐγενῶς ἀποθανεῖν) rather than see their children led into captivity" (14.52.1-2). The same thing could be said of Josephus's account of the deaths of Saul and Jonathan. When Saul and his son realized that they were in a hopeless situation, they died nobly "throwing all their ardor into the fight" (*Antiquities* 6.368; see also *War* 7.380-83).

20. For other examples, see Lycurgus, *Leocrates* 48-49; Xenophon, *Anabasis* 3.1.43-44; Plato, *Menexenus* 246d; Demosthenes, *Funeral Speech* 37; Aristotle, *Virtues and Vices* 4.4; 6.5; Polybius, *Histories* 18.53.3; Dionysius of Halicarnassus 10.45.4-5; 2 Macc. 14:42; 6:28; 4 Macc 6:22, 30; Plutarch, *Alexander* 64.5; *Cato Min.* 15.4; *Otho* 15.4, 6; Diodor of Sicily 14.52.1-2; Josephus, *Antiquities* 6.368; *War* 7.380-83; Aelius Aristides, *Panathenaios* 132.10; Clement of Alexandria, *Stromateis* 6.4.38.

He "ended" his life in a superlative manner ("most gloriously," "most nobly"), that is, as a warrior in the city's army where military prowess translated into honor and praise. His manly courage, moreover, benefited Athens and led to posthumous honors, such as "public burial" and special forms of praise ("great honour").

This sample of terms for "noble death" yields some important points. 1. There was a popular understanding of a heroic or noble death. 2. The context in which death was called "noble" was generally a military one in which Athens' soldiers died in her defense. 3. The calculus of honor and shame (i.e., fight versus flight and death versus life) motivated heroes to die nobly; thus honor was their paramount motive and reward. 4. Comparisons were frequently made: a) manly courage vs cowardice, b) fight versus flight and c) praise and glory versus disgrace and shame. 5. Deaths were noble because they benefited others, generally Athens. 6. Noble deaths were celebrated with posthumous honors: graves built at public expense, annual commemorations in funeral speeches, and immortal fame in history and legend.

1.2 Funeral Orations and Noble Death

The ancients quibbled over who invented the funeral speech, the Greeks or the Romans.[21] But the overwhelming evidence from antiquity about the funeral speech (ἐπιτάφιος λόγος) comes from the classic period of Greek orators who delivered annual orations to honor the dead of Athens' various wars.[22] These

---

21. See Dionysius of Halicarnassus 5.17. Peter L. Schmidt ("Laudatio Funebris," *Der Kleine Pauly* [Stuttgart: Alfred Druckenmüller, 1969] 3.518) remarks that whereas the Greek funeral oration was a civic event, sponsored by the polis to support civic virtues, the Roman *laudatio funebris* was originally a family ceremony honoring the dead members of a family for virtues other than military courage. The Roman funeral ceremony often consisted of the public wearing of the clay images of both the deceased and ancestors of the household; see Polybius, *History* 6.53-54. Thus two different social institutions are in view (polis and family) and two different sets of social values are praised. On the Roman funeral oration, see Fredericus Vollmar, "Laudatio Funebrum Romanorum Historia et Reliquia Editio," *Jahrbuch für Classische Philologie* Supp. 18 (1892): 445-528; Marcel Drury, "*Laudatio Funebris* et Rhétorique," *Revue de Philologie et Littérateur* series 3, 16 (1942): 105-14; and John M. McManamon, *Funeral Oratory and the Cultural Ideas of Humanism* (Chapel Hill: University of North Carolina Press, 1989).

22. Cicero states that an annual funeral oration was delivered in Athens: ". . . in that public oration which it was customary to deliver at Athens in an assembly in honour of those fallen in battle, which was so popular that it had to be read aloud every year, as you know, on that day" (*Orator* 44.151).

The "Noble" Shepherd in John 10

authors explicitly state that the task of a funeral oration is to "enkomiaze"[23] the dead and to "praise them."[24] Funeral orations, then, share the same formal aim as epideictic rhetoric, that is, honor and praise, the pivotal value of the ancient world.

All of the extant examples of Athenian funeral orations closely follow a regular pattern of topics which are the sources of praise, each of which is developed in a remarkably similar manner.[25] We mention this only to underscore the fact that praise and honor were pivotal values already in the times of Thucydides, Plato and Demosthenes, as well as in those of Menander Rhetor and Pseudo-Dionysius. Moreover the content of praise was even then remarkably constant, as evidenced by the stereotyped manner in which conventional sources of honor are developed. Men are praised for their *ascribed honor:* 1) origin in the land of Greece and descent from ancient and noble ancestors, and 2) nurture, education and training in the value codes of Athens. They are praised moreover for their *achieved honor:* 1) excellence of body, soul and fortune. 2) They might, moreover, be compared to famous heroes.[26] This same se-

---

23. For example, Isocrates states that his difficult task is "to eulogize (ἐγκωμιάζειν) in prose the virtues of a man" (*Evagoras* 8; see 11). Hyperides too describes his task as ἐγκωμιάζειν (*Funeral Speech* 7-8, 15). Many centuries later, Menander Rhetor described the funeral speech as pure encomium: ἐπιτάφιος καθαρὸν ἐστιν ἐγκωμίου (2.419.2); see D. A. Russell and N. G. Wilson, *Menander Rhetor* (Oxford: Clarendon, 1981) 172. And Ps.-Dionysius said: "In a word, the *epitaphios* is a praise of the departed. This being so, it is clear that it must be based on the same topics as encomia, viz. country, family, nature, upbringing, actions" (D. A. Russell and N. G. Wilson, *Menander Rhetor*, 374). See Theodore Burgess, *Epideictic Literature* (New York: Garland Publishing Co., 1987) 146-57.

24. For example, Isocrates regards his speech as but part of the honor shown to the dead: "In gratitude we honored (ἐτιμήσαμεν) them with the highest honors and set up their statues" (*Evagoras* 57). Praise is the formal aim of all the funeral speeches: Lycurgus (*Leocrates* 51) states that his speech aims to "pay the highest honors" to the fallen. Similarly, Lycius *(Funeral Oration)* talks of "glorifying and honoring" the dead (3); he says, "Their memory can never grow old, while their honour is every man's envy" (79). Demosthenes *(Funeral Speech)* is the most explicit in his grants of praise: "For knowing that among good men the acquisition of wealth and the enjoyment of the pleasures that go with living are scorned, and that their whole desire is for virtue and words of praise, the citizens were of the opinion that we ought to honour them with such eulogies as would most certainly secure them in death the glory they had won while living" (2).

25. On the Greek funeral oration, see Theodore Burgess, *Epideictic Literature,* 146-56; John E. Ziolkowski, *Thucydides and the Tradition of Funeral Speeches at Athens* (Salem, NH: The Ayer Company, 1985); Nicole Loraux, *The Invention of Athens: The Funeral Oration in the Classical City* (Cambridge, MA: Harvard University Press, 1986).

26. Despite its late date, the rules for a "funeral oration" by Ps.-Dionysius explicitly list the formal categories of the encomium as the grounds for praise in the speech (n. 24 above and D. A. Russell and Nigel Wilson, *Menander Rhetor,* 374-76). On these conventional topics, see

quence of topics and their contents was eventually codified in the encomium genre found in progymnastic literature. Thus the conventionality of the criteria for honor and praise remained constant for centuries,[27] including the common appreciation of what constituted a noble death.

Just as orators structured their funeral orations according to commonplace topics from a shared sense of what constituted a praiseworthy life, so also they praised the death of military heroes according to a common set of canons for a noble death. The data yield seven major criteria. 1. The orators stress how the death of Athens' soldiers *benefited* the city. Hyperides, for example, regularly touts the gift of freedom given Athens and Greece by its fallen soldiers: "Their courage in arms . . . reveals them as the authors of many benefits conferred upon their country and the rest of Greece" (*Funeral Speech* 9; see 15-16, 19, 20-22). Later he says that these soldiers "sacrificed their lives that others might live well" (*Funeral Speech* 26). Similar remarks are made by Thucydides, Plato and Demosthenes.[28] Indeed many of those who fell in defense of Athens were called "saviors."[29]

2. In a variation of the motif of benefit to others, orators argue that Athens' fallen heroes displayed *exceptional justice toward the polis* by their deaths. According to the ancients, justice is one of the four cardinal virtues, the one according to which duties are paid. Ps.-Aristotle says: "To righteousness (δικαιοσύνη) it belongs to be ready to distribute according to desert, and to preserve ancestral customs and institutions and the established laws . . . and to keep agreements." To whom does one owe anything? "First among the claims of righteousness are our duties to the gods, then our duties to the spirits, then those to country and parents, then those to the departed" (Ps.-Aristotle, *Virtues*

Jerome H. Neyrey, "Josephus' *Vita* and the Encomium: A Native Model of Personality," *JSJ* 25 (1994): 177-206; idem, *Honor and Shame in the Gospel of Matthew* (Louisville, KY: Westminster/John Knox, 1998).

27. Although John E. Ziolkowski (*Thucydides and the Traditions of Funeral Speeches at Athens*) argued that the funeral speeches in Thucydides' time did not enjoy common terminology, yet his chart of the fixed element of the rhetoric of praise (pp. 95-97) indicates that there is virtual agreement on the contents of speeches between him and myself.

28. Thucydides, *History* 2.42.3; Plato, *Menexenus* 237a, 242a-b, 246; Demosthenes, *Oration* 38.8, 23; *Funeral Speech 60* 8, 10, 29; see also Lycurgus, *Against Leocrates* 46.

29. Demosthenes, *Oration 37* 8, 23. Iphigenia consoled her mother in a final speech where she catalogues the benefits to Hellas by her death: "The whole might of Hellas depends on me. Upon me depends the passage of the ships over the sea, and the overthrow of the Phrygians. With me it rests to prevent the barbarians from carrying our women off from happy Hellas in the future. . . . All these things I shall achieve by my death, and my name, as the liberator of Hellas, shall be blessed. Indeed, it behooves me not to be too fond of life; you bore me for the common good of all the Hellenes, not for yourself alone" (Euripides, *Iphigenia at Aulis* 1368).

The "Noble" Shepherd in John 10

and Vices, V.2-3).[30] The premier aspect of justice celebrated in the annual memorial for Athens' fallen soldiers was the duty they paid to the polis and its institutions. For example, many orators rehearsed the history of Athens, in particular its struggles to be free of tyranny and its willingness to fight to preserve the ancestral way of life. The fallen who died were duty-bound to be faithful to that political history at the cost of their lives. Demosthenes summarizes this succinctly: "The considerations that actuated these men one and all to choose to die nobly have now been enumerated: birth, education, habituation to high standards of conduct, and *the underlying principles of our form of government in general*" (*Funeral Speech* 27, italics added). Their death, then, is noble not only because it benefited polis and family,[31] but because it demonstrated the virtue of justice as completely as possible.[32]

Since this material will be very important in our consideration of the Johannine shepherd, let us read another sample passage from Lysias.

> Now in many ways it was natural to our ancestors . . . to fight the battles of justice: for the very beginning of their life was just. . . . They were the first and only people in that time to drive out the ruling classes . . . and establish a democracy; by sharing with each other the hopes of their perils they had freedom of soul in their civic life. For they deemed that it was the way of wild beasts to be held subject to one another by force, but the duty of men to delimit justice by law, to convince by reason, and to serve these two in act by submitting to the sovereignty of law and the instruction of reason. (*Funeral Oration* 17-19)

Lysias indicates that current citizens are heirs of a political system based on justice and are accustomed to "fight the battles of justice." And it is their duty to protect this legacy. Hence this defense of fatherland even at the cost of one's life most fully exemplifies justice for them.[33]

---

30. Closer in time to the New Testament is Cicero's definition: "Duty is the feeling which renders kind offices and loving service to one's kin and country. Gratitude embraces the memory of friendships and of services rendered by another, and the desire to requite these benefits" (*Invention* 2.160-61).

31. One of the clearest examples of death resulting from duty to family is that of Antigone, who performed the sacred burial rites for her brother in violation of the decree of her uncle that the dead brother not be buried.

32. It goes without saying that courage (ἀνδρεία) was equally honored, and a noble death is impossible without it. See Lycurgus, *Against Leocrates* 46; Demosthenes, *Funeral Speech*, 17; Isocrates, *Evagoras* 65-66; Hyperides, *Funeral Speech* 15-16.

33. Other examples include Lycurgus, *Leocrates* 50; Lysias, *Funeral Oration* 33, 61, 68, 70; Demosthenes, *Funeral Speech* 11, 18, 19, 23, 27, 36; Isocrates, *Evagoras* 8, 23, 35, 38, 42-44, 52, 66; Hyperides, *Funeral Speech* 11, 16, 19, 24, 26.

3. Athens reveled in its political freedom and despised the world of slaves and the rule of tyrants. Its orators expressed this civic value in another criterion for a noble death, that is, its *voluntary character*.[34] The fallen soldiers were often said to "prefer noble death to a life of servitude" or to "choose" their death. This tradition of a voluntary death[35] is found already in Plato's *Menexenus*, where the speaker's remarks contain most of the conventions of a noble death voluntarily undergone: "We who might have ignobly lived *choose* rather to die nobly before we bring you and those after you to disgrace or before we shame you with our fathers and all our earlier forebears" (*Menexenus* 246d). Again the basic issues are those of honor and shame: honor = "die nobly"; shame = "disgrace." Honor, moreover, comes from voluntary death, that is, from *choosing* one way rather than another; thus those who perish in battle are *not victims* whose fate is decided by others, but courageous soldiers who take fate in their own hands.

Pericles' oration over the war dead contains two versions of this motif, one which celebrates the *preference* of death with honor to life with shame and another which emphasizes the *choice* made in taking up the fight. As regards the first expression Thucydides records:

> [W]hen the moment of combat came, thinking it better to defend themselves and suffer death rather than to yield and save their lives, they fled, indeed, from the shameful word of dishonour, but with life and limb stood stoutly to their task, and in the brief instant ordained by fate, at the crowning moment not of fear but glory, they passed away. (*History* 2.43.4)

Again, the value context is that of honor and shame: "shameful word of dishonor" versus "crowning moment of glory." The author claims that the fallen

---

34. It was also important that animals about to be sacrificed "give their consent"; for this purpose cold water and/or grain were suddenly thrown on the head and face of the animal so that it wagged its head from side to side, which motion was interpreted as voluntary consent to die. See Marcel Detienne, "Culinary Practices and the Spirit of Sacrifice," *The Cuisine of Sacrifice among the Greeks*, ed. M. Detienne and P. Vernant (Chicago: University of Chicago Press, 1989) 9.

35. There is notable Roman evidence for the same topos. Seneca, for example, contrasts the ignoble and unfree death of gladiators with the noble death of a wise man who dies voluntarily: "From the men who hire out their strength for the arena, who eat and drink what they must pay for with their blood, security is taken that they will endure such trials even though they be unwilling; from you, that you will endure them willingly and with alacrity *(volens libensque)*. The gladiator may lower his weapon and test the pity of the people; but you will neither lower your weapon nor beg for life. You must die erect and unyielding *(invictoque)*" (*Epistles* 37.2-3). Indeed Nero is reported to have inquired whether Seneca himself, when faced with extreme royal displeasure, was preparing for a "voluntary death" (*voluntariam mortem*, Tacitus, *Annals* 15.61).

soldiers were formally "thinking" about the honor code of elite Athenians. That is, they appreciated the calculus of shame (i.e. flight, fear of dying, dishonor) and honor ("better to die than yield," "stood stoutly"). Hence their *preference* was clear: flight, saving one's life and fear are dishonorable and disgraceful, but fighting, faithfulness and death are glorious and honorable.[36]

The second aspect of the voluntary character of a noble death is the simple note by the orator in another place that the deceased formally *chose* their fate: ". . . deeming the punishment of the foe to be more desirable than these things (wealth, escape), and at the same time regarding such a hazard as the most glorious of all, they chose (ἐβουλήθησαν) . . ." (Thucydides, *History* 2.42.4). Their death, then, was voluntary; they did not die like slaves or captured troops whose lives are taken from them. They willingly chose their death.[37]

4. On occasion orators declare that, although a warrior died in battle, he died a noble death. In the logic of honor and glory, he can be said to be *undefeated* or to have *conquered* his foe by his dying. For example, Lycurgus writes of the war dead:

> *Unconquered* (οὐχ ἡττηθέντες), they fell in the defense of freedom, and if I may use a paradox, they *triumphed* (νικῶντες) in their death. . . . neither can we say that they have been defeated whose spirits did not flinch at the aggressor's threat . . . since *by the choosing of a noble death* they are escaping slavery. (*Leocrates* 48-49; italics added)

We hear in Lycurgus's speech the cultural horror of death, which means weakness, loss of control and finally "slavery," a shameful status. But a military death, in which manly courage is displayed ("did not flinch") and which was endured for the benefit of Athens ("defense of freedom"), means that in the world of honor and shame the fallen have "triumphed" and "have not been defeated."[38]

---

36. Socrates recounts the conversation between Achilles and his mother Thetis on death: "He [Achilles] made light of danger in comparison with incurring dishonor when his goddess mother warned him, eager as he was to kill Hector, in some such words as these, I fancy. 'My son, if you avenge your comrade Patroclus' death and kill Hector, you will die yourself — Next after Hector is thy fate prepared.' When he heard this warning, he made light of his death and danger, being much more afraid of an ignoble life and of failing to avenge his friends. 'Let me die forthwith,' said he, 'when I have requited the villain, rather than remain here by the beaked ships to be mocked, a burden on the ground'" (Plato, *Apology* 28c-d).

37. Isocrates, *Evagoras* 9.3; see also Plato, *Menexenus* 246d; Demosthenes *Oration* 37 1, 8, 26.

38. Centuries later Plutarch writes: "For the best thing is that a general should be victorious and keep his life, 'but if he must die, he should conclude his life with valour (ἀρετὴν),' as Euripides says; for then he does not suffer death, but rather achieves it" (*Pelopidas and Marcellus* 3.2).

Thus, this small excerpt from Lycurgus contains almost the complete inventory of reasons why a death is called "noble."[39]

5. On occasion funeral orations declare a death "noble" because of some *uniqueness*.[40] Orators assert that "no one" else has ever been able to perform this deed and achieve this honor. In his funeral oration Hyperides articulates the uniqueness of those he praises in this manner: "Never before did men strive for a nobler cause, either against stronger adversaries or with fewer friends, convinced that valour gave strength and courage superiority as no mere numbers could" (*Funeral Speech* 19).[41] Uniqueness is argued in two ways. First, no one before them had a more noble cause for which to fight. Second, a series of comparisons dramatizes their excellence: they faced a foe *stronger than* has ever been faced and they advanced with *fewer* allies than anyone else. Their honor calculus tells them that valour (ἀπετήν) produces strength and courage (ἀνδρείαν), and superiority.

6. A truly noble death was generally identified by the *posthumous honors* paid to the deceased. This esteem might be expressed by public celebration of the dead, such as games or monuments.[42] The very funeral orations which we are examining themselves serve to give glory to the dead first by giving a public evaluation of their worth and later by annual burnishing of their reputation.[43]

---

39. See Demosthenes, *Funeral Speech* 19; 18.192, 207-8.

40. For a full study of the rhetoric of uniqueness, see Jerome H. Neyrey, "'First,' 'Only,' 'One of a Few,' and 'No One Else': The Rhetoric of Uniqueness and the Doxologies in 1 Timothy," *Bib* 86 (2005): 59-87.

41. Isocrates says in praise of Evagoras: "I would say that no one (οὐδεῖς), whether mortal, demigod, or immortal, will be found to have obtained his throne more nobly, more splendidly, or more piously" (*Evagoras* 39). Other instances of uniqueness include Hyperides, *Funeral Speech* 19; Lycurgus, *Leocrates* 15; Demosthenes states in regard to the dead: "How, then, since the whole country unites in according them a public burial, and they alone receive the words of universal praise . . . how can we do otherwise than consider them blessed of fortune?" (*Funeral Oration* 60.33).

42. The Greek celebrations of posthumous honors were well known in antiquity, as Dionysius of Halicarnassus notes: "These writers [Greeks] have given accounts of funeral games, both gymnastic and equestrian, held in honour of famous men by their friends, as by Achilles for Patroclus and, before that, by Herakles for Pelops" (*History* 5.17.4). Isocrates lists the various posthumous honors that might be celebrated to honor Evagoras, adding that his own speech gives greater glory to the dead man: "When I saw you, Nicocles, honouring the tomb of your father, not only with numerous and beautiful offerings, but also with dances, music, and athletic contests, and furthermore, with races of horses and triremes . . ." (*Evagoras* 1).

43. This is illustrated by the following inscription. A public decree, both read aloud at the tomb of a certain Theophilos and subsequently carved in white marble, honors the deceased by the public declaration of his worth: ". . . of very noble ancestral stock, having contributed all good-will towards his country, having lived his life as master of his family, providing many

The "Noble" Shepherd in John 10

Whether games, monuments, or annual funeral orations, the aim was to give a type of eternal glory to the dead. Hence, we frequently find the claim that those being celebrated are in one sense like the gods, because their glory too is now deathless and everlasting. Demosthenes sums it up tidily: "It is a proud privilege to behold them possessors of deathless honours and a memorial of their valour erected by the State, and deemed deserving of sacrifices and games for all future time" (*Funeral Oration* 36).[44]

7. *Immortality* on occasion is said to be the aim and result of a noble death. The common meaning of this point typically finds expression in terms of the undying and immortal fame that is attached to the hero and his exploits.[45]

In summary, this survey of extant Athenian funeral orations yields the following points. 1. Their formal aim is praise and honor[46] of the fallen. Thus the various meanings of "noble death" must be understood in light of this pivotal value. 2. Noteworthy also is the utter conventionality of the topics from which praise is drawn. 3. Seven criteria for a noble death emerge from the speeches: a death is noble which a) benefits others, b) displays justice to the fatherland, c) is voluntarily accepted, d) proves that the fallen died unvanquished and undefeated, e) is unique in some way, f) produces posthumous honors, and g) leads to immortal fame and glory.

1.3 Amplification in the Rhetoric of Praise

Although Athens developed the genre of the funeral speech, Aristotle surprisingly had little specifically to say about a noble death. Yet in his exposition of epideictic rhetoric, he collected the arguments one might use to acknowledge

---

things for his country through his generalship and tenure as agoranomos and his embassies as far as Rome and Germany and Caesar, being amicable to the citizens and in concord with his wife Apphia, now it is resolved that Theophilos be honoured with a painted portrait and a gold bust and a marble statue." *NDIEC* 2 (1982): 58-60.

44. Ziolkowski lists many examples of this motif of posthumous glory (*Thucydides and the Tradition of Funeral Speeches at Athens*, 126-28).

45. For example, see Josephus, *Ant.* 17.152-54.

46. The orators frequently stress that part of the honor of the fallen is the arousal of envy and emulation in those who hear the speech. Lysias most of all employs this rhetorical topic; for example, speaking of the fallen heroes of Athens, he honors them: "Thus the struggles at the Peiraeus have earned for those men the envy of all mankind" (*Funeral Oration* 66; see also 68-73). See also Isocrates, *Evagoras* 6, 70; Hyperides, *Funeral Speech* 31-32; Demosthenes, *Funeral Speech* 60. On the relationship of envy and honor, see Anselm Hagedorn and Jerome Neyrey, "'It Was Out of Envy that They Handed Jesus Over' (Mark 15,10): The Anatomy of Envy and the Gospel of Mark," *JSNT* 69 (1998): 15-38.

someone's claims to honor and nobility, whether ascribed honor (origins and birth) or achieved honor (deeds popularly considered noble). Aristotle's catalogue of topics for amplifying praise bears striking resemblance to the items mentioned frequently in the funeral speeches we have been examining. Thus, we argue, Aristotle's general material on the amplification of praise directly reflects the specific remarks made by orators who eulogized and honored the dead. The funeral orators reflect the actual practice of calling a death noble according to the very criteria Aristotle identified later as criteria for developing praise of the living. The point is, the reasons for labeling a death or a life "noble" are both ancient, widespread and consistent.

Aristotle begins his discussion of the rhetoric of praise and blame with a focus on "virtue and vice": "Let us speak of virtue and vice and honorable and shameful; for these are the points of reference for one praising and blaming" (*Rhet.* 1.9.1). When discussing "virtue," Aristotle lists its subdivision: "justice, manly courage, self-control, magnificence, magnanimity, liberality, gentleness, prudence, and wisdom" (1.9.5), with a focus primarily on courage and justice. At this point, Aristotle catalogues attributes for evaluating actions to determine if they are "honorable" or noble. If we extrapolate from this, we have a precise list of criteria from a native informant on what constitutes a "noble life." The relevant part of Aristotle's analysis goes as follows:

> 16. And things for which the *rewards are an honor* are "noble," especially those that bring honor rather than money; and whatever someone does *by choice*, not for his own sake; 17. and things *absolutely good* and whatever someone has *done for his country*, overlooking his own interest . . . 18. and whatever can belong to a person *when dead more than when alive* (for what belongs to a person in his lifetime has more of the quality of being to his own advantage); 19. and whatever works are done *for the sake of others* (for they have less of the self); and successes gained *for others*, but not for the self and for those who have *conferred benefits* (for that is just); and *acts of kindness* (for they are not directed to oneself); 20. and things that are the opposites of those of which people are shamed . . . 23. And those that give *pleasure to others* more than to oneself; thus, *the just and justice* are honorable. 24. . . . *not to be defeated* is characteristic of a brave man. 25. And *victory and glory* are among honorable things; for they are to be chosen even if they are fruitless, and they make clear a preeminence of virtue. And things that will be *remembered* [are honorable]; and the more so, the more [honorable]. And what *follows a person when no longer alive* (and glory does follow) and things extraordinary and things *in the power of only one person* are more honorable, for [they are] more memorable. (*Rhet.* 1.9.16-25)

The "Noble" Shepherd in John 10

Let us summarize Aristotle's complex criteria according to which he labels an action honorable or praiseworthy. An action is honorable if:

1. it benefits others (17, 19, 23), and is not done for self-interest (16, 17, 18),
2. it is just or demonstrates justice (19, 23),
3. it produces honor (16) and glory (25), or advances one's reputation (21) especially after death (18), and causes one to be remembered (25),
4. it was done voluntarily, by choice (16, 17, 25),
5. it ended in victory; the actor was not defeated (24),
6. it is unique to this particular person or distinctive of a special class of persons (25),[47] and
7. it yielded posthumous honors (25).

1.4 The Encomium: Death as a Source of Honor

Students in the second level of education in the Greco-Roman world learned to compose a series of genres which equipped them to study rhetoric and so enter civic life. Their grammatical handbooks, called *progymnasmata*, codified various genres and their contents, with occasional examples for imitation. We focus on the rules for the encomium, which instructed students how to construct a speech of praise. As noted earlier, many funeral orations state that they are "enkomiazing" someone.

Only Hermogenes, of all the extant progymnastic authors of rules for an encomium, provides criteria for spelling out what might be praiseworthy about a death.[48]

> Then, too, from the manner of his end, as that he died fighting *for his fatherland*, and, if there were *anything extraordinary* under that head, as in the

---

47. In regard to this point Aristotle has more to say. "A praiseworthy person is one who is ... the *only one* or the *first* or *one of a few* or the one *who most* has done something; for all these things are honorable. And [praise can be taken] from the historical contexts ... if a subject has *often had success* in the same way (for that is a great thing and would seem to result not from chance but from the person himself); and if incitements and honors have been *invented and established because of him* ... and if he was the *first* one to receive an *encomium*, as in the case of Hippolochos; and [if for him], as for Hermodius and Aristogeiton, *statues* were set up in the marketplace" (*Rhet.* 1.9.38, italics added).

48. Theon mentions εὐθανασία as one of the external qualities of a person, probably meaning by it an "easy death" free from illness or disease (James Butts, *The "Progymnasmata" of Theon* [unpublished dissertation, Claremont, 1994] 9.19). Herodotus's remark on an "easy death" is important: "[a blest man must be] free from deformity, sickness and all evil, and happy in his children and his comeliness" (1.32).

295

case of Callimachus that even in death he stood. You will draw praise also from the one who slew him, as that Achilles died at the hands of the god Apollo. You will describe also what was done *after his end*, whether funeral games were ordained in his honor, as in the case of Patroclus. (emphasis added)[49]

The perspective is that of warriors and war, which is the preserve of elites and heroes and the arena of honor and shame. Among the criteria for a noble death we find: 1) *benefit* ("fighting for the fatherland"), 2) *uniqueness* ("anything extraordinary"), and 3) *posthumous honors* ("games" and "oracle concerning his bones").[50] Most of the criteria for a noble death described by Hermogenes occurred in earlier Greek rhetorical literature. Hence, they reflect a common cultural consensus.

Theon's remarks below are not said specifically about a noble death; they are a composite instruction on the ways that an orator may "amplify" praise, that is, honor someone. This list is of great importance to us for several reasons. First, Theon's list closely resembles the reasons used in classical funeral orations to argue that a certain death was noble. Second, his list attests to the conventionality and continuity of motifs from the time of Lysias and Isocrates to that of Theon. Of "noble" actions Theon says:

> Noble actions are those which we do *for the sake of others*, and not ourselves; and *in behalf of what is noble*, rather than on account of what is advantageous or pleasant; and on account of which *most people also receive great benefits*. . . . Praiseworthy actions are also those occurring in a timely manner, and if one acted *alone*, or *first*, or when *no one* acted, or *more than others*, or *with a few*, or beyond one's age, or exceeding expectation, or with hard work, or what was done most easily and quickly. (9.25-38, emphasis added)[51]

We note the concern to specify "praiseworthy" deeds: 1) actions "done for the sake of others" and "on account of which most people receive great benefits," 2) actions which are "noble," that is, virtuous, and not advantageous, and 3) unique actions which the actor did "alone or first" or in circumstances which point to leadership or excellence or precocious ability. Thus, the conventional

---

49. Charles S. Baldwin, *Medieval Rhetoric and Poetic* (New York: Macmillan, 1928) 32.

50. Quintilian instructs on what occurs "after death," viz., posthumous honors: "It is not always possible to deal with the time subsequent to our hero's death: this is due not merely to the fact that we sometimes praise him while still alive, but also that there are but few occasions when we have a chance to celebrate the award of divine honours, posthumous votes of thanks, or statues erected at the public expense" (*Inst. Orat.* 3.7.17).

51. Butts, *The "Progymnasmata" of Theon*, 468-71.

criteria found in funeral orations about a "noble" death continue as the measure for praise of the living.

2.0 The Noble Death Tradition and the Greek Literature of Israel

Did the Greek tradition of noble death become part of the rhetorical world of Israelite literature written in Greek?[52] Did Jerusalem learn anything from Athens besides its alphabet? The books of Maccabees indicate that, in addition to the Greek language, Israel also adopted the cultural world of honor and shame and the tradition of praising a noble death for many of the same reasons as did the Greeks.[53]

In general, 1, 2, and 4 Maccabees illustrate the presence of the Greco-Roman understanding of a noble death in both terminology and logic. The Maccabean literature frequently speaks of "dying nobly" (γενναίως ἀπευθανατίζειν)[54] or "ending nobly" (γενναίως τελευτᾶν).[55] Death might also be "glorious" (ἀοίδιμον θάνατον)[56] or "honorable" (μακάριον θάνατον).[57] They cite the same reasons as Greek rhetoric for declaring a death "noble." Death is noble if it benefits the nation or is suffered on its behalf or saves it.[58] For example, Eleazar, called Aravan, charged an elephant he thought was carrying the king and speared it; unfortunately the king was not aboard and the elephant crushed

---

52. Both Seeley (*The Noble Death*, 83-112) and Droge and Tabor (*A Noble Death*, 53-84, 86-96) discuss the Maccabean literature, the latter with an eye to suicide and the former with focus on the background for Paul's soteriology. Neither bring to their task the rich data from Greek rhetoric, and so a new survey of 1, 2, and 4 Maccabees is warranted precisely because they are not only written in Greek but reflect Greek popular understanding of what constitutes a noble death.

53. The fullest treatment of the motif of noble death in 2 and 4 Maccabees is that of Jan Willem Van Henten, *The Maccabean Martyrs as Saviours of the Jewish People* (Leiden: Brill, 1997). In particular he examines the importance of "voluntary" death and death as benefit. He too appreciates the Judean dependence on motifs long ago made sacred in Greek literature (see especially pp. 140-50, 157-59, 213-25).

54. 2 Macc 6:28; see 1 Macc 4:35; 9:10; 4 Macc 6:30.

55. 2 Macc 7:5; see 4 Macc 6:22.

56. 4 Macc 10:1.

57. 4 Macc 10:15; on the translation of μακάριος as "honorable," see K. C. Hanson, "'How Honorable! How Shameful!' A Cultural Analysis of Matthew's Makarisms and Reproaches," *Semeia* 68 (1994): 81-112.

58. Besides speaking about an effective death which benefits the people, van Henten argues persuasively that the author describes the death in 2 Macc 7:33-39 as benefitting the people because it is an atonement sacrifice (*The Maccabean Martyrs as Saviours*, 140-56), and he notes the important Greco-Roman parallels (pp. 156-61).

him as it fell. Nevertheless, the author says of him "So he gave up his life *to save his people* and to win for himself an *everlasting name*" (1 Macc 6:43-44).[59]

The voluntary character of a noble death is expressed in several ways.[60] It may be formally stated that the dying person chose or accepted death or willingly went to it. In regard to Eleazar's death, the author of 2 Maccabees twice states that "[he] *welcoming* death with honor rather than a life with pollutions, *went* to the rack *of his own accord* (αὐθαιρέτως)" (2 Macc 6:19); shortly he records Eleazar saying, "I will leave to the young a noble example[61] of how to die a good death *nobly and willingly*" (2 Macc 6:28).[62] The alternate expression of the voluntary character of a noble death consists of the calculus made by the dying person that noble death is preferable to a shameful escape. Consider 1 Maccabees: "It is better for us to die in battle than to see the misfortunes of our nature and of the sanctuary" (3:59; see 2 Macc 6:19).[63]

Dying unconquered or conquering in death is found abundantly in 4 Maccabees. Of those slain the author says, "By their endurance they *conquered* the tyrant" (1:11). Eleazar won a victory over his torturers: "Although his sacred life was consumed by tortures and racks, he *conquered* the besiegers with the shield of his devout reason" (7:4).[64]

The manner of death conforms to the canons of honor accepted by the audience and so elicits from both observers and hearers the essence of honor: acknowledgment, glory, fame, honor, an everlasting name, renown and the like. For example, 1 Maccabees says of Eleazar, "So he gave his life to save his people and *to win* for himself *an everlasting name*" (6:44). Similarly, when Judas faced the enemy he remarked: "If our time has come let us *die bravely* for our kindred and *leave no cause to question our honor*" (9:10).[65] Thus both Eleazar and Judas are credited with noble motives for dying, namely, benefit to others ("save his people" and "for our kindred") and quest for immortal honor ("everlasting name" and "unquestionable honor").

Noble deaths regularly contain mention of the virtue of those who died, es-

---

59. Although many authors call attention to the sacrificial or atoning significance of the demise of Eleazar and the seven brothers (see also 17:22), yet see Seeley, *The Noble Death*, 97-98.

60. For a more detailed examination of this, see van Henten, *The Maccabean Martyrs as Saviours*, pp. 58, 95-98.

61. On the martyrs as exemplary figures, see van Henten, *The Maccabean Martyrs as Saviours*, 210-43.

62. See also 2 Macc 7:14, 29; 4 Macc 5:23.

63. See also 2 Macc 7:14; 4 Macc 9:1, 4.

64. See also 4 Macc 7:14; 10:7; 11:20-21; 18:22. The same thing is said of Jesus' death in Heb 2:14-15.

65. See also 2 Macc 7:5-6, 29.

pecially their courage and justice. Courage, the manly virtue of endurance of hardships, is often claimed on behalf of the characters in the Maccabean literature. For example, Judas exhorted his army before battle with the remark, "If our time has come, let us *die bravely* (ἐν ἀνδρείᾳ) for our kindred" (1 Macc 9:10). Similarly Eleazar eulogizes the Israelite law by claiming that "it trains us in *courage* (ἀνδρείαν) so that we *endure* any suffering *willingly*" (4 Macc 5:23).[66] But justice emerges as the paramount virtue which warrants our praise of Eleazar and the seven sons.[67] Inasmuch as justice refers to one's duty to God, family/fatherland, and ancestors, the story about the old man and the seven brothers regularly calls attention to the fact that they died explicitly in fulfilment of their duty to one of the three figures mentioned above. One author acknowledges the duty shown to God by death as evidence of the virtue of justice: "They by nobly dying *fulfilled their service to God*" (4 Macc 12:14).[68] Readers regularly hear in this literature that the deaths are noble because they are endured for the sake of ancestral laws. Eleazar boasts that he will leave a noble example to others of how to die a good death "willingly and nobly for the *revered and holy laws*" (2 Macc 6:28).[69] This refers of course to God, the author of the laws, but also to the fatherland or ethnos which collectively keeps those laws rather than Greek ones.[70] Judas' exhortation made his army ready "to die for their laws and their country" (2 Macc 8:21). Finally the Maccabean heroes fulfill their duty toward their kin: "Let us bravely die *for our kindred*" (1 Macc 9:10). All of the Maccabean literature, therefore, acknowledges three virtues in particular as constitutive of a noble death: 1) *courage* to die a painful death, 2) *voluntary death* or *choice* of death, and 3) *justice* or loyalty to God, the laws of the ethnos, the ethnos itself and one's kindred.[71]

The Maccabean literature argues that not only did many Israelites know the Greek language (since the works were composed in Greek for a Greek-speaking Israelite audience), but that their authors learned as well the Greco-Roman canons of honor which earn public praise. The same criteria in Greek rhetoric for labeling a death "noble" occur in Israelite literature as well.[72] As we turn to John 10, we are aware that Greek-speaking audiences are quite likely to

66. See also 2 Macc 6:28, 31; the mother of the seven sons is praised for her display of "manliness," otherwise known as courage: 2 Macc 7:20-21; 4 Macc 1:8.
67. Time and again we are told that they suffer death "for the sake of virtue" (4 Macc 1:8; see 1:10), which must be justice.
68. See also 4 Macc 6:22; 11:20-21.
69. 4 Macc 9:29 reads: "How sweet is any kind of death *for the religion of our ancestors*."
70. See also 2 Macc 8:21; 4 Macc 6:22, 27-28; 9:1.
71. Again, van Henten, *The Maccabean Martyrs as Saviours*, 270-88.
72. For example, Josephus, *Ant.* 17.152-54.

know and appreciate the value code of the dominant culture. What now of the death of the "noble shepherd"?

3.0 The Noble Death of Jesus

3.1 The Noble Shepherd (10:11-18)

As we now examine now the death of Jesus informed by the rhetoric of "noble death," we focus on two passages in John, namely 10:11-18 and 11:46-53. Because of the rich tradition about a "noble" death in the rhetoric of praise, we argue that the adjective qualifying the "shepherd" should also be translated as "noble" (καλός) and not simply "good." The author immediately tells us that the shepherd is labeled "noble" because of his death which benefits the flock: "the 'noble' shepherd lays down his life for his sheep." We observed above that orators most frequently declared the death of fallen soldiers noble because it *benefited* the polis. The same reason is cited here to specify why and how the shepherd is honorable, namely, he benefits his flock by laying down his life on their behalf. Compare the passage in John 10 with Hyperides' remark about the general and soldiers of Athens:

John 10:11: ὁ ποιμὴν ὁ καλὸς τὴν ψυχὴν αὐτοῦ τίθησιν ὑπὲρ τῶν προβάτων.

Hyperides: οἱ τὰς ἑαυτῶν ψυχὰς ἔδωκαν ὑπὲρ τῆς Ἑλλήνων ἐλευθερίας.[73]

The Greek orator praises the soldiers who died in Athens' defense, and he cites the fact that they "died in battle for her" as the clearest proof of their benefaction to the homeland. John cites the same behavior of Jesus-the-shepherd ("lay down his life for his flock") as most beneficial to the flock and as the grounds for praise of the shepherd ("the *noble* shepherd"). The rhetoric of praise, especially that found in funeral orations, provides an adequate background to interpret culturally John's honor claim for the shepherd. There is no question but that the qualifying remark "lay down his life" refers to death.[74]

Part of the argument that the shepherd is "noble" consists in the typical comparison found in funeral orations between heroes and cowards. In John, if the "noble" shepherd lays down his life for his sheep, by comparison the "hire-

---

73. Hyperides, *Funeral Speech* 16.
74. Brown, *The Gospel According to John*, 1.386-87. He notes also that the expression occurs also in 13:37; 15:13; 1 John 3:16.

ling" flees when the wolf attacks. Like comparisons in the rhetoric of praise, two options are compared: 1) manly courage versus cowardice, 2) fight versus flight, 3) death versus life, and finally 4) honor/glory versus shame/disgrace. In this light we read the contrast between the hireling and the noble shepherd as follows. The noble shepherd displays *courage*, *decides* to fight the enemy and thus dies *for the flock*. Therefore, he receives the *acknowledgment* of being "noble" for his honorable deeds. In comparison, the hireling *cowardly flees* from the conflict; by *choosing* to save *his life* he earns only *contempt and disgrace*.[75] We argue that any audience in the world of the fourth Evangelist would understand the implication of "courage" and "cowardice" in this comparison and thus honor the virtuous deed and cast shame on its opposite.

It is sometimes argued that the wolf stands for Satan or the Ruler of the World.[76] If accurate, we recall that in Hermogenes' rules for an encomium, he prescribed that honor may be drawn "from the one who slew him, as that Achilles died at the hands of the god Apollo."[77] The cosmic identification of Jesus' foe as "Ruler of the World," then, serves as grounds for even greater praise of Jesus because he dies battling the ultimate foe.[78] Similarly, the scene where the Jerusalem elite gathered in counsel to destroy Jesus leads to the same conclusion: the elites of Israel rallied together to kill him, a Galilean peasant. They may not be a "noble" foe, but their collective, powerful action against Jesus elevates their conflict between them and Jesus. The best battle the best.

In 10:14 the shepherd is once again declared "noble" because he "knows his own" [sheep]. We suggest that this phrase describes Jesus' *just duty* to his own, and so is an act of virtue. "Knowing" did not surface as a criterion for a noble death in the rhetoric of praise. But it was there in another guise. All "virtuous" actions are noble and worthy of praise, especially courage and justice. A prominent virtue of Athens' soldiers who fell in combat is courage

---

75. The contents of John 10:1-17 contain other comparisons: true and false shepherds (10:1-5), as well as true provider of the sheep and "thieves and bandits" (10:8-10).

76. See Kovacs, "'Now Shall the Ruler of This World Be Driven Out': Jesus' Death as Cosmic Battle in John 12:20-36." She points to three clusters of material (12:20-36; 14:30-31; and 16:8-11) which indicate how the author of the Fourth Gospel elevated Jesus' death by seeing it as combat with the world's most powerful figure, thus giving increased significance to his death. A long tradition exists which identifies the wolf as Satan; vicious wolves, moreover, are often predicted as attacking the fold (Matt 7:15; Acts 20:29-30; *Didache* 16:3; Ignatius, *Philippians* 2:2; *2 Clement* 5:2-4).

77. See Baldwin, *Medieval Rhetoric and Poetic*, 32.

78. A comparable remark is made in Heb 2:14-15, that "through death he might destroy him who has the power of death, that is, the devil, and deliver all those who through fear of death were subject to lifelong bondage." See Harold Attridge, *Hebrews* (Philadelphia: Fortress, 1989) 92.

(ἀνδρεία),[79] which we saw credited to Jesus in the comparison of shepherd with hireling. The shepherd, however, displays another mark of nobility, the virtue of justice. Representing a long tradition, one progymnastic writer defined justice as the virtue whereby people honor their basic obligations. "The parts of justice are piety (εὐσέβεια), fair dealing (δικαιοπραγία) and reverence (ὁσιότης): piety toward the gods, fair dealing towards men, reverence toward the departed."[80] We suggest that in 10:11-18 the Evangelist has two aspects of justice in view: piety to God and fair dealing toward the disciples/sheep.[81] Beginning with the latter, we note that the hireling has no duty to the sheep; they are not his, but belong to another. In no way is he obliged in justice to face the wolf on their behalf; the owner should, but not the hireling. In contrast, the shepherd proclaims that he "knows his sheep," that is, he owns them as his own and assumes responsibility for them. His sheep, moreover, "know" him, thus assuring the reader that duties are understood on both sides. "Knowing" has the sense of acknowledging, being faithful toward and feeling responsibility for.[82] The sheep show their relationship to the shepherd by the fact that they "hear his voice, he calls them by name . . . and the sheep follow him because they know his voice" (10:3-4).[83] The duty of justice which

---

79. In the Athenian funeral speeches, all the orators praise the courage of the fallen, both that of their ancestors and their own: Thucydides, *Histories*, 2.42; Isocrates, *Evagoras*, 29, 42-44; Plato, *Menexenus*, 237-46; Hyperides, *Funeral Speech*, 8-19.

80. Menander Rhetor 1.361.17-25. Another ancient definition of justice is similar: "First among the claims of righteousness are our *duties to the gods, then our duties to the spirits, then those to country and parents, then those to the departed;* among these claims is piety *(eusebeia),* which is either a part of righteousness or a concomitant of it. Righteousness is also accompanied by holiness *(hosiotēs)* and truth and loyalty *(pistis)* and hatred of wickedness" (Ps.-Aristotle, *Virtues and Vices*, 5.2-3, italics added). See also Cicero, *Invention* 2.160-61.

81. John Ashton (*The Understanding of the Fourth Gospel* [Oxford: Clarendon Press, 1992] 328) makes the same point in terms of Israelite religious language: "The Father's 'knowing' the Son is in the Old Testament and Judaic tradition of election, while knowing on the Son's part means acknowledgment: the Son accepts the Father's revelation and his will."

82. Commentators are of many minds on how to understand and translate "know" here; Brown (*Gospel According to John*, 1.396) wisely links 10:14 with the original parable in 10:3-5. Hence "knowledge" is not simply information or recognition but acknowledging someone or accepting a relationship. In Brown's special note on "know" (p. 514) he lists, as illustration of the personal meaning of "know," texts which tell of the world or sinners not knowing the Father or Jesus: 1:10; 16:3; 17:25; 1 John 3:1, 6. "Not knowing" God or Jesus means not accepting them, acknowledging them, or becoming his disciples. This posture refuses a personal relationship which is the basis of duty, which is a key element of justice.

83. Apropos of the shepherd's just duty to the sheep by a noble death, one might also consider how he demonstrates the same duty to the sheep by his noble life. He protects them in a sheepfold and leads them to pasture and to water. He loses none but the one destined to be lost. His virtuous life, then, parallels his virtuous death.

the shepherd owes the sheep is then expressed in the declaration that "I lay down my life for my sheep" (10:15). Thus when Jesus the shepherd said that "I know mine and mine know me" (10:14), he declares his loyalty to the sheep and thus acknowledges his duty in justice to "his own."

The justice of the shepherd points in another direction, *piety* or εὐσέβεια to Jesus' Father who is God. Paralleling the remark made about the reciprocal "knowing" between shepherd and sheep, Jesus declares a similar relationship with the Father: "the Father knows me and I know the Father" (10:15). In addition to what we learned about "knowing" above, we are reminded of Bultmann's remark about the verb "to know," namely, that one of its basic meanings is "acknowledgment," as when the scriptures talk about "knowing God" or "knowing God's name."[84] Although "to know" forms an important part of the way John's Gospel distinguishes insiders from outsiders and ranks those within in terms of what they know, this other meaning of "to know" has to do with social relationships which entail reciprocal duties. Some people form *no* relationship with Jesus: they do *not* acknowledge him (1:10; 16:3; 17:25), whereas God, Jesus and his disciples "know" each other and so indicate intimate levels of loyalty and commitment (6:69; 10:38; 13:31; 17:3, 23). All of this aids in our appreciation of 10:15 as expressing a relationship in which duties are fulfilled, God and Jesus as well as Jesus and his disciples, which encodes what was understood by the virtue of justice. Thus two virtues, justice and courage, mark the behavior of the shepherd, just as they did for Athens' soldiers who died noble deaths. These virtues, moreover, are articulated in the context of the death of the noble shepherd, thus giving further warrant to the "noble" shepherd's death.

In 10:16 Jesus states that he has "other sheep, not of this fold" and so there will be "one flock and one shepherd."[85] This remark, too, becomes more accessible when seen in terms of "noble death." First, it surely benefits the sheep to be safely gathered into one, that is, into close association around the shepherd, who can pasture and protect them all. This represents another example of the duty of the shepherd, that is, his virtue of justice toward the sheep. Second, when or how is this achieved? Comparable remarks in 11:52; 12:23-24, and 32 indicate that Jesus' death occasions these benefits. Caiaphas's prophecy, we are told, really meant "that Jesus would die . . . not for the nation only, but to gather into one the scattered children of God" (11:52). Jesus' death, then, benefits the sheep currently around him and those "scattered." Similarly, in his exhortation to the Greeks whom Philip and Andrew brought to him, Jesus declares that

---

84. Rudolf Bultmann, "γινώσκω," *TDNT* 1.698.
85. See Brown, *The Gospel According to John*, 1.396; Rudolf Schnackenburg, *The Gospel According to John* (New York: Crossroads, 1982) 2.299.

when a seed dies and falls into the ground, it bears much fruit (12:23-24). Finally in an unmistakable reference to his death Jesus says: "When I am lifted up from the earth, I will draw all to myself" (12:32). His death ("lifted up") benefits others by "drawing all to myself." Thus 10:16, especially when seen in relationship to similar remarks in chs 10–12, bears the reading of "noble" death because of benefits rendered and the virtue of justice displayed.

The Father's relationship to Jesus is further developed when we are told, "For this reason my Father loves me, because I lay down my life in order to take it up again" (10:17). Examining this in the light of the rhetoric of noble death, we know that "love" was considered a part of justice in antiquity. Although modern commentators have tended to interpret this verse in light of romantic attachment, in the cultural world of the New Testament love basically referred to group bonds or group glue that held persons together in relationship, especially kinship groups.[86] The Father's "love" contains a strong element of approval, which suggests the pride the Father has in Jesus. Obedient sons, moreover, show justice to their fathers and so honor them. The reason for this "love" is the complex statement that Jesus both lays down his life and takes it back. We have already seen that a noble death warrants praise and honor, which should enlighten our understanding of "lay down my life" in this context.

But the second part, "in order that I may take it again," seems utterly obscure and has no parallel in funeral oratory. No one in the history of humankind has ever come back from the dead. In fact we are called "mortals," i.e., those who die, to distinguish our status from that of God or the gods who are the "immortals." Is Jesus crossing a boundary line here? For a mere mortal to claim such would be ludicrous, and thus shameful (see John 8:52, 56-58). In fact such a claim would violate justice for it would be blasphemy toward God, not piety (see 10:33). How are Jesus' remarks just and so honorable? Jesus claims authorization from God for his speech and actions: "I have received this command from my Father" (10:18). A son who obeys his father honors him; he fulfills the basic justice which offspring owe their parents.

Looking more closely at 10:17-18, we recall how in epideictic rhetoric a death was labeled "noble" because it was voluntary. Both vv 17 and 18 affirm the voluntary nature of Jesus' death. For the third and fourth times, Jesus states that *he* lays down *his own* life.[87]

---

86. John Pilch and Bruce Malina, eds., *Handbook of Biblical Social Values* (updated edition; Peabody, MA: Hendrickson, 1998) 127-28.

87. C. K. Barrett (*The Gospel According to John* [2d ed.; Philadelphia: Westminster, 1978] 374-75) made two useful observations on this phrase. First, it is peculiar to John and 1 John (10:11, 15, 17-18; 13:37-38; 15:13; 1 John 3:16); second, in John ὑπέρ always carries the significance of death (in addition to the citations above, see 6:51; 18:14).

10:11 The good shepherd *lays down his life for his sheep.*
10:15 *I lay down my life for my sheep.*
10:17 The Father loves me because *I lay down my life.*
10:18 I have power *to lay it down.*

He may well declare that his death is God's will or that he goes as it was written of him and other such remarks. But the substance is the same: he chooses, he accepts the command, and he "lays down his life willingly" (ἀπ' ἐμαυτοῦ).[88]

But 10:17-18 state more, for Jesus proudly declares "No one takes it from me." We saw above in the gloss on the "wolf" that, although Jesus confronts a very powerful foe, this foe has no power over Jesus (14:30). In fact, as Jesus faces his death, he declares "I have overcome the world" (16:33). Thus the remarks in 10:17-18 assert two things: 1) Jesus is no victim; he is not mastered by anyone (see 18:4-6);[89] 2) the cause of Jesus' death lies entirely in his own hands, both to "lay it down" and "take it up." Thus it would be fair to say that he dies unvanquished and unconquered, which are marks of a noble death.

Finally, Jesus claims "power" to lay down his life and to take it back. In light of the rhetoric of a noble death, the first half of this expresses for the fourth time that his death is voluntary, namely, "I lay it down." Voluntary deaths are always "noble." The claim to have "power," moreover, belongs to the world of praise and honor. People with "power" are, as we say, movers and shakers. They control their own destiny; they accomplish what they set out to do. This suggests, then, that Jesus stands very high on the scale of people who do difficult deeds and who are masters of their fate. Whence comes this power? "I have received this *command* from my Father" (10:18b). At the very least, 10:18 states that it is God's will that Jesus lay down his life, thus referring to his "obedient

---

88. Scholars have called attention to the voluntary character of 10:17-18; but to my knowledge no one has suggested any Hellenistic parallels to this. Rather they refer to parallels in the Hebrew Scriptures such as David facing the bear and lion in 1 Sam 17:34-35. Thus Brown states: "The similarity [with Old Testament materials] suggests that we need not go outside the OT for the background of this particular aspect of the Johannine picture of the shepherd: it is a combination of elements from the OT descriptions of the shepherd and of the Suffering Servant" (*Gospel According to John*, 1.398).

89. Helen C. Orchard (*Courting Betrayal: Jesus as Victim in the Gospel of John* [JSNTSup 161; Sheffield: Sheffield Academic Press, 1998]) argues just the opposite in her study of the mounting violence against Jesus. While on the one hand one must agree with Orchard that the entire narrative in John describes incessant and increasing hostility to Jesus, on the other hand she brings to the discussion no mention whatsoever of the rhetoric of death in the ancient world. Where I talk of "noble" death, which is articulated in a clear body of ancient rhetorical materials, Orchard speaks of the "victimization" of Jesus in terms of liberation theology and current anecdotes of political martyrs.

death."[90] Hence Jesus claims to be fulfilling the dutiful relationship between himself and the Father, a virtuous or just thing to do.

But the claim to have power "to take it [my life] again" does not register with anything in the Hebrew Bible or the Greek rhetoric of praise. This is nothing else but a claim to be equal to God, that is, to have one of the end-time powers of God.[91] Jesus claims that even though he dies ("I lay down my life"), he will conquer the last enemy ("I take it back again").[92] This remark is but a claim until evidence is provided. But as a claim, it lays hold of the greatest power in the cosmos of which humans could conceive. If the claim is true, then great honor should be accorded Jesus, for he has what no other mortal has. Thus, his death is noble for two reasons: 1) he claims the *greatest* of all powers, namely, power over death; 2) his empowerment is *unique*: no one but his donor has or will have this power.

What, then, in the light of the rhetorical tradition of a noble death does consideration of John 10:11-18 tell us? There seems to be a close affinity on the following points:

Rhetorical Tradition about "Noble Death"	John's Discourse on the Noble Shepherd
1. Death benefited others, especially fellow citizens.	1. Death benefited the sheep, who enjoy a special relationship with the shepherd.
2. Comparison between courage-cowardice, fight-flight, death-life, honor-shame	2. Comparison between shepherd/hireling: courage-cowardice, fight-flight, death-life, honor-shame
3. Manly courage displayed by soldiers who fight and die	3. Manly courage displayed by shepherd who battles wolf and dies
4. Deeds and death unique	4. Power over death and return to life unique to God and Jesus
5. Voluntary death is praised	5. Voluntary death repeatedly claimed: "I lay it down of my own accord"
6. Unconquered in death; victory in dying nobly	6. Not a victim: "No one takes it from me..." "I lay it down; I take it up again"
7. Justice and noble death: soldiers uphold the honor of their families and serve the interests of the fatherland: duties served = justice	7. Justice: the shepherd manifests loyalty to his sheep and his Father/God; he has a command from God: duties served = justice

90. See Brown, *The Gospel According to John*, 1.398.

91. See Jerome H. Neyrey, *An Ideology of Revolt: John's Christology in Social-Science Perspective* (Philadelphia: Fortress, 1988) 22-29, 59-74.

92. The Evangelist does not necessarily share the view of death that Paul had. For Paul death was the enslaving taskmaster who ruled all mortals before the coming of Jesus (Rom 5:14, 17) or the last enemy to be put under Christ's feet (1 Cor 15:26). Similarly, Heb 2:14-16 describes Death as the evil monarch who held all in slavery for fear of it. Both, however, envision some sort of combat between Jesus and death.

The "Noble" Shepherd in John 10

The presence of so many and such important motifs in one Johannine passage warrants comment. First, we trust that the similarities noted in the previous chart are correct. This amplification of the nobility of certain kinds of death is regularly found scattered throughout Greek rhetorical theory and praxis, but is clustered together in John 10:11-18. This amplification of praise suggests that one of the formal strategies in the telling of John 10 is to claim and demonstrate the nobleness of Jesus precisely by his death.[93]

4.0 John 11:45-53

The Evangelist talks again about Jesus' death in 11:45-53, a passage which has received only cursory treatment in commentaries and articles.[94] Bringing our knowledge of the "noble death" tradition to bear, let us examine what is said of Jesus' demise. The narrative context describes a situation caused by Jesus' raising of Lazarus, which is an act of justice or loyalty to a "beloved" friend and which occasions a surge of his reputation and honor (11:45-46). Hence the Pharisees express envy of Jesus' success, because they understand that Jesus' honor means their corresponding loss of prestige (11:47-48).[95] Thus the situation is one of intense conflict, which the opponents magnify by claiming that unless Jesus is cut down to size, a war with Rome will occur. While their envy provides no solution to the conflict, it makes salient the issue at stake: honor — Jesus' or theirs.

After shaming them ("You know nothing . . . you do not understand") the high priest proclaimed, "It is expedient that one man should die for the people and that the whole nation should not perish" (11:50). The Evangelist immediately tells us that this is a prophecy uttered unwittingly, so that the readership

---

93. Yet "shepherd" outside the context of ruler carried with it base and shameful connotation. It is listed among the "despised trades" documented by Joachim Jeremias from mishnaic and talmudic texts (*Jerusalem in the Time of Jesus* [Philadelphia: Fortress Press, 1969] 303-12). On the double meaning of the term see Bruce Malina and Richard Rohrbaugh, *Social-Science Commentary on the Gospel of John* (Minneapolis: Fortress, 1998) 179.

94. Most scholarship has focused on two issues: 1) the background to the prophecy of the high priest (Brown, *The Gospel According to John*, 1.442-43; B. Lindars, *The Gospel of John* [London: Oliphants, 1972] 406-7) and 2) irony (Paul Duke, *Irony in the Fourth Gospel* [Atlanta: John Knox, 1985] 86-90).

95. Similar instances of envy of Jesus' success include John 3:25-30; see also Mark 9:38-41. On the topic of limited good, honor, and envy, see Anselm Hagedorn and Jerome Neyrey, "'It Was Out of Envy that They Handed Jesus Over,'" 20-25. Envy, moreover, is often an important element in Greek funeral orations; see Ziolkowsky, *Thucydides and the Tradition of Funeral Speeches in Athens*, 128.

should examine it for important, ironic information.⁹⁶ First, the word "expedient" indicates achieving profit or advantage.⁹⁷ But as we saw above in Aristotle's exposition of grounds for praise, honorable actions are *not* done for one's own sake (*Rhet.* 1.9.16-17) and have "less of the self" (1.9.19) and are not for one's own advantage (1.9.18). Yet the implications of envy and the actions which follow this conference are indeed to the self-advantage of the elite.

Yet according to the irony of the scene, Jesus' death will yield a noble result which benefits others but not Jesus himself. In contrast to Caiaphas's remark to the Pharisees, profit or advantage truly comes when one man *dies for the nation*. As the death of Athenian soldiers benefited their homeland, Jesus' death too will benefit the *ethnos* of Israel. It will be a noble death because as Aristotle said, "[that is noble] whatever someone has done for his country" (*Rhet.* 1.9.17) and "whatever works are done for the sake of others" (1.9.19).

Third, actions are noble which benefit others, but nobler actions benefit many more. Hence the editorial comment in 11:52 boosts the effect of Jesus' death, thus calling for even greater honor: ". . . and not for the nation only, but to gather into one the children of God who are scattered abroad." The expansion of Caiaphas' prophecy echoes what Jesus said earlier in his role of noble shepherd about achieving "one flock and one shepherd" (10:16; see 12:32). As Raymond Brown has argued, we are touching here the Evangelist's sense of a universal membership,⁹⁸ implying that Jesus' death benefits the whole world, which would make it unspeakably honorable.

5.0 Conclusions and Further Questions

What Have We Learned? First, the data from funeral orations, epideictic rhetoric and encomiums attest to the existence of a formal topos on "noble death."

---

96. Roger David Aus argues that the appropriate background for this narrative is the midrash describing the surrender of Jehoiakim and his son Jehoiachin and of Sheba, the son of Bichri; he identifies six motifs in the midrash that correspond to John 11:46-53: 1) a gathering of the Great Sanhedrin, 2) the destruction of the Temple, 3) rebellion and judgment, 4) one life for others, 5) "what shall we do?" 6) scattering ("The Death of One for All in John 11:45-54 in Light of Judaic Traditions," *Barabbas and Esther and Other Studies in the Judaic Illumination of Early Christianity* [Atlanta: Scholars Press, 1992] 29-63). His treatment of John 11:45-54 could not be more different than mine. It will be up to readers to see whether the rhetoric of noble death accounts for more items here and offers a more satisfying interpretation of this passage, especially in light of the noble death topos in John 10.

97. See Konrad Weiss, "συμφέρω," *TDNT* 9.69-78.

98. Brown, *The Gospel According to John*, 1.442-43.

The ancients indeed articulated the concept and provided the rationale for assessing a death as noble.

Second, the extant literary tradition about "noble death" extends from Thucydides' record of Pericles' funeral speech, through Aristotle and to the school exercises called the progymnasmata which were taught at the time of the early church. This tradition, moreover, was remarkably constant and highly conventional.

Third, the Johannine discourse about the shepherd contains a cluster of seven of the classical criteria for a noble death: 1) death which benefits the sheep, 2) comparison between shepherd-hireling, 3) virtue: the shepherd's manly courage battling the wolf and justice to God and to the sheep, 4) uniqueness of power over death, 5) voluntary character of his death, 6) dying *not* as a victim, and 7) manifestation of the shepherd's justice *for* his sheep and *to* his Father/God.

Fourth, how did the author of the Fourth Gospel come to know this material? We claim that for a person to write Greek as well as the author of the Fourth Gospel, he would have been trained in progymnastic exercises. The Johannine treatment of the "noble" shepherd would be plausible and accessible to someone learning to write Greek through the medium of the progymnastic encomium.

Fifth, it is not our intention to assault the solid argument about the overwhelming Judean background to the Fourth Gospel.[99] Rather, we see no conflict in the assertion that in addition to the Johannine use of Israelite traditions we find compelling evidence of Hellenistic influence on a specific topic such as "noble death." For, the author would have learned to write Greek through the medium of progymnastic exercises, especially epideictic rhetoric as embodied in the encomium.

Sixth, one did not simply learn a genre, but also a code of values and a grammar of worth which was the formal aim of an encomium and epideictic rhetoric. One learned "honor and shame" in terms that would be appreciated by an audience who shared appreciation of them. The acclamation of a "noble death" serves to honor a deceased person. When we recall how Paul combated an assessment of the death of Jesus as "folly" and "scandal" (1 Cor 1:18-25) and how the author of Hebrews declared that Jesus "despised the shame of the cross" (12:2), John like other NT authors emphasizes the ironic honor and sta-

---

99. See Hugo Odeberg, *The Fourth Gospel* (Uppsala: Almquist and Wicksell, 1929); Wayne A. Meeks, *The Prophet-King* (Leiden: Brill, 1967). I myself have argued this repeatedly in a series of articles: "Jacob Traditions and the Interpretation of John 4:10-26," *CBQ* 41 (1979): 419-37; "'I Said: You Are God': Psalm 82:6 and John 10," *JBL* 108 (1989): 647-63; "Jesus the Judge: Forensic Process in John 8, 21-59," *Bib* 68 (1987): 509-41.

tus elevation Jesus experienced through the cross. "Ought not the Christ suffer and so enter into his glory?" (Luke 24:26).

Seventh, other passages in the Fourth Gospel seem to connect with John 10 and the noble death of the Shepherd. It is beyond the scope of this study to present a complete analysis of these, but let us briefly mention some. For example, the exhortation in 15:13 declares: "Greater love has no one than this, than that one lay down one's life for one's friend." This parenetic remark to the disciples echoes Jesus' noble death in 10:11 and 15, and thereby canonizes "laying down one's life for one's friends" as honorable. The comparative here ("greater" love) suggests that such behavior is the highest form of love, thus claiming for it uniqueness and thus maximum worth. A disciple's "laying down his life for his friends" models the death of the Noble Shepherd in these terms: it benefits others, is unique, and is virtuous.[100] Similarly, in a series of remarks Jesus declares that in his death he will be glorified: "The hour has come for the Son of man to be glorified" (12:23; see 13:31 and 17:1). It is generally agreed that "glory" in these remarks refers to a form of posthumous vindication by God (see Acts 2:23-24; 3:14-15; 4:10; 10:39-40) or to Jesus' enthronement with a status and role greater than he enjoyed on earth (see Acts 2:36; Phil 2:6-11).[101] In John the posthumous glory of Jesus is a direct grant of honor from God, which students of honor and shame call "ascribed honor." Nevertheless in the context of this study we consider it posthumous glory, not unlike that bestowed on soldiers who died a noble death.

Moreover, we can compare the remarks about the Noble Shepherd in John 10 with what is said about other "shepherds" of the group. Peter boasts that he would "lay down my life for you" (13:37), an action which this Gospel considers noble and associates with another shepherd, Jesus (10:11, 15). But Peter lacks sufficient courage and justice at this point.[102] Although Jesus shames him for his vain claim (13:38), yet the issue of nobility remains accessible to him as Jesus says: "Where I am going you cannot follow me now; but *you will follow afterwards*" (13:36). In contrast, the Beloved Disciple acts like the shepherd in 18:15-16 when he persuades the maid keeping the door to admit Peter.[103] This closely resembles the parable in 10:1-5 in which the shepherd enters by the door, the

---

100. On the relationship of the parables of the shepherd and the vine, see John F. O'Grady, "Good Shepherd and the Vine and the Branches," *BTB* 8 (1978): 86-96. See also Martin Dibelius, *Botschaft und Geschichte* (Tübingen: Mohr, 1953) 1.204-10.

101. See G. B. Caird, "The Glory of God in the Fourth Gospel: An Exercise in Biblical Semantics," *NTS* 15 (1969): 265-77; Brown, *The Gospel according to John*, 1.470-71; Barrett, *The Gospel according to John*, 450.

102. See chapter 14 below.

103. See chapter 14 below.

gatekeeper opens the door for him, his sheep hear his voice, and he either leads them in or out. The very fact that the Beloved Disciple and Peter enter the dwelling of Jesus' enemy, the high priest, tells us that this is a life-risking scene (i.e., "lay down my life"). But Peter's subsequent cowardice (18:17-18, 25-27) demonstrates his disqualification to be a noble shepherd at this time.

Furthermore, the Gospel concludes with the investiture of Peter with the role of shepherd (21:15-17). In conjunction with this, Jesus predicts the death of Peter (21:18), by which he would "glorify" God (21:19). We ask again: what constitutes a worthy shepherd? Is Peter, who once failed in courage and loyalty toward Jesus, now a "noble" shepherd? The text would suggest that we now reappraise Peter as a person willing to lay down his life, either in imitation of Jesus or to benefit the flock in some way. His triple declaration that he "loves" Jesus qualifies him according to 15:13 as one whose "greater" love leads him to "lay down his life for his friend." "Love," we remember, is a part of justice. This much is clear: worthy shepherds are they who die in service of their flocks, thus highlighting a death which benefits others, is voluntarily accepted, and manifests justice toward a group in one's care. Thus, we have another "noble" shepherd in the Fourth Gospel.

Finally, the scene of Jesus' arrest in 18:1-11 contains many dramatizations of the criteria for a noble death. Throughout the episode, Jesus stands between his disciples and those who would apprehend him, that is, he boldly comes forward like a shepherd who positions himself between the flock and the wolf (18:4-7). Second, by coming forward (18:4) and taking control of the conversation (18:5), Jesus voluntarily enters into the process of his arrest. He is not captured, but allows himself to be taken. Third, like a good shepherd, he benefits his flock by commanding his captors, "Let these men go" (18:8). The Evangelist interprets his remark as the fulfillment of a prophecy which means that the shepherd has benefited the flock by preserving all of those so destined.[104] And at the end of the episode, when the disciples act to protect Jesus, he claims that their zeal is misplaced. Jesus' arrest and death are "the cup which the Father has given me" (18:11); that is, Jesus obeys the will of God here, voluntarily choosing to do this and by it to demonstrate justice by paying his duty to Father and God.[105] This scene, then, both contains many of the criteria for a noble death and seems to be a dramatization of the same materials claimed in John 10:11-18.

Therefore, in addition to the our reading of John 10:11-18 and 11:45-52 in

---

104. See John 6:39; 10:28; 17:12.

105. An analysis of this passage in terms of honor and shame can be found in my article "Despising the Shame of the Cross: Honor and Shame in the Johannine Passion Narrative," *Semeia* 68 (1994): 119-20.

light of the rhetoric of a noble death, other passages and themes in the Gospel seem either to contain direct references to the noble shepherd material or to illustrate one or another of the criteria which serve to qualify a death as noble. In this sense, "noble death" is not just another aspect of John's presentation of the death of Jesus, as are sacrifice or departure. It might be said to emerge as the dominant articulation of Jesus' death in the Fourth Gospel.

12

"I Said: You Are Gods"

Psalm 82:6 and John 10

Biblical texts that called mortals "gods" necessarily attracted attention from commentators and became the focus of ingenious interpretations and studies of eccentric exegetical principles.[1] This is certainly true of Ps 82:6, "I said: 'You are gods.'" The present study examines the use of Ps 82:6 in John 10:34-36. It is my hypothesis that the Fourth Gospel understands Psalm 82 very much the way it was understood in Jewish midrash, for which it might be the earliest extant example. An examination of the understanding and function of Ps 82:6 in John 10:34-36 will necessarily entail a survey of Jewish interpretations of that Psalm to put the Johannine passage in its proper perspective.

1.0 The History of the Interpretation of John 10:34-36

In the 1960s, a debate emerged over the interpretation of Ps 82:6-7 in relation to John 10:34-36, the general lines of which were summarized by Anthony Hanson.[2] He called attention to four different ways in which Psalm 82 was understood in Judean traditions, with reference to 1) angels, 2) Melchizedek, 3) judges, and 4) Israel at Sinai. All four interpretations are attested to in midrashic literature, but which one relates to John 10:34-36?

---

1. For example, Exod 7:1, where God says to Moses, "I make you as god to Pharaoh." This caused no little difficulty to Philo, as he wrestled with its interpretation in *Alleg. Interp.* 1.40; *Sacr.* 9; *Worse* 39-40, 161-62; *Migr.* 84, 169; *Names* 19-20, 125, 128-29; *Dreams* 2.189; *Good Person* 43-44; see also *Post.* 43-44 and *Mos.* 1.158.

2. Anthony Hanson, "John's Citation of Psalm LXXXII Reconsidered," *NTS* 13 (1966-67): 363-67.

Angels. In an early study on Psalm 82, J. A. Emerton[3] argued that in the targum to the Psalms,[4] Qumran,[5] the Peshitta, and the Fathers, *elohim* in Psalm 82 was understood to refer to "angels." Emerton suggests that *elohim* refers to superhuman beings to whom the nations were allotted (e.g., Deut 4:19; Daniel 10), whom the Jews regarded as angels but whom the Gentiles called gods (see 1 Cor 10:20).

Melchizedek. In 11QMelch, Psalm 82 was cited apropos of Melchizedek. The modern editor of 11QMelch described the document as an "eschatological midrash" which cast Melchizedek in the role of judge.[6] Emerton, who had argued that the "gods" mentioned in Psalm 82 were "angels," now saw the Melchizedek = Elohim reference in 11QMelch, strengthening his earlier interpretation of Psalm 82; he suggested that Melchizedek was being identified with the archangel Michael.[7] Hanson conceded that Melchizedek might be called "god," but rejected its relevance for John 10.[8]

Judges. Psalm 82 has also been interpreted in Jewish tradition to refer to the judges of Israel, evidence for which comes from *b. Berakot* 6a and *Midr. Ps.* 82.[9] This interpretation of the psalm enjoyed considerable popularity during a certain period of Johannine scholarship.[10] Returning to the issue of Melchizedek in 11QMelch, Joseph Fitzmyer,[11] who basically agreed with van der Woude's original interpretation of the passage, paraphrased line 10 of this fragment as follows: "Elohim (Melchizedek) has taken his stand in the assembly of El (Yahweh), in the midst of gods (angelic court) he gives judg-

---

3. J. A. Emerton, "Some New Testament Notes," *JTS* 11 (1960): 329-32.

4. See Luis Diez Merino, *Targum de Salmos* (Biblio Poliglota Complutense IV/1; Madrid: Instituto Francisco Suarez, 1982) 142 and 269.

5. See John Strugnell, "The Angelic Liturgy at Qumran — 4QSerek Sirot 'Olat Hassabbat," in *Congress Volume: Oxford 1959* (VTSup 7; Leiden: Brill, 1960) esp. 336-42.

6. The original study was by A. S. van der Woude, "Melchisedek als himmlische Erlosergestalt in den neugefundenen eschatologischen Midraschim aus Qumran Hohle XI," in *Oudtestamentliche Studien* XIV (Leiden: Brill, 1965) 354-73; see also Marinus de Jonge and A. S. van der Woude, "11QMelchizedek and the New Testament," *NTS* 12 (1965-66): 304.

7. J. A. Emerton, "Melchizedek and the Gods: Fresh Evidence for the Jewish Background of John X.34-36," *JTS* 17 (1966): 400-401.

8. Hanson, "John's Citation of Psalm LXXXII Reconsidered," 366.

9. See W. G. Braude, *The Midrash on the Psalms* (New Haven, CT: Yale University Press, 1959) 2.59-60.

10. For example, B. F. Westcott, *The Gospel according to St John* (London: John Murray, 1908) 70; M.-J. Lagrange, *Évangile selon Saint Jean* (Paris: Gabalda, 1948) 290; and R. H. Lightfoot, *St John's Gospel* (Oxford: Clarendon Press, 1956) 209.

11. Joseph A. Fitzmyer, "Further Light on Melchizedek from Qumran Cave 11," *JBL* 86 (1967): 25-41, which is also found in his *Essays on the Semitic Background of the New Testament* (Missoula, MT: Scholars Press, 1974) 245-67.

ment."[12] He understands Melchizedek's role in that text not as an angel but as a judge.[13]

Israel at Sinai. As far back as Billerbeck,[14] it was argued that Ps 82:6-7 was historicized in Israelite traditions to refer to Israel at Sinai when God gave it the Torah, making it holy and so deathless. This midrash, which has become a popular understanding of the use of Ps 82:6-7 in John 10:34-36,[15] implies that Israel experienced a new creation at Sinai. Because God gave Israel the word of Torah, to which it became obedient, Israel became deathless once more as it resumed the "image and likeness of God" given it at creation. James Ackerman, the chief proponent of this argument, suggested that the Johannine Prologue bears striking resemblances to the "Sinai myth," indicating how Wisdom once dwelt on earth with humankind (Ps 82:6), thus making them immortal; but because Wisdom was rejected and returned to heaven, sinful mortals now die (Ps 82:7).[16]

As regards these interpretations and John 10, Hanson rejected the traditions that interpret "god" as either angels or judges.[17] He correctly concluded that only the last interpretation of Psalm 82 (Israel at Sinai) has any bearing on the argument in John 10.[18] All of the studies cited above, however, are deficient for several reasons. First, they tend to argue for an extrinsic interpretation of Psalm 82 in John 10: if Judeans in their scriptures or tradition can call a man "god," then Jesus is not totally out of line in being called a heavenly figure.[19] This type of extrinsic argument shows little respect for the midrashic understanding of Psalm 82 or other texts from scripture about the justification in the first place for calling any human "god," even by extension. Are there intrinsic reasons in the midrash on Psalm 82 which give warrant to such a predication? Second, those who treat the background of Psalm 82, even in passing, do not

---

12. Fitzmyer, "Further Light on Melchizedek," 261-62.
13. Fitzmyer, "Further Light on Melchizedek," 251-53.
14. See Str-B 2.543.
15. For example, see C. K. Barrett, *The Gospel according to St. John* (2d ed.; Philadelphia: Westminster, 1978) 384-85; and Nils Dahl, "The Johannine Church and History," in *Jesus in the Memory of the Early Church* (Minneapolis: Augsburg, 1976) 109-10.
16. See James Ackerman, "The Rabbinic Interpretation of Psalm 82 and the Gospel of John," *HTR* 59 (1966): 186-91.
17. Not all agree with Hanson; for example, see E. Jungkuntz, "An Approach to the Exegesis of John 10:34-36," *CTM* 35 (1964): 556-65.
18. This interpretation has already been urged; see James Ackerman, "Rabbinic Interpretation," 186-91.
19. Jungkuntz ("An Approach to the Exegesis of John 10:34," 556-58) summarizes how many modern commentators see the use of Psalm 82 as either an *ad hominem* argument or simply irrelevant to the narrative's claims.

present an adequate exegesis of the argument in John 10 to see on what grounds Jesus is acclaimed "equal to God" (10:30, 33) and what Psalm 82 has to do with that argument. There are some commentators who deny that Psalm 82 in any way responds to the charges.[20] There is, then, much work left to be done. We turn now to a more detailed exegesis of John 10 to see what is being argued, so that we might assess more clearly the meaning and function of Psalm 82 in relation to that argument.

2.0 The Argument in John 10:28-37

Unless Psalm 82 is used in a purely extrinsic manner in John 10:34-36,[21] we must investigate how it functions as a defense to a specific charge in the forensic dynamics of John 10. The starting place is 10:30, where Jesus claims "I and the Father are one (or equal)." The crowds correctly interpret this to mean that Jesus in some way claims "equality with God." His claim leads them to a judgment, "blasphemy, because you, being a man, make yourself God" (10:33). Several questions arise: In what respect are Jesus and God "one" (or equal)? Is it true that Jesus "makes himself" God? This means that we must examine both the earlier part of John 10 to see in what sense Jesus and God are "equal" and the subsequent defense offered in 10:34-38 to see how Psalm 82 relates to the claims of equality.

2.1 The First Forensic Proceeding (10:1-28a)

After Jesus claimed to be the door and the shepherd (10:1-16), the Gospel describes confusion in the crowd about these claims: Is he a demon or a saint (10:19-21)? So intense is this popular confusion that a formal forensic process is begun in 10:22-27 about Jesus' claims. Since the uneducated crowd ('am hā-'āreṣ, 7:47-49) could not possibly decide these claims, a solemn assembly gathers "in the temple, in the stoa of Solomon" (10:23). There it puts a formal question to Jesus: "Tell us plainly, if you are the Messiah?" (10:24). Thus, 10:1-28a can be seen as a forensic proceeding[22] which formally examines Jesus' claims:

20. For example, Rudolf Bultmann, *The Gospel of John* (Philadelphia: Westminster, 1971) 389.

21. That is, "a play on words"; see, e.g., A. Loisy, *Le quatrième Évangile* (Paris: Emil Nourry, 1921) 335.

22. Some suggestions have been made about the relationship of John 10:22-39 and the trial before the Sanhedrin in the Synoptic Gospels, but no analysis has been made of the Johannine

"I Said: You Are Gods"

Claim: Jesus is the Door, the Noble Shepherd (10:1-18)
Witnesses: He has a demon! No, he is a saint (10:19-21)
Cognitio: Tell us plainly if you are the Christ (10:24)
Defense: Defense becomes accusation: "I told you and you do not believe . . . you do not believe because you do not belong to my sheep" (10:25-27)

Jesus' defense of his claim contains no new material which proves its truth, but is itself a judgment on his judges,[23] an actual demonstration of how his claims work.

10:1-16	*10:27-28a*
1. The (true) sheep *hear* his *voice* (10:3b)	1. My sheep *hear my voice* (10:27a)
2. I *know my own* and my own know me (10:14)	2. I *know them* (10:27b)
3. The sheep *follow him*, for they know his voice (10:4)	3. And they *follow me* (10:27c)

By Jesus' criteria of judgment, then, he proves that his judges are not his sheep nor is he their shepherd. According to the Gospel's logic, these self-confessed non-sheep have rejected Jesus' basic claims to be God's agent and so are convicted of sin and unbelief (see John 3:18, 20; 5:40-45; 9:39-41; 12:46-48). Yet the forensic process is not yet finished.

2.2 The Second Forensic Proceeding (10:28b-39)

In 10:28-30 Jesus makes newer and bolder claims. Although formerly this Gospel claimed that believers by their own judgment come to life and pass beyond death (3:16-19; 5:24), now Jesus asserts that he himself is the giver of eternal life: "I give them eternal life and they never perish" (10:28a). He asserts that "no one

---

passage in terms of the formal elements of a forensic proceeding; see Paul Winter, "Luke xxii 66b-71," *ST* 9 (1955): 112-15; Raymond Brown, *The Gospel according to John* (AB 29; Garden City, NY: Doubleday, 1966) 1. 404-6; and Rudolf Schnackenburg, *The Gospel according to St. John* (New York: Crossroad, 1982) 2.306. On forensic process in John, see J. H. Neyrey, "Jesus the Judge: Forensic Process in John 8,21-59," *Bib* 68 (1987): 509-41.

23. It is vintage Johannine argument to turn a judgment against Jesus into a judgment against his accusers (e.g., 5:31-46; 3:6-12).

shall snatch them out of my hand" (10:28b).[24] Thus, Jesus now functions as the active agent of life, as giver of eternal life and as protector of his sheep even in death. Yet these claims would put him on a par with the all-powerful God.

10:29 states two things about God. First, God is "greater than all" in virtue of God's ruling or executive power as *pantokratōr, despotēs,* and *basileus*.[25] Second, of God it is said, "My Father . . . has given them [the sheep] to me and no one is able to snatch them out of the Father's hand" (10:29). Concerning the latter remark, then, Jesus and God are alike, even equal.

Jesus (10:28)	*The Father (10:29)*
I give them eternal life and they shall not perish forever, and no one shall snatch them out of my hand.	My Father . . . has given them to me and no one is able to snatch them out of the Father's hand.

To underscore the boldness of Jesus' claims, the text emphasizes that "God is greater *than all*" (10:29b), thus raising God above all other creatures, be they of no power or great power. Yet Jesus claims that he is "equal to" God who is "greater than all," when he draws the conclusion in 10:30, "I and the Father are *hen*."

Literally *hen* means "one." But the context suggests that this adjective be translated as "equal to" or "on a par with." Jesus claims far more than mere moral unity with God, which was the aim of every Israelite; such moral unity would never mean that mortals had become "god," as Jesus' remark is understood in 10:31-33. The very argument in John, then, understands *hen* to mean more than moral unity, that is, "equality with God." By way of confirmation, 1 Cor 3:8 indicates that *hen* can mean "equality."[26] In virtue of the comparison noted above, Jesus claims equality with God, who is "greater than all," because there is "no snatching out of their hands." To what does this refer?

In the context of 10:28, Jesus claims both the power to give eternal life so that his sheep do not perish and the power to guard them from being snatched. "Being snatched," then, has to do with life and death, such that Death[27] ulti-

---

24. Robert Aytoun pointed out that 10:28-30 bears striking resemblance to John 17:12 ("No One Shall Snatch Them Out of My Hand," *ExpT* 31 [1919-20]: 475-76). While there are clear parallels, Aytoun did not notice that 10:28-30 speaks about Jesus' power over death, but 17:12 speaks about protecting the disciples from death — two quite different issues.

25. See J. Whittaker, "A Hellenistic Context for John 10,29," *VC* 24 (1970): 241-44.

26. See J. Bernard, *A Critical and Exegetical Commentary on the Gospel according to St. John* (Edinburgh: T. & T. Clark, 1926) 366; and Barnabas Lindars, *The Gospel of John* (London: Oliphants, 1972) 370.

27. One recalls how Paul personifies death in Romans when he says "death reigned" (5:14, 17, 21)

mately has no power over Jesus' sheep. Conversely, this implies that Jesus has such power from God so that he is the one who gives eternal life and rescues the dead from the snares of Death (see John 5:25, 28-29; 6:39, 44, 54; 8:51; 11:25). Since God alone holds the keys of life and death, Jesus claims an extraordinary power which belongs exclusively to God.[28] There is substance, then, to the claim that Jesus and the Father are "equal" (10:30).

I have argued at great length that the Fourth Gospel clearly and formally argues that Jesus is "equal to God" (5:18; 10:33) because God has given him full eschatological power (5:21-29). God gave him power 1) to give eternal life (5:21; 10:28), 2) to judge (5:22, 27; 8:21-30), 3) to be honored as Lawmaker and Judge (5:23), 4) to have life in himself (5:26; 10:17-18), and 5) to raise the dead and judge them (5:28-29). In fact, 5:21-29, a summary of Jesus' eschatological power, functions as a topic statement which the Gospel subsequently develops in chaps, 8, 10, and 11. The claims in 10:28-30, then, continue the exposition of Jesus' full eschatological power.

Our exegesis of 10:22-30 yields the following information. A second forensic process begins in 10:28-30. Jesus is formally on trial, not just concerning whether he is "the Christ" (10:23-24), but especially about his claim to be "equal to God" (10:30, 33). The chief issue that is contested, moreover, concerns ultimate power over death, whereby Jesus is equal to God.

Claim: "I and the Father are 'one.'" (10:30, 33), i.e., *equal power over death* (10:28-30):
"I give them *eternal life*"
"they do not *perish forever*"
"*no one snatches* them out of my hand"

Charge: "Blasphemy, because you, being a man, make yourself equal to God" (10:33)

Defense: Use of Ps 82:6 (10:34-36): their judgment is false, because God makes Jesus to be "Son of God"

Our focus necessarily turns to the defense expressed in 10:34-36. How does the Fourth Gospel understand and use Psalm 82, and does this usage have any relationship to the claims made in 10:28-30? As we begin, let us pay special attention to the form of the charge in 10:33. Jesus is accused of "making himself" equal to God, a charge that dominates many forensic proceedings against him:

---

28. Jewish lore notes that God gave Elijah, Elisha, and Ezekiel the key to three things that are exclusively in God's power — rain, the womb, and the grave; see *b. Ta'anit* 2a; *b. Sanhedrin* 113a; *Midrash Ps.* 78.5; see also Barrett, *Gospel*, 260.

5:18   "... *making himself* God"
10:33 "you, a man, *make yourself* God"
19:7   "he *made himself* the Son of God"
19:12 "who *makes himself* king"[29]

The Evangelist distinguishes two elements of the judgment against Jesus: 1) Does Jesus *make himself* God or equal to God? 2) In what sense is Jesus *equal* to *God* or "god"? The distinction is important, for the Johannine Gospel denies the former half, that is, that Jesus *makes himself* anything, but carefully explains and defends the assertion of his equality with God.

3.0 Psalm 82 as Apologetic Response

In response to the charge of blasphemy, Jesus advances an argument from scripture using Psalm 82. When he cites Ps 82:6 in 10:34, he establishes the mode of argument by comparing two things: if scripture was not in error calling mortals "gods" (Ps 82:6), then neither is there error in calling the one whom God consecrated and sent into the world "the Son of God" (10:35-36).

Jesus' reference to "Son of God" in 10:36 does not weaken the argument by reducing the claim from "god" to "Son of God," because when one continues reading Ps 82:6, the two terms are considered parallel and equivalent there ("I said, 'You are *gods*, all of you, *sons of the Most High*'"). In claiming to be the consecrated "Son of God," he does not claim less than what is claimed by being "god" according to Ps 82:6. On the contrary, he claims more.

Yet how does the Fourth Gospel understand Ps 82:6? One stream of critical opinion takes the citation extrinsically, on a literal level as a mere play on words. If mortals, for whatever reason, can truly be called "gods" according to scripture, then the term is not *a priori* preposterously applied to Jesus. This type of explanation does not ask under what circumstances mortals might be called "gods," and it sees Jesus basically engaging in an evasive maneuver.

Such reasoning, however, does not mesh with the Johannine perspective for several reasons. The Fourth Gospel always criticizes people who take things literally, either Jesus' word or the scriptures.[30] Regularly we find a pattern where

---

29. See Heb 5:5. The substance of this charge is best understood from the perspective of cultural anthropology, which would describe Mediterranean culture in terms of "honor" and "shame"; Jesus' peers interpret his remark as a claim to very great honor, a claim that seems vainglorious for a person who has never studied (John 7:15).

30. On this form in the Fourth Gospel, see Herbert Leroy, *Ratsel und Missverständnis* (Bonn: Peter Hanstein, 1968) 45-47, 53-67.

"I Said: You Are Gods"

Jesus makes a *statement*, which his hearers *misunderstand* because they take it on a literal level, which leads Jesus to issue a *clarification* which exposes the spiritual or inner meaning of his words. It seems improbable, then, that the Fourth Gospel is dealing superficially with Psalm 82, asking readers to take its phrases and argument on a literal or extrinsic level. This is all the more true since the Gospel constantly maintains that spiritual vision is needed to see the inner meaning of texts from the scriptures which Jesus fulfills (see John 2:17, 22; 6:31; 8:56, 58, etc.).

A literal reading of Psalm 82, moreover, seems inconsistent with the more typical pattern of Johannine Christology. Wayne Meeks noted that when something claimed about Jesus causes a reaction from the synagogue, the Johannine community tends not to moderate its claim, but to rephrase it in such a way as to cause even greater offense.[31] Thus, if mortals may be called "god," then Jesus, whom God consecrated and sent into the world, can be called "Son of God," meaning "equal to God." A purely extrinsic reading of Ps 82:6 in regard to John 10:34-36 hardly seems warranted.

How, then, does the Fourth Gospel understand and use Psalm 82? The chief clue to a special reading of Ps 82:6 lies in 10:35, where we observe the way the Gospel interprets Ps 82:6 as part of its argument: "If he called them 'gods' to *whom the word of God came*...." Whoever, then, is called "god" is so named because "the word of God came" to them. Scholars have long argued that this refers to Israel at Sinai when God gave it the Torah, which I think is absolutely correct.[32] Yet what is the shape of the midrash on this and how might it apply to the Fourth Gospel?

B. F. Westcott, for example, argued that when the Fourth Gospel speaks of "those to whom the word of God came," the Evangelist refers to the preexistent Word who regularly gave theophanies to Israel's patriarchs.[33] Although the Fourth Gospel indeed develops an argument that Jesus is the appearing deity of the Hebrew Scriptures,[34] it is not apparent that an allusion is being made to that tradition in John 10, nor is it clear how such an allusion really advances the argument that Jesus is rightly called "god." The Evangelist, moreover, does not

---

31. Wayne Meeks, "The Man from Heaven in Johannine Sectarianism," *JBL* 91 (1972): 70-71.

32. I hasten to add that John 5:37, which alludes to the Sinai theophany, denies that Israel actually saw God: "His (God's) voice you have never heard, his form you have never seen." This text basically argues the repeated claim in the Fourth Gospel that *no one has ever seen God* (3:13; 6:46); it functions to diminish the authority of Israel's previous revealers, such as Moses, Elijah, Abraham, and the prophets by replacing them with Jesus, the unique revealer of God (1:18).

33. Westcott, *Gospel*, 70; a modern version of this is argued by A. T. Hanson, "John's Citation of Psalm lxxxii. John x.33-6," *NTS* 11 (1965-66): 158-62.

34. See J. H. Neyrey, "Jacob Allusions in John 1:51," *CBQ* 44 (1982): 589-94.

propose here the argument which was made in the prologue, that the "Word came unto his own and his own received him not" (1:11). Israel is not being reproached here for rejecting once more God's revelation to it.

4.0. Ps 82:6 in Judean Midrash

The emphasis in John 10:35 is not on Jesus, the preexistent Word, but on "those to whom the word of God came," who are called "gods." Who were these people? Although it is not the only stream of interpretation of Ps 82:6-7 in Israelite literature, there is a clear sense that Ps 82:6-7 was understood in terms of Israel at the Sinai theophany. A second-century midrash goes as follows:

> If it were possible to do away with the Angel of Death I would. But the decree has long ago been decreed. R. Jose says: It was upon this condition that the Israelites stood up before Mount Sinai, on the condition that the Angel of Death should not have power over them. For it is said: *"I SAID: YE ARE GODS"* (Ps 82:6). But you have corrupted your conduct. *"SURELY YE SHALL DIE LIKE MEN"* (Ps 82:7).[35]

Commentary: the occasion is Sinai ("Israel stood up before Mount Sinai"), when God descended on the mountain to give the Torah. According to Exod 20:18-19, when the Israelites saw the mountain blazing with lightning and heard the thundering, they said to Moses: "You speak to us, and we will hear; but let not God speak to us, *lest we die.*" In light of this, the *Mekilta* indicates that God restrained the Angel of Death, so that Israel did not die. And so because Israel became *deathless*, that is, beyond the power of the Angel of Death, Ps 82:6 applied to them, "I said 'You are gods.'" *Gods*, then, because *deathless*. But with the worship of the golden calf, Israel sinned, and suffered once more the penalty for sin, which is death: "You shall die like men" (Ps 82:7).

An important variation of this midrash occurs in *b. 'Abod. Zara* 5a. The context is a discussion of Deut 5:25-26 where Israel received the revelation at Sinai. The author comments that they have seen God and yet still live (recall the discussion of Exod 20:18-19 above); "therefore," they ask, "why should we die?" This question becomes the occasion for comment about the fluctuating power of the Angel of Death.

> R Jose said: The Israelites accepted the Torah only so that the Angel of Death should have no dominion over them, as it is said: *"I SAID: YE ARE GODS*

---

35. *Mekilta de-Rabbi Ishmael*, Tractate *Bahodesh* 9 (trans. Jacob Lauterbach; Philadelphia: Jewish Publication Society of America, 1933) 2.272.

"I Said: You Are Gods"

AND ALL OF YOU SONS OF THE MOST HIGH" (Ps 82:6). Now that you have spoilt your deeds, "YE SHALL DIE LIKE MORTALS" (Ps 82:7).[36]

Commentary: the occasion is Sinai once more; Israel is once again called *god* because *deathless*. But now we find the explicit note that being called *god* and being *deathless* are linked to the reception of Torah. In fact, Israel chose God's Torah for the express purpose that the Angel of Death should not have power over it. Something else, then, is operative here which suggests that receiving God's word (Torah) makes one holy, and if holy, then sinless, and if sinless, then deathless.

A third early midrash can help to clarify the basic lines of this interpretation of Ps 82:6-7. The context is a reflection on Deut 32:20, "I will see what their end will be," which refers to the fickleness and perfidiousness of Israel.

> You stood at Mount Sinai and said, "All that the Lord hath spoken will we do, and obey" (Exod 24:7), (whereupon) "I SAID: YE ARE GODS" (Ps 82:6); but when you said to the (golden) calf, "This is thy god, O Israel" (Exod 32:4), I said to you, "NEVERTHELESS, YE SHALL DIE LIKE MEN" (Ps 82:7).[37]

Commentary: at Sinai Israel received God's word of Torah ("all that the Lord hath spoken") and as a result became holy and sinless (". . .we will do and obey"), for which reason they are called *gods*. Although it is not explicitly stated here, this argument assumes that holiness leads to *deathlessness*, which is a godlike quality, for which reason Israel is called *god*. Yet with Israel's new sin comes death, the typical fate of sinful mortals ("ye shall die like men").

The basic lines of the midrashic understanding of Ps 82:6-7, then, are clear. When Israel at Sinai received God's Torah and obeyed, this resulted in genuine holiness which resulted in deathlessness; hence, Israel could be called *god* because *holy* and so *deathless*. But when disobedient and sinful, Israel deserved the wages of sin, that is, death; hence, Israel could be called *man*.

Yet this type of argument presumes some biblical understanding of death and deathlessness as well as of the nature of humanity and God. In short, the link between obedience-holiness-deathlessness lies back in the Genesis exposition of Adam in God's "image and likeness," an implicit scenario made explicit in the following midrash.[38] The segment is somewhat long, but because of its

---

36. Trans. I. Epstein, *The Babylonian Talmud* (London: Soncino Press, 1935) 19.

37. *Sifre: A Tannaitic Commentary on the Book of Deuteronomy*, Piska 320 (trans. Reuven Hammer; New Haven: Yale University Press, 1986) 329.

38. On this point, see Jacob Jervell, *Imago Dei* (Göttingen: Vandenhoeck & Ruprecht, 1960) 103, 113-19. As Jervell noted, Gen 1:26 ("image and likeness of God") played a more implicit role

importance and the complicated argument in it, it deserves to be cited as fully as possible.

> R. Eleazar the Galilean remarked: The Angel of Death complained to the Holy One, blessed be He: "I have then been created in the world to no purpose!" The Holy One, blessed be He, replied: "I have created you in order that you shall destroy idol-worshipers, but not this people, for you have no jurisdiction over them." That they should live and endure for ever; as it says, "But ye that did cleave unto the Lord your God are alive every one of you" (Deut 4:4). In the same strain it says, "The writing was the writing of God, graven *(haruth)* upon the tables" (Exod 32:16). What is the signification of *"haruth"*? R. Judah says: Freedom *(heruth)* from foreign governments; R. Nehemiah says: From the Angel of Death; and Rabbi says: From suffering. See then the plan the Holy One, blessed be He, had made for them! Yet forthwith they frustrated the plan after forty days. Accordingly it says, "But ye have set at nought all my counsel" (Prov 1:25). The Holy One, blessed be He, said to them: "I thought you would not sin and would live and endure for ever like Me; even as I live and endure for ever and to all eternity; I SAID: YE ARE GODS, AND ALL OF YOU SONS OF THE MOST HIGH (Ps 82:6), like the ministering angels, who are immortal. Yet after all this greatness, you wanted to die! INDEED, YE SHALL DIE LIKE MEN (Ps 82:7) — Adam, i.e. like Adam whom I charged with one commandment which he was to perform and live and endure for ever"; as it says, "Behold the man was as one of us" (Gen 3:22). Similarly, "And God created man in His own image" (Gen 1:27), that is to say, that he should live and endure like Himself. Yet [says God] he corrupted his deeds and nullified My decree. For he ate of the tree, and I said to him: "For dust thou art" (Gen 3:19). So also in your case, "I SAID YE ARE GODS"; but you have ruined yourselves like Adam, and so *"INDEED, YE SHALL DIE* like Adam." (Num. Rab. 16.24)[39]

The typical features of the midrashic understanding of Ps 82:6-7 are clearly evident: 1) Sinai and the giving of the Torah, 2) Israel's obedience ("cleaving unto the Lord"), 3) deathlessness or immortality ("freedom from the Angel of Death" . . . "live and endure for ever like Me"), and hence 4) Israel being called *god* (Ps 82:6). This midrash makes explicit the generally assumed doctrine of the relation of sin and death found primarily in Genesis 1–3, for it points out

---

in the explanations of deathlessness; the more frequently cited text in this regard was Gen 3:22 ("the man has become like one of us").

39. The translation is from *Midrash Rabbah,* ed. H. Freedman and M. Simon (London: Soncino Press, 1939).

that God created Adam "in His image and likeness," that is, *deathless*. Adam was deathless because holy and obedient ("I charged with one commandment which he was to perform and live and endure for ever"). Adam died precisely because he sinned and lost God's holiness and "image." This midrash also makes clear that interpreters of Ps 82:6-7 saw Sinai as a new creation, when the obedience, holiness, and deathlessness of Adam were restored to Israel, thus linking the Adam myth with the Sinai myth, as the following diagram suggests.

Adam in Paradise	*Israel at Sinai*
1. created in holiness	1. reconstituted in holiness
2. and so deathless	2. and so deathless
3. yet sinned (ate fruit)	3. yet sinned (worshiped calf)
4. and so died	4. and so died

The midrashim we are examining all presume a complex yet traditional explanation of the source of death. Good biblical doctrine states that God created Adam in a state of holiness. He was, moreover, created in God's "image and likeness," which Wisdom 2:23 explains as a state of deathlessness:

God made man for incorruption
and made him in the image of his own eternity.

Deathlessness (or "eternity") was conditioned upon holiness. God said, "On the day you eat it you shall die" (Gen 2:17; 3:3). The tempter deceived Eve by saying that if she broke God's commandment "You shall *not* die" (Gen 3:4), which was a lie. To the sinful Adam God said, "You are dust and to dust you shall return" (Gen 3:19).

Although we have surveyed only four instances of the midrashic understanding of Psalm 82, many more can be found in Israelite literature. Yet as we investigate those other citations of Psalm 82, they only confirm what has just been shown. In general, it can be stated that when Psalm 82 is cited in Judean midrash, writers generally understand that Israel is called god because of its holiness and/or its deathlessness.[40]

Evidently some midrashim contain a fully developed exposition of the Psalm, while others have but fragments of an explanation. Yet even the earliest midrash cited above, the *Mekilta*, implies as much as it states, probably because it reflects a very common tradition which is presumably well known. Not all of

---

40. Besides the three examples cited, other instances of the use of Ps 82:6 would include *Exod. Rab.* 32.7; *Lev. Rab.* 4.1; 11.3; *Num. Rab.* 16:24; *Pirqe Rabbi Eliezer* 47; *Pesiq. Rab.* 1.2; 14.10; 33.10; *Tanhuma B Lev* 7:5; *Pesiqta de Rab Kahana* 4; *Eliyyahu Zuta* 4; *Eliyyahu Rabbah* 24.

the elements of the midrash, moreover, need be explicitly mentioned when the Psalm is interpreted, for midrash is like an iceberg. As much is implied as is visible. With this survey of midrashic interpretation of Ps 82:6 in mind, we return to John 10:34-36. Does the Fourth Gospel interpret Ps 82 in a midrashic manner, and, if so, how much of the midrash does it know?

5.0 Midrash in John 10:34-36

If the Fourth Gospel understands Psalm 82 in a midrashic manner, we would want to see where John 10:34-36 stands in regard to three issues which regularly arise in the midrashim. First, the historical occasion of Psalm 82 is regularly seen to be Israel's reception of God's word at Sinai. Second, the midrash does not call Israel *god* for purely extrinsic reasons, but links godlikeness with holiness and so deathlessness. Finally, even the simple midrash assumes some biblical notion of death and deathlessness, which implies an understanding of Genesis 1–3 or some popular myth of the origin of death in the world. With these points in mind let us return to John 10.

As we noted above, the Fourth Gospel seems to understand Psalm 82 in a midrashic sense as referring to Israel at Sinai. For the Evangelist interprets the psalm "I said, 'You are gods'" as addressed to "those to whom the word of God came" (10:34-35). People, then, are not called *god* gratuitously, but with extreme qualification, *gods* because *the word of God* came to them. Although deathlessness is not explicitly mentioned in 10:34, I would argue that it is evident in two ways. First of all, Jesus and God both are said to have power over death: to give life and to protect people from being snatched. The disciples then are *deathlessness* because of the favor of God and Christ to them; we assumed that such benefaction is given to disciples who are holy. Hence *deathlessness* is linked with *holiness*. We know that it is not the mere physical hearing of the Word of God, but hearing in obedience which constitutes holiness. Such is the hearing that is celebrated in John 5:24; 8:37; 9:27. This Gospel, moreover, clearly sees an intrinsic link between hearing in faith and passing to eternal life.

The focus on holiness, moreover, continues in the application of Ps 82:6 to Jesus himself in 10:36. If Israel, who became holy, may be called *god*, then it is not blasphemy if Jesus, whom God consecrated and sent as his agent into the world, is called *god* and Son *of God*. Holiness or sinlessness again serves as the ground for calling someone Israel, or in this case, calling Jesus *god*.

Throughout the Fourth Gospel. Jesus' holiness or sinfulness has been a formal topic of debate. As regards his alleged sinfulness, the author of the Gospel repeatedly takes note of the popular judgment of Jesus as a sinner (9:16, 24), a judgment based on his two healings on the Sabbath (5:1-17; 9:1-7). His enemies, moreover, charge him with being thoroughly evil, that is, possessed of a demon (7:20; 8:48; 10:20). Here in 10:33 and 36 he is charged with a new sin, blasphemy, for claiming to be "equal to God."

Yet the Fourth Gospel denies any sin on Jesus' part. John 10:36 represents but the most recent evidence of this defense, as it proclaims that God *consecrated* Jesus. After all, God's judgment of Jesus must surely have greater weight than that of his peers (see 5:16; 7:12, 20; 8:48; 10:33; 18:29-30). We have heard, moreover, of God's evaluation of Jesus elsewhere, that "The Father loves the Son" (3:35; 5:30). Sinners, of course, find no place in God's presence, yet Jesus was "face to face" with God (1:1-2) and in God's "bosom" (1:18). And Jesus will return to God's presence at the completion of his mission (13:3; 17:5, 24). God, then, judges Jesus to be sinless and worthy to stand in the divine presence. Nor could anyone convict Jesus of sin (8:46). Even his working on the Sabbath must be perceived precisely as obedience to God's will (5:30; 7:21-23). In fact, Jesus' very ability to open the eyes of the blind testifies to his closeness to God (9:31-33). Jesus' holiness (6:69) and his consecration (10:36) attest to his preeminent sinlessness.

Divine consecration of Jesus, moreover, suggests a picture of him as one totally set aside for God's purposes[41] and completely obedient to God's will. This radical image of commissioning evoked for Rudolf Schnackenburg the sense of a person sealed with the Holy Spirit,[42] a comment that makes us recall the testimony of the Baptizer in 1:30-31. John testified that he saw God's Spirit not only descend on Jesus but "remain on him" (1:32-33), which suggests that divine power and holiness were no passing phenomenon for Jesus. Because of the dwelling of the Holy Spirit on Jesus, John testifies that he is "the Son of God" (1:34), a figure whose task was to purify others with the Spirit which remained in him (1:33). Jesus, then, is no sinner, but God's Holy One.

Thus far we have noted that 10:34-35 understands Ps 82:6 to attest that obedience to God's word leads to holiness and godlikeness. As we saw with the midrashim, this interpretation presumes some notion of deathlessness linked with holiness. Yet it is important to pay attention to where and how Ps 82:6 functions in the forensic structure of 10:28-36. The Fourth Gospel uses Psalm 82 as a refutation of part of a charge. Jesus' judges judged wrongly when they accused him of *making himself* God or equal to God, because God Himself *makes* Jesus Son of God, just as God *made* Israel "god" by delivering the Torah to it. At a minimum, then, Jesus refutes the essence of the charge by maintaining that

---

41. So Barrett, *Gospel*, 385.
42. Schnackenburg, *Gospel*, 2.311.

God makes him what he is, namely, a consecrated servant, agent, and apostle, a person totally set apart by God for sacred duty.[43] The apology based on Psalm 82, then, argues two things: it refutes the charge that Jesus *makes himself* "Son of God," even as it affirms that he is "on a par" with God in power over death, both that of disciples and his own. But if it confounds his accusers (10:31-33), does it explain or support the claims made in 10:28-30 which precipitated the forensic controversy in the first place?

We claimed above that Jesus is "equal to God" because of his "power over death." In regard to this, Ps 82:6 supports that claim in such a way that Jesus is rightly called *god*.

> *Claim:* Equal to God; power over death: "I give them *eternal life*, and they will *never perish*. No one will *snatch* them out of my hand" (10:28)
> *Judgment:* Blasphemy: you, a man, *make yourself* a god (10:33) = radical sinfulness
> *Defense:* Charge refuted: it is God who *makes Jesus* "Son of God" because of his holiness (Ps 82:6//John 10:34-36) = radical holiness

Ps 82:6, then, functions to prove that the judges' judgment is false. Jesus' claim to extraordinary power (to give life, to keep from perishing and protect from snatching) is defended because Ps 82 has already declared that some holy people were acclaimed *god*, and Jesus himself is one of those people. The very claim by Jesus that this power has been given Jesus in 5:21-29 was contested then (5:17-18) even as it is now. But in both cases Jesus defends himself against the charge that he is a sinful person deserving of death for blasphemy. He never claimed that they never die and are laid in tombs (11:38-44). But he claims power over ultimate death,[44] which is the basis for the claim that "I and the Father are 'equal' or 'on a par.'" Jesus, then, is holy and God-favored and God has given him power over death, his own (10:17-18) and that of others (10:28-30). Thus the full import of the claims made in 10:28-30 argue that Jesus is himself deathless and acts with power over disciples ("my sheep"). In this sense Ps 82:6 can illuminate the claims to power over death with Jesus' implication that "I said, you are gods" indeed refers to him. The issue is power over death, in which regard Jesus is "god" or "equal to God." The citation of Ps 82, then, is a very satisfactory

---

43. See Peder Borgen, "God's Agent in the Fourth Gospel," in *Religions in Antiquity*, ed. Jacob Neusner (Leiden: Brill, 1968) 137-48; and more recently George W. Buchanan, "Apostolic Christology," *SBLSP* 1986: 172-82.

44. Even when made deathless, Israel always remained vulnerable to the Angel of Death who was poised to have power over them. Of Jesus, however, this Gospel claims that he is no mere mortal, but a heavenly figure. He has power over the Angel of Death.

explanation for Jesus' "equality with God." according to the Fourth Gospel. Ps 82:6 may function to prove the judges' judgment wrong (he does *not* "make himself" anything; God makes him "Son of God"), but it is not exploited as an adequate explanation for the Johannine assertion that Jesus has power over death (10:28-30). Ps 82:6 functions only to prove that the judges' judgment is false.

What then of the forensic claims themselves? Jesus and God are "equal" in terms of power over death. Yet is Jesus himself deathless? Whence comes his power over death? Friend and foe both know that he died on the cross. Friends proclaim that his death was God's will and plan (Acts 2:23; 4:28) and that he was fully obedient to God, even unto death (Phil 2:8; Mark 14:35-36). The Fourth Gospel, moreover, proclaims a more remarkable thing about God's involvement in Jesus' death. In 10:17-18 Jesus asserts that God loves him precisely because he dies: "For this reason the Father loves me, that I lay down my life, that I may take it again" (10:17). Death is usually a sign of God's wrath, not love. Jesus' death, then, is clearly not the result of sin, as the midrash on Ps 82:7 argues. Nor is Jesus the helpless victim whose life is taken from him, either by men or the Angel of Death. For, as he declares, "No one takes it from me, but I lay it down of my own accord" (10:18a).

Furthermore, his death occurs in strict obedience to God, not as punishment for sinfulness on his part: "This commandment I have received from my Father (10:18b). In 10:28-30, moreover, Jesus claims to be equal to God in having God's own power over death. Jesus, then, while not literally *deathless* himself, has full power over death (see 8:51, 53, 58).

Indisputably Jesus dies, but the Fourth Gospel steadfastly maintains that Jesus has power over death, both his own and that of his followers. We noted earlier how this Gospel proclaims that Jesus has God's eschatological power to the full, one aspect of which is to "give life" to others (5:21; 10:28) and to "raise the dead" (5:25, 28-29; 11:25). Yet Jesus has power over his own death, to lay down his life and *to take it back* (10:17-18); this power was received when God gave him to "have life in himself" (5:26), just as God has life in Himself. And so Jesus is proclaimed *deathless* in a special way: although he dies, he has complete power over his own death. He raises himself from death to life and he raises his followers from death as well.

Ps 82:6 in the midrashim explains deathlessness, but in a way that is different from the claims made in the Fourth Gospel about Jesus' power over death. But power over death claimed in 10:28-30 is the borrowed meaning of Ps 82. Yes, Jesus has power over death and so is deathless, and yes, Jesus is not a sinner for claiming to be "on a par with God" because God consecrated him and sent him into the world. Admittedly, John equates "deathlessness" with the power given Jesus and radical holiness with his being on a par with God and consecrated by God.

6.0 Summary, Conclusions and Further Questions

6.1 Summary

John 10:34-36 can be said to understand Ps 82:6 and use it in specific ways.

1. According to 10:34-35, Ps 82:6 ("I said, 'You are gods'") is understood to refer to Israel at Sinai when it received the Torah ("to whom the word of God came," 10:35).

2. Implied in this understanding is the intimate link between holiness :: deathlessness :: godlikeness. The Fourth Gospel cites only an abbreviated form of this, deathlessness :: holiness :: godlikeness.

3. Ps 82:6b ("sons of the Most High") is cited by Jesus when he calls himself "Son of God" (10:36), and it refers to his godlikeness in terms of holiness (see "consecrated and sent").

4. Ps 82:6 indeed touches the substance of the claims made in 10:28-30 which precipitated the forensic process in 10:31-39. It functions as an adequate refutation of the erroneous judgment of Jesus' judges, who charged that he, "a man, *makes himself* equal to God." This judgment is false because God *makes him* "Son of God." In essence, God has given Jesus power over death.

5. According to the apology in 10:34-36, holiness is linked with godlikeness in ways that are appropriate to human beings. Jesus would be a mere human being even if acclaimed "god/Son of God," as was Israel. But the forensic argument in John 10 claims much more. No mere human being, Jesus is a heavenly figure who is "equal to God." His equality rests not on holiness but on divine powers intrinsic to him, that is, full eschatological power.

6. Jesus' claims in regard to power over death always remain important in John 10. In this Gospel, his deathlessness[45] does not formally derive from sinlessness/holiness as in the case of the midrash on Ps 82:6, but from an apprecia-

---

45. The Fourth Gospel has very conflicting material about "deathlessness." Concerning disciples, one might literally take statements such as 3:16; 5:24; 6:50, 54 to mean that true disciples do not die; some characters in the narrative are said to believe just this (8:51-53; 11:21, 32). It is even suggested that the Beloved Disciple would not die (21:23). Yet the Gospel seems to have quickly corrected that literal reading of Jesus' words. Concerning Jesus himself, however, his followers could never claim "deathlessness" for him, given his evident demise on the cross. Yet they did claim that he overpowered death (8:28; 13:1-3). His resurrection from death is seen as his own act of power (10:17-18), thus affirming his power over death, if not deathlessness itself in another form.

tion of the full eschatological power which God gave him over death (5:21-29; 10:17-18). In 5:18 and 10:30, Jesus may be called "equal to God" for a much greater reason than ever justified calling Israel *god*, namely, because of powers intrinsic to him. Power over death is the specific content of "equal to God."

7. If we are correct that Ps 82:6 is understood in 10:34-36 in line with its basic midrashic interpretation, then the remark in 10:28-29 that "no one shall snatch them out of my hand" probably echoes what the midrash discusses in terms of the Angel of Death whose power over God's people was restrained. The Angel of Death will not snatch Jesus' followers/sheep either from his hand or God's hand.

8. Although the midrashim studied above were written considerably later than the Fourth Gospel, the understanding of Ps 82:6 in John 10:34-36 belongs in that same trajectory of interpretation. It might be the earliest extant witness of that tradition is John 10, although not the most complete example.

6.2 Further Questions

This study has not by any means exhausted the inquiry into John 10:31-39. But it does raise new questions. It focuses on the formal forensic process which structures the narrative in 10:21-28a and 28b-39, highlighting especially the claims made by Jesus. The use of Psalm 82 in 10:34-36 only deflects the judges' false judgment; a full exposition of Jesus' claims in 10:28-30 and their adequate apology in 10:37-38 remains to be examined. The relationship of 10:28b-30 to issues of Jesus' eschatological power in 5:21-29; 8:21-59; 11:1-41 remains to be considered.

The use of midrashic traditions is not confined to 10:34-36.[46] Appreciation of John's use not only of the scriptures but especially their midrashic understanding will go a long way toward clarifying the context of the Johannine community. Finally, if there is substance to the argument about two forensic processes narrated in 10:21-28a, 28b-39, this might provide further clues to the historical development of the Johannine community. It would stand as another piece of evidence for a development from a "low" Christology ("Messiah") to "high" Christology ("equal to God").

---

46. For example, concerning the Johannine use of midrashic traditions about Jacob, see J. H. Neyrey, "Jacob Traditions and the Interpretation of John 4:10-26," *CBQ* 41 (1979): 419-37.

13

"In Conclusion..."

John 12 as a Rhetorical "Peroratio"

1.0 Introduction, Topic, and Hypothesis

Most commentators on John 12:37-50 label it a "conclusion" or "epilogue." By this they mean that the final part of John 12 contains two differing sets of information: 1) a "summary" of the ministry of Jesus and its non-reception or 2) a review of major motifs and themes. Commentators, however, tend to distinguish 12:37-43 from 44-50. The former verses indicate that the story of Jesus' ministry "which he set forth as a series of semeia, or significant actions, is a story of man's refusal of divine life and light. Those who saw and heard did not respond with faith, or, if in their hearts they were convinced, they would not confess it for fear of the consequences, and so were self-condemned."[1] The remaining verses (12:44-50) serve as a resume of leading themes of the discourse in John 2–12.

> No new theme is introduced; yet the passage is no mere *cento* of phrases from the earlier chapters. It rings the changes afresh upon the themes of life, light and judgment, restating the central purpose of what has already been said on these themes.[2]

In this regard, the "summary" spoken about refers both to the explicit parallels between 3:16-19 and 12:37-50[3] and more widely to the discourses in the Book of

---

1. C. H. Dodd, *The Interpretation of the Fourth Gospel* (Cambridge: Cambridge University Press, 1953) 379.
2. Dodd, *The Interpretation of the Fourth Gospel*, 379-80.
3. On the links between 3:16-19 and 12:46-48, see Raymond E. Brown, *The Gospel according*

Signs. Back when scholars were wrestling with Bultmann's displacement theory, 12:44-50 was detached from 12:37-43 as misplaced remarks. But it is time to bring fresh thinking to the assessment of John 12:37-50. We think that John Ashton got it right when he remarked that it is an epilogue in the proper sense,[4] rounding off and summing up the preceding revelation. Moreover, we will argue that the conversation in John 12:37-50 should be taken as a rhetorical unit, that is, as a genuine "conclusion."

Much more can be said about this material in John 12. First, the labels "conclusion" and "epilogue" have been used in casual, non-technical ways. Rare is the commentator who mentions the formal rhetorical "conclusion" (*peroratio* or ἐπίλογος) about which classical rhetoricians have so much to say. Furthermore, what about John 12:1-36? Is it also part of the "conclusion"? It depends on how one understands "conclusion" in ancient rhetoric. Must 12:37-43 be separated from 44-50? Again, it depends on what one knows about classical "conclusions."

The thesis argued here is that interpreters must become familiar with the discourse of ancient rhetoric on the shape and function of the "conclusion" (*peroratio* or ἐπίλογος). Rules for a "conclusion" instruct students not simply to summarize an argument; more importantly, they instruct a speaker to play to the emotions of the audience, ascribing praise and blame to the characters and thus persuading the audience to do likewise. This formal theory, then, serves as an appropriate template to follow the argument in John 12:31-50. The result will be a richer, more detailed, and more accurate interpretation of the argument at the end of the Book of Signs. It should be pointed out that scholars have no trouble labeling 1:1-18 as a prologue (προοίμιον), meaning that it contains a studied presentation of major themes and topics to be developed in the rest of the narrative.[5] Similarly, the same courtesy should be given to the *peroratio* or ἐπίλογος which concludes what the prologue began.

---

to John (Garden City, NY: Doubleday, 1966) 1.147, 490; Brown's treatment depends on M.-E. Boismard, "L'évolution du thème eschatologique dans les traditions johanniques," *RB* 68 (1961): 507-14.

4. John Ashton, *Understanding the Fourth Gospel* (Oxford: Clarendon Press, 1991) 541-45.

5. Robert Kysar, "The Contributions of the Prologue of the Gospel of John to New Testament Christology and Its Historical Setting," *CurrTM* 5 (1978): 348-64; J. A. T. Robinson, "The Relation of the Prologue to the Gospel of John," *NTS* 9 (1963): 120-29; and R. Alan Culpepper, "The Pivot of John's Prologue," *NTS* 27 (1980): 1-31.

2.0 What Is a "Conclusion"?

Put simply, it ends or terminates a discourse. In terms of what makes an effective conclusion, ancient rhetoricians present a broad consensus on its main components. Aristotle's definition of the conclusion shaped the understanding of it for centuries to come and so deserves consideration.

> The epilogue is composed of four parts: 1. to dispose the hearer favorably towards oneself and unfavorably towards the adversary; 2. to amplify and depreciate (to praise and to blame), 3. to excite the emotions of the hearers, 4. to recapitulate. (*Rhet.* 3.19.1)

The first three items (dispose hearer favorably/unfavorably; amplify/depreciate; and excite emotions) are all of a package. Characters are paraded before the audience for the purpose of judging them, which is achieved by the author's evocation of emotional reactions toward them. "Disposing" and "amplifying" rest not just on an intellectual evaluation of characters, but on creating an argument from πάθος. Aristotle earlier spoke of what makes for a favorable/unfavorable assessment of speaker or adversary (*Rhet.* 1.9) and for amplification or depreciation (i.e., "praise and blame," *Rhet.* 2.19) and which emotions to excite (pity, indignation, anger, hate, jealousy, emulation, quarrelsomeness, *Rhet.* 2.1-11). In Aristotle, "recapitulation" seems like a step-child to the argument from emotions, which is given extended attention. In subsequent tradition, the "four" parts eventually become "two," arousal of emotions and recapitulation.

Before Cicero, an anonymous compendium of rhetoric appeared, *Rhetorica ad Herennium*, in which Aristotle's four elements of a conclusion are simplified to three.

> Conclusions, among the Greeks called *(epilogi)* are tripartite, consisting of the Summing Up, Amplification, and Appeal to Pity. . . . The *Summing Up* gathers together and recalls the points we have made. . . . *Amplification* is the principle of using Commonplaces to stir the hearers. . . . We shall stir Pity in our hearers by recalling the vicissitudes of fortune; by comparing the prosperity we once enjoyed with our present adversity, by enumerating and explaining the results that will follow for us if we lose the case; by entreating those whose pity we seek to win . . . by disclosing the kindness, humanity, and sympathy we have dispensed to others. . . . The *Appeal to Pity* must be brief, for nothing dries more quickly than a tear. (2.47-50)

In Aristotle recapitulation stood last, but here, first. Aristotle's appeal to the emotions specifies that one should arouse hearers to "certain emotions" (pity, indignation, anger, hate, envy, etc.), indeed very conflict-promoting emotions, whereas here the emotions are softer in kind and designed to bring "a tear" to the eye.

Cicero repeats much of what was seen in the *Rhetorica ad Herennium* about a conclusion, in particular an enumeration of its three parts: "The conclusion is the end and termination of the whole oration. It has three parts, the *summing up*, the *indignatio* or exciting indignation or ill-will against the opponents, and the *conquestio* or the arousing of pity and sympathy" (*De Inventione* 1.52.98). Immediately we recognize new labels for the second and third parts. "Amplificatio" is now *indignatio*, and appeal to emotions becomes *conquestio*. This is no mere quibble over words, for the character of the second and third parts has changed. As regards *summing up*, we find nothing out of the ordinary: "As a general principle for *summing up*, it is laid down that since the whole of any argument cannot be given a second time, the most important point of each be selected, and that every argument be touched on as briefly as possible, so that it may appear to be a refreshing of the memory of the audience, rather than a repetition of the speech" (*De Inventione* 1.52.98). "Indignation" aims to arouse "*great hatred* against a man, or great *dislike* of some proceeding" (*De Inventione* 1.53.100). Like opening a valve, Cicero proscribes restraint; rather, "*it is possible to give vent to indignation from all those topics* which we have suggested." Finally, his *conquestio* closely resembles Herennius's appeal to pity: "The *conquestio* (lament or complaint) is a passage seeking to arouse the pity of the audience. In this, the first necessity is to make the auditor's spirit gentle and merciful, that others may be more easily moved by the *conquestio*" (*De Inventione* 1.55.106).

Quintilian's code of rhetoric tailors the common notion of a conclusion even further. It has two, not three or four parts: "The next subject that I was going to discuss was the *peroratio* which some call the completion and others the conclusion. There are two kinds of peroration, for it may deal either with *facts* or with the *emotional aspects* of the case" (*Inst. Orat.* 6.1.1). "Facts" have to do with repetition, and "emotions" with accusation and defense. His understanding of repetition (i.e., "facts") seems broader than anything previously seen: "The repetition and grouping of the facts, which the Greeks call ἀνακεφαλαίωσις, and some of our own writers call enumeration, serves both to refresh the memory of the judge and to place the whole case before his eyes" (*Inst. Orat.* 6.1.2). At first Quintilian seems cautious about appeal to the emotions, noting that this strategy was "forbidden to Athenian orators." But he takes up the topic, stating that the prosecution and the defense "appeal to different emotions." "The accuser has to rouse the judge, while the defender has to soften him." In principle, "it is the duty of both parties to seek to win the judge's goodwill and to divert it from their opponent, as also to excite or assuage his emotions" (*Inst. Orat.* 6.1.11). The emotions proper to exciting shame and condemnation are "envy, hatred and anger." Conversely, an accused person appropriately appeals to his honor, that is, to "his worth, his manly pursuits, the scars from wounds received in battle, his rank and the services rendered by his ancestors" (*Inst. Orat.* 6.1.21).

What, then, do we know when we know this? First, a "conclusion" is indeed a recapitulation, a crisp and succinct enumeration of major points of the speech. Second, it is also the occasion to arouse emotions appropriate to either accuser or defendant. An accuser, who seeks to bring the judge to make a decision about the accused, arouses strong emotions such as anger, hatred, and envy in an effort to put the accused in as unfavorable light as possible. Conversely a defendant speaks in such a way as to make the judge favorably disposed to him, and so he appeals to "pity," which he will arouse by enumerating his own honorable deeds, or as Herennius remarked, "by disclosing the kindness, humanity, and sympathy we have dispensed to others." Thus an accuser will write a strong *indignatio*, but a defendant, a *conquestio*. It is the consideration of the πάθος[6] or the exciting of the emotions that we particularly bring to a more rhetorical interpretation of John 12:1-50.

3.0 Recapitulation and Enumeration in John 12

As we saw, scholars occasionally describe the end of John 12 as a "conclusion," that is, a summing up of the previous narrative. But there is little agreement about the specific content of the "conclusion," i.e., what is recapitulated or enumerated. Some make a firm distinction between 12:36-43 and 44-50, identifying the former as a comment on the mission to Israel or on the blindness of Israel, but considering the latter as a resume of themes, a précis of what has been revealed or "an anthology of representative sayings." Thus 12:31-43 is a summary of the story, and 12:44-50 equals a resume of sayings, particularly about judgment. We think such distinctions to be overly subtle and that further consideration of the rhetorical *peroratio* can better explain how the whole of 12:31-50 is a unified argument. What, then, is being recapitulated or summarized in 12:31-50? A fuller assessment of the parallels and links between 12:31-50 and material in John 2–11 provides the data needed to judge this issue.

---

6. Literature on the rhetoric of πάθος is indeed scant. See Mario M. DiCicco, *Paul's Use of Ethos, Pathos, and Logos in 2 Corinthians 10–13* (Lewiston, ME: Mellen Biblical Press, 1995) 113-87; Thomas H. Olbricht and Jerry L. Sumney, eds., *Paul and Pathos* (Atlanta, GA: Scholars Press, 2001); and Jakob Wisse, *Ethos and Pathos from Aristotle to Cicero* (Amsterdam: Adolf M. Hakkert, 1989).

"In Conclusion..."

3.1 Recapitulation of Judgments

We begin with the most frequently cited parallel to 12:31-50, namely the judgment materials in 3:16-19 vis-à-vis 12:31-36 and 3:17-19 vis-à-vis 12:45-50.[7] The judgmental language in 12:36-50, which appeared much earlier in the discourse with Nicodemus, is clearly repeated in the conclusion to the Book of Signs. In 12:31-50 the author brings back the following items from the dynamic of the previous narrative: 1. "Jesus," 2. "the light," 3. "comes," 4. "to provoke a judgment by those who see him," 5. "but many fail to come to the light and walk in darkness," 6. and so "bring judgment on themselves." It matters that 3:16-21 occurs after a failure of a "ruler of the Judeans" (3:1) to understand Jesus, whereas 12:26-50 concludes Jesus' labors in Jerusalem where elites plot to dishonor him. Thus from the prologue of the narrative (1:11)[8] to its conclusion in John 12, people have rejected the light. This, we suggest, provides the lens for evaluating all of the materials in 12:36-50.

3:19-21	12:31-36
1. This is the *judgment* (3:19)	1. Now is the *judgment* (12:31)
2. The *light* has come *into the world* (3:19b)	2. The *light* is with you for a little longer (12:35a)
3. Those who *do what is true* come to the *light*, so that it may be clearly seen that their *deeds* have been *done* in God (3:21)	3. *Walk* while you *have the light*, so that the darkness may not overtake you (12:35b)
4. For all who *do evil* hate the light and *do not come* to the light, so that their deeds may not be exposed (3:20)	4. If you *walk* in the darkness, you *do not know* where you are going (12:35c)

This comparison argues that Jesus himself occasions the judgment, even a schism of contrasting judgments about him (7:40-43; 9:16; 10:19-21; 11:36-37; and 12:29). Some accept him, his agency and his word, but many do not. For the former there is praise, for the latter, dishonor. But the judgment rests in the hands of those to whom Jesus spoke; for, "as you sow, so shall you reap" — for better or worse.

The subsequent passage, 12:45-50, repeats much of the judgmental material seen earlier in John 3, but highlights different aspects of judgment.

---

7. Brown, *The Gospel according to John*, 490; M.-E. Boismard, "L'évolution du thème eschatologique," 507-14; and Dodd, *The Interpretation of the Fourth Gospel*, 379-83.
8. See Sjef van Tilborg, *Imaginative Love in John* (Leiden: Brill, 1993) on 1:11.

3:17-19, 34-36	12:45-50
1. *God sent the Son* into the world (3:17)	1. Whoever believes, believes not in me but in him *who sent me*. Whoever sees me sees him *who sent me* (12:44-45)
2. This is the judgment: *the light has come into the world,* and people loved *darkness* rather than light (3:19)	2. I have come *as light into the world,* so that everyone who believes in me should not remain in the *darkness* (12:46)
3. God did *not* send the Son into the world *to condemn* the world, but in order that the *world* might be *saved through him* (3:17)	3. *I do not judge anyone.* I came *not to judge the world,* but to *save the world* (12:47)
4. *He whom God has sent speaks the words of God* (3:34)	4. I have *not spoken on my own;* the Father who sent me has himself given me what to say and what to speak (12:49)
5. Whoever believes in the Son has *eternal life* (3:36)	5. His commandment is *eternal life* . . . I speak just as the Father has told me (12:50)

If John 3:19-21/12:31-36 focused on "judgment," i.e., *whether* people choose darkness over light, then 3:17-19, 34-36/12:45-50 recapitulate *who* is to be judged. The reward for right judgment is eternal life. Thus, the conclusion in 12:36-50 is a recapitulation of the fundamental dynamic of the narrative: judgment depends upon reaction to Jesus, the light, who speaks God's word. As we shall shortly see, when judgment is described, certain emotions necessarily arise in the hearts of the audience. Those judged are to be scorned, even hated. In the Fourth Gospel there is "zero tolerance" for those who choose darkness over light.

3.2 Recapitulation of Those Who Judge

Both 12:35-36 and 12:45-50 repeat materials characteristic of an early pattern in the Gospel, that those who hear and see Jesus are judging him. Whether they declare him a saint or a sinner, they make a momentous judgment. For, when judges judge, they are themselves subject to judgment depending on whether they judge justly and not according to appearances (7:24; 8:15). For "with the judgment you make you will be judged, and the measure you give will be the measure you get" (Matt 7:2). Moreover, this chapter contains an extensive range of judgments about Jesus. *Judgment*, therefore, is the apt conclusion to John 1–12 because it summarizes the role and status of Jesus as "light of the world," concludes the trial of the Word which had been formally conducted since John 5, and articulates the criteria for praise and blame. But something more is found here, namely, the claim that God has sent Jesus, so that rejecting Jesus means rejecting God — a most serious affair (12:44-45). If "eternal life" emerges as the reward for believers, "eternal death" will be the sanction for those who refuse belief.

From a rhetorical point of view, the author has placed an *inclusio* around the Book of Signs which first establishes the topic of belief/judgment in the prologue of the narrative (1:5, 11) and then resumes it after numerous characters have had their opportunities to make their judgments. This is a summary statement of the on-going process which each character has passed through, now with a concluding judgment of the judges themselves.

If 12:31-50 qualifies as a recapitulation of narrative and argument, we are convinced that the extraordinary parade of Johannine *dramatis personae* who make a final appearance here functions in the conclusion as a rhetorical enumeration.[9] They make a strategic re-appearance illustrating varying types of "judgments" about Jesus, hence their presence serves the recapitulation by viewing and evaluating their reactions to him. To appreciate why these characters are highlighted, we must link them with their former appearance — another aspect of recapitulation. 1. *The Beloved of Bethany* were the object of Jesus' catechesis and his greatest sign (11:1-44). Now Mary's kindness exposes Judas the traitor (12:3-6), whom we already know to be a liar (6:64-65, 70-71). Lazarus' return to life provokes a new wave of envy against Jesus (12:9-11), for which he, alas, will die (again). 2. *Judas Iscariot* has constantly appeared as the most sinister person around Jesus; not only is he the one who will betray Jesus (6:64, 71), he is on the side of the Evil One: "One of you is a devil" (6:70).[10] Now we learn that he is not only a liar, but a thief and a dissembler (12:5-6). 3. *The Chief Priests* continue the role they assumed in 11:45-52 when they tried Jesus *in absentia* and sentenced him to death out of envy (12:19). Here, their envy of Jesus becomes violence also against Lazarus because of the sign value of his return to life (12:9-11); they too are murderers (8:44). 4. *The crowds* mentioned in

---

9. Not all characters reappear in John 12; missing are the mother of Jesus, Nicodemus, the Samaritan woman, the royal official, the man at the pool, the brothers of Jesus, and the man born blind.

10. Ronald A. Piper, "Satan, Demons and the Absence of Exorcisms in the Fourth Gospel," in *Christology, Controversy, and Community,* ed. David G. Horrell and Christopher M. Tuckett (Leiden: Brill, 2000) 253-78.

12:9, 12, 17, 18, 29 and 34, play diverse and conflicting roles as far back as the Bread of Life Discourse. Some "follow" Jesus (6:2, 24), but not as disciples; others are impressed by his signs (7:31). Mostly, the crowds are portrayed as divided in their judgment of Jesus, some praising him and others judging him (7:40-43; 9:16; 10:19-21; 11:36-37), the same pattern found in 12:29. Most of these are hostile outsiders (7:20), fixated on signs; others give no indication that they want to became disciples. 5. *Pharisees* have been Jesus' enemies from the start. Nicodemus, a Pharisee, came to Jesus at night and ridiculed Jesus' remarks (3:3, 5), only to be ridiculed in turn (3:10-12). Pharisees sought to arrest Jesus (7:32); they tried Jesus *in absentia* (7:47-52), the same pattern repeated in 11:45-52 and 12:19. Hence, along with the chief priests, they have become murderers. 6. *Philip, Andrew and the Greeks*. This episode resembles the recruitment of disciples in 1:36-51, but with some twists. Initially Andrew recruited his brother, Simon, and Philip brought Nathanael. In that sequence of the narrative, their recruitment was most praiseworthy. But here Greeks are not recruited, but come forward on their own; yet they need brokers, such as Andrew and Philip, to get to Jesus. Normally volunteers are set in their place by Jesus (Luke 9:57-62), the same strategy found in 12:23-25. 7. *Father-God*. Jesus just prayed to his Father at Lazarus' tomb (11:41-42), and prays again in 12:27-28. These two prayers, which differ in type and content, also tell us about the Father of Jesus.[11] At Lazarus' tomb, Jesus' prayer contains *thanksgiving* ("I thank you for you have heard me"), is *self-focused* ("I knew that you hear me always") and expresses *petitions* ("I have said this on behalf of the people standing by, that they may believe that you sent me"). But in 12:27-28 Jesus prays only one type of prayer: *petitionary* ("Father, save me from this hour" . . . "Father, glorify your name"). The first prayer occurs in the circle of those standing at Lazarus' tomb, but the latter one speaks directly to God about the voluntary character of Jesus' death (10:17-18). Thus Father-God authorizes Jesus' works of power, even as it is his will that Jesus undergo a life-producing death (12:24-25). 8. *Many, even of the Authorities*. From Nicodemus's appearance, they either come to Jesus at night or fear to acclaim him Christ in public. Among these we include the parents of the man born blind (9:22) and many, even of the authorities (12:42-43).

We have surveyed these characters within the framework of a judgment scenario which in 3:16-19 and 34-36 and 12:31-50 brackets the Book of Signs. Did people come into the light or remain in the darkness; what kind of acknowledgment did they show to Jesus, what adherence to him? Thus in a recapitulation

---

11. On types of prayer, see Jerome H. Neyrey, "Prayer, in Other Words: A Social-Science Model for Interpreting Prayers," *Social Scientific Models for Interpreting the Bible: Essays by The Context Group in Honor of Bruce J. Malina*, ed. John J. Pilch (Leiden: Brill, 2001) 349-80.

"*In Conclusion . . .*"

of their reaction to Jesus, we learn a classification system for evaluating what judgments people make and how they are rated by the Jesus group.

Judgment: Insiders Walking into the Light	Judgment: Outsiders Walking away from the Light
1. The Beloved of Bethany, "hard core" disciples: Lazarus favored with the premier sign; Martha, with extraordinary revelation from Jesus; Mary touches Jesus	1. People dominated by shame and fear: Parents of the man born blind; many even of the authorities
2. Philip and Andrew continue their earlier role of recruitment; significant roles in the multiplication of the loaves	2. Crowds critical of Jesus when the mass divides: some criticize Jesus, judge him unfavorably, and report gossip about him
3. Crowds acclaiming Jesus at a schism; some speak well of Jesus, give a favorable interpretation to his actions in the face of criticism	3. Judas the Iscariot: from the beginning Jesus knew who would betray him; exposed as thief, liar and soon, as murderer

This canvas of the *dramatis personae* argues that much, much more is being recapitulated in John 12 than just 3:16-19, 34-36. This in turn suggests that we are mistaken to split 12:31-43 from 43-50, because both blocks of material together summarize the judgment process dramatized in John 3–11.

4.0 Appeal to the Emotions[12]

Typically "appeal to the emotions" serves as a second but equally important element of a conclusion. "Appeal to emotions" serves as a significant rhetorical element in the conclusion, for it solidifies our judgment of the characters in John 12 in three ways. First, the audience has already been instructed on the correct emotional evaluation of the Trio from Bethany, whom Jesus labels "beloved." He even defends Mary against criticism. We are expected to evaluate them according to basic emotions such as love and hate. Second, balancing the praise

---

12. What is meant by "emotions" in rhetorical literature? First of all, we are considering "emotions," not "passions" or "desires." At the end of his address, the speaker seeks to "alter judgments" in those overseeing the case, trying to put them in a certain frame of mind (Aristotle, *Rhet.* 1.2.5; 2.1.8); these "emotions of the soul" are intended to shape an evaluation of the situation and prompt an appropriate response. See Wisse, *Ethos and Pathos from Aristotle to Cicero*, 65-75.

given to the Beloved of Bethany, the theme of judgment returns in John 12:31-50 which leads us to hold in contempt certain villains, such as the "ruler of this world" (12:31), hypocritical believers (12:42-43), and those who "do not receive my sayings" (12:47-48). The judgment, moreover, extends to the "murderers" who appear on stage: Judas, the chief priests, and the Pharisees. Third, the narrative presents characters in contrasting pairs, inviting us to praise one and blame the other: 1) Judas criticizes Mary; 2) the chief priests determine to kill Lazarus; 3) the crowds acclaiming Jesus drive the Pharisees to further envy of Jesus; 4) some declare that an angel spoke to Jesus, but others dismiss the noise as thunder; 5) Jesus says one thing about his death, but "crowds" use his reference to his death as grounds to dismiss him as the Christ (12:32-34); and finally 6) hostile unbelievers exercise control over hypocritical believers too fearful to acknowledge Jesus publicly (12:42-43). Andrew and Philip may be juxtaposed to the Greeks seeking Jesus; they were recruited, but the Greeks seem to be volunteering, not an honorable thing. And because "judgment" dominates John 12, the audience is urged to judge all of the persons in the six pair of contrasting characters. In this case, the author seeks to evoke in the audience an appropriate emotional response about them.

4.1 Rhetorical Theory about the Emotions

In order to see this in John 12, we need to know what "emotions" could and should be aroused. Thus our task requires us to make a brief inventory of emotions in antiquity, especially those most likely to be aroused here. In his *Rhetoric*, Aristotle, our primary informant,[13] instructed speakers to build an argument by attending to *pathos* (2.2-11), *ethos* (2.12-17) and *logos* (2.18-26).[14] "The emotions (πάθη)," he states, "are those things through which, by undergoing change, people come to differ in their judgments and which are accompanied by pain and pleasure, for example, anger, pity, fear and other such things and their opposites" (*Rhet.* 2.1.8). Emotions, he continues, come in pairs, i.e., binary opposition.[15] The following catalogue, drawn from Aristotle, *Rhet.* 2.2-9, is repeated in Cicero, *Orator* 131 and *De Oratione* 2.185.

---

13. See W. W. Fortenbaugh, *Aristotle on Emotion* (London: Duckworth, 1975) 12-22.
14. For a convenient view of these three items functioning in a rhetorical context, see DiCicco, *Paul's Use of Ethos, Pathos, and Logos*, 36-164. For a more restricted study, see Olbricht and Sumney, *Paul and Pathos*.
15. See G. E. R. Lloyd, *Polarity and Analogy: Two Types of Argumentation in Early Greek Thought* (Cambridge: Cambridge University Press, 1966).

"In Conclusion..."

Anger (ὀργή)	Mildness (πραότης)
Hate (μῖσος, ἔχθρος)	Love (φιλία)
Fear (φόβος)	Confidence (θάρσος)
Shame (αἰσύχνη)	Benevolent (χαρίζεσθαι)
Indignation (νέμεσις)	Pity (ἔλεος)
Envy (φθόνος)	Emulation (ζῆλος)

Later, Quintilian distilled the Aristotelian catalogue into two classes of emotions:

> Emotions fall into classes; the one is called πάθος by the Greeks and is rightly and correctly expressed in Latin by *adfectus* (emotion): the other is called ἦθος, a word for which in my opinion Latin has no equivalent; it is however rendered by *mores* (morals) and consequently the branch of philosophy known as ethics is styled *moral* philosophy. (*Inst. Orat.* 6.2.8, emphasis added)

Although Quintilian labels his two classes of emotions πάθος and ἦθος, he repeats the ancient system of classification by opposing violent and benevolent emotions:

> They explain πάθος as describing the more violent emotions and ἦθος as designating those which are calm and gentle: in one case the passions are violent, in the other subdued, the former command and disturb, the latter persuade and induce a feeling of goodwill. (*Inst. Orat.* 6.2.9-12)

Therefore we are advised to view the emotions as binary opposites, that is, as "violent or calm/gentle," which traditionally consist of six violent emotions (anger, hate, fear, shame, indignation, and envy) juxtaposed to six calm ones (mildness, love, confidence, benevolence, pity and emulation).

Yet we must still overcome a modern problem by learning what cultural meanings the ancients gave these emotions. We cannot presume that our meaning matches those of the ancients. Finally, it would be unwise to expect to find all of these emotions evoked in John 12. We take what we are given. What then are these emotions? What arouses them? To what kind of person are they directed? The following definition and commentary come directly from Aristotle's exposition in *Rhet.* 2.2-11.

4.2 Positive Emotions, Especially "Love"

What, then, are the meanings given by the ancients to the positive emotions: mildness, love, benevolence, and pity? Aristotle, as always, provides us with crisp, native meanings to them.

1. *Love* (φιλία) means "wanting for someone what one thinks are good things for him, not what benefits oneself." Ideally, love is mutual: it may also be the emotion we show to those who have benefited us. Love, moreover, means that people share the same loves and hates. My friend's enemies are my enemies.
2. *Benevolence* (χάρις). Having χάρις means offering a service to one in need for no other reason than as a boon to the recipient. The person receiving the χάρις is either greatly in need or in need of what is great and difficult.
3. *Pity* (ἔλεος) means pain at an apparently destructive or unpleasant evil happening to one who does not deserve it and which a person might expect either himself or his own to suffer. Pity is directed toward those closely related to one's household.

Because we hypothesize that "love" will be the dominant positive emotion aroused in the presentation of insiders, we should give it special attention, especially because it is the antithesis of "hate." To be certain "love" is by no means the romantic love dominant in Euro-American cultures, but has a strong element of commitment, loyalty and faithfulness in it. In attempting to see how the audience of the Fourth Gospel is expected to respond to characters in John 12, we should look quickly at "love" in the Fourth Gospel to see in what situations love is the appropriate reaction. We can profitably recover John's understanding of "love" by asking three questions: 1) Who loves whom? 2) What is love? and 3) Who does not love whom?

Who loves whom? The Gospel emphasizes that Jesus *loved* Lazarus (11:3) and the sisters (11:5). Jesus also loves the inner core of the disciples, loving them just as the Father has loved him (13:1; 15:9). The Father, too, is a great lover, for he loves Jesus (15:9) and those who love his Son (14:21). Finally, the core disciples are commanded to love one another (13:34-35; 15:12-13).

What is love? "Love" relationships in the Fourth Gospel are based on and expressed by several criteria, such as "Those who love me will *keep my word*" (14:23) or "If you love me you *will keep my commandments*" (14:15; see 15:10, 12, 14, 17). Love admits of degrees: "No one has greater love than this, to lay down one's life for one's friends" (15:13).

Who does not love whom? "Love" characterizes the relationships within the Jesus circle, but in two places we learn of people who emphatically do *not* belong to it, because they have no love for the Father (5:42); and because God is not their Father, they do not love Jesus (8:42; see 14:24). Love, then, reflects acceptance of Jesus' relationship to God.

"Love" serves as a marker for insider relationships (the Father, Jesus and the disciples). Only in the Farewell Address does Jesus issues commands, such as to "love," "keep on believing" (14:1) and "abide" (15:4-9). In fact, he commands the disciples to "abide in my love" (15:9-10). In a sense, all three commands blend into each other, such that together they suggest loyalty, faithfulness, attachment and constancy. Let us now consider the positive emotions appropriate to the characters in John 12.

The author would surely have us feel the emotion of love or "friendly feeling" for Bethany's Beloved Three. When they are introduced to us, we are schooled in the appropriate emotion to have toward them: if "beloved by Jesus" (11:3, 5), insiders should be attached to them as well. In 12:1-7, the same emotion is appropriate for them because of the friendship they show to Jesus: Martha served the meal, Mary displayed exquisite etiquette to Jesus, and Lazarus seated Jesus at the honorable place at his side. No doubt the author wants us to react to them with "love" or "friendly feeling." They received a χάρις both when they were greatly in need and when in need of what is great and difficult (Aristotle, *Rhet.* 2.3.4).

Lazarus is targeted for assassination (12:9-11), at which news we are expected to show "pity" for him. He does not deserve this; moreover, the animus against him is directed because of Jesus — he has done nothing to deserve death. Finally, inasmuch as Lazarus is targeted to die because of Jesus, his fate is pitiable in the eyes of disciples, some of whom will share the same fate (16:1-2; 21:19). Perhaps Lazarus also models the criterion for would-be disciples who are told formally that if they love their lives, they will die; but if they hate their lives, they will live (12:24-25). In addition to "love," the audience should experience "pity" for him because of his undeserved misfortune.

Crowds who go out to meet Jesus (12:12-18) are ambivalently portrayed. Yes, they publicly acknowledge Jesus: "Blessed is he who comes in the name of the Lord, even the King of Israel!" (12:13-15). Yet that is tempered by the observation that part of the group consists of people who were present when Jesus raised Lazarus and who, like spies or informers, bring news of this to Jesus' enemies (11:45-46). Nevertheless their public acknowledgment of Jesus stands in opposition to the silence of others who fear to confess him lest they be thrown out of synagogue (12:42-43). We suggest that a mild positive emotion is aroused toward them by the author, but no "friendly feeling." They are fringe people, not genuine insiders; they blow hot and cold. Although not blamed, they receive very modest praise.

The appropriate emotions toward Philip, Andrew and the Greeks are difficult to assess. The scene in 12:20-26 appears to be positive: Greeks want to see Jesus, but is this "recruitment" or "volunteering"? Earlier when Andrew recruited Peter and Philip recruited Nathanael, the expected reaction was thoroughgoing praise of them. But Philip and Andrew are not recruiting these Greeks, only facilitating access to Jesus. This is a different role, Jesus' reaction to which is not praise at all. If we are intended to remember that "no one can come to me unless the Father draws him" (6:44), then we are left with the question whether the Greeks are, in fact, recruited (by God or the disciples) or whether they are volunteering.[16] But is volunteering a praiseworthy and honorable thing? Volunteering, along with gifts, compliments, and requests, are considered positive challenges in the scenario of honor and shame.[17] All such put Jesus on the spot. He may not want such volunteers; moreover, if he takes them, he risks being indebted to them for their services. As he did with the volunteers in Matt 8:19-22 and Luke 9:57-62, he discourages them by making severe demands on them and by delivering a severe warning: "Unless a grain of wheat falls into the earth and dies, it remains just a single grain; but if it dies, it bears much fruit. Those who love their life lose it, and those who hate their life in this world will keep it for eternal life" (12:24-25). We are not told if they accepted this, so the audience is left without data to conclude that they are genuine followers. But if Jesus' word indeed caused fear in them, then they are not genuine candidates for discipleship. What emotion does the author want us to have toward them? Nothing positive is being praised. Not foes, but yet not friends either. No news is probably bad news.

Negative Emotions, Especially "Hate." If "love" is aroused toward noble characters, we should investigate if "hate" is the emotion aroused for characters negatively portrayed in John 12. We recall that the rhetorical tradition about emotions understood them as binary opposites.[18] Thus, "love" balances "hate" and "mildness" contrasts with "anger." Again, what did the ancients mean by the negative emotions "anger," "hate," "indignation" and "envy"?

---

16. For a social-science description of "volunteering" and why it is a honor challenge, see Jerome H. Neyrey, "Call and Commitment in the New Testament," *Horizon* 31 (2006): 26; see also Bruce J. Malina, *The New Testament World. Insights from Cultural Anthropology* (3rd ed.; Louisville, KY: Westminster John Knox, 2001) 33-36.

17. Similar to volunteering, requests are also considered as positive challenges, albeit mild. See C. H. Giblin, "Suggestion, Negative Response, and Positive Action in St. John's Portrayal of Jesus (2:1-11; 4:46-54; 7:2-14; 11:1-44)," *NTS* 26 (1980): 197-211.

18. Inevitably modern readers will ask about the morality of hating another. In heroic Greece, we are told, it was considered a virtue to hate one's enemies; W. B. Stanford, *Sophocles: "Ajax"* (Salem, NH: Ayer Co., 1985). Although the dramatists portrayed excessive hate as the cause of destruction to some heroes, hatred was a regular factor of social life: see Mary W. Blundell, *Helping Friends and Harming Enemies* (Cambridge: Cambridge University Press, 1989), and Elaine Fantham, "'Envy and Fear the Begetter of Hate': Statius' *Thebaid* and the Genesis of Hatred," in *The Passions in Roman Thought and Literature*, ed. Susanna Braund and Christopher Gill (Cambridge: Cambridge University Press, 1997) 185-212. The strongest criticism of hate came from the Stoics, not because of its social harm but because it was a passion and so was unreasonable.

"In Conclusion . . ."

Anger (ὀργή) means a desire for revenge for a real or imagined slight. "Slight" (ὀλιγωρία), the judgment that someone appears valueless, has three kinds: disdain (καταφρόνησις), spitefulness (ἐπηρεασμός), and insult (ὕβρις).

Hate/Enmity (μῖσος, ἔχθος) goes much further than anger.[19] Anger, a response to injury which seeks revenge or vengeance, is cured in time because retaliation may lead to mildness (πραότης). But no possible means exists to moderate or erase hatred. It endures! Instead of retaliation, hatred seeks to cause only evil to the offender.[20]

Indignation (νέμεσις) describes the pain someone feels at the *undeserved* good fortune of another, and so differs from envy which is pain at another *deserved* good fortune.

Envy (φθόνος), like indignation, is pain at the sight of another prospering; the one who envies does not seek the fortune or prosperity of another, only desires that the possessor NOT have it.[21]

As we did with "love" in the Fourth Gospel, let us repeat the process with "hate."

Who hates whom? Some hate the light (3:20); the world hates Jesus (7:7; 15:18, 24) as well as his disciples (15:18). Whoever hates Jesus also hates the Father (15:23-24). Finally, disciples themselves must "hate": "He who hates his life in this world will keep it for eternal life" (12:25). Thus "hate" suggests radical animosity between Jesus and company and "the world," an alarming concept. "Hate" means a radical boundary line.

Why do people hate? In some cases, those in darkness refused to come into the light "lest their deeds be exposed" (3:20). Hence we see evil persons fearing loss of face. Similarly, in 12:43 we observe potential disciples failing to be forthright about Jesus because they too are afraid to lose face: "They loved

---

19. Quintilian makes an excellent point about "hate": "There are two kinds of *invidia* (hatred, envy), to which the two adjectives *invidius* (envy) and *invidiosus* (hatred) apply. . . . For though some things are hateful in themselves such as parricide, murder, poisoning, other things have to be made to seem hateful. This latter contingency arises when we attempt to shew that what we have suffered is of a more horrible nature than what are generally regarded as evils" (*Inst. Orat.* 6.2.21-22).

20. "Hate" is directed to Jesus (3:20; 7:7; 15:18), his disciples (15:18-24; 17:14). The world is not just "angry" at Jesus and company, but hates them and wishes to destroy them utterly. Fundamentally, Jesus and company do not belong to this world, which hates those who are not its own. Furthermore, Jesus tells would-be disciples that "He who hates his life in this world will keep it for eternal life" (12:25). "Hate" here suggests willingness to be crushed by evil, an acceptance of hate from others.

21. See Jerome H. Neyrey and Anselm C. Hagedorn, "'It Was Out of Envy that They Handed Jesus Over' (Mark 15:10): The Anatomy of Envy and the Gospel of Mark," *JSNT* 69 (1998): 15-56.

the praise of men more than the praise of God." Cowards deserve hate. Finally, disciples themselves are hated because they "do not belong to the world" (15:18-19).

Who cannot be hated? The brothers of Jesus cannot be hated by the world because they belong to it and try to manipulate Jesus (7:7).

5.0 To Hate or Not to Hate?

5.1 Hate in the New Testament

Even as we claim that hate is an appropriate emotion toward certain characters in John 12, we are confronted with an immediate problem. We have sayings of Jesus which seem to preclude "hate" by his disciples: "You have heard that it was said, 'You shall love your neighbor and hate your enemy.' But I say to you, love your enemies" (Matt 5:43-44). Other remarks, however, indicate a less rigid meaning of hate. Jesus himself said, "If any one comes to me and does not hate his own father and mother and wife and children and brothers and sisters, he cannot be my disciple" (Luke 14:26; John 12:25). Jesus, then, commands disciples to "hate" their closest kin. Jesus also tells the Ephesians that he too hates: "You hate the works of the Nicolaitans, which I also hate" (Rev 2:6). Furthermore, God loves and hates: "Jacob I loved, Esau I hated" (Mal 1:2-3; Rom 9:13). Proverbs provides a list of things that God himself hates: "There are six things which the Lord hates: haughty eyes, a lying tongue, and hands that shed blood, a heart that devises wicked plans, feet that make haste to run to evil, a false witness who breathes out lies, and a man who sows discord among brothers" (6:16-19). Furthermore, hate is what the disciples regularly receive from others: hated by outsiders (Matt 10:22; 24:9; Mark 13:13) and by apostates (Matt 24:10). "Hate," then, is both given and received, but is it part of the repertoire of Christian behavior? What does it mean? The data suggest that hate is by no means a proscribed emotion.

5.2 The Old Testament on "Hate"

A brief survey of the uses of "hate" in the Scriptures indicates a spectrum of attitudes to it. 1. Hate = *voluntary separation from someone or something,* as in "I hate the company of the evildoers" (Ps 26:5) and "hating father, mother, wife and children" (Luke 14:26). Conversely, evil people separate themselves from the group: "Those who hate reproof, walk in the sinner's steps" (Sir 21:6).

2. Hate = *virtuous choice, as in loving good and hating evil:* "The Lord loves those who hate evil" (Ps 97:10; see Ps 45:7) and "Hate what is evil but hold fast to what is good" (Rom 12:9). 3. Hate = *the fate of the wicked, often a desire for vengeance:* "I will repay those who hate me" (Deut 32:41, 43). "Those who hated me I destroyed" (Ps 18:40; see Ps 21:8).[22] "Those who hate me may be put to shame" (Ps 86:17; Ps 68:1). 4. Hate = *hostility and enmity received,* as in "Consider how many are my foes, and with what hatred they hate me" (Ps 25:19); "Let not those [my foes] wink the eye who hate me without cause" (Ps 35:19).[23] Thus, we discover a spectrum in the understanding of "hate." It has positive meanings: separation and choice: it is good to hate the company of evildoers and to love virtue and hate iniquity, as well as negative meanings: the fate of those who hate and show hostility/enmity. "Hate," then, because it is a positive choice for good, is acceptable behavior. Everyone hates, even God.

5.3 Hate in the Greco-Roman World

Aristotle offers a rare definition of "hate." First he describes it from its opposite, "friendliness." If "friendliness" is "wanting for someone what one thinks is good for him" (*Rhet.* 2.4.2), then "hate" desires evil for someone.[24] Second, Aristotle contrasts it with its close cousin, "anger."

---

22. In the Scriptures, then, revenge and hate are praised as virtues (Deut 7:1-9; 20:16; 32:41; Pss 26:5; 137:7-9; 139:19-22). In this case, you "hate" an enemy, especially someone who has done you a harm.

23. There are four more usages of "hate" that are worth considering. 1) *Hyperbole.* Jacob is said to have "loved Rachel more than Leah" (Gen 29:30) such that Leah considered herself "hated" (29:33). Inasmuch as Jacob begat a flock of children through her, this suggests that what is called "hate" is close to "love less." 2) *From love to hate.* Amnon once "loved" his sister Tamar; but after he raped her, "the hatred with which he hated her was greater than the love with which he had loved her" (2 Sam 13:15). Amnon's hatred springs not from some injury to him by Tamar, but from his change in family loyalty to her after he injured her. 3) *No loyalty.* A man cannot serve two masters, for he will love one and hate the other (Matt 6:24). If "love" suggests faithfulness, then "hate" means an absence of loyalty and allegiance. 4) *Ethnic love and hate.* Tacitus writes of the Judeans: "The Jews are extremely loyal toward one another, and always ready to show compassion, but toward every other people they feel only hate and enmity" (*Histories* 5.5). Again, this appears to be a matter of loyalty and compassion to insiders and suspicion and separation from outsiders.

24. The antithetical character of emotions is a constant in any discussion of them. For example, Cicero says that the aim of a speaker is to make the jury "angry or appeased, to feel ill will or to be well disposed . . . scorn or admiration, hatred or love, desire or loathing" (*Orator* 131; see also 2.185).

Anger	Hate
1. Curable in time	1. Not curable in time[25]
2. Desires that another suffer pain	2. Desires that another suffer evil
3. Accompanied by pain	3. Not accompanied by pain
4. May feel pity after retaliation	4. Never feels pity, under any circumstance
5. Wants object of anger to suffer	5. Wants objects of hate not to exist

Whom, then, do we hate? According to Aristotle, we hate those who belong to a detested class of people, such as "a thief and a spy" or an "enemy" (ἐχθρός), who is both a personal as well as a national enemy, with whom no cessation of hostilities or truce is possible. Yet, as Elaine Fantham notes, "For Aristotle, emotions such as anger and hatred could be 'reasonable,' warranted by certain types of provocation and useful in ensuring the defense of innocence and punishment of evil."[26] Finally, a popular maxim instructed Greeks to "help one's friends and harm one's enemies," that is, to seek revenge for a injury suffered.

Plutarch's treatise "Envy and Hatred" provides an analysis of hate closer to the meaning that is found in early Christian literature. As regards its origin, "Hate arrives when a person is bad either in general or toward oneself (i.e., an aggressor). It is men's nature to hate when they think they have been wronged. Men view with disgust all who in any other way are given to wrong doing or to wickedness." Thus, we hate those who have wronged us. Hatred, moreover, may in fact be virtuous: "Many are hated with justice, as those we call 'deserving of hate.' Hatred of wickedness is among the things we praise." Plutarch provides an interesting example of virtuous hating.

> Those who brought false charges against Socrates, being held to have reached the limit of baseness, were so hated and shunned by their countrymen that no one would lend them light for a fire, answer their questions, or bathe in the same water, but poured it out as polluted, until the men hanged themselves, finding the hatred unendurable.

---

25. Following the universal penchant to distinguish items, Cicero provides a useful description of aggressive emotions: "*Anger* is the lust of punishing the man who is thought to have inflicted an undeserved injury; *rage* on the other hand is anger springing up and suddenly showing itself, termed in Greek θύμωσις; *hate* is inveterate anger; *enmity* is anger watching for an opportunity for revenge; *wrath* is anger of greater bitterness conceived in the innermost heart and soul" (*Tusculan Disputations* 4.9.21). Hatred is "inveterate": it never ceases or moderates.

26. Fantham, "'Envy and Fear the Begetter of Hate': Statius' 'Thebaid' and the Genesis of Hatred," 185-212.

He approves of the hatred by the polis, which not only separates the good from the wicked, but is assuaged only by the death of the wicked (for the death of Socrates).

5.4 Summary

What have we learned about "hate"? 1) Who hates? All persons, including Jesus and God, hate. 2) What is hate? Hate enjoys a wide spectrum of meaning: from the mild "love less," to a taste for vengeance and then to a desire for evil. When juxtaposed with "love," "hate" suggests a refusal to show loyalty, faithfulness and allegiance.[27] 3) Can hate be virtuous? Yes, for it serves to make a voluntary separation from wickedness and from one's family who block one's allegiance to Jesus. It encourages the detestation of types and classes of people, such as thieves and the like. We hypothesize that in John 12 the author seeks to arouse "hate" in a meaning closest to Aristotle's definition of it noted above. Strong, robust, give-no-quarter "hate."

6.0 Hate and the Fourth Gospel

The verb "to hate" is not found in John 12, but that does not mean that hatred is absent. Except for "beloved," none of the other emotions we surveyed are identified, but that does not mean that others are not operative. When assessing each character in John 12, readers ancient and modern are required to judge what kind of character each is, that is, whether they belong to the world below or to the world of Jesus, what actions have been done or not done by them, what relationship they have to Jesus or do not have. On the basis of this the author wants his audience to react. The premier question is "Are they friends or foes?" Let us now begin assessing what emotions the author wants to arouse in us in regard to various characters who come before us in John 12. Paraded before us are Judas, the chief priests, Pharisees, those who intimidate believers. What is urged? Hate? Anger? Indignation?

Judas Iscariot. We are told in 12:4-6 that Judas was a liar and a thief. While claiming concern for the poor, as keeper of the purse he "used to take what was put into it." This comes on top of an earlier revelation that Judas belongs to the world of devils ("one of you is a devil," 6:70), an identification to be repeated

---

27. Joel Green (*The Gospel of Luke* [Grand Rapids, MI: Eerdmans, 1997] 565) defined "hate" as "a disavowal of primary allegiance to one's kin."

shortly in 13:2 ("the devil had already put it into the heart of Judas Iscariot to betray him"). Already identified as Jesus' "betrayer" (6:64, 71), he will shortly demonstrate this by aiding those who wish to kill Jesus. He is, then, a liar, a thief, and a murderer (8:44). The appropriate emotional reaction to Judas is hate (μῖσος) not anger (ὀργή). Anger seeks conspicuous retaliation, which can change into "mildness" ("Let mildness be defined as a settling down and quieting of anger," *Rhet.* 2.3.2). No possible satisfaction can be gotten from Judas for his behavior because he belongs to the world of Satan, whom one should also hate. No calming of anger is possible. Hate, moreover, comes from perceiving another as being a certain type of person: "everyone hates the thief and the sycophant" (*Rhet.* 2.4.31). Judas is clearly a liar, a thief, and a murderer. Anger is curable and of limited duration, but not hate, which admits no cure and which rages indefinitely. Indeed hatred of Judas would be a virtue.

Chief Priests. As we strive to learn what emotions we should have to the Chief Priests, we are invited to learn what emotions drive them in 11:47-48. They sentenced Jesus to death out of indignation (νέμεσις), not envy (φθόνος). Envy is aroused against someone, a peer, who *legitimately* has some good or fortune, which pains the one envying to see. The one who envies labors to cut that success down to size. An indignant person, however, is pained at seeing someone, generally a social inferior, enjoy *unworthy* success. The chief priests certainly do not acknowledge that Jesus deserves legitimate respect, thus act out of envy; for in their eyes he is a deceiver, a law-breaker and a blasphemer. *Indignation* drives actions against Jesus, as well as their plot to kill Lazarus, and so destroy the chief source of Jesus' rising honor (12:9-11, 19). But should the audience of the Gospel "hate" them? Their judgment of Jesus warrants negative emotions. While they are portrayed as acting out of base self-interest, the audience knows them only as Jesus' constant critics, even those who seek to arrest him and kill him. As the Gospel goes, they are Jesus' consummate enemies. Hatred of them would be a virtue in John's group.

Turning to the audience in John 12, what emotion(s) are being aroused in them? What emotions are appropriate to the audience who perceive the High Priests as murderers? At first, *anger* appears to be the appropriate emotion because of their plans to murder Jesus and Lazarus. Since anger means retaliation, this may be suggested ironically in the remark they make about Jesus' success: "The Romans will come and destroy both our holy place and our nation" (11:48) — God's retribution. The very thing they seek to forestall will come about by their very actions. But the Johannine audience seems never to consider revenge an option in its conflicts with the Jerusalem elites, but rather complete and permanent separation. *Anger*, then, is not what is aroused. However, they represent a class of persons that all should hate, namely, murderers, such as Ishmael, Cain and his father (the devil), and those who plot to stone Jesus (8:44). They are, then, evil characters, of whom Jesus says, "They have hated me without cause" (15:25). Guilty of indignation toward Jesus, they seek moreover to destroy Jesus, that is, to murder him. The audience should hate them.

Pharisees. In the narrative, the Pharisees continually judged Jesus: as an improper witness (8:13), a "sinner" (9:16, 24), and as a nowhere man (9:29). Twice they conducted trials of Jesus, albeit illegal because in both instances Jesus was absent (7:45-52; 11:46-48). Moreover they agreed with the chief priests to put Jesus to death (11:53), even ordering those who knew of Jesus' whereabouts to report to them (11:57). Readers were schooled to judge them as unjust judges who judge according to appearances or out of indignation, which recurs in the conclusion.

> If we let him go on thus, every one will believe in him (11:48)
> You see that you can do nothing; look, the world has gone after him (12:19).

The appropriate emotion toward them is the same as for the high priests, namely, hate. There is an irreconcilable enmity between them and Jesus, which can only be assuaged with the death of Jesus. This enmity will never end nor can it be excused or erased. In John's logic, they will remain indignant and murderous. Hate is the appropriate reaction to them.

Certain "Authorities" (12:42) try to prohibit people from publicly acknowledging Jesus. It seems safe to include both Pharisees and Chief Priests in this remark. They declare a rule (do not acclaim Jesus as Messiah) to which they attach a penalty (expulsion from the synagogue). In harming others or causing them to stumble, they harm the Jesus group as well. If these "authorities" are Pharisees and chief priests, this behavior only adds to the judgment of them as deserving hate.

Those Silenced by the Authorities. They too are the subject of critical judgment by the Evangelist. They lack courage to speak publicly of Jesus or to come to him in the daylight or openly. To these the author would have us feel "anger-as-slight." *Slight* (ὀλιγωρία), the emotion we feel toward what is worthless, comes in three flavors: "contempt" (καταφρόνησις), "spite" (ἐπηρεασμός), and "insult" (ὕβρις). We judge that the author is trying to appeal to the emotion of "anger-as-slight and contempt." Again Aristotle, "One who shows contempt belittles; people have contempt for those things that they think of no account" (*Rhet.* 2.1.4). Contempt, then, means withdrawing honor or worth from some person. Those who show contempt are thus shaming (αἰσύχνη) and bringing another into dishonor.

The Crowds. Finally, as we noted, the crowds typically divide in their evaluations of Jesus. What emotion is appropriate to those who misunderstand or challenge Jesus at this point? To them the heavenly voice which spoke to Jesus is only "thunder" (12:29). A second misunderstanding occurs when they challenge Jesus (12:32-34). Thus the crowds in 12:29 and 34 should be treated as having no worth, and so deserve contempt. They are not enemies as are the Pharisees and Chief Priests, nor do they plot Jesus' death. Not hate, but contempt is appropriate to them.

7.0 Summary, Conclusions, and Further Questions

Since a good conclusion highlights the major points of an argument, we know now what a rhetorical conclusion is, its parts, and its purposes. The point of judgment is whether it is an appropriate model for reading and interpreting John 12. This pushes the argument one step further, what is a good or appropriate model? Rhetoric is rhetoric; all writers in antiquity employed some of the arts of communication and persuasion. "Conclusion" seems appropriate because it is rooted in ancient rhetoric; this is the way the ancients thought and wrote. It is also appropriate in the sense that, like all models, it surfaces data — especially data that other models do not — and provides a system in which to interpret the data discovered. Hence, using this rhetorical model, we are by no means imposing a meaning on John 12, but surfacing its data and synthesizing it in a way suitable to ancient discourse.

Given this argument, what can we say about the educational level of the author of the Fourth Gospel? It would seem that the person who composed and wrote John 1–12 was minimally schooled in the middle stages of education where the progymnasmata were taught, but might also have had more elite training in rhetoric. The use of classical rhetoric here is hardly unique in the Fourth Gospel, for he knows the topos on "noble death"[28] and the contents of the encomium and vituperation.[29]

If John 1:1-18 is a prologue which finds its conclusion in John 12, then what about John 13:1-3 and a second conclusion? It would seem that John 20–21 would serve that rhetorical role, for all the major characters in John 13–19 return to the scene, such as the Beloved Disciple, Mary Magdalene and Peter. As

---

28. Jerome H. Neyrey, "The 'Noble' Shepherd in John 10: Cultural and Rhetorical Background," pp. 282-312 in the present volume.

29. Jerome H. Neyrey, "Encomium vs Vituperation: Contrasting Portraits of Jesus in the Fourth Gospel," pp. 3-28 in the present volume.

"In Conclusion..."

we see them in John 20–21, we are instructed once more how to think about them in terms of their relationship to Jesus, either confirming them as elites or as redeeming them from their folly. By the end of the story, we know that all of them "love" Jesus, and so the audience is instructed to "love" them. These sketchy ideas, however, need to be worked out in some detail. But if they make rhetorical sense, then the second pair of prologue and conclusion would indeed confirm the presence and function of the first pair.

14

The Footwashing in John 13:6-11

Transformation Ritual or Ceremony?

Introduction and Hypothesis

Scholars often note the complications in the narrative of the footwashing in John 13:4-20.[1] The Evangelist first narrates Jesus' washing of Peter's feet along with conversation with Peter (13:4-11), but he reports a discourse about footwashing, which is addressed to all of the disciples (13:12-20). Upon inspection, the remarks in 13:12-20 hardly serve as an adequate or proper explanation for the events in 13:6-11.[2]

The similarities between 13:6-11 and 12-20 remain deceptive,[3] and the differences deserve attention.[4]

---

1. The distinction between 13:6-11 and 12-20 has become a commonplace in Johannine scholarship; see Fernando Segovia, "John 13:1-20: The Footwashing in the Johannine Tradition," *ZNW* 73 (1982): 31; Arland Hultgren, "The Johannine Footwashing (13:1-11) as Symbol of Eschatological Hospitality," *NTS* 28 (1982): 539-40; Karl Kleinknecht, "Johannes 13, die Synoptiker und die 'Methode' der Johanneischen Evangelienüberlieferung," *ZTK* 82 (1985): 366-68.

2. R. Bultmann (*The Gospel of John* [Philadelphia: Westminster, 1971] 466-67) insisted that there are two interpretations of the footwashing, 13:6-11 and 12-20. Similar observations can be found in Edwyn Hoskyns, *The Fourth Gospel* (London: Faber and Faber, 1947) 436-39; M.-E. Boismard, "Le lavement des pieds (Jn, XIII, 1-17)," *RB* 71 (1964): 5-24; Georg Richter, "Die Fusswaschung Joh 13,1-20," *Studien zum Johannesevangelium* (Regensburg: Pustet, 1977) 42-57; and Herold Weiss, "Footwashing in the Johannine Community," *NovT* 21 (1971): 301-2.

3. For example, Jesus "washes the feet" of disciples (13:5, 10, 14). Peter calls him "Lord" (13:6), a label which Jesus uses about his role and status (13:13, 14). At the end of both interpretations, someone is cryptically identified as a misfit in the group (13:10-11, 18). And in both cases, the disciples are reminded of the special meaning of some special word, either Jesus' own remark (13:10b-11) or a citation of Psalm 41 (13:18). In both a contrast is made between "now" and "then," contrasting present ignorance with future understanding (13:7, 19).

4. Commentators distinguish the two interpretations in 13:6-11 and 12-20 in three basic ways:

1. Simon Peter emerges as Jesus' only conversation partner in 13:6-9, whereas all the disciples are addressed collectively in 13:12-20.
2. Peter is emphatically told "You do *not* know" (13:7) but will understand later, whereas all of them are clearly "in the know" during the interpretation: "You know what I have done" (13:12). "I have given you an example" (13:15) which leads to happiness, "If you know these things, blessed are you if you do them" (13:17).[5]
3. Jesus tells Peter, "Unless I wash . . ." (13:8), whereas they "ought" to wash others' feet (13:14) — quite different notions of obligation.
4. Jesus' action will make Simon and others "pure" (13:10-11), whereas their performance of this toward others will make them "happy" (13:17).
5. The final word in 13:10 identifies someone who is not pure, "You are clean, but not every one of you," which is applied to Jesus' betrayer in a form of Gnostic midrash by the author himself: "He knew who was to betray him; that was why he said, 'You are not all clean'" (13:11). In contrast, during the interpretation following the footwashing Jesus alludes to a traitor, "I am not speaking of you all; I know whom I have chosen" (13:18); in a prophecy-fulfillment mode, he quotes Ps 41:9 about a treacherous table companion. "Clean" and "chosen" are quite different things, as are Jesus' own words and a snatch of psalm.
6. Even the "now–later" distinction functions differently: Peter does not understand *now*, but will *later* (13:7), whereas all of them are told *now,* so that *later* when the prophecy comes true, they will remain faithful (13:19). 13:6-11 and 12-20 are not doublets.

I suggest that the footwashing in 13:6-11 signifies something quite different from the action described in 13:12-20. Surely some event on Jesus' part warrants the notice of it as an "example," which Jesus commands be repeated (13:15, 17).[6] But what the narrator describes in 13:6-11 is a distinctively Johannine conversa-

---

Boismard ("Le lavement," 6-8, 18-20) contrasted sacramental with moral interpretations (see also Rudolf Schnackenburg, *The Gospel According to St. John* [New York: Crossroad, 1982] 3.21); Georg Richter (*Die Fusswaschung im Johannesevangelium* [Regensburg: Pustet, 1967] 252-78) distinguished a christological interpretation from a sacramental interpretation; Bultmann (*The Gospel of John*, 467) juxtaposed a cleansing by hearing the revealer's word with a gesture of humility.

5. It is generally agreed that 13:12-20 do not give Peter the knowledge that Jesus said in 13:7 he lacks; see Hoskyns, *The Fourth Gospel*, 438.

6. Commentators who concern themselves with the growth of the Fourth Gospel identify 13:4-5 as the "action" which is then interpreted; see Robert T. Fortna, *The Gospel of Signs: A Reconstruction of the Narrative Source Underlying the Fourth Gospel* (SNTSMS 11; Cambridge: Cambridge University Press, 1970) 155-56.

tion[7] about an unrepeatable action. What Jesus does to Simon and says to him about "purification" in 13:6-11 simply does not match what is discussed in 13:12-20, an action of hospitality which is presumably repeated when the Johannine group gathers.

Notions of "ritual" and "ceremony" drawn from cultural anthropology can serve as an important lens for sharpening our perception of 13:6-11 and explaining the differences between the two accounts of Jesus' symbolic action. "Ritual" refers to rites of status transformation, such as baptism, marriage, ordination, death, in which individuals change status and role. "Ceremony" refers to rites which confirm roles and statuses, such as anniversaries, temple rites, annual games, feast days, and the like. In 13:6-11 Peter is urged to undergo a status transformation *ritual* to become "wholly clean" and so have a special *inheritance* or place with Jesus. In 13:12-20, however, the disciples are told to practice a *ceremony* in which their role and status are confirmed by their acts of hospitality to group members. As I hope to show, Peter's footwashing *ritual* has to do with his transformation into the role of an elite, public witness to Jesus with accompanying risk of death — a one-time event, whereas the *ceremony* which the disciples will perform to members of their circle confirms their role and status as leaders of the group — an action to be repeated regularly. The author describes two different rites in 13:4-11 and 12-20, and the use of materials from anthropology offers a fruitful way of clarifying the social dynamics of the narrative.

1.0 Cultural Anthropology: Transforming Rituals and Confirming Ceremonies

Among others, Victor Turner observes the difference between rites which transform and which confirm:

> I consider the term 'ritual' to be more fittingly applied to forms of religious behavior associated with social *transitions*, while the term 'ceremony' has a

---

7. The Johannine redactional elements include: 1) Simon Peter as a "representative character" (see R. F. Collins, "Representative Figures in the Fourth Gospel," *DR* 94 [1976]: 26-46, 118-32); 2) statement-misunderstanding-clarification (see Jerome H. Neyrey, *An Ideology of Revolt* [Philadelphia: Fortress, 1988] 42, 234, numbers 10 and 11); 3) dialogue with a disciple (see R. Schnackenburg, *The Gospel According to St. John*, 3.18); 4) knowing vs. not knowing; 5) purification (2:6; 15:3); 6) "unless. . ." demands; 7) laying down and taking up (see R. E. Brown, *The Gospel according to John XIII–XXI* [AB 29a; Garden City: Doubleday, 1970] 551); and 8) now vs. then.

closer bearing on religious behavior associated with religious *states*. . . . Ritual is transformative, ceremony confirmatory.[8]

The following diagram should aid us in comparing and contrasting status change *rituals* and *ceremonies* which confirm status.[9]

Transformation Ritual	Characteristic	Confirming Ceremony
1. Irregular pauses	**Frequency**	1. Regular pauses
2. Unpredictable, when needed	**Calendar**	2. Predictable, planned for
3. From present to future	**Time Focus**	3. From past to present
4. Professionals, who legitimately cross boundaries	**Presided over by**	4. Officials, who are entrusted with maintaining the system
5. Transformation in role/status — elevation or degradation	**Function**	5. Confirmation of role/status in institutions of kinship or politics

Frequency: Both transformations and ceremonies represent pauses in life's rhythms. Certain pauses occur irregularly (sickness, purification, marriage, etc.) which allow us to assume new and different roles and statuses. Other pauses, which occur routinely in our lives, we call *ceremonies* (meals, birthdays, anniversaries, holidays, etc.). These do not effect change of role or status, but confirm them.

Calendar: Transformational pauses occur unpredictably; we undergo them when necessary or timely. No one plans to be ill or unclean; but when sickness or pollution occurs, rituals for changing from those states are needed. Some rituals are unrepeatable status changes, such as birth and parenthood and death. On the other hand, ceremonial pauses occur on fixed calendar dates, such as Sabbath, Passover, Tabernacles, Dedication, Pentecost, etc. These we anticipate and plan for.

---

8. Victor Turner, *The Forest of Symbols: Aspects of Ndembu Ritual* (Ithaca: Cornell University Press, 1967) 95 (emphasis added); see also Raymond Firth and John Skorupski, *Symbol and Theory: A Philosophical Study of Theories of Religion in Social Anthropology* (Cambridge: Cambridge University Press, 1976) 164.

9. This represents a systematization of Bruce Malina, *Christian Origins and Cultural Anthropology: Practical Models for Biblical Interpretation* (Atlanta: John Knox Press, 1986) 139-43. See also Jerome Neyrey, *Paul in Other Words* (Louisville: Westminster John Knox Press, 1990) 76-80, and Mark McVann, "Rituals of Status Transformation in Luke-Acts: The Case of Jesus the Prophet," in *The Social World of Luke-Acts: Models for Interpretation*, ed. Jerome H. Neyrey (Peabody, MA: Hendrickson Publishers, 1991) 334-36.

Time Focus: Transformational pauses take us from present needs to the future, as we change our current status and are transformed so as to assume a new role in the future. Ceremonies, however, look to the past and celebrate its influence on the present. Past relationships, roles and statuses continue to exist even into the present and influence present social dynamics.

Presiding: Different kinds of people preside over transformations and ceremonies. *Professionals* (physicians, prophets, lawyers, police, etc.) preside over or direct status transformations. These are the "limit breakers" whom society allows to deal with marginal people as they cross fixed social lines.[10] *Officials* (father and mother, high priest, elders) preside at Shabbat or Passover meals, offer sacrifice in the Temple and serve as judges at trials. They preside over or direct the appropriate *rites* in their institutions to maintain relationships and societal order.

Function: Ceremonies leave in place the lines of the maps of society, because they function to *confirm* the values and structures of society, to *affirm* its purity system and to *celebrate* the orderly classification of persons, places and things in the cosmos.[11] For example, birthdays, anniversaries, pilgrimage feasts and the like confirm the roles and statuses of individuals in the group as well as the group's collective sense of holy space and holy time which pertain to its festivals. Ceremonies look to the stability of the lines of society's maps. Conversely, transformation rituals attend precisely to those lines, but focus on their crossing. Rituals are stable ways of dealing with necessary *instability* and *change* in the system: a boy and a girl cross lines to become husband and wife in marriage; sick people cross lines and become healthy (Lev 14; Mark 1:44); sinners become purified (Luke 18:13-14). The converse is also true: a seemingly innocent person may become guilty through a ritual trial. The status of those who cross lines is thereby *changed,* either as a status elevation or degradation. If ceremonies look to the center of the map and the stable lines which make up the map, rituals look to the map's boundaries. These should be stable, but may be legitimately crossed.

---

10. "Limit breaker" is the term Bruce Malina (*Christian Origins and Cultural Anthropology,* 144-54) uses to identify the professional whom society authorizes to lead people across lines and boundaries usually judged dangerous.

11. On "purity systems" and "symbolic universes," see Jerome H. Neyrey, "The Symbolic Universe of Luke-Acts: 'They Turn the World Upside Down,'" in *The Social World of Luke-Acts,* ed. Neyrey, 271-304.

The Footwashing in John 13:6-11

2.0 Footwashing (13:6-11) as a Ritual of Status Transformation

Using our model of a ritual, let us examine Jesus' washing of Peter's feet.

1. *Frequency:* This ritual occurs just once in the Fourth Gospel.[12] Since the meal had begun when Jesus rose to wash his disciples' feet, this ritual occurs as an irregular pause in a ceremonial meal.
2. *Calendar:* The narrator locates the general meal in the context of Passover, a fixed calendar date (13:1). Because the footwashing in 13:4-11 is not a fixed element of Passover or any other known Jewish meal, it is an irregular, unpredictable pause; it arises then because it was needed ("Unless. . .").
3. *Time Focus:* The present footwashing looks to the future: "Unless I wash you, you have no part in me (now and in the future)" (13:8). The narrator evokes no past action of Jesus here, as in 13:14-15; rather future association with Jesus depends on what is presently happening.
4. *Presiding:* Jesus presides over the ritual. Were this an act of hospitality which welcomed guests to a ceremonial meal, Jesus would be an official of the kinship institution which celebrated its commitment through commensality. But his washing of Peter's feet has nothing to do with hospitality or meal participation. This action will make Peter "wholly clean," a status which he cannot now enjoy, unless Jesus performs this ritual. Jesus, then, acts here as a professional, not an official. He allows Peter to cross from one status ("already bathed") to a better status ("wholly clean").
5. *Purpose:* Whatever role and status Peter enjoyed prior to 13:6, Jesus requires that he undergo this ritual for two reasons. First, unless he accepts this, "You will have no part in me." Second, when completed, Peter will be "wholly clean." As regards the former purpose, this footwashing resembles other status transformation rituals in the Fourth Gospel, all of which are presented under the rubric of "unless":

   3:3   *Unless* one is born anew, he cannot see the kingdom of God.
   3:5   *Unless* one is born of water and the spirit, he cannot enter the kingdom of God.

---

12. It should be contrasted with two others in which Jesus is the recipient of the action. In Luke 7:37-38 a woman interrupts a meal to wet his feet with her tears; Luke interprets this as a *ceremonial* act of hospitality which the host failed to extend to Jesus (7:44-46); such actions should confirm his status as "honored guest." In John 12:1-8, Mary interrupted Jesus' meal with the family to anoint Jesus' feet (12:2-3). Although this is an anointing and not a "footwashing," we label it as a *status transformation ritual* because it constitutes part of Jesus' burial ritual (12:7). Ceremonial hospitality can be extended repeatedly, not so ritual anointing for burial.

6:53   *Unless* you eat the flesh of the Son of Man and drink his blood, you have no life in you.
8:24   *Unless* you believe that 'I AM,' you will die in your sins.
12:24 *Unless* a grain of wheat falls into the earth and dies, it remains alone.
13:8   *Unless* I wash you, you have no part in me.
15:4   As the branch cannot bear fruit by itself, *unless* it abides in the vine, neither can you, *unless* you abide in me.

John 3:3 and 5 refer to the status transformation of entrance, most likely baptism.[13] Outsiders become insiders by virtue of this entrance ritual, which replaces circumcision. Jesus demands of prospective disciples in 8:24 that they acclaim him by a confession of his heavenliness, thus changing status from outsiders or even luke-warm disciples to that of first-class insiders. Later even this confession is deemed an insufficient ritual; something extra is required. Like grains of wheat, disciples must be willing to die (12:24; see 16:1-2; Mark 8:34-37). Finally, Jesus tells Peter, who is already a member of the circle, that still more is needed; his current status is inadequate, and although he has "bathed," he is not yet "wholly clean."

All of these "unless" statements of Jesus, then, should be seen as indicative of status transformation rituals. Some represent the radical change of status from outsider to insider (3:3, 5). Others indicate a change of insider status, from less complete to more complete and from imperfect to perfect follower. Indeed, there seems to be a sense of escalation in these statements: first, mere membership (3:3, 5), then elite confession (8:24), and then elite behavior (12:24).

In regard to the first purpose of the footwashing, therefore, let us examine the range of meanings for "portion" *(meros)*. Often it means 1) a region or place (Matt 2:22; 15:21; Mark 8:10; Acts 2:10; Eph 4:9; Rev 16:19), 2) a party or faction (Acts 23:9; Josephus, *Wars* 1.143), 3) an inheritance (Rev 21:8; 22:19), or 4) a member of the body (Eph 4:16). All of these meanings find a ready equivalent in the Johannine symbolic world: 1) *meros* as place: Jesus speaks about "where" he is going and the mansions awaiting his disciples (14:2); 2) *meros* as party or faction: scholars now recognize many factions within the Johannine church, among them the elite (12:24) and the cowards (9:22; 12:42);[14] 3) *meros* as inheri-

---

13. See Ignace de la Potterie, "'To Be Born Again of Water and the Spirit' — The Baptismal Text of John 3,5," *The Christian Lives by the Spirit* (Staten Island, NY: Alba House, 1971) 1-36; David Rensberger, *Johannine Faith and Liberating Community* (Philadelphia: Westminster Press, 1988) 57-59, 66-70.

14. See Raymond E. Brown, *The Community of the Beloved Disciple* (New York: Paulist Press, 1979) 26-47, 71-88.

tance, such as "peace" bequeathed (14:27), the Holy Spirit sent by Jesus (15:26) or the positive results of affiliation: "bring forth much fruit" (15:2-6); and 4) *meros* as membership: belonging to Jesus' group, i.e., vine and branch (15:1-7).[15] In the logic of Johannine symbols all of these meanings seem to overlap. As member of Jesus' party and of a special circle, one is in the right place and gains special benefits. Some transformation rituals give one the status of basic membership or being a "part"; others convey new and better status as members of an elite inner circle.

According to the story's logic, we understand Peter as a disciple who has passed one loyalty test (6:67-69) and so enjoys basic membership and is part of the general circle of disciples (see 9:28). The "part" Jesus offers in 13:8 would seem to be a new and better status. Yet the Gospel says that if Peter rejects this, he will have "*no* part" in me, which is a typically unqualified Johannine ultimatum.[16] The footwashing, then, stands as the last of the transformation rituals we have seen. Is it thereby the climax, the quintessential way to first-class status in the group?

As regards the second stated purpose of this ritual, what does it mean to be "wholly clean"?[17] Although purity and cleanness concerns are frequently evident in the other Gospels, they remain important in the Fourth Gospel as well. For example, the six stone jars at Cana stood there "for the Jewish rites of *purification*" (2:6).[18] According to this Gospel's logic, Jesus replaces former rites, feasts, places of worship, etc. with new and better ones (mere water becomes quality wine).[19]

---

15. In the *Martyrdom of Polycarp* we find a remark that has much to commend it as an explanatory parallel to Jesus' remarks on "portion" and "wholly clean": "I bless you that I may share, among the number (*meros*, as in 'share the lot') of martyrs, in the cup of Your Christ. . . . And may I be received among them before You, as a rich and acceptable sacrifice. . . . I glorify You through the everlasting and heavenly high priest" (14.2-3).

16. For example, failure to be born again means "not entering the kingdom of God" (3:5); failure to confess Jesus as "I AM" means "dying in one's sins" (8:24); failure to fall into the ground and die means "bearing no fruit" (12:24); failure to allow Jesus' washing means "to have no part in me" (13:8).

17. "Clean" is one aspect of the semantic word field that has to do with purity and pollution; see Jerome H. Neyrey, "Unclean, Common, Polluted and Taboo," *Forum* 4.4 (1988): 72-82, and *Paul, in Other Words* (Louisville: Westminster John Knox Press, 1990) 54-55. Generally "clean" either has to do with the removal of pollution or consecration for entrance or participation in a holy rite.

18. These presumably include the washing of hands and perhaps vessels; see Mark 7:2-4; the volume of the six jars correlates with a house filled with wedding guests needing to wash their hands before the wedding feast.

19. See Jerome H. Neyrey, *An Ideology of Revolt*, 130-41. See James VanderKam, "John 10 and the Feast of the Dedication," in *Of Scribes and Scrolls*, ed. Harold Attridge, John Collins, and Thomas Tobin (New York: University Press of America, 1990) 203-14.

Moreover, the purification envisioned here is a status transformation ritual, suggesting that Jesus provides not just the fluid, but the ritual of purification as well.[20] Shortly after this, the narrator presents a discussion of water birth between Jesus and Nicodemus (3:3-5) and among the disciples of John (3:25-27). The baptism about which Jesus informs Nicodemus is a status transformation ritual effecting membership ("enter the kingdom of God," 3:5). When the scene shifts to "the land of Judea" where Jesus and his disciples baptized (3:22-23), the reader then hears of "a discussion between John's disciples and a Judean over *purification*" (3:25). They do not discuss the ritual of baptism and purification so much as the rivalry between Jesus and the circle of the Baptizer. "Purification," then, arises in situations of comparison, rivalry and conflict.[21]

Excursus: Cultural Meanings of Foot-washing in Antiquity

We begin with consideration of the work of John C. Thomas, who identified three different functions of foot-washing in the ancient world: cultic settings, domestic hygiene or comfort, and hospitality.[22] The last meaning, hospitality, is attested to as part of the role of a widow (1 Tim 5:10; see also Luke 7:44-46); people are frequently given water to wash their own feet, a matter of hygiene and comfort after a dusty journey (Gen 18:4; 19:2; 24:32; 43:24; Judges 19:21; 2 Sam 11:8). As part of their cultic behavior, priests wash before offering sacrifice (Exod 30:17-21; 40:30-32); likewise warriors in a Holy War washed their feet to symbolize that they were assuming duties requiring ritual purity.[23]

---

20. Schnackenburg (*The Gospel According to St. John*, 3.21) calls attention to John 7:38 and 19:34, where he interprets fluids from Jesus in terms of a purificatory rite, namely baptism.

21. In two ways the author linked the Cana sign (2:1-11) and the discussion about purification (3:25-30): 1) Both have to do with purification *(katharismos)*. 2) At Cana the lesser figure, the steward, praises the greater figure, the bridegroom, because what comes later is better than what came first: "You have kept the good wine till now" (2:10). Likewise, at Aenon near Salim, the lesser figure, the Baptizer, praises the greater figure, Jesus. The Baptizer has insisted that Jesus "comes after me" (1:15, 27, 30), yet ranks "before me." Thus what comes later in time (i.e., Jesus) is better than what came first (i.e., John): "He must increase, but I must decrease." These linkages reinforce each other and together state that Jesus' fluids and rituals of purification are superior to all that went before, be they Jewish rites of purification or the Baptizer's baptizing. Jesus replaces them both.

22. John C. Thomas, *Foot-Washing in John 13 and the Johannine Community* (Sheffield: Sheffield Academic Press, 1991) 27.

23. See James Swetnam's review of Richter's *Die Fusswaschung* in *Bib* 49 (1968): 441-43. While no evidence of Holy War is found in John 13, the suggestion of ritual purification before confronting mortal danger has much to recommend it.

Purification as a formal theme drops from the narrative until the allegory of the vine in John 15. There Jesus states that the vine-dresser "takes away" unfruitful branches, but "prunes" fruitful ones (15:2). "Pruning" may be an adequate translation here, but the actual verb used is "to cleanse" or "to purify." Hence more cleansing lies in store for disciples, despite the fact that they were already cleansed in baptism. In 13:10 Jesus affirmed that some have already "bathed and do not need to wash"; nevertheless they still need to have their feet washed so as to become "wholly clean." Likewise in 15:3 Jesus affirms, "You are already made clean by the word which I have spoken to you"; nevertheless they will be made "clean" when pruned/cleansed by the vine-dresser. In 15:1-3, then, a status transformation ritual is envisioned, whereby an already "clean" disciple will take on a new status of "clean" (i.e., a branch which bears more fruit), when cleansed by the vine-dresser. This is not like baptism, an entrance ritual whereby an outsider becomes an insider. Rather this transforms ordinary insider status to that of elite or perfect insider status. According to the logic of 15:1-3, this status transformation occurs through suffering (see 16:1-2).

All of these references to purification should have a bearing on how we interpret "wholly clean" in 13:10. At a minimum, Jesus' washing of Peter's feet is a *washing*. Like other washings in the Fourth Gospel, it formally aims at *purification*. Like other washings, it too is a status transformation ritual, not a mere entrance ritual, but a ritual whereby an insider gains a new status, a more perfect role. Peter will be *wholly* clean, something impossible without this ritual. The comparison of 13:6-10 with 15:1-3 suggests that this footwashing is more than a mere water washing; perfect *"purification"* comes about by public confession and even risk of death (16:1-2).[24]

3.0 Footwashing (13:12-20) as a Confirming Ceremony

If 13:6-11 describes a ritual of status transformation, a different type of ritual action is portrayed in 13:12-20. Because this does not involve change of role or status but rather confirmation of them, let us read 13:12-20 according to the model of ceremony.[25]

---

24. J. A. T. Robinson's interpretation is worth remembering ("The Significance of the Foot-Washing," *Neotestamentica et Patristica* [NovTSup 6; Leiden: E. J. Brill, 1962] 144-47). He noted the parallel with Mark 10:32-45 and its offer of "baptism" to James and John; Jesus' "way of the cross/way of glory" must be imitated by his disciples. Robinson also links Peter's remarks in John 13:37 about willingness to follow Jesus even unto death.

25. Although we focus on only one ceremony (13:12-20), the Fourth Gospel notes two other types which correspond to two key social locations: 1) the Temple and pilgrimage feasts to the

1. *Frequency:* Jesus mandates in 13:12-15 that the feet of church members be washed, presumably as a standard part of ceremonial gatherings. Whereas Peter would be washed once and then be "wholly clean," the feet of the members of the group would be washed again and again. How often? If this footwashing is, as I suspect, an act of hospitality which welcomes people to a ceremonial meal (see Luke 7:44-46; 1 Tim 5:10), then it would be repeated whenever the group gathered. We simply do not know how frequently they gathered, whether only at Passover (13:1) or at Sabbath or the first day of the week (Acts 20:7).[26] But as often as they gathered, this ceremony of hospitality would be appropriate.

2. *Calendar.* This footwashing is expected with every gathering, and should occur regularly at the beginning as a welcoming act of hospitality. It is not the emergency ritual which Peter received but once on the eve of a crisis. In 13:12-20 the washing has an established place in the sequence of events; it is always done at the beginning of the gathering.

3. *Time Focus:* It harkens to the past example of Jesus which should be presently imitated by the group's leaders. Jesus calls attention to his past action as the warrant for its continuation in the present: "Do you know what I have done to you? . . . I have given you an example. If I have washed your feet, you also ought to wash one another's feet" (13:12, 14). Present roles and relationships among the Johannine group depend on the past action and example of Jesus.

4. *Presiding:* Jesus describes his actions as those of an official of the group who establishes a precedent to be followed. If foot-washing belongs in the orbit of hospitality and hospitality denotes commensality, then Jesus pre-

---

nation's shrine and 2) the household and meals. As regards the Temple, Jesus participates in certain feasts such as Passover (2:13ff.; 13:1ff.), Tabernacles (7:2–8:20), Dedication (10:22), and an unnamed feast (5:1ff.). Ideally these should confirm his membership, role, and status in the political institution, but in the Fourth Gospel he challenges and replaces the feasts, thereby disrupting their function as confirming ceremonies. As regards the household, Jesus confirms his association with circles of intimate friends (12:1-8; 13:1–17:26; 21:9-13) and general disciples (6:1-15). Meals confirm his special role as host and provider when he feeds others, or his status as honored guest when they fete him. This sketch suggests that according to this Gospel ceremonies are not functioning properly on the public level of participation in the nation's ongoing socialization, which indeed is challenged by Jesus. But on the level of private associations in households they do function to confirm membership, as well as specific roles and statuses. On the importance of the Temple-household distinction, see John H. Elliott, "Temple versus Household in Luke-Acts: A Contrast in Social Institutions," in *The Social World of Luke-Acts*, ed. Neyrey, 212-38.

26. See W. Rodorf, *Sunday: The History of the Day of Rest and Worship in the Earliest Centuries of the Christian Church* (Philadelphia: Westminster, 1968).

sides over that ceremony. It would be unthinkable that the disciples wash the feet of members had not Jesus done so previously.

5. *Purpose:* The purposes of the footwashing in 13:12-16 are manifold. Jesus confirms his own role and status by this act: "You call me 'Teacher' and 'Lord'; and you are right, for so I am" (13:13). Then he alludes to himself as "Master" (13:16). Yet the appropriate act of this Teacher-Lord-Master is to wash the feet of disciples and servants, thus offering them hospitality. By presiding at this ceremonial washing, Jesus confirms his unique role as Teacher-Lord-Master and his exalted status, even if the action done is "humble" in their eyes. Only the person of this exalted role and status within the group is expected to perform this action.

So when those whose feet Jesus has washed in turn wash the feet of others, they do so as leaders of the group who imitate Jesus. They have roles and status vis-à-vis the group comparable to those Jesus had, who was of superior role and exalted status. Hence, Jesus' word legitimates their behavior. In their ceremonial actions they are like the master; they are not "greater than their master" so as to avoid this action. Rather as "servants" they imitate their "master": "A servant is not greater than his master; nor is he who is sent greater than he who sent him" (13:16). They too will be officials presiding at this hospitality ceremony. And their performance of this action will serve to confirm their role as leaders and teachers of Jesus' group. Moreover, they wash the feet of members of the church, and so the status of those washed is confirmed as authentic members of this Jesus synagogue.

Using a model of rituals and ceremonies, then, we conclude that Jesus' washing of Peter's feet in 13:6-11 should be understood as a ritual of status transformation. In contrast, the explanation of Jesus' action in 13:12-20 has nothing to do with transformation, but rather confirms already existing roles and statuses. We might clarify this by comparing the stated purposes of each passage. In 13:4-11, Jesus demands of Peter this final action so as to become "wholly pure." Yet in 13:12-20, Jesus demands that all the disciples imitate his action and so confirm their role and status as leaders and teachers of the group of disciples. "Purification" simply is not "imitation."

Meals are quintessential ceremonies where status is confirmed by the sheer fact of commensality (likes eat with likes) and roles are confirmed by virtue of seating arrangements, portions served, and conversational roles.[27] The full meal ceremony includes, not just footwashing, but commensality and symposium.

---

27. See Jerome H. Neyrey, "Ceremonies in Luke-Acts: The Case of Meals and Table Fellowship," in *The Social World of Luke-Acts,* ed. Neyrey, 261-87.

The narrator states that a meal was in progress ("during supper," 13:2). The footwashing mentioned in 13:12-15, we have argued, is a ceremonial act of hospitality welcoming members to the group's meal; it confirms membership status as well as specific roles within the group. Characteristic of meals, only members should be present, for likes eat with likes.[28]

4.0 Who Participates in These Rituals and Ceremonies?

Students of ritual actions regularly concern themselves with ritual elements such as elders, initiands, sacra, etc. But we ask different questions: Who gets elevated to what role or status in the status transformation ritual in 13:6-11? Was the ritual successful in transforming role and status? Yet we ask these questions in light of recent studies which argue that readers must attend to the whole of the story in John 13.[29] And so we focus on Peter, asking whether he was successfully transformed by the status elevation ritual and how this is portrayed.

4.1 Comparison: Peter, Judas and the Beloved Disciple

The narrator highlights three specific characters in 13:1-38: 1) Peter (13:6-10, 24, 36-38), 2) Judas (13:11, 18, 24-29), and 3) the Beloved Disciple (13:23-26). But Peter stands out as the most involved character in all the segments of this story. Since the work of Collins,[30] readers have become more sensitive to the representative or symbolic character of the *dramatis personae* of the Fourth Gospel. This material directly pertains to our analysis of status transformation rituals, for it indicates the precise status of the characters who undergo ritual transformation.

Peter. One of the major techniques of characterization in the Fourth Gospel is comparison and contrast,[31] a technique used frequently in the presentation of

---

28. After the meal in 6:1-15 and the discourse about food in 6:25-59, some break commensality with Jesus because they find his bread too stale (6:60); but others remain, who share commensality (6:67-68).

29. In particular, Francis J. Moloney, "A Sacramental Reading of John 13:1-38," *AusBR* 34 (1984): 1-16; idem, "A Sacramental Reading of John 13:1-38," *CBQ* 53 (1991): 242-48; F. Manns, "Le lavement des pieds: essai sur la structure et la signification de Jean 13," *RevScRel* 55 (1981): 159.

30. "Representative Figures in the Fourth Gospel," *DR* 94 (1976): 26-46, 118-32; idem, *These Things Have Been Written* (Grand Rapids: Wm. B. Eerdmans, 1991) esp. 38-46.

31. New Testament scholars are increasingly studying the rhetorical device called *synkrisis* or comparison, especially as this is found in the encomia of the progymnasmata; see James

Peter. On the narrative level, he is contrasted in 13:6-11 with Judas, just as he was in 6:67-71. If Jesus washes him he will be "wholly clean," which juxtaposes him with Judas, who is "not clean." Yet he is also contrasted with the Beloved Disciple. In seeking to know the traitor's identity, Peter asks the BD to ask Jesus.[32] Peter's alleged primacy among the Twelve stands in contrast with the status of the Beloved Disciple. He is "in the know," Peter is not; he enjoys the place of honor next to Jesus, whereas Peter reclines further away. As we shall see, the BD and Peter will be contrasted first as 1) shepherd and sheep (18:15-16), 2) loyal disciple (19:26-27) versus disloyal coward (18:17, 25-27) and finally 3) as the fast runner who believes versus the slow disciple who does not believe (20:3-8).

Peter and Jesus converse once more about discipleship and loyalty. Jesus' remark to Peter in 13:36 resembles that of 13:7. Peter cannot follow Jesus now, just as he does not know now what Jesus is doing. But "you will follow *afterward*," just as "*afterward* you will understand." *Afterward* indicates that the process begun here is not completed, because the essential qualifications are not present yet, namely, "follow" and "understand." Thus Peter remains in a liminal stage, incomplete both in knowledge and virtue. The narrator, then, compares and contrasts Peter with both Judas and the Beloved Disciple. The BD knows and follows most closely — not so Peter. Judas disguises himself and plots malice — not so Peter, who fails the test for courage and public loyalty. Yet the narrative says that Peter is only delayed on route to special status: "You will know *afterward* and follow *afterward*." Hence he is a figure still in a liminal state, a figure whose status and role have not yet been transformed. While he is not an elite figure, neither is he a hostile outsider.

Judas. The narrator identifies him as the person into whose heart the devil had already put it to betray Jesus (13:2),[33] an identity already noted in 6:70-71 where loyal and disloyal disciples are separated. He is then labeled "not clean"

Butts, *The Progymnasmata of Theon: A New Text with Translation and Commentary* (dissertation, Claremont, 1986) 494-512; Christopher Forbes, "Comparison, Self-Praise and Irony: Paul's Boasting and the Conventions of Hellenistic Rhetoric," *NTS* 32 (1986): 1-8; Peter Marshall, *Enmity at Corinth: Social Conventions in Paul's Relations with the Corinthians* (WUNT 2.23; Tübingen: J. C. B. Mohr, 1987) 53-56, 325-29, 348-65; D. A. Russell, "On Reading Plutarch's Lives," *Greece and Rome* 13 (1966): 150-51; P. A. Stadter, "Plutarch's Comparison of Pericles and Fabius Maximus," *GRBS* 16 (1975): 77-85.

32. Compare this with a parallel process in 12:20-23. Certain "Greeks" ask to see Jesus. They ask Philip, who asks Andrew, who takes them to Jesus. Hence certain people in this Gospel function as mediators or brokers of access and information, thus indicating their special role and status.

33. On the social import of accusations of demon possession, see Bruce J. Malina and Jerome H. Neyrey, "Jesus the Witch," *Calling Jesus Names* (Sonoma, CA: Polebridge Press, 1988) 3-32.

(13:10b-11). Even if Jesus washed his feet, Judas certainly will not be transformed to elite status, especially as that means public loyalty to Jesus even to the loss of one's life. He is out to kill Jesus. According to characterization technique, then, we view Judas as deceiving, disloyal and demonic.

According to 13:12-15 Jesus' ceremonial washing of his disciples' feet confirms both membership status and specific roles. But this cannot apply to Judas. After giving the mandatum, Jesus excepts Judas from this role and status: "I am not speaking to you all; I know whom I have chosen" (13:18). Indeed he identifies Judas as the one who violates the basic laws of commensality: "He who ate my bread has lifted up his heel against me" (13:18b).[34] Although Jesus identifies his deceiving enemy, Judas' role remains hidden to all but one. When Jesus declared that "One of you will betray me" (13:21), the disciples were "uncertain of whom he spoke." Peter seeks the mediation of the Beloved Disciple to learn from Jesus the identity of the deceiving, disloyal member (13:23-24). The traitor shares Jesus' table: "It is he to whom I shall give this morsel when I have dipped it" (13:26). "He who eats my bread" and yet "raises his heel against me" is the one to whom Jesus gives the bread dipped (13:26-27), again deceptive commensality. Even when Jesus told him "What you are going to do, do quickly" (13:27b), the other disciples are deceived by Judas' disguise: "Now no one at the table knew why he said this to him. Some thought that, because Judas had the money box, Jesus was telling him, 'Buy what we need for the feast'; or that he should give something to the poor" (13:28-29). Judas remained a deceiving, disloyal and dangerous member of the group. He certainly did not participate in the status transformation ritual (for he was *not* made "clean") nor was he confirmed as a group member in the ceremony (for he violated commensality).

Beloved Disciple. He appears for the first time at a moment of crisis. With no prior clues to his characterization, we quickly learn that he is "the one whom Jesus loved," whose intimacy is symbolized by "lying close to the breast of Jesus" (13:23). He asks for and receives from Jesus secret information hidden from all others: "Lord, who is it?" (13:25). In this, he acts as Peter's broker or mediator: what Peter lacks, the Beloved Disciple has or can get.[35] He is, then, the consummate insider with access to unique knowledge of deviants in the group. Finally, he follows Jesus most closely, both to Caiaphas's house and to the cross, displaying public loyalty at the risk of his life.

Thus, when we survey the characterization of Peter, Judas and the Beloved

---

34. Is a play on words intended with the reference to a "heel" lifted against Jesus? Instead of footwashing as solidarity, someone's foot is raised in aggression.

35. When the Beloved Disciple acts as shepherd to Peter in 18:15-16, he again acts as broker who allows Peter's entry where he would otherwise be excluded.

Disciple in regard to roles and statuses relative to the rituals and ceremonies described in John 13, we find the following contrasts:

Person	Ritual or Ceremony	Characterization
Peter	1. still a candidate for status transformation 2. group membership barely confirmed	failed loyalty
Judas	1. no status transformation whatsoever: "One of you is *not* clean" 2. group membership denied: "I am *not* speaking of you all"	hostile disloyalty
Beloved Disciple	1. elite status transformation 2. elite group membership confirmed	courageous loyalty

4.2 Peter in Other Rituals and Ceremonies

This examination of Peter's transformation ritual in 13:6-11 leads us to inquire about parallel passages where he is either the subject of other rituals of status transformation or participant in other ceremonies. The Evangelist consistently presents Peter as an initiand in rituals of status change, both elevating and demoting him.[36]

Let us focus on "the Noble Shepherd" materials. These involve Peter and shape how we should read the footwashing in 13:6-11. Jesus, the group leader, enjoys the ceremonial role of the Noble Shepherd. When he calls the sheep by name and leads them out or when he lays down his life for them, he acts as the Noble Shepherd and so confirms his role.

As regards "laying down one's life for the sheep," Peter protests that this too is his role. After Judas' exit (13:21-30), Peter and Jesus again converse. When compared with Jesus' conversation with Peter in 13:6-11, this exchange gives the impression not only of parallelism between the two conversations, but continuation of the first one.

13:6-8
1. *Question by Peter*
"Lord, do you wash my feet?" (13:6)

13:36-38
1. *Question by Peter*
"Lord, where are you going?" (13:36)

---

36. Peter's call to become Jesus' disciple (1:40-42) is the first such status transformation ritual. Yet unlike Luke 5:1-11; Mark 1:16-20; Matt 16:17-19, Peter is not called first (a comment on his *status*), and although given a name change, the *role* signified by the new name is not specified.

13:6-8	13:36-38
2. *Answer from Jesus* Jesus answered and said to him: "What I am doing you do not know now, but afterward you will understand" (13:7)	2. *Answer from Jesus* Jesus answered him: "Where I am going you cannot follow now, but afterward you will follow" (13:36b)
3. *Peter's Boast* Peter said to him: "You shall never wash my feet" (13:8)	3. *Peter's Boast* Peter said to him: "Lord, why cannot I follow you now? I will lay down my life for you" (13:37)
4. *Response from Jesus* Jesus answered him: "Unless I wash you, you have no part in me" (13:8)	4. *Response from Jesus* Jesus answered: "Will you lay down your life for me? Amen, amen, I say to you, the cock will not crow, until you have denied me three times" (13:38)

The two conversations are similar in terms of topics discussed and rituals of status transformation mentioned. In both, Jesus tells Peter that he does *not know* and *cannot follow* Jesus *now*; but *afterward* he will understand or follow. When Peter speaks in 13:36, he remains a candidate for the elite status which that "foot-washing" symbolized. He boasts loyalty unto death, claiming that he is no longer a candidate for elite status, but has genuinely been transformed into an elite disciple. Peter's boast of loyalty, moreover, implies another claim to an elite role, namely the role of a "noble shepherd, who lays down his life for his friends":

The Noble Shepherd (10:11)	Peter, the Shepherd? (13:37)
The good shepherd lays down his life for the sheep	I will lay down my life for you

Jesus has just commanded that his disciples "love one another" (13:34-35). He shortly defines "love" in terms of what the noble shepherd does: "Greater love has no one than this, that a man lay down his life for his friends" (15:13).[37] *Shepherds*, then, *love by laying down their lives for their sheep/friends*. Peter indeed claims in 13:37 the status of an elite disciple and the particular role of "noble

---

37. Jesus is presented as the model of love. In the prologue to the Book of Glory, the narrator says of Jesus, "Having loved his own who were in the world, he loved them *eis telos* (perfectly? loyally? 13:1)." "Loyalty" is a constitutive element of this "love" (see 17:11-12, 15).

shepherd." But has he been ritually transformed to this elite status and role? Does anyone acknowledge it?

Jesus challenges Peter's claim to this new status, and in doing so instigates, not a ritual of status elevation, but of status degradation. He predicts that Peter, far from being the noble shepherd, will instead act like a hireling, who sees the wolf coming, leaves the sheep and flees (10:12). If this is true, then the narrator issues a serious challenge to Peter's role vis-à-vis the church. According to Johannine logic, the hireling has no relationship with the sheep: "He who is a hireling, whose own the sheep are not. . . . He flees because he is a hireling and cares nothing for the sheep" (10:12-13). Whatever the community of this Gospel knew of the traditional role and status of Peter, that would be severely challenged by Peter's association here with the hireling and not the shepherd role. He would be degraded by this ritual of status transformation, hardly elevated.

Who, then, is the noble shepherd? According to this Gospel, the Beloved Disciple fills that ceremonial role. Returning to Jesus' parables of shepherds, doors, and sheep in 10:1-4 and 11-13, we learn that the authentic shepherd enters the door; the doorkeeper recognizes and admits him, and he calls the sheep by name. This is precisely what the Beloved Disciple does in 18:15-18.

Parabolic Description of the Noble Shepherd	Johannine Description of the Beloved Disciple
1. *Shepherd Enters by the Door* "He who enters by the door is the shepherd of the sheep" (10:2)	1. *Beloved Disciple Enters by the Door* "As this disciple was known to the high priest, he entered . . . while Peter stood outside at the door" (18:15).
2. *Gatekeeper Recognizes Him* "He who enters by the door is the shepherd of the sheep. To him the gatekeeper opens" (10:2-3).	2. *Gatekeeper Recognizes Him* "So the other disciple, who was known to the high priest, went out and spoke to the maid who kept the door" (18:16).
3. *He Leads the Sheep In/Out* "He calls his own sheep by name and leads them out. When he has brought out all his own, he goes before them, and the sheep follow him" (10:3-4).[38]	3. *He Leads the Sheep In* "Peter stood outside the door. . . . The other disciple spoke to the maid who kept the door and brought Peter in" (18:16).

38. According to the parable, the sheep know the voice of the shepherd (10:4-5); this seems to be ironically illustrated in 18:15-18 when the maid recognizes the voice of Peter and identifies him as a follower of Jesus, an association he denies.

In fact, using the perspective of this study, we should label the actions described in 18:15-18 as a ceremony. The respective roles of Beloved Disciple and Peter are confirmed as shepherd and sheep within the institution of the fictive kinship group of the Fourth Gospel. Far from being either shepherd or noble, Peter acts out the inferior role of sheep.

Yet the conflict over who is the group's shepherd ends only when the Gospel ends. In ch. 21 the Evangelist presents Peter once more in terms of rituals of status transformation. The scene opens with Peter assuming his ceremonial role as fisherman: "I am going fishing" (21:3). The fact that six others join him suggests that Peter's role as leader of Jesus' followers is ceremonially confirmed, which is in accord with gospel tradition (see Luke 5:1-11). He is not commissioned as "fisher of men," as in the synoptic stories, but that is not far from the author's mind. Peter's ideal role, moreover, is not Fisherman, but Shepherd. The opening scene, then, conditions the reader to examine the role and status of Peter. The fishing ceremony confirms a traditional role, but there is no transformation of status here.

Jesus then serves a ceremonial meal confirming his role as host and provider, that is, of shepherd who feeds his flock. After it, he addresses Peter in a way which signals a radical transformation of his status. *Afterward* is finally *now*. The reader knows that Peter is the weak figure who failed thrice in loyalty (13:38; 18:17, 25-27). Despite his claims to the contrary (13:36-38), he has been presented, neither as "noble" nor as "shepherd," but as a cowardly hireling. Now Jesus questions Peter, and in doing so transforms his status to that of loving/loyal disciple and his role to that of shepherd by formally commissioning him (21:15-17).

Question:	*Answer:*	*Status Transformation:*
"Simon, son of John, do you love me more than these?"	"Yes, Lord, you know that I love you."	"Feed my lambs" "Tend my sheep" "Feed my sheep"

This Gospel labors to affirm that Peter finally becomes the group's Shepherd (and *not* the Beloved Disciple). Through ritual loyalty oaths, Peter's status transformation occurs, which Jesus formally acknowledges as he invests Peter with the role and status of Shepherd of all the sheep.[39] Hence it is now legitimate for Peter to act as "shepherd." But is he a "noble" shepherd?

---

39. We note that just as Jesus acted as the host of the ceremonial meal just finished (21:13), so Peter will assume that role too, as Jesus tells him, "*Feed* my lambs.... *Feed* my sheep" (21:15, 17). Whether we understand Jesus' command literally (Peter as host at genuine community

The scene concludes with Jesus' prediction of Peter's death (21:18-19). Earlier Peter had boasted that he would lay down his life for Jesus, only to have this challenged (13:38). Now Jesus' prediction serves to acknowledge Peter's earlier claim. But is this too a status transformation ritual? Does it add anything to the role and status of Peter?

At this point, we should ask about the relationship of 13:6-11 to 21:18-19. In the former passage, Jesus would make Peter "wholly clean." But at that point, can Peter be "clean," much less "wholly" clean, for he will fail in loyalty (13:36-38)? Jesus, moreover, told Peter, "What I am doing you do not know now, but afterward you will understand" (13:7). When did Peter finally know? Why did the narrative juxtapose at this point Peter (13:6-10a) with the disloyal traitor (13:10b-11)? These questions call attention to the problem of understanding fully what is being communicated in 13:6-11. It narrates an incomplete ritual, whose completion lies later and whose meaning will only be understood "afterward." But when?

The questions raised about 13:6-11 are fully answered in 21:18-19. Now Peter can become "wholly clean" though a death whereby "God will be glorified" (21:19). The failure in loyalty is replaced by a declaration of "love" (21:15-17); the un-grasped meaning of Jesus' actions is met with full understanding of Jesus' words in 21:19.

On the level of ritual analysis, Peter is the initiand of two contrasting status transformation rituals in chapter 13. On the one hand, Peter should experience status elevation by becoming "wholly clean" (13:10); yet he experiences status degradation by exposure as a hireling, not a shepherd. What are we to think of him? He remains a candidate for status transformation because the ritual remains incomplete. Jesus twice tells him that completion of the ritual lies in the future ("afterwards you will know," 13:7; "you will follow afterward," 13:36). He is commissioned to be the official and unchallenged Shepherd ("Feed my lambs . . . Feed my sheep," 21:15-17). Likewise his status as "noble" shepherd is acknowledged; he can truly "follow Jesus" and "lay down his life for him" (13:37). His death will seal his status as an elite disciple, courageous, loyal and perfect. In his death, he will become "wholly clean."

5.0 Conclusions

By itself the use of cultural anthropology cannot fully interpret the symbolic meaning of the footwashing in 13:6-11; nor was its use intended to ignore the

---

meals) or symbolically (Peter as shepherd who pastures the flock), Jesus designates him as a ceremonial official.

study of background materials[40] and redactional inquiry.[41] But the use of this anthropological model greatly aids in distinguishing what Jesus intends for Peter in 13:6-10 (a status change) and what his example means for the disciples in 13:12-20 (a confirmation of their roles).

Such a model of rites of status change and status confirmation greatly aids our general reading of the Fourth Gospel. This Gospel records precious few successful ceremonies. Since attention is focused on boundary crossings and status changes (i.e. "unless . . ."), we are urged to focus attention on the social conflict within the Johannine community; this is aided by noting the shifting demands made of disciples, which are expressed in terms of new rites of status change and transformation. This model, moreover, greatly clarifies the rivalry between the symbolic figures Peter and the Beloved Disciple, when we see the latter successfully if temporarily acting as the ceremonial Noble Shepherd. The figure of Peter, moreover, remains in a state of change and uncertainty until the final ritual in 21:15-19. Who assumed *which role* in virtue of *which ritual* of change? Such questions open up the text in fresh ways which are eminently compatible with traditional critical methods.

---

40. The Torah speaks of two kinds of footwashings: 1) a ceremonial act of hospitality to travelers before they eat (Gen 18:4; 24:32; Judg 19:21) and 2) a ritual purification of priests before they enter and minister to the Lord (Exod 30:19-21; 40:31). Philo gives a moral meaning to priestly footwashing, namely, blamelessness or walking in the way of the Lord (*Mos.* 2.138; *QE* 1.2); when a sacrificial animal's feet are washed, it is transformed from a creature who walks on earth to one who walks in God's realm (*Spec.* 1.206); see Herold Weiss, "Foot Washing in the Johannine Community," *NovT* 21 (1979): 315-17.

41. On the relationship of the footwashing in 13:6-11 to Jesus' death, see Hoskyns, *The Fourth Gospel,* 435; Brown, *The Gospel according to John,* 2.551; J. D. G. Dunn, "The Washing of the Disciples' Feet in John 13,1-20," *ZNW* 61 (1970): 249.

15

Worship in the Fourth Gospel

A Cultural Interpretation of John 14–17

1.0 State of the Question and Hypothesis

As the title indicates, this chapter examines John 14–17 as "worship." It employs a model of worship developed in cultural studies as an appropriate and proper way to interpret the same phenomenon in the Fourth Gospel, in particular, John 14–17. Our initial problem, however, is to define worship, not just to describe it or catalogue its elements. Take for example the remarks of Henton Davies on Old Testament worship:

> Worship is homage... the attitude and activity to recognize and describe the worth of the person or thing to which homage is addressed. Worship is thus synonymous with the whole of a reverent life, embracing piety as well as liturgy. The range of meaning, therefore, is very great.[1]

Three elements are noteworthy: 1) object of worship = a worthy figure; 2) purpose of worship = to honor the deity ("to recognize the worth of the person to whom homage is addressed"); 3) forms of worship = reverent life, piety and liturgy. If this definition emphasizes the value of honor, it also excludes any notion of worship as communication of the Worthy One to the worshipers. Nor does it take up issues such as where and how worship occurs. There is, then, much more to be done to understand worship, without which many, many texts will remain opaque to us.

Curiously, discussions of worship in the Fourth Gospel are rare,[2] and in

---

1. Henton Davies, "Worship in the Old Testament," *IDB* 4.879.
2. Oscar Cullmann (*Early Christian Worship* [London: SCM Press, 1953]) describes "basic

most commentaries it does not even rate a place in the topical index. Yet the author of the Fourth Gospel formally attends to matters of worship when he himself raises certain topics: 1) *where* to worship? 2) *how* to worship? 3) *of what* does worship consist? 4) *when* to worship? and 5) *who* participates?

Where? At Jesus' inaugural visit to Jerusalem's Temple, he upsets its sacrificial worship system ("he drove . . . the sheep and oxen out of the temple") and its revenue collection. In defense, he declares: "Destroy this temple, and in three days I will raise it up" (2:19), which his opponents misunderstand, for they think that he refers to a physical building, a fixed sacred space. The truth is, "He spoke of the temple of his body" (2:21), an entirely different concept of space. The Samaritan woman asked Jesus-the-prophet to settle a dispute about *where* to worship, "this mountain . . . or in Jerusalem?" (4:20). Jesus gives a sweeping answer: "neither on this mountain nor in Jerusalem . . ." (4:21). Thus Jesus broadly negates all fixed places of worship. Finally, he declares that "in my Father's house there are many rooms. . . . I go to prepare a place for you" (14:2). On the one hand, these locations ("house," "rooms," "place") suggest a "where" for worship, but they do not refer to any fixed sacred space. James McCaffrey argues that we not consider these as geographical spaces at all: "The text describes the redemptive work of Christ in terms which pertain to the family and its intimate personal relationships."[3] Thus *where* one worships remains throughout the Gospel a major issue, for which we propose a model of fixed and fluid sacred space drawn from cultural anthropology.

How? True worshipers will perform actions that do not consist of sacrifice or require temple clergy, tithes, and revenues. Neither will they worship in fixed sacred space, nor in the manner of the Temple. At least this seems to be the substance of Jesus' remark: "True worshipers will worship the Father in spirit and truth" (4:23).[4] This remark, however, is mute on specific forms of worship. Inasmuch as so much attention is given to prayer(s) in John 14–17, prayer would seem to be a most promising place to start.

When? Although Jesus attended certain feast days in Jerusalem, scholars argue that he replaced with himself both the feasts and the benefits sought from

---

characteristics of the early Christian worship service" in the first quarter of his book, and then with a sacramental focus treats the various episodes in the Fourth Gospel which have to do with water/baptism, bread/Eucharist, Sabbath, and Temple. On occasion, one finds a treatment of worship in the Fourth Gospel as part of a larger work, for example, David E. Aune, *The Cultic Setting of Realized Eschatology in Early Christianity* (Leiden: Brill, 1972) 45-135.

3. James McCaffrey, *The House with Many Rooms: The Temple Theme of Jn. 14,2-3* (Rome: Pontifical Biblical Institute, 1988) 21.

4. For example, Herman Ridderbos, *The Gospel according to John* (Grand Rapids, MI: Eerdmans, 1997) 163.

them. Jesus is now the benefit of benefits sought at festive worship: he is the bread come down from heaven (6:33-51), the Passover lamb (19:33-34), the rains/water (7:37-38) and the sun/light (8:12) sought at Tabernacles. But where is the evidence that Johannine disciples kept a calendar of this sort? Balancing these replacements, we learn that special significance was given to the "first day of the week" (20:1) and the "eighth day" (20:26).

Who? Worship, of course, is directed to God. And God, who is spirit, seeks worshipers who worship in spirit and truth. Clearly, then, both God and a worshiping group are envisioned. But other figures function in this worship, namely, Jesus, in whose name the disciples petition God, and the Paraclete, who mediates Jesus' words to the group. But those who refuse or are afraid to acknowledge Jesus as sent from God are *not* true worshipers (8:24; 17:3). Is there any formal pattern to relationship among those who worship?

What, then, do we know? Oddly, we know where *not* to worship, how *not* to worship, and perhaps when *not* to worship. But the Gospel does not tell us of what worship consists, nor does it define roles and statuses of members of the worshiping group. Much more needs to be learned about worship so as to interpret the Fourth Gospel. First, our task begins with "worship" itself. While descriptive catalogues of early Christian "worship" are helpful, we search for a formal definition of it and a cultural model which will help us interpret its forms. From this perspective, we will interpret four forms of worship: prayer, prophecy, homily, judgment. Second, since the author puts so much emphasis on *where* the group worships, we need a model which compares and contrasts fixed and fluid sacred spaces. This will aid us in interpreting Jesus' remarks about "my Father's house" and "many rooms" (μοναί, 14:2). And in this light we will examine other aspects of *where* worship occurs: "being in" and "dwelling in." Third and finally, in attempting to understand the structural relationships between God, Jesus, Spirit and the group in worship, we turn to the model of patron-broker-client. The roles of God-patron and group-clients are clear, but modern scholarship often misunderstands the structural place of Jesus and the Paraclete in Johannine worship. Some clarification, then, is needed.

2.0 Worship in the Early Church

2.1 Early Worship Described and Catalogued

As we saw earlier, scholarly surveys[5] of early Christian worship agree that: 1) the early church borrowed heavily from synagogue worship both in form and con-

---

5. The sources consulted are: Oscar Cullmann, *Early Christian Worship*; C. C. Richardson,

tents, especially prayer and the study of the Scripture; 2) its activities were not tied to particular places, but could be practiced virtually anywhere; and 3) the central forms of worship were verbal.[6] Because of its comprehensiveness, David Aune's description is worth examining:

> Christian worship had a primarily verbal character, and in this respect it was similar to synagogue Judaism.... Yet Christians did have religious gatherings where various types of rituals were practiced. Christians gathered to eat together, to baptize new members, to read Scripture, to listen to God speaking through other Christians, to experience healing, to pray and sing hymns and thanksgivings to God. These activities were not tied to particular places, but could be practiced virtually anywhere.[7]

Aune, following Delling, Cullmann and Martin, identifies a variety of activities which fall under the genus "worship": 1) prayers, creeds and confessions, doxologies, hymns, songs and psalms, 2) prophecy (oracles of judgment, salvation, and the like), 3) sermons and homilies and 4) public reading of Scripture.[8] To this Cullmann added another, namely, remembering specifically the words and deeds of Jesus.

> The proclamation of the message of salvation had a fixed place not only in the early missionary preaching, but also in the worship services of the community. Intimately associated with it particularly in the assemblies of the community is the transmission of Jesus' words and narratives concerning him.[9]

As impressive as Aune's description of worship is, it does not address or answer many issues. For example, Aune's first element of worship, "prayer," seems

---

"Worship in New Testament Times, Christian," *IDB* 4.883-94; Gerhard Delling, *Worship in the NT* (London: Darton, Longman and Todd, 1962); Ralph P. Martin, *Worship in the Early Church* (London: Marshall, Morgan and Scott, 1964); Ferdinand Hahn, *The Worship of the Early Church* (Philadelphia: Fortress, 1973); David E. Aune, "Worship, Early Christian," *ABD* 6.973-89.

6. Early Christian worship differed from worship in the Greco-Roman world in that it had no temples, cult statues, or regular sacrifices. Thus David Aune ("Worship, Early Christian," 973) states: "Christian worship had a primarily verbal character, and in this respect it was similar to synagogue Judaism."

7. Aune, "Worship, Early Christian," 973.

8. The prototype of worship in the New Testament is found in Acts 2:42 ("they devoted themselves to the apostles' teaching and fellowship, to the breaking of the bread, and the prayers"), the letters of Paul (1 Cor 11:20ff.; 14:1-36), Pliny's letter to Trajan (*Epistle* 10.96), and reconstructions of early synagogue worship.

9. Cullmann, *Early Christian Worship*, 48-49.

fixated on *forms* of prayer to the exclusion of *classifications* of prayer according to their purpose. More attention, we think, should be given to the variety of reasons why one prays, the effect one wishes to have on God and the relationship that should be repaired or strengthened. Aune's description, while it identifies an entrance ritual, baptism, does not include other rituals of transformation or exit rituals. Ceremonial eating together is noted, but is there place for other ceremonies?

The importance of this material for our project lies in having a complete index of verbal forms of worship before we begin our reading of John 14–17. Thus, at this point, we know several important things: 1) worship is "primarily *verbal*"; 2) members "pray and sing hymns and thanksgivings"; 3) they not only speak to God in prayer, but also *listen to God* through the Scriptures, the words of Jesus, or Spirit-inspired utterances; and 4) these activities are *not* tied to *particular places*.

2.2 Worship Defined, Not Described

What is worship? Why include this or that action? Although descriptions of worship are ready to hand, definitions or models of it are rare. Most social science dictionaries either exclude it or discuss it under the term "religion." We suggest a social science definition of prayer by Bruce J. Malina, which lends itself to being readily adapted to describe all forms of worship.

> [Worship is] . . . a socially meaningful symbolic act of communication, bearing directly upon persons perceived as somehow supporting, maintaining, and controlling the order of existence of the one praying, and performed with the purpose of getting results from or in the interaction of communication.[10]

The underlying model is that of "communication theory," which Malina derived from social science experts in this field.[11] The model contains five elements: 1) a sender who sends 2) a message, 3) by means of some channel, 4) to a receiver, 5) for the purpose of having some effect. Malina's model explains how in the worshiping action of prayer 1) worshipers-senders send a 2) communication-message, 3) via some channel (script, verbal, material of-

---

10. Bruce J. Malina, "What Is Prayer?" *TBT* 18 (1980): 215.

11. David K. Berlo, *The Process of Communication* (New York, NY: Holt, Rinehart and Winston, 1960) 47-60; Everett M. Rogers and F. Floyd Shoemaker, *Communication of Innovations: A Cross-Cultural Approach* (New York, NY: Free Press, 1971) 11, 18-19, 251-52.

fering),[12] 4) to God, the object of prayer and worship, 5) for a purpose: to have some effect on the deity.

In worship, however, communication comes also from God, which indicates that our communication model should include a second direction which accounts for a flow of communication from God to mortals, who now listen instead of speak. The amplified communications model now looks like this.

	Worship as *speaking* to God	Worship as *listening* to God
sender:	mortals	God
message:	petitions, praise, etc.	information, rebuke, exhortation, etc.
channel:	voiced prayer, incense, sacrifice	Jesus, Holy Spirit or group member
receiver:	God	Christian group
effect:	see many types of prayer below	reform, inform, confirm, exhort

Since our definition of worship controls what we label as "worship" in a document, let us be clear about the object of worship, its purpose, and its forms of communication. Christians communicate with the "living and true God" and in turn listen to God's word(s). Worship's manifold purpose includes communication with God seeking to have various effects, such as thanksgiving, praise, petition, confession and the like.[13] And as speech from God, worship consists of listening to various types of communication from God: prophecy, the Jesus tradition, Scripture and homilies. These are spoken for the purpose of exhortation, enlightenment, judgment and the like. Now let us take this model of worship and examine Jesus' discourse in John 14–17.

---

12. As well as verbal means of communication (1 Tim 2:1), we know of pious Jews who insert slips of paper into the seams of the Old Wall on which are written various messages; I have personally observed both in Turkey and in Native American lands trees whose every branch has white cloths tied to it; and we are all acquainted with Buddhist prayer wheels and windsocks. Offerings in the Temple (animals, bread, libations, and incense) are material communications.

13. Philo provides an exceptional collection of varieties of verbal communication with God: "Under the head of the preservation offering is embraced what is called the praise-offering (αἰνέσεως) . . . (the blessed person) has as his bounded duty to requite God . . . with hymns (ὕμνοις) and benedictions (εὐδαιμονισμοῖς) and prayers (εὐχαῖς) and sacrifices (θυσίαις) and the other expressions of gratitude (εὐχαριστίαις) as religion demands. *All these collected and summed up have obtained the single name of praise* (αἰνέσεως)" (*Spec.* 1.224, emphasis added; see *Plant.* 135).

3.0 Worship in John 14–17

Most readers are comfortable with understanding John 14–17 in terms of its form-critical classification as a Farewell Address.[14] Yet the various prayers of Jesus throughout John 14–17 and especially the so-called "high priestly" prayer in John 17 suggest that "worship" is not a misleading category for interpreting John 14–17. We propose to examine these chapters in terms of the two directions of worship: 1) *speaking* to God (i.e., prayers) and 2) *listening* to God (i.e., prophecy, homily, and oracles of salvation/judgment).

3.1 Types of Prayer in Antiquity[15]

Bruce Malina provides readers with a sophisticated taxonomy of prayers. All prayer is a communication of mortals to God, but prayer differs from prayer in terms of the effect it seeks to have on God, ranging from petition to praise. Malina suggested the following taxonomy of prayers: 1) petitionary, 2) regulatory, 3) interactional, 4) self-focused, 5) heuristic, 6) imaginative, 7) acknowledgment/appreciation.

Petitionary prayer ("I need...") is a request for goods and services. For example, "Now, Lord, look upon their threats, and grant to your servants to speak your word with all boldness" (Acts 4:29). Elsewhere Jesus instructs the disciples how to make petitionary prayer: "Ask, and it will be given you; seek, and you will find; knock, and it will be opened to you" (Matt 7:7).

Regulatory prayer ("Do as I tell you...") seeks to control the activity of God, commanding God to order people and things about on behalf of the one praying.[16] Scholars distinguish the verb "to pray (for)" (εὔχομαι) from "to pray against" (ἀράομαι), the latter being conveniently translated as "to curse."[17] The former expresses one's wishes for oneself, and the latter one's wishes regarding others. Illustrative of the curse is the prayer against a rival in the hippodrome:

---

14. Fernando Segovia (*The Farewell of the Word* [Minneapolis: Fortress, 1991] 5) provides the most exhaustive treatment of this material.

15. Malina, "What Is Prayer?" 214-20; Bruce J. Malina and Richard L. Rohrbaugh, *Social-Scientific Commentary on the Gospel of John* (Minneapolis: Fortress Press, 1998) 246-47.

16. Included here are curses, spells, incantations and the like. See Christopher A. Faraone and Dirk Obgink, eds., *Magika Hiera: Ancient Greek Magic and Religion* (New York: Oxford University Press, 1991); Hans Dieter Betz, ed., *The Greek Magical Papyri in Translation* (2d ed.; Chicago: University of Chicago Press, 1986); Martin Meyer and Richard Smith, eds., *Ancient Christian Magic: Coptic Texts of Ritual Power* (San Francisco: Harper, 1994).

17. Simon Pulleyn, *Prayer in Greek Religion* (Oxford: Clarendon, 1997) 70-77.

"Bind, tie down, fetter, strike with a javelin, overturn, finish off, destroy, kill, crush Eucherius the charioteer and all the horses."[18]

Interactional prayer ("Where are you when I need you?") resembles the lament found in the Psalter. It is a petition expressed in desperate terms to God who seems to be slow to act. The pray-er asks a question of God, which is not a request for information, but a protest at God's seeming inactivity:

> Why do you hide your face? Why do you forget our affliction? (Ps 44:24)
> How long, O Lord? Will you forget me forever? (Ps 13:1)
> O God, why do you cast us off forever? (Ps 74:1)

Hence, the pray-er complains to God: "Why are you doing this or allowing it to happen"[19] and requests the restoration of a previously good relationship with God.

Self-focused prayer ("I gave them your word. . . . I kept them safe") describes persons identifying their individual selves to God.[20] The posture toward God may be a confession of a task finished or of superiority. Occasionally we find that in the psalms God is addressed, not in petition or praise, but in innocent confidence:

> O LORD, my heart is not lifted up, my eyes are not raised too high; I do not occupy myself with things too great and too marvelous for me. But I have calmed and quieted my soul, like a weaned child with its mother; my soul is like the weaned child that is with me. (Ps 131:1-2; see also Pss 40:10-11; 62:1-2, 5-6; and 108:1)

Examples of this type of prayer may be found in the literatures of ancient Egypt, Israel, and the Greco-Roman world as well as in the New Testament. The following communication/prayer was given by the deceased to the Egyptian guardians of the gates of the underworld; innocent persons declare their innocence.

> Behold, "*Sati-merfiti*, Lord of Justice,"
> I have brought you justice;
> I have not committed evil against men.

---

18. Pulleyn, *Prayer in Greek Religion*, 83. H. S. Versnel itemizes many of the types we are covering here, including "Offensive, indecent and improper prayers" in his *Faith, Hope and Worship: Aspects of Religious Mentality in the Ancient World* (Leiden: Brill, 1981) 21-26.

19. Patrick Miller, *They Cried to the Lord: The Form and Theology of Biblical Prayer* (Minneapolis, MN: Fortress, 1994) 71.

20. Versnel (*Faith, Hope and Worship*, 6-8, esp. n. 70) discusses what we call "self-focused" under the label "*Gebetsegoismus*," thus drawing on an old German conversation.

I have not mistreated cattle.
I have not done violence to a poor man.
I have not defamed a slave to his superior.
I have not made anyone sick.
I have not killed.
I have not had sexual relations with a boy.
I have not defiled myself.
I have neither increased or decreased the grain measure.
I am pure! I am pure! I am pure! I am pure![21]

Luke presents a comparison of two types of prayer in 18:9-14, a Pharisee praying a self-focused prayer in contrast to the petitionary prayer of a tax collector. As Gerald Downing noted in his study of this passage, the self-focused prayer should not ipso facto be labeled a bad prayer, for it was one commonly prayed in the Greco-Roman world.[22] Furthermore, we have several examples of this prayer from the Talmud.

> I thank you, O Lord my God, that you have given me my lot with those who sit in the seat of learning, and not with those who sit at the street corners; for I am early to work, and they are early to work; I am early to work on the words of the Torah, and they are early to work on things of no moment. I weary myself and they weary themselves; I weary myself and profit by it, while they weary themselves to no profit. I run, and they run; I run toward the life of the Age to Come, and they run towards the pit of destruction. (*b. Berakot* 28b)[23]

As we shall see, this and petitionary prayer are the dominant types of prayer prayed by Jesus in John 17.

Heuristic prayer ("Tell me why . . . ?") is best illustrated by Job, who searches relentlessly to know God's ways. Many times Job asks heuristic ques-

---

21. James B. Pritchard, *Ancient Near Eastern Texts* (Princeton, NJ: Princeton University Press, 1950) 34. The citation in our text is only a selection from the whole confession.

22. F. Gerald Downing, "The Ambiguity of 'The Pharisee and the Tax Collector' (Luke 18:9-14) in the Greco-Roman World of Late Antiquity," *CBQ* 45 (1992): 80-99.

23. Joachim Jeremias, *The Parables of Jesus* (New York: Scribner, 1963) 142. He points to another example of this type of prayer: "I (who study the law) am a creature of God, and my fellow man is a creature (of God). My work is in the city, his in the field; I rise early to my work, he rises early to his. Just as he cannot excel in my work, so I cannot excel in his. Perhaps you will say, I do much and he does little (for the Torah). But we have learned . . . he who offers much and he who offers little are equal, provided that each directs his heart to heaven" (*b. Berakot* 17a).

tions to God to learn God's ways (3:11-15; 6:8-13; 9:1-10; 12:2-25). Similarly, H. S. Versnel indicates that the gods were called upon at times in a detective capacity: "Did D steal the gown?" "Has so and so kidnapped my slave?" He goes on to describe questions asked of various oracles.[24] Perhaps the best illustration of heuristic prayer is found in Plutarch's treatise on oracles, in which he informs us the kinds of questions put to the god:

> The interrogations are on slight and commonplace matters, like the hypothetical questions in school: if one ought to marry, or to start on a voyage, or to make a loan; and the most important consultations on the part of States concern the yield from crops, the increase of herds, and public health. (Plutarch, *Oracles at Delphi* 408C)

Imaginative/contemplative prayer ("I was caught up to the second heaven") occasionally describes those praying who find themselves having out of body experiences.[25] They might be taken up to the heavens (2 Cor 12:1-3) or receive visions on earth.[26] They may pray in "tongues" to God, a language known only to them, when an interpreter is present (1 Cor 14:6-26).

Acknowledgment prayer ("I bless you . . . I name you Sovereign Lord") is speech addressed to God which 1) acknowledges God's sovereignty or glory, 2) praises and declares God's worthiness or 3) expresses gratitude for divine benefaction. God in the Christian Scriptures cannot be ascribed honor, because there is no person above God to bestow honor on God. The issue is that of *acknowledging* God's *claims* to worthiness and respect. "Acknowledgment" may be found on the pray-ers' lips, or expressed by their posture (bend the knee; prostration) or in their hearts. Although all prayers of acknowledgment "inform" God of something, they do not give God new knowledge, but rather acknowledge God's claims.

> *Know* that the Lord is God; he made us and we are his (Ps 100:3)
> I will *confess* you among the gentiles and *sing* to your name (Rom 15:9//Ps 18:49)
> Let all the earth *fear* the Lord . . . *stand in awe* of him (Ps 33:8).

---

24. Versnel, *Faith, Hope and Worship*, 6-8.
25. John J. Pilch, "Altered States of Consciousness in the Synoptics," *The Social Setting of Jesus and the Gospels*, ed. Wolfgang Stegemann, Bruce J. Malina, and Gerd Theissen (Minneapolis, MN: Fortress, 2002) 103-16; idem, "Holy Men and Their Sky Journeys" *BTB* 35 (2005): 106-11.
26. John J. Pilch, "Appearances of the Risen Jesus in Cultural Context: Experiences of Alternate Reality," *BTB* 28 (1998): 52-60.

Honoring the name of God is another type of acknowledgment commonly found in the psalms: "O Lord, our Lord, how majestic is your *name* in all the earth" (Ps 8:1). Honoring the name of a deity was a phenomenon found throughout the Greco-Roman world, as is instanced by Seneca:

> You may address the author of this world by *different names*... call him Jupiter Best and Greatest, and the Thunderer and the Stayer.... Any name you choose will be properly applied to him if it connotes some force that operates in the domain of heaven — *his titles may be as countless as are his benefits.* (Seneca, *Benefits* 4.7.1, emphasis added)

Finally, the Psalter again provides a variety of different ways in which Israel glorified, praised and exalted God. Alleluia!

> The heavens declare the *glory* of God (Ps 19:1)
> Great is the Lord and greatly to be *praised* in the city of our God (Ps 48:1)
> *Clap your hands,* all peoples. *Shout* to God with *loud songs of joy* (Ps 47:1)
> *Sing* to the Lord; *bless* his name; *declare his glory* among the nations (Ps 96:2-3)

In interpreting the prayer contained in John 14-17, we must pay attention, not only to petitionary and self-focused prayer, but to acknowledgment prayer as well.

3.2 Petitionary Prayer in John 14–16

No one can read John 14–17 without noting Jesus' repetitive instructions to "ask" the Father for some benefit, which in the taxonomy we are using means *petitionary* prayer. The New Testament employs a variety of verbs in the context of prayerful petitioning. In one sense they all mean "to ask for," but they differ in the urgency with which the request is made. Most frequently readers find petitionary request expressed in 1) "to ask with urgency, beg" (δέομαι) and 2) "to speak to, make requests" (προσεύχομαι). John's petitions, however, are expressed by different words, 1) "to ask with urgency even to the point of demanding" (αἰτέω) and 2) "to ask, request" (ἐρωτάω), but without any change of meaning. Except for Martha's remark that Jesus could petition God for Lazarus (11:22), the other eleven instances of petitionary prayer all occur in the Farewell Address, which thus constitute a distinct body of materials on this type of prayer.

14:13-14	"Whatever you *ask* in my name, I will do it . . . if you *ask* anything in my name . . ."
14:16	"I will *pray* the Father and he will send another Counselor"
15:7	"If you abide in me and my words abide in you, *ask* whatever you will . . ."
15:16b	"whatever you *ask* the Father in my name . . ."
16:23-24	"In that day you will *ask* nothing of me . . . if you *ask* anything of the Father . . ."
16:26	"In that day you will *ask* in my name"

In addition to the insistent instructions of Jesus, we note several things. First, the object of the petitions is both vastly expansive ("whatever" and "anything") and specific ("the Counselor"). Second, while the Patron being petitioned is always God, Jesus maintains his role as broker by indicating that the petitions will be made "in my name." He himself will initiate the process by petitioning on their behalf ("I will ask . . ."). Petitionary prayer, moreover, is only one type of prayer found in John 14–16. When we turn to John 17, we observe a prayer composed of many types.

3.3 Jesus' Multi-Purposed Prayer in John 17

Malina's taxonomy of prayer provides the means to distinguish different types of prayer occurring in John 17. In general, we consider that John 17 contains two basic forms of prayer: 1) petitionary and 2) self-focused, as the chart below indicates:[27]

John 17	Prayer Text	Classification
v. 2	Glorify thy Son so that the Son may glorify thee . . .	petitionary
v. 3	This is eternal life, that they (ack)know(ledge) you the only true God, and Jesus Christ whom you have sent.	acknowledgment

---

27. It is a commonplace among commentators to divide John 17 into three sections: 17:1-8 = Jesus' prayer for himself; 17:9-19 = Jesus' prayer for his disciples; and 17:20-26 = Jesus' prayer for those whom his disciples will recruit. See Raymond E. Brown, *The Gospel According to John* (Garden City, NY: Doubleday, 1970) 2.748-51; and with minor variations, see C. H. Talbert, *Reading John: A Literary and Theological Commentary on the Fourth Gospel and the Johannine Epistles* (New York: Crossroad, 1992) 224-31. As accurate as this literary division may be, it obscures the different types of prayers which occur throughout 17:1-26. Hence a different kind of model is needed which can do just that.

Worship in the Fourth Gospel

John 17	Prayer Text	Classification
v. 5	Glorify me in your own presence with the glory which I had with you before the world was made.	petitionary
v. 6	I have manifested Your NAME to the men whom you gave me out of the world.	self-focused
vv. 6-8	Yours they were, and you gave them to me, and they have kept your word. Now they know that everything you have given me is from you; for I have given them the words which you gave me, and they have received them and know in truth that I came from you; and they have believed that you sent me.	self-focused
v. 9	I am praying for them; I am not praying for those in the world, but for those whom You have given me, for they are yours.	self-focused + petitionary
v. 10	All mine are thine; and thine are mine; and I am glorified in them.	self-focused
v. 11	Keep them in your NAME, which you have given to me, that they may be one, even as we are one.	petitionary
v. 12	While I was with them, I kept them in your NAME, which you have given me; I have guarded them and none of them is lost but the son of perdition.	self-focused
vv. 13-14	But now I am coming to you; and these things I speak in the world, that they may have my joy fulfilled in themselves. I have given them your word, and the world has hated them because they are not of the world, even as I am not of the world.	self-focused
v. 15	I do not pray that you should take them out of the world, but keep them from the Evil One.	petitionary
v. 16	They are not of the world, even as I am not of the world.	self-focused
v. 17	Sanctify them in your truth.	petitionary

vv. 18-19	As You sent me into the world, so I have sent them into the world. For their sake I consecrate myself, that they also may be consecrated in truth.	self-focused
vv. 20-21	I do not pray for these only, but also for those who believe in me through their word that they may all be one; even as You, Father, are in me and I in You, that they may be in us, so that the world may believe that You have sent me.	self-focused + petitionary
vv. 22-23	The glory which you have given me, I have given them, that they may be one, even as we are one, I in them and You in me, that they may be perfectly one, that the world may know that you have sent me and have loved them even as you have loved me.	self-focused
v. 24	Father, I desire that they also, whom You have given to me, may be with me where I am, to behold my glory which You have given me in your love for me before the foundation of the world.	petitionary
vv. 25-26	O just Father, the world has not known you; but I have known you; and these know that you have sent me. I made known to them Your NAME, and I will make it known that the love with which you have loved me may be in them, and I in them.	self-focused

We observe that Jesus *petitions* God frequently (17:1, 5, 11, 15, 17, 20-21, 24), the form of which is easily discerned: 1) a verb of "asking" in the imperative mood, and 2) a request for a specific benefaction from God (glory, unity, special relationship, etc.). We see, moreover, another type of prayer, which Malina calls *self-focused* (17:6-8, 9, 10, 12, 13-14, 16, 18-19, 20, 22-23, 25-26), whose shape is also clearly expressed: 1) a first-person speech: "I made manifest . . . ," "I kept them in your name" . . . "I have given them your word" (vs. second person in petitionary prayer), which 2) celebrates the record of Jesus' past good deeds (vs future benefactions in petitionary prayer). In John 17 Jesus tells God that he has fulfilled his apostleship and done what God sent him to do:

> I have glorified you on earth (v. 4).
> I have manifested your name (vv. 6, 26).

I have given them the words which you have given me (vv. 8, 14).
I have kept them in your name (v. 12a).
I have guarded them (v. 12b).
I have sent them into the world (v. 18).
I have consecrated myself (v. 19).
I have given them the glory which you have given me (v. 22).
I have "known" you (v. 25).

Unlike petitionary prayer, Jesus declares to God before his disciples his perfect fulfilment of the mission he was sent to accomplish:[28] 1) he has *glorified* God on earth, 2) *manifested* to the disciples the divine *Name* and *kept* them in it, 3) *given* the divine *words* to them and 4) *extended* his work by sending them into the world.[29]

Labeling John 17 as a "high priestly" is clearly anachronistic, although the label does convey the sense that Jesus enjoys the role of mediator or broker, a topic which will be shortly developed.[30] Similarly, the prayer celebrates his effectiveness in the role of channel of God's benefaction to the disciples. Benefits came through Jesus and will continue to come through him.

Jesus' self-focused prayer may also be seen as a claim to the virtue of piety or justice. Throughout the Greco-Roman world, justice was thought of as the noble fulfilment of one's basic duties. Ps.-Aristotle states:

> First among the claims of righteousness are our duties to the gods, then our duties to the spirits, then those to country and parents, then those to the departed; among these claims is piety (εὐσέβεια), which is either a part of righteousness or a concomitant of it. Righteousness is also accompanied by holiness (ὁσιότης) and truth (ἀλήθεια) and loyalty (πίστις) and hatred of wickedness. (*Virtues and Vices*, 5.2-3)

---

28. It has long been a staple of commentaries on John 17 to compare and contrast it with the "Our Father" in the Synoptics. See William O. Walker, "The Lord's Prayer in Matthew and John," NTS 28 (1982): 237-56.

29. Although he seems to consider "prayer" only as "petitionary" speech, Ernst Käsemann (*The Testament of Jesus: A Study of John in the Light of Chapter 17* [London: SCM Press, 1968] 5) commented on the variety of Jesus' speech in John 17, yet he writes: "This is not a supplication, but a proclamation directed to the Father in such manner that his disciples can hear it also. The speaker is not a needy petitioner but the divine revealer and therefore the prayer moves over into being an address, admonition, consolation and prophecy."

30. Raymond Brown (*The Gospel According to John*, 2.747) said: "If Jesus is a high priest here, it is not primarily in the sense of one about to offer sacrifice, but more along the lines of the high priest described in Hebrews and in Rom viii 34 — one who stands before the throne of God making intercession for us."

The distinction of the triple focus of justice is found regularly in the philosophical and rhetorical literature of antiquity,[31] and also in John 17. Here Jesus acknowledges that he has fulfilled his *duties to God* ("I have glorified you . . . manifested your name . . . given them your words") and his *duties to "kin"* ("I have kept them . . . guarded them, etc.").[32] Thus the Just Jesus celebrates his virtuous completion of the duties he owes to God, who is Father and Patron, as well as to "kin."

Yet in 17:3 we find still a third type of prayer, namely, *acknowledgment:* "This is eternal life, that they know You, the only true God, and Jesus Christ whom You have sent." Instead of a petition, we find here an honorable acknowledgment of God in traditional words. This prayer consists of two elements: 1) we read "to know" in the sense of "to ac*know*ledge," that is, to honor, and confess the worth, sovereignty and excellence of God.[33] The first part of 17:3 resembles the confession known as the Shema, the premier prayer of the synagogue (see Mark 12:29, 32; Deut 6:4). Thus acknowledgment of the "only true God" is an appropriate confessional honoring of God. But 17:3 also includes 2) confession of "Jesus Christ whom you have sent." So the complete honoring of God consists of the acknowledgment both of the unique God of Israel and of God's unique agent, Jesus.[34] While "confession" and "creed" are no strangers to New Testament scholarship, rarely do we find them discussed as "prayer."[35]

---

31. Other samples of this include *Rhetorica ad Herennium*: "(justice is shown) if we contend that alliances and friendships should scrupulously be honored; if we make it clear that the duty imposed by nature towards parents, gods, and fatherland must be religiously observed; if we maintain that ties of hospitality, clientage, kinship, and relationship by marriage must inviolably be cherished; if we show that neither reward nor favour nor peril nor animosity ought to lead us astray from the right path; if we say that in all cases a principle of dealing alike with all should be established" (3.3.4). Similarly, Menander Rhetor (*Menander Rhetor* [trans. D. A. Russell and N. G. Wilson; Oxford: Clarendon, 1981]): "The parts of justice are piety, fair dealing and reverence: piety toward the gods, fair dealing towards men, reverence toward the departed. Piety to the gods consists of two elements: being god-loved and god-loving. The former means being loved by the gods and receiving many blessings from them, the latter consists of loving the gods and having a relationship of friendship with them" (1.1361.17-25).

32. It should be noted that God is addressed as "Just Father" (17:25), indicating that God too has duties toward Jesus and his disciples.

33. See Robert Picirelli, "The Meaning of 'Epignosis,'" *EvQ* 47 (1975): 85-93; see also Jerome H. Neyrey, *2 Peter, Jude* (New York: Doubleday, 1993) 149. See Tit 1:16, where "know" is juxtaposed with "deny," Rom 1:20-21, where "knowing" does *not* lead to "acknowledging," and Jas 2:19, where knowing that God is one does *not* lead the demons to honor God.

34. In John 5:23, Jesus declared that God had given all judgment to the Son "so that all may honor the Son even as they honor the Father. Who does not honor the Son does not honor the Father who sent him."

35. Representative of these is Cullmann (*Early Christian Worship*, 22), who asserts "We may

John 17:3 is situated in a continuous address to God which petitions God for the disciples, who as clients should make the prayer-confession in v. 3 to their heavenly Patron while acknowledging that Jesus is the true agent sent from heaven.[36] The disciples' "knowing" of Israel's "only, true God" is not simply knowledge, but acknowledging and honoring God and the deity's existential plans. This prayer, moreover, is not possible in Temple and synagogue (e.g., 9:22; 12:42).[37]

4.0 Listening to God

According to our model of communication, a *sender* sends a *message* via some *channel* to a *receiver* to have an *effect*. In the case of prayer, the senders are the Johannine members who send a message via Jesus-as-channel to God; but in the case of prophecy, the process is reversed as God speaks to mortals, not listens to them. In prophecy, 1) God, the *sender*, 2) sends a *verbal message*, 3) through the *channel* of Jesus, the "Spirit of Truth," or a disciple-prophet, 4) to the *receiver*s, the members of the Johannine group, 5) for the *purpose* of communicating to them special information. But in the Fourth Gospel, the sender of esoteric information also seems to be Jesus. While in general Jesus remains mediator and broker of God's benefaction, in regard to prophecy he functions as the source or sender. This may be because most of the prophetic materials concern themselves with remembering Jesus' words which are themselves mediated by the Spirit who will bear witness to Jesus (15:26).[38] This may be an idiosyncratic quirk from a maverick Gospel.

---

assume with certainty that *Confessional formulae* were recited in the early Christian service of worship. The verbs ὁμολογεῖν and ἐξομολογεῖσθαι (Rom 10:9; Phil 2:11, etc.) connect above all with the confession that Christ is the Lord, in the same way as the early liturgical prayer *Maranatha* is concerned with his second coming." See also Ralph Martin, *Worship in the Early Church*, 52-65; Gerhard Delling, *Worship in the New Testament*, 77-91; and David Aune, "Worship, Early Christian," 981.

36. Peder Borgen, "God's Agent in the Fourth Gospel," *Religions in Antiquity*, ed. Jacob Neusner (Leiden: Brill, 1968) 137-48; George W. Buchanan, "Apostolic Christology," *SBLSP* 1986: 172-82.

37. John 9:22 and 12:42 tell us that those who make the confession found in 17:3 will be expelled from the synagogue. Confessional prayers are sometimes 1) thanksgivings or doxologies, such as Matt 11:25//Luke 10:21; 1 Tim 1:16; 6:12-16, 2) protestations of loyalty, such as Matt 10:32//Luke 12:8, or 3) the honorific acknowledgment of Jesus' new role and status (Rom 10:9-10; 1 Cor 12:3; Phil 2:11).

38. M. Eugene Boring, *The Continuing Voice of Jesus* (Louisville, KY: Westminster John Knox, 1991) 38.

We need, however, a catalogue of the varieties of prophetic speech to alert us to what types of prophetic oracles are possible and their respective purposes. At the end of his study of prophecy in early Christianity and the Hellenistic world, David Aune offers the following catalogue of "basic forms of Christian prophetic speech": 1) oracles of assurance; 2) prescriptive oracles; 3) announcements of salvation; 4) announcements of judgment; 5) legitimation oracles; and 6) eschatological theophany oracles.[39]

4.1 "Prophet" in the Fourth Gospel

The Fourth Gospel occasionally records people favorable to Jesus acclaiming him as a prophet (4:19; 6:14; 7:40 (52); 9:17), generally because of his wisdom or powers; thus he is the traditional "prophet mighty in word and deed." But prophet/prophecy in John 14–17, while it focuses on the words of Jesus, also foresees events already in the process of occurring and predictions of future events.[40] Among the many remarks about "going away" and "coming back" (14:3, 18-19; 16:16), we find three statements that serve a special purpose which surpasses the mere communication of esoteric information. Some predictions by Jesus serve a prophylactic purpose of confirming loyalty in times of conflict. For example, after repeating the remark "I go away and I will come to you," Jesus states the reason for telling this to his disciples: "Now I have told you before it takes place, so that when it does take place, you may believe" (14:28-29). Similarly, after Jesus discloses the bleak future awaiting the disciples (16:1-2), he explains once again the prophylactic purpose of the prediction: "I have said these things to you, that when their hour comes you may remember that I told you of them" (16:4).[41] The Fourth Gospel would have us read these statements as communication from Jesus in the course of his career, which, when remembered, ameliorate a forthcoming crisis by

---

39. David E. Aune, *Prophecy in Early Christianity and the Ancient Mediterranean World* (Grand Rapids, MI: Eerdmans, 1983) 320-25.

40. In their remarkable commentary, Bruce J. Malina and Richard L. Rohrbaugh (*Social-Science Commentary on the Synoptic Gospels* [Minneapolis, MN: Fortress, 2003] 361-63) call attention to the expectation that those about to die experienced an altered state of consciousness whereby the person in transition belonged to both worlds, present and to come; hence they knew of coming events, which they told to their clan: "At the advent of death, men become more divine, and hence can foresee the forthcoming" (Xenophon, *Cyropaedia* 7.7.21; see also Plato, *Apology* 39c; Homer, *Iliad* 16.849-50).

41. Besides announcing a traitor, Jesus states the purpose of this communication: "I tell you this now, before it takes place, that when it takes place, you may believe that I am he" (13:19). The prediction of Peter's future death given by the Risen Jesus (21:18-19) likewise functions as a prophecy given to offset the shock of future suffering.

indicating a providential knowledge of, if not control of, forthcoming, painful events. Thus, the purpose of this prophetic communication is exhortation to faithfulness, courage and the like. Oracles of assurance? Salvation?

In a similar vein, when Jesus tells the disciples that they will be hated (15:18-25), he adds, "Remember the word that I said to you, 'A servant is not greater than his master'" (15:20). An earlier word in 13:16 reads: "A servant is not greater than his master, nor is he who is sent greater than him who sent him." But this remark occurs in the context of the mandate of Jesus that the disciples wash one another's feet: if Jesus (master) did so, then disciples (servants) must do likewise. Although in 15:18-25 the words are the same, the context has changed. Now "hate" is the fate of both master and servants. Thus past words can be prophetic of forthcoming events, especially trials awaiting the disciples. And in both cases, they communicate assurance and encouragement.

4.2 Missing Information: Statement, Misunderstanding, Clarification

Prophecy may also be understood as the communication of esoteric information needed to understand Jesus' cryptic words. Throughout the Fourth Gospel the author regularly casts Jesus' discourse with friend and foe in terms of a pattern known as "statement, misunderstanding, and clarification." Jesus makes a statement ("You know the way where I am going," 14:4), which is misunderstood ("Lord, we do not know where you are going, how can we know the way?" 14:5), which prompts Jesus to offer a clarification ("I am the way, the truth, and the life," 14:6).

Statement	*Misunderstanding*	*Clarification*
14:1-4	14:5	14:6
14:7	14:8	14:9-11
14:18-21	14:22	14:23-24
16:16	16:17-18	16:19-24
16:25-27	16:29-30	16:31-33

Although instances of this pattern occur regularly throughout the Gospel, we observe a density of them in chs. 14 and 16, which is Jesus' final address to his inner circle of disciples. Previously this pattern served as catechetical enlightenment of enlighten-able disciples, such as the Samaritan Woman, but also as a wall which shuts out unenlightenable disciples, such as Nicodemus and the Jerusalem crowds. Here, insiders and core disciples require special information about the cryptic world of Jesus, which is provided for them eventually, we suggest, by prophets speaking in the name of Jesus. Although we will take up the topic of the "Spirit of truth" enlightening or reminding the disciples, the Spirit is presumed in this discussion as a broker of Jesus. Thus, this pattern functions to make and maintain boundaries; it informs, but by doing so marks and confirms certain persons as elite insiders.

The quest for esoteric information may be observed also in the pattern of questions and answers found in John 14–16. In addition to the question of Thomas noted above (14:5), Judas, not the Iscariot, asked "How is it that you will manifest yourself to us, and not to the world?" (14:22). In several places Jesus himself anticipates and asks their question to facilitate his next remarks. Although Jesus' question to Philip has much of the reproach in it (14:9), it issues in a remarkable revelation of Jesus' union with God (14:10-11), surely a singular favor. Similarly, Jesus questions the failure of the disciples to ask about a cryptic remark (16:5). At the very least, this pattern indicates that Jesus' speech is filled with esoteric information and double-meaning words, which the receivers do not fully perceive at first and which require explanation. Here at least, Jesus can lead the disciples into fuller insight by his subsequent clarifying statements. But in terms of group worship, a prophet during the group worship would presumably access the questions and provide an enlightened answer.[42] As regards function, the providing of special, esoteric knowledge both designates and confirms elite membership.

Furthermore, this Gospel records Jesus declaring that "I have said this to you in figures; the hour is coming when I will no longer speak to you in figures" (16:25). Does this cover only the metaphor of hard times resembling childbirth (16:20-24) or also the cryptic statements about "going away" and "coming back"? Minimally, a communication is given to the disciples which is admittedly "in figures," liable to "misunderstanding," or containing double meanings. But the veil will be lifted when in the future a prophet remembers, studies, examines, and interprets Jesus' words.

4.3 Homily

Scholars who write on early Christian sermons or homilies draw on two sources: the ancient synagogue service and summary remarks like Acts 2:42 ("devoted to the apostles' teaching, fellowship, breaking of the bread, and

---

42. The classic example of later reception of the esoteric meaning of earlier speech of Jesus is found 2:19, 21-22. Only "when he was raised from the dead, his disciples remembered that he had said this; and they believed the scripture and the word Jesus had spoken." But this insight must be mediated by someone in the group, namely, the prophet.

prayers").⁴³ "Teaching" likely has some affinity with homilies/sermons given in synagogues, which tended to be concerned with exegesis of Scripture or legal precision over what is proscribed and prescribed. Two types of homily have been observed by the experts, the *proem* and the *yelammedenu*. The *proem* form takes its name from *proemium* or introduction. It introduced the Scripture readings to the group from the Torah or Prophets. The *proem* was a verse chosen by the speaker, which is not found in either reading, so as such it is not an exegesis or explanation of either. Rather the speaker chose the *proem* to be remote from the readings, but by his pursuit of some inner connection between this verse and the Scriptural readings he might suggest explanations and clarifications of them so that when the homily concluded, hearers would have a taste for it, a hint of its hidden meanings, and an intellectual satisfaction.⁴⁴

The second form, the *yelammedenu*, takes its name from the introductory formula of many sermons found in the collection named *Tanchuma*. Each sermon begins with "Let our rabbis teach us [about] . . . ," which means "Let our teacher instruct us" *(yelammedenu)*. This is followed by an answer introduced by "Thus our rabbis taught us . . ." In general it might be said that these synagogue homilies tend to be instructions, teachings and interpretations.⁴⁵

Homilies and sermons written for a Greco-Roman audience deserve consideration. We build on the works of Lawrence Wills and C. Clifton Black, who have pioneered research on these materials. Wills's survey of New Testament and early Christian speeches led to this conclusion:

> 1. An indicative or exemplary section *(exempla)* in the form of scriptural quotations, authoritative examples from the past and present or reasoned exposition of theological points; 2. a conclusion, based on the *exempla* and indicating their significance to those addressed (often expressed with a participle and "what then," "therefore," "by this," or some such particle or conclusion); and 3. an exhortation (usually in the imperative or hortatory subjunctive, often accompanied by "then").⁴⁶

---

43. Everett Ferguson, *Early Christians Speak* (Austin, TX: Sweet Publishing Company, 1971) 86-87; Cullmann, *Early Christian Worship*, 12-14, 28-29; Delling, *Worship in the New Testament*, 92-103; Martin, *Worship in the Early Church*, 66-76; Richardson, "Worship in New Testament Times," 887-89; Aune, "Worship, Early Christian," 983.

44. Joseph Heinemann, "The Proem in the Aggadic Midrashim — A Form Critical Study," *Scripta Hierosolymitana* 22 (1971): 100-122.

45. J. W. Bowker, "Speeches in Acts: A Study in Proem and Yelammedenu Form," *NTS* 14 (1967): 96-111.

46. Lawrence Wills, "The Form of the Sermon in Hellenistic Judaism and Early Christianity," *HTR* 77 (1984): 278-80.

His parade piece is Acts 13:14-41 in which the speaker begins with a reprise of salvation history from Exodus to Conquest to the good news about Jesus (13:16-33) and concludes with a citation of Scripture which is interpreted to refer to Jesus (13:33-37). After this the speaker draws a conclusion as though he were finishing a syllogism: "Therefore through this man, forgiveness of sins is proclaimed . . . and by him everyone is freed from everything from which you could not be freed by the law of Moses" (13:38-39). This conclusion about Jesus' mediation implies that the hearers should ally themselves with Jesus to share in his powers. After urging acceptance, the author exhorts the audience not to fail to act, lest the dire prophecy of Hab 1:5 be fulfilled (13:40-41).

C. Clifton Black basically endorses Wills's study, but considers the material in terms of the three types of classical rhetoric, but especially deliberative.[47] For him, deliberative rhetoric embraces "speeches that entail consideration of future action, a choice between two or more forms of conduct, based on self-interest or future benefit."[48] For example, he analyzes Peter's Pentecostal remarks as deliberative rhetoric: "Repent, and be baptized every one of you in the name of Jesus Christ for the forgiveness of your sins; and you shall receive the gift of the Holy Ghost" (Acts 2:38).

Black also considers Acts 13 not only as deliberative rhetoric but in terms of the traditional parts of a speech. There is no *captatio benevolentiae* here; but one does find *narratio* in the detailed recitation of God's saving acts to Israel (13:16-26), a *propositio* (13:26), followed by a *probatio* or demonstration (13:27-37). In this the author demonstrates that "the significance of Jesus, formerly ignored by the inhabitants of Jerusalem, has been vindicated by the resurrection and corroborated by the Scriptures."[49] The speech ends with a classic *conclusio* or epilogue (13:38-41), which recapitulates the basic argument (13:38-39) and arouses the emotions (13:40-41).

What do we know if we know this? Some text, perhaps only an metaphor, serves to focus attention and provide direction for the discourse. Deliberative rhetoric or exhortation seems to be a large part of discourse: either moral reform or progress, behavior urged which is representative of the group. The examples surveyed suggest that they are not haphazard remarks, but highly crafted speech, even following the canons of classical rhetoric.

Although neither the Jewish nor the Greco-Roman types of homily apply exactly to materials in John 15–16, we find, nevertheless, two exhortations side-

---

47. C. Clifton Black, "The Rhetorical Form of the Hellenistic Jewish and Early Christian Sermon: A Response to Lawrence Wills," *HTR* 81 (1988): 1-18.
48. Black, "The Rhetorical Form of the Hellenistic Jewish and Early Christian Sermon," 5.
49. Black, "The Rhetorical Form of the Hellenistic Jewish and Early Christian Sermon," 8-9.

by-side. In 15:1-8 and 9-17 the audience is exhorted in the type of rhetoric called deliberative to choose and keep on choosing loyalty to Jesus and his Father. In terms of our communication model, "teaching" or "exhortation" or "instruction" is diagramed as follows: 1. a *sender* (God), 2. sends a *message* (teaching, exhortation), 3. via some *channel* (Jesus → Spirit → teacher), 4. to *receivers* (Johannine group), 5. to have some *effect* on them (to confirm and to urge loyalty). We focus, then, on 15:1-8 and 9-17 because these exhortations most closely accord with the elements of deliberative rhetoric.

In regard to 15:1-8, the topic of the exhortation is introduced in the metaphor: "I am the vine, my father is the vine dresser" (15:1).[50] The entire passage exhorts the disciples to choose to "remain" in the vine. This exhortation occurs seven times, sometimes in the imperative mood and sometimes in a conditional clause, surely indicative of the choice to be made.

> *Abide* in me as I abide in you. Just as the branch cannot bear fruit by itself unless it *abides* in the vine, neither can you unless you *abide* in me. I am the vine, you are the branches. Those who *abide* in me and I in them bear much fruit, because apart from me you can do nothing. Whoever does not *abide* in me is thrown away like a branch and withers; such branches are gathered, thrown into the fire, and burned. If you *abide* in me, and my words *abide* in you, ask for whatever you wish, and it will be done for you. (15:4-7)

Seven occurrences! The exhortation builds on current relationships and urges the disciples to maintain them in the future, the value of which relationships provides the argument from advantage. The relationships are: Jesus = vine, the disciples = the branches, while the Father = the vine dresser (15:1-2, 5). The telltale signs of an argument from advantage suggests that we consider this material an example of deliberative rhetoric which "appeals for action *on the basis of future benefits.*"[51] "Remaining" brings sweet advantage, just as "*not* remaining" leads to bitterness. A branch which remains and is cleansed by the vine dresser "bears much fruit" (15:2), a phrase which is repeated 3 times (15:4, 5, 8) to underscore the advantage that comes from "remaining." Similarly, branches which "remain" may petition God for "whatever you will" and expect God's positive response (15:7) — advantage indeed! In contrast, we are told of the sanctions imposed on those who do "*not* remain." They are taken away (15:2), and worse, "are cast forth . . . wither . . . thrown into the fire and burned" (15:6).

---

50. Many have seen the mention of "vine" as a reference to various Old Testament texts that use this metaphor for Israel. If this is so, then the "vine" would function like a citation or reference to a text which is subsequently developed. See Raymond E. Brown, *The Gospel according to John* (Garden City, NY: Doubleday, 1970) 2.669-72.

51. Black, "The Rhetorical Form of the Hellenistic Jewish and Early Christian Sermon," 5.

We find clear argumentative patterns here. "Unless the branch remains..." is a necessary condition frequently found in the Fourth Gospel: "unless" one is born of the Spirit or eats the flesh of the Son of Man or is washed by Jesus, one does not experience the benefit of God. So, too, here the advantage of "remaining" is also cast in the form of an "unless" argument: "A branch cannot bear fruit *unless* it remains in the vine, neither can you, *unless* you remain in me" (15:4)[52] Similarly, in 15:6-7 conditional sentences articulate the deliberative character of "remaining" and "*not* remaining": "*Unless* disciples remain, they are cast forth . . . *if* you remain in me and my words remain in you, you may ask for whatever you wish."

The speaker, moreover, provides reasons for the right choice. On the positive side, the "cleansing" of the vine (a euphemism for something like testing gold in a furnace?) serves the purpose of causing the branches to bear more fruit, clearly an advantage. And Jesus gives the reason why branches must "remain" in the vine: *"for"* without me you can do nothing" (15:5). Because we observe an argument being made, not merely information being imparted, we consider 15:1-8 an example of deliberative rhetoric, which places before the disciples the decision of "remaining," a deliberation richly rewarded or severely sanctioned.

A second exhortation follows immediately, which begins with a command to *remain* ("*Remain* in my *love*," 15:9) and ends with a command to *love* ("*Love* one another," 15:17). Evidently the focus here is on *love*, although 15:9-17 are linked with 15:1-8 by means of four more references to *remain* (15:9-10, 16). Thus 15:1-8 and 9-17 should be seen as parallel and linked exhortations, the first one expressing a vertical series of relationships between vine dresser, vine and branches, and the second one horizontal relationships between "one another." As was the case with 15:1-8, the exhortation in 15:9-17 is argued by: 1) imperatives, urging: "Love one another!"; 2) conditional sentences explaining this "love," such as "*if* you keep my commandments, you will abide in my love" (15:10); and 3) analogies which clarify the topic: "*as* the Father has loved me, so have I loved you" (15:9).

In language expressive of the argument from advantage, the author first tells the disciples that "remaining" and "loving" elevate their status from that of "servants" to "friends." This echoes the contrasting statuses of dead versus fruitful branches in 15:1-8, with the comparison now made between "servants" and "friends." Jesus' final argument here reminds the disciples of their debt in justice to him, which he is calling in through this exhortation: "You did not choose me, but I chose you and appointed you that you should go and bear fruit and that your fruit should remain" (15:16). The verbs indicate the extent of Jesus' benefaction which creates the debt of justice: "chose," "appointed," "bear fruit" and "fruit remain." To this he now appends one more benefaction, effec-

---

52. Other "unless" demands include 3:3, 5; 6:53; 8:24; 12:24; 13:8.

tive petitionary prayer: "Whatever you ask the Father in my name, he will give it to you" (15:16b), surely a significant advantage.

Therefore, this material is clearly exhortatory, and it resumes the most important behaviors urged in the Fourth Gospel, *remaining* and *loving*. Because of its exhortatory character, it stands apart from all other parts of the Farewell Address. But is "homily" or "sermon" the appropriate classification here? And do such things belong in worship? The type of rhetoric in 15:1-17 is deliberative, that is, it exhorts the hearers to make choices which affect their future, and the argument rests primarily on pointing out the advantage to those choosing to *remain* and *love*. Such rhetoric is not exclusive to homily or sermon and may occur in many types of public speaking, especially speeches to the Roman senate or the Greek assembly. Yet it is very compatible with sermon and homily (see Heb 3:1–4:13; 6:1-12), which are admittedly parts of Christian worship.[53]

4.4 Study of the Words of Jesus

It is indisputable that the disciples in their worship told the story of Jesus once more and examined his words and parables. This is, moreover, where the speeches of Acts all end: what God has done to Jesus. But John 14–17 do not contain the splendid narratives found earlier or elsewhere; on the contrary, they contain only his words, although the self-focused prayer in John 17 does summarize his mission. But as has been the case from John 2 onward, the meaning of his words is by no means clear. For example, "Destroy this temple . . ." was heard as "this [Herodian] temple." Only after his resurrection, "his disciples remembered that he had said this; and they believed the scripture and the word that Jesus had spoken" (2:22). We have seen above the pattern of statement-misunderstanding-clarification, which demonstrates that many, even of the inner circle, failed to understand Jesus' words correctly, but required an interpreter either then or in the future. This material has been studied according to the sociology of secrecy, which study argues that it was a regular feature of the Fourth Gospel to have Jesus conceal and reveal. Secrecy, as we saw in an earlier chapter, is the "mandatory or voluntary, but calculated concealment of information, activities or relationships."[54] Put simply, knowledge is controlled. Not all people know everything at the same time; being "in the know" serves as an

---

53. Harold W. Attridge, "Paraenesis in a Homily (λόγος παρακλήσεως): The Possible Location of, and Socialization in, the 'Epistle to the Hebrews,'" *Semeia* 50 (2004): 211-26.

54. S. K. Tefft, "Secrecy as a Social and Political Process," in *Secrecy: A Cross-Cultural Perspective*, ed. S. K. Tefft (New York: Human Sciences Press, 1980) 320.

important marker of insider status.⁵⁵ Readers of John are already familiar with certain types of secrecy: riddles, irony, parables, footnotes and asides. When was the veil lifted? When did the disciples get the correct understanding of Jesus' words? How far afield are we to suggest that Jesus' words were studied by the group at its gathering and given attention comparable to the Scriptures?

Enter the Paraclete, the Spirit of Truth. In John 14–16 this figure is described four times, every time as the broker of special knowledge about Jesus. First of all, we note that most of the time this Paraclete/Spirit of truth reminds about Jesus, glorifies Jesus, takes what is Jesus' and declares it to the disciples. The Paraclete, then, attends primarily to the Jesus story and the words of Jesus. We know, moreover, that this Paraclete spoke through someone in the group, a prophet. But the Spirit has other functions as well.

Category	*14:26*	*15:26*	*16:7-10, 13*
Title or Name	Paraclete Holy Spirit	Paraclete Spirit of Truth	16:7 Paraclete 16:13 Spirit of Truth
Source and Relationship to Father and Jesus	whom the Father will send in my name	whom I shall send to you from the Father . . . who proceeds from the Father	16:7 I will send him
Functions	1. he will teach you all things	1. _____	1. he will guide you into all the truth . . . he will declare to you the things that are to come
	2. bring to your remembrance all that I have said to you	2. he will bear witness to me	2. he does not speak on his own authority . . . he will glorify me, for he will take what is mine and declare it to you

4.5 Judgment

Few scholars who list the various elements of Christian worship include mention of "judgment" as part of it. All the more, then, are David Aune's reflections worth our attention. In *The Cultic Setting of Realized Eschatology in Early Christianity*, he argued that two elements of eschatology, declarations of salvation

---

55. Elizabeth Brandt, "On Secrecy and the Control of Knowledge: Taos Pueblo," in *Secrecy: A Cross-Cultural Perspective*, ed. S. K. Tefft (New York: Human Sciences Press, 1980) 125-34.

and judgment, have their proper place in "the worship, preaching and teaching of that community."[56]

This cultic "coming" of the Son of man to save and to judge, to bless and to curse, was a corporate worship experience which the Johannine community conceptualized in terms of the traditional Christological expectation of the Son of man.[57]

Aune cites with approval Käsemann's "Sentences of Holy Law" as illustrative of cultic judgment speech.[58] "Announcements of judgment and salvation," then, are not foreign to Christian worship. They were, moreover, types of sanctioned speech.

For example, we recall Paul's judgment of the man in an incestuous marriage in 1 Cor 5. Paul calibrates the timing of the judgment of the sinner to occur within a group meeting ("when you are assembled"), at which he speaks with pneumatic authority and declares that he enjoys the "power of the Lord," that is, authority to censure the man. Found guilty of corruption, the man is publicly expelled from the group (5:3-5).[59] Similarly, Matt 18:15-17 records a group ritual in which an errant member progressively receives correction; should the correction fail, "the church" declares him an outsider. Both of these examples envision a community assembly, at which takes place an oracle of judgment.

This material, we suggest, pertains to John 16:7-11, which we interpret as a form of judgment oracle. In terms of Johannine logic, the Paraclete will play a forensic role, similar to the presentation of Jesus in his various trials in the Gospel.[60]

---

56. Aune, *The Cultic Setting of Realized Eschatology in Early Christianity*, 121; this is continuously argued in 45-135.

57. Aune, *The Cultic Setting of Realized Eschatology in Early Christianity*, 126.

58. Ernst Käsemann, "Sentences of Holy Law in the New Testament," *New Testament Questions of Today* (Philadelphia: Fortress Press, 1979) 66-81. His location of this material in worship contexts is based on Hans Lietzmann, *Mass and the Lord's Supper: A Study in the History of the Liturgy* (Leiden: E. J. Brill, 1979) 186, and Gunther Bornkamm, "Das Anathema in der urchristlichen Abendmahlsliturgie," *TLZ* 75 (1950): 227-30.

59. In addition, see the curse "anathema" in 1 Cor 16:22; Gal 1:8-9; Rom 9:3.

60. Frequently in his defense Jesus, the accused, became the accuser; and his judges are judged:
   – "I know that *you do not have the love of God* within you" (5:42; see vv. 43-47).
   – "*Do not judge by appearances*, but judge with right judgment" (7:24).
   – "*You judge according to the flesh*" (8:15; see vv. 16-18).
   – "You know *neither me nor my Father*" (8:19).
   – "*You are from below*, I am from above; *you are of this world*, I am not of this world" (8:23).
   – "*You are of your father the devil*, and your will is to do your father's desires" (8:44).
   – "The reason you do not hear them [the words of God] is that *you are not of God*" (8:47).

Unlike 1 Corinthians 5 and Matt 18:15-17, no one is cast out of the group; on the contrary the group itself is experiencing expulsion from the synagogue (9:22, 34; 12:42; 16:1-2). The judgment oracle, then, serves to make and maintain boundaries with "the world" by emphasizing in dualistic terms how and why the Johannine group is right and therefore does not belong in the world. The following list drawn from the Farewell Address illustrates the studied emphasis on group boundaries:

Jesus and His Disciples	*The World*
. . . you know him for he dwells in you and will be in you (14:17b)	the Spirit of Truth whom the world cannot receive because it neither sees him or knows him (14:17a)
. . . but you will see me (14:19b)	the world will see me no more (14:19a)
how is it you will manifest yourself to us (14:22a)	. . . and not to the world (14:22b)
Peace I leave with you, my peace I give to you (14:27a)	. . . not as the world gives peace do I give to you (14:27b)
. . . he has no power over me (14:30b)	the ruler of this world is coming (14:30a)
. . . [the world] has hated me . . . because you are not of the world, but I chose you out of the world, therefore the world hates you (15:18-19)	If the world hates you, know that it has hated me before it hated you. If you were of the world, the world would love its own (15:18-19)
You will weep and lament . . . (16:20a)	. . . but the world will rejoice (16:20b)
. . . I am leaving the world and going to the Father (16:28b)	I came from the Father and have come into the world (16:28a)
. . . fear not, I have overcome the world (16:33b)	In the world you have tribulation (16:33a)

The discourse in the Farewell Address, then, makes and maintains boundaries with "the world" to emphasize the chasm that separates the disciples from the synagogue and to make any crossing back impossible. Thus in this context we read 16:7-11 as an oracle of judgment.

The task of the Paraclete in 16:8 consists of some form of judgment, whether we translate the Greek verb which is used here as "convict" or "convince."[61] On the one hand, the Johannine group will surely have much to criticize the synagogue for, at least to confirm the synagogue's utter depravity. Thus they are equipped with ready arguments to judge the synagogue and so prove it hopelessly wrong. On the other hand, this criticism serves also to firm up the group's own beliefs of its superiority and so its necessary separation from the world. Thus the Paraclete will prove *to the disciples* that the *synagogue/world* is guilty of sin, (false) righteousness, and (false) judgment.[62] "Of sin," because the world did not believe in Jesus. "Of [false] righteousness," because the synagogue judged Jesus a sinner and deceiver, yet Jesus will shortly be in the presence of the all holy God.[63] "Of [false] judgment," because it persecutes and judges Jesus, and by doing so it brings judgment upon itself.[64] Thus, we argue that part of the worship described in the Farewell Address includes oracles of judgment, that is, a *communication* sent from *God* through the *channel* of the Paraclete to the *disciples* for the *purpose* of shoring up the disciples even as it condemns their adversaries.

5.0 Not on This Mountain nor in Jerusalem. But Where?

This important question was the subject of chapter 3 of this book. There is no need to repeat that material, although it may profit to remember three specific points: 1) fluid vs. fixed sacred space; 2) my Father's " house" with many rooms; and 3) "being in" and "dwelling in."

---

61. See Tricia Gates Brown, *Spirit in the Johannine Writings: Johannine Pneumatology in Social-Science Perspective* (New York: T. & T. Clark, 2003) 221-27.

62. On this reading of John 16:8-11, see D. A. Carson, "The Function of the Paraclete in John 16:7-11," *JBL* 98 (1979): 547-66. See also Brown, *The Gospel according to John*, 2.705.

63. When Jesus qualifies "righteousness" by saying that he is going to the Father, this expresses the right relationship to God: acting as God's agent, fulfilling God's commands to speak God's word and to lay down his life. As one who has always done his duty to God, he is welcome in God's presence. But many see their duty to God as putting Jesus to death and exterminating his disciples (16:1-2). Thus, their relationship with God is tragically wrong; their true duties are left unfulfilled; they dishonor God with wrongdoing.

64. On the principle that "as you judge, so you are judged" (Matt 7:2), the enemies of the group share the judgment of the ruler of this world. And those who judge unjustly will be judged by the same judgment (7:24; 8:15; 9:16, 24). Instead of judging Jesus justly as God's agent, they judge him according to appearances (7:24) as having a demon (8:48; 10:20). But Jesus has already judged this ruler: "now shall the ruler of this world be cast out" (12:31).

5.1 Fixed vs. Fluid Sacred Space (4:21-24)

Jesus' declaration that his body would be the new and true Temple (2:19-22) is followed by a conversation with a Samaritan woman about the right place to worship, Mount Gerizim or Mount Zion (4:20), which mountains Jesus declassifies as sacred places of worship.[65] Thus, the Johannine disciples have no *fixed sacred space* in contrast with Samaritan and Israelite temples which are permanently fixed atop certain mountains. Nor does the local synagogue serve as the site of their worship, for public confession of Jesus as the Christ results in expulsion from that assembly (9:22, 12:42-43). But if *not* Mount Gerizim *nor* Jerusalem *nor* the synagogue, then where?[66] One of the dominant themes discussed in John 14–17 treats of the issue of where worship will take place.

"Not on this mountain, nor in Jerusalem" negates all fixed sacred space for the Johannine group, that is, temples and their elaborate systems that surround them (priests, offerings, tithes, revenues, temple building with its adornment and maintenance, and hosts of diverse persons to staff it, perform in it, and guard it). Needless to say, ethnic temples are clear examples of fixed sacred space, which is expressed by classifying them as the "navel" or "center" of the cosmos. But fluid sacred space refers to the place where the group meets. "The group is the central location of importance, whether the Body of Christ, the church, for Christians, or the synagogue gathering for Jews, or the philosophical 'schools.' . . . Discourse within these groups, whether the words of a portable Torah, the story of Jesus, or the exhortations of the philosopher-teacher, becomes the mobile, portable, exportable focus of sacred place."[67] The following chart compares and contrasts the two with clarity.

FIXED: Temple	FLUID: Group
1. topological, actual space	1. place where the group meets
2. place enduring over time	2. space of opportunistic, occasional group meetings
3. major mode of worship: sacrifice	3. major mode of worship: verbal forms
4. focus on altar	4. focus on sacred writings
5. hierarchical arrangement of persons by birth	5. significant individuals whose competency is based on spirit giftedness or closeness to the group's hero

---

65. See Tod D. Swanson, "To Prepare a Place: Johannine Christianity and the Collapse of Ethnic Territory," *JAAR* 62 (1994): 248-51.

66. Although the disciples remain in the world, Jesus repeatedly tells them that they do not belong to "this world" and that they are "not of this world" (17:9, 14, 15, 16).

67. Bruce J. Malina, *Christian Origins and Cultural Anthropology* (Atlanta: John Knox Press, 1986) 38.

Fixed sacred space means 1) a temple building and compound, 2) which is sanctified by ancient reverence, 3) in which worship is primarily animal sacrifice, 4) with focus on its altar; 5) presiding over this are priests born into classes whose bloodlines are perfect.[68] In contrast, fluid sacred space is 1) no particular location, but the worshiping group, 2) when assembled as convenient; 3) its major form of worship is verbal and 4) focused in sacred writings, not by means of sacrifices; 5) its leaders are not so because of birth and pedigree, but because of spirit investment. For members of the Fourth Gospel's audience, where the group is, there is the place of worship.

5.2 In My Father's House There Are Many Rooms (14:2)

McCaffrey wrote a monograph on 14:2, focusing on two elements: 1) "in my Father's house there are many rooms" and 2) "I am going to prepare a place for you."[69] He focused on the term "in my Father's *house*," which suggests intimate kinship relationships,[70] such as Father and son, God and disciples, vine dresser, vine and branches — "many rooms."[71] And when Jesus states that "I go to prepare a place for you," he goes not as an architect but as a broker of relationships which will secure access to God through Jesus himself. Thus we consider it an excellent way to read 14:2-3 in terms of personal relationships and not in terms of buildings or space.

Jesus next states that he "goes away and comes back" — he goes "to prepare a place for you" and then says that "I will come back and will take you to myself." He states as his purpose that "where I am you also may be." After brokering his relationship with the Father, he returns to solidify his relationship with God's clients. He does not say that he will take the disciples to the "Father's house," but rather he will facilitate his brokerage by maintaining a favored relationship with the disciples. Thus, I would extend the sense of "relationship" to the "place" which Jesus prepares. As tortured as it may sound, Jesus is in two "places" at once: in heaven (in relationship with God, wherever God is) and on earth (in relationship with disciples, wherever they gather). Balancing his remark that he has access to God's presence, he also "takes the disciples to myself." Thus they too have access to God's house, but only in relation to Jesus.

---

68. Because birth by blood or water avails nothing and because the flesh is of no avail, the Fourth Gospel sees no value in any form of hereditary roles or statuses.

69. James McCaffrey, *The House with Many Rooms: The Temple Theme in Jn. 14,2-3* (Rome: Pontifical Biblical Institute, 1988).

70. McCaffrey, *The House with Many Rooms*, 29-32.

71. See John 17:20-22; also Tod D. Swanson, "To Prepare a Place," 244-45, 248-51, 257-60.

Later Jesus amplifies the meanings we argue for "Father's house" and "place": "If a man loves me, he will keep my word, and my Father will love him, and we will come to him *and make our home* with him" (14:23). Once more, the key to this "geography" is relationship: 1) a disciple *loving* Jesus and *keeping* his word, 2) the Father *loving* this disciple, and 3) the Father and Son *coming to him* and making a "*home*" with him. Again Jesus functions as the key link, the broker or mediator between God and the clients. The purpose or utility of this relationship comes from the benefaction the Patron then shows the client, namely, "We will make *our home* with him."

Later Jesus petitions God for a benefaction which relates to the Johannine statement studied above, namely, that "place" = relationship: "Father, I desire that they also, whom you have given me, may be with me *where I am*, to behold my glory which you have given me in your love for me before the foundation of the world" (17:24). The related figures include "Father," "I," "they whom you gave me," that is, the same persons described in terms of patron-broker-client relationship above. What can "be with me where I am" mean? Several times in John 17 Jesus recognizes the *non*-relatedness of the disciples to "the world": While "they are in the world (17:11) . . . they are not of the world" (17:14). Nevertheless, Jesus does not ask that they be removed *from the world:* "I do not pray that you should take them out of the world, but that you should keep them from the evil one" (17:15). Thus the petition that "they be with me where I am" is no heavenly ascent nor a mere spatial relocation. Rather, the directional and spatial patterns we observe suggest that such language is best understood in terms of relationships.

5.3 "Being In" and "Dwelling In"

We find in John 14–15 a number of remarks by Jesus describing his relationship with both the Father and the disciples, which are seemingly expressed in spatial terms. His relationship with the Father is either "I am *in* the Father and the Father is *in* me" (14:10, 11, 20) or "the Father *dwells in* me" (14:10b). Similarly, Jesus' relationship with the disciples parallels that between him and God: "I *in* my Father and you *in* me and I *in* you" (14:20). Although one might initially think that "in" is a spatial term, the disciples do not travel to another place nor does "being in" necessarily imply spatial location.

Similarly with "dwell in." In terms of Jesus' relationship with God, we are told that "the Father *dwells* in me" (14:10b). The same verb is used 10 times in 15:4-10 to express the relationship of Jesus with the disciples. On the one hand, the disciple must "dwell" in or remain in or sustain loyalty to Jesus: "The branch cannot bear fruit unless it '*dwells*' in the vine" (15:4). Conversely, if a branch *"dwells"* in the vine, the vine curiously will *"dwell"* in the branch: *"Dwell in me and I in you"* (15:4, 5b). An alternate way of expressing this indicates the basis for this type of dwelling: "If you '*dwell*' in me and my words '*dwell*' in you . . ." (15:7). The words of Jesus *"dwelling"* in someone point to a relationship of loyalty and faithfulness. Finally, the Spirit will *"dwell"* in you and *"be"* in you (14:17). When we ask what type of relationships are envisioned, several types seem suitable here: 1) kinship relationships (father, son, household) and 2) patron-broker-client relationships.

6.0 Summary, Conclusions, and Further Questions

Summary. This study began by providing a current descriptive inventory of worship. In addition to which we developed a social science model of worship based on communication theory which adequately explains how both prayer and other types of worship (prophecy, homily, etc.) all belong together as diverse aspects of worship. The communications model identifies and interprets the two directions of communication: 1) worshipers sending a message to the deity for a specific purpose and 2) the deity sending a message to the worshipers for various purposes via various persons in the group. The model identifies both the medium of the communication and the channel along which it is sent, as well as a wide variety of purposes for the communication.

In regard to prayer, the communication model provided a rich taxonomy of prayer, which advances our understanding of the various effects that prayer seeks to have on the deity. While we are all familiar with the purpose of petitionary prayer, we found the taxonomy of prayer particularly helpful in identifying petitionary and self-reflective prayers in John 14–17. Moreover, the communication model allowed for a nuanced reading and understanding of other forms of worship, which in the model describe the communication of the deity with worshipers. We identified the following such types of communication in John 14–17, namely, prophecy (oracles of assurance and of judgment), homily and study of the words of Jesus.

In examining the issue of "where" the Johannine group worshiped, we were greatly aided by the use of a model of fixed versus fluid sacred space. Fluid sacred space, unlike fixed spaces as found in temples, does not embody the system of temple personnel such as we find in Jerusalem's temple.[72] But we can go fur-

---

72. See Joachim Jeremias, *Jerusalem in the Time of Jesus* (Philadelphia, PA: Fortress Press, 1969) 21-27, 127-221; K. C. Hanson and Douglas E. Oakman, *Palestine in the Time of Jesus* (Minneapolis, MN: Fortress Press, 1998) 131-60.

ther than the standard rejections of Mounts Gerizim and Zion and their facile replacements of "spirit and truth." The model of fluid sacred space urges us to examine how both the person of Jesus and the persons of the group become the sacred space. Jesus does not take his disciples out of the world, even though he has prepared a place (i.e., "relationship") for them. The key element in understanding the "where" of worship for the Johannine group lies in appreciating how the Risen Jesus continues to offer christophanies to the group, especially in the revealing the sacred name "I AM" to them. In short, God draws near to the group through Jesus, and the disciples are drawn near to God through Jesus, especially as the figure who bridges the heavenly and earthly worlds. Thus we look to relationships as the "where" of worship.

Finally, scholars agree on the prayer aspect of the section of the Fourth Gospel labeled as a "Farewell Address." But it also contains materials which have never been considered as elements of worship but have remained in the shadows for want of an adequate model to identify them. When one adds to discussions of worship both a communications model and notions of fluid vs. sacred space, then we find that a surprising amount of material in John 14–17 can then be seen to be part of a large discourse on worship in the Fourth Gospel. A familiar text is thus freshly interpreted precisely because new models of reading and interpretation suggest new data.

Further Questions. Because we have focused on John 14–17, our investigation of worship is not complete in two ways. First, how are we to interpret pilgrimage feasts to Jerusalem? How do we understand baptism (3:22-26) and eating the bread of life (6:32-56)? As Aune earlier stated, worship consists of "various types of rituals. . . . Christians gathered to eat together, to baptize new members, to experience healing."[73] The very presence of the foot washing in 13:12-17 suggests a ceremonial welcome of group members by its officials. This is the raw material of a study of group worship. The details of a purificatory ritual described in 20:23 are absent, although Jesus authorizes those on whom he breathed to "forgive" and "retain" sins. What, then, still needs to identified and interpreted? The inquiry is just beginning. Second, the more forms of worship that are identified, the more need we have of a consideration of roles and statuses within the group. How might the patron-broker-client model assist us in interpreting the roles of elite members of the group, if this is possible? Third, if we have focused only on John 14–17, then are there other data in the Gospel about various forms of worship and various aspects of it (time, place, ritual)? We claimed to find most of the elements of worship described by those who make surveys of what constitutes early Christian wor-

---

73. See Aune, "Worship, Early Christian," 973.

ship. What, however, have we *not* found in John 14–17? Finally, the worship models exposed here can only benefit from their application to other worship materials in the New Testament.

16

"Despising the Shame of the Cross"

Honor and Shame in the Johannine Passion Narrative

1.0 Introduction

New Testament authors share the general perception of crucifixion in the Greco-Roman world as "shame" (Heb 12:2). Various classical authors give us a sense of the typical process of crucifixion, which at every step entailed progressive humiliation of the victim and loss of honor.[1]

1. Crucifixion was considered the appropriate punishment for slaves (Cicero, *In Verrem* 2.5.168), bandits (Josephus, *War* 2.253), prisoners of war (Josephus, *War* 5.451) and revolutionaries (Josephus, *Ant.* 17.295).[2]
2. Public trials served as status degradation rituals, which labeled the accused as a shameful person.
3. Flogging and torture, especially the blinding of eyes and the shedding of blood, generally accompanied the sentence (Josephus, *War* 5.449-51 & 3.321; Livy 22.13.19; 28.37.3; Seneca, *On Anger* 3.6; Philo, *Flacc.* 72; Diodor of Sicily 33.15.1; Plato, *Gorgias* 473bc; *Republic* 2.362e). Since even according to Judean practice (*Makshirin* 3.12) scourging was done both to the front and back of the body, the victims were nude; often they befouled themselves with urine or excrement (3.14). Roman practice would be decidedly more humiliating.
4. The condemned were forced to carry the cross beam (Plutarch, *Delay* 554B).

---

1. Martin Hengel, *Crucifixion* (London: SCM, 1977) 22-32.
2. Hengel, *Crucifixion*, 46-63.

5. The victims' property, normally clothing, was confiscated; hence they were further shamed by being hung nude (see Diodor of Sicily 33.15.1).
6. The victim lost power and thus honor through pinioning of hands and arms, esp. the mutilation of being fixed to the cross (Philo, *Post.* 61; *Dreams* 2.213).
7. Executions served as crude forms of public entertainment, where the crowds ridiculed and mocked the victims (Philo, *Spec.* 3.160), who were affixed to crosses in odd and whimsical manner, including impalement (Seneca, *Consolation to Marcia* 20.3; Josephus, *War* 5.451).
8. Death by crucifixion could be slow and protracted. The powerless victims suffered bodily distortions, loss of bodily control, and gross enlargement of the penis.[3]
9. Ultimately they were deprived of life and thus the possibility of gaining satisfaction or vengeance.
10. In many cases, victims were denied honorable burial; corpses were left on display and devoured by carrion birds and scavenger animals (Pliny, *Natural History* 36.107-8).

Victims would thus experience themselves as progressively humiliated and entirely stripped of public respect or honor.

The issue, however, lies not in the brutal pain endured. For among the warrior elite, at least, the endurance of pain and suffering was the mark of *andreia* or manly courage (e.g. Hercules' labors; Paul's hardship catalogues: e.g. 2 Cor 6:3-10; 11:23-33). Silence by the victim during torture was itself a mark of honor (see Isa 53:7; Cicero, *In Verrem* 2.5.162; Josephus, *War* 6.304). Mockery, loss of respect, and humiliation were the bitter parts, with loss of honor the worst fate. Although the Gospels record in varying degrees the physical torture of Jesus, they all focus on the various attempts to dishonor him by spitting on him (Mark 14:65//Matt 26:67; see Mark 10:33-34), striking him in the face and head (Mark 14:65//Matt 26:67), ridiculing him (Mark 15:20, 31; Matt 27:29, 31, 41), heaping insults upon him (Mark 15:32, 35-36; Matt 27:44), and treating him as though he were nothing (Luke 23:11; see Acts 4:11).

This study of the Johannine passion narrative views it precisely through the lenses of honor and shame. We suggest that despite all the shameful treatment of Jesus, he is portrayed, not only as maintaining his honor, but even gaining glory and prestige.[4] Far from being a status degradation ritual, his pas-

---

3. Leo Steinberg, *The Sexuality of Jesus in Renaissance Art and in Modern Oblivion* (New York: Pantheon/October, 1983) 82-108.

4. Bruce J. Malina and Jerome H. Neyrey, *Calling Jesus Names: The Social Value of Labels in Matthew* (Sonoma, CA: Polebridge, 1988) 95-131.

sion is seen by the author and his audience as a status elevation ritual. This hypothesis entails a larger consideration, namely, the importance of honor and shame as pivotal values of the Mediterranean world.[5] We presume that the original audience would have perceived Jesus' passion in these terms.

Modern readers, however, are not cognizant of these pivotal cultural values. We understand neither the grammar of honor nor appreciate the social dynamics in which it plays so important a part. If we would interpret the narrative of Jesus' death from the appropriate cultural point of view, we must attempt to see things through the lenses of ancient Mediterranean culture, which were those of honor and shame. In the cultural world of the New Testament, Jesus' death by crucifixion was acknowledged as a most shameful experience. Paul merely expressed what others perceived when he labeled the crucified Christ as a *stumbling block* to Judeans and *foolishness* to Greeks (1 Cor 1:23). The author of Hebrews explicitly calls the cross "shame" (12:2).

The Gospels acknowledge that prophets are denied honor in their own villages (Mark 6:4//Matt 13:57). They tell of messengers sent to a vineyard, who are wounded in the head and treated shamefully (Mark 12:4). But the early Christians counted this type of public shame as honor: "... rejoicing that they were counted worthy to suffer dishonor for the name" (Acts 5:41). Honor and shame, then, are integral parts not only of the language patterns which describe the fate of Jesus and his disciples, but a basic element in the way the Christian storyteller perceives and deals with suffering, rejection and death.

2.0 A Brief Grammar of Honor and Shame

Greeks, Romans and Judeans all considered honor and shame as pivotal values in their cultures.[6] From Homer to Herodotus and from Pindar to Paul,[7] men lived and died in quest of honor, reputation, fame, approval and respect. Lexical definitions offer a wide range of overlapping meanings for "honor": 1) the price or value of something, 2) respect paid to someone, 3) honorary office, 4) dignity

---

5. Bruce J. Malina, *The New Testament World: Insights from Cultural Anthropology* (3rd ed.; Atlanta: John Knox, 2001) 27-57.

6. Arthur W. H. Adkins, *Merit and Responsibility: A Study in Greek Values* (Oxford: Oxford University Press, 1960); David Gilmore, ed., *Honor and Shame and the Unity of the Mediterranean* (Special Publication of the American Anthropological Association 22; Washington, DC: American Anthropological Association, 1987).

7. Gregory Nagy, *The Best of the Achaeans* (Baltimore: The Johns Hopkins University Press, 1979) 222-42; Paul Friedrich, "Sanity and the Myth of Honor: The Problem of Achilles," *The Journal of Psychological Anthropology* 5 (1977): 281-305.

or status, 5) honors or awards given someone.[8] Paul Friedrich offers a social grammar of honor based on Greek epic poetry: "The structure of Iliadic honor can be stated in part as a larger network that includes propositions about honor and nine honor-linked values: power, wealth, magnanimity, personal loyalty, 'precedence,' sense of shame, fame or 'reputation,' courage, and excellence."[9]

A detailed grammar of honor can be found in Malina and Neyrey.[10] But a summary of it may aid readers unfamiliar with the topic. Honor comes to someone either by *ascription* by another (birth, adoption, appointment) or by one's own *achievement*. Achieved honor derives from benefaction (Luke 7:5; Diodor of Sicily 6.1.2), military prowess, success at athletic games, and the like. In the warrior culture of Greece and Rome, honor accrues to prowess in battle (see David and Goliath) or endurance in labors (Heracles; see 2 Tim 4:7-8). Yet most commonly honor is acquired in the face-to-face game of challenge and riposte which makes up much of the daily life of individuals in villages and cities.

Honor resides in one's name, always an inherited name. Sons enjoy the honor of their father's name and membership in his clan. Hence, they are regularly identified as "the son of so-and-so" (e.g. 1 Sam 9:1-2; Ezra 7:1-6). Yet individuals might be called by honorific names such as "Rabbi" (Matt 23:7) or "Prophet" (John 9:17) or "Christ" (John 7:26). These labels, which are claims to precedence and honor, are likely to be bitterly contested.

Honor resides in certain public roles, statuses and offices. Fathers enjoy great honor in their households, which is sanctioned in the Ten Commandments. Most notably, honor was attached to offices such as king and high priest, as well as governor, proconsul and other civic or imperial offices. In the great tradition of the aristocrats, the hierarchical ranking of honor was clearly known.[11] But in the little tradition of peasants and artisans, such ranking was a matter of considerable debate and controversy, which we can observe in the squabbles over the seating at dinner tables (Luke 14:7-11).

Honor has "a strong material orientation."[12] That is, honor is expressed and measured by one's possessions which must needs be on display. Wealth in general denotes honor, not simply the possession of wealth, but its consumption and display: e.g. banquets, fine clothes, weapons, houses, mounts, etc.

---

8. Johannes Schneider, "τίμη," *TDNT* 8.169-80.

9. Friedrich, "Sanity and the Myth of Honor," 290.

10. Bruce J. Malina and Jerome H. Neyrey, "Honor and Shame in Luke-Acts: Pivotal Values of the Mediterranean World," in *The Social World of Luke-Acts: Models for Interpretation*, ed. Jerome H. Neyrey (Peabody, MA: Hendrickson, 1991) 25-66.

11. Peter Garnsey, *Social Status and Legal Privilege in the Roman Empire* (Oxford: Clarendon Press, 1970) 221-71.

12. Schneider, "τίμη," 170.

Hence it is not surprising to hear Josephus describing as "honor" the benefactions Vespasian bestowed on him: "raiment and other precious gifts" (*War* 3.408). Similarly he describes the honors given Daniel: "(The king) gave him purple to wear and put a chain of linked gold about his neck" (*Ant.* 10.240). Finally Josephus records Haman's suggestion to the Persian king on how to honor a friend: "If you wish to cover with glory the man whom you say you love, let him ride on horseback wearing the same dress as yourself, with a necklace of gold, and let one of your close friends precede him and proclaim throughout the whole city that this is the honour shown to him whom the king honours" (*Ant.* 11.254).

Anthropologists describe the physical body as a microcosm of the social body.[13] The values and rules pertinent to the macrocosm are replicated in the way the physical body is perceived and treated. Let us examine how the body replicates honor. 1) *The head, face* and *eyes* are particular loci of personal honor and respect. A head is honored when crowned or anointed. Servants and courtiers honor monarchs by avoiding looking them in the face by means of the deep oriental bow. Comparably, to slap someone on the mouth, spit in his face, box his ears or strike his head shames this member and so gives "affront" (Matt 26:67; Luke 22:63-64; Mark 15:17-20). It is not by accident that the body parts mentioned in the *talio* are *eye* and *tooth* — the central features of the face (Exod 21:24; Lev 24:20; Matt 5:38). How honorable are certain things that happen before the eyes (Mark 12:11), but how shameful to be forced to see the slaughter of one's family. 2) *Clothing* covers the dishonorable or shameful parts of the body (1 Cor 12:23-24), namely the genitals and the buttocks. Clothing, moreover, symbolizes honor: "Men are the glory of God and their clothes are the glory of men" *(Derek Eretz Zuta)*. Elites signal their status by their clothing and adornment (Luke 7:25; see *m. Yoma* 7.5). Purple clothing was a particular mark of honor, worn by kings (Judg 8:26), priests (Exod 28:4-6; 39:1, 28-29; 1 Macc 10:20; 11:58), and nobles at court (Ezek 23:6; Esth 8:15; Dan 5:7).[14] Uniforms signal rank or office. Philo provides a striking example of the way clothing replicates honor in his description of Pharaoh's investiture of Joseph with symbols of status: ". . . royal seat, sacred robe, golden necklace, setting him on his second chariot, bade him go the round of the city with a crier walking in front who proclaimed the appointment" (Philo, *Jos.* 120). The costuming of Jesus in a purple robe and a crown of thorns mocks him with the normal trappings of honor.

---

13. Mary T. Douglas, *Purity and Danger: An Analysis of the Concepts of Pollution and Taboo* (London: Routledge and Kegan Paul, 1966).

14. Meyer Reinhold, *History of Purple as a Status Symbol in Antiquity* (Brussels: Latomus, 1970) 7-21, 48-61.

"Despising the Shame of the Cross"

Being stripped of clothing, moreover, eliminates all marks of honor and status; it also indicates a loss of power to cover and defend one's "shameful parts." 3) *Bodily postures* express honor. Masters sit at table, while servants stand and wait upon them (Luke 17:7-8; see 13:29). Twenty-four elders stand around the throne where God is seated; they fall down before him in worship (Rev 4:10). *Proskynein* describes the posture whereby someone bends low to kiss another, either on the hand or the foot; thus it comes to mean bowing before or showing respect for someone (Josephus, *Ant.* 11.209).

Yet in the perception of the ancients, honor, like all other goods, existed in quite limited supply.[15] There was only so much gold, so much strength, so much honor available. When someone achieved honor, it was thought to be at the expense of others. Philo, for example, condemns polytheism, because in honoring others as deities, the honor due to the true God is diminished: "God's honour is set at naught by those who deify mortals" (*Drunkenness* 110; see Josephus, *Ant.* 4.32; *War* 1.559). When John's disciples lament to their master that Jesus is gaining more disciples and honor, they understand that Jesus' gain must be John's loss. John confirms this, "He must increase, but I must decrease" (John 3:30).[16] Thus claims to honor by someone tend to be perceived as threats to the honor of others, and thus need be challenged, not acknowledged. In fact, two Gospels state that it was out of envy that Jesus' enemies have handed him over (Mark 15:10//Matt 27:18; see John 11:47-48).

Thus far we have discussed "honor," but what is "shame"? Contempt, loss of face, defeat, and ridicule all describe shame, the opposite of honor. The grammar of honor presented above can be reversed to describe "shame." Shame can be *ascribed* or *achieved*. In terms of *ascribed* shame, a magistrate may declare someone guilty and so worthy of public flogging (2 Cor 11:23-25); a king may mock and treat one with contempt (Luke 23:11). God may declare one a "Fool!" (Luke 12:20). Thus elites and those in power may declare someone honorless and worthy of contempt: ". . . exclude, revile, and cast out your name as evil" (Luke 6:22). Yet shame may be *achieved* by one's folly or by cowardice and failure to respond when challenged. One may refuse to participate in the honor-gaining games characteristic of males, and thus bring contempt on oneself.

The bodily grammar for honor works also for shame. If the honorable parts of the body, the head and face, are struck, spat upon, slapped, blindfolded or otherwise maltreated, shame ensues. If the right arm, symbol of male power

---

15. George Foster, "The Image of Limited Good," in *Peasant Society: A Reader*, ed. J. Potter, M. Diaz, and G. Foster (Boston: Little, Brown and Company, 1967) 300-323.

16. Jerome H. Neyrey and Richard L. Rohrbaugh, "'He Must Increase, I Must Decrease' (John 3:30): A Cultural and Social Interpretation," pp. 123-42 in the present volume.

and strength, is bound, tied or nailed, the resulting powerlessness denotes shame. If one is publicly stripped naked, flogged, paraded before the crowds, and led through the streets, one is shamed. Shame results when one's blood is intentionally spilled, but especially when one is killed by another.

3.0 Irony: Turning Shame into Honor

Since there are two parties competing in the passion narrative, there are two perceptions of what is occurring. The enemies of Jesus bind, slap, spit upon, blindfold, flog, strip, and kill Jesus; their actions are all calculated to "mock" and "revile" him. In their eyes they have shamed Jesus and so destroyed him. But the Gospel, while it records these actions and gestures of shame, tells quite a different story. In the Evangelist's eyes, Jesus' shame and humiliation is truly the account of his glory: "Ought not the Christ suffer and so enter into his glory" (Luke 24:26; see Acts 14:22; Heb 2:10). Indeed, in the Fourth Gospel, his death is regularly described as glory and glorification (John 7:39; 12:28; 17:5; see 21:19). Or, to paraphrase Paul, foolishness, weakness and shame in human eyes are wisdom, strength and honor in God's eyes (1 Cor 1:20, 25).

Rhetoricians give advice to would-be orators on "alchemy," that is, how to turn shame into honor. Noteworthy are the remarks of Theon:

> If he has none of the aforementioned good qualities, one must say that although he met with misfortune he was not humbled, not unjust despite his poverty, nor slavish despite being in need, and although he comes from a small city, he became illustrious, just as both Odysseus and Democritus did, and although he was raised under a bad form of government, he was not perverted but to them as a whole he was superior, as Plato in the oligarchy. It is also praiseworthy if someone, though he comes from a humble household, became great, as Socrates, the son of Phaenarete the midwife and Sophroniscus the sculptor did. It is also worthwhile to admire the one who, though he comes from a handicap or bad circumstances, is able to do something good. For virtue shines forth especially in misfortune. (Theon 9.65-76)[17]

Thus the story of Jesus' shame is ironically understood by his disciples as his "lifting up," his exaltation, his enthronement and so his honor. The issue might

---

17. Aelius Theon, *The Progymnasmata of Theon: A New Text with Translation and Commentary*, trans. James Butts (unpublished dissertation, Claremont, 1986) 474-75. See also Aristotle, *Rhet.* 1.9.28-29; Quintilian, *Inst. Orat.* 3.7.5-6.

"Despising the Shame of the Cross"

be rephrased: Who gets to judge whether the crucifixion is honor or shame? If the public verdict rests with the Judeans, then Jesus is shamed. But if God gives a riposte to those who shame Jesus or if Jesus demonstrates power by his death, then the community of believers renders Jesus a grant of honor.

This ironic perspective is part and parcel of the principle that Jesus constantly narrates, that last is first, least is greatest, dead is alive, shame is honor.[18] Hence, two perspectives need to be distinguished as we read the account of Jesus' crucifixion: in the eyes of outsiders and enemies, his crucifixion is unqualified shame! But in the eyes of his disciples, it is ironic honor! Let us now take these abstract notions of honor (and shame) and use them as an exciting and illuminating lens for perceiving the passion narrative of Jesus, the honorable one.

4.0 Honor and Shame in John 18–19

4.1 Arrest (18:1-11)

Although capture and arrest normally denote dishonor, the narrative in the Fourth Gospel presents a scene of honor both displayed and maintained. First of all, honor means power and control.[19] In this regard, when the cohort approaches Jesus, he steps forward to take charge of the events. By claiming that "Jesus knew all that was to befall him" (18:4), the narrator signals Jesus' control of the situation (see 19:28). Moreover, he questions the powerful forces gathered against him: "Whom do you seek?" In the cultural scenario of honor and shame, the questioner generally acts in the challenging or commanding position (see Mark 11:27-33).[20]

At his remark "I am he," the soldiers "drew back and fell to the ground" (18:6), leaving Jesus standing. Honor is thus signaled by bodily posture: he stands, they fall down. Falling to the ground characterizes the posture appropriate in the presence of a glorious or honorable person, such as God (Ezek 1:28; 44:4) or a superior person (Dan 2:46; Rev 1:17). At a minimum, Jesus enjoys such a prominent and honorable status that armies fall at his feet. Even if Dodd is correct that the narrator is drawing on psalms describing how one's foes

---

18. Paul D. Duke, *Irony in the Fourth Gospel* (Atlanta: John Knox Press, 1985) 95-116, 126-38.
19. Ignace de la Potterie, *The Hour of Jesus: The Passion and Resurrection of Jesus according to John* (New York: Alba House, 1989) 29.
20. It has been argued that questions in all genres tend to be aggressive weapons. See Jerome H. Neyrey, "Questions, *Chreiai*, and Challenges to Honor: The Interface of Rhetoric and Culture in Mark's Gospel," *CBQ* 60 (1998): 657-81.

stumble and fall when attacking,[21] nevertheless some vindication or riposte to a challenge is evident.

The narrator repeats the sequence of events in 18:7-8, which doubles the impression of Jesus' strength and honor. His control of the situation extends even to his command about the safe departure of his disciples: "Let these others go" (18:8). Weak people do not tell soldiers what to do. This proves, moreover, that his word of honor is trustworthy: "This was to fulfill the word which he had spoken, 'I did not lose a single one of those you gave me'" (18:9). Thus the narrator presents Jesus firmly in control: knowing all that will happen, asking questions, controlling events, giving commands, and receiving profound respect from his would-be assailants. He is without doubt the most honorable person in the situation.

Jesus' commanding posture reminds the reader of the Noble Shepherd discourse, where he disavowed that he was a victim and claimed power even over death: "No one takes my life from me, but I lay it down of my own accord. I have power to lay it down, and I have power to take it again" (10:18). Since power is one of the public indices of honor, Jesus' ability to protect his sheep as well as his power to lay down his life indicate that he suffers no shame whatever here. Nothing happens against his will; he is in no way diminished.

Yet others in the narrative see the scene differently. Simon Peter draws his sword and strikes at one of the arresting crowd, which we must interpret as his riposte to the perceived challenge to Jesus' honor. In other circumstances, his action would be labeled an honorable act, namely, the defense of one's leader against an honor challenge. Jesus himself states this: "If my kingdom were of this world, my servants would fight, that I not be handed over to the Jews" (18:36). Normally failure to respond to a challenge is shameful, but here Jesus explains that it is precisely out of honor that he refuses to resist, that is, out of respect for the will of his Father: "Shall I not drink the cup which the Father has given me?" (18:11). Peter's riposte, then, is unnecessary; for, as obedient son, Jesus' honor is not threatened. Indeed, it belongs to the virtue of *andreia* or courage to endure what must be endured.[22] And courage of this sort is an honorable thing.

---

21. Charles H. Dodd, *Historical Tradition in the Fourth Gospel* (Cambridge: Cambridge University Press, 1963) 76-77.

22. David Seeley, *The Noble Death: Graeco-Roman Martyrology and Paul's Concept of Salvation* (Sheffield: JSOT Press, 1990) 117-41.

4.2 Jewish Investigation (18:12-14, 19-24)

Outsiders see only that Jesus has lost power: "The cohort seized Jesus and bound him" (18:12). His captors take him to the private chambers of Annas, a very powerful enemy, who questions Jesus. Recall that questions are generally challenges. When questioned, Jesus delivers a bold response: "I have spoken openly to the world; I have always taught in the synagogues and in the temple, where all Jews come together" (18:20). Jesus claims that he has acted as an honorable man, always appearing in the appropriate male space, the public arena, and speaking boldly and clearly. His "bold speech" denotes courageous and honorable public behavior (see 1 Thess 2:2). In contrast, this Gospel declares as shameful people who are afraid to speak openly about the Christ (9:22-23; 12:42; see Phil 1:20).

The narrative interprets Jesus' bold speech as a riposte to Annas's challenging questions. Jesus commands his interrogator, "Ask those who have heard me. They know what I said" (18:21). This occasions a severe counter-challenge from one of the officers standing by, who "struck Jesus with his hand" (v. 22; see 19:3). The gesture was surely a slap in the face, thus giving an "affront" to Jesus. It is similar to the blows given Jesus according to the synoptic accounts (Matt 26:67; Mark 14:65; Luke 22:63-64; see Matt 5:39). But Jesus is not silenced or humbled as was Paul, when struck by Annas's servant (Acts 23:4-5). He gives an appropriate riposte, "If I have spoken wrongly, bear witness to the wrong; but if I have spoken rightly, why do you strike me?" (18:23). Thus he withstands the insult and continues to speak boldly, even having the last word.

4.3 Roman Trial (18:28-19:16)

The very fact of being put on trial is itself an honor challenge, simply because the accused experience their claims to honor (name, worth, reputation) to be publicly challenged. We modern people at times have idealized trials as occasions not only to clear one's name, but to put the system itself on trial, that is, to challenge the challenger. Our judicial process, moreover, functions on the presumption of innocence. Not so the ancients, where guilt was presumed. It was inherently shameful to be seized and publicly charged with wrongdoing, "This man . . . is an evildoer" (18:30).

The trial episode (18:28–19:16) can be described as an extended game of charge and refutation or challenge and riposte. This occurs on several levels. First, those who deliver Jesus engage in their own challenge-riposte game with Pilate. Pilate *claims* the honor of procurator and magistrate as he questions them ("What accusation?" 18:29). They *challenge* him by asserting their own power ("If this man were not an evildoer . . . ," v. 30), which leads to Pilate's *riposte* ("Take him yourselves . . . ," v. 31). For the moment Pilate wins, as they are forced to admit their own powerlessness and Pilate's power: "It is not lawful for us . . ." (v. 31). This challenge-riposte game between Pilate and the Judeans will continue in 18:39-40 and 19:6, 12-16. But the main contest focuses on the formal process of Jesus before Pilate, which is itself an elaborate game of challenge and riposte.

Commentators who note the alternation of scenes in the trial from outside to inside suggest that the scenes are arranged in a chiastic shape.[23]

1. *Outside* (18:28-32)
   Judeans demand death

2. *Inside* (18:33-38a)
   Pilate questions Jesus
   about kingship

3. *Outside* (18:38b-40)
   Pilate finds Jesus not guilty;
   choice of Barabbas

7. *Outside* (19:12-16a)
   Judeans obtain death

6. *Inside* (19:9-11)
   Pilate talks with Jesus
   about power

5. *Outside* (19:4-8)
   Pilate finds Jesus not guilty;
   "Behold the man"

4. *Inside* (19:1-3)
   Soldiers scourge Jesus:
   typical judicial warning

Commentators, moreover, are wont to contrast these scenes as "public" (outside) and "private" (inside). Yet the designation "private/inside" is misleading here, for we should not imagine Pilate and Jesus having a tete-à-tete.[24] And even if the narrative action occurs "within" the Roman compound, it is still a "public" place occupied by Roman soldiers, and not the "private" world of the household (cf. 12:1-8; 13:3-5). Dodd's remark that there are two stages, "a front stage and a back,"[25] seems more accurate. It helps to articulate that all events

---

23. Raymond E. Brown, *The Gospel according to John* (AB 29A; Garden City, NY: Doubleday, 1970) 2.859; Charles H. Giblin, "John's Narration of the Hearing before Pilate (John 18,28-19,16a)," *Bib* (1986): 221-39.

24. For a fulsome study of the meanings of "public" and "private" in antiquity, see Jerome H. Neyrey, "'Teaching You in Public and from House to House' (Acts 20:20): Unpacking a Cultural Stereotype," *JSNT* 26 (2003): 69-102; idem, "Jesus, Gender and the Gospel of Matthew," in *New Testament Masculinities, Semeia* 45 (2003): 43-66.

25. Dodd, *Historical Tradition in the Fourth Gospel,* 96.

here are "public" and so honor is always at risk. Yet the narrative distinction between "going within" and "going out" serves to distinguish the various scenes and different audiences. The "outside" scenes are the honor contests between Pilate and the Judeans. The "inside" scenes, however, comprise the *cognitio* of the trial between judge and the accused. They also are public in that they occur in the public forum of the Roman courtyard or praetorium, whether this be the fortress Antonia (Josephus, *Ant.* 15.292) or the new palace of Herod.[26] The "outside" crowds are informed of the results of the "inside" contest, which affects their challenge-riposte game with Pilate. The honor-shame dynamic, then, occurs on both "stages," but between different sets of contestants.

Trials under Roman jurisdiction have a formal structure which is helpful to note.[27]

Formal Elements of a Roman Trial	*first*	*second*
1. arrest	18:1-11	
2. charges	18:28-32	19:7
3. judge's *cognitio*	18:33-38a	19:8-11
4. verdict	18:38b	19:12
5. judicial warning	19:1-6	
6. sentence		19:13-16

This structure indicates that Jesus' trial went through two cycles. It helps, moreover, to clarify the roles of Pilate, Jesus and the crowds, especially in terms of the formal elements of an honor contest. The crowds, who function as the witnesses or accusers in the forensic process, *challenge* Jesus' *claims*. Pilate, the judge, examines these challenges and determines whether Jesus' claims are honorable or not, often giving a *riposte* to Jesus' critics. Jesus, who is on trial, is *challenged* precisely as to his honorable status.

Yet forensic process is only one formal way of describing the action in the narrative. Each of the two confrontations ("inside": Jesus vs Pilate; "outside": Pilate vs. crowds) is similarly structured in terms of the social dynamics of honor challenges (claim–challenge–riposte–public verdict). Even as we spell out the forensic process which formally structures the narrative as a whole, we must attend to the specific differences in the challenge–riposte dynamics of the "inside" and "outside" scenes of the story, for which the following diagram might prove useful.

---

26. Pierre Benoit, "Prétoire, Lithostroton et Gabbatha," *RB* 59 (1952): 545-49.
27. A. N. Sherwin-White, *Roman Society and Roman Law in the New Testament* (Oxford: Clarendon, 1963); idem, "The Trial of Christ," *Historicity and Chronology in the New Testament* (Theological Collections 6; London: SPCK, 1965) 97-116.

	Inside Forum: The Trial of Jesus before Pilate	Outside Forum: The Struggle between Pilate and the Crowd
claim:	Jesus' status	Pilate's authority
challenger:	Pilate	the crowds
riposte:	Jesus' defense of being a king	Pilate solicits the crowd's disloyalty to God and loyalty to Caesar
public verdict:	innocent	Pilate's title over the cross

Charges (18:29-33). This Gospel mentions that Roman soldiers participated in the seizure of Jesus (18:3); their presence indicates that Jesus was in some sense arrested. The charges against him which Pilate investigates are formal *challenges* to his *claims* to honor and status: "Are you the *King of the Jews?*" (18:33; see also 19:7, 14, 19). From the beginning, Jesus has been acclaimed as a most honorable person, and so enjoys a singular portion of *ascribed honor.* On the basis of God's own prompting, John the Baptizer acclaimed him "Son of God" (1:34). Disciples acknowledge him as "the Messiah" (1:41) and "Son of God and King of Israel" (1:49). Even a leader of the Judeans accepts him as "a teacher come from God" (3:2). According to the story, various people acclaim him "savior of the world" (4:42), "prophet" (6:14; 9:17), "king" (6:15; 12:13-15), and "Christ" (7:26). In the game of honor and shame, all of this constitutes a claim of honor, the public identity and reputation of Jesus, which is now challenged in this trial.

Cognitio (18:33-38). The judge's *cognitio* of Jesus in his judicial quarters serves as the forum where Jesus' honor claims are both *challenged* and *defended.* On the level of rhetoric, Pilate asks questions which challenge Jesus, whose riposte is initially the clever strategy of answering a question with a question (see Mark 11:28-33; 12:14-16). Pilate challenges with a question: "Are you the King of the Jews?" Jesus parries with his own question: "Do you say this of your own accord . . . ?" Pilate asks more questions: "Am I a Jew?" . . . "What have you done?" . . . "So you are a king then?" . . . "What is truth?" On the narrative level, then, Pilate is perceived as asserting his own honor claims as the embodiment of Roman authority by his rhetorical posture as the figure whose duty it is to ask questions and so challenge others. This initial exchange flashes with honor challenges. Pilate asks a question, presumably concerning the charge against Jesus. By questioning Pilate, Jesus might be said to be giving a riposte: "Do you say this of your own accord . . . ?" (18:34). Pilate's response is not only scorn ("Am I a Jew?"), but a mockery of Jesus. How shameful, he points out, that "Your own nation and the chief priests have handed you over" (18:35). Thus, judge and accused, besides going through the formalities of a forensic process, spar and take the measure of each other — very un-forensic behavior.

"Despising the Shame of the Cross"

This sparring game quickly fades, for the narrator wishes to portray Jesus giving a solemn *riposte* to the challenges to his identity and authority. Pilate challenges Jesus' "kingship," a very noble and honorable status, which Jesus vigorously defends. Twice he proclaims, "My kingship is not of this world" (18:36, 37). If his kingship is not of this world, it must belong to another world (8:23), that is, God's world, which is eternal, unchanging, and truly honorable. Although this "world" was once a worthy recipient of divine favor (3:16; 4:42; 10:36; 12:47), it quickly proved hostile to Jesus. He became an alien here in this world and met only challenge and opposition (1:9-10).[28] The world's hostility, then, constitutes an ongoing challenge to Jesus' honor. But the assertion that his kingdom is not of this world implies that he belongs to a better kingdom, which must triumph over the hostility experienced here. Although challenged on earth, Jesus belongs to a kingdom where he is honored as he should be (5:23; 17:5, 24; see 8:23).

This Gospel speaks of a ruler of this world, who will be Jesus' chief challenger. But even this powerful figure "has no power over me" (14:30); he will be cast out (12:31) and judged (16:11). Thus Jesus boasted to his disciples, "I have overcome the world" (16:33). This powerful challenger appears at times to be Satan.[29] But as the passion narrative progresses, even the Roman emperor will qualify as a rival of God, "a ruler of this world" (19:12, 15). Yet if Jesus' kingship were of this world, his followers would do the honorable thing and "fight, that I not be handed over to the Judeans" (18:36, e.g. 18:10). The vindicator of his kingship, then, must be a most powerful person also "not of this world," namely God. He will give the riposte for King Jesus (12:28; 17:1). But the claim that Jesus is a king stands defended: "You say that I am a king; for this I was born, and for this I have come into the world" (18:37). Jesus makes another *claim* that pertains to his kingship, "Everyone who is of the truth hears my voice" (18:37). This directly echoes the remarks about the shepherd in 10:3-4, 26-27. If "shepherd" is a metaphor for king (i.e. David, the Royal Shepherd), then Jesus reaffirms his honor as king. Good and honorable people, he says, acknowledge his honor claim by "hearing my voice." Whether scornful or cynical,[30] Pilate's retort, "What is truth?," indicates that he rejects this claim.

Verdict (18:38b). The source of Jesus' honor, while not made explicit here, will shortly be made clear to the court (19:8-11). Yet the reader knows that Jesus enjoys maximum *ascribed honor* from the most honorable person in the uni-

---

28. Wayne A. Meeks, "The Man from Heaven in Johannine Sectarianism," *JBL* 91 (1972): 67-70.

29. Rudolf Schnackenburg, *The Gospel according to St. John* (New York: Crossroad, 1982) 2.391.

30. Brown, *The Gospel according to John*, 2.869.

verse, namely, God (see 5:36-38; 12:27-28). All that Jesus is, has and does comes from God (5:19-29). The reader knows that he comes from God and is returning to God (13:1-3; 17:1-5), where he will be glorified with the glory he had before the creation of the world. At this point in the trial, Jesus has given an adequate *riposte* to the *challenge* to his honor; he is a king and defends that *claim*. On the narrative level, Pilate's forensic verdict of innocence tells the reader, at least, that Jesus' claims are publicly judged to be honorable: "I find no crime in him" (18:38). Honor defended is honor maintained. Yet the *public verdict* in this honor contest remains unclear, for the crowds do not accept this.

In acknowledging a custom, Pilate offers to those who have just challenged Jesus' honor the release of this same "King of the Jews" (18:39). This should be interpreted as Pilate's personal *challenge* to the crowd.[31] Their challenge to Jesus had just been rejected (18:38), and now Pilate taunts them by inviting them to accept Jesus in the fullness of his honor claim, "Will you have me release to you the 'King of the Jews'?" (18:39). Pilate asks Jesus' challengers publicly to accept a *riposte* to their challenge, and so to admit defeat in this game. His question, then, continues the honor-shame contest between himself and the crowd (see 18:29-31). Yet, the crowds give a counter-challenge to Jesus' honor claim and Pilate's gambit: "Not this man!" The shame of being disowned by one's own occurs again (18:35; see 1:11); Jesus' enemies prefer the release of Barabbas, a thief or social bandit, to him (18:40). The contest between Pilate and the crowd continues as a stalemate.

Judicial Warning (19:1-5). Pilate gives Jesus a "judicial warning," such as Paul received when five times lashed and three times beaten with rods (2 Cor 11:24-25; see Acts 5:41). Judicial warnings were intended to inflict pain but especially to humiliate and disgrace troublemakers. In essence, Jesus is beaten and mocked. Even if the technical terms "mock" and "mockery" do not occur here (see Matt 27:29; Mark 15:20), native readers whose world is structured around honor and shame know what is going on. To be mocked is by far more painful than physical beating because it produces the most dreaded of all experiences, shame.

As regards his body, Jesus is shamed by being stripped naked, bound and beaten in the public forum of the Roman soldiers. His head, the most honorable member of his body, is mocked with a "plaited crown of thorns." His body is dressed in purple, the royal color. Many of the soldiers "struck him with their hands," surely on the face or head, and sarcastically acclaimed his honor, "Hail, King of the Jews" (19:3). Each of these ritual gestures has been shown to be a

---

31. David Rensburger, *Johannine Faith and Liberating Community* (Philadelphia: Westminster, 1988) 92-94.

characteristic element in the honoring of Persian and Roman rulers. Alföldi's study[32] lists the following elements of a coronation: *proskynēsis*/bending the knee (11-16, 45-70); acclamation, especially as *dominus* (38-45, 209-10); crown (17-18, 128-129, 263-67); clothing (143-56, 175-84, 268-70); scepter (156-57, 228-35); throne (140-41, 159-61). Thus a mock coronation ritual occurs,[33] whose primary function is to shame Jesus, the alleged King of the Judeans.

But if the actors in the drama are portrayed as shaming Jesus, it does not follow that readers of this Gospel concur. On the contrary, insiders have been repeatedly schooled in irony to see Jesus' death is his "lifting up" to heaven (3:14; 8:28; 12:32) or his "glorification" (12:23; 13:31-32; 17:1, 5). The grain of wheat dies and falls into the ground, but thereby lives and bears fruit. In short, the Gospel inculcates an ironic point of view such that death and shame mean glory and honor. The mock coronation of Jesus, which in the eyes of outsiders means shame, truly betokens honor to insiders. In terms of Jesus' honor, it functions as a status elevation ritual. Although ironically invested with imperial honors, Jesus nonetheless is acclaimed as honorable, especially in his shame.[34] David Rensberger describes this scene as Pilate's humiliation of the Judeans by the sarcastic presentation of a Roman's interpretation of Judean messianic hopes.[35]

New Charges/New Cognitio (19:7, 9-11). Pilate then brings forth this Jesus who has been mocked and dishonored. I do not know when modern readers started thinking that such a presentation was supposed to inspire sympathy for Jesus, because in the culture of the Levant such a scene would provoke laughter and derision. Crowds regularly gathered at public executions to participate in the mockery (see Matt 27:38, 39, 41). The crowds react here in predictably cultural ways by continuing their dishonoring of Jesus: "Crucify him! crucify him!" (19:6). Rejection by one's *ethnos* and delivery to the Romans would be shame enough (18:35, 40); now his own people call for his shameful death.

With Pilate's verdict of Jesus' innocence, the trial should be over ("I find no crime in him," 19:5, 6). But a new charge is made, which constitutes a new *challenge by* Jesus. "By our law he ought to die, for he made himself the Son of God" (19:7). The crowds consider this "claim" to be so serious a charge as to warrant the death sentence. And so a new trial ensues to deal with the new charge.

---

32. Andreas Alföldi, *Die monarchische Repräsentation im römischen Kaiserreiche* (Darmstadt: Wissenschaftliche Buchgesellschaft, 1970).

33. Josef Blank, "Die Verhandlung vor Pilatus Jo 18:28-19:16 im Lichte johanneischer Theologie," *BZ* 3 (1959): 60-81; Wayne A. Meeks, *The Prophet-King: Moses Traditions and the Johannine Christology* (NovTSup 14; Leiden: E. J. Brill, 1967) 69-72.

34. Duke, *Irony in the Fourth Gospel*, 132-33.

35. Rensberger, *Johannine Faith and Liberating Community*, 93-94.

Let us view this new charge from the perspective of honor and shame. In antiquity people were constantly "making themselves" something, that is, claiming a new and higher status or role (Acts 5:36). Hence the public accusation that Jesus *makes himself* something functions as a *challenge* to a perceived empty *claim*, a common phenomenon in antiquity.[36] This sort of challenge to Jesus, moreover, occurred regularly throughout the narrative: "... *making himself* equal to God" (5:18) ... "Who do you *make yourself* to be?" (8:53) ... "You, a mortal, *make yourself* God" (10:33) ... "He *made himself* the Son of God" (19:7) ... "every one who *makes himself* a king ..." (19:12). In the course of this narrative, the author has consistently dealt with this charge by *dividing the charge from the challenge:* 1) it is denied that Jesus "makes himself" anything, but 2) it is defended that he is indeed such-and-such. For example, Jesus claims in 5:19-29 that he is "equal to God." This is no empty claim, for he insists that God has granted him both creative and executive powers and the honor attached to them. The Father 1) *shows* him all that God is doing; 2) has *given* all judgment to the Son (5:22), 3) *has granted* the Son also to have life in himself (5:26), and (4) *has given* him authority to execute judgment (5:27). Thus, Jesus does *not* "make himself" anything, for that would be a vainglorious claim and thus false honor. But he truly is "equal to God," "King" and "Son of God," because these honors, roles and statuses are ascribed to him by the most honorable person in the cosmos, namely, God.

Moreover, it is not accidental in the Gospel traditions that Jesus himself rarely claims to be anything, prophet, king, Son of God, etc. These are ascribed to him by God (13:31; 17:5, 24; see Mark 1:11; 9:7) and acknowledged by others: (Son of God, 1:34, 49; Christ, 1:41; 10:24; King, 1:49; 6:15; 12:13; Savior, 4:42; and Prophet, 4:19; 6:14). Thus the tradition steadfastly maintains that Jesus is an honorable person in two respects: he does not seek honor by making vain claims to such-and-such a status, but he is regularly ascribed great honor by others. The reader, then, has been schooled how to interpret this new charge against Jesus, rejecting any sense of a vainglorious claim and affirming the truth of the honor ascribed to Jesus.

The new forensic charge requires a new *cognitio* by the judge (19:8-11). Pilate asks the appropriate question in terms of honor and shame: "Where are you from *(pothen)*?" (19:8). True and lasting honor is ascribed honor, which is a

---

36. In Theophrastus's *Characters,* one figure exposed for shame is the *alazōn* (number 23): he "makes himself to be more than he is." Similar is the *mikrotimos,* the person with an "ignoble desire for prestige" (number 21). Another person is the braggart *(kenodoxos),* as Epictetus said: "Let him who makes pretense to things which in no wise concern him be a braggart" (*Dissertations* 3.24.43); see 4 Macc 2:15. Examples of vainglory are Simon (Acts 8:9) and Herod (Acts 12:22-23); see also Josephus, *War* 2.55, 60; *Ant.* 17.272, 278.

function of one's father/clan and one's place of origin.[37] Concerning place of origin, honor was earlier denied Jesus because he is from Nazareth, from which no good comes (1:46; see Titus 1:12). In contrast, Paul claims honor by coming from Tarsus, "no mean city" (Acts 21:39), and Jerusalemites claim honor from being born there (Ps 87:5-6). Concerning father and clan, it is a universal phenomenon in the Bible that when characters are introduced or described, they are always identified as the "son of so-and-so" or the "daughter of so-and-so." For an individual's honor is bound with that of his or her father. The rules in the *progymnasmata* for writing an encomium all stress that writers begin their praise of someone by noting that person's family and place of origin.[38] All of the extant texts of the *progymnasmata* on writing an encomium start with praise for *eugeneia*, which consists in noting 1) origin *(genos)*, 2) race *(ethos)*, 3) country *(patris)*, 4) ancestors *(progonoi)*, and 5) parents *(pateres)*. Hence Pilate tests Jesus' honor with the appropriate question, "From whence do you come," which may refer either to his "place of origin" (8:23) or his parents (6:41-42). But the question directly touches Jesus' honor.

Jesus now remains silent (19:9). He neither defends himself nor offers a riposte to the challenge. Silence in the face of accusation is very difficult to assess; but in an honor and shame context it would probably be read as a shameful thing (see Neh 6:8). To fail to give a riposte to a challenge is to accept defeat and so loss of honor. Yet readers have already been socialized in just this aspect of Jesus' honor, and so the riposte has been given in advance. Knowledge of *whence* Jesus comes and *whither* he goes has been a major issue throughout the narrative. Outsiders either do not know (3:8; 8:14, 9:29) or falsely think they know (6:41-42; 7:27-28). Many times Jesus proclaims the correct answer, namely, that he comes down from heaven (6:38) or that he descends from heaven and ascends back there (3:13; 6:62). Insiders like the blind man accurately deduced the true "whence" of Jesus because of his power to heal (9:30). And finally the reader is told that Jesus comes from God and returns to heaven (13:1-2). Thus readers can answer Pilate's question; they know "whence he is," namely, a person whose parent is none other than God and whose "country of origin" is none less than heaven. His exalted honor, then, is secure in their eyes.

The narrative suggests that Jesus' silence in fact *challenges* Pilate's power, who then responds with new questions: "Will you not speak to me? Do you not

---

37. Malina and Neyrey, "Honor and Shame in Luke-Acts," 32-40; Bruce J. Malina and Jerome H. Neyrey, "First-Century Personality: Dyadic, Not Individualistic," in *The Social World of Luke-Acts*, ed. Neyrey, 85-87.

38. See Bruce J. Malina and Jerome H. Neyrey, *Portraits of Paul: An Archaeology of Ancient Personality* (Louisville, KY: Westminster John Knox, 1996) 23-33; Jerome H. Neyrey, *Honor and Shame in the Gospel of Matthew* (Westminster/John Knox, 1998) 70-89.

know that I have power to release you and I have power to crucify you?" (19:10). "Power," an expression of honor, is at stake. Although Jesus gives no *riposte* to this new challenge concerning his origin, he does in turn offer a counter-challenge to Pilate's claim of power: "You would have no power over me unless it were given you from above" (19:11). Hence Pilate's power is a relative thing, for the truly powerful figure is not Caesar, from whom Pilate enjoys ascribed honor, but God, from whom all power flows (John 10:29). Emperors, kings and governors all owe their power and honor to God (Rom 13:1; 1 Tim 2:2; 1 Pet 2:13-17). This narrative, moreover, asserts that it is God's will and purpose that Jesus undergo this trial (John 12:27). God commanded that he "lay down his life and take it again" (10:17-18). Inasmuch as sons are commanded to "Honor their father" (Exod 20:12; Deut 5:16; Mark 10:19), the presentation of Jesus as the obedient one (Heb 5:8; see Mark 14:36//Matt 26:39//Luke 22:42) marks his actions here as honoring his Father and thus warranting the honor of an obedient son.

In fact, Jesus ironically states that even Pilate is behaving honorably because he acts in accord with the power given him from above. The dishonorable people are those "who have delivered me over to you" (19:11); they are the sinners. Thus in the confrontation between him and Pilate, Jesus remains successful; he suffers no loss of honor. In fact, he seems to have gained an ally of sorts in Pilate, his judge, "who sought to release him."

Final Verdict and Sentence (19:12-16). In the next scene, the grand public tableau of the trial, the two sets of contestants play another episode of challenge and riposte. In terms of the Pilate-vs-Jesus contest, Pilate's move "to release him" functions as a definitive *riposte* to the various *challenges* made by the crowds to Jesus' *claims* to honor. Pilate thrice declares Jesus innocent, and so Jesus cannot be shown to be "making himself" anything. But in terms of the Pilate-vs.-crowd contest, the latter issues one final *challenge,* not so much to Jesus' claims, but to Pilate's *riposte*. The trial has reached the moment of solemn judicial verdict and sentence. But the scene as narrated contains a fundamental ambiguity. The text states that "he (Pilate) brought Jesus out and sat down at the judgment seat" (19:13). Controversy surrounds the verb "sat down" *(ekathisen),* which may be read transitively (i.e., Pilate *sat* Jesus *down* on the judgment seat) or intransitively (i.e., Pilate *sat* himself *down* on the seat).[39] Grammatical studies support both readings. Those who argue that Jesus was seated point to the irony of the powerless Jesus assuming the powerful role of judge. This reading would follow

---

39. Ignace de la Potterie ("Jesus King and Judge according to John 19:13," *Scripture* 13 [1961]: 97-98) cites these texts: "And they clothed him with purple and set him on the seat of Judgment, saying, 'Judge righteously, King of Israel'" (*Gospel of Peter* 7) and "They tormented him and set him on the judgment seat, and said, 'Judge us'" (Justin, *1 Apology* 35).

"Despising the Shame of the Cross"

the gospel axiom that last is first, weakest is greatest, the judged one is the judge, etc. Indeed it would be an extraordinary piece of irony for the dishonored Jesus to assume this position of great honor (see Luke 24:26).

But the literal reading of the passage portrays Pilate's *riposte* to the crowd's *challenge* to him. As judge and magistrate in charge of these affairs, including the exercise of the *jus gladii*, Pilate now assumes all of the trappings of his office. Honor is replicated in bodily posture as Pilate *seats* himself on his official seat, the *bēma*, while the other participants *stand* (19:13). Exercising his authority, Pilate issues a proclamation to the crowds: "Behold your king!" Rhetorically, this remark is a command ("Behold!") and an insult ("your king," see 18:39). It ostensibly upholds the original claims of Jesus by dismissing the challenges of the crowd. Thus the judge has rendered this final verdict of innocence (18:38; 19:4, 12), which functions as a riposte to the crowd's challenges to Jesus' honor. But the claim that Jesus is a king is no more acceptable to the crowds now than it was earlier.

Finally the two strands of the honor contests coincide. The crowds *challenge* Pilate's verdict, even as they shame Jesus: "Away with him . . . crucify him" (19:15a). Pilate had previously noted the shame of being disowned by one's own *ethnos* (18:35), which shameful action is now repeated. Ostensibly Pilate has lost the game, and his honor has been diminished. But he makes one last move, a final *riposte* to the power of the crowd.

Inasmuch as "king" has been the contested claim throughout the trial, Pilate demands of the crowd a formal judgment in the case: "Shall I crucify your 'king'?" (19:15b). Questions, of course, are challenging, and the response to this question brings maximum shame on Jesus' antagonists: "We have no king but Caesar" (19:15c). Their remark is an act of supreme dishonor to their heavenly Patron and Sovereign. At the conclusion of the Greater Hallel we find the following prayer:

> From everlasting to everlasting thou art God;
> Beside thee we have no king, redeemer, or savior;
> No liberator, deliverer, provider;
> None who takes pity in every time of distress or trouble.
> We have no king but thee.[40]

It is the crowd who proves to be the "friend of Caesar,"[41] thus shaming God and God's anointed king. David Rensberger notes that Pilate has once more humili-

---

40. Meeks, *The Prophet King*, 77.

41. Josephus described some aristocrats as "persons of power among the Friends of the King" (*Ant.* 12.298); he notes that Antiochus wrote to his "Governors and Friends" (*Ant.* 12.134). See P. A. Brunt, "'Amicitia' in the Late Roman Republic," *Proceedings of the Cambridge Philological Society* 191 (1965): 1-20; Ernst Bammel, "*Philos tou Kaisaros*," *TZ* 77 (1952): 205-10.

ated his opponents by having them publicly deny their claims to a political messiah.[42] Yet no reader would fail to note that God too is now shamed and must vindicate the divine honor. The advantage seems to lie with the crowd who bends Pilate to its will and succeeds in dishonoring Jesus ("Crucify him!").

A judicial sentence is pronounced, but one which is fraught with irony. Pilate, the official judge, apparently yields in this game of push and shove; his sentence is hardly honorable or just. Jesus' accusers, who earlier claimed that they had no legitimate authority to put a man to death (18:31), finally succeed in a plot that began in 5:18 and was solemnized at a rump trial in 11:50-53. Their success in having Jesus killed would be a mark of honor for them in the eyes of observers. But readers of the narrative know that this "sentence" is fully within the control of Jesus (12:32-33; 10:17-18) and the will of God. The sentence of a shameful death, then, is but an apparent loss of honor.

4.4 Title (19:19-22)

The game of push and shove continues over the public title attached to Jesus' cross. Pilate's inscription, "Jesus of Nazareth, King of the Jews," may be read as a final ironic riposte by the narrator in defense of Jesus' honorable status, comparable to Caiaphas's ironic "prophecy" about Jesus' death (11:51). It is also Pilate's act of authority in defense of his own embattled status. The title, which may be construed as another honor claim, is once again challenged by the Jerusalem elite, who urge a more shameful version: "This man said, 'I am King of the Jews.'" Again, they charge that Jesus vaingloriously assumes honors not rightfully his (19:7, 12); "he makes himself" this. This time Pilate wins: "What I have written, I have written" (19:22). He has the last word.

4.5 Crucifixion (19:17-37)

The normal sequence of events which accompany crucifixion was listed at the beginning of this study. In view of that, the shameful elements narrated in the crucifixion of Jesus in the Fourth Gospel are the stripping of Jesus' clothing,[43]

---

42. Rensberger, *Johannine Faith and Liberating Community*, 96.

43. Ancient sources suggest that Jesus was probably stripped naked on several occasions: 1) according to *m. Makširin* 3.12 victims were scourged naked, both front and back, and occasionally befouled themselves with urine or excrement (3.14); 2) the victim's clothing was confiscated; 3) victims were further shamed by being crucified naked (see Diodor of Sicily 33.15.1). On the shame of imposed nudity, see Jerome H. Neyrey, "Nudity," in John J. Pilch and Bruce J. Malina,

the crucifixion itself, with Jesus' position as the middle figure in a triptych of criminals, themselves shameful persons (19:18). The mocking title over the cross publicly challenges Jesus' claim to honor and status. He is apparently crucified naked, for his clothing is confiscated by his executioners (19:23-24). The Synoptics all record various persons "mocking" him (Mark 15:27-32; Matt 27:38-43; Luke 23:35-36), which is absent from the Fourth Gospel's account. Yet the very scene is one of public humiliation (John 19:20). Yet this hardly exhausts the shame to which victims were subjected.

The narrator instructs his audience to perceive this scene in terms of honor. First, Jesus does the honorable thing by his mother. Presumably a widow, her only son is dying. In that culture, she has no male (husband or son) to defend her; she will suffer a tragic loss of honor with this death. But Jesus defends her honor by adopting as "brother" the Beloved Disciple, and by ensuring that his new kinsman will defend his mother's honor by "taking her into his own house" (19:27; see Acts 1:14).

Playing the role of a victim is shameful, especially when one's life is taken away. The eye of the imagination sees this in Jesus' death, but the ear hears differently in the narrative. Jesus is presented as the figure in control of events. He *knows* that all is now completed (v. 28) and he *chooses* to die; "It is finished" (v. 30). Death is noble or honorable when voluntary. Because the narrative has prepared us for this scene, we are not reading these honorable ideas into the text. Back in the exposition of the role of the Noble Shepherd in John 10, Jesus explicitly described the honorable character of his death. First, he knows it, and so manifests control over his life: "I lay down my life" (10:17); "I lay it down of my own accord" (10:18). Second, he is no victim; no one shames him by taking his life: "No one takes it from me" (10:18); no one shames him by having power over him: "I have power to lay it down and I have power to take it again" (10:18b). Just as he manifested control and power at his arrest, so he is presented here as doing the same thing. Honor is thus maintained.

Finally his body is mutilated, a shameful act (recall the treatment of Hector's body by Achilles; see 1 Sam 31:9-10; 2 Sam 4:12; Josephus, *Ant.* 20.99). The soldiers intend to break his legs and thus hasten death. Yet Jesus is spared this because he has already died. Moreover, the text puts an honorable interpreta-

---

eds., *Handbook of Biblical Social Values* (Peabody, MA: Hendrickson, 1998) 136-42. Roman custom showed no quarter, so we assume that they stripped Jesus naked twice. But was the same true for Judeans? The following passage from the *b. Sanhedrin* 6.3 provides some evidence, albeit conflicting: "When [the condemned person] was at a distance of four cubits from the place of stoning they stripped off his garments. They covered a man in front and a woman both in front and behind: this is the view of R. Judah: but the Sages say, A man is stoned naked, but a woman is not stoned naked."

tion on this by comparing Jesus' body to the paschal lamb, none of whose bones were broken (Exod 12:46; John 19:36). He dies, then, "unblemished." Nevertheless his chest is pierced, the wanton mutilation of a corpse. Yet as Josephine Ford has shown, the piercing of Jesus' side yields both blood and water, which in rabbinic lore constitutes a kosher object.[44] And so the narrator rescues Jesus' honor by indicating that this mutilation was controlled by God's prophecy through Zech 12:10.

4.6. Jesus' Burial (19:38-42)

Under other circumstances, the bodies of the crucified might be left to rot on the cross and become food for scavengers (see Rev 19:17-18). This final shame precludes reverential burial by kin, which is both a mark of honor and a religious duty. Yet in our narrative, purity concerns demand some rapid disposal of the corpses; and so the body of Jesus is immediately buried. The narrator simply states that all happened according to "Judean burial customs" (19:40).[45]

This Gospel narrates that Jesus' body received quite an honorable burial, despite the shame of his death. Joseph and Nicodemus bring a prodigious quantity of spices, "a mixture of myrrh and aloes, about a hundred pounds," enough spices for a royal burial (see 2 Chron 16:14 and Josephus, *Ant.* 17.199).[46] They perform the honorable burial ritual, "binding the body in linen cloths with the spices, as is the burial custom of the Judeans" (19:40). A new tomb is at hand, where they honorably lay Jesus. Despite the shame of crucifixion, some honor is maintained by this burial.

5.0 Conclusions and Final Observations

Does a modern reader know anything new by reading with this lens? Does appreciation of honor and shame demand a reinterpretation of older scholarly opinions on various passages? What difference does it make to read John 18–19 in this light? All valid questions, which may not have simple answers.

---

44. Josephine M. Ford, "'Mingled Blood' from the Side of Christ (John xix.34)," *NTS* 15 (1969): 337-38.
45. S. Safrai, "Death, Burial and Mourning," in *The Jewish People in the First Century*, ed. S. Safrai and M. Stern (Philadelphia: Fortress, 1976) 2.773-87.
46. Dennis D. Sylva, "Nicodemus and His Spices (Jn. 19.39)," *NTS* 34 (1988): 148-51.

"Despising the Shame of the Cross"

5.1 Honor and Shame: A Native's Point of View

Honor and shame are not foreign categories imposed by modern readers upon an alien, ancient culture, but values rooted in the very cultural world of Jesus and his disciples, whether Roman, Greek, or Judean. In studying honor and shame, we have learned what these ancient people value, how they strive either to gain honor or to maintain their reputation, and how honor is replicated in the presentation and treatment of the physical body. When we appreciate the typical form of a challenge/riposte encounter, we gain greater clarity into the common social dynamics of the male half of the gender-divided world of the first century in all its agonistic flavor. Appreciation of the ancient psychology of honor and shame offers an authentic cultural and historical sensitivity to the social dynamics of ancient persons. In looking through this lens, we see what the natives see.

5.2 Honor and Shame: Pivotal Values

Anthropologists claim that honor and shame constitute the pivotal values of the cultural world of the eastern Mediterranean, which includes Jesus and his disciples. When we examine a pivotal value of a given culture, we learn about its place in the larger system of behaviors, institutions, and structures in the social fabric of that world. By "value," we mean:

> The word "value" describes some general quality or direction of life that human beings are expected to embody in their behavior. A value is a general, normative orientation of action in a social system. It is an emotionally anchored commitment to pursue and support certain directions or types of actions.[47]

But a pivotal value in a culture implies a larger system within that culture. It colors the way roles and statuses are understood within institutions; it directs behaviors in certain ways; it forms the unspoken context or horizon behind vast areas of social interaction, which is known by the natives, if by no one else. When we appreciate the importance of "honor" vis-à-vis the ancient world, we are thereby capable of recognizing the systematic contours of the social dynamics of that period and of understanding its pervasive importance in the lives of the ancient author and his characters.

---

47. Pilch and Malina, *Handbook of Biblical Social Values*, xiii.

5.3 Honor and Shame: Structural Implications

Pivotal values do not exist in splendid isolation from the cultural systems in which they are embedded. Knowledge of the value of honor and shame invites readers into the larger cultural system in which we take note of the following replications and incarnations of this value. Scholars agree that the ancient Mediterranean was a gender-divided world, with specific places, tasks, tools and behaviors for males and females. Reading John 18–19 in the light of honor and shame makes salient the male half of that world: a public world where males constantly behave in ways which seek to gain or maintain honor. It is a world of swords and sharp speech, power and posturing, in short, a pervasively agonistic world. Since it is an entirely public world, each gesture, all clothing, every word communicates a claim to precedence. In short, formal reflection about honor and shame spells out for the initiated what is implicit in the cultural world of the ancient documents, even as it introduces readers new to cultural issues to the basic and pervasive social dynamics of antiquity.

5.4 Honor and Shame: What Is Common, Not What Is Different

Anthropology focuses on what is common to a specific culture and what is shared by most of its members; it operates at a higher level of abstraction than historical studies which ferret out specific local and temporal differences. Thus it deals in generalities, common patterns, stereotypes, and the like. Whereas historical studies regularly concern themselves with what is "new" or "different" in certain circumstances, cultural studies ask what is typically going on. Thus cultural studies may not scratch the historian's itch for novelty. Historical critics might justifiably ask how the Johannine use of honor and shame values differs from that expressed in Cicero, Plutarch, Dio Chrysostom or Josephus — a valid request, which deserves a study of its own.

Moreover, it may appear to some that honor and shame as expressed in the challenge–riposte form is a social dynamic so prevalent as to become a catch-all generalization. Mediterranean anthropologists go so far as to claim that every social interaction outside the home or kinship circle is likely to be a contest for honor acquisition or its maintenance. "Challenges" are expressed by positive actions, such as compliments, gifts, petitions, etc., as well as by negative ones, such as questions, verbal attacks, physical affronts, etc. One might ask whether Jesus ever appears in a public situation without some sort of challenge arising. Even forensic processes such as Jesus' trial are structured around honor; uses of power are never simply "power," but exercises in honor. Honor may be a minor factor in western social transactions, but it is the major value in Mediterranean ones and major values should surface with great regularity and be replicated in many areas.

5.5 Honor and Shame: A Reader's Responsibility

Knowledge of honor and shame, moreover, equips a person to be a more informed and culturally attuned reader. Nuances of social interaction and their meanings are made clearer. But the issue is not quantity of new insight, but rather quality. The value of using this model lies in its ability to ensure readers that they are seeing with the eyes of a native and so they become insiders in a cultural world quite different from their own. Learning about honor and shame and reading with this lens make us better readers, namely, readers who listen as closely and accurately as possible to ancient speakers and writers. This duty of readers is all the more important when modern, western readers attempt to understand communication from another culture. Thus readers who seek to avoid ethnocentrism must strive to appreciate the pivotal values of the world of writers removed from them in time and space. Honor and shame is just such a pivotal value and full appreciation of it ensures that contemporary readers are in tune with the characteristic modes of perceiving and acting embodied in ancient, foreign documents. The ubiquitous and perhaps generalized description of social interactions in terms of challenge/riposte simply is a fact of that ancient world.[48] Readers are surely better off knowing the incidence of this dynamic and its importance. Thus it is hardly an oversimplification to view every scene of Jesus' passion in the light of the ongoing game of push and shove.

5.6 Honor and Shame: From Hunch to Knowledge

Scholarship is rich in imaginative hunches. But hunches are not arguments, nor probabilities, nor sure foundations for further research. The formal knowledge of honor and shame articulated here serves to promote scholarly hunches into the realm of provable arguments; impressions yield to probability. Thus the quality of scholarly interpretation improves immeasurably.

Finally, this brief study cannot do certain things. Although it presented a

---

48. Readers are alerted again to a study which examines the interplay of rhetoric (questions), responsive chreiai and challenge-riposte dynamics, a good index of the pervasiveness of agonistic behavior in antiquity: Neyrey, "Questions, *Chreiai*, and Challenges to Honor," 657-81.

concise grammar of honor, historically oriented readers would desire a fuller exposition of this value in the Hellenistic and Jewish worlds of antiquity. This study simply cannot satisfy that legitimate interest in the space allowed. Nor can it show in any detail just how a cultural reading using honor and shame would nuance older scholarly interpretations, some of which display remarkably intuitive hunches and others of which are totally ignorant of this value. Again, space does not allow. Rather it is the strength of all the articles in this study to fill in the gaps that escape the size and scope of individual articles.

PART THREE

Jesus vis-à-vis God: Agent or Equal?

17

"My Lord and My God"

The Heavenly Character of Jesus in John's Gospel

1.0 Introduction and Hypothesis

A disciple of Jesus calls him "Lord and God" (20:28; see 1:1-2), while his enemies charge that Jesus "makes himself 'equal to God'" (5:18) and "makes himself God" (10:33). What is the scope of these remarks about Jesus? What content goes into the confession of Jesus as "Lord and God" and what is meant by claiming that Jesus is "equal to God"? In what ways is Jesus properly called "god"?

All of the topics in this chapter have been treated earlier in the exposition of chs. 5–11. But the discussion was necessarily piecemeal in each chapter; that is, suited to the piece of the Gospel that was examined. At the risk of repeating the materials to excess, we gather the fragments in the Fourth Gospel which address the heavenly character of Jesus and attempt to present them as an integrated, coherent exposition of what the Evangelist meant by calling Jesus "god," "equal to God," an eternally existing being, and a figure who appeared to patriarchs. The benefit of this study lies in: 1) surfacing and collecting the diverse elements about the heavenly character of Jesus, which are generally *not* treated in commentaries, and 2) appreciating how they are redundant claims for Jesus, and 3) assessing how they form a coherent whole according to the ancient discussion of what constitutes a "true" deity.

2.0 The Content of the High Christological Confession

2.1 Jesus as the Appearing Deity

The Gospel absolutely maintains that "*no one* has ever seen God" (1:18; 6:46) — except the Son, of course. Nor has anyone ever ascended to heaven to see God or receive revelations (3:13) — except the Son. The Israelites neither saw God's shape nor heard his voice (5:37). No, neither Abraham, nor Moses, nor Elijah, nor any of Israel's prophets or visionaries has ever seen God. But since Scripture says that "God" appeared to them, what are we to think about the theophanies in the Bible? John's Gospel argues in several places that the appearing deity was not God (whom no one has ever seen) but Jesus.[1]

Abraham, for example, saw Jesus' day (8:56). As has been shown,[2] this might refer to an experience of Abraham during his life on earth, such as the theophany at the Covenant of the Pieces (Gen 15) or his reception of the three heavenly visitors (Gen 18).[3] Although Abraham is credited with prophetic visions of the future, John's text is not referring to a vision of Jesus-who-is-to-come-as-the-Messiah, for the text continues with the extraordinary claim that Jesus was not a mere future figure revealed to Abraham but rather a contemporary of Abraham, nay an eternal divine figure: "before Abraham came into being, I AM" (8:58). Although the Johannine text insists that Abraham did not see God, he saw an appearing figure nonetheless. Abraham, the contingent one, saw Jesus, the eternally existing figure, in his visions as the one who bears the name of God, "I AM."

Likewise in John 12:41 it is stated that Isaiah "saw his glory." Although Isaiah prophesied about future events (see Sir 48:24-25), it is commonly argued that John's text refers to a time in the prophet's life when he saw his glory, viz. the vision in the temple (Isaiah 6). Isaiah did not see God; but since the theophany was genuine, he must have seen the heavenly Jesus, the glory of God, the true Shekinah who pitched his tent there.

We made a similar argument earlier apropos of 1:51. Jesus promises his dis-

---

1. For a full exegetical exposition of this argument, see my article "The Jacob Allusions in John 1:51," *CBQ* 44 (1982): 589-94.

2. See Nils Dahl, "The Johannine Church and History," *Jesus in the Memory of the Early Church* (Minneapolis: Augsburg, 1976) 108-9.

3. In a recent article, L. Urban and P. Henry ("'Before Abraham Was I AM': Does Philo Explain John 8:56-58?" *Studia Philonica* 6 [1979-80]: 166-93) argued on the basis of 8:56 ("Abraham rejoiced") for Genesis 17 and the theophany to Abraham concerning the birth of Isaac. But the issue in Genesis 18 of Abraham's hospitality to the heavenly visitor (see John 8:38) seems equally likely.

ciples that they will see a heavenly vision; they will look into heaven, even to the throne of God, and view the Son of Man there with angels ascending and descending upon him. This verse, which clearly alludes to Jacob's vision in Gen 28:12, promises that the disciples will see what Jacob saw: a vision of an appearing, heavenly figure. Jacob never saw God, although he had a genuine theophany. Therefore Abraham, Jacob and Isaiah saw the appearing Jesus in their theophanies.

The author of the Fourth Gospel was not the only one to engage in this type of exegesis of the Scriptures. Justin Martyr, for example, employed it in his *Dialogue with Trypho*, when he argued with his Jewish opponent that it was Jesus who appeared to the Patriarchs. After systematically demonstrating that Jesus appeared to Abraham (*Dialogue* 56, 59), to Moses (56, 59, 60, 120), and to Jacob (58, 60, 86, 126), Justin summarized his claim to have shown that

> ... neither Abraham, nor Isaac, nor Jacob, nor any other man, saw the Father and ineffable Lord of all, but (saw) him who was according to his will his Son, being God, and the Angel because he ministered to his will. (*Dialogue* 127)

The structure of Justin's argument, moreover, is like that in the Fourth Gospel: 1) no one has ever seen God, 2) therefore the Patriarchs, who received genuine theophanies according to the Scriptures, saw Jesus, 3) who is properly called "God."

For completely other reasons, Philo likewise argues that the theophanies in the Scriptures were not visions of God (material persons cannot see the immaterial God). Therefore, they were revelations of God's Logos or of a Power of God. In Gen 17:1, for example, Abraham did not see God but only a Power of God (*Names* 15, 17). Despite his request to God to "show me Thyself" (Exod 33:13 LXX), Moses saw only "the back of God," which is one of "the powers that keep guard around you" (*Spec.* 1.45-46). In Gen 28:12, Jacob saw one of the powers of God (*Dreams* 1. 70). But in another theophany (Gen 31:13), Jacob is told that the appearing figure is *not* God but "god who appeared to you *in place of God*" (*Dreams* 1.228). Are there two gods? No, Philo can distinguish between *ho theos* and *theos*:

> Accordingly the holy word in the present instance has indicated Him who is truly God by means of the article saying "I am the God" (Gen 31:13) while it omits the article when mentioning him who is improperly so called, saying "Who appeared to you in one place" not "of the God," but simply "of God." (*Dreams* 1.229)

The point is, *ho theos* never appears in theophanies according to Philo, for no one can see God. The appearing figure is *theos*, one of God's powers, even the Logos, who is "improperly called god."[4]

2.2 Jesus Is "Equal to God"

In John 5 Jesus worked a miracle on the Sabbath (5:1-15), which led to a charge that he had "violated the Sabbath" (5:16), which charge prompted an apologetic defense of his action and his person (5:30-47). At a later time in the history of the Johannine community, a new controversy between church and synagogue developed over the high christology of the Johannine group, viz. its confession of Jesus as a heavenly figure. This later controversy is reflected in 5:17-29, where a new charge is brought against Jesus ("he makes himself equal to God," 5:18), which charge prompts a new apology (5:19-29).

As the following synopsis shows, the new charge in 5:18 is not simply a doublet of the old charge in 5:16. The prosecution[5] by the Jews is heightened ("they sought to kill him") and a new and more cogent reason for this is offered ("he makes himself equal to God"). The key to understanding the new apology (5:19-29) is to deal critically with the new charge. Part of it is erroneous and must be rejected ("he makes himself"), but part of it is true ("equal to God") which requires defense and careful explanation.

As response to the charge "he makes himself God" (5:19), Jesus disowns acting independently of God, much less contrary to God's law, for "of himself the Son can do nothing." Rather he does "what he sees the Father doing," which does not mean that he spies on God and steals heavenly secrets (e.g., Prometheus). On the contrary, "the Father loves the Son and shows him all that he does" (5:20). Thus the charge is untrue that Jesus arrogantly assumes power or status (". . . making himself"); for as the defense argues, God *loves* the Son and God *shows* the Son what he does. That is, God *makes him equal*. But as regards the second part of the charge, Jesus' equality with God is clearly maintained: "What the Father does, the Son does likewise" (5:19b) and the Father shows him "all that he himself does" (5:20a).

In 5:21-29, while the Gospel denies false honor claims by Jesus, it affirms the second part. First it is argued that Jesus has *not* arrogated to himself any power, for whatever powers he enjoys have been *given* him by God:

---

4. Once again, Neyrey, "Jacob Allusions in John 1:51," 592-93.
5. See A. E. Harvey, *Jesus on Trial* (Atlanta: John Knox, 1976) 50-51.

5:22   The Father judges no one, but *has given* all judgment to the Son.
5:26   As the Father has life in himself, so he *has given* the Son also to have life in himself.
5:27   . . . and *has given* him authority to execute judgment.

Again, it is not true that Jesus "makes himself" anything.

Second, 5:21-29 indicate quite clearly in what sense Jesus is "equal to God," viz., Jesus has God's full eschatological power:

1. *make alive*: As the Father raises the dead and gives them life, so the Son *makes alive* whom he wills (5:21);
2. *judgment*: The Father has given all *judgment* to the Son (5:22);
3. *honor*: . . . that all may *honor* the Son just as they *honor* the Father (5:23);
4. *dead hear and live*: The *dead* will *hear* the voice of the Son of God and those who *hear* will *live* (5:25);
5. *life in himself*: As the Father has *life in himself*, so he has granted the Son also to have life in himself (5:26);
6. *judgment*: . . . and has given him authority to execute *judgment*, because he is the Son of Man (5:27); and
7. *dead raised and judged*: All in the tombs will hear his voice and come forth, those who have done good, to the *resurrection* of *life*, and those who have done evil to the *resurrection* of *judgment* (5:28-29).

Since Jesus enjoys the same honor as God, the same authority, and the same extraordinary powers, he is undeniably "equal to God." And this equality is definitely not Jesus' vainglorious self-extension; rather it is God's will that he be so recognized and honored.

In summary, the claim that Jesus "makes himself" anything is rejected. God loves him, shows him all he does. God gave him all judgment, to have life in himself, to exercise power to raise the dead and judge them. And God wills that he be honored equally with him. Contrary to the charge in 5:18, the proper statement should be "God makes him equal to Himself."

Equality with God, however, is emphatically maintained by showing how Jesus has God's two basic powers, creative and judgmental power (5:19-29).[6] Raising the dead, judging, and having life in oneself refer to God's eschatologi-

---

6. C. H. Dodd (*The Interpretation of the Fourth Gospel* [Cambridge: University Press, 1968] 322-23) argued that two powers are alluded to, but he described them inaccurately as *zōopoiein* and *krinein*; comparably, R. Schnackenburg, *The Gospel according to St. John* (New York: Crossroad, 1982) 2.106. These studies need to be corrected in the light of the present discussion of God's two powers, creative and eschatological.

cal power. If eschatological power is ascribed to Jesus in 5:21-29, what can be said of the power credited to him in 5:19-20? It would not seem to refer to either executive leadership or eschatological power. I suggest that 5:19-20 refers to God's grant of creative power to Jesus.

In 5:17 Jesus claimed that "my Father is working still and I am working." That statement functions as an apology for *not* resting on the Sabbath; it implies that God did not stop creating on the seventh day but continued working.[7] Apropos of the healing in 5:1-9, Jesus defends himself by claiming two things: 1) God continues to work on the Sabbath, hence Jesus is imitating God's continued creative work by his healing on the Sabbath, and 2) God shows him all that he does, empowering him for works of creation and providence. And all of God's deeds of creation/providence Jesus does likewise. The Gospel has already attributed all creation to the Logos (1:1-3) and we should see 5:1-9 and 17-20 as the continuation of that theme. Jesus has God's full creative power, just as he has God's complete eschatological power.

What is the significance of insisting that Jesus has God's *two powers?* Jewish discussions of God focused on God's two measures *(middoth)* of kindness and justice (see Ex 34:6-8).[8] Since all theology dealt with God's operations in the world, these two measures encompassed all of God's actions in the world. The same is true of Hellenistic theology, where the deity is fundamentally described in terms of his providence (kindness/justice) which is manifested by creation/maintenance of the world and by justice.[9] Philo, however, expresses this most clearly in his exposition of God's two powers: *dynamis poiētikē* and *dynamis basilikē*.[10] Through the *dynamis poiētikē* God "creates and operates the world" (*QG* 4.2); and by the *dynamis basilikē* contains "authority, legislation, punishment," as well as governance (hence "kingly"/*basilikē*). The same dual aspect of God's total powers may also be found in Rom 4:17 where Abraham's great faith was belief in God who 1) called being out of non-being (creative power) and 2) made the dead alive (eschatological power).[11] Creation and eschatology,

---

7. See Philo *Cher.* 88-89; *Alleg. Interp.* 1.5; *Gen. Rab.* 11.10; *Exod. Rab.* 30.6.

8. See A. Marmorstein, *The Old Rabbinic Doctrine of God* (New York: Ktav, 1969) 41-53; E. E. Urbach, *The Sages* (Jerusalem: Magnes Press, 1975) 448-61.

9. This, of course, resembles the doctrine of God's providence as this is discussed in Greco-Roman philosophy; see my dissertation, "The Form and Background of the Polemic in 2 Peter" (unpublished, Yale University, 1977) 179-208.

10. See *Alleg Interp.* 2.68; *Cher.* 27-28; *Sacr.* 59; *Plant.* 86-87; *Heir* 166; *Flight* 95, 100; *Dreams* 1.159-63; *Abr.* 124-25; *Mos.* 2.99; *Embassy* 4, 6; *QE* 2.62, 64-66, 68. See also Harry Wolfson, *Philo* (Cambridge: Harvard University Press, 1948) 1.218-225, and Erwin R. Goodenough, *By Light, Light* (New Haven: Yale University Press, 1935) 24-29.

11. See Halvor Moxnes, *Theology in Conflict: Studies in Paul's Understanding of God in Romans* (NovTSup 53; Leiden: Brill, 1980) 231-82.

then, encompass all of God's actions. John's Gospel, moreover, reflects just this tradition of God's two basic powers in 5:19-29 when it attributes creative (5:19-20) and eschatological (5:21-29) power to Jesus.[12]

In Philo and the Rabbis, moreover, the two powers of God are associated respectively with God's two names.[13] For Philo, the beneficent, creative power *(dynamis poiētikē)* is called *Theos* ("God," the equivalent of Elohim in the LXX) and the royal, punishing power *(dynamis basilikē)* is called *Kyrios* ("Lord," the equivalent of the tetragrammaton in the LXX). For example, in explaining the Cherubim (Exod 25:18), Philo identifies the two powers of the Deity and names them accordingly:

> I should myself say that they (the Cherubim) are allegorical representations of the two most august and highest potencies *(dynameis)* of Him that is, the creative and the kingly. His creative potency is called God *(Theos)*, because through it He placed and made and ordered this universe, and the kingly is called Lord *(Kyrios)*, being that with which He governs what has come into being and rules it steadfastly with justice. (*Mos.* 2.99)[14]

The Rabbis likewise associated the two powers with God's two names, although for them sometimes the creative power was linked with the tetragrammaton and judgment with Elohim.[15] But the tradition is clear that God's two powers are linked respectively with God's two names. Is this true in John?

In the Gospel's prologue, where Jesus is credited with creative power, he is called *Theos* (1:1-3). Ch. 5 also deals with Jesus' creative "working," in which context Jesus is alleged to be "equal to God" (*ison tō theō*, 5:18). *Theos,* then, is the appropriate name for Jesus when he exercises creative power. *Kyrios,* however, is much more difficult to deal with; for while Jesus is often acclaimed *Kyrios* in John, this title is constantly open to the minimalist interpretation of "sir" or "master." There is, however, one climactic confession in the Gospel in which Jesus is acclaimed "My Lord *(Kyrios)* and my God *(Theos)*" (20:28).

---

12. It should be noted that whereas Philo and the rabbis speak of God's "executive" power, John has already broadened this category to include eschatological issues, such as resurrection, judgment, and "having life in himself," and so the second power of God is perceived as eschatological power.

13. The study by Alan Segal and Nils Dahl ("Philo and the Rabbis on the Names of God," *JSJ* 9 [1978]: 1-28) presents a contemporary discussion of this material; see also A. Marmorstein, "Philo and the Names of God," *JQR* 22 (1931-32): 295-306.

14. For other places in Philo where the two powers of God are called by God's two names respectively, see *Plant.* 86-87; *Abr.* 124-25; *Dreams* 1.160, 163; and *QE* 2.62.

15. For a summary of the differences between Philo and the Rabbis, see Segal and Dahl, "Philo and the Rabbis on the Names of God," 1-3.

Surely at this point *Kyrios* should be treated as a cultic title, its full force acclaiming Jesus as a heavenly figure.[16] But what is intended by acclaiming Jesus as *Kyrios* after his resurrection? Is his exercise of a certain power implied and acknowledged?

Creative power is not only claimed but demonstrated (1:1-18; 5:1-9, 19-20) and so Jesus is rightly called *Theos*. Eschatological power is initially only claimed in 5:18, 21-29, and its demonstration remains the task of the rest of the Gospel, especially the next several chapters. As is characteristic of the Fourth Gospel, a sentence or statement is frequently made which serves as the text, topic or agenda of subsequent discussion. 5:18, 21-29 is just such a topic statement.[17] As the following chart shows, the seven items contained in 5:18-29 are formally explained and treated in chs. 8, 10, and 11. The following chart appeared in the discussion of this material in John 5, but we repeat it here because of its influence on our comprehensive reading of this material.

Eschatological Power	John 6	John 8	John 10	John 11
1. *Equal to God:* ". . . making himself equal to God" (5:18)			10:30, 33	
2. *Son gives life:* "Just as the Father raises the dead and gives them life, so also the Son gives life to whomever he wishes" (5:21)	6:27, 33, 47-50, 54, 57, 58	8:51	10:28	11:25a
3. *Judgment:* "The Father . . . has given all judgment to the Son" (5:22); "he has given him authority to execute judgment, because he is the Son of Man" (5:27)		8:21-30	10:29	
4. *Equal honor:* "all honor the Son just as they honor the Father. Who does not honor the Son does not honor the Father" (5:23)		the name "I AM"	(10:31; 10:39)	11:4
5. *The dead hear and live:* "the dead will hear the voice of the Son of God, and those who hear will live" (5:25)			(10:3-5)	11:43-44
6. *Life in himself:* "just as the Father has life in himself, so he has granted the Son also to have life in himself" (5:26)	6:51	8:24, 28, 58	10:17-18	11:25a

---

16. See Rudolf Bultmann, *The Gospel of John* (Philadelphia: Westminster, 1971) 695.

17. See my article "John III — A Debate over Johannine Epistemology and Christology," *NovT* 23 (1981): 115-17.

"My Lord and My God"

Eschatological Power	John 6	John 8	John 10	John 11
7. *Resurrection and life:* "all who are in their graves will hear his voice and come out — those who have done good, to the resurrection of life, and those who have done evil, to the resurrection of condemnation" (5:28-29)	6:40, 44, 54			11:25-26

What was claimed in 5:21-29, then, was formally discussed and even demonstrated, the greatest demonstration surely being Jesus' self-resurrection, his proof that he "has life in himself." It is after this demonstration that the Evangelist records that the title *Kyrios* is properly given to Jesus, "My Lord and my God" (20:28), indicating that by then Jesus has demonstrated that he has God's eschatological power and may be called by the name associated with that power, *Kyrios*.

From this investigation of ch. 5, we draw the following conclusions:

1. Jesus is properly called "equal to God," because
2. he has God's *two basic powers* (creative/eschatological);
3. he is properly called *Theos* in virtue of having God's creative power, and *Kyrios* in virtue of God's executive or eschatological power.
4. Jesus does *not* falsely "*make himself*" anything, for
5. God gave him these powers and so wants Jesus to be honored even as God is honored.

2.3 Jesus Eternal and Imperishable

It has often been remarked that according to 17:6 and 11-12, "the name" which God gave Jesus is not "God" or "Lord," but "I AM."[18] When we turn to 8:24, 28 and 58, where Jesus manifests that name, we must continue to ask what is understood by this name, "I AM." It is a commonplace of Johannine scholarship to indicate that "I AM" reflects the usage of LXX Isaiah, indicating that it is a condensed version of the name manifested to Moses at the burning bush in Exod 3:14.[19] As important as this observation is, we continue to ask how "I AM" was popularly interpreted in contemporary Jewish materials such as LXX,

---

18. See Raymond E. Brown, *The Gospel according to John* (AB 29; Garden City: Doubleday, 1970) 1.756.

19. For a survey of the issues and evidence, see Philip Harner, *The "I AM" of the Fourth Gospel* (Philadelphia: Fortress, 1970); see also R. E. Brown, *The Gospel according to John*, 1.533-38, and R. Schnackenburg, *The Gospel according to St. John* (New York: Crossroad, 1982) 79-89.

Philo, and the targums. First, the LXX interpreted the name of God in Exod 3:14 to mean "the Existent One," already understanding that name in reference to a divine mode of being:

Exod 3:14 (MT)
God said to Moses:
"I AM WHO I AM."

Exod 3:14 (LXX)
God said to Moses:
"I AM THE EXISTENT ONE"
(*egō eimi ho ōn*)

And he said:
"Say this to the
children of Israel:
'I AM
has sent me to you.'"

And he said:
"Say this to the
Children of Israel:
'THE EXISTENT ONE (*ho ōn*)
has sent me to you.'"

Secondly, Philo repeats the LXX interpretation of "I AM" as *"the Existent One,"* always drawing a distinction between God's genuine existence and that of creatures which exist in semblance only.[20] Yet as Martin Hengel[21] has observed, a genuine Hellenistic influence is already introduced into the interpretation of the sacred name, in which non-contingent being is contrasted with contingent being, and eternal with temporal existence.

Tgs. Yer. I, II, and *Neof.,* moreover, all interpret the "I AM" of Exod 3:14 in ways which bring out a sense of God's past and future eternity, as the following chart indicates:[22]

Tg. Yer. I
And the Lord
said to Moses:

Tg. Yer. II
And the Memra of the Lord
said to Moses:

Tg. Neof.
And the Lord
said to Moses:

"He who spoke and
the world was;
who spoke and
all things were."

"He who said to the world,
'Be!' and it was; and who
Shall yet say to it 'Be!'
and it will be."

"I AM WHO I AM."

20. See *Worse* 160; *Change* 11; *Dreams* 1.230-31; *Mos.* 1.66, 74-76; see also Wolfson, *Philo,* 210.

21. I am presupposing a background for the LXX understanding of God's name like Hengel's "The 'Interpretatio Graeca' of Judaism" in his *Judaism and Hellenism* (Philadelphia: Fortress, 1974) 1.255-67; on this issue see also Morton Smith, "The Image of God, Notes on the Hellenization of Judaism with Especial Reference to Goodenough's Work on Jewish Symbols," *BJRL* 40 (1957-58): 473-512.

22. I am indebted here for the collection of these texts, their translation, and the interpretation to Martin McNamara, *The New Testament and the Palestinian Targum to the Pentateuch* (AnB 27; Rome: Biblical Institute Press, 1966) 97-112.

"My Lord and My God"

| And he said: "Say this to the children of Israel: 'I AM has sent me to you.'" | And he said: "Say this to the children of Israel: 'I AM HE WHO IS AND WHO WILL BE has sent me to you.'" | And he said: "Say this to the children of Israel: 'He who spoke and the world was from the beginning and shall say again to it "Be!" and it shall be — he has sent me to you.'" |

A cursory examination of these texts suggests two lines of interpretation. All the targums understand "I AM" to refer to a special quality of God's being, viz., God's past and future eternity. And they all link the special name with God's actions or powers: creation in the past and eschatological new creation in the future. And so, the "I AM" of Exod 3:14 was popularly understood to contain remarks about God's two powers as well as God's eternity both past and future.

Stepping aside from Jewish sources, considerable light can be shed on this material from comparable discussions about the nature of a true deity in Greco-Roman literature. For example, Sextus Empiricus records the popular idea about god as "eternal *(aidion)* and imperishable *(aphtharton)* and perfect in happiness."[23] Diogenes Laertius, in reporting Stoic doctrine about god, notes that the deity must be "everlasting *(aidion)* and the artificer of each thing throughout the whole extent of matter." Later he remarks that, as the deity is a principle, it belongs to principles to be "without generation *(agenētous)* or destruction *(aphthartous).*"[24] Occasionally we find formal discussions of the attributes of a true deity by which they are compared and contrasted with heroic mortals who were apotheosized at their death,[25] which discussions have a direct bearing on the point of this inquiry. Examples of this discussion may be found in Plutarch,[26] although the clearest illustration of this topos comes from Diodor of Sicily:

> As regards the gods, men of ancient times have handed down to later generations two different conceptions: Certain of the gods, they say, are *eternal* and *imperishable (aidious kai aphthartous)* ... for each of these *genesis* and *duration* are *from everlasting to everlasting.* But the other gods, we are told, were terrestrial beings who attained immortal honors and fame because of their benefactions to mankind, such as Heracles, Dionysus, Aristaeus, and the oth-

---

23. *Against the Physicians* 1.46.
24. Diogenes Laertius, *Zeno* 7.134; see comparable discussions in Cicero, *De Natura Deorum* 1.10.25, 24.68.
25. See Charles H. Talbert, *What Is a Gospel?* (Philadelphia: Fortresss, 1977) 25-52.
26. *On the Malice of Herodotus* 857D; *Pelopidas* 16.

ers who were like them. (*Library of History* 6.1.2; see also 1.12.10-13.1, emphasis added)

Greco-Roman god-talk as well as Israelite targumic and Philonic understandings of God in the expansions attached to the interpretation of Exod 3:14 agree on these significant points: 1) a true deity must be genuinely eternal, uncreated, without beginning *(aidios)* or imperishable and eternal *(aphthartos);* 2) a true deity, who is uncreated, has creative power; and this deity, who is imperishable, exercises judgment over all created, perishable beings.

This range of material, I am suggesting, has a direct bearing on the meaning of "I AM" in John 8:24, 28, and 58. First, in 8:28, "I AM" is linked with survival of death: "When you have lifted up the Son of Man, you will know that I AM." Death (being "lifted up") is not the last word for Jesus; for despite his death, the Gospel claims that he has power over death (10:17-18). Hence, "I AM" means eternal existence for the Imperishable One. And in 8:58, "I AM" is linked both with eternal existence in the past and with imperishable existence in the future. Concerning the latter focus, a contrast is made between Jesus and Abraham, a point that occupies the discussion in 8:51-58. First, it is asked if Jesus is "greater than our father Abraham *who died*" (8:53), a remark in response to Jesus' claim that those who keep his word "never die." Jesus is contrasted with Abraham *who died* and with the prophets *who died;* and so, being "greater than Abraham, *who died,*" lies in Jesus' superior existence. If "greater than . . . ," his greatness will lie in *not dying.* Second, Jesus goes on to describe how, in fact, he is "greater than Abraham," indicating that he existed already prior to Abraham and that his mode of being is different from that of Abraham, for he *is (eimi)* whereas Abraham *came into being (ginesthai).* 8:58, then, suggests that Jesus is both ancient and eternal in the past and eternal and imperishable in the future. It suggests that Jesus is uncreated *(eimi)* in contrast to beings who are created *(ginesthai).* Together, the "I AM" statements in 8:28 and 58 reflect the content given to God's name in the Jewish understandings of Exod 3:14, as well as the substance of the discussions about true deity in Hellenistic literature, i.e. eternal and ungenerated existence in the past, imperishable existence in the future — such is the nature of Israel's God and any true deity.

This discussion of the content of "I AM" correlates with other aspects of the high christology in the Fourth Gospel.

1. "I AM," of course, is the name of the *appearing deity* in the Scriptures. Inasmuch as Jesus is proclaimed as having appeared to patriarchs and prophets, he was also truly functioning as "I AM," the appearing figure.
2. Jesus has God's two powers, creative and eschatological. Inasmuch as he

"was" in the beginning,[27] he was *not* created but is the creator of all in virtue of God's creative power (1:1-5). He is truly eternal-in-the-past. And inasmuch as he has "life in himself" (5:26; 10:17-18), he is imperishable in virtue of the fullness of eschatological power which he enjoys. He is truly eternal-in-the-future.

The content of "I AM" in John 8, then, meshes integrally with the other aspects of Jesus' "equality with God" according to the exposition of the Fourth Gospel.

3.0 Apologetic Aspects of the High-Christological Confession

This exalted confession was indisputably controversial, which probably led the community to explain it in more apologetic or provocative terms.

Johannine Christians are monotheists: this Gospel does not claim that Jesus is Yahweh or that he replaces God. Jesus himself would seem to be endorsing monotheism, echoing the Shema (Deut 6:4-5), when he addresses Israel's deity, "This is eternal life, that they know Thee, *the only true God* . . ." (17:3). Yet the Johannine community is also calling Jesus "god."

Jesus is not blaspheming when he claims to be "equal to God." It is God who "makes him" what he is: 1) God commissioned him to reveal his name; 2) God gave him his two powers; and 3) God sent him into the world as his apostle and agent, equal to himself.[28]

Jesus is not a rival of Yahweh, a pretender to the throne. All that he says and does is done in obedience to the will of him who sent Jesus (see 5:23; 7:16-18; 8:38; 17:4).

Jesus is not a recent invention of Christian imagination; he is not a new figure in cosmic or national history. He was face to face with God in the beginning, before anything was created. Although in glory, he was continuously active in Israel's salvation history: he created the cosmos, and he gave theophanies to Israel's patriarchs.[29] Therefore his current appearance in our midst is continuous with his past activity.

---

27. It is probably relevant to include here the references to Jesus being "*before* John" in 1:15, 30.

28. See Peder Borgen, "God's Agent in the Fourth Gospel," *Religions in Antiquity*, ed. Jacob Neusner (Leiden: Brill, 1968) 137-47.

29. For comparable assertions of Jesus' activity in Israel's past history, see 1 Cor 10:4; Jude 5.

18

"I Am the Door" (John 10:7, 9)

Jesus the Broker in the Fourth Gospel

1.0 Why This Study? Introduction and Hypothesis

The Fourth Gospel seems to be immune to interpretation via the ancient model of patron-client relationships. Peder Borgen applied the Semitic model of "agent" to Jesus.[1] But he does not tell us what makes for a good agent or whether the agent labors on behalf of those to whom he is sent. George W. Buchanan presented Jesus as an "apostle," according to an understanding of "agency" as a legal phenomenon. He considered the "agency" of angels, kings, apostles, and especially Jesus, the one uniquely "sent" from God.[2] Again, what makes for a successful apostle? Does the apostle also represent the interests of those to whom he is sent? Previous study of God as Benefactor-Patron has been mostly limited to studies of the Greco-Roman world,[3] with only few New Testament studies going this route.[4] Tricia G. Brown has written thus far the

---

1. Peder Borgen, "God's Agent in the Fourth Gospel." in *Religions in Antiquity*, ed. Jacob Neusner (Leiden: Brill, 1968) 137-48; A. E. Harvey, "Jesus as Agent," in *The Glory of Christ in the New Testament*, ed. L. D. Hurst and N. T. Wright (Oxford: Clarendon Press, 1987) 239-50. See Karl H. Rengstorf, *Apostleship* (London: Adam and Charles Black, 1952) 11-24.

2. George W. Buchanan, "Apostolic Christology," SBLSP 1986: 172-82. Moreover, Charles A. Gieschen (*Angelomorphic Christology: Antecedents and Early Evidence* [Leiden: Brill, 1998] 293) remarks: "John never calls Jesus an angel, [yet] this analysis of evidence has demonstrated that angelomorphic terminology, traditions, and functions are an integral part of his Christology."

3. See Jerome H. Neyrey, "God, Benefactor and Patron: The Major Cultural Model for Interpreting the Deity in Greco-Roman Antiquity," *JSNT* 27 (2005): 471-83; Arthur Darby Nock, "Soter and Euergetes," in his *Essays on Religion and the Ancient World* (Cambridge, MA: Harvard University Press, 1972) 720-35.

4. See Stephen C. Mott, *The Greek Benefactor and Deliverance from Moral Distress* (unpub-

"I Am the Door" (John 10:7, 9)

only monograph on patron-client relationships in the Fourth Gospel; she focuses on the role of the Spirit as the sub-broker of Jesus.[5] But few indeed are the studies of the Fourth Gospel in terms of the patron-broker-client model.

Hence many questions are not even asked, much less answered. How does someone become a broker? What makes a person a good broker? Are brokers one-way agents (patron to clients) or two-way (patron to clients and clients to patron)? What do brokers broker? Previous studies of "agency" do not and cannot function at a high enough level of abstraction to answer these questions. Something more is needed, namely, a more complete model of patron-broker-client relations, a worthy and needed contribution.

The basic hypothesis argued here is that Jesus as the Broker belongs to two worlds, the world of God-Patron and that of disciples-clients. In one direction, he serves as a bridge between patron and clients, as a go-between whom God sends to mediate knowledge, power, loyalty and material benefaction to his clients. Correspondingly he brokers the interests of the clients by praying for them and urging them to pray "in my name." Jesus himself regularly insists that he is not acting on his own or representing another patron, but serves as the agent or broker sent by God to speak and to act. To argue this, we must perform these tasks: 1) review the model of patron-client relationships, 2) investigate the Judean and Greco-Roman background of a "broker," 3) describe the role of broker in the light of the social sciences, and 4) examine the role of Jesus the Broker in the Fourth Gospel.

2.0 The Classical Model of Patron-Client Relations

We presume that scholars are well informed about the model of patron-client relations by this time.[6] But some important features deserve repeating. Typical

---

lished dissertation, Harvard, 1971) 74-82 and 345-53; Bruce J. Malina, "Patron and Client: The Analogy behind Synoptic Theology," in his *The Social World of Jesus* (London: Routledge, 1996) 143-74; Bruce J. Malina and Richard L. Rohrbaugh, *Social-Science Commentary on the Gospel of John* (Minneapolis, MN: Fortress, 1998) 115-19.

5. Tricia Gates Brown, *Spirit in the Writings of John* (New York, NY: T. & T. Clark International, 2003).

6. See Richard P. Saller, *Personal Patronage under the Early Empire* (Cambridge: Cambridge University Press, 1982); S. N. Eisenstadt and L. Roniger, *Patrons, Clients and Friends: Interpersonal Relations and the Structure of Trust in Society* (Cambridge: University of Cambridge Press, 1984); and Ernst Gellner and John Waterbury, eds., *Patrons and Clients in Mediterranean Societies* (London: Duckworth, 1977). See also John H. Elliott, "Patronage and Clientage," in *The Social Sciences and New Testament Interpretation*, ed. Richard L. Rohrbaugh (Peabody, MA: Hendrickson, 1996) 144-56.

pairings in patron-client relationships might include God-man, saint-devotee, godfather-godchild, lord-vassal, landlord-tenant, and so forth. We know, moreover, the characteristics of a typical patron-client structure[7]: 1) *asymmetrical relationship* between parties of different status;[8] 2) *interpersonal obligation*, focusing on personal loyalty or attachment;[9] 3) *favoritism*;[10] 4) *reciprocity:* as goods and services are exchanged, clients incur *debts* and obligations to the patron;[11] 5) *"kinship glaze"* reduces the crassness of the relationship;[12] and 6) *honor* is everywhere present. Whereas human patron-client relationships tend to be asymmetrical, reciprocal, often including favoritism, focused on honor, and held together by "good will" or faithfulness,[13] the same is said to characterize the relationship of divine patrons and mortal clients.

---

7. Eisenstadt and Roniger, *Patrons, Clients and Friends*, 48-49.

8. See Gellner and Waterbury, *Patrons and Clients*, 4; Saller, *Personal Patronage under the Early Empire*, 1-2.

9. John Rich ("Patronage and Interstate Relations in the Roman Republic," in *Patronage in Ancient Society*, ed. Andrew Wallace-Hadrill [London: Routledge, 1990] 128) describes the importance of loyalty/faithfulness in the patron-client relation: "In one of the most important of its many uses *fides* means 'protection.' The weaker party is said 'to be in the *fides*' of the stronger. At the formation of such a relationship, the weaker party is said to give himself into or entrust himself to the *fides* of the stronger and the stronger to receive the weaker into his *fides*."

10. Richard Saller, "Patronage and Friendship in Early Imperial Rome: Drawing the Distinction," in *Patronage in Ancient Society*, ed. Wallace-Hadrill, 52-53. Plutarch states: "There are favors that involve causing no offence, such as giving a friend preferential help in obtaining a post, putting some prestigious administrative function into his hands, or a friendly embassy" (*Precepts for Politicians* 19-20).

11. Richard Saller, *Personal Patronage under the Early Empire*, 21, 27-29; see also Stephen C. Mott, "The Power of Giving and Receiving: Reciprocity in Hellenistic Benevolence," *Current Issues in Biblical and Patristic Interpretation*, ed. Gerald F. Hawthorne (Grand Rapids, MI: Eerdmans, 1975) 60-71.

12. Dionysus of Halicarnassus on Roman reform of Greek relationships: "The Athenians called their clients *'thetes'* or 'hirelings,' because they served for hire, and the Thessalians called theirs *'penestai'* or 'toilers,' by the very name reproaching them with their condition" (2.9). So he recommended that the poor and lowly be described by a "handsome designation," namely "patronage."

13. Patron-client relationships could be coercive and exploitative: Paul Millett, "Patronage and Its Avoidance in Classical Athens," in *Patronage in Ancient Society*, ed. Wallace-Hadrill, 15-47; Peter Flynn, "Class, Clientelism, and Coercion: Some Mechanisms of Internal Dependency and Control," *Journal of Commonwealth and Comparative Politics* 12 (1974): 129-56.

"I Am the Door" (John 10:7, 9)

2.1 Fathers as Patrons[14]

We need first to consider the relationship of an earthly father-patron and his son-client because this served as the model for "Father" and "Son" in the Fourth Gospel. What, then, were these "reciprocal relationships of human life" like? Seneca discussed these very relationships in his *Benefits*, the best exposition of this we have. As regards *fathers*, they are indeed patron and benefactor: "Can there be any greater benefits than those that a father bestows upon his children?" (Seneca, *Benefits* 2.11.5). Fathers bestow power (to protect their sons), inducement (food, clothing, support), but especially commitment (loyalty, fidelity to them).[15] Most importantly, fathers provide strict and severe upbringing and the education and socialization of their sons: "Do you see how parents force their children in the stage of tender infancy to submit to wholesome measures? Though the infants struggle and cry, they tend their bodies with loving care, and fearing that their limbs may become crooked from too early liberty, they swathe them in order that they may grow to be straight.... And so the greatest benefits are those that while we are either unaware or unwilling, we receive from our parents" (Seneca, *Benefits* 6.24.1-2). As regards *sons*, their duties to their fathers must be learned in the school of hard knocks (see Heb 5:8; 12:5-11), and so fathers only occasionally see the fruit of their labors:

> Our parents almost always outdo us.... When at last with age we have acquired wisdom, it begins to be evident that we ought to love them for the very things that keep us from loving them — their admonitions, their strictness, and their careful watch over our heedlessness — they are snatched from us. Few reach the age when they can reap some true reward from their children. (Seneca, *Benefits* 5.5.2-4)

---

14. Patrons elected to become such and did so for their own advantage. In Greece, benefactors were pressured into performing a λειτουργία. On the burdensomeness of these, see Naphtali Lewis, *Inventory of Compulsory Public Services of Ptolemaic and Roman Egypt* (New Haven: American Society of Papyrologists, 1968). See also S. R. Llewelyn, "The Development of the System of Liturgies," *NDIEC* 7 (1994): 93-111.

15. The analogy of fathers and sons as patrons and clients is evident here: "In order to choose our duties to them [parents] easily, we should have this summary statement at hand, namely, that our parents are the images of the gods, and by Zeus, domestic gods, benefactors, kinsmen, creditors, lords and the warmest of friends.... They are lenders of the most valuable things, and take back only things which will benefit us when we repay them. For what gain is so great to a child as piety and gratitude to his parents?" (Hierocles, "How to Conduct Oneself toward One's Parents," *Stob.* 3.52).

Sons are expected to live up to the customs of the ancestors, to be obedient, to manifest loyalty, and thus honor their fathers. But the education was often achieved by the rod.

In Israelite terms, the duties of an earthly father include socializing his son into the traditional values and roles which he himself learned.[16] A father circumcised his son, "redeemed" his firstborn (Exod 13:13; Luke 2:22-24) and continually provided nourishment and protection. The personal name of sons included the identity of their fathers ("Simon, *son of Jonah*" and "James and John, *sons of Zebedee*") as well as their trades, roles, and statuses. Sons of priests are themselves priests (1 Sam 23:6); sons of kings are likely to be kings themselves (1 Kgs 1:32-37). Ideally sons are "chips off the old block," embodying the virtue, identity, and status of their fathers.[17]

The rights of a father center around the honorable acknowledgment of his role and status by his sons. This is enshrined in the commandment: "Honor your father and mother" (Exod 20:12; Deut 5:16; Mal 1:6; Eph 6:1-3). Children particularly manifest this honor by their obedience to their fathers (Gen 27:8, 13, 43; Col 3:20; Eph 6:1), and the support given to them in their old age (Sir 3:11-16). Conversely the father can be shamed when a son curses him (Exod 21:17; Lev 20:9), dishonors him (Deut 27:16), robs him (Prov 28:24), mocks him (Prov 30:17), strikes him (Exod 21:15), or disobeys him (Matt 21:28-31).

The rights and duties of earthly fathers serve as the model for considering the heavenly Patron as Father. The Patron Father, too, gives life to his clients, nurtures them, socializes them into his ways, provides them knowledge of how his family works, and provides them with their primary identity as "sons of God." Conversely, earthly clients of this Patron Father owe him honor, obedience and respect. This will be manifest in acceptance of his words, his will, and his agents; faith (as obedience and loyalty) will be their primary way of honoring their Patron Father.

Names for earthly fathers are all connected with generating children in some fashion ("father," "parents," "ancestor," "patriarch," and "elder"). In the Greco-Roman world the high god, Zeus, was often addressed as "Father." Dio Chrysostom states: "At that time, the Creator and Father (δημιουργὸς καὶ πατὴρ) of the World . . ." (*Oration* 36.60); Cicero comments: ". . . the poets call

---

16. See Jerome Neyrey, "Father," *The Collegeville Pastoral Dictionary of Biblical Theology*, ed. Carroll Stuhlmuller (Collegeville, MN: Liturgical Press, 1996) 315-19. See also John J. Pilch, "'Beat His Ribs While He Is Young' (Sir 30:12): A Window on the Mediterranean World," *BTB* 23 (1993): 101-13.

17. After instructing a father to "whip his son often" and "discipline him," Sirach explains the importance of such training: "The father may die, and yet he is not dead, for he has left behind him one like himself" (30:4).

"I Am the Door" (John 10:7, 9)

him 'father of gods and men'" (*Nature of the Gods* 1.64). Of particular interest is this comment by Dio: "Yet all these poets in precisely the same fashion call the first and greatest god Father of the whole rational family. . . . Some do not hesitate even to call him Father in their prayers" (Dio Chrysostom, *Oration* 36.35-36).

Similar paternal language was ascribed to the Roman Emperor, who was not only *pater familias*, but *pater patriae*.[18] On the one hand Caesar extended his authority to the Empire, analogous to the authority of individual fathers to their families. On the other hand, he "kinifies" the relationship by trying to soften or mask the harsh realities of imperial power.[19]

2.2 "Broker": Bridging Patron and Client

Inaccessible eastern potentates (patrons) utilized their viziers to broker their plans to the world outside the palace and to gather information for him about the state of affairs of the empire.[20] Petitioners employed the services of persons well placed in the circles of power as for example, Pliny, who brokered the concerns of friends and relatives to Caesar.[21] A "priest" in Rome was called a "ponti-fex," that is, a bridge-maker, for he functioned as the bridge linking gods/patrons and mortals/clients.[22] A broker is, then, a mediator, a bridge, a go-between, an ambassador, etc. But besides examples and instances of a broker, we need an adequate definition of broker and brokerage, which will encompass the vast array of specific examples of "broker" that we shall shortly see: "A social broker, by definition, is a professional manipulator of people and informa-

---

18. T. R. Stevenson, "The Ideal Benefactor and the Father Analogy in Greek and Roman Thought," *CQ* 42 (1992): 429-36. See P. H. Swan, *The Augustan Succession: An Historical Commentary on Dio Cassius' Roman History Books 55-56* (Oxford: Oxford University Press, 2004) 55-56.

19. See W. K. Lacey, "Patria Potestas," *The Family in Ancient Rome: New Perspectives*, ed. Beryl Rawson (Ithaca, NY: Cornell University Press, 1986) 121-44.

20. John T. Green (*The Role of the Messenger and Message in the Ancient Near East* [Atlanta, GA: Scholars Press, 1989] xvi-xvii) distinguishes five types of messenger (ambassador, emissary-courier, envoy, herald and harbinger); he argues that the concept of messenger was constant and did not change (40-41).

21. Examples of Pliny's brokerage are common in his letters, but see 10.2, 4, 5, 6, 12, 26, 51. See also Tor Hauken, *Petition and Response: An Epigraphic Study of Petitions to Roman Emperors 181-249* (Stavenger: MHS, 1994).

22. See Gottlob Schrenk, "ἱερεύς," *TDNT* 3.267. See also Hans Gärtner, "Pontifex," *Paulys Realencyclopädie der Classischen Altertumswissenschaft*, supp. vol. 15, 331-96, especially the list of pontifices maximi on p. 346.

tion who brings about communication for personal benefit."[23] A broker is a special type of entrepreneur who knows whom to contact for resources he does not have and which are desired by others.[24] In addition, we would also want to know the characteristics of a successful broker.[25]

There are, then, a series of questions about a broker which can focus our understanding. 1) How does a person become a broker? 2) What does he broker?[26] 3) What makes for a successful broker? 4) Why a broker at all or this broker? Is he special or necessary? 5) What does the broker receive for his services? It profits us to consider certain figures in the ancient world who were understood as brokers. Their presentation can provide clarity and support for our subsequent interpretation of the Fourth Gospel in terms of a full patron-broker-client model.

2.3 Israelite Brokers[27]

Moses functioned as the consummate broker[28] between God and Israel in three episodes in his career: 1) Israel's arrival at Sinai, 2) Israel's worship of the golden calf, and 3) Moses' own death. When Israel arrived at Sinai, the people begged Moses to be their mediator with God: "You speak to us and we will hear; but let not God speak to us, lest we die" (Exod 20:19). Philo interprets this to mean that God respects human incapacity to receive "unmixed and exceedingly great" benefaction without a mediator:

---

23. Malina, "Patron and Client," 152. See also P. G. Davis, "Divine Agents, Mediators, and New Testament Christology," *JTS* 45 (1994) 484-85.

24. Jeremy Boissevain, *Friends of Friends: Networks, Manipulators, and Coalitions* (New York, NY: St. Martin's Press, 1974) 147-48.

25. The characteristics of a successful broker are found in the work of Boissevain, *Friends of Friends*, 148-63.

26. For further discussion of first and second order goods, see Boissevain, *Friends of Friends*, 147-48; Malina, "Patron and Client," 151-54. Israel's great prophets, Moses and Elijah, did not themselves possess the power, manna and quail, oil and flour, etc. which they delivered to God's clients; they were but channels or bridges through which these benefactions came from Israel's Patron.

27. It has been pointed out that there is no simple term for "mediator" in the Old Testament, but as A. Oepke said, "Though the word is not used, mediatorship is at the heart of Old Testament religion" ("μεσίτης," *TDNT* 4.614).

28. Abraham was also appreciated as an intercessor for the people with God; see Gen 18:22-33; 20:17. See Ronald H. Nash, "The Notion of Mediator in Alexandrian Judaism and the Epistle to the Hebrews," *WTJ* 40 (1977): 95.

"I Am the Door" (John 10:7, 9)

> It was our attainment of a conception of this that once made us address to one of those *mediators* (μεσιτῶν) the entreaty "Speak to us and let not God speak to us, lest we die" (Exod 20:19). For if He, without *ministers* (ὑπηρέταις), holds out to us ... benefits unmixed and exceeding great, we are incapable of receiving them. (*Dreams* 1.143, emphasis added; see *Post*. 143)

Elsewhere Philo distinguishes the relationship of patron (God) and client (Moses) from that of patron (God)–broker (Moses)–clients (Israel): "Now wise men take God for their guide and teacher, but the less perfect take the wise man; and therefore the Children of Israel say: 'Talk to us, and let not God talk to us, lest we die'" (*Heir* 19). Whereas Moses is that "wise" man who has God as patron ("guide and teacher"), Israel is the "less perfect" (client) who needs a "wise man" (Moses, now as broker) to mediate between the Patron and his clients.

On the occasion of the golden calf, Moses acted the role of intercessor between sinners and the sinless God (Exod 32:32). Using a wide variety of synonyms, Philo articulated clearly Moses' role as mediator/broker between the offended deity and the offending people:

> Yet he took the part of *mediator* (μεσίτης) and *reconciler* (διαλλακτὴς) and did not hurry away at once, but first made prayers and supplications, begging that their sins might be forgiven. Then, when this *protector* (κηδεμὼν) and *intercessor* (παραιτητὴς) had softened the wrath of the Ruler, he wended his way back in mingled joy and dejection. (Philo, *Mos*. 2.166, emphasis added)

This incident stands behind the remark in John 5:45. Israel presumes that Moses will continue to mediate on its behalf,[29] but Jesus claims that, on the contrary, Moses will condemn unbelievers.[30]

When Moses died, the people lamented that they had lost their intercessor, mediator, and premiere go-between with God. Thus, Josephus remarks, Israel was in tears both for Moses' sake and their own:

> They were in tears and displaying deep regret for their general, alike remembering the risks which he had run and all that ardent zeal of his for their salvation, and despondent concerning the future, in the belief that they would never more have such a ruler and that *God would be less mindful of them,*

---

29. While we use the term "broker" or "mediator" for Moses, others consider only his role as "intercessor" with God for the people; this is the perspective of David Crump, *Jesus the Intercessor: Prayer and Christology in Luke-Acts* (Grand Rapids, MI: Baker Books, 1992) 204-30.

30. On Moses as intercessor, see Wayne Meeks, *The Prophet-King: Moses Traditions and Johannine Christology* (Leiden: Brill, 1967) 118, 137, 160-61, 200-204.

since it was Moses who had ever been the intercessor (παρακαλῶν). (*Ant.* 4.194, emphasis added)[31]

In addition to Moses as broker, Philo identifies another broker, namely, the Logos. While Moses evidently serves as the bridge between God-Patron and Israel-client, nothing was said about why and how he qualifies as a broker, much less a successful one. But in his description of the Logos, Philo provides this important information.

> To His Word, His chief *messenger* (πρεσβευτάτῳ), the Father (Πατὴρ) has given the special prerogative, to stand on the border and separate creature from the Creator. This same Word both pleads with the immortal as *suppliant* (ἱκέτης) for afflicted mortals and acts as *ambassador* (πρεσβευτὴς) of the ruler to the subject. He glories that 'and I stood between the Lord and you' (Deut 5:5), *that is neither uncreated as God, nor created as you, but midway between the two extremes* (μέσος τῶν ἄκρων), *a surety to both sides* (ἀμφοτέροις ὁμηρεύων). (*Heir* 205-6, emphasis added)

The ancients did not have a technical term, much less a scientific definition for the role of this figure, and so they described him in terms of familiar mediators: "messenger," "suppliant," and "ambassador." Moreover, he is positioned "in the middle," that is, on the border which separates mortals from the Immortal One. Far from being a barrier, the Logos "stands between the Lord and them" precisely as a bridge, not a wall.[32] He both "pleads with the Immortal as suppliant for afflicted mortals" and acts as ambassador of the ruler to the subject, i.e., "two-way" mediation. But of great importance is Philo's description of this mediator sharing the worlds of both Sender and subject. "Standing between the Lord and you," he belongs to the world of God, although not uncreated as God is; and he belongs to the world of those created, although not created as they are. Hence, he is ideally positioned "midway between the extremes," a participant in both worlds who facilitates the interests of both parties.[33]

---

31. Yet despite Philo and Josephus, there is evidence of the opposite position, namely, that God does not use mediators or brokers; see Judah Golden, "Not by Means of an Angel and Not by Means of a Messenger," *Religions in Antiquity*, ed. Jacob Neusner (Leiden: Brill, 1974) 412-24.

32. See Lala Kalyan Kumar Dey, *The Intermediary World and Patterns of Perfection in Philo and Hebrews* (Missoula, MT: Scholars Press, 1975) 7-30.

33. In Philo's *Mos.* the patriarch's role as broker has many names: mediator, intercessor, priest, judge, defense attorney, defender, and savior. Similarly Philo provides another example of the two-way bridge that brokers play between God and the people: "The sacred record calls them 'angels' or messengers, employing an apter title, *for they both convey the biddings of the Father to His children and report the children's need to their Father.* In accordance with this they are

"I Am the Door" (John 10:7, 9)

2.4 Greco-Roman Brokers

The catalogue below indicates that the Greco-Roman world considered a variety of roles and services as brokerage between patrons and clients. Whether agents, ambassadors, diviners, priests, or prophets, all serve as go-betweens between patrons and clients.

ἄγγελος (messenger, envoy)[34]
ἀπόστολος (ambassador)
διάκονος (attendants, diviners, heralds)[35]
διαλλάκτικος (conciliator, reconciler)
δικαστής (judge)
ἔγγυος (security)
ἐντυγχάνω (to appeal, obtain an audience)
ἐξαίτησις (intercessor)
ἐπιδιακρίνω (to decide as umpire)
ἐπίτροπος (agent, representative)
ἱερεύς (priest)
ἱκέτης (suppliant)
λειτουργός (minister, performer of state duties)
μεσίτης (mediator)[36]
παραιτητής (intercessor)
παράκλητος (a broker, a mediator)
πρεσβευτής (an ambassador)
προφήτης (one who speaks for God)
ὑπηρέτης (petty official, attendant)

---

represented by the lawgiver *as ascending and descending:* Not that God, who is already present in all directions, needs informants, but as a boon to us in our sad case to avail ourselves of the services of 'words' acting on our behalf as mediators, so great is our awe and shuddering dread of the universal Monarch and the exceeding might of His sovereignty" (*Dreams* 1.140-43, emphasis added).

34. Margaret Mitchell, "New Testament Envoys in the Context of Greco-Roman Diplomatic and Epistolary Conventions: The Example of Timothy and Titus," *JBL* 111 (1992): 644-51.

35. John N. Collins (*Diakonia: Re-Interpreting the Ancient Sources* [Oxford: Oxford University Press, 1990) 73-148) understands διάκονος as more than a mere table-serving role. His data warrant calling the διάκονος a "go-between" or middleman. Other διάκονοι function as those who transmit messages, such as Hermes and Iris, as well as earthly sibyls, prophets, interpreters of dreams, heralds, and couriers.

36. See Oepke, "μεσίτης," 598-624; C. Becker, "μεσίτης," *NIDNTT* 1.372-76. Harold Attridge, *Hebrews* (Philadelphia, PA: Fortress, 1989) 221.

Political Realm. Kings were often thought of as stand-ins for the deity:[37] "The king, regarded as god or the son of god, serves as a mediator of the people before the godhead, receiving divine laws and offering national sacrifices."[38] Other political brokers are the λειτουργός (minister, performer of state duties) and the πρεσβευτής (ambassador). We read, moreover, of ἄγγελοι (messengers, envoys) delivering messages from kings and receiving messages for the king. Similarly, an ἀπόστολος (envoy, embassy) is occasionally sent from city to city: "Alyttes straightway sent a herald (κήρυκα) to Miletus . . . offering to make a truce. So the envoy (ἀπόστολος) went to Miletus" (Herodotus 1.21).

Legal or Forensic Realm. An intermediary (μεσίτης) may be an arbiter in legal transactions who is linked with a κριτής or appointed by one. A judge (δικαστής) appointed by a city acts as broker of justice between polis and populace (Herodotus 1.96). Finally an ἔγγυος, a type of intermediary, acts as the guarantor who accepts legal obligation for a bond or payment. He himself is the surety of the contract.[39]

Religious Realm. In this area one finds diviners, priests, oracles, prophets and the like. Plato describes the general role of a Hellenic priest: "According to the orthodox view they understand how to offer our gifts to the gods in sacrifices in a manner pleasing to them, and they know, too, the right forms of prayer for petitioning the gods to bestow blessings on us. Both of these expert activities are parts of the art of ministration, are they not?" (Plato, *Statesman* 290c-d). Greece's famous oracles include a patron-god who gives illumination or knowledge to a client through brokers. The brokers are the oracle herself and the interpreter of the oracle's messages, i.e., a prophet: "The voice is not that of a god, nor the utterance of it, nor the diction, nor the meter, but all these are the woman's; he puts into her mind only the visions, and creates a light in her soul in regard to the future; for inspiration is precisely this" (Plutarch, "Oracles at Delphi," 397C).[40] In summary, with the exception of Iris, the oracles and their prophets, Greco-Roman mediators are males, not surprising given the radical gender-division of ancient society.

---

37. E. R. Goodenough ("The Political Philosophy of Hellenistic Kingship," *Yale Classical Studies* 1 [1928]: 64-67) describes how a king rules in place of God; his duties in his realm are threefold: military leadership, the dispensation of justice, and the cult of the gods.

38. A. Oepke, "μεσίτης," 609. J. Scharbert in his comparative study of intercession in antiquity (*Heilsmittler im Alten Testament und im Alten Orient* [Freiburg: Herder, 1964] 21-67), listed kings and priests as the premiere mediators in the ancient Near East.

39. Nash, "The Notion of Mediator in Alexandrian Judaism and the Epistle to the Hebrews," 114-15.

40. See David E. Aune, *Prophecy in Early Christianity and the Ancient Mediterranean World* (Grand Rapids, MI: Eerdmans, 1983) 23-48.

"I Am the Door" (John 10:7, 9)

3.0 Patron and Broker in the Fourth Gospel

With what we know about the patron-broker-client relationship, how a broker emerges, what he does and what makes him a successful broker, we focus now on the Fourth Gospel.

3.1 The Patron, Who is God/Father

The premier name of the Patron/God in the Fourth Gospel is "Father," whose patronage consists entirely of sending his ambassador, Jesus, to Israel. The Patron's "sending" is expressed by two terms (ἀποστέλλω, πέμπω), which, despite similarities, exhibit important differences. In regard to ἀποστέλλω, we note the following patterns:

1. *The Patron's Sending:* "*God sent* the Son into the world" (3:17, 34).
2. *The Client's Duty: Acknowledgment of the Father's Sending:* "The *Father who sent* me has born witness to me . . . you do not *believe* him whom *he sent*" (5:36-38). "This is the work of God that you *believe* him whom *he has sent*" (6:29). "They have *received* the words you gave me and *know* in truth that I came from you, and they have *believed* that *you have sent me*" (17:8); ". . . that the world may *believe* that *you sent me*" (17:21, 23).

In the key of honor and shame, the Patron-Father makes an honor claim, namely, that Jesus is his ambassador and agent. Such claims are honored by acknowledging the agent/ambassador. The familiar legal principle states that whoever receives the agent receives not just the agent but the one who sent him (John 13:20; Matt 10:40). Hence when the clients acknowledge that God sent Jesus, they honor the Patron-Father who sent him. The converse is also true: dishonoring the agent means dishonoring the Sender: "I honor my Father, and you *dishonor* me" (8:49).[41]

The case is different for the second verb, πέμπω, which is more closely linked with specific tasks that the agent must do.

1. *Do the Will of the Sender.* "My food is to *do the will* of him *who sent me*" (4:34); "I seek not my own will but *the will* of him *who sent me*" (5:30); "I have come from heaven not to do my own will but *the will* of Him *who sent*

---

41. God mandates equal honor for Jesus: ". . . all may honor the Son, even as they honor the Father. Who does not honor the Son does not honor the Father who sent him" (5:23).

me" (6:38); "This is *the will* of him *who sent* me, that I lose none of all that he has given me" (6:39).
2. *What the Sender Gives Jesus to Do:* "My *teaching* is not mine but his *who sent me"* (7:16); "We must *do the works* of him *who sent me"* (9:4).
3. *The Sender Himself Testifies to Agent:* "The Father *who sent me* has *borne witness to me"* (5:37); "The Father *who sent me bears witness to me"* (8:18).
4. *Acknowledging Jesus/Broker Means Acknowledging the Patron-Sender:* "*Who believes in me believes* not in me but in him *who sent me"* (12:44).

Consideration of the Patron/Father will be resumed when we present a more detailed inventory of what the Patron gives the broker. But with this we know that the essential figures are Patron/Father and Son/Broker and that the honor, role, and status of the Son is that of "agent" of God.

3.2 Jesus the Broker

Adequately to interpret Jesus the Broker in the Fourth Gospel, we need to consider these five items in our model. How does a broker *become a broker?* What makes for a *successful broker? What* does he *broker?* What makes this broker *special or necessary?* What tariff does the *broker get for his services?* About these, the Fourth Gospel has much to say.

How does someone become a broker? In this case it is a matter of ascribed honor: God "sent" him as agent and ambassador. God-Patron authorized Jesus as his broker when "on him God has set his seal" (6:27) and "consecrated and sent [him] into the world" (10:36). God's dedicatory "sealing" and "consecrating" indicates that Jesus is the chosen broker who is set aside exclusively for God's tasks. How does he become the broker of God's clients? He has a formal relationship with the world: he is the "lamb of God who takes away the sins of the world" (1:36). He was sent to save it (3:17) and is in fact the Savior of the world (4:42). At some point, the clients relate to Jesus as sheep to a shepherd (10:1-4); he is the door through which they exit and enter and find pasture (10:9); they acknowledge only his voice, not that of a stranger (10:5). So precious are they to him that he will act the part of the "noble shepherd" and lay down his life for them (10:11, 15). The sheep depend upon the shepherd, which clearly is the intention of Jesus as broker.

The most striking example of this relationship is the allegory of the vine and branches. The branches have life and bear fruit only if they remain in the vine. The Patron plays the role of the vinedresser, whereas Jesus is the vine. The vine belongs to the vinedresser, one set of relationships, but the branches remain in the vine (another set). The issue is settled in the Farewell Address, where Jesus teaches the disciples to pray "in my name."

What makes a broker successful? Brokers are successful for several reasons. First, they belong to the worlds of both Patron and clients, and so can represent the interests of both. As we saw above in regard to Moses and the Logos, successful brokers have a foot in the worlds of both Patron and clients. Jesus the Broker first "descends" from the heavenly world and later "ascends." He was at home in the world of his Patron but subsequently descended from there to the world of his clients. For example, the two prologues of the Gospel (1:1-18 and 13:1-3) state that the heavenly Word came from God into the world (1:10) and later prepared to "depart out of this world to the Father" (13:1). During his Farewell Address, this same Word tells the clients that "I go away," and "I go to the Father" (16:5, 17; 14:28), stressing his belonging to God's world. He petitions his Patron "Glorify me in your own presence with the glory which I had with you before the world was made" (17:5). Jesus the Broker, who uniquely belongs to the world of the Patron, has also pitched his tent among us (1:14).

Conversely, most people do not know "whence" Jesus comes and "whither" he goes, and so cannot accept him as broker. Some reduce Jesus to a person of this world only, removing Jesus from the world of the Patron and reducing him to the status of a mere (deceiving) mortal. Yet some know Jesus' "whence" and "whither," and thus are positioned to accept him as a broker belonging to their world and God's (e.g., the man born blind).

Jesus belongs equally and fully to the world of the clients.[42] Many characters in the Gospel, however, reduce Jesus to a lowly figure of this world, and so cannot imagine how he could be favored by the heavenly one. He comes from Nazareth (1:46) or Galilee (7:41, 52); his father was an undistinguished laborer (6:41-42). Evidence abounds that he belongs to their world: he hungers (4:8, 31-34), thirsts (4:7), grows weary (4:6) and is disturbed in spirit (12:27-28). In the eyes of outsiders, he belongs entirely to this earthly world, and to its least honorable parts.

The fact that Jesus belongs to both worlds is explicitly claimed in the remark in the prologue: "the Word became flesh and dwelled among us" (1:14). Moreover, he performs signs on ill, dying and dead persons in a gesture which expresses his solidarity with those of this earthly world. Furthermore, the relationship of broker and clients is a qualitatively rich relationship, not a fickle one (15:9-17).

---

42. Hebrews argues the same point: "Since the children share flesh and blood, he himself likewise shared the same things. . . . he had to become like his brothers in every respect . . . to make a sacrifice of atonement for the sins of the people" (2:14-17).

The successful broker, moreover, belongs to both worlds *at the same time* by virtue of his relationships. "In my Father's house are many rooms. . . . And when I go and prepare a place for you, I will come again and will take you to myself, that where I am you may be also" (14:2-3). The relationship of the Patron-Father and his Broker-Son is secure, and so is that of the Broker and his clients. After securing a relationship for the clients in God's household, he returns to them and maintains the relationship. This, moreover, is a relationship the clients may rely on: "Do you not believe that I am in the Father and the Father in me? . . . the Father who dwells in me does his works. Believe me that I am in the Father and the Father in me; or else believe me for the sake of the works themselves" (14:10-11). This relationship must be highly significant for it to be mentioned many, many times (14:20, 23; 17:21, 23). Alternately the relationship of the Broker and his clients receives much attention. "I am the vine, you are the branches. He who abides in me, and I in him, he it is that bears much fruit, for apart from me you can do nothing" (15:5). "In that day you will know that I am in my Father, and you in me, and I in you" (14:20). Not only does he belong to both worlds, he bridges them in his own person.

A final, significant reason for success rests on the broker's ability to maintain his relationship with Patron and clients. In short, he must have or develop a lasting bond of reliability, loyalty and faithfulness between himself and each party. First, let us examine the unity between Patron and Broker. The author tells us that the Patron Father "loves" the Son, indicating just such a loyal and reliable relationship: "The Father loves the Son and has given all things into his hands" (3:35). For his part, the Broker Son shows loyalty to his Patron Father by virtue of obeying his commands. "I do not seek my own will but the will of him who sent me" (5:30; 6:38; 4:34). The absolute loyalty of the Broker to his Patron-Father constitutes the topic of John 17 where Jesus gives an audit of his actions prior to his death:

I have glorified you on earth (v. 4).
I have manifested your name (vv. 6, 26).
I have given them the words which you have given me (vv. 8, 14).
I have kept them in your name, I have guarded them (v. 12).
I have consecrated myself (v. 19).
I have given them the glory which you have given me (v. 22).

Similarly, the Broker maintains bonds of loyalty with his clients by "loving" them. This bond of loyalty is never more important than when Jesus enters into his death. We are told that "having loved his own who were in the world, he loved them perfectly" (13:1). I follow Bruce Malina in interpreting "love" in this context as "group glue" or faithfulness.[43] In fact, upon departure Jesus gives a commandment that replicates the "love" between him and the clients in the relationship of client with client: "A new commandment I give to you, that you love one another; even as I have loved you, that you also love one another" (13:34). "Solidarity" between broker and clients is also highlighted. In that same ch. 17, Jesus speaks more broadly of his relationship to his disciple-clients. He tells the Father

> I have kept them in your name . . . (v. 12).
> These things I speak in the world, that they may have my joy fulfilled in them (v. 13).
> Keep them from the evil one (v. 15).
> For their sake I consecrate myself, that they may be consecrated in truth (v. 19).

In John 14–17, we find much discourse on the unity between Patron, Broker and Clients. They are glued together in an utterly reliable relationship, as the following citations indicate:

> He who has my commandments and keeps them, he it is who loves me; and he who loves me will be loved by my Father (14:21).
> If a man loves me, he will keep my word, and my Father will love him, and we will come to him and make our home with him (14:23).
> As the Father has loved me, so have I loved you; abide in my love (15:9).
> I in them and you in me, that they may become perfectly one, so that the world may know that you have sent me and have loved them even as you have loved me (17:23).

"Love," then, is the mark of reliability in these relationships: the Patron with the Broker, the Broker with the clients, and the Patron and Broker with the clients.

The term abide/remain (μένειν) images the same sense of loyal and reliable relationships. As regards Patron and Broker, the Patron sent a Holy Spirit which "remained" on Jesus (1:32-33); in contrast, when God's Spirit comes on others, it is a limited and transient relationship. Similarly, the Patron is "in" the Broker and the Broker is "in" the Patron: "The words that I say to you I do not speak on my own authority; but the Father who 'remains' in me does his works" (14:10). Because of the loyalty of Broker to Patron, "the Father 'remains' in me." Similarly, we are told that clients "remain" with Jesus (1:38-39) or he "remains" with

---

43. Bruce J. Malina, "Faith/Faithfulness," in *Handbook of Biblical Social Values*, ed. John J. Pilch and Bruce J. Malina (Peabody, MA: Hendrickson, 1998) 72-75.

them (2:12; 4:40). The point of the exhortation about vine and branches centers on just this broker-client relationship expressed by "remaining." First, it is hardly insignificant that "remain" occurs ten times in 15:1-11. "Remaining," of course, means "remaining" in me or the vine (15:4-7) or in my love (15:9-10). If the relationship is secure and reliable, then the Broker assures his clients that "you should bear fruit and your fruit should 'remain'" (15:16).

What does he broker? We could make an exhaustive list of each and every benefaction that Jesus brokers, but then we would still have to collect, digest and classify these data. Or, we could employ a model developed by Talcott Parsons and adjusted by Bruce Malina which abstracts these benefactions and classifies them according to four comprehensive categories: 1) *power*,[44] 2) *commitment*,[45] 3) *inducement*, and 4) *influence*.[46] Because of their *power*, kings can protect and deliver their subjects. *Inducement* refers to gifts of seed, food, dowries for daughters, and hospitality. As regards *influence*, teachers give instruction to students; those who consult sibyls, oracles or prophets seek for influence-as-knowledge and influence-as-access. Finally *commitment* refers to faithfulness, loyalty, obedience, as well as to fictive-kin bonds, and grants of honor and respect.

Although brokers generally have only second-order goods, i.e., access to the patron's first-order goods, the Evangelist argues in the Fourth Gospel that Jesus himself has these first-order goods. On the one hand we are told that "the Father loves the Son and has *given all things* into his hand" (3:35) and again "the Father loves the Son and *shows him all* that he himself is doing" (5:20). "All" is certainly inclusive and comprehensive. But to get specific about what God gives Jesus, we use the Parsons-Malina model to process data in the Fourth Gospel and classify them appropriately. Note, moreover, that Jesus cannot broker what he himself has not received from the Patron-Father. In effect, whatever Jesus has received from God-Patron he in turn brokers to others.

POWER:

1. Power = signs: "Never since the world began has it been heard that any one opened the eyes of a man born blind. If this man were not from God, he could do nothing" (9:32-33).
2. Power = over death: "... and I will raise him up at the last day" (6:39, 44, 54); "Lazarus, come out" (11:43); "I have power to lay down my life and I have power to take it back" (10:17-18).

---

44. Parsons, *Politics and Social Structure*, 352-404, originally published as "On the Concept of Political Power," *Proceedings of the American Philosophical Society* 107 (1963): 232-62.
45. Parsons, *Politics and Social Structure*, 439-72.
46. Parsons, *Politics and Social Structure*, 405-29.

"I Am the Door" (John 10:7, 9)

COMMITMENT:

1. Kinship: Father, Son, and other offspring: "To all who received him . . . he gave power to become children of God" (1:12).
2. Relationships: "When I prepare a place for you, I will come and take you to myself" (14:3); "We will come to him and make our home with him" (14:23).
3. Loyalty/Obedience: "I do not seek my own will but the will of him who sent me" (5:30); "This is the will of him who sent me, that I lose nothing he has given me . . . this is the will of my Father, that every one who sees the Son and believes should have eternal life" (6:39-40).
4. Love: "As the Father has loved me, so have I loved you; abide in my love . . . you will abide in my love, just as I abide in his love" (15:9-10); ". . . that the love with which thou [Father] hast loved me may be in them, and I in them" (17:26); "Love one another as I have loved you. Greater love . . . than a man lay down his life for his friends" (15:12-13).

INDUCEMENT:

1. Abundant wine (2:7-10), water (4:14; 7:37-38), bread (6:1-13), light (8:12).
2. Everything (14:14).

INFLUENCE:

1. Jesus as Word: "In the beginning was the Word and the Word was with God" (1:1-2).
2. Witness to his relationship with God: "He bears witness to what he has seen and heard" (3:32; 8:18).
3. Delivers God's teaching: "My teaching is not mine, but his who sent me" (7:16-17); "I do nothing on my own authority but speak thus as the Father taught me" (8:28).
4. Jesus as teacher in synagogue (6:59; 18:20) and Temple: "Jesus went up to the Temple and taught" (7:14; see 7:28); "Teacher" = "a teacher come from God" (3:2; see 11:28) and "Rabbi"= "Rabbi, you are the son of God" (1:49; see 1:38; 4:31).
5. Speaks God's words: "He whom God sent utters the words of God" (12:49); "The words which you hear are not mine but the Father's" (14:24); "I have given them your word" (17:14).
6. Sees and reveals God: "[No one] has seen the Father except him . . . he has seen the Father" (6:46); "No one has ever seen God; the only Son, in the bosom of the Father, has made him known" (1:18).

7. Reveals name:[47] "I manifested your name . . ." (17:6); "I made known to them your name and I will make it known" (17:26).

In terms of comprehensiveness, the model indicates that Jesus is mediator of all four categories of benefits. There is an emphasis, however, on *commitment* (kinship, relationships, loyalty and love) and *influence* (Jesus as Word, witness, teacher, and revealer). In short, Jesus is not a broker of this or that benefaction, but a complete broker rich in all of God's favors. Moreover, the Gospel makes it clear that God gives these to Jesus, making Jesus an exceptional broker and the disciples blessed clients. Moreover, if God gives them, then Jesus is and remains a broker; he does not displace the Patron.

What do we know if we know this? Precisely because he is the Broker of Brokers, Jesus is himself most richly endowed with the things that are God's: unique powers associated only with God, the closest possible relationship with God the Patron, and unique knowledge of God. Because he is given God's first-order good, he has the where-with-all to function as a superior broker. Indeed, his relationship with God the Patron is his "capital,"[48] that is, the source of all other endowments.

Is this broker unique or necessary? The author claims that Jesus is unique as a broker. "Unique" is my term for what the ancient rhetoricians attempted to show in their amplification of praise of a person. Aristotle expressed uniqueness this way: ". . . amplification, for example, if the subject is the *only* one or the *first* or *one of a few* or the one who *most* has done something" (*Rhet.* 1.9.38). In the Fourth Gospel, Jesus is not only the unique, but the necessary broker:

No one has ever seen God . . . the *only*[49] Son has made him known (1:18).
No one has ascended into heaven *but* he who descended from heaven (3:13).
No one has seen the Father, *except* him who is from God (6:46).

His being *first* or *only* is not a personal achievement of Jesus' prowess in arms, athletics, etc., the typical grounds for personal honor. Rather because of God's

---

47. The broker's name is also important, for the clients must petition the patron using the broker's name: "Whatever you ask in my name, I will do it, that the Father may be glorified in the Son; if you ask anything in my name, I will do it" (14:13-14, 26; 15:16).

48. Boissevain, *Friend of Friends*, 147-48, 156-61.

49. Many translate μονογενής as "only" or "single"; see Paul Winter, "Μονογενὴς παρὰ Πατρός," *ZRG* 5 (1953): 335-65; Gerard Pendrick, "Μονογενής," *NTS* 5 (1995): 587-600, whose data overwhelmingly indicate that its proper translation is "the only one of its kind" or "unique." But see also J. V. Dahms, "The Johannine Use of *Monogenes* Reconsidered," *NTS* 29 (1983): 222-32.

pleasure, Jesus *alone* descends from God's world, he *alone* has seen God and he *alone* makes God known. His honor, then, is all the more significant because of his being a unique Broker. But his uniqueness is not simply that of a descending figure who makes the Patron known but because of his ascending role as Broker. He brokers the unique and necessary way to the Patron: "*No one* comes to the Father *except* by me (John 14:6; see Acts 4:12).

What does the broker get for his services? The Patron who sent him will glorify him with the glory which he had before the creation of the world (17:5). As Jesus explains, the most important thing his Patron can give him is "glory": "Jesus said, 'Now is the Son of man glorified, and in him God is glorified; if God is glorified in him, God will also glorify him in himself, and glorify him at once'" (13:31-32). Because Jesus glorifies and honors his Father Patron especially in his death, Jesus expects that this Patron will "glorify him" and "glorify him at once." Yes, the broker receives a tariff from the patron, but reader are hard pressed to find any tariff from the clients.

Does a broker show favoritism, as patrons do? In the Farewell Discourse in John 13–17, we find statements celebrating the favoritism of Jesus for his disciples. He gives them warnings of future hard times, thus strengthening them: "I tell you this now, before it takes place, that when it does take place you may believe that I AM" (13:19; see 14:29; 16:1-2, 31-33). He exhorts them not to be troubled: "Let not your hearts be troubled" (14:1); "I will not leave you desolate, I will come to you" (14:18); "Peace I leave with you, my peace I give to you" (14:27; see 16:20-24). It seems, moreover, that he has love for the few who are loyal to him: "Love one another; even as I have loved you" (13.34). Jesus asks on behalf of the few, who in turn ask in his name: "Whatever you *ask* in my name, I will do it. . . . If you *ask* anything in my name, I will do it" (14:13-14); "I will *pray* the Father and he will send another Counselor" (14:16); "If you abide in me and my words abide in you, *ask* whatever you will . . ." (15:7); ". . . so that whatever you *ask* the Father in my name, he may give it to you" (15:16b); "In that day you will *ask* nothing of me . . . if you *ask* anything of the Father, he will give it to you in my name" (16:23). In short, the disciples alone are the recipients of his benefactions: "In my Father's house there are many rooms. . . . I go to prepare a place *for you*" (14:2); "'I will love him and *manifest myself to him.*' Judas (not the Iscariot) said, 'How is it that you will manifest yourself to us and *not to the world?*'" (14:21-22); "I have manifested thy name to them" (17:6; see 17:11-12, 26). Finally, it is clear that Jesus prays only for his disciples, not for the rest: "I am praying *for them;* I am *not praying* for the world but for those whom thou hast given me" (17:9; see 17:11-12, 26). Favoritism is manifested in the simple fact that only the elite few hear this discourse; only they have Jesus' warnings of future trials and his exhortations to peace; only for them does Jesus pray.

4.0 Summary

As regards models, readers are reminded of the model of patron-client relationships. Hardly a modern invention, it functioned widely in the ancient world. But in this study, we expanded this classical model to include understanding of the role of broker who links or bridges patron and client. Jesus-the-Broker has both a descending and an ascending role vis-à-vis God's clients. "Descending" means that he belongs to God's world and mediates heavenly benefaction to God's earthly clients; as an "ascending" broker, he belongs to the world of the clients and functions as intercessor between them and the heavenly Patron. Jesus acts, in short, as a two-way broker.

As models go, the patron-broker-client model proves more helpful in understanding the Fourth Gospel than theories about "agency." Borgen's and Buchanan's considerations of Jesus' relationship to God in terms of "agency" or "apostle," certainly valid, are simply incomplete. First, our patron-broker-client model can surface much more data in the Gospel than their "agent" model. Moreover it provides a conceptual glue that holds together diverse materials in the narrative in a cogent and coherent whole. Furthermore, their model only describes a one-way agency, but does not account for the agent playing a two-way role. A better conceptual tool is needed to account for the "descending" and "ascending" role of Jesus. As a model, it exposes various items that typically occur in patron-broker-client relations which allow us to surface materials in the Fourth Gospel that would otherwise not be noticed or if observed, not put into relationship. It makes, indeed, a whole out of the pieces, and in this case, the whole is greater than the sum of its parts. And so, the model passes the test of discovery, integration and utility. If the success of a model depends on how much and how well it accommodates the data, by this standard the patron-broker-client model is judged highly successful. The model which best accommodates the data in the Gospel and integrates it into a coherent whole is the patron-broker-client model.

Philo's examples of Moses' brokerage are exceptionally valuable because they are very strong arguments for the existence of the "broker" role and embody the qualifications for his success. Although Philo is only expanding on passages from Exodus, in doing so he casts the figure and role of Moses as a mediator (μεσίτης), a minister (ὑπηρέτης), a reconciler (διαλλακτής), a protector (κηδεμών), intercessor (παραιτητής), and advocate (παρακαλῶν). Similarly, the Logos plays the role of broker: as messenger (πρεσβευτάτῳ), suppliant (ἱκέτης), and ambassador (πρεσβευτής). Most importantly, Philo states the prime qualification for a successful broker: quoting Deut 5:5 ("and I stood between the Lord and you"), Philo understands that the Logos belongs to both worlds, but not wholly in each: "that is neither uncreated as God, nor created as you, but midway between the two extremes (μέσος τῶν ἄκρων), a surety to both sides (ἀμφοτέροις ὁμηρεύων)." This manner of thinking, then, fully existed in antiquity and was a concept ready to hand for the author of the Fourth Gospel to describe Jesus' role.

This study, moreover, describes what a broker is and does. The cluster of five questions about a broker provided us with the proper lenses with which to examine Jesus, his words and deeds. He is a broker because God "sent" him. He is successful because he belongs to the world of both patron and client. He faithfully serves the interests of both. Because of God's largesse, Jesus is equipped to mediate God's power, kinship, material benefaction, and in particular wisdom and knowledge. As a broker, Jesus is positioned such that he forms unique relationships: 1) God in Jesus, 2) Jesus in the disciples, and 3) God and Jesus dwelling in the disciples. Jesus, we are told, is the unique and necessary broker because he is the "only" son and because "no one can come to the Father except through me." And finally, Jesus truly receives a tariff from God, his glorification or return to former glory. He seems not to receive any tariff from the disciples.

Finally, this model should help readers consider the role of Jesus in the Pauline letters and Hebrews. When a doxology is prayed or when an author talks about God's patronage, glory, honor and praise are given to God *through Jesus Christ*. Romans alone provides these examples:

> "I thank my God *through* Jesus Christ . . ." (1:8).
> "We have peace with God *through* our Lord Jesus Christ" (5:1).
> "*Through* him we have obtained access to this grace" (5:2).
> "To the only wise God be glory for evermore *through* Jesus Christ!" (16:27).

Furthermore, the utility of this model invites us to examine other places where Jesus is called "mediator" or "intercessor." Some New Testament authors formally label Jesus as a "mediator" (μεσίτης), such as "For there is one God; there is also *one mediator* between God and humankind, Christ Jesus, himself human" (1 Tim. 2:5) and "But Jesus has now obtained a more excellent ministry, and to that degree he is *the mediator* of a better covenant" (Heb 8:6; see 9:15; 12:24). Jesus is, moreover, acclaimed as "priest," one who bridges the world of God and of mortals: "Consider Jesus, the apostle and *priest* of our confession" (Heb 3:1); he is, moreover, the perfect priest because God declares him to be *"a priest forever"* (7:17, 21). Jesus' role as a "priest forever" is elegantly explained later:

> But he holds his priesthood permanently, because he continues forever. Consequently he is able for all time to save those *who approach God through him*, since he always lives to make intercession for them. (7:24-25, emphasis added)

Finally, we think that all expressions of Jesus "seated at the right hand of God" understand his session there precisely as a broker. Acts certainly does, for Luke links Jesus' heavenly session with his dispensation of God's Spirit:

> Being therefore exalted at the right hand of God, and having received from the Father the promise of the Holy Spirit, he has poured out this that you both see and hear. For David did not ascend into the heavens, but he himself says, "The Lord said to my Lord, 'Sit at my right hand.'" (Acts 2:33-34)

Jesus as broker, then, is a common interpretation of his role in the Christian Scriptures. But it is the Fourth Gospel that uses this model most extensively.

Index of Topics

Abraham, ix, 236-37, 244
  born and died a contingent being, 452
  hospitality of, 239
  saw Jesus' day, 245-46, 442
  sons
    Isaac, free son, 234, 236
    Ishmael, slave son, 234, 236-37
Aelius Theon
  Progymnasmata, 296, 418
Agonistic societies, 126, 139, 140, 214-17, 435
Aphthonius
  Progymnasmata, 12
Aristotle
  Politics, 352-53, 391, 472
  Rhet., 4-5, 8, 10, 136, 137, 212, 213, 288-89, 294-95, 308, 334, 342-43, 345, 349, 352-53, 391, 472

Background
  Cultural, xi
  Greco-Roman, x-xi
  Judean, ix-x
Beloved Disciple, 278-79
  compared with Simon, 373
  role: son to mother, 52
  status: exceptionally high, 53
  sub-broker to disciples, 52
  what he knows, 368-69

Broker, 455-64
  brokers in Greco-Roman world, 463-64
  brokers in Israelite tradition, 460-62, 474
  how does one become a broker? 465-66
  Jesus as broker, 466-73
  Logos as broker, 462
  model of, 459-60
  Moses as broker, 460-61
  what makes a good broker, 470

Challenge-riposte exchange, 217-18, 222
  questions as challenges, 364-65, 423-24, 426, 429-31, 435
Chreia, 192-93, 226
Cicero
  De Inventione, 11, 335
  De Natura Deorum, 458-59
  De Officiis, 36-37
  De Oratore, 137, 152, 342, 343
  In Verrem, 412, 413
  Orator, 286, 342
  Tusculan Disputations, 136-37
Comparison
  form taught in the *progymnasmata*, 106
  Samaritan Woman and Mary Magdalene, 166

Beloved Disciple and Simon Peter, 373
Jesus and Abraham, 22-23
Jesus and Moses, 23
Conclusion, rhetorical form, 333, 336-54
  emotions aroused, 341-48
  hate and anger compared, 350
  negative emotions, 346-54
  positive emotions, 343, 344-45
  recapitulation, 337-41
  review of *dramatis personae,* 339
Cornelius Nepos, *praef.,* prepared expressly for the use of students learning to read at sight, 150

David, 131, 223
Death, Jesus' power over, 242-43, 310, 326
Demosthenes
  Funeral Oration, 12-13, 288, 289, 293
Dio Chrysostom
  Oration, 151, 458, 459
Diodor of Sicily
  World History, 34, 412, 413, 415, 451
Diogenes Laertius
  Zeno, 451
Double meaning words
  find, 205, 207
  know, 203-4, 206, 208
  lift up, 98, 427
  remain, 234-35
  seek, 199, 204-5, 207, 210, 232, 238, 242
  sexual double entendres, 143
  whence, whither, 206, 261-62, 428
Dwell in, 77-78, 82, 408, 409
  See Remain

Envy, 136-41, 307, 339
  avoiding, 138-39
  expressions, 137
  Jesus envied, 131-34
  See Agonistic societies; Limited good

Footwashing
  as confirming ceremony, 365
  as status transformation ritual, 361-64
  Beloved Disciple, successful transformation, 370, 371-72

model of ritual to assess footwashing, 358-60
  parallel footwashings, 356-58
  Simon Peter, failure of transformation, 369-70, 371-72, 375
Friend, 125-26, 141, 276, 400, 431
Fronto
  Correspondence, 130

Gender
  female, 143-44, 170,
  gender-divided space, 48, 60, 144-45
  gender-divided world, 146-49
  male, 160, 195, 435-36
  stereotypes, 144
Gideon, 131
glory, 179, 218, 226, 310, 473, 475
  God glorifies Jesus, 245
  See Honor
God
  as patron, 465
  as teacher, 220
  loved by Jesus, 245
  loving Jesus, 179, 304, 327, 344, 444-45
  monotheism, 453
  mortals called "gods," 313
  name "I AM" used by Jesus
    makes Jesus equal, 180, 444
  names of God, 447
  works on the Sabbath, 180, 190, 201-2
God's two powers, 180
  creative, 180
  end-time, 180, 187, 188, 318
  names of, 182
Gossip, 42, 168-69, 170, 266, 269

Hate, 194, 223
  See Conclusion
Healings
  as credential, 172-74
  form of, 173-74, 188
Hierocles
  On Duties, 61, 146, 148
High and low context societies, 154
Hippocrates
  Air, Water and Places, 8
Honor, 24-25, 38, 128-30, 132-33, 134-35,

Index of Topics

141, 173, 174, 180-81, 187, 192-93, 212-14, 282-83, 290, 307-8, 310, 334, 342, 412-18
  achieved, 221, 224, 287, 415, 487
  ascribed, 140, 178-81, 214, 219-21, 226, 245, 250, 415, 417, 425, 435-38, 445, 473
  See Challenge-riposte exchange; Envy

Jacob, 94-95, 107, 121-22
  and Esau, 131
  deity appeared to, 90, 443
  gave a well, 108-10
  supplanter, 111
Jesus
  as agent of God, 206
  as appearing figure of OT, 91-92, 246, 442-43, 452
  as broker, 466-73
  as eternal in the past, imperishable in the future, 449-51
  as "I AM," 92, 186-87, 231-32, 245-47
  as judge, 176, 186, 198, 227, 232-35, 248, 250
  as witness, 230
  Christ/Messiah, 73, 88, 92, 161, 208, 316, 415, 424, 428
  consecrated, 327, 328
  deceiver, 68, 260
  equal to God, 97, 172, 178, 179, 316-18, 328-30, 441, 444-49
  greater than . . . , 107, 243, 245
  has life in himself, 186-87, 188, 189, 250
  king, 424-26, 428, 431-32
  lamb of God, 88
  Lord and God, 441, 447-48
  makes himself something, 97, 172, 178-79, 223, 319-20, 327-29, 330, 427-28, 444
  noble shepherd, 300-307, 420, 425, 433
  possessor of God's two powers
    creative, 180, 446
    end-time, 181-82, 184, 319, 328, 445-48
  prophet, 68, 73, 113-14, 160-61, 174, 394-95, 415, 424, 428
  rabbi/teacher, 19, 67, 471

  replacement of Israel's holy figures, places, and objects, 195, 209
  revealer, exclusive, 101, 269-71
  savior of the world, 424, 428
  Son of God, 320, 328, 330, 424, 427-28
  Son of man, 95-96
  speaks God's words, works God's works, 238
  taught by God, 220
John the Baptizer, 22, 40, 124, 176, 216, 263-64, 269
Josephus
  Ant., 64, 112, 114, 129, 173-74, 198, 412, 416, 417, 432, 433-34, 461
  Life, 11, 128-29, 216
  War, 64, 129, 150, 198, 362, 412-13
Judas
  hatred for, 352, 368, 369-70
Judgment
  according to the flesh, 231, 261
  judge justly, 208, 219
  judges are judged, 224, 338
  judgment divided, 199, 202, 204, 211, 221, 225, 317, 337
  no judgment until face-to-face with accuser, 225
  wrong judgment, 200, 202, 210
Justin
  Dialogue with Trypho, 93, 112, 443
  1 Apology, 439
Juvenal
  Satires, 153

Knowledge, gnosis, and inner meaning, 88
  earthly, fleshly knowledge, 243
  knowledge of/acknowledging God, 243-44
  not in the know, 163
  selective revelation, 260, 266-69, 276-77
  See Double meaning words
  statement-misunderstanding-clarification, 158, 160

Lazarus, 188-89, 345
Limited good
  Greco-Roman illustrations, 127

479

Israelite and Christian illustrations, 130
model of, 126-27, 135-36, 179, 214-17, 307
See Envy
Livy
    Ab Urbe Condita, 152
Lucian
    The Cock, 149-50
    Lover of Lies, 174
Lycurgus
    Leocrates, 291
Lysias
    Funeral Oration, 289
    On the Murder of Eratosthenes, 149

Man born blind, 45-46, 275
Martha, 45-47, 188, 274-75
Mary Magdalene, 27, 41, 47-50, 188, 274-75, 279
Menander Rhetor, 9, 11, 21, 219, 220
Moses, 117, 322, 474
    as accuser, 178, 201
    as broker, 460-61
Murder and lying
    Judas a liar and murderer, 339
    lying, 207, 224, 239, 240, 241, 243, 251
    murder, 201, 207, 224, 237, 240, 245, 339-40
    murderers from the beginning, 207

Nathanael, 88-90, 222, 273-74
Nicodemus, 43, 206, 209, 272, 286-93
Noble death
    commonplace in ancient world, 297-99
    elements of, 24-25, 284-93, 433-34,

Patron-client relationship, 454-59
    fathers as patrons, 457-58
Pausanias
    Descriptions of Greece, 62
Philo
    Alleg. Interp., 257
    Cher., 259
    Dreams, 94, 95, 120, 121, 413, 450, 460-61
    Drunkenness, 120
    Flacc., 412

Flight, 93, 120
Heir, 461, 462
Joseph, 416
Mos., 183, 447, 450, 461, 475
Names, 93, 240, 450
Post., 93, 120, 148, 152, 413
QG, 120, 182, 446
Rewards, 94
Sobr., 240
Spec., 61, 93, 149, 152, 413
Virt., 148
Worse, 450
Plato
    Gorgias, 412
    Menexenus, 10, 290
    Republic, 412
    Statesman, 464
Pliny
    Natural History, 413
Plutarch
    Camillus, 152
    Delay of the Divine Judgment, 412
    Dinner of the Seven Wise Men, 34
    Envy and Hatred, 350
    In Praise of Women, 151-52
    Letter to Apollonius, 34
    Lycurgus and Numa, 153, 161
    Old Men in Public Affairs, 128
    On Being a Busybody, 137
    On the Malice of Herodotus, 451
    Oracles at Delphi, 384, 464
    Parallel Lives, 106
    Pelopidas, 147
    Sayings of the Spartans, 149, 152
Praise. See Honor
Prayer, 340
    petition, 387-88, 390
    self-focused, 388, 390
Progymnasmata, 106, 429
Psalm 82, midrash on, 322-26
Purification, 363-65, 375, 412

Quintilian
    Inst. Orat., 5, 11, 26-27, 335-36, 343

Recruitment, 49, 340
    versus volunteering, 346

Index of Topics

Remain, 64, 66, 76, 169, 234-35, 327, 345, 469-70
  abide in, 399
  dwell in, 408-9
Rhetorical patterns
  chiasm, 234, 237
  chreia, 139-41, 214-17
  conclusion, 333-36
  deliberative rhetoric, 398-99, 401
  farewell address, 276, 404, 405, 410, 467
  topos on "noble death," 286-300, 306
Rituals, 358-61, 366, 371-73
  ceremonies which confirm, 365-68
  comparison of rituals, 357
  status transformation, 361-65, 413
Rivalry, 124-25
  See Envy; Limited good
Role, 31-33, 162
  family roles of Jesus, 32
  non-importance of roles in John, 55

Samaritan woman, 39-43, 164-69, 274, 275
Satan, the devil
  father of liars and murderers, 238-39, 241
Secrecy
  asides, 266-67
  deception, ambiguity, evasion, lying, 252-53, 260-61
  double meaning remarks, 252, 261, 401-2
  espionage against Jesus, 263-64, 265-66
  information control, 253
  Jesus knows hearts, 270
  Jesus revealer and concealer, 252
  keep/reveal secrets, 251
  lying, 251
  model of, 253-58, 280
  not in the know, 253, 258, 271-72, 277-78
  selected disclosure, 260, 266-69, 273-75, 276-77
  speaking in public or in private, 252
  special meaning of words, translations, 267
  status dependent on knowledge, 255, 258

  why people do not know, 268
Seneca
  Benefits, 387, 457
  Consolation to Marcia, 413
  On Anger, 412
Sextus Empiricus
  Against the Physicians, 451
Simon Peter, 29, 50, 310-11
  comparison to Beloved Disciple, 373
  disclosure to, 277-78
  role and status of, 51
  shepherd, successor to Jesus, 311, 368-75
Space, 58-86
  classifications of, 48-72
  communication and control, 64
  fixed-fluid, 62-64, 70-72, 82, 406-7
  honorable-shameful, 62
  "my Father's house," 74-76
  public-private, 48-61, 145-47, 199
  sacred-profane, 61
  symbolic: Galilee and Jerusalem, 58, 65-67
Status, 31, 33-38
  criteria, 53-55
Statement-misunderstanding-clarification, 47, 223-34, 242-43, 252-53, 261-62, 274, 276, 321, 395-96
Stereotypes, 9, 26, 149-55

Temple, 64, 70, 75, 229
Territoriality
  See Space
Thucydides
  Histories, 151-52, 291
Trials, 172-73, 191, 195
  elements of a trial, 175, 189, 191, 195, 196-98, 200, 203, 209, 210, 228-29, 247-48, 316-20, 423
  judges are judges, 176, 177, 178
  trial before Pilate, 421-32
  See Judgment

"Unless . . . ," 363-64, 400

Valerius Maximus
  Memorable Deeds and Sayings, 152
Vices

fear to speak publicly, 275
having no love, 177
lack of courage, 57
lying, 201, 240
murder, 201, 240
unfaithfulness, 58, 374
Virtues
aggressive-cooperative virtues, 35
courage, 49, 413, 420, 421
faithfulness/loyalty, 64, 176, 218, 469
holiness, 176
justice, 288, 302

Whence and whither, 206, 208, 230, 270, 429, 467
whence, 18, 45, 49-50, 72-73, 206, 224
whither, 45, 50, 73-74, 206, 231, 279
Witness, 175-77
false testimony, 211
Jesus as authorized witness, 230, 244
role of, 176, 197-98, 200, 209
World, 78-80, 194, 249-50

Xenophon
Oeconomicus, 61, 148-49, 151

Index of Passages in John's Gospel

Passage	Pages	Passage	Pages	Passage	Pages
1:1-2	19, 88, 106, 222, 327, 441, 446, 447, 471	1:29	40, 216, 222	1:50	88, 274
		1:30	40, 107, 125, 222, 246	1:51	44, 50, 87, 88, 89, 90, 91, 92, 99-101, 105, 106, 442
1:1-5	453	1:31	268		
1:1-18	49, 74, 183, 206, 467	1:33	40, 77, 107, 268, 317, 327, 469	2:1-12	32, 44, 471
				2:2	431
1:6	40, 176	1:33-34	22, 40, 41, 107, 176, 222, 428	2:4	264, 273
1:7	40			2:6	164
1:8	22, 176, 216	1:34	424	2:9	268
1:9	17, 18, 73, 107, 425	1:35	168, 268	2:11	43, 226, 268, 273
1:9-10	250, 425	1:35-51	43, 87, 90, 101, 105, 161, 168, 273	2:12	66, 75, 470
1:10	303, 425			2:17	321
1:11	15, 322, 427	1:36	168, 216, 222, 466	2:18	264
1:12-13	241, 471	1:38	19, 23, 66, 67, 267, 469, 471	2:18-20	76
1:14	17, 18, 19, 49, 467			2:19	70, 378
1:15	22, 40, 125, 176, 216, 222, 246	1:39	89, 186, 469	2:19-22	406
		1:40	32	2:20	71
1:17	23	1:40-42	266	2:21	71, 378
1:17-18	107	1:41	32, 141, 207, 267, 273	2:22	267, 321, 401
1:18	18, 19, 49, 72, 74, 91, 176, 222, 269, 327, 441, 471, 472			2:23-25	249, 270, 274
		1:42	89	3:1-2	35, 73, 209, 337
		1:43	43, 207	3:2	32, 50, 67, 68, 83, 263, 272, 471
1:19-28	41, 67, 125, 141, 176, 264	1:44	168, 266		
		1:45	72, 89, 207, 273, 274	3:3	75, 231, 232, 236, 241, 340, 361
1:22	264				
1:23	22, 263	1:46	273, 274, 467	3:4	273
1:25	264	1:47	89, 270, 274	3:5	75, 231, 232, 236, 241, 361, 364
1:26-27	125, 222	1:49	19, 88, 222, 273, 424, 428		
1:28-29	169			3:6	14, 78, 272

INDEX OF PASSAGES IN JOHN'S GOSPEL

3:8	14, 78, 206, 429	4:15	159, 162, 268		180, 184, 193, 195,
3:9	272, 273	4:16	39, 40, 45, 53, 156,		250, 331, 426, 444,
3:10	271		160-62, 163, 166		446
3:12	206, 265, 269, 272,	4:17	156, 160, 161, 162,	5:18-29	97, 172, 173, 178,
	273, 340		166		182, 198, 250, 426,
3:13	17, 23, 49, 73, 88,	4:18	39, 160		444, 446, 447
	91, 98, 270, 275,	4:19	70, 162, 274, 394,	5:19-20	20, 179, 183, 188,
	429, 442, 472		428		188, 444
3:14	25, 96, 97, 427	4:19-20	112, 114, 161	5:20	19, 20, 97, 444
3:16	19, 79	4:20	58, 117, 161, 378,	5:21	179, 184, 319, 329,
3:16-19	332, 337, 340, 341		406		445
3:17	79, 338, 465, 466	4:20-24	268	5:21-29	319, 328, 331
3:18	19, 317	4:21	70, 117, 378	5:22	168, 198, 250, 428,
3:19	272, 337, 338	4:21-24	58, 117, 118, 121,		444
3:20	317, 337, 347		274	5:23	38, 97, 179, 184,
3:21	337	4:23	70, 74, 118, 121,		187, 218, 250, 319,
3:22-30	123, 124, 140, 410		274		425, 453
3:25	124, 216, 364	4:25	160, 161, 267, 269	5:24	68, 317, 326
3:25-30	127, 128	4:25-26	113, 117, 274	5:25	184, 189, 319, 329,
3:26	125, 216, 364	4:26	161, 268, 269		445
3:27	125, 140, 364	4:27	43, 156, 162	5:26	179, 184, 185, 319,
3:27-30	140, 317	4:28	157, 266, 274		329, 428, 445, 453
3:28	125	4:28-30	266	5:27	91, 97, 179, 184,
3:29	22, 126, 141	4:29	41, 42, 156, 157,		186, 198, 428, 445
3:30	123, 141, 216		161, 166, 273, 274	5:28	169
3:31	17	4:31	19, 67, 266, 471	5:28-29	74, 184, 250, 319,
3:31-34	20	4:34	465, 468		329, 445
3:32	471	4:38	40, 43, 53, 163	5:30	22, 68, 175, 327,
3:34	68, 269, 337, 465	4:39-42	145, 169, 170		465, 468, 471
3:34-36	338, 340, 341	4:40	66, 169, 470	5:31-40	41, 172, 177, 178,
3:35	19, 21, 327, 468,	4:41	169		444
	470	4:42	41, 53, 70, 79, 107,	5:32	222
4:1	263		121, 161, 164, 169,	5:35	175, 222
4:2	108		273, 428, 466	5:36	176, 465
4:6	467	4:44	38, 193, 218	5:37	176, 177, 442, 466
4:7	159, 467	4:47	263	5:38	68, 107, 176, 178,
4:7-14	42, 158, 162	5:1-10	374, 446		426, 444, 464
4:8	467	5:1-15	57, 172, 174, 180,	5:39	90, 177, 178
4:9	70, 155, 156, 159,		183, 202, 327, 443	5:41	22
	164, 274, 267	5:3-5	403	5:42	177, 178, 270, 344
4:10	109, 113, 157, 268,	5:10	195, 196, 222	5:43	19, 177
	274	5:15	175, 198	5:44	22, 38, 177, 265
4:10-26	145, 170	5:16	164, 172, 174, 177,	5:45	178
4:11	109, 159		178, 196, 222, 327,	5:46	23, 177
4:12	87, 107-9, 159, 274		444	5:46-47	90, 177, 274
4:13	111	5:17	19, 172, 180, 446	5:47	265
4:14	111, 159, 476	5:18	22, 40, 106, 178,		

Index of Passages in John's Gospel

6:1-15	174, 471	6:60	98	7:24	201, 202, 203, 229, 230, 263, 338
6:2	340	6:61	199	7:25	186, 201, 204
6:4	267	6:62	17, 50, 98, 429	7:26	415, 424
6:5-7	43, 44	6:63	98	7:26-27	50, 72, 196, 198, 203, 230, 429
6:6	270	6:64	19, 271, 339, 352		
6:8-9	43	6:65	339	7:27	262
6:10	44	6:67-69	277	7:27-29	14, 89, 206, 211, 223
6:12	44	6:67-71	43, 363, 369		
6:14	32, 107, 394, 424, 428	6:69	303, 327	7:28	17, 18, 206, 209, 210, 224, 230, 271
6:15	32, 424, 428	6:70	79, 271, 339, 351, 369	7:29	20, 204, 210, 224
6:24	340			7:30	209, 210, 224, 229
6:25	19, 67	6:71	267, 271, 339, 352, 369	7:31	73, 204, 223, 225, 340
6:26	270				
6:27	22, 448, 466	7:1	193, 196, 199, 204, 207, 210	7:32	195, 196, 204, 208, 209, 210, 227, 340
6:28	264				
6:29	465	7:1-7	15	7:33-34	73, 204, 205, 206, 207, 210, 231
6:30	264	7:1-10	262		
6:32	107	7:2	194, 228, 267	7:35	25, 58, 73, 205, 206, 272
6:33	79, 186, 448	7:3	32, 194		
6:38	17, 20, 22, 49, 73, 429, 466, 468	7:5	32, 194, 222	7:36	73, 204, 207, 208, 264
		7:6	223		
6:39-40	185, 186, 379, 470	7:7	222, 250, 347, 348	7:37	194, 195, 205, 229, 230, 272
6:40	186, 449	7:8	223, 260		
6:41-42	14, 49, 73, 98, 199, 206, 378, 429, 467	7:9	66	7:37-39	222, 228, 229, 379, 471
		7:10	260		
6:42	262	7:11	199, 207	7:40	68, 225, 340, 394
6:43	79, 185, 448	7:12	16, 68, 198, 199, 200, 209, 210, 211, 218, 221, 222, 225, 260, 327	7:41	260
6:43-51	272, 378			7:41-42	14, 73, 89, 208, 209, 210, 211, 262, 337, 467
6:44	168, 319, 346, 448, 449				
6:45	25, 272	7:13	69, 199, 203, 210	7:43	68, 221
6:46	176, 471, 472	7:14	194, 471	7:44	182, 195, 198, 210
6:47	185, 448	7:15	16, 68, 133, 200, 210, 220, 222, 230, 262, 265	7:45	189, 208, 209, 224, 265
6:48	186				
6:49	185			7:46	68, 209, 210, 225
6:50-51	17, 79, 98, 185, 378	7:16-17	20, 68, 195, 200, 206, 210, 223, 230, 453, 471	7:47	16, 69, 198, 209, 210, 218, 225, 260, 316
6:51	448				
6:52	265			7:47-52	316, 340, 353, 394
6:53	362	7:18	22, 68, 218, 223, 229, 230, 453	7:49	209, 225, 316
6:53-54	185, 231, 232			7:50	209
6:54	185, 186, 319, 449, 470	7:19	186, 196, 201, 204	7:51	198, 209, 210, 225, 273
		7:20	201, 211, 218, 224, 327		
6:57	185	7:21	202		
6:58	17, 98, 185, 186, 448	7:21-23	196, 198, 203, 204, 207, 327	7:52	14, 32, 50, 73, 90,
6:59	66, 471				

485

	177, 196, 211, 223, 225, 263, 274, 467		244, 252, 260, 339, 353	9:31 9:33	275 49, 73, 275
8:12	79, 195, 200, 228, 229, 441	8:45 8:46	241, 271 265, 327	9:34 9:35	275, 404 275
8:13-18	41, 176, 195, 200	8:47	204, 234, 269, 271	9:35-37	269
8:14	14, 74, 229, 239, 271, 429	8:48	16, 38, 242, 260, 465	9:35-38 9:36	101, 275 250, 268
8:15	186, 195, 196, 201, 224, 228, 229, 239, 261, 319, 338	8:51 8:52	245, 255 16, 23, 234, 260, 271	9:39 9:39-41 10	79, 269 272, 275, 317 299
8:17-18	175, 229, 230, 452	8:53	22, 234, 243, 264,	10:1-4	466
8:18	353, 466, 471		272, 329	10:1-16	316, 317
8:19	206, 229, 230, 270, 271, 272	8:54 8:55	20, 22, 38, 245 204, 206, 243, 252,	10:2 10:3	373 301, 310, 317, 373,
8:20	70, 195, 229		260, 271		425
8:21	233, 242, 448	8:56	321, 442	10:4	317
8:21-59	186, 210, 227, 230, 236, 244	8:58	23, 92, 98, 187, 245, 321, 329, 442,	10:4-5 10:5	272 466
8:22	25, 74, 206, 231, 233, 272	8:59	448, 452 16, 69, 198, 199,	10:6 10:9	261, 271 207, 466
8:23	18, 78, 231, 242, 246, 247, 249, 250,	9:2	237, 245, 252, 262 19, 67	10:11	50, 300, 305, 310, 372, 466
	272, 425	9:2-3	267	10:12	83, 273
8:24	19, 231, 232, 243, 247, 248, 250, 272,	9:4 9:5	35, 466 79	10:14 10:15	283, 301, 303, 317 15, 83, 303, 310,
	362, 379, 448, 452	9:7	265		466
8:26	186, 227, 228, 231	9:12	275	10:16	303, 308
8:28	25, 98, 186, 227, 228, 231, 275, 427,	9:15 9:16	265 16, 24, 68, 164,	10:17	20, 21, 304, 305, 329, 433
	452, 471		260, 326, 337, 340,	10:17-18	181, 187, 189, 304,
8:30	204, 235, 247, 253, 272	9:17	353 32, 41, 68, 264,		305, 319, 328, 329, 420, 430, 448, 453,
8:31	169, 234, 248		275, 394, 415, 424		470
8:31-37	235, 236	9:19	265	10:19-20	68, 316, 317, 337,
8:32	43, 234, 248	9:20-22	275		340
8:33	237, 243, 265	9:21	261, 264, 265	10:20	260, 327
8:34	234, 235	9:22	35, 45, 66, 69-70,	10:21	68
8:35	75, 77, 243, 245		84, 275, 340, 362,	10:22	62, 199, 267
8:37	98, 234, 235, 237, 238, 239, 271	9:24	393, 404, 406, 421 45, 260, 275, 326,	10:24-27 10:25	271, 272, 425 19, 41, 271
8:38	97, 234, 237, 453		352	10:26	271, 425
8:40	98, 234, 237, 238, 239, 242	9:25 9:26	45, 275 264, 265	10:26-27	205, 271, 272, 316, 317, 425
8:41	234, 239, 241, 243	9:27	265, 326	10:28	317, 318, 329
8:42-43	240, 442	9:28	363	10:28-29	185, 187, 317, 319,
8:43	271	9:29	262, 353, 429		328, 329, 331
8:44	201, 207, 237, 241,	9:30-36	45, 176, 269, 275	10:29	318, 430, 448

486

Index of Passages in John's Gospel

10:30	19, 318, 319, 331, 448	11:49-51	33, 198, 216	13:1	361, 366, 467, 468
10:31	16, 448	11:51	432	13:1-3	49, 74, 296, 426, 429, 467
10:33	22, 40, 98, 178, 304, 319, 320, 327, 428, 441, 448	11:52	303, 308	13:2	368, 369
		11:53	353	13:4-11	356, 357, 358, 361, 365, 367, 369, 371
		11:57	263		
10:34	322	12:1-2	46, 161	13:5	43
10:34-36	313, 319, 326, 327, 328, 330	12:1-8	66, 84, 345, 352	13:6	371
		12:3-6	339, 351	13:6-8	51, 357
10:35	322	12:9	263, 340	13:7	278, 357, 369, 372, 375
10:36	425, 466	12:9-11	46, 339, 345, 352		
10:39	199, 208, 448	12:12	349	13:8	372
11:1	32, 66	12:13	32, 428	13:9	357
11:1-44	174, 331, 339	12:16	25, 267	13:10	357, 365, 375
11:2	267	12:16-18	345, 424	13:10-11	276, 357, 370
11:3	42, 46, 266, 345	12:17-18	340	13:11	357, 368
11:4	448	12:19	339, 340, 352, 353	13:12	277, 357, 366
11:5	84, 275, 345	12:20	164, 273	13:12-17	276, 366, 370
11:8	19	12:21-22	266	13:12-20	20, 356, 357, 358, 365, 367, 371, 376, 375, 376, 398
11:14	268	12:21-23	42, 43, 44, 168, 273		
11:16	43	12:23-26	273, 303, 304, 340, 345, 346	13:13-14	19, 67, 361, 367
11:17	188			13:14	357, 366
11:20	47, 161, 166	12:25	347, 348	13:15	53, 357, 361
11:20-27	158, 252	12:27	20, 349, 426, 430, 467	13:16	367, 395, 398
11:21	243			13:17	277, 357, 374, 398
11:22	274	12:28	168, 425, 426, 467	13:18	270, 271, 276, 357, 368, 370, 398
11:23	270, 274	12:29	340, 354		
11:24	274	12:31	79, 337, 425	13:19	270, 276, 357, 398, 473
11:24-25	49	12:32	25, 83, 146, 304, 427		
11:25	268			13:20	465
11:26	449	12:34	77, 98, 264, 265, 275, 340, 354	13:21	270, 271, 370
11:27	47			13:21-30	276, 277, 278, 398
11:28	19, 42, 166, 266, 471	12:35	337	13:23	53, 84, 368, 370
		12:36	69, 252, 262	13:24	278, 368, 370
11:28-30	166, 2775	12:37	271	13:24-25	270
11:36-37	337, 340	12:37-50	269, 332, 333, 336, 337, 339	13:25	52, 270, 278, 370
11:37	243			13:27	211, 370
11:38-44	448, 470	12:40	272	13:31-32	25, 38, 98, 276, 427, 473
11:41-42	340, 345	12:41	92, 442		
11:43-44	448, 470	12:42	35, 66, 69-70, 84, 272, 340, 353, 362, 393, 404, 406, 421	13:34-35	276, 344, 372, 468, 473
11:45-52	124, 125, 140, 199, 210, 307, 311, 339, 340				
		12:43	347, 406	13:36	97, 267, 371, 372
11:46-47	263	12:44-45	339, 466	13:36-38	51, 276, 368, 374, 375
11:47	264	12:46	169, 317, 338		
11:47-48	216, 307, 352	12:47	69, 317, 338, 425	13:37	265, 278, 310, 369
11:48	352, 323	12:48	68, 317	13:38	310, 372, 374, 375

487

14:1	345, 473	15:4-7	76, 77, 169, 345, 399, 470	16:31	395, 473
14:1-4	276, 395, 468			16:32	74, 276, 395, 473
14:2	18, 74, 75, 83, 362, 378, 407, 473	15:5	399, 400, 409, 468	16:33	276, 277, 305, 404, 425
		15:6	77, 399		
14:2-3	25, 74, 75	15:7	77, 388, 399, 409, 473	17:1	25, 38, 390, 425, 427
14:3	76, 277, 394, 471				
14:3-6	276	15:9	19, 21, 76, 344, 345, 400, 469	17:1-5	426
14:4-5	43, 276			17:2	388
14:5	395, 396	15:9-10	66, 77, 345, 399, 471	17:3	303, 379, 388, 453
14:6	276, 277, 395, 472			17:4	38, 390, 453, 468
14:7	395	15:10	344, 400	17:5	18, 25, 50, 74, 97, 206, 327, 389, 425, 427, 428, 467, 473
14:8	395	15:11	270		
14:9	276, 395, 396	15:12-17	276, 277, 344, 399, 400, 467, 471		
14:10	76, 77, 395, 408, 468			17:6	19, 247, 268, 270, 270, 277, 389, 390, 468, 472, 473
		15:13	311, 344		
14:11	408, 468	15:14-15	277		
14:13-14	388, 471	15:14-17	276	17:7-8	270, 277, 389, 390
14:15	276, 388, 473	15:15	270	17:8	391, 465, 468
14:16-17	276, 388, 473	15:16	77, 400, 470, 473	17:9	79, 389, 390, 473
14:17	76, 77, 344, 395, 404, 409	15:18	277, 347	17:10	389, 390
		15:18-19	348, 404	17:11	277, 389, 408
14:18-22	267, 394, 395, 473	15:20	277, 395	17:11-12	9, 247, 268, 473
14:19	394, 404	15:23-24	347	17:12	277, 389, 390, 468, 469
14:20	77, 408, 468	15:25	353		
14:21	22, 276, 344, 469, 473	15:26-27	276, 393, 402	17:13	53, 389, 390, 469
		16:1-2	66, 345, 362, 365, 394, 404, 473	17:14	68, 79, 277, 389, 390, 391, 408, 468
14:21-22	268, 277, 473				
14:21-24	276	16:1-4	270, 276	17:15	66, 389, 469
14:22	260, 265, 395, 396, 404, 473	16:2	263	17:16	389, 390
		16:3	303	17:17	277, 389
14:23	22, 276, 344, 395, 408, 468, 469, 471	16:4	276, 277, 394	17:18	40, 44, 48, 390
		16:5	74, 276, 396, 402, 467	17:19	390, 391, 468, 469
14:24	395			17:20	390
14:25	45, 76, 267, 277, 402	16:7-15	41, 276, 402, 403, 404	17:21	77, 390, 465, 468
				17:22	390, 391, 468
14:27	363, 404	16:13-14	267, 402	17:23	77, 303, 390, 465, 468
14:28	467	16:16	276, 394, 395		
14:28-31	276, 394	16:17-18	264, 276, 395, 467	17:24	21, 25, 327, 390, 408, 425
14:29	270, 395, 473	16:20	276, 404		
14:30	305, 395, 404, 425	16:21-24	276, 277, 388, 396, 473	17:25	277, 303, 390, 391
15:1	107, 365, 399			17:26	19, 21, 247, 268, 270, 277, 390, 468, 471, 472, 473
15:1-10	276, 277, 399, 400, 470	16:25	396		
		16:25-30	277, 395		
15:2	77, 365, 399	16:26	388	18:1-11	228, 311, 423, 424, 428
15:3	68, 365	16:28	404	18:3	
15:4	66, 231, 399, 400, 408, 409	16:29-30	261, 270, 395, 404	18:4	311
		16:30	270	18:4-6	305

Index of Passages in John's Gospel

Passage	Pages	Passage	Pages	Passage	Pages
18:7	420	19:5	427	20:16	19, 32, 67, 267, 269, 279
18:8	311, 420, 429	19:6	422, 427		
18:10	267, 425, 428	19:7	22, 40, 179, 320, 422, 423, 424, 427, 428, 432	20:17	54, 71, 84, 166, 168, 266, 270
18:11	311, 428			20:18	166, 279
18:12	421			20:19	64, 71
18:14	267	19:9	206, 429	20:19-21	269
18:15	273	19:9-11	422, 423, 425, 427	20:20-26	431
18:15-18	52, 64, 278, 369, 373, 374	19:10	34, 340	20:21-23	40, 43, 44, 45, 48, 53, 71, 269
		19:11	430		
18:16	373	19:12	33, 179, 320, 423, 425, 428, 431, 432	20:23	48
18:17	369				
18:17-18	311	19:12-16	422, 427, 430	20:24-25	266
18:20	60, 67, 195, 228, 252, 268, 421, 471	19:13-16	423	20:24-29	43, 45, 84, 269
		19:15	431	20:25	42, 71, 165, 168
18:21	421	19:18	433	20:26	64, 379
18:22	50, 451	19:20	164, 433	20:27	71
18:23	429	19:22	432	20:28	71, 88, 96, 106, 183, 441, 447
18:25-27	311, 369	19:23	433		
18:28	62, 422	19:25	32	20:29	52
18:28-32	422, 423, 424, 427	19:26-27	32, 55, 84, 278, 369, 433	20:31	226
				21:1-2	43, 71
18:29	228, 264	19:28	419, 433	21:1-19	45, 50
18:30	260, 421, 422	19:33	379	21:2	32, 43
18:33	424	19:34	110, 379	21:3	374
18:33-37	32, 228, 422, 423, 424	19:35	268	21:6	207
		19:36	69, 434	21:7	52, 278
18:34	424	19:39	209, 268, 273	21:11	51
18:35	264, 424, 426, 431	19:40	267, 434	21:12	264
18:36	420, 425	19:40-41	33	21:15-18	48, 54, 71, 165, 311, 375, 376
18:37	49, 271, 272, 425	20:1-18	279		
18:37-38	205	20:2	84, 279	21:17	84
18:38	207, 423, 426, 431	20:4-5	278, 369	21:18	278, 311
18:39	228, 426, 431	20:8	52, 278, 369	21:18-19	54, 375
18:40	427	20:11-17	166	21:19	278, 311, 345, 375
19:1-4	228, 422, 423	20:13	279	21:20-23	185, 243, 264
19:3	421, 326	20:14	279	21:22	54
19:4	207, 422, 431	20:15	279	21:24	268

www.ingramcontent.com/pod-product-compliance
Lightning Source LLC
Chambersburg PA
CBHW021113300426
44113CB00006B/131